Macworld®
Photoshop® 5 Bible

Deke McClelland

IDG Books Worldwide, Inc.
An International Data Group Company

Foster City, CA ✦ Chicago, IL ✦ Indianapolis, IN ✦ New York, NY

Macworld® Photoshop® 5 Bible

Published by
IDG Books Worldwide, Inc.
An International Data Group Company
919 E. Hillsdale Blvd., Suite 400
Foster City, CA 94404
www.idgbooks.com (IDG Books Worldwide Web site)

Library of Congress Catalog Card No.: 98-71154

ISBN: 0-7645-3231-6

Printed in the United States of America

10 9 8 7 6 5 4 3 2 1

1E/SZ/QW/ZY/FC

Distributed in the United States by IDG Books Worldwide, Inc.

Distributed by Macmillan Canada for Canada; by Transworld Publishers Limited in the United Kingdom; by IDG Norge Books for Norway; by IDG Sweden Books for Sweden; by Woodslane Pty. Ltd. for Australia; by Woodslane (NZ) Ltd. for New Zealand; by Addison Wesley Longman Singapore Pte Ltd. for Singapore, Malaysia, Thailand, Indonesia, and Korea; by Norma Comunicaciones S.A. for Colombia; by Intersoft for South Africa; by International Thomson Publishing for Germany, Austria, and Switzerland; by Toppan Company Ltd. for Japan; by Distribuidora Cuspide for Argentina; by Livraria Cultura for Brazil; by Ediciencia S.A. for Ecuador; by Ediciones ZETA S.C.R. Ltda. for Peru; by WS Computer Publishing Corporation, Inc., for the Philippines; by Unalis Corporation for Taiwan; by Contemporanea de Ediciones for Venezuela; by Computer Book & Magazine Store for Puerto Rico; by Express Computer Distributors for the Caribbean and West Indies. Authorized Sales Agent: Anthony Rudkin Associates for the Middle East and North Africa.

For general information on IDG Books Worldwide's books in the U.S., please call our Consumer Customer Service department at 800-762-2974. For reseller information, including discounts and premium sales, please call our Reseller Customer Service department at 800-434-3422.

For information on where to purchase IDG Books Worldwide's books outside the U.S., please contact our International Sales department at 650-655-3200 or fax 650-655-3297.

For information on foreign language translations, please contact our Foreign & Subsidiary Rights department at 650-655-3021 or fax 650-655-3281.

For sales inquiries and special prices for bulk quantities, please contact our Sales department at 650-655-3200 or write to the address above.

For information on using IDG Books Worldwide's books in the classroom or for ordering examination copies, please contact our Educational Sales department at 800-434-2086 or fax 317-596-5499.

For press review copies, author interviews, or other publicity information, please contact our Public Relations department at 650-655-3000 or fax 650-655-3299.

For authorization to photocopy items for corporate, personal, or educational use, please contact Copyright Clearance Center, 222 Rosewood Drive, Danvers, MA 01923, or fax 978-750-4470.

is a trademark under exclusive license to IDG Books Worldwide, Inc., from International Data Group, Inc.

ABOUT IDG BOOKS WORLDWIDE

Welcome to the world of IDG Books Worldwide.

IDG Books Worldwide, Inc., is a subsidiary of International Data Group, the world's largest publisher of computer-related information and the leading global provider of information services on information technology. IDG was founded more than 25 years ago and now employs more than 8,500 people worldwide. IDG publishes more than 275 computer publications in over 75 countries (see listing below). More than 90 million people read one or more IDG publications each month.

Launched in 1990, IDG Books Worldwide is today the #1 publisher of best-selling computer books in the United States. We are proud to have received eight awards from the Computer Press Association in recognition of editorial excellence and three from *Computer Currents*' First Annual Readers' Choice Awards. Our best-selling ...*For Dummies*® series has more than 50 million copies in print with translations in 38 languages. IDG Books Worldwide, through a joint venture with IDG's Hi-Tech Beijing, became the first U.S. publisher to publish a computer book in the People's Republic of China. In record time, IDG Books Worldwide has become the first choice for millions of readers around the world who want to learn how to better manage their businesses.

Our mission is simple: Every one of our books is designed to bring extra value and skill-building instructions to the reader. Our books are written by experts who understand and care about our readers. The knowledge base of our editorial staff comes from years of experience in publishing, education, and journalism — experience we use to produce books for the '90s. In short, we care about books, so we attract the best people. We devote special attention to details such as audience, interior design, use of icons, and illustrations. And because we use an efficient process of authoring, editing, and desktop publishing our books electronically, we can spend more time ensuring superior content and spend less time on the technicalities of making books.

You can count on our commitment to deliver high-quality books at competitive prices on topics you want to read about. At IDG Books Worldwide, we continue in the IDG tradition of delivering quality for more than 25 years. You'll find no better book on a subject than one from IDG Books Worldwide.

John Kilcullen
CEO
IDG Books Worldwide, Inc.

Steven Berkowitz
President and Publisher
IDG Books Worldwide, Inc.

Eighth Annual
Computer Press
Awards ➤1992

Ninth Annual
Computer Press
Awards ➤1993

Tenth Annual
Computer Press
Awards ➤1994

Eleventh Annual
Computer Press
Awards ➤1995

IDG Books Worldwide, Inc., is a subsidiary of International Data Group, the world's largest publisher of computer-related information and the leading global provider of information services on information technology. International Data Group publishes over 275 computer publications in over 75 countries. More than 90 million people read one or more International Data Group publications each month. International Data Group's publications include: **ARGENTINA:** Buyer's Guide, Computerworld Argentina, PC World Argentina; **AUSTRALIA:** Australian Macworld, Australian PC World, Australian Reseller News, Computerworld, IT Casebook, Network World, Publish, Webmaster; **AUSTRIA:** Computerwelt Österreich, Networks Austria, PC Tip Austria; **BANGLADESH:** PC World Bangladesh; **BELARUS:** PC World Belarus; **BELGIUM:** Data News; **BRAZIL:** Annuário de Informática, Computerworld, Connections, Macworld, PC Player, PC World, Publish, Reseller News, Supergamepower; **BULGARIA:** Computerworld Bulgaria, Network World Bulgaria, PC & MacWorld Bulgaria; **CANADA:** CIO Canada, Client/Server World, Computerworld Canada, InfoWorld Canada, NetworkWorld Canada, WebWorld; **CHILE:** Computerworld Chile, PC World Chile; **COLOMBIA:** Computerworld Colombia, PC World Colombia; **COSTA RICA:** PC World Centro America; **THE CZECH AND SLOVAK REPUBLICS:** Computerworld Czechoslovakia, Macworld Czech Republic, PC World Czechoslovakia; **DENMARK:** Communications World Danmark, Computerworld Danmark, Macworld Danmark, PC World Danmark, Techworld Denmark; **DOMINICAN REPUBLIC:** PC World Republica Dominicana; **ECUADOR:** PC World Ecuador; **EGYPT:** Computerworld Middle East, PC World Middle East; **EL SALVADOR:** PC World Centro America; **FINLAND:** MikroPC, Tietoverkko, Tietoviikko; **FRANCE:** Distributique, Hebdo, Info PC, Le Monde Informatique, Macworld, Reseaux & Telecoms, WebMaster France; **GERMANY:** Computer Partner, Computerwoche, Computerwoche Extra, Computerwoche FOCUS, Global Online, Macwelt, PC Welt; **GREECE:** Amiga Computing, GamePro Greece, Multimedia World; **GUATEMALA:** PC World Centro America; **HONDURAS:** PC World Centro America; **HONG KONG:** Computerworld Hong Kong, PC World Hong Kong, Publish in Asia; **HUNGARY:** ABCD CD-ROM, Computerworld Szamitastechnika, Internetto online Magazine, PC World Hungary, PC-X Magazin Hungary; **ICELAND:** Tolvuheimur PC World Island; **INDIA:** Information Communications World, Information Systems Computerworld, PC World India, Publish in Asia; **INDONESIA:** InfoKomputer PC World, Komputek Computerworld, Publish in Asia; **IRELAND:** ComputerScope, PC Live!; **ISRAEL:** Macworld Israel, People & Computers/Computerworld; **ITALY:** Computerworld Italia, Macworld Italia, Networking Italia, PC World Italia; **JAPAN:** DTP World, Macworld Japan, Nikkei Personal Computing, OS/2 World Japan, SunWorld Japan, Windows NT World, Windows World Japan; **KENYA:** PC World East African; **KOREA:** Hi-Tech Information, Macworld Korea, PC World Korea; **MACEDONIA:** PC World Macedonia; **MALAYSIA:** Computerworld Malaysia, PC World Malaysia, Publish in Asia; **MALTA:** PC World Malta; **MEXICO:** Computerworld Mexico, PC World Mexico; **MYANMAR:** PC World Myanmar; **NETHERLANDS:** Computer! Totaal, LAN Internetworking Magazine, LAN World Buyers Guide, Macworld Netherlands, Net, WebWereld; **NEW ZEALAND:** Absolute Beginners Guide and Plain & Simple Series, Computer Buyer, Computer Industry Directory, Computerworld New Zealand, MTB, Network World, PC World New Zealand; **NICARAGUA:** PC World Centro America; **NORWAY:** Computerworld Norge, CW Rapport, Datamagasinet, Financial Rapport, Kursguide Norge, Macworld Norge, Multimediaworld Norge, PC World Ekspress Norge, PC World Nettverk, PC World Norge, PC World ProduktGuide Norge; **PAKISTAN:** Computerworld Pakistan; **PANAMA:** PC World Panama; **PEOPLE'S REPUBLIC OF CHINA:** China Computer Users, China Computerworld, China InfoWorld, China Telecom World Weekly, Computer & Communication, Electronic Design China, Electronics Today, Electronics Weekly, Game Software, PC World China, Popular Computer Week, Software Weekly, Software World, Telecom World; **PERU:** Computerworld Peru, PC World Profesional Peru, PC World SoHo Peru; **PHILIPPINES:** Click!, Computerworld Philippines, PC World Philippines, Publish in Asia; **POLAND:** Computerworld Poland, Computerworld Special Report Poland, Cyber, Macworld Poland, Networld Poland, PC World Komputer; **PORTUGAL:** Cerebro/PC World, Computerworld/Correio Informático, Dealer World Portugal, Mac*In/PC*In Portugal, Multimedia World; **PUERTO RICO:** PC World Puerto Rico; **ROMANIA:** Computerworld Romania, PC World Romania, Telecom Romania; **RUSSIA:** Computerworld Russia, Mir PK, Publish, Seti; **SINGAPORE:** Computerworld Singapore, PC World Singapore, Publish in Asia; **SLOVENIA:** Monitor; **SOUTH AFRICA:** Computing SA, Network World SA, Software World SA; **SPAIN:** Communicaciones World España, Computerworld España, Dealer World España, Macworld España, PC World España; **SRI LANKA:** Infolink PC World; **SWEDEN:** CAP&Design, Computer Sweden, Corporate Computing Sweden, Internetworld Sweden, it.branschen, Macworld Sweden, MaxiData Sweden, MikroDatorn, Nätverk & Kommunikation, PC World Sweden, PCaktiv, Windows World Sweden; **SWITZERLAND:** Computerworld Schweiz, Macworld Schweiz, PCtip; **TAIWAN:** Computerworld Taiwan, Macworld Taiwan, NEW ViSiON/Publish, PC World Taiwan, Windows World Taiwan; **THAILAND:** Publish in Asia, Thai Computerworld; **TURKEY:** Computerworld Turkiye, Macworld Turkiye, Network World Turkiye, PC World Turkiye; **UKRAINE:** Computerworld Kiev, Multimedia World Ukraine, PC World Ukraine; **UNITED KINGDOM:** Acorn User UK, Amiga Action UK, Amiga Computing UK, Apple Talk UK, Computing, Macworld, Parents and Computers UK, PC Advisor, PC Home, PSX Pro, The WEB; **UNITED STATES:** Cable in the Classroom, CIO Magazine, Computerworld, DOS World, Federal Computer Week, GamePro Magazine, InfoWorld, I-Way, Macworld, Network World, PC Games, PC World, Publish, Video Event, THE WEB Magazine, and WebMaster; online webzines: JavaWorld, NetscapeWorld, and SunWorld Online; **URUGUAY:** InfoWorld Uruguay; **VENEZUELA:** Computerworld Venezuela, PC World Venezuela; and **VIETNAM:** PC World Vietnam.
5/7/98

Credits

Acquisitions Editor
Andy Cummings

Development Editors
Amy Thomas
Susannah Pfalzer

Technical Editor
Marc Pawliger

Copy Editor
Tracy Brown

Project Coordinator
Susan Parini

Book Designer
Murder By Design

Graphics and Production Specialists
Laura Carpenter
Linda Marousek
Hector Mendoza
Elizabeth Pauw
Dina F Quan

Quality Control Specialists
Mick Arellano
Mark Schumann

Proofreader
C² Editorial Services

Indexer
Richard Shrout

About the Author

Deke McClelland is a contributing editor to *Macworld* and *Publish* magazines. He has authored more than 40 books on desktop publishing and the Macintosh computer, and his work has been translated into more than 20 languages. Deke also hosts "Digital Gurus," a syndicated TV show about personal computing, from his home base in Colorado. He started his career as artistic director at the first service bureau in the United States.

Deke won a Society of Technical Communication Award in 1994, an American Society for Business Press Editors Award in 1995, and the Ben Franklin Award for Best Computer Book in 1989. He also won the prestigious Computer Press Association Award in 1990, 1992, 1994, and 1995.

Deke is author of the following books published by IDG Books Worldwide, Inc.: *CorelDRAW 8 For Dummies*, *FreeHand 8 Bible*, *Photoshop 5 For Windows 95 Bible*, *Photoshop 5 For Dummies*, *Photoshop Studio Secrets*, and *Web Design Studio Secrets*.

There's nothing I'd rather do

than nothing but nothing with you

lie on my back and watch cheesy TV

black-and-white game shows

are my idea of heaven

if you lie down next to me.

E. P.

Foreword

If you are reading this foreword, it probably means that you've purchased a copy of Adobe Photoshop 5.0. For that, I and the rest of the Photoshop team at Adobe thank you.

If you own a previous edition of the *Photoshop Bible*, you probably know what to expect. If not, get ready for an interesting trip.

I have long felt that the best way to learn Photoshop is through exploration. Rather than just offering a set of canned effects, Photoshop offers a broad collection of tools for a wide range of imaging tasks. Becoming a skilled Photoshop user involves getting to know these tools, how they interact, and when to use them. The best way I've found to do that is through use, exploration, and play.

Photoshop 5.0 contains a number of features designed to allow you to change your mind repeatedly while working on an image. Those features should make it easier to explore the product without fear. On the other hand, because Photoshop allows one to do so much, it can be difficult to know where to begin. It's like opening a watch maker's tool chest: the screwdrivers are pretty obvious, but what about all these other strange and mysterious instruments?

This is where Deke McClelland comes in.

In Deke's hands, Photoshop goes from being just a toolbox to being a strange and wonderful land all its own. The *Photoshop Bible* is a guided tour through that land with a guide who has been over the territory many times. (I've been involved with Photoshop for seven years, and for essentially as long as I can remember, I've had Deke looking over my shoulder.)

Deke takes you through most of Photoshop and covers a lot of areas in impressive depth. Not only does he show you the features in Photoshop — after all, you've got the manual to do that — he shows you how to use them to solve issues that look almost like real-world problems. This is the *Photoshop Bible* not the *Photoshop Encyclopedia*; it tells stories rather than just present information. Those stories take the form of looking at complex problems — like dealing with hair (believe me, it can be difficult in ways you've never imagined) — and showing how you can use Photoshop's tools to solve those problems.

A second thing you'll get from this book is a lot of commentary. Deke isn't shy about letting you know how he feels about various features. I don't always agree with Deke's opinions on these matters, but I think his openness about his opinions makes the book much richer. If you become a routine user of Photoshop, you will almost certainly develop your own opinions, some of which will probably match Deke's and some of which probably won't. It's valuable to get his opinions during the tour, however, because, even if you end up disagreeing with them, they give you more to think about.

Finally, the most invigorating aspect of this book is the enthusiasm Deke brings to the tour. You'll note that I included "play" in my list of strategies for coming to know Photoshop, and I think just having fun with the program is really one of the best things you can do when starting out. Deke almost relentlessly conveys that sense of excitement and fun, and for that I thank him.

So, fasten your seat belts, put on your pith helmets, and get ready. It's a fascinating trip ahead.

Mark Hamburg

Principal Scientist and Architect for Adobe Photoshop

Adobe Systems Incorporated

May 1998

Preface

I have no idea where you are as you read this. You might be sitting in front of your computer, lounging on a beach in Martinique, or curled up under the covers with a flashlight. But there's a chance you're standing in a bookstore with a clerk behind you asking if you need any help. If so, you're at what we in the book biz like to call the *point of purchase* (POP). From my perspective, the POP is a dangerous place, fraught with ambiguities and temptations. There's a chance — however infinitesimal — that you might put this book back where you found it and buy a competing title. I shudder to think of it.

So for the benefit of you POPers, I'm about to lay it on a bit thick.

This book is not only the number-one selling guide to Adobe Photoshop, but one of the two or three most successful books on any electronic publishing topic ever printed. You can find dozens of localized translations throughout the world. The Dutch translation has been known to come out before the English edition, and I just received an e-mail from my German translator urging me to get her manuscript ASAP. The *Photoshop Bible* is the most widely accepted text book for college courses. It is also the only third-party book that has been edited for technical accuracy by members of Photoshop's programming team (for which I am duly grateful).

Now, we all know "bestseller" doesn't necessarily translate to "best" — I needn't remind you that Air Supply sold a lot of albums in its day. But the *Photoshop Bible* seems to have touched a chord. Based on the letters I've received over the years, most readers find the book informative, comprehensive, and entertaining. (Okay, one woman summed it up as "violent, satanic, and blasphemous" — cross my heart, it's true — but now that we've removed all the backward lyrics, I think we've addressed that problem.) Knowing that people not only buy the book, but actually *read* it and find it pleasurable, gives me more satisfaction than I can say.

The driving philosophy behind *Macworld Photoshop Bible* is simple: Even the most intimidating topic can be made easy if it's explained properly. This goes double when the subject of the discussion is something as modest as a piece of software. Photoshop isn't some remarkable work of nature that defies our comprehension. It's nothing more that a commercial product designed by a bunch of regular people like you for the express purpose of being understood and put to use by a bunch of regular people like you. If I can't explain something that's inherently so straightforward, then shame on me.

I've made it my mission to address every topic head on — no cop-outs, no apologies. Everything's here, from the practical benefits of creating accurate masks to the theoretical wonders of designing your own custom filters. I wasn't born with this knowledge, and there are plenty of times when I'm learning with you. But if I don't know how something works, I do the research and figure it out, sometimes discussing features directly with the programmers, sometimes taking advantage of other sources. My job is to find out the answers, make sure those answers make sense, and pass them along to you as clearly as I can.

I also provide background, opinions, and humor. A dry listing of features followed by ponderous discussions of how they work doesn't mean squat unless I explain why the feature is there, where it fits into your workflow, and — on occasion — whether it's the best solution. I am often cranky, excited, and just plain giddy as I explain Photoshop, and I make no effort to contain my criticisms or enthusiasm. This book is me walking you through the program as subjectively as I would explain it to a friend.

But before I brag any more about the book, it's possible you're not even sure what Photoshop is, much less why you'd need a book on the subject. Just so we're all clear, let's take a peek at the program.

What Is Photoshop?

Photoshop 5 is a professional-level image editor that runs on a Power Macintosh computer or a Pentium-based PC equipped with Windows 95, 98, NT 4, or later. By *image editor*, I mean that Photoshop enables you to edit photos and artwork scanned to disk. You can then post the resulting images on the Internet or print them on paper.

Here's an example: Your job is to take a picture of your company's high-and-mighty CEO, touch up the crow's feet, fix the hair, and publish the Chief's smiling face on the cover of the annual report. No problem. Just shoot the photo, have it scanned to disk, open Mr. or Mrs. CEO inside Photoshop, and away you go. Photoshop arms you with all the digital wrinkle cream, toupee relaxer, jowl remover, and tooth polisher that you could ask for. The head honcho looks presentable no matter how badly the company is doing.

Photoshop, then, is about changing reality. It follows in the footsteps of a rich procession of after-camera tools. Despite all the hand-wringing you may have heard about the veracity of photographs in the digital age, image editing has been around almost as long as photography itself. Witness the editorial image below, lifted from the hallowed pages of a 1917 issue of *The Geographic* (predecessor to *National Geographic*). The men on the left are authentic, but I'm a bit skeptical about that fellow inside the van. Today's editing techniques may be more sophisticated, but they're hardly anything new.

Photograph by Paul Thompson

A WAGON-LOAD OF HELMETS OR CASQUES FOR FRENCH
SOLDIERS LEAVING THE FACTORY

In 1917, *The Geographic* tendered this image as a genuine photograph, and very likely many readers thought nothing of it. One day, future generations will think the same of our work.

Photoshop goes beyond just reducing the distance between two Giza pyramids on the cover of *National Geographic* or plopping a leaning Tom Cruise, photographed in Hawaii, onto the supportive shoulder of Dustin Hoffman, photographed in New York, for a *Newsweek* spread (both duller-than-fiction applications of image-editing software). Photoshop brings you full-tilt creativity. Picture a diver leaping from the summit of Mount Kilimanjaro, or a bright violet zebra galloping toward a hazel-green sunset, or an architectural rendering with wallpaper that looks exactly like the surface of the moon. Photoshop lets you paint snapshots from your dreams. The sky's the limit.

About This Book

If you're familiar with previous editions of this book, this one represents your everyday average exhaustive renovation. I've added detailed discussions on the subjects of color management, image history, text editing, photo restoration, spot colors, automated effects, and three-dimensional transformations. Three chapters (6, 10, and 14) and an appendix (Appendix A) were rewritten from the ground up. And the shortcut table in Chapter 3 has grown by 30 percent, making it (as in past editions) the most comprehensive of its kind.

Images, color, and otherwise

More than half the figures and images in this book are new. If only for the sake of variety, I've changed out images that have been staples of previous editions and traded them out for new photographs from stock-image vendors Digital Stock and PhotoDisc, as well as stuff that I've shot myself with the latest digital cameras.

As in the past, the book includes 32 pages of color images, with hundreds of color images and artwork available for your perusal on the CD. Of course, that still leaves a lot of grayscale images, which begs the question, why isn't this book printed in full color throughout? The answer is an irrefutable matter of economics. A full-color book of this size would cost nearly $150. With volume discounts, we could probably pull it off at something in the $90 to $100 range. But even so, that's a little steep for a book that's going to sit on your desk and get coffee stains and pen marks all over it. So we opted to forego full color throughout and concentrate on giving you what you really need: Tons of useful information at an affordable price.

That silver Frisbee in the back of the book

In the back of this book, you'll find a CD-ROM containing Photoshop plug-ins, hundreds of pieces of original artwork, and lots of stock photography in full, natural color. I've included most of the pivotal images from this book so that you can follow along with my examples if you see fit. And the CD is cross-platform, so you can open it on a Mac or on a PC equipped with Windows 95, 98, or NT.

Cross-Reference

Read Appendix C, "Using the CD-ROM," for a complete listing of the contents of the CD.

The Guts of the Book

I wrote *Macworld Photoshop Bible* to serve as the ultimate guide to retouching and enhancing scanned images in Photoshop. After you finish reading this book, it is my sincere hope not only that you will understand virtually every nook and cranny of Photoshop, but also that you will know how to apply your vast expanse of knowledge to real-world design situations.

Moderately experienced artists and designers are likely to benefit the most from this book. However, even snooty power users will learn gallons of stuff they never imagined they could from a book with such a chatty introduction.

Artists and designers? Snooty power users? Does this mean you have to dye your hair black and hang out at espresso bars to understand what's going on? At your age, no way. In fact, the *Photoshop Bible* is designed to appeal to all sexes, income brackets, and experience levels. I leave no stone unturned, I assume no future knowledge, and I treat you with the respect a dedicated student deserves. In a few hours, you'll be fixing, enhancing, and printing images in style. (Hang in there, you can do it. Honest.)

To enhance your enjoyment of learning Photoshop, I've sliced the process into 5 tasty parts and then diced those parts into a total of 20 digestible chapters. Bon appetite, my sweet.

Part I: Welcome to Photoshop 5 Part I includes all the basic stuff you need to know about Photoshop. I explain the revised Photoshop 5 interface, give you an overview of the low-level functions that have changed, and show you how to work with Photoshop from the keyboard. Whether you're new to Photoshop or an old hand, you'll find a lot you didn't know in these first three chapters.

Note

If you're experienced with Photoshop and you're familiar with the previous edition of this book, read the last section of Chapter 1 and skim through Chapters 2 and 3. Then skip to Chapter 6 and keep reading.

Part II: Understanding Digital Imagery Part II examines the core image editing process, taking you from composition and construction to color theory and output. You learn how to change the size and resolution of an image, how to define colors and navigate among color channels, and finally how to print the image to paper or film.

Part III: Painting and Retouching Images Every month or so, some fraudulent photo sparks a new flame of public scorn and scrutiny. Now it's your chance to give people something to talk about. These chapters show you how to exchange fact with a modicum of fantasy.

Part IV: Selections, Layers, and Text

Selections are Photoshop's most important capability. They enable you to limit the area that you edit, as well as lift foreground images and combine them with other backgrounds. I also cover text in this section, because text in Photoshop is no more than character-shaped selection outlines.

Part V: Filters and Special Effects Making manual artistic enhancements is all very well and good, but it's easier to let your computer do the work. These chapters show ways to produce highly entertaining and effective results using fully automated operations.

Part VI: Corrections, Composites, and the Web Here's where you learn what you can do with Photoshop's most powerful color correction commands, how to composite images using overlay modes and channel operations, and how to create images specifically for the World Wide Web.

Appendixes

Three appendixes follow Chapter 20. Appendix A explains how to prepare and upgrade your hardware to get the most out of Photoshop; Appendix B provides complete information on the photographers, image collections, and news services that contributed images to this book. Appendix C explains the expansive contents of the CD-ROM in the back of the book.

Last but not least is an astonishingly comprehensive index. It'll knock your socks off, should you happen to be wearing any.

Conventions

Every computer book seems to conform to a logic all its own, and this one's no exception. Although I try to avoid pig latin — ellway, orfay hetay ostmay artpay — I do subscribe to a handful of conventions that you may not immediately recognize.

Vocabulary

Call it computerese, call it technobabble, call it the synthetic jargon of propeller heads. The fact is, I can't explain Photoshop in graphic and gruesome detail without reverting to the specialized language of the trade. However, to help you keep up, I can and have italicized vocabulary words (as in *random-access memory*) with which you may not be familiar or which I use in an unusual context. An italicized term is followed by a definition.

If you come across a strange word that is *not* italicized (that bit of italics was for emphasis), look it up in the index to find the first reference to the word in the book.

Commands and options

To distinguish the literal names of commands, dialog boxes, buttons, and so on, I capitalize the first letter in each word (for example, *click on the Cancel button*). The only exceptions are option names, which can be six or seven words long and filled with prepositions like *to* and *of*. Traditionally, prepositions and articles (*a, an, the*) don't appear in initial caps, and this book follows that time-honored rule, too.

When discussing menus and commands, I use an arrow symbol to indicate hierarchy. For example, *Choose File ⇨ Open* means to choose the Open command from the File menu. If you have to display a submenu to reach a command, I list the command used to display the submenu between the menu name and the final command. *Choose Image ⇨ Adjust ⇨ Invert* means to choose the Adjust command from the Image menu and then choose the Invert command from the Adjust submenu.

Version numbers

A new piece of software comes out every 15 minutes. That's not a real statistic, mind you, but I bet I'm not far off. As I write this, Photoshop has advanced to Version 5.0. But by the time you read this, the version number may be seven hundredths of a percentage point higher. So know that when I write *Photoshop 5,* I mean any version of Photoshop short of 6.

Similarly, when I write *Photoshop 4,* I mean Versions 4.0 and 4.0.1; *Photoshop 3,* means Versions 3.0, 3.0.1, 3.0.3, 3.0.4, and 3.0.5; *Photoshop 2.5* means 2.5 and 2.5.1; you get the idea.

Icons

Like just about every computer book currently available on your green grocer's shelves, this one includes alluring icons that focus your eyeballs smack dab on important information. The icons make it easy for folks who just like to skim books to figure out what the heck's going on. Icons serve as little insurance policies against short attention spans. On the whole, the icons are self-explanatory, but I'll explain them anyway.

The Caution icon warns you that a step you're about to take may produce disastrous results. Well, perhaps "disastrous" is an exaggeration. Inconvenient, then. Uncomfortable. For heaven's sake, use caution.

The Note icon highlights some little tidbit of information I've decided to share with you that seemed at the time to be remotely related to the topic at hand. I might tell you how an option came into existence, why a feature is implemented the way it is, or how things used to be better back in the old days.

The Photoshop 5 icon explains an option, command, or other feature that is brand spanking new to this latest revision. If you're already familiar with previous versions of Photoshop, you might just want to plow through the book looking for Photoshop 5 icons and see what new stuff is out there.

This book is bursting with tips and techniques. If I were to highlight every one of them, whole pages would be gray with triangles popping out all over the place. The Tip icon calls attention to shortcuts that are specifically applicable to the Photoshop application. For the bigger, more useful power tips, I'm afraid you'll have to actually read the text.

The Cross-Reference icon tells you where to go for information related to the current topic. I included one a few pages back and you probably read it without thinking twice. That means you're either sharp as a tack or an experienced computer-book user. Either way, you won't have any trouble with this icon.

I thought of including one more icon that alerted you to every new bit of information—whether or not Photoshop 5-dependent—that's included in this book. But I found myself using it every other paragraph. Besides, that would have robbed you of the fun of discovering the new stuff.

How to Bug Me

Even in its fifth edition, scanned by the eyes of hundreds of thousands of readers and scrutinized intensely for months at a time by myself and my editors, I bet someone, somewhere will still manage to locate errors and oversights. If you notice those kinds of things and you have a few spare moments, please let me know what you think. I always appreciate readers' comments.

If you want to share your insights, comments, or corrections, please visit my Web site, the infamous *http://www.dekemc.com*. There you'll find news and excerpts about my books, tips for various graphics products, and other goofy online stuff. Let me know what you think. To e-mail me, click on the Contact Deke button. Don't fret if you don't hear from me for a few days, or months, or ever. I read every letter and try to implement nearly every constructive idea anyone bothers to send me. But because I receive hundreds of reader letters a week, I can respond to only a small percentage of them.

Note

Please, do not write to ask me why your copy of Photoshop is misbehaving on your specific computer. I was not involved in developing Photoshop, I am not paid by Adobe, and I am not trained in product support. Adobe can answer your technical support questions way better than I can, so I leave it to the experts.

Now, without further ado, I urge you to turn the page and advance forward into the great untamed frontier of image editing. But remember, this book can be a dangerous tool if wielded unwisely. Don't set it on any creaky card tables or let your children play with it without the assistance of a stalwart adult, preferably an All-Star Wrestler or that guy who played the Incredible Hulk on TV. And no flower pressing. The little suckers would be pummeled to dust by this monstrously powerful colossus of a book.

Acknowledgments

Thank you to the following people and companies for their assistance in providing me with the information and product loans that I needed to complete this book.

Marc Pawliger, Christie Cameron, and Mark Hamburg at Adobe Systems

Josh Weisberg at Intergraph

Bruce Berkoff at Umax

Wynne Ahern at A&R Partners

William Hollingworth at Mitsubishi

Roger Kasten and Jack Putnam at Newer Technology

Charles Smith at Digital Stock

Sophia McShea at PhotoDisc

Burton Holmes at Burton Holmes Associates

Scott Rawlings and Steve Sechrist at Wacom

Myke Ninness and Kevin Hurst at Extensis

Skip Elsheimer and JB Popplewell at Alien Skin Software

Barry Burns and Sumeet Pasricha at Andromeda

Chris Mills at Ulead Systems

Chuck Duff and Dawn Ginn at Digital Frontiers

Travis Anton and Cindy Johnson at BoxTop Software

Sid Fish and Carolyne Walton at Altamira Group

Michael Schumaker and Kirk Lyford at Vivid Details

Robin Shiverick at Chroma Graphics

Ted Cheney at ImageXpress

Mark Feldman at Xaos Tools

Renee Cooper at Miramar Systems

Kris Atkins, Kristina Ross, and Steve Zahm at DigitalThink

Additional kudos to the artists who contributed their work to this book: Robert Bowen, Ron Chan, Helen Golden, Wendy Grossman, Dorothy Krause, Bonny Lhotka, Kent Maske, Judith Moncrieff, Bud Peen, Jeff Schewe, Karin Schminke, Gordon Studer, Richard Tuschman, and Nanette Wylde.

Save the Best for Last

Extra special thanks to my fabulous editor Amy Thomas, the great overseers Andy Cummings and Walt Bruce, CD mistress Lisa Sontag, long-time image providers Mark Collen, Denise McClelland, and Russell McDougal, page layout supervisor Laura Carpenter, and background champions Ted Padova, Katrin Eismann, Steve Roth, and Steve Broback. Finally, thanks to John Kilcullen, and Matt Wagner for getting this book up and running lo these many years ago.

Finally, thanks to you, the reader. You're what makes this big, thick, exhaustive tome possible.

Contents at a Glance

Contents

Part V: Filters and Effects   559

Chapter 17: Constructing Homemade Effects 683

Part VI: Corrections, Composites, and the Web   729

Chapter 18: Mapping and Correcting Colors 731

Welcome to Photoshop 5

I

Getting to Know Photoshop

What Is Photoshop?

Adobe Photoshop is the most popular image-editing application available for use on Macintosh and Windows-based computers. Despite hefty competition from programs such as Macromedia xRes and Live Picture, Adobe Systems, Inc., reports that Photoshop's sales account for more than 80 percent of the image-editing market. (This estimate includes Painter from MetaCreations, an image-creation program that does not strictly compete with Photoshop.) This makes Photoshop four times more popular than all its competitors combined.

Photoshop's historically lopsided sales advantage provides Adobe with a clear incentive to reinvest in Photoshop and regularly enhance — even overhaul — its capabilities. Meanwhile, other vendors have had to devote smaller resources to playing catch-up. Although competitors provide interesting and sometimes amazing capabilities, the sums of their parts remain inferior to Photoshop.

As a result, Photoshop rides a self-perpetuating wave of industry predominance. It hasn't always been the best image editor, nor was it the earliest. But its deceptively straightforward interface combined with a few terrific core functions made it a hit from the moment of its first release. Nearly a decade later — thanks to substantial capital injections and highly creative programming on the part of Adobe's staff and Photoshop originator Thomas Knoll — it has evolved into the most popular program of its kind.

If you're already familiar with Photoshop and you just want to scope out its new capabilities, skip to the section "Fast Track to Version 5."

Image-Editing Theory

Like any *image editor*, Photoshop enables you to alter photographs and other scanned artwork. You can retouch an image, apply special effects, swap details between photos, introduce text and logos, adjust color balance, and even add color to a grayscale scan. Photoshop also provides the tools you need to create images from scratch. These tools are fully compatible with pressure-sensitive tablets, so you can create naturalistic images that look for all the world like watercolors and oils.

Bitmaps versus objects

Image editors fall into the larger software category of painting programs. In a painting program, you draw a line, and the application converts it to tiny square dots called pixels. The painting itself is called a bitmapped image, but bitmap and image are equally acceptable terms. Every program discussed so far is a painting program.

Photoshop uses the term *bitmap* exclusively to mean a black-and-white image, the logic being that each pixel conforms to one *bit* of data, 0 or 1 (off or on). In order to avoid ad hoc syllabic mergers such as *pix-map* — and because forcing a distinction between a painting with exactly two colors and one with anywhere from 4 to 16 million colors is entirely arbitrary — I use the term bitmap more broadly to mean any image composed of a fixed number of pixels, regardless of the number of colors involved.

What about other graphics applications, such as Adobe Illustrator and Macromedia FreeHand? Illustrator, FreeHand, CorelDraw, and others fall into a different category of software called *drawing programs*. Drawings comprise *objects*, which are independent, mathematically-defined lines and shapes. For this reason, drawing programs are sometimes said to be *object-oriented*. Some folks prefer the term *vector-based*, but I really hate that one because *vector* implies the physical components direction and magnitude, which generally are associated with straight lines. Besides, my preference suggests an air of romance, as in, "Honey, I'm bound now for the Object Orient."

The ups and downs of painting

Painting programs and drawing programs each have their strengths and weaknesses. One strength of a painting program is that it offers an extremely straightforward approach to creating images. For example, although many of Photoshop's features are complex — *exceedingly* complex on occasion — its core painting tools are as easy to use as a pencil. You alternately draw and erase until you reach a desired effect, just as you've been doing since grade school. (Of course, for all I know, you've been using computers since grade school. If you're pushing 20, you probably managed to log in many happy hours on paint programs in your formative years. Then again, if you're under 20, you're still in your formative years. Shucks, we're *all* in our formative years. Wrinkles, expanding tummies, receding hairlines . . . if that's not a new form, I don't know what is.)

In addition to being simple to use, each of Photoshop's core painting tools is fully customizable. It's as if you have access to an infinite variety of crayons, colored pencils, pastels, airbrushes, watercolors, and so on, all of which are entirely erasable. Doodling on the phone book was never so much fun.

The downside of a painting program is that it limits your *resolution* options. Because bitmaps contain a fixed number of pixels, the resolution of an image—the number of pixels per inch—is dependent upon the size at which the image is printed, as demonstrated in Figure 1-1. Print the image small, and the pixels become tiny, which increases resolution; print the image large, and the pixels grow, which decreases resolution. An image that fills up a standard 13-inch screen (640 × 480 pixels) prints with smooth color transitions when reduced to, say, half the size of a postcard. But if you print that same image without reducing it, you may be able to distinguish individual pixels, which means that you can see jagged edges and blocky transitions. The only way to remedy this problem is to increase the number of pixels in the image, which dramatically increases the size of the file on disk.

Figure 1-1: When printed small, a painting appears smooth (left). But when printed large, it appears jagged (right).

Cross-Reference Bear in mind that this is a very simplified explanation of how images work. For a more complete description that includes techniques for maximizing image performance, refer to the "How Images Work" section of Chapter 4.

The downs and ups of drawing

Painting programs provide tools reminiscent of traditional art tools. A drawing program, on the other hand, features tools that have no real-world counterparts. The process of drawing might more aptly be termed *constructing*, because you actually build lines and shapes point by point and stack them on top of each other to create a finished image. Each object is independently editable — one of the few structural advantages of an object-oriented approach — but you're still faced with the task of building your artwork one chunk at a time.

Nevertheless, because a drawing program defines lines, shapes, and text as mathematical equations, these objects automatically conform to the full resolution of the *output device*, whether it's a laser printer, imagesetter, or film recorder. The drawing program sends the math to the printer and the printer *renders* the math to paper or film. In other words, the printer converts the drawing program's equations to printer pixels. Your printer offers far more pixels than your screen — a 300 dots-per-inch (dpi) laser printer, for example, offers 300 pixels per inch (dots equal pixels), whereas most screens offer 72 pixels per inch. So the printed drawing appears smooth and sharply focused regardless of the size at which you print it, as shown in Figure 1-2.

Figure 1-2: Small or large, a drawing prints smooth, but it's a pain to create. This one took more than an hour out of my day, and as you can see, I didn't even bother with the letters around the perimeter of the design.

Another advantage of drawings is that they take up relatively little room on disk. The file size of a drawing depends on the quantity and complexity of the objects the drawing contains. Thus, the file size has almost nothing to do with the size of the printed image, which is just the opposite of the way bitmapped images work. A thumbnail drawing of a garden that contains hundreds of leaves and petals consumes several times more disk space than a poster-sized drawing that contains three rectangles.

When to use Photoshop

Thanks to their specialized methods, painting programs and drawing programs fulfill distinct and divergent purposes. Photoshop and other painting programs are best suited to creating and editing the following kinds of artwork:

✦ Scanned photos, including photographic collages and embellishments that originate from scans

✦ Images captured with any type of digital camera

✦ Realistic artwork that relies on the play between naturalistic highlights, midranges, and shadows

✦ Impressionistic-type artwork and other images created for purely personal or aesthetic purposes

✦ Logos and other display type featuring soft edges, reflections, or tapering shadows

✦ Special effects that require the use of filters and color enhancements you simply can't achieve in a drawing program

When to use a drawing program

You're probably better off using Illustrator, FreeHand, or some other drawing program if you're interested in creating more stylized artwork, such as the following:

✦ Poster art and other high-contrast graphics that heighten the appearance of reality

✦ Architectural plans, product designs, or other precise line drawings

✦ Business graphics, such as charts and other "infographics" that reflect data or show how things work

✦ Traditional logos and text effects that require crisp, ultrasmooth edges

✦ Brochures, flyers, and other single-page documents that mingle artwork, logos, and standard-sized text (such as the text you're reading now)

If you're serious about computer graphics, you should own at least one painting program and one drawing program. If I had to rely exclusively on two graphics applications, I would probably choose Photoshop and Illustrator. Adobe has done a fine job of establishing symmetry between the two programs, so that they share common interface elements and keyboard shortcuts. Learn one and the other makes a lot more sense.

On the other hand, if you don't care if your drawing program and image editor share a common interface, then FreeHand is currently more powerful than Illustrator. It offers a better realized collection of features, including better blending, tracing, and lens-effect tools. It also works remarkably well in combination with Photoshop. The only downside is that knowing Photoshop doesn't prepare you as well for FreeHand as it does for Illustrator.

For those who are interested, I write cradle-to-grave books on both FreeHand and Illustrator. I authored the *FreeHand Bible* — which comes from this same publisher, IDG Books Worldwide — and *Real World Illustrator*. (Occasionally a reader asks me why I didn't write IDG Books's *Illustrator Bible*, perhaps hoping for a salacious insight into the publishing world. Sadly, the reason is altogether mundane: I already had a signed contract to write the *Real World* book when IDG Books offered the *Bible* to me. Fortunately for IDG Books Worldwide and the industry at large, a talented first-time author named Ted Alspach stepped in. The result is a fine resource — which, to its credit, has made me work much harder.

The Computer Design Scheme

If your aspirations go beyond image editing into the larger world of computer-assisted design, you'll soon learn that Photoshop is just one cog in a mighty wheel of programs used to create artwork, printed documents, and presentations.

The natural-media paint program Fractal Design Painter emulates real-world tools such as charcoal, chalk, felt-tip markers, calligraphic pen nibs, and camel-hair brushes as deftly as a synthesizer mimics a thunderstorm. Three-dimensional drawing applications such as Infini-D, Strata StudioPro, and Ray Dream Designer enable you to create hyper-realistic objects with depth, lighting, shadows, surface textures, reflections, refractions — you name it. These applications can import images created in Photoshop as well as export images you can then enhance and adjust with Photoshop.

Page-layout programs such as Adobe PageMaker and QuarkXPress let you integrate images into newsletters, reports, books (such as this one), and just about any other kind of document you can imagine. If you prefer to transfer your message to slides, you can use Microsoft PowerPoint to add impact to your images through the use of charts and diagrams.

With Adobe Premiere and After Effects, you can merge images with video sequences recorded in the QuickTime format. You even can edit individual frames in Premiere movies with Photoshop. Macromedia Director makes it possible to combine images with animation, QuickTime movies, and sound to create multimedia presentations you can show on a screen or record on videotape.

Finally, you can publish your images over the World Wide Web. You can code HTML pages in any word processor, or mock up pages in a drag-and-drop editor such as Adobe PageMill or Symantec Visual Page. (If you want my opinion, avoid Microsoft FrontPage like the plague.) You can even integrate images into simple GIF animations using any number of shareware programs available over the Internet. The Web is single-handedly breathing new life and respectability into low-resolution images, as I explore in Chapter 20.

Photoshop Scenarios

All the programs I mentioned above are well-known industry standards. But they also cost money — sometimes lots of money — and they take time to learn. The number of programs you decide to purchase and how you use them is up to you. The following list outlines a few specific ways to use Photoshop alone and in tandem with other products:

✦ After scanning and adjusting an image inside Photoshop, use PageMaker or QuarkXPress to place the image into your monthly newsletter and then print the document from the page-layout program.

✦ After putting the finishing touches on a lovely tropical vista inside Photoshop, import the image for use as an eye-catching background inside PowerPoint. Then save the document as a self-running screen presentation or print it to overhead transparencies or slides from the presentation program.

✦ Capture an on-screen image by pressing ⌘-Shift-3 or using a screen capture utility. Then open the image inside Photoshop. That's how the screens in this book were produced.

✦ If you want to annotate the image, import it into Illustrator or FreeHand, add arrows and labels as desired, and print it from the drawing program.

✦ Paint an original image inside Photoshop using a pressure-sensitive tablet. Use the image as artwork in a document created in a page-layout program, or print it directly from Photoshop.

✦ Snap a photo with a digital camera. As I write this, the best midrange cameras come from Kodak, Olympus, and Epson. Correct the focus and brightness in Photoshop (as explained in Chapters 15 and 18). Then add the photo to your personal Web site or print it out from a color printer.

✦ Scan a surface texture, such as wood or marble, into Photoshop and edit it to create a fluid repeating pattern (as explained in Chapter 10). Import the image for use as a texture map in a three-dimensional drawing program. Render the 3-D graphic to an image file, open the image inside Photoshop, and retouch as needed.

✦ Create a repeating pattern, convert it to the system software's built-in 256-color palette inside Photoshop, and drag and drop it into the Desktop Pictures control panel.

✦ Take a problematic drawing that keeps generating errors and save it as an EPS file. Then open the file inside Photoshop to render it as a high-resolution bitmap. Place the image in a document created in a page-layout program or print it directly from Photoshop.

✦ Start an illustration in a drawing program and save it as an EPS file. Open the file in Photoshop and use the program's unique tools to add textures and tones that are difficult or impossible to create in a vector-based drawing program.

✦ Record a QuickTime movie in Premiere and export it to the FilmStrip format. Open the file inside Photoshop and edit it one frame at a time by drawing on the frame or applying filters. Finally, open the altered FilmStrip file in Premiere and convert it back to the QuickTime format.

Obviously, few folks have the money to buy all these products, and even fewer have the energy or inclination to implement every one of these ideas. But quite honestly, these are just a handful of projects I can list off the top of my head. There must be hundreds of uses for Photoshop that involve no outside applications whatsoever. In fact, so far as I've been able to figure, there's no end to the number of design jobs you can handle in whole or in part using Photoshop.

Photoshop is a versatile and essential product for any designer or artist who owns a personal computer. Simply put, this is the software around which virtually every other computer graphics program revolves. I, for one, wouldn't remove Photoshop from my hard drive for a thousand bucks. (Of course, that's not to say I'm not willing to consider higher offers. For $1,500, I'd gladly swap it to a Jaz cartridge.)

Fast Track to Version 5

If it seems like you've been using Photoshop for the better part of your professional career and you're itching to strap on the new version and ride, the following list explains all. Here I've compiled a few of the most prominent features that are new to Photoshop 5, in rough order of importance. I also point you to the chapter where you can rocket on to more information:

✦ **Multiple undos (Chapter 10):** They said it couldn't be done, but users kept on asking for it. Finally, Adobe gives the gift that keeps on undoing. Photoshop 5 keeps track of your most recent actions in the History palette. You can revert to any previous state in the list merely by clicking on it. Or if you prefer, you can paint back to a previous state with the new history brush. The implementation is nontraditional, but it amounts to the best implementation of multiple undos that I've ever seen. We're not just talking multiple undos, we're talking time travel.

✦ **Editable text layer (Chapter 14):** Text in Photoshop has remained virtually undisturbed since Version 1. You click with the tool, enter type into a dialog box, hit the Enter key, and take what you get. Photoshop 5 still makes you edit type inside a dialog box, but now you can mix typefaces, sizes, and other formatting attributes within a single block. You can also adjust tracking and baseline shift and preview changes in the image window. But best of all, text remains forever editable until you rasterize it. It's a bold new day for type.

✦ **Revised RGB and CMYK color matching (Chapter 6):** Adobe has re-engineered much of the way that Photoshop makes conversions between the basic color spaces. You now identify an RGB source for matching foreign monitors (great for Web folks) and a CMYK destination for printing. These profiles then get embedded into an image when you save it. Color matching is always a tricky business, and the new methods are likely to cause considerable confusion. But if you take the time to calibrate your system properly — as documented at length in Chapter 6 — Photoshop 5's new color matching capabilities rock. (I know, you may hate them now, but you'll come to love them.)

✦ **Spot-color separations (Chapter 7):** Yes, it's true, you can add Pantone and other spot colors to any image, not just duotones. Just add a channel to the image, specify the color and ink solidity, and fill the channel with whatever you deem appropriate. Photoshop 5 not only prints the channel onto a separate plate, but does a decent job of previewing the effect on screen. You can also convert duotones to multichannel images and edit the channels independently.

✦ **DCS 2.0 format support (Chapter 4):** If you can add spot channels to an image, you need to be able to save the result in the DCS 2.0 file for placement into PageMaker or QuarkXPress. True to form, Photoshop 5 does just that, giving you the option of saving a single large file or a separate file for each channel.

✦ **Layer effects (Chapter 13):** Everyone has a way of making drop shadows, but you don't need it anymore. Photoshop 5 automates the creation of a variety of stacking effects, including shadows, glows, and bevels. If you're considering scoffing, don't. These effects are not only well implemented, but they're fully editable from one session to the next. And if you apply one or more effects to a text layer, they update automatically when you edit the text.

✦ **3-D transformation filter (Chapter 16):** Photoshop 5 adds a new filter — Render ➪ 3D Transform — that wraps a selected image around a three-dimensional primitive, such as a cube or sphere. The bad news: You have no control over lighting and it doesn't render the image onto a new layer. The good news: It's fun and even moderately useful when matching 2-D images to 3-D environments.

✦ **Better scripts (Chapter 3):** Adobe has made a series of minor modifications to Photoshop's Actions palette. You can now organize scripts into groups, assign a wider range of keyboard shortcuts, and adjust playback speed. Photoshop 5 also lets you record more operations. It's virtually perfect.

✦ **Magnetic selection tools (Chapter 11):** Photoshop 5 offers two new selection tools that make it a little easier to select complicated images. The magnetic lasso and magnetic pen are designed to automatically snap to the contours of a foreground image. They take a little time to get used to — and they don't always work the way you might hope — but they're wonderful additions to the basic lasso and pen.

✦ **Less guesswork with GIFs (Chapter 20):** You can now preview the effects of the Indexed Color command! Adobe has also improved its color-reduction algorithms a little, but it's the preview that will make a difference in the quality of your Web pages.

✦ **New image saving options (Chapter 4):** Photoshop 5 introduces a handful of new saving options. You can choose whether to save upper or lowercase extensions at the end of file names, which is great for Web designers. When you choose Save a Copy, you can select to dump all nonimage data — including paths, guides, file info, and anything that might balloon the file size. If you're the cross-platform type, you can save a Windows-compatible thumbnail preview with your file. And finally, Photoshop can open and save FlashPix files.

✦ **Improved Hue/Saturation command (Chapter 18):** You now have precise control over the range of colors you want to adjust inside the Hue/Saturation dialog box. You can add and subtract colors by clicking in the image window with an eyedropper, and adjust the "fuzziness" between modified and unmodified colors. Colorization is also handled better. All in all, it's a substantial improvement.

✦ **Freeform path tool (Chapter 11):** Hate drawing paths? Then Photoshop 5 brings glad tidings. The new freeform path tool lets you draw a path as simply as dragging your mouse across the screen.

✦ **Align layers (Chapter 13):** Attention Web designers, you can now align and distribute layers in Photoshop 5. Just link the layers you want to align or distribute and choose the desired command from the Layer menu. The active layer serves as the anchor for the alignment.

✦ **Transform paths and selection outlines (Chapter 11):** In the past, the only way to scale or rotate a path was to transform the entire image. To transform a selection outline independently of its pixels, you had to visit the quick mask mode. Now, you can access path-specific transformation functions under the Edit menu. To transform a selection outline, choose Select ➪ Transform Selection.

✦ **Replay last transformation (Chapter 13):** After transforming a layer, selection, or path, you can apply that exact transformation to another element simply by pressing ⌘-Shift-T. Simple, useful, awesome.

✦ **Automated channel mixing (Chapter 6):** A new command under the Image ➪ Adjust submenu lets you merge the contents of color channels. It's great for fixing problem scans and creating custom RGB-to-grayscale conversions.

✦ **More gradient styles (Chapter 9):** For ages now, you've been able to select between two gradient patterns — linear and radial. Photoshop 5 adds three more — wrap-around, reflected, and diamond.

✦ **Measure tool (Chapter 13):** If you've been measuring images with the line tool set to a weight of 0, you can stop. The measuring tool does the same thing but better, even permitting you to move endpoints after setting the basic line.

✦ **Color sampler (Chapter 5):** Do you find the eyedropper too limiting? Wish you could sample and compare multiple colors at once? Now you can with the new color sample tool. Together with the Info palette you can examine the colors of five regions of an image at the same time.

✦ **Reselect (Chapter 11):** Photoshop now offers a separate undo buffer that holds the most recent selection outline. The upshot is that you can deselect an area, perform a variety of modifications, and then restore the selection several actions later by choosing Select ➪ Reselect. Your selections are now safer than ever before.

✦ **Position the transformation origin (Chapter 13):** Previous versions of Photoshop rotated selections and layers around their centers. Now you can specify the precise origin of a rotation or any other transformation. It's a small precision thing, but some folks (myself included) will really appreciate it.

✦ **Toolbox reorganization (Chapter 2):** As with Photoshop 4, Version 5 is witness to yet another toolbox reorganization. Some tools have new keyboard equivalents. To access the alternative tools, you press Shift along with the key.

✦ **Revised rubber stamp (Chapter 10):** The hall-of-mirrors effect introduced in Photoshop 2.5 is a thing of the past. The rubber stamp now clones like it did in the good old days, which is infinitely better. Tell ya more in Chapter 10.

✦ **Page left, page right (Chapter 2):** It's a relatively little known fact that you can scroll up and down inside an image by pressing the Page Up and Page Down keys. But what about left and right? ⌘-Page Up goes left and ⌘-Page Down goes right.

Photoshop 5 also introduces a new breed of helper plug-in that automates certain kinds of operations and walks you step-by-step through others. Plug-ins that automate tasks appear as commands under the File ⇨ Automate submenu. Step-by-step Wizards appear under the Help menu. I discuss these plug-ins at different stages in the book. If you need help with a specific command, consult the index.

If you have access to a 48-bit drum scanner — which scans 65,000 brightness levels per color channel — then Photoshop 5 provides more reason to rejoice. You can now crop, resample, rotate, filter, and even clone inside 48-bit images with the rubber stamp tool. For most folks, 48-bit color is overkill. But for the very few who need it, Photoshop provides expanded support.

All in all, this is a meaty list of new features. In fact, I don't think I've seen an Adobe upgrade this dramatic since Photoshop 3, and there's *never* been one quite this thorough. Good job, Adobe!

Naturally, that makes my job all the more difficult. (Shame on you, Adobe!) Nonetheless, I've risen to the challenge, making every effort to document the new features with clarity and in their proper context. Just remember to keep an eye peeled for the Photoshop 5 icon and you'll be over the hump and back into the image-editing groove in no time.

✦ ✦ ✦

Inside Photoshop

A First Look at Photoshop 5

These days, most computer applications speak a common graphical language, and Photoshop is no exception. It subscribes to the basic structure of on-screen nouns and verbs proposed and first spoken by the operating system. As a result, Photoshop may seem tolerably comprehensible the first time you meet it. Without any prior knowledge of its origins or behavior, you should be able to pick up a paintbrush and specify a color in a matter of a few seconds, simply based on the rudimentary vocabulary that you've picked up from other programs. After years of staring into cathode ray tubes, you can't help but get the picture.

But Photoshop has its own special dialect, one that differs from every other program out there. The dialect is so distinct that it's only peripherally understood by other applications, including those from Adobe, the very siblings that Photoshop grew up with. Photoshop has its own way of turning a phrase, it speaks its words in a different order than you might expect, and yes, it uses a lot of strange and sometimes unsettling jargon that it has picked up on the street. Photoshop is always and will forever be a foreigner unnaturally introduced to your hard drive. For all you may think you share in common, it doesn't know you and you don't know it.

Even you experienced users — you hearty few who have carried on more conversations with Photoshop than you have with most of your friends and family — may find yourselves stumbling when negotiating with Version 5. The program speaks differently every time it upgrades. In fact, it's wrong to think of Photoshop 5 as an older, wiser version of its former self. This is a completely new beast, bearing about as much resemblance to Photoshop 1.0 as you bear to a fellow human located on the exact opposite end of the earth.

So in this chapter, I introduce to you the Fifth Beast, insubordinate child of its ancestors, spoiler of photographic traditions, and speaker of the new language that you now have to learn. These pages represent a low-level primer you need to ingest before you can utter so much as a coherent "gack!" Granted, it comes to you second hand — I am a non-native myself, with my own peculiar dialect as you'll discover — but given that Photoshop 5 itself is the only native speaker on the planet, this foreigner's perspective will have to do.

See Photoshop Run

Shortly after you launch Photoshop, the splash screen appears. Shown at the top of Figure 2-1, the splash screen explains the launching process by flashing the names of plug-in modules as they load and listing the various initialization procedures.

You can access the splash screen by choosing About Photoshop from the Apple menu. To make the splash screen go away, just click on it.

Splash screen tricks

In a typical program, there isn't much reason to revisit the splash screen. But Photoshop 5 offers a few splash-screen-related tips and tricks:

✦ Press ⌘ while choosing the About Photoshop command, and you display digital photographer Jeff Schewe's top-secret Strange Cargo screen, pictured at the bottom of Figure 2-1.

✦ After a few seconds, the list of programmers and copyright statements at the bottom of the screen starts to scroll. Press the Option key to make the list scroll more quickly.

✦ Photoshop 3 introduced us to Adobe Transient Witticisms — a series of arbitrary gags invented by Photoshop's sleep-deprived, espresso-swilling programmers — and they've been a staple ever since. To see the Witticisms, wait for the credit messages to scroll by one complete cycle. Then click above the words Adobe Photoshop on the standard splash screen, or below the graphic on the Strange Cargo screen.

✦ If you're inclined to dig a little deeper, then Marc Pawliger — my technical editor and one of Photoshop's key developers — provides the following hint: "If you call the cat by name she'll speak to you. Do it again and maybe you'll get a glimpse of her. If you're good, she may even burp for you (but you have to ask)." The trick is knowing the name of the cat. Luckily, it's disclosed in the Adobe Transient Witticisms. Keep your eye peeled for the name of something that has not died. (I guess that rules out Kenny.)

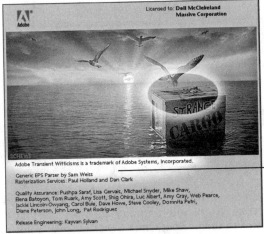

Click here for Witticisms

Figure 2-1: Photoshop 5's splash screens feature genuine Adobe Transient Witticisms and more.

On-line studios resource

Click on the icon at the top of the toolbox to open yet another variation on the splash screen titled Adobe Studios. Pictured in Figure 2-2, this screen provides access to Adobe's Internet-based resources, which include technical support, tips and tricks, and information about upgrades and related products. If you have Internet access, click on a button under the eye to automatically launch your default browser and dial into Adobe's Web site.

Figure 2-2: Adobe offers a series of online support options for Photoshop 5.

To keep the Adobe Studios links up to date, you might want to click on the Refresh button when you first display the screen. (If it gets hung up, dial up your Internet account manually and then return to the Adobe Studios screen and click on Refresh again.) Then click on Refresh every couple of weeks or so to keep the links fresh.

If you work in a corporation or other environment where you have a sustained Internet connection, you can instruct Photoshop to update its links automatically. Just click on the Configure button, and then select Once a Day, Once a Week, or Once a Month from the Refresh pop-up menu. (You can do this as a dial-up user as well, but I for one am not crazy about Photoshop using my modem without my permission.)

The Photoshop Desktop

After the launch process is complete, the Photoshop desktop consumes the foreground. Figure 2-3 shows the Photoshop 5 desktop as it appears when an image is open and all palettes are visible.

Many of the elements that make up the Photoshop desktop are well-known to folks familiar with the Macintosh environment. For example, the menu bar provides access to menus and commands. You can drag the title bar to move the image window. And the scroll bars let you look at hidden portions of the image.

Figure 2-3: The Photoshop 5 desktop as it looks on a 17-inch screen.

Other potentially less familiar elements of the Photoshop desktop work as follows:

✦ **Image window:** Like any halfway decent product, Photoshop lets you open multiple images at a time. Each open image resides inside its own window. Click on the zoom box in the upper right corner of the image window to resize the window to fit the image. Also worth noting are two special boxes in the lower left corner of the image window. The magnification box tells you the current view size, and the preview box lists how much room the image takes up in memory.

For complete information on the magnification box, read the "Navigating in Photoshop" section later in this chapter. I explain the preview box in the very next section.

Cross-Reference

✦ **Toolbox:** The toolbox offers 20 tool icons. The tools are organized into logical groups, starting with the selection tools on top; then the painting and editing tools; the path, type, and fill tools, and the two navigation tools at the bottom. To select a tool, click on its icon. Then use the tool by clicking or dragging with it inside the image window.

The lower third of the toolbox features three sets of controls. The color controls let you change the colors that you paint with; the mask controls let you enter and exit the quick mask mode, and the image window controls let you change the state of the foreground window on the desktop.

✦ **Floating palettes:** Photoshop 5 offers a total of 11 palettes, one up from Version 4. (This number excludes the toolbox, which is technically a palette as well.) Each palette is said to be "floating," which means that it's independent of the image window and of other palettes. Palettes can be grouped together as panels or dragged apart to float separately according to your tastes. Read "The floating palettes" section later in this chapter for more information.

The Preview box

The preview box is Photoshop's way of passing you a memo marked FYI. No biggie, nothing to fret about, just a little bit of info you might want to know. As an unusually obliging piece of software, Photoshop likes to keep its human masters informed on the latest developments.

The document size

By default, the preview box contains two numbers divided by a slash. The first number is the size of the base image in memory. The second number takes into account any additional layers in your image.

Photoshop calculates the first value by multiplying the height and width of the image (both in pixels) by the *bit depth* of the image, which is the size of each pixel in memory. Consider a typical full-color 640 × 480-pixel image. A full-color image takes up 24 bits of memory per pixel (which is why it's called a 24-bit image). There are 8 bits in a byte, so 24 bits translates to 3 bytes. Multiply that by the number of pixels and you get 640 × 480 × 3 = 921,600 bytes. Because there are 1,024 bytes in a kilobyte, 921,600 bytes is exactly 900K. Try it yourself — open a 640 × 480-pixel RGB image and you'll see that the first number in the preview box reads 900K. Now you know why.

But it's the second value, the one that factors in the layers, that represents the real amount of memory that Photoshop needs. If the image contains one layer only, the numbers before and after the slash are the same. Otherwise, Photoshop measures the opaque pixels in each layer and adds approximately 1 byte of overhead per pixel to calculate the transparency. The second number also grows to accommodate paths, masks, spot-color channels, undoable operations, and miscellaneous data required by the image cache.

Now obviously, it's not necessary that you be able to predict these values (which is lucky, because predicting the second value is virtually impossible). Photoshop asks no help when calculating the values in the preview box, and any help you might care to offer will be summarily ignored. But it's a good idea to know what's going on as you start piling layers on top of an image. The larger the preview numbers grow, the more work Photoshop has to do and the slower it's likely to perform.

Image position

Click and hold on the preview box to display a pop-up window that shows the position of the image on the printed page. The preview also shows the approximate placement of crop marks and other elements requested in the Page Setup dialog box (File ➪ Page Setup).

Press Option and mouse down on the preview box to view the size and resolution of the image.

You can also ⌘-click the preview box to see the tile sizes. Photoshop uses *tiles* to calculate pixel manipulations. If you confine your work to a single tile, it will probably go faster than if you slop a little over into a second tile. But who cares? Unless you're some kind of tile-reading robot, this technical information is rarely of any practical use.

Click the right-pointing arrowhead next to the preview box to display a pop-up menu of five options. The first option — Document Sizes — is selected by default. This option displays the image size values described in the previous section.

The prefix displayed before the values in the preview box indicates which of the options is active: Doc shows that Document Sizes is selected; Scr, Scratch Sizes, and Eff, Efficiency. When the Timing option is active, an *s* appears after the numerical value. If a tool name appears in the preview box, you know the final option, Current Tool, is active.

The following sections explain how the three remaining options work.

Memory consumption and availability

When you select Scratch Sizes, Photoshop changes the values in the preview box to represent memory consumption and availability. The first value is the amount of room required to hold the currently open images in RAM. The second value indicates the total amount of RAM that Photoshop has to work with. For the program to run at top efficiency, the first number must be smaller than the second.

In the old days, the number before the slash was generally equal to between 3 and 5 times the size of all open images, including layers. But thanks to the advent of multiple undos, this value can grow to more than 100 times as big as any one image. This is because Photoshop has to store each operation in memory on the off chance that you may want to undo to a previous point in time. For each and every action, Photoshop nudges the first value upward until you reach the ceiling of undoable operations.

The second value is simply equal to the amount of memory available to your images after the Photoshop application itself has loaded. For example, suppose you've assigned 100MB of RAM to Photoshop. The code that makes up the Photoshop application consumes about 15MB, so that leaves 85MB to hold and edit images.

If the second value is bigger than the first, then all is happiness and Photoshop is running as fast as your particular brand of computer will permit. But if the first value is larger, Photoshop has to dig into its supply of *virtual memory*, a disk-bound adjunct to RAM. Virtual memory makes Photoshop run more slowly because the program must swap portions of the image on and off your hard disk. The simple fact is, disks have moving parts and RAM does not. That means disk-bound "virtual" memory is slower than real memory.

To increase the size of the value after the slash, you have to get more RAM to your images in one of the following ways:

✦ Purchase more RAM and install it in your computer. The fact that an adequate supply of memory is the single best way to make Photoshop run more quickly makes RAM a very good long-term investment.

✦ Quit other applications so that only Photoshop is running.

✦ Quit Photoshop and remove any filters that you don't need from the Plug-Ins folder (which resides in the same folder as the Photoshop 5 application). Don't throw the filters away, just move them to a location outside the Plug-Ins folder so they won't load into RAM when you launch Photoshop.

✦ Quit Photoshop. Then select the Photoshop application icon at the Finder desktop level, press ⌘-I, and raise the Preferred Size value.

For more information on getting Photoshop to run at top form on your computer, read Appendix A.

Operating efficiency

When you select the Efficiency option, Photoshop lists the amount of time it spends running operations in RAM compared with swapping data back and forth between the hard disk. A value of 100 percent is the best-case scenario. It means Photoshop never has to rely on virtual memory. Low values indicate higher reliance on the hard disk and, as a result, slower operations. Adobe recommends that if the value falls below 75 percent, you should either assign more memory to Photoshop or purchase more RAM for your computer.

The Efficiency option is a reality check. If it seems Photoshop is dragging its feet, and you hear it writing a little too often, you can refer to the Efficiency rating to see if things are as bad as you suspect. Keep in mind, hearing Photoshop occasionally write to disk is not, in and of itself, cause for concern. All versions of Photoshop since 3.0 automatically copy open images to a disk buffer in case virtual memory is later warranted. In fact, this is the reason Adobe added the Efficiency option to Version 3.0.1 — to quash fears that a few sparks from your hard drive indicated anything less than peak performance.

Clocking Photoshop

If you select Timing, the preview box tells how long Photoshop took to perform the last operation (including background tasks, such as transferring an image to the system Clipboard). Adobe may have added this option to help testing facilities run their Photoshop tests. But built-in timing helps you as well.

For example, suppose you're trying to decide whether to purchase a new computer. You read a magazine article comparing the newest super-fast system. You can run the same filters with the same settings on your computer and see how much slower your results are, all without picking up a stopwatch.

At the risk of starting interoffice feuding, the Timing option also provides you with a mechanism for testing your computer against those of coworkers and friends. The Timing option serves as a neutral arbitrator, enabling you and an associate to test identical operations over the phone. Like Efficiency, Timing is a reality check. If you and your associate own similarly configured computers and your Timing values are vastly different, something's wrong.

The active tool

The final option — Current Tool — is new to Photoshop 5. It merely tells you which tool you've selected from the toolbox. Why do you need such a condescending option? Surely you're not so far gone that you need Photoshop telling you what you already know! Adobe's intention is not to drum you over the head with redundant information, but rather to offer you a helping hand if you find the new tool configuration confusing. Also, if you use multiple monitors and you keep the toolbox on the second monitor, the Current Tool helps keep you apprised of current events.

Still, my guess is that this option will prove as rarely useful to everyday image editing as Timing. Use it if you're having problems when first using Photoshop 5, then set it back to Document Sizes, Scratch Sizes, or Efficiency. The original three continue to be the best.

The tools

The new Photoshop 5 toolbox shows only 20 of its 46 tools at any one time. The other tools are hidden inside pop-up menus. Any tool icon that includes a tiny right-pointing triangle harbors a pop-up menu with one or more alternate tools. As demonstrated in Figure 2-4, just drag on a tool to display the pop-up menu.

You can also Option-click a tool icon to switch to the next tool in the pop-up menu.

Figure 2-4: Drag from any tool icon
with a triangle to display a pop-up
menu of alternates.

Also, when you hover your cursor over a tool, Photoshop tells you the name of the
tool and how to select it from the keyboard. I explain more about keyboard
shortcuts in Chapter 3.

If you find the tool tips irritating, you can turn them off using File ⇨ Preferences ⇨
General (⌘-K). I explain more about this and other preference settings in the
"General preferences" section later in this chapter.

If you're familiar with Photoshop 4, you may notice that several tool icons have
moved to new places in the toolbox. Version 5 also adds 13 new tools — a 40
percent increase over the previous version. But these are largely cosmetic
changes — the new tools are mostly variations on the old and the old tools work
just as they did in Photoshop 4. The magnetic selection tools and the history
brush might be a little challenging the first few times you use them, but otherwise
the new tools are a breeze.

I've catalogued each tool in the following lengthy list, with tool icons, pithy
summaries, and the chapter to which you can refer for more information. No need
to read the list word for word; just use it as a reference to get acquainted with the
new program. Incidentally, unless otherwise noted, each of the following
descriptions tells how to use the tool inside the image window. For example, if an
item says drag, you click the tool's icon to select the tool, and then drag in the
image window; you don't drag on the tool icon itself.

Rectangular marquee (Chapter 11): Drag with this tool to enclose a portion of the image in a rectangular marquee, which is a pattern of moving dash marks indicating the boundary of a selection.

Shift-drag to add to a selection; Option-drag to delete from a selection. The same goes for the other marquee tools, as well as the lassos and magic wand.

Elliptical marquee (Chapter 11): Drag with the elliptical marquee tool to enclose a portion of the window in an oval marquee.

Single-row marquee (Chapter 11): Click with the single-row marquee to select an entire horizontal row of pixels that stretches all the way across the image. You can also drag with the tool to position the selection. You'll rarely need it, but when you do, here it is.

Single-column marquee (Chapter 11): Same as the single-row marquee, except the single-column marquee selects an entire vertical column of pixels. Again, not a particularly useful tool.

Crop (Chapter 4): Drag with the crop tool to enclose the portion of the image you want to retain in a rectangular boundary. The crop boundary sports several square handles you can drag to resize the cropped area. Drag outside the boundary to rotate it; drag inside to move it. Press Return to apply the crop or Escape to cancel.

Move (Chapter 11): Drag to move a selection or layer. In fact, the move tool is the exclusive means for moving and cloning portions of an image. (You can also ⌘-drag selections with other tools, but only because ⌘ temporarily accesses the move tool.)

Lasso (Chapter 11): Drag with the lasso tool to select a free-form portion of the image. You can also Option-click with the lasso to create a straight-sided selection outline.

Polygonal lasso (Chapter 11): Click hither and yon with this tool to draw a straight-sided selection outline (just like Option-clicking with the standard lasso). Each click sets a corner point in the selection.

Magnetic lasso (Chapter 11): As you drag with the magnetic lasso tool, the selection outline automatically sticks to the edge of the foreground image. Bear in mind, however, that Photoshop's idea of an edge may not jibe with yours. Like any automated tool, the magnetic lasso sometimes works wonders, other times it's more trouble than it's worth.

The magnetic lasso automatically lays down points as you drag. If you don't like a point and you want to get rid of it, press the Delete key.

Magic wand (Chapter 11): Click with the magic wand tool to select a contiguous area of similarly colored pixels. To select discontiguous areas, click in one area and then Shift-click in another.

Airbrush (Chapter 8): Drag with the airbrush tool to spray diffused strokes of color that blend into the image, just the thing for creating shadows and highlights.

Tip

Paintbrush (Chapter 8): Drag with the paintbrush tool to paint soft lines, which aren't as jagged as those created with the pencil, but aren't as fluffy as those created with the airbrush.

Rubber stamp (Chapter 10): The rubber stamp tool copies one portion of the image onto another. Option-click the part of your image you want to clone, and then drag to clone that area to another portion of the image.

Pattern stamp (Chapter 10): In previous versions of Photoshop, the rubber stamp tool let you paint with a pattern. Now this job falls to a new tool called the pattern stamp. Define a pattern using Edit ➪ Define Pattern, then paint away.

History brush (Chapter 9): Remember how you used to be able to revert an image to its saved or snapshot appearance using the rubber stamp? Well, no more. Now you have a dedicated history brush that reverts the image to any of a handful of previous states throughout the recent history of the image. To specify the state that you want to revert to, click in the first column of the History palette. It's like an undo brush, except way, way better.

Eraser (Chapter 10): Drag with the eraser tool to paint in the background color or erase areas in a layer to reveal the layers below. Option-drag to access the "magic" eraser, which reverts the image to a previous state just like the history brush.

Four styles of erasers exist in all—paintbrush, airbrush, pencil, and square (called "block"). You can cycle through them by Option-clicking the eraser tool icon in the toolbox.

Pencil (Chapter 8): Drag with the pencil tool to paint jagged, hard-edged lines. It's main purpose is to clean up individual pixels when you're feeling fussy.

Line (Chapter 9): Drag with the line tool to create a straight line. Click the Start or End option in the Line Tool Options palette to add arrowheads.

Blur (Chapter 8): Drag with the blur tool to diffuse the contrast between neighboring pixels, which blurs the focus of the image. You can also Option-drag to sharpen the image.

Sharpen (Chapter 8): Drag with this tool to increase the contrast between pixels, which sharpens the focus. Option-drag when this tool is active to blur the image.

Smudge (Chapter 8): The smudge tool has moved to a subordinate position in Photoshop 5, but it still works the same. Just drag with the tool to smear colors inside the image.

Dodge (Chapter 8): Drag with the dodge tool to lighten pixels in the image. Option-drag to darken the image.

Burn (Chapter 8): Drag with the burn tool to darken pixels. Press Option to temporarily access the dodge tool and lighten pixels.

Sponge (Chapter 8): Drag with the sponge tool to decrease the amount of saturation in an image so the colors appear more drab, and eventually gray. You can also increase color saturation by changing the setting in the Sponge Options palette from Desaturate to Saturate.

Pen (Chapter 11): Click and drag with the pen tool to set points in the image window. Photoshop draws an editable path outline — much like a path in Illustrator — that you can convert to a selection outline or stroke with color.

Magnetic pen (Chapter 11): The magnetic pen tool works just like the magnetic lasso. You drag along the edge of an image and Photoshop automatically adjusts the selection outline to fit that edge. The only difference is that the magnetic pen results in an editable path.

Freeform pen (Chapter 11): Photoshop 5 now lets you draw freehand paths just by dragging with this tool. It's easy, it works, and it's about time.

Insert point (Chapter 11): Click a segment with this tool to insert a point in the path.

Remove point (Chapter 11): Click a point to remove the point without interrupting the outline of the path. Photoshop automatically draws a new segment between the neighboring points.

Direct selection (Chapter 11): I like to call this the *arrow tool* because it looks like an arrow and the word *arrow* requires less typing. But whatever you call it, you use this tool to edit a path drawn with one of the pens. You can drag points or control handles. Or Option-click on a path to select all its points and move the path as a whole.

Convert point (Chapter 11): Points in a path come in different varieties, some indicating corners and others indicating smooth arcs. The convert point tool enables you to change one kind of point to another. Drag a point to convert it from a corner to an arc. Click on a point to convert it from an arc to a sharp corner.

Type (Chapter 14): Click with the type tool to display the updated Type Tool dialog box, which is where you enter and format text. Note: You can't use the type tool to edit existing text as you would in a page-layout or drawing program; it's for type creation only.

Photoshop 5 creates editable type on a special kind of layer. To edit the type, just double-click on the type in the Layers palette and Photoshop redisplays the Type Tool dialog box. Then you can edit the type or change its formatting. Very cool.

Type mask (Chapter 14): As with the standard type tool, clicking with the type mask tool brings up the Type Tool dialog box. But when you exit the dialog box, Photoshop draws the letters as transparent selection outlines. If you don't want to add a new layer, this is the type tool to use.

Vertical type (Chapter 14): Want to create type that reads from top to bottom, the Japanese way? Then this is the tool to use. It's really just a way of creating consistency between regionalized Western and Eastern versions of Photoshop, but it may very well come in handy.

Vertical type mask (Chapter 14): This tool works just like the type mask tool, except that the letter outlines are arranged in vertical columns.

Measure (Chapter 13): The new measure tool lets you measure distances and directions inside the image window. Just drag from one point to another and note the measurement data in the Info palette. You can also drag the endpoints or your line to take new measurements.

Gradient (Chapter 9): Drag with this tool to fill a selection with a gradual transition of colors, commonly called a *gradient*. In Photoshop 5, the gradient tool creates linear gradients only. Use one of the other gradient tools to access a different style.

Radial Gradient (Chapter 9): The first of four new gradient style tools, the radial gradient creates spotlight transitions, starting from the center and flowing outward in concentric circles to the perimeter of the selection.

Angle Gradient (Chapter 9): This tool creates a wrap-around gradient that looks something like a cone viewed from above (which is why this style is more commonly called a *conical gradient*). It works best with gradients that begin and end with the same color.

Reflected Gradient (Chapter 9): Drag with this tool to create a linear gradient that begins and ends with the same color. Too bad you can't combine this tool with the angle gradient tool.

Diamond Gradient (Chapter 9): A diamond gradient is like a radial gradient, but instead of filling a selection with concentric circles of color, it fills with concentric diamonds.

Paint bucket (Chapter 9): Click with the paint bucket tool to fill a contiguous area of similarly colored pixels with the foreground color or a predefined pattern.

Eyedropper (Chapter 5): Click with the eyedropper tool on a color in the image window to make that color the foreground color. Option-click on a color to make that color the background color.

Color sampler (Chapter 5): Click on as many as four pixels in an image to evaluate the colors of those pixels in the Info palette. After you set a point, you can move it by dragging it to a different pixel.

Hand (Chapter 2): Drag inside the image window with the hand tool to scroll the window so you can see a different portion of the image. Double-click the hand tool icon to magnify or reduce the image so it fits on the screen in its entirety.

Zoom (Chapter 2): Click with the zoom tool to magnify the image so you can see individual pixels more clearly. Option-click to step back from the image and take in a broader view. Drag to enclose the specific portion of the image you want to magnify. And, finally, double-click the zoom tool icon inside the toolbox to restore the image to 100 percent view size.

Tip

You can modify the performance of any tool by adjusting the settings in the Options palette. To display this palette, double-click the tool icon in the toolbox. Or, just press the Return key when the tool is active. Only a handful of tools including the type, measure, and hand tools lack palette options.

The toolbox controls

Well, that pretty much wraps it up for the 46 tools. It was a breathtakingly dull tale, but one that had to be told. But the excitement isn't over yet. Gather the kittens and hold onto your mittens as we explore the nine controls that grace the lower portion of the toolbox:

Foreground color: Click on the foreground color icon to bring up the Color Picker dialog box. Select a color and press Return to change the foreground color, which is used by the pencil, paintbrush, airbrush, and gradient tools.

Note

I'm not sure why, but many users make the mistake of double-clicking the foreground or background color icons when they first start using Photoshop. A single click is all that's needed. Experienced users don't even do that — they stick to the more convenient Color palette.

Background color: Click on the background color icon to display the Color Picker and change the background color, which is used by the eraser and gradient tools. Photoshop also uses the background color to fill a selected area on the background layer when you press the Delete key.

Switch colors: Click on the switch colors icon to exchange the foreground and background colors.

Default colors: Click on this icon to change the foreground color automatically to black and the background color to white.

Tip

At any time, you can quickly make the foreground color white by clicking on the default colors icon and then clicking on the switch colors icon.

Marching ants: Click this icon to exit Photoshop's quick mask mode and view selection outlines as animated dotted lines that look like marching ants, hence the name. (Adobe calls this the "standard" mode, but I think marching ants mode better describes how it works.)

Quick mask: Click here to enter the quick mask mode, which allows you to edit selection boundaries using painting tools. The marching ants vanish and the image appears half covered by a translucent layer of red, like a rubylith in traditional paste-up. The red layer covers the deselected—or masked—portions of the image. Paint with black to extend the masked areas, thereby subtracting from the selection. Paint with white to erase the mask, thereby adding to the selection.

The quick mask mode is too complex a topic to sum up in a few sentences. If you can't wait to find out what it's all about, check out Chapter 12.

Standard window: Click this icon to display the foreground image in a standard window, as shown earlier in Figure 2-3. Every image appears in the standard window mode when you first open it.

Full screen with menu bar: If you can't see enough of your image inside a standard window, click this icon. The title bar and scroll bars disappear, as do all background windows, but the menu bar and palettes remain visible, as shown in Figure 2-5. (You can still access other open images by choosing their names from the Window menu.) A light gray background fills any empty area around the image.

By default, the empty area outside an image is shown as gray when working in either the standard window or full screen with menu bar modes. To change it to a different color—such as black—select a color and Shift-click in the gray area with the paint bucket tool.

Absolute full screen: If you still can't see enough of your image, click on the rightmost of the image window controls to see the photo set against a neutral black background. (You can't change the color of this backdrop—it's always black.) The menu bar disappears, limiting your access to commands, but you can still access many commands using keyboard shortcuts. Only the toolbox and palettes remain visible.

If you need access to a menu command when working in the absolute full screen mode, press Shift-F to display the menu bar. Press Shift-F again to hide it.

If Photoshop's screen elements get in the way of seeing an image, you can hide all palettes—including the toolbox—by pressing the Tab key. To bring the toolbox back into view, press Tab again.

You can hide the palettes but leave the toolbox up on screen by pressing Shift-Tab. Press Shift-Tab again to bring the palettes back. (Pressing Tab while the palettes are gone hides the toolbox.)

Figure 2-5: Click on the middle icon at the bottom of the toolbox to hide the title bar and scroll bars.

The floating palettes

You can count on Photoshop's palettes to change in subtle but disquieting ways from one version to the next. Still, the palettes include a core of basic elements that ensure their long-term service and reliability. For example, each palette offers most or all of the elements labeled in Figure 2-6, just as it has since Version 3. Some palettes lack scroll bars, others lack size boxes, but that's just to keep you from getting too stodgy.

Many palette elements are miniature versions of the elements that accompany any window. For example, the close button and title bar work identically to their image-window counterparts. The title bar lacks a title—I have a lobbyist in Washington working on getting the name changed to "untitled bar" as we speak—but you can still drag it to move the palette to a different location on screen.

Tip

Photoshop automatically snaps palettes into alignment with other palettes. To snap a palette to the edge of the screen, Shift-click its title bar. You can also Shift-drag the title bar to move the palette around the perimeter of the screen, or to snap the palette from one edge of the screen to the other. (This tip also works with the toolbox.)

Figure 2-6: Most palettes include the same basic elements as the Brushes palette, shown here.

Four elements are unique to floating palettes:

✦ **Palette options:** Each floating palette offers its own collection of options. These options may include tools, icons, pop-up menus, slider bars, you name it.

✦ **Palette menu:** Click the right-pointing arrowhead icon to display a menu of commands specific to the palette. These commands enable you to manipulate the palette options and adjust preference settings.

✦ **Panel tabs:** Click on a panel tab to switch from one panel to another inside a palette. (You can also switch panels by selecting the palette commands from the Window menu, but it's more convenient to click a tab.)

✦ **Collapse button:** Click on the collapse button to decrease the amount of space consumed by the palette. If you previously enlarged the palette by dragging the size box, your first click reduces the palette back to its default size. After that, clicking the collapse button hides all but the most essential palette options.

In most cases, collapsing a palette hides all options and leaves only the panel tabs visible. But in the case of the Options, Color, and Layers palettes, clicking the collapse button leaves a sliver of palette options intact, as demonstrated in the middle example of Figure 2-7. To eliminate all options for these panels — as in the last example — Option-click the collapse button. You can also double-click one of the panel tabs or in the empty area to the right of the tabs. These tricks work even if you've enlarged the palette by dragging the size box.

Click here

Option-click here
or double-click here

Figure 2-7: The Options palette shown at full size (top), partially collapsed (middle), and fully collapsed (bottom)

Tabbing through the options

I mentioned earlier that you can hide the palettes by pressing Shift-Tab and hide both palettes and toolbox by pressing Tab. But this keyboard trick doesn't work if an option box is active.

For example, suppose you click inside the R option box in the Color palette. This activates the option. Now press Tab. Rather than hiding the palettes, Photoshop advances you to the next option box in the palette, G. To move backward through the options, press Shift-Tab.

To apply an option box value and return focus to the image window, press Return. This deactivates the palette options. If an option box remains active, certain keyboard tricks — such as pressing a key to select a tool — won't work properly. Photoshop either ignores the shortcut or beeps at you for pressing a key the option box doesn't like. For more information on shortcuts, read Chapter 3.

Tip

You can also return focus to the palette options from the keyboard. When you press Return, Photoshop displays the Options palette for the active tool. Assuming the Options palette for that tool offers an option box, Photoshop highlights the contents of the option box. You can then tab around to reach the option you want to change, enter a new value, and press Return to get out.

Shuffling panels

Photoshop enables you to separate and group panels into palettes as you see fit. To separate a panel into its own palette, drag the panel tab away from the palette, as demonstrated in the left example in Figure 2-8. To combine a panel with a different palette, drag the panel tab onto the palette so the palette becomes highlighted, and then release. The middle and right examples in the figure show off this technique.

Figure 2-8: Dragging a panel off a palette (left) results in a new panel (middle). Dragging a panel onto another palette (middle) adds that panel to the palette (right).

If you use Illustrator, you've probably gone nuts combining palettes together using "docking." Unfortunately, you can't dock in Photoshop. Rats!

Tip   If you ever completely muck up the palettes — or a palette somehow gets stuck under the menu bar — press ⌘-K and click on the Reset Palette Locations to Default button in the Preferences dialog box. For more information, read the "General preferences" section later in this chapter.

Navigating in Photoshop

All graphics and desktop publishing programs provide a variety of navigational tools and functions that enable you to scoot around the screen, visit the heartlands and nether regions, examine the fine details, and take in the big picture. And Photoshop is no exception. In fact, Photoshop's navigation tools would make Magellan drool (were he inclined to edit an image or two).

The view size

You can change the view size—the size at which an image appears on screen—so you can either see more of an image or concentrate on individual pixels. Each change in view size is expressed as a zoom ratio, which is the ratio between screen pixels and image pixels. Photoshop displays the zoom ratio as a percentage value in the title bar. The 100 percent zoom ratio shows one image pixel for each screen pixel (and is therefore equivalent to the old 1:1 zoom ratio in Photoshop 3 and earlier). A 200 percent zoom ratio doubles the size of the image pixels on screen, and so on.

Actual pixels

Photoshop calls the 100 percent zoom ratio the *actual-pixels* view. This is the most accurate view size because you can see the image as it really is. Reduced view sizes drop pixels; magnified view sizes stretch pixels. Only the actual-pixels view displays each pixel without a trace of screen distortion.

You can switch to this most accurate of view sizes at any time using one of the following techniques:

✦ Choose View ➪ Actual Pixels.

✦ Press ⌘-Option-0. (That's a zero, not the letter O.)

✦ Double-click the zoom tool icon in the toolbox.

Fit on screen

When you first open an image, Photoshop displays it at the largest zoom ratio (up to 100 percent) that permits the entire image to fit on screen. Assuming you don't change the size of the image, you can return to this "fit-on-screen" view size in one of the following ways:

✦ Choose View ➪ Fit on Screen.

✦ Press ⌘-0.

✦ Double-click the hand tool icon in the toolbox.

Strangely, any of these techniques may magnify the image beyond the 100 percent view size. When working on a very small image, for example, Photoshop enlarges the image to fill the screen, even if this means maxing out the zoom to 1,600 percent. Personally, I prefer to use the fit-on-screen view only when working on very large images.

Well, actually, I almost never use the fit-on-screen view because it's too arbitrary. Photoshop does the best job of previewing an image when you can see all pixels— that is, 100 percent view size. Short of that, you want the screen pixels to divide evenly into the image pixels. This means view sizes like 50 percent or 25 percent, but not 75 percent or 66.7 percent. And you never know what it's going to be with the fit-on-screen view.

Print size

You can switch to yet another predefined view size by choosing View ➪ Print Size. New to Photoshop, this command displays the image on screen at the size it will print. (You set the print size using Image ➪ Image Size, as I explain in Chapter 4.)

That's the theory, anyway. In practice, the "print-size" view isn't particularly reliable. Photoshop assumes your monitor displays exactly 72 pixels per inch. Although this is the commonly accepted Macintosh screen resolution, in reality it's pure nonsense. Monitor resolutions vary all over the map. And high-end monitors let you change screen resolutions without Photoshop even noticing.

The long and the short is this: Don't expect to hold up your printed image and have it exactly match the print-size view on screen. It's a rough approximation, designed to show you how the image will look when imported into QuarkXPress, PageMaker, or some other publishing program — nothing more.

The zoom tool

Obviously, the aforementioned zoom ratios aren't the only ones available to you. You can zoom in as close as 1,600 percent and zoom out to 0.2 percent.

The easiest way to zoom in and out of your image is to use the zoom tool:

✦ Click in the image window with the zoom tool to magnify the image in preset increments — from 33.33 percent to 50 to 66.67 to 100 to 200 and so on. Photoshop tries to center the zoomed view at the point where you clicked (or come as close as possible).

✦ Option-click with the zoom tool to reduce the image incrementally — 200 to 100 to 66.67 to 50 to 33.33 and so on. Again, Photoshop tries to center the new view on the click point.

Drag with the zoom tool to draw a rectangular marquee around the portion of the image you want to magnify. Photoshop magnifies the image so the marqueed area fits just inside the image window. (If the horizontal and vertical proportions of the marquee do not match those of your screen — for example, if you draw a tall, thin marquee or a really short, wide one — Photoshop favors the smaller of the two possible zoom ratios to avoid hiding any detail inside the marquee.)

✦ If you like, you can instruct Photoshop to resize the window when you click with the zoom tool. Press Return when the zoom tool is active to display the Zoom Options palette, then select the Resize Windows to Fit check box.

To access the zoom tool temporarily when some other tool is selected, press and hold the ⌘ and spacebar keys. Release both keys to return control of the cursor to the selected tool. To access the zoom out cursor, press Option with the spacebar. These keyboard equivalents work from inside many dialog boxes, enabling you to modify the view of an image while applying a filter or color correction.

The zoom commands

You can also zoom in and out using the following commands and keyboard shortcuts:

✦ Choose View ➪ Zoom In or press ⌘-plus (+) to zoom in. This command works exactly like clicking with the zoom tool except you can't specify the center of the new view size. Photoshop merely centers the zoom in keeping with the previous view size.

✦ Choose View ➪ Zoom Out or press ⌘-minus (–) to zoom out.

Photoshop's Zoom commands resize the window as they magnify. To override this, throw in the Option key. Press ⌘-Option-plus to zoom in without resizing the window; press ⌘-Option-minus to zoom out without resizing the window.

If you want to swap the performance of the zoom shortcut keys — so ⌘-plus and minus no longer resize the window and ⌘-Option-plus and minus do — install the Swap Zoom Key extension plug-in found on the Photoshop CD.

The Magnification box

Another way to zoom in and out without changing the window size is to enter a value into the magnification box, located in the lower-left corner of the Photoshop window. Select the magnification value, enter a new one, and press Return. Photoshop zooms the view without zooming the window.

In Figure 2-9, I started with a specially sized window at actual-pixels view. I then entered two different zoom ratios into the magnification box — 156.7 percent and 60.4 percent — alternately enlarging and reducing the image within the confines of a static window.

You might like to know several other things about the magnification box:

✦ You can enter values in the magnification box as percentages, ratios, or "times" values. To switch to a zoom value of 250 percent, for example, you can enter *250%*, *5:2*, or *2.5x*.

✦ You can specify a zoom value in increments as small as .01 percent. So if a zoom value of 250.01 doesn't quite suit your fancy, you can try 250.02. I seriously doubt you'll need this kind of precision, but isn't it great to know it's there?

When you press Return after entering a magnification value, Photoshop changes the view size and returns focus to the image window. If you aren't exactly certain what zoom ratio you want to use, press Shift-Return instead. This changes the view size while keeping the magnification value active; this way you can enter a new value and try again.

Figure 2-9: To zoom an image without changing the window size, enter a zoom ratio into the Magnification box and press Return.

Magnification box

Creating a reference window

In the ancient days, paint programs provided a cropped view of your image at the actual-pixels view size to serve as a reference when you worked in a magnified view. Because it's so doggone modern, Photoshop does not, but you can easily create a second view of your image by choosing View ➪ New View, as in Figure 2-10. Use one window to maintain a 100 percent view of your image while you zoom and edit inside the other window. Both windows track the changes to the image.

Figure 2-10: You can create multiple windows to track the changes made to a single image by choosing the New View command from the View menu.

Scrolling inside the window

In the standard window mode, you have access to scroll bars, just as you do in just about every other major application. But as you become more proficient with Photoshop, you'll use the scroll bars less and less. One way to bypass the scroll bars is to use the keyboard equivalents listed in Table 2-1. If you're using a computer without an extended keyboard — such as a PowerBook — try out the Control key equivalents in the third column.

Table 2-1		
Scrolling from the Keyboard		
Scrolling Action	**Extended Keyboard**	**Other Keyboard**
Up one screen	Page Up	Control-K
Up slightly	Shift-Page Up	Control-Shift-K
Down one screen	Page Down	Control-L
Down slightly	Shift-Page Down	Control-Shift-L

(continued)

Table 2-1 *(continued)*		
Scrolling Action	**Extended Keyboard**	**Other Keyboard**
Left one screen *	⌘-Page Up	⌘-Control-K
Left slightly *	⌘-Shift-Page Up	⌘-Control-Shift-K
Right one screen *	⌘-Page Down	⌘-Control-L
Right slightly *	⌘-Shift-Page Down	⌘-Control-Shift-L
To upper left corner	Home	Control-A
To lower right corner	End	Control-D

* Indicates shortcuts that are new to Photoshop 5.

I've heard tales of artists who use the Page Up and Page Down shortcuts to comb through very large images at 100 percent view size. This way, they can make sure all their pixels are in order before going to print.

Personally, however, I don't use the Page key tricks very often. I'm the kind of merry lad who prefers to scroll by hand. Armed with the grabber hand — as old timers call it — you can yank an image and pull it in any direction you choose. A good grabber hand is better than a scroll bar any day.

To access the hand tool temporarily when some other tool is selected, press and hold the spacebar. Releasing the spacebar returns the cursor to its original appearance. This keyboard equivalent even works from inside many dialog boxes.

The Navigator palette

I saved the best for last. Shown in Figure 2-11, the Navigator palette is the best thing to happen to zooming and scrolling since Photoshop was first introduced. If you routinely work on large images that extend beyond the confines of your relatively tiny screen, you'll want to get up and running with this palette as soon as possible.

If the Navigator palette isn't visible, choose Window ➪ Show Navigator. You can then use the palette options as follows:

✦ **View box:** Drag the view box inside the image thumbnail to reveal some hidden portion of the photograph. Photoshop dynamically tracks your adjustments in the image window. Isn't it great?

But wait, it gets better. Press ⌘ to get a zoom cursor in the Navigator palette. Then ⌘- drag to resize the view box and zoom the photo in the image window.

You can also Shift-drag to constrain dragging the view box to only horizontal or vertical movement.

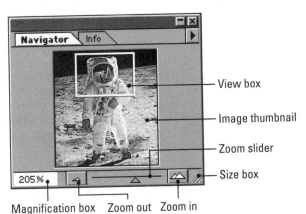

Figure 2-11: The Navigator palette is the best thing to happen to zooming and scrolling since Photoshop 1.0.

✦ **Box color:** You can change the color of the view box by choosing the Palette Options command from the palette menu. My favorite setting is yellow, but it ultimately depends on the colors in your image. Ideally, you want something that stands out. To lift a color from the image itself, move the cursor outside the dialog box and click in the image window with the eyedropper.

✦ **Magnification box:** This value works like the one in the lower-left corner of the image window. Just enter a new zoom ratio and press Enter.

✦ **Zoom out:** Click the zoom out button to reduce the view size in the same predefined increments as the zoom tool. The difference is this button doesn't alter the size of the image window. So it works like the zoom tool used to work.

✦ **Zoom slider:** Give the slider triangle a yank and see where it takes you. Drag to the left to zoom out, drag right to zoom in. Again, Photoshop dynamically tracks your changes in the image window. Dang, it's nice to zoom on the fly.

✦ **Zoom in:** Click the big mountains to magnify incrementally the view of the image without altering the window size.

✦ **Size box:** If you have a large monitor, you don't have to settle for that teeny thumbnail of the image. Drag the size box to enlarge both palette and thumbnail to a more reasonable size.

Customizing the Interface

Every program gives you access to a few core settings so you can modify the program to suit your personal needs. These settings are known far and wide as *preferences*. Photoshop ships with certain recommended preference settings already in force — known coast-to-coast as *factory defaults* — but just because these settings are recommended doesn't mean they're right. In fact, I disagree with quite a few of them. But why quibble when you can change the preferences according to your merest whim?

You can modify preference settings in two ways: You can make environmental adjustments using File ➪ Preferences ➪ General, or you can change the operation of specific tools by adjusting settings in the Options palette. Photoshop remembers environmental preferences, tool settings, and even the file format under which you saved the last image by storing this information to a file called Adobe Photoshop 5 Prefs in the Adobe Photoshop Settings folder inside the same folder that contains the Photoshop application.

To restore Photoshop's factory default settings, delete the Adobe Photoshop 5 Prefs file when the application is *not* running. The next time you launch Photoshop, it creates a new preferences file automatically.

Deleting the preferences file is also a good idea if Photoshop starts acting funny. Photoshop's preferences file has always been highly susceptible to corruption, possibly because the application writes to it so often. Whatever the reason, if Photoshop starts behaving erratically, quit the program, delete the Adobe Photoshop 5 Prefs file, and relaunch Photoshop. You'll have to reset your preferences, but a smooth-running program is worth the few minutes of extra effort.

Photoshop 5 saves actions and color settings separately of the Prefs file. Actions go in the Actions Palette file and color settings go in the Color Settings file, both located in the Adobe Photoshop Settings folder. This means you can now delete your Prefs file without any worry about harming your scripts and color conversions.

After you get your preferences set as you like them, you can prevent Photoshop from altering them further by locking the file. Go to the Finder desktop, select the Adobe Photoshop 5 Prefs file, and choose File ➪ Get Info (⌘-I). Then select the Locked check box inside the Info dialog box. From now on, Photoshop will start up with a consistent set of default settings.

That's a good tip, and I include it in the name of comprehensive coverage. But personally, I don't lock my Prefs file because I periodically modify settings and I want Photoshop to remember the latest and greatest. Instead, I make a backup copy of my favorite settings. After a few weeks of working in the program and getting things to a more or less acceptable level, copy the preferences file to a separate folder on your hard disk (someplace you'll remember!). Then, if the preferences file becomes corrupt, you can replace it quickly with your backup.

The preference panels

Photoshop includes a long list of commands in the File ➪ Preferences submenu. As it turns out, you needn't choose any of these commands if you'll remember a simple keyboard shortcut: ⌘-K. This shortcut brings up the Preferences dialog box, which provides access to eight panels of options, representing every one of the File ➪

Preferences commands. Select the desired panel from the pop-up menu in the upper left corner of the dialog box, as demonstrated in Figure 2-12. Or press the ⌘ key equivalent for the panel as listed in the pop-up menu. You can also click the Prev and Next buttons to cycle from one panel to the next.

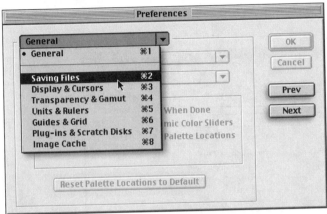

Figure 2-12: Select a panel of options from the pop-up menu, or click the Prev and Next buttons to advance from one panel to the next.

Tip

Photoshop always displays the first panel, General, when you press ⌘-K. If you prefer to go to the panel you were last using, press ⌘-Option-K.

To accept your settings and exit the Preferences dialog box, press Return. Or press Escape to cancel your settings. Okay, so you already knew this, but here's one you might not know: Press and hold the Option key to change the Cancel button to Reset. Then click the button to restore the settings that were in force before you entered the dialog box.

The following sections examine each of the Preferences panels, in the order they appear in the Figure 2-12 pop-up menu. I explain how each option works, and include what I consider the optimal setting in parentheses. (The figures, however, show the default settings.) Out of context like this, Photoshop's preference settings can be a bit confusing. In future chapters, I'll try to shed some additional light on the settings you may find most useful.

General preferences

The General panel, shown in Figure 2-13, contains a miscellaneous supply of what are arguably the most important Preferences options.

✦ **Color Picker (Photoshop):** When you click on the foreground or background color control icon in the toolbox, Photoshop displays one of two color pickers: its own or the one provided by the operating system. If you're familiar with other Macintosh graphics programs, the system's color picker may at first seem more familiar. But while Apple's new multipaneled color picker offers a slew of options, Photoshop's is better suited to photographic work.

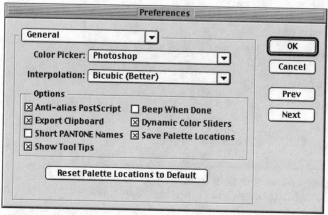

Figure 2-13: The General panel provides access to the most important environmental preference settings. I agree with most of these default settings, but in most image editing situations, it's better to turn Export Clipboard off.

✦ **Interpolation (Bicubic):** When you resize an image using Image ➪ Image Size or transform it using Layer ➪ Free Transform or one of the commands in the Layer ➪ Transform submenu, Photoshop has to make up — or *interpolate* — pixels to fill in the gaps. You can change how Photoshop calculates the interpolation by choosing one of three options from the Interpolation submenu.

If you select Nearest Neighbor, Photoshop simply copies the next-door pixel when creating a new one. This is the fastest setting, but it invariably results in jagged effects.

The second option, Bilinear, smoothes the transitions between pixels by creating intermediate shades. Photoshop averages the color of each pixel with four neighbors — the pixel above, the one below, and the two to the left and right. Bilinear takes more time but, typically, the softened effect is worth it.

Still more time intensive is the default setting, Bicubic, which averages the color of a pixel with its eight closest neighbors — one up, one down, two on the sides, and four in the corners. The Bicubic setting boosts the amount of contrast between pixels to offset the blurring effect that generally accompanies interpolation.

Tip

The moral is this: Select Bicubic to turn Photoshop's interpolation capabilities on, and select Nearest Neighbor to turn them off. The Bilinear setting is a poor compromise between the two — too slow for roughing out effects, but too remedial to waste your time.

✦ **Anti-alias PostScript (on):** Photoshop enables you to import object-oriented graphics from such programs as Illustrator, FreeHand, and Adobe Dimensions. Either copy the objects in Illustrator or Dimensions and paste them into Photoshop, or drag the objects from Illustrator and drop them into an open Photoshop image window. Either way, the Anti-alias PostScript option softens the edges of PostScript objects. If you prefer jagged edges, turn off this check box.

✦ **Export Clipboard (off):** When selected, this option tells Photoshop to transfer a copied image from the program's internal Clipboard to the operating system's Clipboard whenever you switch applications. This enables you to paste the image into another running program. Turn this option off if you plan to use copied images only within Photoshop and you want to reduce the lag time that occurs when you switch from Photoshop to another program. Even with this option off, you can paste images copied from other programs into Photoshop.

✦ **Short Pantone Names (off):** As most digital artists are already aware, Pantone is a brand name assigned to a library of premixed spot-color printing inks. Photoshop supports the most recent Pantone naming conventions. Most modern publishing programs support these longer color names, but a few older versions do not. If you run into problems separating spot-color Photoshop images when printing from another program, turn this option on. Otherwise, leave it off, as by default. (When exporting straight grayscale, RGB, or CMYK images, this check box is irrelevant.)

✦ **Show Tool Tips (on):** When on, this option displays little labels and keyboard shortcuts when you hover your cursor over a tool or palette option. The tool tips don't impede Photoshop's performance, so I see no reason to turn off this option.

✦ **Beep When Done (off):** You can instruct Photoshop to beep at you whenever it finishes an operation that displays a Progress window. This option may be useful if you doze off during particularly time-consuming operations. But I'm a firm believer that computers should be seen and not heard.

✦ **Dynamic Color Sliders (on):** When selected, this option instructs Photoshop to preview color effects within the slider bars of the Color palette. When the option is turned off, the slider bars show the same colors regardless of your changes. Unless you're working on a slow computer, leave this option on. On a fast machine, Photoshop takes a billionth of a second longer to calculate the color effects and it's well worth it.

✦ **Save Palette Locations (on):** When this option is selected, Photoshop remembers the location of the toolbox and floating palettes from one session to the next. If you turn off this check box, Photoshop restores the default palette positions the next time you restart the program.

✦ **Reset Palette Locations to Default:** Occasionally palettes go haywire. They can get stuck under menu bars. And, if you change monitor resolutions, a palette can even disappear off the screen. If this happens, click this button and Photoshop will restore the palettes to their original "safe" positions.

Saving files

When in the Preferences dialog box, press ⌘-2 to advance to the Saving Files panel, shown in Figure 2-14. Every one of these options affects how Photoshop saves images to disk. The following list explains how the options work and the recommended settings:

Figure 2-14: The Saving Files options panel, along with the truth-in-advertising version in back. I prefer to set the Image Previews option to Ask When Saving. And by all means, turn that God-forsaken check box off!

✦ **Image Previews (Ask When Saving):** Photoshop saves previews so that you can see what an image looks like before opening or importing it. You can select as many as four kinds of image previews:

The Icon option creates a tiny preview icon that you can view from the Finder desktop. In my opinion, this option is hardly worth the extra 1.5K of disk space, and too many custom icons can cause problems with older versions of the system software.

There are now two Thumbnail options, one for the Mac and one for Windows. When selected, Photoshop creates a postage-stamp preview that displays inside the Open dialog box when you select a file. The Macintosh Thumbnail option saves the preview in a part of the file known as the *resource fork*, but Windows doesn't recognize resource forks. So if you ever plan on previewing the image on a PC, you should select the Windows Thumbnail option as well.

The third option, Full Size, creates a 72-dpi preview that can be used for placement inside a page-layout program.

The problem with previews is that they slightly increase the size of the file. This is fine when doing print work — a little thumbnail isn't going to add that much — but when creating Web graphics, every byte counts. That's why I prefer to select Ask When Saving from the Image Previews pop-up menu. This adds a check box to the Save dialog box so that you can decide when to save previews and when to not on an image-by-image basis.

✦ **Append File Extension (Ask When Saving):** This option appends a three-character extension to the end of a file name to make your images compatible with Windows and DOS programs. For example, a layered composition saved in the Photoshop format gets a *.psd* extension. I personally like to set this option to Ask When Saving; that way, I can decide whether to include a PC-style extension from inside the Save dialog box on a file-by-file basis.

Tip

Actually, you can set the Append File Extension option to Never and still be able to access extensions when saving images. Just press the Option key when selecting a file format and Photoshop automatically slaps on an extension. I tell more in Chapter 4.

✦ **Use Lower Case (on):** This option decides whether the three-character extensions at the end of file names are upper- or lowercase. Lower is the better because it ensures compatibility with other platforms, particularly Unix, the primary operating system for Web servers. (Unix is case-sensitive, so a file called *Image.psd* is different than *Image.PSD*. Lowercase extensions eliminate confusion.)

✦ **Include Composited Image with Layered Files (OFF!):** This option is pure evil. If you never change another preference setting, you should turn this one off. I know, I know, if it was so awful, Adobe wouldn't have it on by default. But believe me, this option should be named Double My File Sizes Because I'm an Absolute Fool, and even Adobe's designers will tell you that you probably want to go ahead and turn it off.

Okay, so here's the long tragic story: the Double My File Sizes check box ensures backward compatibility between Photoshop 5 and programs that support the Photoshop file format but don't recognize layers. It's a nice idea, but it comes at too steep a price. In order to ensure compatibility, Photoshop has to insert an additional flattened version of a layered image into every native Photoshop file. As you can imagine, this takes up a considerable amount of disk space, doubling the file size in the most extreme situations.

So turn this check box off. And when you want cross-application compatibility, save an extra TIFF version of your file (as explained in Chapter 4).

Display & Cursors

Press ⌘-3 to saddle up to the Display & Cursors options, which appear in Figure 2-15. These options affect the way colors and cursors appear on screen. Here's how the options work, along with recommended settings:

✦ **Color Channels in Color (off):** An individual color channel contains just 8 bits of data per pixel, which makes it equivalent to a grayscale image. Photoshop provides you with the option of colorizing the channel according to the primary color it represents. For example, when this option is turned on, the red color channel looks like a grayscale image viewed through red acetate. Most experts agree the effect isn't helpful, though, and it does more to obscure your image than make it easier for you to see what's happening. Leave this check box turned off and read Chapter 6 for more information.

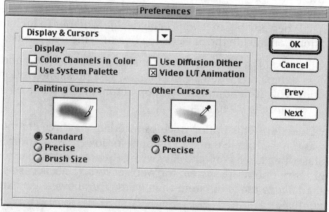

Figure 2-15: The Display & Cursors options control the way images and cursors look on screen. Shown here are the default settings, but I turn Use Diffusion Dither on, Video LUT Animation off, and I select the Brush Size radio button.

✦ **Use System Palette (off):** If you're working on an 8-bit monitor that displays no more than 256 colors at a time, this option matters to you. Otherwise, give it the slip.

To simulate the 16-million-color spectrum on a 256-color screen, Photoshop automatically jumbles colored pixels using a technique called *dithering*. By default, Photoshop selects 256 colors best suited to your image. In doing so, however, it must switch to a new set of 256 colors every time you bring a new document to the foreground. If you want all open documents to conform to the same set of colors — namely, the so-called "system palette" built into your system — select this check box. But for the most accurate display, leave the option turned off and live with the periodic screen fluctuations.

✦ **Use Diffusion Dither (on):** Here's another option for you folks working on 8-bit screens. While the previous option controls the colors used, this option controls the pattern of dithered pixels. Photoshop offers a naturalistic "diffusion" dither that looks nice on screen. But because the diffusion dither follows no specific pattern, you sometimes see distinct edges between selected and deselected portions of your image after applying a filter or some other effect. You can eliminate these edges and resort to a more geometric dither pattern by turning off this check box.

Turning off the Use Diffusion Dither check box is an awfully drastic (not to mention ugly) solution, though. The better way to eliminate the occasional visual disharmony is to force Photoshop to redraw the entire image. You can press ⌘-Option-0 or perform some other zoom function.

✦ **Video LUT Animation (off):** If you've ever worked inside one of Photoshop's color correction dialog boxes — such as Levels or Curves — and turned off the Preview check box, you've seen Photoshop's video look-up table animation in progress. Photoshop changes the look-up table (LUT) on the fly according to your specifications, in effect applying the color correction to the entire screen. It's not a real preview — in fact, it's pretty lousy. Video LUT Animation doesn't account for selections, and it doesn't properly preview CMYK images. I go into more detail on this option in Chapter 18, but for now, turn this check box off.

✦ **Painting Cursors (Brush Size):** When you use a paint or edit tool, Photoshop can display one of three cursors. The default Standard cursor looks like a paintbrush, airbrush, finger, or whatever. These cursors are great if you have problems keeping track of what tool you selected, but otherwise they border on childish.

The Precise and Brush Size options are more functional. The Precise option displays a cross-shaped cursor — called a crosshair — regardless of which tool is active. The crosshair is great because it prevents the cursor from blocking your view as you edit. Meanwhile, the Brush Size option shows the actual size and shape of the active brush in the Brushes palette. Most artists prefer this final setting to the others because it comes the closest to showing the cursor the way it really is.

When Standard or Brush Size is selected, you can access the crosshair cursor by pressing the Caps Lock key. When Precise is selected from the Painting Cursors options, pressing Caps Lock displays the brush size.

✦ **Other Cursors (Standard):** Again, you can select Standard to get the regular cursors or Precise to get crosshairs. I prefer to leave this option set to Standard because you can easily access the crosshair cursor by pressing Caps Lock. The Precise option locks you into the crosshair whether you like it or not.

Transparency & Gamut

Press ⌘-4 to switch to the Transparency & Gamut panel shown in Figure 2-16. The options in this panel change how Photoshop displays two conceptual items — transparent space behind layers and RGB colors that can't be expressed in CMYK printing.

Figure 2-16: The options in this panel affect how Photoshop represents transparency and out-of-gamut colors. For the most part, you just want to select colors that you don't often see inside your images.

The options are arranged into two groups — Transparency Settings and Gamut Warning — as explained in the following sections.

Transparency settings

Just as the Earth spins around in empty space, a Photoshop image rests on a layer of absolute transparency. By default, Photoshop represents this transparency as a gray checkerboard pattern. (What better way to demonstrate nothingness? I might have preferred a few lines from a Jean-Paul Sartre play, but no matter.) You may get a brief glimpse of this checkerboard when you first open an image or switch to Photoshop from another application.

When you view a layer independently of others, Photoshop fills the see-through portions of the layer with the checkerboard. So having the checkerboard stand out from the layer itself is essential. You can customize the size of the checkers and the color of the squares using the Grid Size and Grid Colors pop-up menus. You can also click the color swatches to define your own colors.

Tip

To lift colors from the image window, move your cursor outside the Preferences dialog box to get the eyedropper. Click a color to change the color of the white checkers; Option-click to change the gray ones.

If you own a TrueVision NuVista+ board or some other 32-bit device that enables chroma keying, you can select the Use Video Alpha check box to view a television signal in the transparent area behind a layer. Unless you work in video production, you needn't worry about this option.

Gamut warning

If Photoshop can display a color on screen but can't accurately print the color, the color is said to be *out of gamut*. You can choose View ➪ Gamut Warning to coat all out-of-gamut colors with gray. I'm not a big fan of this command — View ➪ Preview ➪ CMYK (⌘-Y) is much more useful — but if you use it, you don't have to accept gray as the out-of-gamut coating. Change the color by clicking the Gamut Warning Color swatch, and lower the Opacity value to request a translucent coating.

Units & Rulers

The Units & Rulers panel is the fifth panel in the Preferences dialog box, hence, you reach the panel by pressing ⌘-5. Shown in Figure 2-17, this panel offers options that enable you to change the predominant system of measurement used throughout the program.

Figure 2-17: Go to the Units & Rulers panel to change the system of measurement. I prefer to use Pixels as opposed to Inches.

Whenever the rulers are visible, the Units & Rulers panel is only a double-click away. Choose View ➪ Show Rulers (⌘-R) to see the rulers on screen and then double-click either the horizontal or vertical ruler.

Rulers

Start by selecting the desired unit of measure from the Units pop-up menu. When you're first learning Photoshop, going with inches or picas is tempting, but experienced Photoshop artists use pixels. Because you can change the resolution of an image at any time, the only constant is pixels. An image measures a fixed number of pixels high by a fixed number of pixels wide — you can print those pixels as large or as small as you want. (To learn more about resolution, read Chapter 4.)

You can also change the unit of measurement from the Info palette. Click on the little crosshair to display a pop-up menu then select the desired option. It's much easier than slogging through a multipaneled dialog box like Preferences.

Column size

The Column Size options enable you to size images according to columns in a newsletter or magazine. Just enter the width of your columns and the size of the gutter into the Width and Gutter option boxes. Then use File ➪ New or Image ➪ Image Size to specify the number of columns assigned to the width of the image. I explain these commands in more detail in Chapter 4.

Point/pica size

The last option in the Units & Rulers panel may be the most obscure of all Photoshop options. In case you aren't familiar with points and picas, exactly 12 points are in a pica, and about 6.06 picas are in an inch.

Well, because picas are almost evenly divisible into inches, the folks who came up with the PostScript printing language decided to bag the difference and to define a pica as exactly ⅙ inch. This makes a point exactly 1/72 inch.

But a few purists didn't take to it. They found their new electronic documents weren't quite matching their old paste-up documents and, well, I guess life pretty much lost its meaning. So Adobe had to go back and add the Traditional (72.27 points/inch) option to keep everyone happy.

I prefer the nontraditional PostScript definition of points. This way, a pixel on screen translates to a point on paper when you print an image at 72 ppi (the standard screen resolution). Call me a soulless technodweeb, but computer imaging makes more sense when you can measure points and pixels without resorting to a calculator. The old ways are dead; long live the 1/72-inch point!

Guides & Grid

Someone at Adobe said, "Let the preference settings continue." And, lo, there is Guides & Grid, which can be accessed by all who press ⌘-6 and viewed by all who cast an eye on Figure 2-18. This panel lets you modify the colors of the guides and specify the size of the grid.

Figure 2-18: Use these options to adjust the size of the grid and change the way both the grid and ruler guides appear on screen.

You can display the Preferences dialog box and go directly to the Guides & Grid panel by double-clicking a guide with the move tool or ⌘-double-clicking with another tool. (To create a guide, drag from the horizontal or vertical ruler into the image.)

I explain these options in more detail in Chapter 13 but, for the moment, here are some brief descriptions.

Guides

Select a color for horizontal and vertical ruler guides from the Color pop-up menu. To lift a color from the image, move your cursor outside the Preferences dialog box and click in the image window with the eyedropper. You can also view guides as solid lines or dashes by selecting an option from the Style pop-up menu.

Grid

Select a color for the grid from the Color menu, or Option-click in the image window to lift a color from the image. Then decide how the grid lines look by selecting a Style option. The Dots setting is the least intrusive.

The Gridline Every value determines the increments for the visible grid marks on screen. But the Subdivisions value sets the real grid. For example, if you request a grid mark every two inches with four subdivisions — as in Figure 2-18 — Photoshop snaps selections and layers in half-inch increments (two inches divided by four).

Plug-ins & Scratch Disk

Press ⌘-7 to advance to the panel shown in Figure 2-19. Each time you launch Photoshop, the program searches for plug-in modules and identifies one or more scratch disks. You have to tell Photoshop where the plug-ins can be found and where the temporary scratch files should go.

Figure 2-19: Tell Photoshop where to find plug-ins and where to put scratch files using these options.

Plug-ins folder

By default, the plug-ins are located in a folder called Plug-Ins, which resides in the same folder as the Photoshop application. But you can rename this folder and put it anywhere you like. You can even organize your plug-ins into multiple folders, loading one folder of plug-ins one day, and another folder the next.

If you do change the location of the plug-ins, tell Photoshop where to find them by clicking the Choose button and locating the desired folder on disk.

Scratch disks

By default, Photoshop assumes you have only one hard disk, so Photoshop stores its temporary virtual memory documents — called *scratch files* — on the same disk that contains your system software. If you have more than one drive available, though, you might want to tell Photoshop to look elsewhere. In fact, Photoshop 5 can now use up to four drives.

For example, one of my computers is equipped with two internal hard drives:

✦ A 2GB drive, Gold Leader, contains the system and most of the workaday documents I create.

✦ The other drive is a 4GB device partitioned into two 2GB segments. These are formatted as PowerShrine.1 and PowerShrine.2. (Let's face it, I spend most of my time praying my computer will work, so I decided to make this official.) PowerShrine.2 contains all my applications while PowerShrine.1 remains largely empty except for a few large miscellaneous files — QuickTime movies, digital camera snapshots, weird plug-ins — that I haven't gotten around to backing up yet.

PowerShrine.1 has the most free space, so I selected it from the First pop-up menu. On the off chance that my images get so huge that Photoshop fills up PowerShrine.1 and has to look elsewhere for scratch space, I selected PowerShrine.2 from the Second pop-up menu and my main system drive Gold Leader from the Third. That's the end of my drives, so Fourth remains set to None.

Adobe advises against using removable media — such as SyQuest, MO, and Zip drives — as a scratch disk. Removable media is typically less reliable and slower than a permanent drive. (A Jaz cartridge is more stable than Zip or the others, but still not as reliable as a fixed hard drive.) Using a removable drive on an occasional basis isn't the end of the world, but if you use it regularly you may end up crashing more often, in which case you'll probably want to add a new hard drive.

Changes affect the next session

As the note at the bottom of the Plug-ins & Scratch Disks panel warns, the settings in this panel don't take effect until the next time you launch Photoshop. This means you must quit Photoshop and restart the program.

There's nothing more frustrating than knowing that the options in this dialog box are set incorrectly before you've even started up Photoshop. It means you have to launch Photoshop, change the settings, quit Photoshop, and launch the program again. What a waste of time!

That is, it *would* be a waste of time if there wasn't a workaround. Fortunately, you can access the plug-ins and scratch disk settings during the launch cycle. After double-clicking on the Photoshop application icon, press and hold the ⌘ and Option keys. After a few seconds, Photoshop greets you with a message requesting that you locate the Plug-Ins folder. After you do so, press and hold the ⌘ and Option keys again and in a moment, a screen of the scratch disk options appears. Specify the disks as desired and press Return. Your new settings now work for the current session — no restarting necessary.

Image cache

Ever since Photoshop 3 came out, Adobe has received a fair amount of flack from high-end users who demand faster image handling. Programs like Live Picture and xRes take seconds to apply complex operations to super-huge photographs, while Photoshop putters along for a minute or more. Granted, Live Picture and xRes aren't nearly as capable as Photoshop, but they are faster.

The good news is that Photoshop sports a caching scheme that speeds operations at reduced view sizes. You can adjust this feature by pressing ⌘-8 in the Preferences dialog box. This displays the Image Cache panel, shown in Figure 2-20.

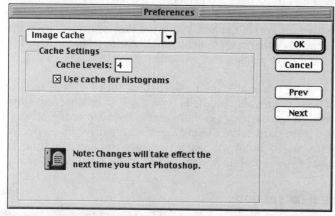

Figure 2-20: Photoshop's new caching capabilities speed the processing of very large images.

Cache levels

Photoshop has been criticized for its lack of a "pyramid-style" file format, such as Live Picture's IVUE or xRes' LRG. Both IVUE and LRG store an image several times over at progressively smaller and smaller image sizes, called *downsamplings*. For example, the program would save a full view of the image, a 50 percent view, a 25 percent view, and so on. Live Picture or xRes can then load and edit only the portion of the image visible on screen, greatly accelerating functions.

Photoshop's alternative is image caching. Rather than saving the downsamplings to disk, Photoshop generates the reduced images in RAM. By default, the Cache Levels value is set to 4, the medium value. This means Photoshop can cache up to four downsamplings — at 100, 50, 25, and 12.5 percent — which permits the program to apply operations more quickly at reduced view sizes. For example, if you choose a color correction command at the 50 percent view size, it previews much faster than normal because Photoshop has to modify a quarter as many pixels on screen.

However, Photoshop must cache downsamplings in RAM, which takes away memory that could be used to hold the image. If you have lots of RAM (128MB or more) and you frequently work on large images (20MB or larger), you'll probably want to raise the value to the maximum, 8. The lost memory is worth the speed boost. If you have little RAM (say, 16MB or less) and you usually work on small images or Web graphics (4MB or smaller), you may want to reduce the Cache Levels value to 1 or 2. When files are small, RAM is better allocated to storing images rather than caching them.

Use cache for histograms

The Use Cache for Histograms check box tells Photoshop whether to generate the histograms that appear in the Levels and Threshold dialog boxes based on the cached sampling or the original image. As I explain in Chapter 18, a *histogram* is a bar graph of the colors in an image. When you choose a command like Image ➪ Adjust ➪ Levels, Photoshop must spend a few seconds graphing the colors. If you turn the Use Cache for Histograms check box on, Photoshop graphs the colors in the reduced screen view, which takes less time, but is also less accurate. Turn the check box off for slower, more accurate histograms.

Generally speaking, I say leave the option on. A histogram is merely a visual indicator and most folks will be unable to judge the difference between a downsampled histogram and a fully accurate one.

Again, if you're working in very large images and you have the Cache Levels value maxed out at 8, you should probably leave this check box selected. But if you have to reduce the Cache Levels value, turn off the check box. Histograms are the first thing that can go.

Note

This option is *not* responsible for the Histogram irregularities that popped up in Photoshop 4. The fact that the Threshold dialog box sometimes lifted its histogram from the active layer only was a bug, not a function of Use Cache for Histograms. Even so, this option has received a lot of flack it did not deserve. My opinion is that, on balance, this is a positive feature that should be left on.

Annotating an Image

If you work for a stock agency or you distribute your work by some other means, you might be interested in Photoshop's image-annotation feature. You can attach captions, credits, bylines, photo location and date, copyright, and other information, as prescribed by the IPTC (International Press Telecommunications Council). We're talking official worldwide guidelines here.

Choose File ➪ File Info to display the six-paneled File Info dialog box, shown in Figure 2-21. You switch from one panel to another by pressing ⌘-1 through ⌘-6 or choosing the panel name from the Section pop-up menu. The first panel, the Caption panel, appears in Figure 2-21.

Figure 2-21: You can document your image in encyclopedic detail using the wealth of options in the File Info dialog box.

Although sprawling with options, this dialog box is pretty straightforward. For example, if you want to create a caption, travel to the Caption panel and enter your caption into the Caption option box, which can hold up to 2,000 characters. The Keywords panel enables you to enter a list of descriptive words that will help folks find the image if it's part of a large electronic library. Just enter the desired word and press Return (or click the Add button) to add the keyword to the list. Or you can replace a word in the list by selecting it, entering a new word, and pressing Return (or clicking Replace). Likewise, you can delete a selected keyword by clicking Delete. Browser utilities enable you to search images by keyword, as do some dedicated image servers.

The Categories panel may seem foreign to anyone who hasn't worked with a news service. Many large news services use a system of three-character categories to file and organize stories and photographs. If you're familiar with this system, you can enter the three-character code into the Category option box and even throw in a few supplemental categories up to 32 characters long. Finally, use the Urgency pop-up menu to specify the editorial timeliness of the photo. The High option tells editors around the world to hold the presses and holler for their copy boys. The Low option is for celebrity mug shots that can be tossed in the morgue to haul out only if the subject of the photograph decides to do something diverting, like lead police on a nail-biting tour of the Los Angeles freeway system.

The Copyright & URL panel enables you to add a copyright notice to your image. If you check the Mark as Copyrighted check box, a copyright symbol (©) will appear in the window title bar and in the preview box at the bottom of the image window. This symbol tells people viewing the image they can go to the Copyright & URL panel to get more information about the owner of the image copyright.

You can also include the URL for your Web site, if you have one. Then, when folks have your image open in Photoshop, they can come to this panel and click the Go to URL button to launch their Web browsers and jump to the URL.

File information is saved with an image regardless of the format you use. Photoshop merely tacks the text onto the image's resource fork. Because you cannot format the text in the File Info dialog box, it consumes little space on disk—1 byte per character—meaning that you can fill in every option box without adding 1K.

You can also save the information from the File Info dialog box by clicking the Save button. Or open information saved to disk previously by clicking Load. To add the information from a saved file to the information you've already entered into the File Info dialog box, click the Append button.

File Info settings can be recorded as a script in Photoshop 5. Using the Actions palette, you can create a script that adds your specific copyright, byline, and URL to an image. After recording the script, you can automatically add the information to an entire folder of files using File ⇨ Automate ⇨ Batch. For more information on the Actions palette and Batch command, read the last half of Chapter 3.

✦　　✦　　✦

Shortcuts and Scripts

Keystrokes and Modifiers

Unlike most graphics programs, Photoshop invests a lot of its capabilities in the keyboard. Literally hundreds of functions are available exclusively at the press of a key. For example, Photoshop provides no command that adds the next selection outline you draw to the previous one. There is no command that hides all palettes, nor is there an option that brings up the last-used color correction settings. Every one of these options is out of your reach if you don't know the right key. The keyboard may seem like an unlikely artistic tool, but it is both a powerful and an essential ally in Photoshop.

There are three basic varieties of keyboard tricks. Some keystroke combinations produce immediate effects. For example, pressing ⌘ and Delete together fills the selection with the background color. Other keys change the behavior of a tool or command. Pressing Shift while dragging with the lasso tool adds the lassoed area to the previous selection. As a result, Shift, Option, ⌘, and Control are known collectively as *modifiers*.

The third variety is shortcuts that you invent for yourself. Known generically as *scripts*, these custom shortcuts may include a sequence of commands that Photoshop can play over and over again in a specified order and with specified settings. You create scripts using the Actions palette, which I explain at length later in this chapter. After creating a script, you can assign a keyboard equivalent to it, or you can play the script by ⌘-double-clicking on it. Even the shortcuts have shortcuts.

Experienced users will discover that many of the shortcuts they enjoyed using in Photoshop 4 have changed in Version 5. The changes are not nearly as extensive as they were last time around. (For those who have blotted this painful episode from their minds, upgrading from Version 3 to Version 4 required some significant gray-matter retooling.) But if you're used to speeding through Photoshop in a blaze of keystrokes and mouse clicks, be prepared for some occasional miscommunications with Version 5.

Or just read this chapter and avoid the headache. With a keen mind and a little practice, you'll be driving your new Model 5 Photoshop at speeds that would land your butt in jail in the real world.

Hidden Shortcuts and Modifiers

Shortcuts permit you to initiate operations without resorting to the laborious task of choosing commands from menus or clicking on a tool icon until your arm falls off. Some shortcuts are fairly obvious. For example, Photoshop lists keyboard equivalents for its commands next to the command in the menu. You can choose File ➪ New by pressing ⌘-N, choose Edit ➪ Undo by pressing ⌘-Z, choose Select ➪ All by pressing ⌘-A, and so on. But most of Photoshop's shortcuts are hidden. And, wouldn't you know it, the hidden ones are the most essential.

Control-clicking

One of the best hidden tricks in Photoshop is Control-clicking. Go ahead, try it: Press the Control key, then click and hold the mouse button inside the image window. Up pops a menu of commands tailored to your current activity. For example, if you Control-click with the lasso tool while a selection is active, you get the list of commands shown in Figure 3-1. Although you can apply other commands to a selection, these are some of the most common.

The Control-click pop-up menu is *context-sensitive*, which means it changes to suit the active tool and the current state of the image (selected or not). You can also access context-sensitive pop-up menus inside many of the palettes. Figure 3-2 shows me Control-clicking on a layer in the Layers palette.

Control-clicking without the Control key

With Apple's OS 8, Control-clicking is now a standard element of the operating system. But Adobe added Control-clicking to Photoshop about a year prior to the introduction of OS 8. In fact, Adobe developed this feature specifically to satisfy users of the Windows environment, where the two-button mouse reigns supreme. Rather than pressing Control while clicking, you simply click with the right mouse button.

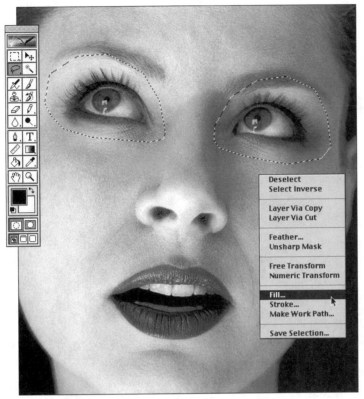

Figure 3-1: If you get stuck, Control-click to bring up a pop-up menu of helpful commands.

If you envy this dual button action—right-clicking is admittedly easier than Control-clicking—you can purchase a two-button mouse from a company like Kensington or Mouse Systems and set the second mouse button to Control-click. There are even keyboards that have two-button touchpads built into them.

But my favorite solution is the one most likely to appeal to artists. Any tablet manufactured in the last couple of years by Wacom (*www.wacom.com*) includes a four-button stylus. These buttons are the pen nib, an eraser, and two side switches. As shown in Figure 3-3, you can modify the performance of either side switch. I personally set one switch to double-click and the other to Control-click.

Figure 3-2: You can also Control-click on items in the Layers, Channels, Paths, Brushes, Color, and History palettes.

Figure 3-3: You can set the side switch of a Wacom stylus to Control-click so you don't have to waste your valuable time pressing the Control key manually.

Toolbox shortcuts

Usability has always been one of Photoshop's great strengths. One of the ways Photoshop expedites your workflow is to let you select tools from the keyboard. This way, you can use one tool, press a key, and immediately start in with another tool without losing your place in the image.

Tip

Best of all, the shortcuts work even when the toolbox is hidden. The only reason I even look at the toolbox is to monitor which tool is selected, so I don't get confused.

Figure 3-4 tells the whole, wonderful story. Press the appropriate key, as shown in the figure—no ⌘, Option, or other modifiers required. Many of the shortcuts make sense. M selects the marquee tool, L is for lasso tool. But then there are the weird ones, like K for paint bucKet, O for dOdge, R for bluR, and my favorite, I for I-dropper.

Figure 3-4: Press these keys to select tools and activate controls. Press Shift with the bold keys to toggle between alternative tools.

Photoshop **5.0**

The toolbox shortcuts have changed quite a bit in Photoshop 5 (more than they did in Photoshop 4). The Y, U, A, N, and J keys all do something different. Y used to select the pencil, now it selects the new historY tool. U used to select the smudge tool, now it selects the new measUre tool. A changes from the airbrush to the direct selection (or Arrow) tool, N changes from line to peNcil, and J goes from doing nothing to selecting the airbrush. (That's right, folks, it's the new air-Jordan-brush tool. Okay, so it's a lame joke, but maybe it'll help you remember.)

But that's not all that changes. In Photoshop 5, none of the old tool keys acts as a toggle. For example, pressing M repeatedly used to switch between the rectangular and elliptical marquee tools. Now pressing M *always* takes you to the last marquee tool that you used, no matter how many times you press it.

To toggle to an alternative tool, you have to press the Shift key. These Shift-key combos appear in bold in Figure 3-4, but here's a brief rundown:

✦ **M** selects the rectangular marquee tool. Press Shift-M to toggle between the rectangular and elliptical marquees.

✦ **L** selects the standard lasso tool we all know and love from the ancient days of MacPaint. Shift-L switches between the lasso, polygon lasso, and new magnetic lasso.

✦ **S** gets the cloning rubber stamp tool. Shift-S cycles between the cloning and pattern stamp tools.

✦ **E** selects the paintbrush-type eraser. Shift-E changes between the four styles of eraser — paintbrush, airbrush, pencil, and block. You can monitor the active style by pressing Return to display the Eraser Options palette.

✦ **N** selects the pencil. Shift-N toggles between the pencil and the line tool.

✦ **R** selects the blur tool. Shift-R switches between the blur, sharpen, and smudge tools.

✦ **O** activates the dodge tool. Shift-O toggles between the dodge, burn, and sponge tools.

✦ **P** gets you the pen tool. Shift-P switches between the pen and its two new flavors, magnetic pen and freeform pen.

✦ **T** selects the standard type tool. Shift-T cycles through type mask and the two vertical type tools.

✦ **G** permits you to draw linear gradients. Shift-G accesses the other gradient styles — radial, angle, reflected, and diamond.

✦ **I** selects the eyedropper. Shift-I goes between the eyedropper and the new color sampler.

The control toggles — X, Q, and F — work as before. X swaps between the foreground and background colors. Q takes you in and out of the quick mask mode. F takes you from one image window mode to the next.

Palette shortcuts

Photoshop also lets you access a few palette options from the keyboard. I've documented these options in Figure 3-5. But the figure is sufficiently peculiar that I thought I'd back it up with the following list. And as with the tool keys, each of these shortcuts works even when the palette is hidden:

✦ Press the bracket keys [and] to decrease and increase the brush shape when a paint or edit tool is selected.

Figure 3-5: These shortcuts work even when the palettes themselves are hidden. To display a palette, press one of the big superimposed keys (F5 through F9 and Return).

✦ Press Shift-[to select the first brush shape (generally the single-pixel brush). Press Shift-] to select the last brush shape.

✦ When a paint, edit, or fill tool is selected, press a number key to change the Opacity, Pressure, or Exposure setting assigned to that tool in the Options palette. Lowered values result in translucent strokes and fills. Press 1 to change the value to 10 percent, 2 for 20 percent, all the way up to 0 for 100 percent. Or enter the exact value — such as 15 percent — by typing 1-5 right in a row.

✦ When any other tool is selected — whether a selection, navigation, type, or eyedropper tool — pressing a number key changes the Opacity value assigned to a floating selection or layer. Again, press one number to modify the Opacity setting in 10-percent increments; press two numbers to specify an exact Opacity setting.

✦ When a paint or edit tool is active, you can cycle through the brush modes by pressing Shift-plus (+) or minus (–). Shift-plus takes you down the brush mode pop-up menu and Shift-minus takes you back up.

✦ When some other tool is selected, Shift-plus and minus affect the blend mode applied to the active layer. You can also access a particular blend mode by pressing Shift and Option with a letter key. For example, Shift-Option-M selects the Multiply mode and Shift-Option-S selects Screen.

✦ Press the forward slash key (/) to turn on and off the Preserve Transparency check box. This is easily one of the least-known shortcuts in all of Photoshop. But it's useful, as I explain further in Chapter 13.

✦ Press Option-] to ascend through the layers. Press Option-[to descend.

✦ Press Shift-Option-] to activate the top layer in the image. Press Shift-Option-[to go all the way down to the bottom of the stack (usually the Background layer).

The Great Grandmother of All Shortcut Tables

Saddam Hussein is not a popular fellow. As an International Ambassador of Evil who specializes in Bloodthirsty Dictatorship, he incites scorn, disgust, hatred, and world-wide irritation. Theologians speculate that a private parking space awaits Saddam in Hell, right between Stalin and the guy who invented Amway.

But you have to give Saddam credit for that "mother of all battles" thing. English isn't even the guy's first language, yet he added a wonderful catch phrase to it. I'm sure we'll be joking about the mothers of all this and that for years to come. That Saddam, what a sense of humor.

Even so, the phrase doesn't quite do justice to Table 3-1. Here's a list covering every keystroke and modifier available to Photoshop 5, a whopping 400 in all! And for the second edition running, I've done something you won't find in any other book: I've created a table that tells you both the old Photoshop 4 keyboard shortcut and the new Photoshop 5 equivalent. If the shortcut is new to Version 5 — as nearly 25 percent them are — I've indicated it in **bold type** so you can more quickly scan the list.

Note

By the way, don't press Shift just because a key combination involves a character that normally requires the Shift key. Just press the key with the shortcut character on it. For example, the shortcut for the Zoom In command is ⌘-plus (+). Technically, + is the shifted version of equal (=), so a literal person might think you have to press ⌘-Shift-=. But the literal person would be wrong. The plus sign is used because it implies zooming while the equal sign does not. So when you see ⌘-plus (+), just press ⌘-=.

Naturally, a shortcut won't make much sense if you aren't familiar with the feature it facilitates. I explain both features and their shortcuts in context in later chapters. The intent of the table is to serve as a reference you can revisit as your knowledge of Photoshop grows. The more you learn, the more useful the table becomes.

So fold the corner of this page, tag it with a sticky note, or stab it with a bayonet. This isn't your everyday average mother of all shortcuts table. This table is so huge and all-encompassing, it skips two whole generations. Table 3-1 is a great grandmother — the kind who doesn't tolerate sass from a merciless tyrant no matter how big his secret stockpile might be.

Table 3-1
Photoshop's Hidden Shortcuts and Modifiers

Operation	Old Photoshop 4 shortcut	New Photoshop 5 shortcut
Menu commands		
Actual Pixels	⌘-Option-zero (0)	⌘-Option-zero (0)
Auto Levels	⌘-Shift-L	⌘-Shift-L
Bring Layer Forward	⌘-]	⌘-]
Bring Layer to Front	⌘-Shift-]	⌘-Shift-]
Clear	Delete	Delete
Close	⌘-W	⌘-W
Color Balance	⌘-B	⌘-B
Color Balance, with last settings	⌘-Option-B	⌘-Option-B
Copy	⌘-C or F3	⌘-C or F3
Copy Merged	⌘-Shift-C	⌘-Shift-C

(continued)

Table 3-1 *(continued)*

Operation	Old Photoshop 4 shortcut	New Photoshop 5 shortcut
Menu commands		
Curves	⌘-M	⌘-M
Curves, with last settings	⌘-Option-M	⌘-Option-M
Cut	⌘-X or F2	⌘-X or F2
Desaturate	⌘-Shift-U	⌘-Shift-U
Defloat	⌘-E	**They killed the feature!**
Fade Filter	⌘-Shift-F	⌘-Shift-F
Feather Selection	⌘-Shift-D or Shift-F6	**⌘-Option-D** or Shift-F6
Fill	Shift-Delete or Shift-F5	Shift-Delete or Shift-F5
Fill from history	*new feature*	**⌘-Option-Delete**
Filter, repeat last	⌘-F	⌘-F
Filter, repeat with new settings	⌘-Option-F	⌘-Option-F
Fit on Screen	⌘-zero (0)	⌘-zero (0)
Free Transform	⌘-T	⌘-T
Gamut Warning	⌘-Shift-Y	⌘-Shift-Y
Grid, show or hide	⌘-quote (")	⌘-quote (")
Group with Previous Layer	⌘-G	⌘-G
Guides, show or hide	⌘-semicolon (;)	⌘-semicolon (;)
Hide Edges	⌘-H	⌘-H
Hide Path	⌘-Shift-H	⌘-Shift-H
Hue/Saturation	⌘-U	⌘-U
Hue/Saturation, with last settings	⌘-Option-U	⌘-Option-U
Image Size	F11	F11
Inverse Selection	⌘-Shift-I or Shift-F7	⌘-Shift-I or Shift-F7
Invert	⌘-I	⌘-I
Layer Via Copy	⌘-J	⌘-J
Layer Via Cut	⌘-Shift-J	⌘-Shift-J

Operation	Old Photoshop 4 shortcut	New Photoshop 5 shortcut
Menu commands		
Levels	⌘-L	⌘-L
Levels, with last settings	⌘-Option-L	⌘-Option-L
Lock Guides	⌘-Option-semicolon (;)	⌘-Option-semicolon (;)
Merge Down	⌘-E	⌘-E
Merge Visible	⌘-Shift-E	⌘-Shift-E
New	⌘-N	⌘-N
New, with default settings	⌘-Option-N	⌘-Option-N
New Layer	*new feature*	**⌘-Shift-N**
Numeric Transform	⌘-Shift-T	*none*
Open	⌘-O	⌘-O
Page Setup	⌘-Shift-P	⌘-Shift-P
Paste	⌘-V or F4	⌘-V or F4
Paste Into	⌘-Shift-V	⌘-Shift-V
Preferences	⌘-K	⌘-K
Preferences, last panel	⌘-Option-K	⌘-Option-K
Preview CMYK	⌘-Y	⌘-Y
Print	⌘-P	⌘-P
Quit	⌘-Q	⌘-Q
Redo	⌘-Z	⌘-Z
Reselect	*new feature*	**⌘-Shift-D**
Revert	F12	F12 or **click first item in History palette**
Rulers, show or hide	⌘-R	⌘-R
Save	⌘-S	⌘-S
Save As	⌘-Shift-S	⌘-Shift-S
Save a Copy	⌘-Option-S	⌘-Option-S
Select All	⌘-A	⌘-A
Select None	⌘-D	⌘-D
Send Layer Backward	⌘-[	⌘-[

(continued)

Table 3-1 *(continued)*

Operation	Old Photoshop 4 shortcut	New Photoshop 5 shortcut
Menu commands		
Send Layer to Back	⌘-Shift-[	⌘-Shift-[
Step Backward	*new feature*	**⌘-Option-Z**
Step Forward	*new feature*	**⌘-Shift-Z**
Snap to Grid	⌘-Shift-quote (")	⌘-Shift-quote (")
Snap to Guides	⌘-Shift-semicolon (;)	⌘-Shift-semicolon (;)
Transform Again	*new feature*	**⌘-Shift-T**
Undo	⌘-Z or F1	⌘-Z or F1
Ungroup Layers	⌘-Shift-G	⌘-Shift-G
Zoom In	⌘-plus (+)	⌘-plus (+)
Zoom Out	⌘-minus (−)	⌘-minus (−)
Navigation		
Scroll image with hand tool	spacebar-drag or drag in Navigator palette	spacebar-drag or drag in Navigator palette
Scroll up or down one screen	Page Up or Page Down	Page Up or Page Down
Scroll up or down slightly	Shift-Page Up or Shift-Page Down	Shift-Page Up or Shift-Page Down
Scroll up or down exactly one frame in Filmstrip file	Shift-Page Up or Shift-Page Down	Shift-Page Up or Shift-Page Down
Scroll left or right one screen	*none*	**⌘-Page Up or ⌘-Page Down**
Scroll left or right slightly	*none*	**⌘-Shift-Page Up or ⌘-Shift-Page Down**
Switch to upper-left corner	press Home	press Home
Switch to lower-right corner	press End	press End
Magnify to custom zoom ratio	⌘-spacebar-drag or ⌘-drag in Navigator palette	⌘-spacebar-drag or ⌘-drag in Navigator palette
Zoom in without changing window size	⌘-spacebar-click or ⌘-Option-plus (+)	⌘-spacebar-click or ⌘-Option-plus (+)
Zoom in and change window size to fit	⌘-plus (+)	⌘-plus (+)

Operation	Old Photoshop 4 shortcut	New Photoshop 5 shortcut
Navigation		
Zoom out without changing window size	Option-spacebar-click or ⌘-Option-minus (–)	Option-spacebar-click or ⌘-Option-minus (–)
Zoom out and change window size to fit	⌘-minus (–)	⌘-minus (–)
Zoom to 100%	⌘-Option-zero (0) or double-click zoom tool icon	⌘-Option-zero (0) or double-click zoom tool icon
Fit image on screen	⌘-zero (0) or double-click hand tool icon	⌘-zero (0) or double-click hand tool icon
Apply zoom value but keep magnification box active	Shift-Return	Shift-Return
Cycle through full screen and normal window modes	F	F
Toggle display of menu bar in full screen modes	*new feature*	**Shift-F**
Painting and editing		
Display Options palette	Return or double-click tool icon	Return or double-click tool icon
Display crosshair cursor	Caps Lock	Caps Lock
Revert image with magic eraser	Option-drag with eraser	Option-drag with eraser
Select pencil, paintbrush, or airbrush	press Y, B, or A	**press N, B, or J**
Cycle through eraser styles	Option-click eraser tool icon or press E	Option-click eraser tool icon or **Shift-E**
Specify an area to clone	Option-click with rubber stamp	Option-click with rubber stamp
Cycle through rubber stamp options	Option-click rubber stamp tool icon or press S	Option-click rubber stamp tool icon or **Shift-S**
Cycle through focus tools	Option-click focus tool icon or press R	Option-click focus tool icon or **Shift-R**

(continued)

Table 3-1 *(continued)*

Operation	Old Photoshop 4 shortcut	New Photoshop 5 shortcut
Painting and editing		
Sharpen with the blur tool or blur with the sharpen tool	Option-drag	Option-drag
Dip into the foreground color when smearing	Option-drag with smudge tool	Option-drag with smudge tool
Cycle through toning tools	Option-click toning tool icon or press O	Option-click toning tool icon or **Shift-O**
Darken with the dodge tool or lighten with the burn tool	Option-drag	Option-drag
Paint or edit in a straight line	click and then Shift-click	click and then Shift-click
Change opacity, pressure, or exposure in 10% increments	press number (1 through 0)	press number (1 through 0)
Change opacity, pressure, or exposure in 1% increments	press two numbers in a row	press two numbers in a row
Select brush mode	Control-click with paint or edit tool	Control-click with paint or edit tool or **Shift-Option-letter**
Cycle through brush modes	*none*	**Shift-plus (+)** or **Shift-minus (–)**
Reset to Normal brush mode	*none*	**Shift-Option-N**
Display or hide Brushes palette	F5	F5
Cycle through brush shapes	press bracket, [or]	press bracket, [or]
Switch to first shape in Brushes palette	Shift-[	Shift-[
Switch to last shape in Brushes palette	Shift-]	Shift-]

Operation	Old Photoshop 4 shortcut	New Photoshop 5 shortcut
Painting and editing		
Delete shape from Brushes palette	⌘-click brush shape	⌘-click brush shape
Create new brush shape	click in empty area of Brushes palette	click in empty area of Brushes palette
Edit brush shape	double-click brush shape	double-click brush shape
Applying colors		
Lift foreground color from image	Option-click with paint tool or click with eyedropper	Option-click with paint tool or click with eyedropper
Lift background color from image	Option-click with eyedropper	Option-click with eyedropper
Sample color in image	*new feature*	**click with color sampler tool**
Delete color sample	*new feature*	**Option-click on target with color sampler tool**
Display or hide Color palette	F6	F6
Lift foreground color from color bar at bottom of Color palette	click color bar	click color bar
Lift background color from color bar	Option-click color bar	Option-click color bar
Cycle through color bars	Shift-click color bar	Shift-click color bar
Specify new color bar	Control-click color bar or ⌘-click for dialog box	Control-click color bar or ⌘-click for dialog box
Lift foreground color from Swatches palette	click swatch	click swatch
Lift background color from Swatches palette	Option-click swatch	Option-click swatch
Delete swatch from palette	⌘-click swatch	⌘-click swatch
Replace swatch with foreground color	Shift-click swatch	Shift-click swatch
Add new swatch to palette	click in empty area of palette or Shift-Option-click swatch	click in empty area of palette or Shift-Option-click on swatch

(continued)

Table 3-1 *(continued)*

Operation	Old Photoshop 4 shortcut	New Photoshop 5 shortcut
Applying colors		
Fill selection or layer with foreground color	Option-Delete	Option-Delete
Fill layer with foreground color but preserve transparency	Shift-Option-Delete	Shift-Option-Delete
Fill selection on background layer with background color	Delete	Delete
Fill selection on any layer with background color	⌘-Delete	⌘-Delete
Fill layer with background color but preserve transparency	Shift-⌘-Delete	Shift-⌘-Delete
Fill selection with source state in History palette	*new feature*	**⌘-Option-Delete**
Display Fill dialog box	Shift-Delete or Shift-F5	Shift-Delete or Shift-F5
Type		
Edit text layer	*new feature*	**double-click on T in Layers palette or click on type with type tool**
Select word in Text Tool dialog box	double-click on word	double-click on word
Select word to left or right	*none*	**⌘-Shift-left or right arrow**
Select all text	*none*	**⌘-A**
Increase type size two pixels (or points)	*none*	**⌘-Shift-greater than (>)**
Decrease type size two pixels	*none*	**⌘-Shift-less than (<)**
Increase type size 10 pixels	*none*	**⌘-Shift-Option-greater than (>)**
Decrease type size 10 pixels	*none*	**⌘-Shift-Option-less than (<)**

Operation	Old Photoshop 4 shortcut	New Photoshop 5 shortcut
Type		
Tighten leading two pixels	*none*	**Option-up arrow**
Expand leading two pixels	*none*	**Option-down arrow**
Tighten leading 10 pixels	*none*	**⌘-Option-up arrow**
Expand leading 10 pixels	*none*	**⌘-Option-down arrow**
Kern together × 2/100 em	*new feature*	**Option-left arrow**
Kern apart × 2/100 em	*new feature*	**Option-right arrow**
Kern together × 1/10 em	*new feature*	**⌘-Option-left arrow**
Kern apart × 1/10 em	*new feature*	**⌘-Option-right arrow**
Raise baseline shift two pixels	*new feature*	**Shift-Option-up arrow**
Lower baseline shift two pixels	*new feature*	**Shift-Option-down arrow**
Raise baseline shift 10 pixels	*new feature*	**⌘-Shift-Option-up arrow**
Lower baseline shift 10 pixels	*new feature*	**⌘-Shift-Option-down arrow**
Exit Type Tool dialog box	Enter	Enter or **⌘-Return**
Left-align text	*new feature*	**⌘-Shift-L**
Center-align text	*new feature*	**⌘-Shift-C**
Right-align text	*new feature*	**⌘-Shift-R**
Magnify view in Text Tool dialog box	*new feature*	**⌘-plus (+)**
Zoom out in Text Tool dialog box	*new feature*	**⌘-minus (–)**
Selections		
Select everything	⌘-A	⌘-A
Deselect everything	⌘-D	⌘-D
Restore selection after deselecting	*new feature*	**⌘-Shift-D**

(continued)

Table 3-1 (continued)

Operation	Old Photoshop 4 shortcut	New Photoshop 5 shortcut
Selections		
Hide or show marching ants	⌘-H	⌘-H
Feather the selection	⌘-Shift-D or Shift-F6	**⌘-Option-D** or Shift-F6
Reverse the selection	⌘-Shift-I or Shift-F7	⌘-Shift-I or Shift-F7
Cycle through all marquee tools (including crop tool)	Option-click marquee tool icon	Option-click marquee tool icon
Toggle between rectangular and elliptical marquees	press M	**Shift-M**
Draw out from center with marquee tool	Option-drag	Option-drag
Constrain marquee to square or circle	press Shift while drawing shape	press Shift while drawing shape
Move marquee as you draw it	press spacebar	press spacebar
Cycle through lasso tools	Option-click lasso tool icon or press L	Option-click lasso tool icon or **Shift-L**
Add corner to straight-sided selection outline	Option-click with lasso tool or click with polygonal lasso	Option-click with lasso tool or click with polygonal lasso
Add point to magnetic selection	*new feature*	**click with magentic lasso tool**
Delete last point added with magnetic lasso tool	*new feature*	**Delete**
Increase or reduce magnetic lasso width	*new feature*	**press bracket, [or]**
Close polygon or magnetic selection	double-click with respective lasso tool or press Return	double-click with respective lasso tool or press Return
Close magnetic selection with straight segment	*new feature*	**Option-double-click or Option-Return**
Cancel polygon or magnetic selection	press Escape	press Escape

Operation	Old Photoshop 4 shortcut	New Photoshop 5 shortcut
Selections		
Add to selection	Shift-drag or Shift-click with selection tool	Shift-drag or Shift-click with selection tool
Subtract from selection	Option-drag or Option-click with selection tool	Option-drag or Option-click with selection tool
Retain intersected portion of selection	Shift-Option-drag or Shift-Option-click with selection tool	Shift-Option-drag or Shift-Option-click with selection tool
Add character outlines to a selection	Shift-click with type mask tool	Shift-click with type mask tool
Cut letter-shaped holes into a selection	Option-click with type mask tool	Option-click with type mask tool
Retain areas where character outlines and selection intersect	Shift-Option-click with type mask tool	Shift-Option-click with type mask tool
Select move tool	press V or press and hold ⌘	press V or press and hold ⌘
Move selection	drag with move tool or ⌘-drag with other tool	drag with move tool or ⌘-drag with other tool
Constrain movement vertically or horizontally	press Shift while dragging selection	press Shift while dragging selection
Move selection in 1-pixel increments	⌘-arrow key	⌘-arrow key
Move selection in 10-pixel increments	⌘-Shift-arrow key	⌘-Shift-arrow key
Clone selection	Option-drag selection with move tool or ⌘-Option-drag with other tool	Option-drag selection with move tool or ⌘-Option-drag with other tool
Clone selection in 1-pixel increments	⌘-Option-arrow key	⌘-Option-arrow key
Clone selection in 10-pixel increments	⌘-Shift-Option-arrow key	⌘-Shift-Option-arrow key
Clone selection to different image	⌘-drag selection from one window and drop it into another	⌘-drag selection from one window and drop it into another
Move selection outline independently of its contents	drag with selection tool	drag with selection tool

(continued)

Table 3-1 *(continued)*

Operation	Old Photoshop 4 shortcut	New Photoshop 5 shortcut
Selections		
Move selection outline in 1-pixel increments	press arrow key when selection tool is active	press arrow key when selection tool is active
Move selection outline in 10-pixel increments	Shift-arrow key when selection tool is active	Shift-arrow key when selection tool is active
Copy empty selection outline to different image	drag selection from one window into another with selection tool	drag selection from one window into another with selection tool
Change opacity of floating selection	press number (1 through 0) when selection tool is active	⌘-**Shift-F**
Paste image into selection	⌘-Shift-V	⌘-Shift-V
Paste image behind selection	⌘-Shift-Option-V	⌘-Shift-Option-V
Layers		
Display or hide Layers palette	F7	F7
View single layer by itself	Option-click eyeball icon in Layers palette	Option-click eyeball icon in Layers palette
Create new layer and set blend options	Option-click page icon at bottom of Layers palette	Option-click page icon at bottom of Layers palette or ⌘-**Shift-N**
Create new layer and bypass blend options	click page icon at bottom of Layers palette	click page icon at bottom of Layers palette or ⌘- **Shift-Option-N**
Clone selection to new layer	⌘-J	⌘-J
Convert selection to new layer and leave hole behind	⌘-Shift-J	⌘-Shift-J
Convert floating selection to new layer	double-click Floating Selection item in Layers palette or ⌘-Shift-J	⌘-Shift-J
Duplicate layer to new layer	drag layer name onto page icon or ⌘-A, ⌘-J	drag layer name onto page icon or ⌘-A, ⌘-J
Ascend one layer	Option-]	Option-]

Operation	Old Photoshop 4 shortcut	New Photoshop 5 shortcut
Layers		
Descend one layer	Option-[	Option-[
Ascend to top layer	Shift-Option-]	Shift-Option-]
Descend to background layer	Shift-Option-[	Shift-Option-[
Go directly to layer that contains specific image	⌘-Option-Control-click image with any tool	⌘-Option-Control-click image with any tool
Preserve transparency of active layer	press slash (/)	press slash (/)
Convert layer's transparency mask to selection outline	⌘-click layer name in Layers palette	⌘-click layer name in Layers palette
Add transparency mask to selection	⌘-Shift-click layer name	⌘-Shift-click layer name
Subtract transparency mask from selection	⌘-Option-click layer name	⌘-Option-click layer name
Retain intersection of transparency mask and selection	⌘-Shift-Option-click layer name	⌘-Shift-Option-click layer name
Move entire layer	drag with move tool or ⌘-drag with other tool	drag with move tool or ⌘-drag with other tool
Move entire layer in 1-pixel increments	⌘-arrow key	⌘-arrow key
Move entire layer in 10-pixel increments	⌘-Shift-arrow key	⌘-Shift-arrow key
Bring layer forward one level	⌘-]	⌘-]
Bring layer to front of file	⌘-Shift-]	⌘-Shift-]
Send layer backward one level	⌘-[	⌘-[
Send layer to back, just above the background layer	⌘-Shift-[	⌘-Shift-[

(continued)

Table 3-1 *(continued)*

Operation	Old Photoshop 4 shortcut	New Photoshop 5 shortcut
Layers		
Link layer with active layer	click in front of layer name	click in front of layer name
Unlink layer from active layer	click on chain icon in front of layer name	click on chain icon in front of layer name
Unlink all layers from active layer	Option-click on brush icon in front of active layer name	Option-click on brush icon in front of active layer name
Change opacity of active layer in 10% increments	press number (1 through 0) when selection tool is active	press number (1 through 0) when selection tool is active
Change opacity of active layer in 1% increments	press two numbers in a row when selection tool is active	press two numbers in a row when selection tool is active
Edit blend options for layer	double-click layer name in Layers palette	double-click layer name in Layers palette
Select blend mode	*none*	**Shift-Option-letter**
Cycle through blend modes	*none*	**Shift-plus (+)** or **Shift-minus (–) when selection tool is active**
Reset to Normal blend mode	*none*	**Shift-Option-N**
Adjust "fuzziness" in Layer Options dialog box	Option-drag slider triangle	Option-drag slider triangle
Merge layer with next layer down	⌘-E	⌘-E
Merge linked layers	⌘-E	⌘-E
Merge all visible layers	⌘-Shift-E	⌘-Shift-E
Copy merged version of selection to Clipboard	⌘-Shift-C	⌘-Shift-C
Clone contents of layer into next layer down	⌘-Option-E	⌘-Option-E
Clone contents of linked layers to active layer	⌘-Option-E	⌘-Option-E
Clone contents of all visible layers to activate layer	⌘-Option-Shift-E	⌘-Option-Shift-E
Group neighboring layers	Option-click horizontal line in Layers palette or ⌘-G	Option-click horizontal line in Layers palette or ⌘-G

Operation	Old Photoshop 4 shortcut	New Photoshop 5 shortcut
Layers		
Ungroup neighboring layers	Option-click dotted line in Layers palette or ⌘-Shift-G	Option-click dotted line in Layers palette or ⌘-Shift-G
Switch between layer effects in Effects dialog box	*new feature*	**⌘-1 through ⌘-5**
Switch between layer effects outside dialog box	*new feature*	**Control-click on ƒ in Layers palette**
Edit layer effect	*new feature*	**double-click on ƒ**
Move shadow when Effect dialog box is open	*new feature*	**drag in image window**
Disable last layer effect	*new feature*	**Option-double-click on ƒ**
Disable specific layer effect	*new feature*	**Option-choose command from Layer ⇨ Effects submenu**
Create adjustment layer	⌘-click page icon at bottom of Layers palette	⌘-click page icon at bottom of Layers palette
Save flattened copy of layered image	⌘-Option-S	⌘-Option-S
Channels and masks		
Switch between independent color and mask channels	⌘-1 through ⌘-9	⌘-1 through ⌘-9
Switch to composite color view	⌘-tilde (~)	⌘-tilde (~)
Activate or deactivate color channel	Shift-click channel name in Channels palette	Shift-click channel name in Channels palette
Create channel mask filled with black	click page icon at bottom of Channels palette	click page icon at bottom of Channels palette
Create channel mask filled with black and set options	Option-click page icon at bottom of Channels palette	Option-click page icon at bottom of Channels palette
Create channel mask from selection outline	click mask icon at bottom of Channels palette	click mask icon at bottom of Channels palette

(continued)

Table 3-1 (continued)		
Operation	Old Photoshop 4 shortcut	New Photoshop 5 shortcut
Channels and masks		
Create channel mask from selection outline and set options	Option-click mask icon at bottom of Channels palette	Option-click mask icon at bottom of Channels palette
View channel mask as Rubylith overlay	click top eyeball in Channels palette or press tilde (~)	click top eyeball in Channels palette or press tilde (~)
Convert channel mask to selection outline	⌘-click channel name in Channels palette or ⌘-Option-number (1 through 0)	⌘-click channel name in Channels palette or ⌘-Option-number (1 through 0)
Replace channel mask with selection outline	new feature	**⌘-Control-click channel name in Channels palette**
Add channel mask to selection	⌘-Shift-click channel name	⌘-Shift-click channel name
Subtract channel mask from selection	⌘-Option-click channel name	⌘-Option-click channel name
Retain intersection of channel mask and selection	⌘-Shift-Option-click channel name	⌘-Shift-Option-click channel name
Enter or exit quick mask mode	press Q	press Q
Toggle quick mask color over masked or selected area	Option-click quick mask icon in toolbox	Option-click quick mask icon in toolbox
Change quick mask color overlay	double-click quick mask icon	double-click quick mask icon
View quick mask independently of image	click top eyeball in Channels palette or press tilde (~)	click top eyeball in Channels palette or press tilde (~)
Create layer mask filled with white	click mask icon at bottom of Layers palette	click mask icon at bottom of Layers palette
Create layer mask filled with black	Option-click mask icon	Option-click mask icon
Create layer mask from selection outline	click mask icon	click mask icon

Operation	Old Photoshop 4 shortcut	New Photoshop 5 shortcut
Channels and masks		
Create layer mask that hides selection	Option-click mask icon	Option-click mask icon
Switch focus from layer mask to image	⌘-tilde (~)	⌘-tilde (~)
Switch focus from image to layer mask	⌘-backslash (\\)	⌘-backslash (\\)
View layer mask independently of image	Option-click layer mask thumbnail in Layers palette or press backslash (\\) then tilde (~)	Option-click layer mask thumbnail in Layers palette or press backslash (\\) then tilde (~)
View layer mask as Rubylith overlay	Shift-Option-click layer mask thumbnail or press backslash (\\)	Shift-Option-click layer mask thumbnail or press backslash (\\)
Disable layer mask	Shift-click layer mask thumbnail	Shift-click layer mask thumbnail
Toggle link between layer and layer mask	click between layer and mask thumbnails in Layers palette	click between layer and mask thumbnails in Layers palette
Convert layer mask to selection outline	⌘-click layer mask thumbnail or ⌘-Option-backslash (\\)	⌘-click layer mask thumbnail or ⌘-Option-backslash (\\)
Add layer mask to selection	⌘-Shift-click layer mask thumbnail	⌘-Shift-click layer mask thumbnail
Subtract layer mask from selection	⌘-Option-click layer mask thumbnail	⌘-Option-click layer mask thumbnail
Retain intersection of layer mask and selection	⌘-Shift-Option-click layer mask thumbnail	⌘-Shift-Option-click layer mask thumbnail
Add spot color channel	*new feature*	**⌘-click page icon at bottom of Channels palette**
Paths		
Select pen tool	press P	press P
Cycle between standard, freeform, and magnetic pen tools	*new feature*	**Shift-P**
Select insert point tool	press P	**press plus (+)**

(continued)

Table 3-1 *(continued)*

Operation	Old Photoshop 4 shortcut	New Photoshop 5 shortcut
Paths		
Select remove point tool	press P	**press minus (–)**
Add corner to path	click with pen tool	click with pen tool or **Option-click with freeform pen tool**
Add smooth arc to path	drag with pen tool	drag with pen tool
Add cusp to path	drag with pen tool, then Option-drag same point	drag with pen tool, then Option-drag same point
Add point to magnetic selection	*new feature*	**click with magentic pen tool**
Delete last point added with standard or magentic pen tool	Delete	Delete
Draw freehand path segment	*new feature*	**drag with freeform pen tool or Option-drag with magnetic pen tool**
Switch to polygonal Lasso	*new feature*	**Option-click**
Toggle to Convert Direction tool from Pen Tool	*new feature*	**Option**
Toggle to Convert Direction tool from Direct Select Tool	*new feature*	**⌘-Option over anchor point**
Increase or reduce magnetic pen width	*new feature*	**press bracket, [or]**
Close magnetic selection	*new feature*	**Double-click with magnetic pen tool** or **click on first point in path**
Close magnetic selection with straight segment	*new feature*	**Option-double-click** or **Option-Return**
Cancel magnetic or freeform selection	*new feature*	**press Escape**
Select arrow (direct selection) tool	press P or press and hold ⌘ when pen tool is active	**press A** or press and hold ⌘ when pen tool is active
Select insert or remove point tool	press P	**press plus (+)** or **minus (–)**

Operation	Old Photoshop 4 shortcut	New Photoshop 5 shortcut
Paths		
Move selected points	drag point with arrow tool or ⌘-drag with pen tool	drag point with arrow tool or ⌘-drag with pen tool
Select multiple points in path	Shift-click point with arrow or ⌘-Shift-click with pen	Shift-click point with arrow or ⌘-Shift-click with pen
Select entire path	Option-click path with arrow or ⌘-Option-click with pen	Option-click path with arrow or ⌘-Option-click with pen
Clone path	Option-drag path with arrow or ⌘-Option-drag with pen	Option-drag path with arrow or ⌘-Option-drag with pen
Convert corner or cusp to smooth arc	control-drag point with arrow or ⌘-Control-drag with pen	**⌘-Option-drag point with arrow or Option-drag with pen**
Convert arc to corner	control-click point with arrow or ⌘-Control-click with pen	**⌘-Option-click point with arrow or Option-click with pen**
Convert arc to cusp	control-drag handle with arrow or ⌘-Control-drag with pen	**⌘-Option-drag handle with arrow or Option-drag with pen**
Insert point in path	⌘-Option-click segment with arrow tool or Control-click with pen tool	**click segment with pen tool or Option-click with remove point tool**
Remove point from path	⌘-Option-click point with arrow tool or Control-click with pen tool	**click point with pen tool or Option-click with insert point tool**
Convert path to selection outline	⌘-click path name in Paths palette or press Enter when selection or path tool is active	⌘-click path name in Paths palette or press Enter when selection or path tool is active
Add path to selection	⌘-Shift-click path name or Shift-Enter	⌘-Shift-click path name or Shift-Enter
Subtract path from selection	⌘-Option-click path name or Option-Enter	⌘-Option-click path name or Option-Enter
Retain intersection of path and selection	⌘-Shift-Option-click path name or Shift-Option-Enter	⌘-Shift-Option-click path name or Shift-Option-Enter
Apply brushstroke around perimeter of path	press Enter when paint or edit tool is active	press Enter when paint or edit tool is active

(continued)

Table 3-1 *(continued)*

Operation	Old Photoshop 4 shortcut	New Photoshop 5 shortcut
Paths		
Revert around perimeter of path	press Option-Enter when eraser tool is active	press Option-Enter when eraser tool is active or **Enter when history brush is active**
Save path for future use	double-click Work Path item in Paths palette	double-click Work Path item in Paths palette
Hide path (it remains active)	⌘-Shift-H	⌘-Shift-H
Deactivate path	click in empty portion of Paths palette	click in empty portion of Paths palette
Crops and transformations		
Select crop tool	press C	press C
Move cropping boundary	drag inside boundary	drag inside boundary
Resize cropping boundary	drag boundary handle	drag boundary handle
Rotate cropping boundary	drag outside boundary	drag outside boundary
Accept crop	double-click inside boundary or press Return	double-click inside boundary or press Return
Cancel crop	press Escape	press Escape
Transform selection or layer numerically	⌘-Shift-T	none
Freely transform selection or layer	⌘-T	⌘-T
Duplicate selection and freely transform	⌘-Option-T	⌘-Option-T
Move image in Free Transform mode	drag inside boundary	drag inside boundary
Move transformation origin	*new feature*	**drag crosshair target**
Resize image	drag boundary handle	drag boundary handle
Resize with respect to origin	*new feature*	**Option-drag boundary handle**
Rotate image (always with respect to origin)	drag outside boundary	drag outside boundary
Scale with respect to center point	*new feature*	**Option-drag corner**

Operation	Old Photoshop 4 shortcut	New Photoshop 5 shortcut
Crops and transformations		
Skew image	⌘-drag side handle	⌘-drag side handle
Skew image along constrained axis	⌘-Shift-drag side handle	⌘-Shift-drag side handle
Skew image with respect to origin	*new feature*	**⌘-Option-drag side handle**
Skew image along constrained axis with respect to origin	*new feature*	**⌘-Shift-Option-drag side handle**
Distort image	⌘-drag corner handle	⌘-drag corner handle
Symmetrically distort opposite corners	⌘-Option-drag corner handle	⌘-Option-drag corner handle
Constrained distort for perspective effect	⌘-Shift-drag corner handle	⌘-Shift-drag corner handle
Constrained distort for symmetrical perspective effect	⌘-Shift-Option-drag corner handle	⌘-Shift-Option-drag corner handle
Apply specific transformation in Free Transform mode	Control-click in image window	Control-click in image window
Accept transformation	double-click inside boundary or press Return	double-click inside boundary or press Return
Cancel transformation	press Escape	press Escape
Replay last transformation	*new feature*	**⌘-Shift-T**
Duplicate selection and replay last transformation	*new feature*	**⌘-Shift-Option-T**
Rulers, measurements, and guides		
Display or hide rulers	⌘-R	⌘-R
Display or hide Info palette	F8	F8
Change unit of measure	drag from X,Y pop-up in Info palette or double-click ruler	drag from X,Y pop-up in Info palette or double-click ruler
Select measure tool	*new feature*	**press U**
Measure distance and angle	drag with line tool set to Weight of 0	**drag with measure tool**

(continued)

Table 3-1 *(continued)*

Operation	Old Photoshop 4 shortcut	New Photoshop 5 shortcut
Rulers, measurements, and guides		
Move measure line	*new feature*	**drag measure line**
Change length and angle of measure line	*new feature*	**drag point at either end of measure line**
Measure angle between two lines (protractor option)	*new feature*	**Option-drag endpoint**
Display or hide guides	⌘-semicolon (;)	⌘-semicolon (;)
Create guide	drag from ruler	drag from ruler
Move guide	drag guide with move tool or ⌘-drag with other tool	drag guide with move tool or ⌘-drag with other tool
Toggle horizontal guide to vertical or vice versa	press Option while dragging guide	press Option while dragging guide
Snap guide to ruler tick marks	press Shift while dragging guide	press Shift while dragging guide
Toggle guide magnetism	⌘-Shift-semicolon (;)	⌘-Shift-semicolon (;)
Lock or unlock guides	⌘-Option-semicolon (;)	⌘-Option-semicolon (;)
Display or hide grid	⌘-quote (")	⌘-quote (")
Toggle grid magnetism	⌘-Shift-quote (")	⌘-Shift-quote (")
Edit guide color and grid increments	⌘-double-click guide	⌘-double-click guide
Filters		
Repeat filter with last-used settings	⌘-F	⌘-F
Repeat filter with different settings	⌘-Option-F	⌘-Option-F
Scroll preview box in corrective filter dialog boxes	drag in preview box or click in image window	drag in preview box or click in image window
Zoom preview box in corrective filter dialog boxes	⌘-click and Option-click	⌘-click and Option-click

Operation	*Old Photoshop 4 shortcut*	*New Photoshop 5 shortcut*
Filters		
Increase selected option-box value by 1 (or 0.1)	up arrow	up arrow
Decrease value by 1 (or 0.1)	down arrow	down arrow
Increase value by 10 (or 1)	Shift-up arrow	Shift-up arrow
Decrease value by 10 (or 1)	Shift-down arrow	Shift-down arrow
Adjust Angle value (where offered) in 15° increments	Shift-drag in Angle wheel	Shift-drag in Angle wheel
Reset options inside corrective filter dialog boxes	Option-click Cancel button or Option-Escape	Option-click Cancel button or Option-Escape
Clone light in Lighting Effects dialog box	Option-drag light	Option-drag light
Delete Lighting Effects light	press Delete	Press Delete
Adjust size of footprint without affecting angle of light	Shift-drag handle	Shift-drag handle
Adjust angle of light without affecting size of footprint	⌘-drag handle	⌘-drag handle
Switch between arrow tools in 3D Transform dialog box	*new feature*	**press V** or **A,** or **⌘-Tab**
Select 3D cube, sphere, or cylinder tool	*new feature*	**press M, N,** or **C**
Edit shape with pan camera or trackball	*new feature*	**press E** or **R**
Delete selected 3D Transform shape	*new feature*	**delete**

(continued)

Table 3-1 *(continued)*

Operation	Old Photoshop 4 shortcut	New Photoshop 5 shortcut
Advanced color corrections		
Add point in Curves dialog box	click on graph line	click on graph line
Add specific color as new point on composite curve	*new feature*	**⌘-click in image window**
Add color as new point on independent channel curves	*new feature*	**⌘-Shift-click in image window**
Nudge selected curve point	*new feature*	**press arrow key**
Select next curve point	*new feature*	**⌘-Tab**
Select previous curve point	*new feature*	**⌘-Shift-tab**
Delete curve point	*new feature*	**⌘-click point**
Select multiple curve points	*new feature*	**Shift-click point**
Deselect all points	*new feature*	**⌘-D**
Move Hue/Saturation range to new location	*new feature*	**click in image window**
Add colors to Hue/Saturation range	*new feature*	**Shift-click** or **drag in image window**
Subtract colors from Hue/Saturation range	*new feature*	**Option-click** or **drag in image window**
Edit all colors in Hue/Saturation dialog box	*new feature*	**⌘-tilde (~)**
Edit predefined color range	*new feature*	**⌘-1 through ⌘-6**
Undoing operations		
Undo or redo last operation	⌘-Z	⌘-Z
Undo operation prior to last one	*new feature*	**⌘-Option-Z**
Redo undone operation	*new feature*	**⌘-Shift-Z**

Operation	Old Photoshop 4 shortcut	New Photoshop 5 shortcut
Undoing operations		
Undo to specific point	*new feature*	**click on item in History palette**
Duplicate previously performed operation	*new feature*	**Option-click on item in History palette**
Select state to revert to with history brush	*new feature*	**click in front of item in History palette**
Create snapshot from active state	*new feature*	**click page icon at bottom of History palette**
Create duplicate image from active state	*new feature*	**click . . . box icon at bottom of History palette**
Revert to saved image	F12	F12 or **click first item in History palette**
Miscellaneous		
Display or hide all palettes, and toolbox	Tab	Tab
Display or hide palettes except toolbox	Shift-Tab	Shift-Tab
Hide toolbox	Tab, Shift-Tab	Tab, Shift-Tab
Move a panel out of a palette	drag panel tab	drag panel tab
Snap palette to edge of screen	Shift-click palette title bar	Shift-click palette title bar
Fully collapse palette	Option-click collapse box or double-click panel tab	Option-click collapse box or double-click panel tab
Display or hide Actions palette	F9	F9
Play script	⌘-double-click on item in Actions palette	⌘-double-click on item in Actions palette
Permanently delete item from palette that includes trash can	Option-click trash can	Option-click trash can
Preview how image sits on printed page	click preview box	click preview box
View size and resolution of image	Option-click preview box	Option-click preview box

(continued)

	Table 3-1 (continued)	
Operation	*Old Photoshop 4 shortcut*	*New Photoshop 5 shortcut*
Miscellaneous		
Change the preference settings	⌘-K	⌘-K
Display last used Preferences dialog box panel	⌘-Option-K	⌘-Option-K
Bring up dialog box with last-used settings	Option-choose command from Image ⇨ Adjust submenu	Option-choose command from Image ⇨ Adjust submenu
Duplicate image and bypass dialog box	Option-choose Image ⇨ Duplicate	Option-choose Image ⇨ Duplicate
Cancel the current operation	⌘-period or Escape	⌘-period or Escape
Activate Don't Save or Don't Flatten button	Press D	Press D

Creating Scripts

So much for the shortcuts built into Photoshop. But while Table 3-1 may be the longest shortcuts list you've ever seen in your life, it's possible the list isn't long enough. You still must choose quite a few common commands from the menus. Canvas Size, Unsharp Mask, Variations, CMYK Color, and Color Range are a few of the commands I dearly wish included keyboard equivalents. Frankly, I use all five a heck of a lot more often than Show Rulers, Color Balance, and Gamut Warning, all of which Photoshop has endowed with shortcuts.

Photoshop's answer is the Actions palette, which lets you define your own keyboard shortcuts. But the Actions palette does more than simply let you assign a keyboard equivalent to a command. You can record an entire sequence of commands and operations as a single *script*. You can also *batch-process* images, which means to apply a script to an entire folder of files while you go off and have one of those power lunches you've heard so much about. If you spend a lot of your time performing repetitive tasks, scripts can help you automate your workaday routine; then you can devote your creative energies to something more important, like take a nap.

Photoshop 5.0

For you Action-eers who are familiar with scripting from Photoshop 4, prepare yourself for some improvements. First, the Actions palette is more sensitive, permitting you to record blend modes, opacity settings, and other options that the previous Actions palette ignored. You can also save and load scripts in groups. And finally, you can assign the ⌘ key as a shortcut modifier, effectively doubling the number of keystrokes from 30 to 60. (In the last edition I wrote "I for one could use twice as many custom shortcuts" and now I got 'em. Isn't the free market awesome?)

Cross-Reference

For examples of real scripts, read Chapters 15 and 18. Both chapters contain recipes for correcting pictures you've shot with a digital camera or downloaded from the Web.

Recording a script

Choose Window ➪ Show Actions or press F9 to view the Actions palette. The icons along the bottom of the palette — labeled in Figure 3-6 — allow you to record operations and manage your recorded scripts. A script can include only a single command, as in the case of the RGB Color and Grayscale items listed near the middle of the palette in the figure. Or you can record many operations in a row, as in the case of the Sharpen JPEG example.

Figure 3-6: The Actions palette lets you record a sequence of operations and assign a keyboard shortcut.

In Photoshop 5, you can organize scripts into groups, which Adobe calls "sets." (I'm not a big fan of this term—what's wrong with "groups"?—but now I'm nit-picking, aren't I?) Sets are useful when saving scripts—you save an entire set at a time—and they help keep things tidy. A set appears as a folder in a gray bar. Scripts are indented below the set and operations are indented below the scripts. It's a simple directory hierarchy, with which we're all amply familiar from the operating system.

If you've ever used a macro editor, such as QuicKeys or Tempo, the Actions palette isn't much different. (If you've never even heard of these utilities, not a problem. No experience required.) Here's a basic rundown of how you record a script:

Steps: Recording a Script

1. **Select a set for your new script.** Just click on the set that makes sense. Or create a new set by clicking on the little folder icon at the bottom of the Actions palette. Naturally, Photoshop asks you to name the set.

If you don't want Photoshop to bother you with such trivialities as set naming, Option-click on the folder icon to bypass the New Set dialog box.

2. **Create a new script.** This is very important. Much as you might like to click on the record button and go, you have to first make a script to hold the recorded operations. Click on the new script icon—the one that looks like a little page. Photoshop responds with the New Action dialog box, shown in Figure 3-7.

To skip this dialog box, use that Option key again. (In this case, I don't recommend it, but it is an option.) Option-clicking on the new script icon takes you directly to Step 7.

Figure 3-7: You can assign a name, function key, and color to a new script.

If you accidentally start recording and decide against it, just press ⌘-Z to both cancel the operation and undo the new script. This new undo feature is hot, hot, hot.

3. **Enter a name for your script.** Something descriptive, up to 31 characters long.

4. **Assign a keyboard shortcut.** You can also assign a function key, F1 through F15, with or without Shift and ⌘. From then on, you can play the script simply by pressing the assigned function key combination.

When assigning function keys, it's possible to overwrite one of the predefined shortcuts in Table 3-1. By default, F1 is assigned to the Undo command. F2 through F4 choose Cut, Copy, and Paste. Shift- F5, F6, and F7 are assigned to the Fill, Feather, and Inverse commands. As far as I'm concerned, all of these shortcuts are up for grabs, because the commands have alternative shortcuts. (You can press ⌘-Z for Undo, for example.)

But you might hesitate before assigning F5 through F9. These display palettes, as shown back in Figure 3-5, and there are no alternative shortcuts. Also worth noting, Photoshop won't let you assign a function key that's already assigned in the Actions palette. To assign F11 or F12, for example, you have to first release the key from its current assignment (Image Size or Revert, respectively).

5. **Select a designer color.** The color affects the appearance of the script in the Actions palette's button mode, which I discuss in the "Playing scripts and operations" section later in this chapter.

6. **Press Return to start recording.** The circular record icon at the bottom of the Actions palette turns red to show you Photoshop is now observing your every action.

7. **Perform the desired operations.** If you want to assign a keystroke to a single command—such as Unsharp Mask—choose that command, enter some settings, and press Return. If you want to record a sequence of operations, work through the sequence as you normally would.

But whatever you do, relax. There's no hurry and no pressure to perform. Feel free to take all day to figure out what you're doing. You can start to choose a command and then change your mind. You can even enter a dialog box and cancel out of it. Like a kindly great grandmother (there's that relative again!), Photoshop turns a blind eye to your hesitations and false starts. Even if you mess up, just keep going. Photoshop lets you insert and reorder operations later.

(continued)

Photoshop 5.0

As I mentioned before, Photoshop 5 is more sensitive to your actions than its predecessor. But just how sensitive may come as a surprise. Where Version 4 recorded only commands (and numerical settings inside those commands), the new Photoshop records layer movements, transformations, links, opacity settings, blend modes, changes to the foreground and background colors, tool settings, and — get this — shapes and positions of free-form selection outlines. You can even record a state in the History palette, which is to say that a script may undo a specific number of operations performed on an image.

Not recorded are paint and edit tools operations, zooms and scrolls, and any command under the View or Window menu. (However, you can force Photoshop to record a command under the View or Window menu, as explained later in the "Editing a script" section.)

After you complete the operation, Photoshop adds it to the Actions palette. The program constantly keeps you apprised of what it's recording. If you perform an action and Photoshop doesn't add it to the palette, you've been officially ignored.

8. **When you're finished, click on the stop button.** That's the square icon at the bottom of the Actions palette. Congratulations, you've now successfully recorded a script.

Tip

Photoshop not only records your operations in the Actions palette, it also applies them to whatever image you have open. (If you open an image while recording, Photoshop adds the Open command to the script.) For this reason, it's usually a good idea to have a dummy image open. When you're finished recording, you can choose File ⇨ Revert (F12) to restore the original, unmolested image.

If your script includes a Save operation, try to use File ⇨ Save As or File ⇨ Save a Copy. This way, the original file will remain intact.

Editing a script

If you take it slow and easy, you have a good chance of recording your script right the first time. But no matter if you flub it. Photoshop offers the following options to help you get it exactly right:

✦ **Adding more operations:** To add more operations at the end of a script, select the script and click on the round record icon. Then start applying the operations you want to record. When you finish, click again on the stop icon. If you selected the script before recording, Photoshop automatically adds the new operations to the end of the script. Or you can click on a specific operation name and then begin recording. In this case, the new operation appears immediately after the operation you clicked.

✦ **Moving an operation:** To change the order of an operation, drag the operation up or down in the list. You can even drag an operation from one script into another if you like.

✦ **Copying an operation:** To make a copy of an operation, Option-drag it to a different location. Again, you can Option-drag operations between scripts.

✦ **Investigating an operation:** If you can't remember what setting you entered in a dialog box, or you don't recognize what an operation name like Set Current Layer means, click on the triangle before the operation name to expand it. Figure 3-8 shows an example of a Set Current Layer operation expanded to show that Photoshop has set the layer to 30 percent opacity.

Note

(Now do you see why I think "set" is a bad name for those folder/group things that hold scripts? Commands have settings, the Actions palette records an operation as being "set," and now you can group operations into sets. These terms may be set in stone, but they don't sit well with me.)

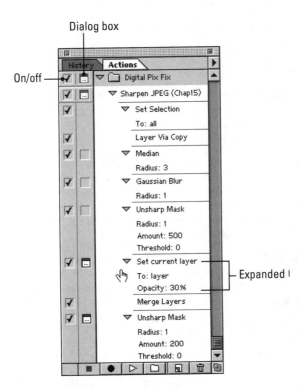

Figure 3-8: Click on the little triangles to expand the operations and view their settings.

✦ **Changing a setting:** If an operation name includes an embossed square to the left of it — in the column marked *Dialog box* in Figure 3-8 — it brings up a dialog box. When you expand the operation, Photoshop tells you the settings entered into that dialog box. In the case of the Median item in the figure, for example, the Radius value in the Median dialog box has been set to 3. To change the setting, double-click on the operation name, revise the settings in the dialog box, and press Return.

Photoshop will go ahead and apply the settings to your image. If this is a problem, press ⌘-Z to undo the operation. This reverses the settings applied to the image, but has no effect on the changed settings in the script. The Actions palette ignores Edit ➪ Undo. (You can force the palette to accept the Undo command, however, as I'll explain shortly.)

✦ **Leaving a setting open:** Not all images are alike, and not all images need the same settings applied to them. If you want to enter your own settings as the script plays, click on the faint square in front of the operation name in the dialog box column. A little dialog box icon appears, which shows that you must be on hand when the script is played. In Figure 3-8, for example, a dialog box icon appears before the Set Current Layer item. When I play the script, Photoshop leaves the Layer Options dialog box up on screen until I enter an Opacity value and press Return. Then the program continues playing until it reaches the next dialog box icon or the end of the script.

Option-click in front of an operation name in the dialog box column to display a dialog box icon in front of that one operation and hide all others. To bring up dialog boxes for everybody, Option-click on the same dialog box icon again, or click on the red dialog box icon in front of the script name.

✦ **Forcing Photoshop to record a command:** If Photoshop ignored one of the commands you tried to record, choose Insert Menu Item from the Actions palette menu. Photoshop displays the dialog box shown in Figure 3-9, which asks you to choose a command. Go ahead and do it — the dialog box won't interfere with your progress. Then press Return to add the command to the script. In Figure 3-9, for example, I'm forcing a script to display the rulers.

If you want to force Photoshop to record a dimmed command, enter the name of the command and click on the Find button. For example, when you first enter the Insert Menu Item dialog box, the Undo command may read Cannot Undo in gray. Typing *Undo* and clicking on Find gets around the problem.

✦ **Inserting a stop:** A *stop* is a pause in the action. You can't do anything when the script is paused — not in Photoshop anyway. You can switch to a different application, but Photoshop's options are off limits until you cancel or complete the script. The only real purpose of a stop is to give you the chance to see how the operations have progressed so far. To add a stop, choose the Insert Stop command from the Actions palette menu. Then enter the message you want to appear when the stop occurs. Select the Allow Continue check box to enable you to continue the script during playback.

Figure 3-9: This dialog box forces Photoshop to record your command, whether it likes it or not.

✦ **Changing the name and function key:** To change the name, shortcut, or color assigned to a script, double-click on the script name. Up comes the Action Options dialog box, which contains the same options as appeared back in Figure 3-7. Change the settings as you like. Any function keys assigned to other scripts appear dimmed.

✦ **Deleting an operation:** To delete an operation, drag it to the trash can icon at the bottom of the Actions palette. Or easier still, select the operation you want to delete, and then Option-click on the trash can icon. (You can also merely click on the icon, but Photoshop will display an irritating alert message. Option-clicking skips the message.)

Playing scripts and operations

When it comes time to play your script, you can play all of it or just a single operation. The simplest way to play back an entire script is to press the function key you assigned to it.

If you don't like to fill your brain with ephemeral nonsense like what function key does what, you might prefer to switch to the button mode. To do so, choose the Button Mode command from the Actions palette menu, as shown in Figure 3-10. You can now see the colors you assigned to the scripts, as well as the function keys. Just click on the button for the script you want to play.

But the button mode has its drawbacks. All you can do is click on buttons. You can't edit scripts, you can't change the order of scripts, you can't assign new function keys to scripts, and you can't play individual operations. This is a great mode if you want to protect your scripts from less adept users, but it's an awful mode if you want to modify your scripts and create new ones.

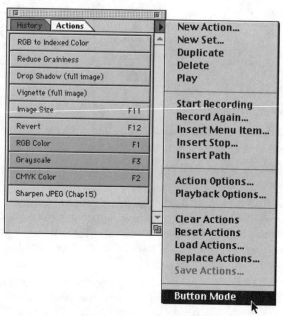

Figure 3-10: Choose the Button Mode command to view each script as an independent button.

So, choose the Button Mode command again to return to the normal palette setup. Then try some of these less-restrictive script-playing techniques:

✦ To play a selected script, click on the play icon at the bottom of the palette. You can also play a script by ⌘-double-clicking on the script name.

✦ To play a script from a certain operation on, select that operation name in the palette, and then click on the play icon.

✦ To play a single operation and no more, drag the operation name onto the play icon. Or ⌘-double-click on the operation name.

✦ You can tell Photoshop which operations to play and which to skip using the check marks in the on/off column (labeled back in Figure 3-7). Click on a check mark to turn off the corresponding operation.

✦ Option-click on a check mark to turn that one operation on and the rest off. To turn all the operations in the script on again, Option-click on the check mark again, or click on the red check mark by the script name.

✦ If you want to modify the speed at which Photoshop plays a script, choose the Playback Options command from the Actions palette menu. You have three options — play the script at top speed (Accelerated), permit Photoshop to redraw the screen image after each step (Step by Step), or add timed pauses between operations. The latter two options are useful if you want to show a script to a coworker or play a script for a presentation. But for routine work, stick with the default Accelerated setting.

If a script makes a mess of your image, it's no problem thanks to Photoshop 5's multiple undos. Switch to the History palette and click on the state in the list that comes directly before the first operation in your script. (The History palette doesn't list operations the same way the Actions palette does — so much for consistency — but with a little effort you can figure it out.) In a flash, you're back to your original image.

For complete information on the History palette, read Chapter 10.

Saving a set

In Photoshop 5, you save and load scripts in sets. It may sound like a bother, but it's way better than it used to be. Photoshop 4 saved all Actions in the palette, which meant that you ended up with a lot of duplicate scripts when you loaded a saved Actions file.

To save a set, first click on the set name in the Actions palette. Then choose Save Actions from the palette menu. Photoshop asks you for a destination and file name. Nothing out of the ordinary.

Scripts are 100 percent cross-platform. But if you want to be able to open a set of saved scripts in Photoshop for Windows, you have to include the three-character extension *.atn* at the end of the file name. Otherwise, the Windows Actions palette won't recognize the file.

Incidentally, the contents of the Actions palette is stored in the Adobe Photoshop 5.0 Prefs file. If this file becomes corrupted (as I explained in Chapter 2), you lose your scripts. So it's a good idea to save your sets to disk whenever you create a new script.

Batch-Processing Images

Batch-processing is one of those scary terms you hear bandied about by experts on a fairly regular basis. But it's actually relatively easy, especially with Photoshop's Batch command.

The following steps walk you through the task of batch-processing a bunch of files. This isn't the only way to batch-process files — Photoshop offers several additional variations you can experiment with on your own. But these steps represent the best way.

Steps: Batch-Processing Files

1. **Round up the images that you want to apply the script to.** You can put all the images in a single folder. Or, if you own a digital camera from which Photoshop can open images directly—anything from the $1,300 Olympus D-600L to the $200 Kodak DC20—plug the camera into your Mac and turn it on.

2. **Create a folder to collect the images once Photoshop is done processing them.** If you're opening images from a folder, you can have Photoshop save to the same folder, but this will save over the original files. It's a good precaution to save the files elsewhere so you can refer to the originals if you're not pleased with the scripted results.

3. **Select the script that you want to apply from the Actions palette.** This step isn't absolutely necessary, but frees you from having to select a script inside the Batch dialog box, which is less convenient.

4. **Choose File ⇨ Automate ⇨ Batch.** Photoshop displays the dialog box shown in Figure 3-11 with the script you selected all set to go. (See how convenient that is?) Don't be put off by the glut of options—the Batch dialog box is a peach once you get to know it.

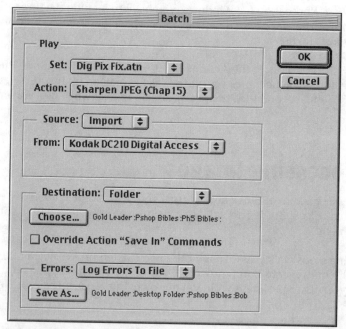

Figure 3-11: Here I have the Batch command all set up to import images from a Kodak DC210 digital camera, run the Sharpen JPEG script on them, and save each image to a folder on my hard drive.

5. **Select a source for the images.** Select Import from the Source pop-up menu if you want to acquire the images from a digital camera. Then select the acquire module you generally use to communicate with the camera from the From pop-up menu. (This requires a Photoshop-compatible plug-in, provided with the camera.)

   To open images from a folder, select Folder from the Source pop-up menu. Then click on the Choose button and locate the folder on disk.

6. **Select the destination folder.** First, select the Folder option from the Destination pop-up menu. Then click on the Choose button and locate the destination folder on disk.

   The Destination pop-up menu offers two other options — None, which collects the images on screen without saving them, and Save and Close, which saves the images over the originals and closes them. One clogs up RAM and slows performance, while the other eliminates your backup images. I'd steer clear of both.

   If the folder contains subdirectories, and you want to open and batch process images inside those subdirectories, select the Include All Subdirectories check box. Otherwise don't.

7. **Press Return.** Photoshop begins batch-processing your images, starting with the first image in alphabetical order.

Note

The Batch dialog box includes two Override check boxes that you can generally ignore. These apply only to scripts that include Open and Save As operations, in which case, the check box tells Photoshop to ignore the operation in favor of the Batch dialog box's own opening and saving functions. But because most scripts don't include Open or Save commands, these check boxes are seldom applicable.

You might want to watch the first image from start to finish to make sure everything goes smoothly, particularly the save operation. (Photoshop should close each image after it finishes saving it.) But after the first image, you should probably leave Photoshop and your computer alone to work their wonders. A watched pot never boils and a watched batch defeats the purpose. You're supposed to be out there engaging in interesting carbon-based activities while Photoshop slaves away in your absence. So get out of here!

Tip

If you're looking for maximum performance, there are two ways to crank batch processing up to its top speed. First, turn down the image cache. Press ⌘-K, ⌘-8 to display the Image Cache panel of the Preferences dialog box, then change the Cache Levels value to 1. Second, turn off the History palette's automatic snapshot feature. Choose History Option from the History palette menu. Then deselect the Automatically Create First Snapshot check box. Both steps work wonders in improving Photoshop's response time.

✦   ✦   ✦

Understanding Digital Imagery

Image Fundamentals

How Images Work

Think of a bitmapped image as a mosaic made from square tiles of various colors. When you view the mosaic up close, it looks like something you might use to decorate your bathroom. You see the individual tiles, not the image itself. But if you back a few feet away from the mosaic, the tiles lose their definition and merge together to create a recognizable work of art, presumably Medusa getting her head whacked off or some equally appetizing thematic classic.

Similarly, *images* are colored pixels pretending to be artwork. If you enlarge the pixels, they look like an unrelated collection of colored squares. Reduce the size of the pixels, and they blend together to form an image that looks to all the world like a standard photograph. Photoshop deceives the eye by borrowing from an artistic technique older than Mycenae or Pompeii.

Of course, differences exist between pixels and ancient mosaic tiles. Pixels come in 16 million distinct colors. Mosaic tiles of antiquity came in your basic granite and sandstone varieties, with an occasional chunk of lapis lazuli thrown in for good measure. Also, you can resample, color separate, and crop electronic images. We know from the time-worn scribblings of Dionysius of Halicarnassus that these processes were beyond the means of classical artisans.

But I'm getting ahead of myself. I won't be discussing resampling, cropping, or Halicarnassus for several pages. First, I'll address the inverse relationship between image size and resolution.

Size versus resolution

If you haven't already guessed, the term *image size* describes the physical dimensions of an image. *Resolution* is the number of pixels per linear inch in the final printed image. I say linear because you measure pixels in a straight line. If the resolution of an image is 72 *ppi*—that is, pixels per inch—you get 5,184 pixels per square inch (72 pixels wide × 72 pixels tall = 5,184).

Assuming the number of pixels in an image is fixed, increasing the size of an image decreases its resolution and vice versa. An image that looks good when printed on a postage stamp, therefore, probably looks jagged when printed as an 11 × 17-inch poster.

Figure 4-1 shows a single image printed at three different sizes and resolutions. The smallest image is printed at twice the resolution of the medium-sized image; the medium-sized image is printed at twice the resolution of the largest image.

Figure 4-1: These three images contain the same number of pixels, but are printed at different resolutions. Doubling the resolution of an image reduces it to 25 percent of its original size.

One inch in the smallest image includes twice as many pixels vertically and twice as many pixels horizontally as an inch in the medium-sized image, for a total of four times as many pixels per square inch. Therefore, the smallest image covers ¼ the area of the medium-sized image.

The same relationships exist between the medium-sized image and the largest image. An inch in the medium-sized image comprises four times as many pixels as an inch in the largest image. Consequently, the medium-sized image consumes one-fourth the area of the largest image.

Changing the printing resolution

When printing an image, a higher resolution translates to a sharper image with greater clarity. Photoshop lets you change the resolution of a printed image in one of two ways:

✦ Choose Image ➪ Image Size to access the controls that enable you to change the pixel dimensions and resolution of an image. Then enter a value into the Resolution option box, either in pixels per inch or pixels per centimeter.

A good idea (although not essential) is to turn off the Resample Image check box, as demonstrated in Figure 4-2. If you leave it on, Photoshop may add or subtract pixels, as discussed in the "Resampling and Cropping" section later in this chapter. By turning it off, you instruct Photoshop to leave the pixels intact but merely change how many of them print per inch.

Figure 4-2: Turn off the Resample Image check box to maintain a constant number of pixels in an image and to change only the printed resolution.

✦ Alternatively, you can ask Photoshop to scale an image during the print cycle. Choose File ➪ Page Setup (Ctrl+Shift+P) and enter a percentage value into the Reduce or Enlarge option box. Lower values reduce the size of the printed image and thereby increase the resolution; higher values lower the resolution.

Both the Resolution and Reduce or Enlarge settings are saved with an image. Together, the two determine the printed resolution. Photoshop divides the Resolution value in the Image Size dialog box by the Reduce or Enlarge percentage from Page Setup. For example, if the image resolution is set to 72 ppi and you reduce the image to 48 percent, then the final printed image has a resolution of 150 ppi (72 divided by .48).

Note

At the risk of boring some of you, I'll briefly remind the math haters in the audience that whenever you use a percentage in an equation, you first convert it to a decimal. For example, 100 percent is 1.0; 64 percent is .64; 5 percent is .05, and so on.

Tip

To avoid confusion, most folks rely exclusively on the Resolution value and leave Page Setup's Reduce or Enlarge value set to 100 percent. The only exception is when printing tests and proofs. Because ink-jet and other consumer printers offer lower-resolution output than high-end commercial devices, you may find it helpful to proof images larger so you can see more pixels. Raising the Reduce or Enlarge value lets you accomplish this without upsetting the Resolution value. Just be sure to restore the value to 100 percent after you make your test print.

Changing the page-layout resolution

The Reduce or Enlarge value has no effect on the size and resolution of an image imported into an object-oriented application, such as QuarkXPress or Illustrator. But these same applications do observe the Resolution setting from the Image Size dialog box.

Specifying the resolution in Photoshop is a handy way to avoid resizing operations and printing complications in your page-layout program. For example, I preset the resolution of all the images in this book so the production team had only to import the images and print away.

Tip

Always remember: Photoshop is as good or better at adjusting pixels than any other program you work with. So prepare an image as completely as possible in Photoshop before importing the image into another program. Ideally, you should never have to resize, rotate, or crop an image in any other program.

That tip is so important I'm going to repeat it: *Never* resize, rotate, or crop an image in Illustrator, FreeHand, CorelDraw, PageMaker, or QuarkXPress. Get your image fully ready to go in Photoshop, and then place it in the drawing or page-layout program, position it on the page, and leave it alone.

So what's the perfect resolution?

After all this explanation of pixels and resolution, you might be thinking, "Okay, this is all very interesting, but what's my bottom line? What Resolution value should I use?" The answer is frustrating to some and freeing to others: Any darn resolution you like. It's true—there is no right answer; there is no wrong answer. The images in this book vary from 100 ppi for screen shots to 300 ppi for color plates. I've seen low-resolution art that looks great and high-resolution art that looks horrible. As with all things, quality counts for more than quantity. You take the pixels you're dealt and you make the best of them.

That said, there are a few guidelines, which I'll share only if you promise to take them with a grain of salt:

✦ Most experts recommend that you set the Resolution value to somewhere between 150 percent and 200 percent of the *screen frequency* of the final output device. The screen frequency is the number of halftone dots per linear inch, measured in *lpi* (short for *lines per inch*). So ask your commercial printer what screen frequency he uses—generally 120 lpi to 150 lpi—and multiply that times 1.5 or 2.

✦ Want to be more specific? For high-end photographic print work, it's hard to go wrong with a Resolution value of 267 ppi. That's 200 percent of 133 lpi, arguably the most popular screen frequency. When in doubt, most professionals aim for 267 ppi.

✦ What if you don't have enough pixels for 267 ppi? Say that you shoot a digital snapshot that measures 768 × 1,024 pixels and you want to print it at 6 × 8 inches. That works out to a relatively scant 128 ppi. Won't that look grainy? Probably. Should you add pixels with Image Size or some other command? No, that typically won't help. You have a finite number of pixels to work with, so you can print the image large and a little grainy, or sharp and small. The choice is yours.

✦ What if you have a photograph or slide and you can scan it at any resolution you want? Flat-bed scanners typically offer two maximum resolutions: a true optical maximum and an interpolated digital enhancement. The lower of the two values is invariably the true optical resolution. Scan at this lower maximum setting. Then use Image ➪ Image Size to resample the image down to the desired size and resolution, as explained in the "Resampling and Cropping" section near the end of this chapter.

Orson Welles claimed that he relied on his inexperience when creating *Citizen Kane*. He didn't know the rules of film making, so he couldn't be hampered by them. When his assistants and technicians told him, "You can't do that," he ignored them because he didn't know any better.

I feel the same about resolution. Take the pixels you have and try to make them look the best you can. Then print the image at the size you want it to appear. If you focus the function of your image first and fret about resolution and other technical issues second, you'll produce better art.

The Resolution of Screen Images

Regardless of the Resolution and Reduce or Enlarge values, Photoshop displays each pixel on screen according to the zoom ratio (covered in Chapter 2). If the zoom ratio is 100 percent, for example, each image pixel takes up a single screen pixel. Zoom ratio and printer output are unrelated.

This same rule applies outside Photoshop as well. Other programs that display screen images — including multimedia development applications, presentation programs, and Web browsers — default to showing one image pixel for every screen pixel. This means when creating an image for the screen, the Resolution value has no affect whatsoever. I've seen some very bright people recommend that screen images should be set to 72 ppi on the Mac or 96 ppi for Windows, and while there's nothing wrong with doing this, there's no benefit either. When publishing for the screen, the Resolution value is ignored.

So all that counts is the 100-percent view. That means you want the image to fit inside the prospective monitor when you choose View ➪ Actual Pixels (⌘-Option-zero) inside Photoshop. I say *prospective* monitor because although you may use a 17-inch monitor when you create the image, you most likely need the final image to fit on a 13-inch display. So even though your monitor probably displays as many as 1,024 × 768 pixels, most Web and screen artists prepare for the worst-case scenario, 640 × 480 pixels. This is the 13-inch VGA standard, shared by some of the first color Macs and PCs, most laptops, an endless array of defunct computers, and even televisions.

Of course, a 640 × 480-pixel image would consume an entire 13-inch screen. If you want the image to share the page with text and other elements, the image needs to be smaller than that. A typical screen image varies from as small as 16 × 16 pixels for icons and buttons to 320 × 240 pixels for a stand-alone photograph. Naturally, these are merely guidelines. You can create images at any size you like.

For more information on creating images specifically for the World Wide Web, read Chapter 20.

How to Open, Duplicate, and Save Images

Before you can work on an image in Photoshop — whether you're creating a brand new document or opening an image from disk — you must first load the image into an image window. Here are the four basic ways to create an image window:

✦ **File ➪ New:** Create a new window by choosing File ➪ New (⌘-N). After you fill out the desired size and resolution specifications in the New dialog box, Photoshop confronts you with a stark, white, empty canvas. You then face the ultimate test of your artistic abilities — painting from scratch. Feel free to go nuts and cut off your ear.

✦ **File ➪ Open:** Open an image saved to disk or CD-ROM by choosing File ➪ Open (⌘-O). Of the four ways to create an image window, this method is the one you'll probably use most often. You can open images scanned in other applications, images purchased from stock photo agencies, slides and transparencies digitized to a Kodak Photo CD, or an image you previously edited in Photoshop.

✦ **Edit ➪ Paste:** Photoshop automatically adapts a new image window to the contents of the Clipboard (provided those contents are bitmapped). So if you copy an image inside a different application or in Photoshop, and then choose File ➪ New, Photoshop enters the dimensions and resolution of the image into the New dialog box. All you must do is accept the settings and choose Edit ➪ Paste (⌘-V) to introduce the image into a new window. This technique is useful for editing screen shots captured to the Clipboard or for testing effects on a sample of an image without harming the original.

   Photoshop automatically pastes an image to a new layer, preventing you from saving the file in any but the native Photoshop format (as I explain later in this chapter). To flatten the pasted image so you can save it in some other format, choose Layer ➪ Merge Down or press ⌘- E.

✦ **File ➪ Import:** If you own a scanner or digital camera, it may include a plug-in module that lets you to transfer an image directly into Photoshop. Just copy the module into Photoshop's Plug-Ins folder and then run or relaunch the Photoshop application. To initiate a scan or to load an image into Photoshop, choose the plug-in module from the File ➪ Import submenu.

For example, to load an image from my Polaroid PDC-2000 — an aging but still very good camera under $2,000 — I cable the camera to my Mac's SCSI port. Then I turn the camera on and choose File ➪ Import ➪ PDC-2000. A dialog box appears showing thumbnails of all the images I've shot, as in Figure 4-3. I select the images I want to edit, click the Transfer button, and the images open directly inside Photoshop.

Figure 4-3: The Polaroid PDC-2000 module lets me view images stored in the camera's memory and open them up directly inside Photoshop.

Creating a new image

Whether you're creating an image from scratch or transferring the contents of the Clipboard to a new image window, choose File ➪ New or press ⌘-N to bring up the New dialog box shown in Figure 4-4. If the Clipboard contains an image, the Width, Height, and Resolution option boxes show the size and resolution of this image. Otherwise, you can enter your own values in one of five units of measurement: pixels, inches, centimeters, picas, or points. If you're uncertain exactly what size image you want to create, enter a rough approximation. You can always change your settings later.

Although Photoshop matches the contents of the Clipboard by default, you can also match the size and resolution of other images:

✦ Press Option when choosing File ➪ New, or press ⌘-Option-N to override the contents of the Clipboard. Photoshop displays the size and resolution of the last image you created, whether it came from the Clipboard or not. Use this technique when creating many same-sized images in a row.

✦ You can also match the size and resolution of the new image to any other open image. While the New dialog box is open, choose the name of the image you want to match from the Window menu. It's that simple.

Figure 4-4: Use the New dialog box to specify the size, resolution, and color mode of your new image.

Units of measure

The Width and Height pop-up menus contain the five common units of measure mentioned earlier: pixels, inches, centimeters, points, and picas. But the Width pop-up menu offers one more, called Columns. If you want to create an image that fits exactly within a certain number of columns when it's imported into a desktop publishing program, select this option. You can specify the width of a column and the gutter between columns by pressing ⌘-K and ⌘-5 for the Units & Rulers preferences. Then enter values into the Column Size option boxes.

The Gutter value affects multiple-column images. Suppose you accept the default setting of a 15-pica column width and a 1-pica gutter. If you specify a one-column image in the New dialog box, Photoshop makes it 15 picas wide. If you ask for a two-column image, Photoshop adds the width of the gutter to the width of the two columns and creates an image 31 picas wide.

The Height pop-up menu in the New dialog box lacks a Column option because vertical columns have nothing to do with an image's height.

Tip

You can change the default unit of measure that appears in the Width and Height pop-up menus by pressing ⌘-K, ⌘-5, and selecting a different option from the Units pop-up menu. Easier still, bring up the Info palette by pressing the F8 key. Then click or drag on the little cross icon in the palette's lower-left corner. Up comes a pop-up menu of units, as demonstrated in Figure 4-5.

Figure 4-5: You can select a default unit of measure from the coordinates pop-up menu in the lower-left corner of the Info palette.

New image size

In most cases, the on-screen dimensions of an image depend on your entries in the Width, Height, and Resolution option boxes. If you set both the Width and Height values to 10 inches and the Resolution to 72 ppi, the new image will measure 720 × 720 pixels. The exception occurs if you choose pixels as your unit of measurement, as in Figure 4-5. In this case, the on-screen dimensions depend solely on the Width and Height options, and the Resolution value determines the size at which the image prints.

Color mode

Use the Mode pop-up menu to specify the number of colors that can appear in your image. Choose Bitmap to create a black-and-white image and choose Grayscale to access only gray values. RGB Color, CMYK Color, and Lab Color all provide access to the full range of 16 million colors, although their methods of doing so differ.

Cross-
Reference

RGB stands for red, green, blue; CMYK for cyan, magenta, yellow, black, and Lab for luminosity and two abstract color variables: a and b. To learn how each of these color modes works, read the "Working in Different Color Modes" section of Chapter 5.

Background color

The New dialog box also provides three Contents radio buttons that enable you to change the color of the background for the new image. You can fill the new image with white, with the current background color (assuming, of course, the background color is something other than white), or with no color at all. This last setting, Transparent, results in a floating layer with no background image whatsoever. This can be useful when editing one layer independently of the rest of an image, or when preparing a layer to be composited with an image. (For an in-depth examination of the more nitty-gritty aspects of layering, see Chapter 13.)

If you do select a transparent background, you must later flatten the layer by choosing Layer ➪ Flatten Image if you want to save the image to any format other than native Photoshop. The advantage of the Transparent setting, however, is that Photoshop doesn't create a new layer when you press ⌘-V to paste the contents of the Clipboard. In the long run, this doesn't make much difference — you still must flatten the image before you save it — but at least you needn't fuss around with two layers, one of which is completely empty.

Incidentally, just because you create an image with a transparent background doesn't mean you can automatically import a free-form image with transparency intact into an object-oriented program like Illustrator or QuarkXPress. In order to carve a transparent area out of the naturally rectangular boundaries of an image, you have to use the pen tool to create a clipping path. I explain how in the "Retaining transparent portions of an image" section of Chapter 11.

Naming the new image

The New dialog box provides a Name option. If you know what you want to call your new image, enter the name now. Or don't. It doesn't matter. Either way, when you choose File ➪ Save, Photoshop asks you to specify the location of the file and confirm the file's name, just as in previous versions. So don't feel compelled to name your image anything. The only reason for this option is to help you keep your images organized on screen. Lots of folks create temporary images they never save; Photoshop offers a way to assign temporary images more meaningful names than *Untitled-4, Untitled-5, Untitled-6,* and so on.

Opening an existing image

If you want to open an image stored on disk, choose File ➪ Open or press ⌘-O to display the Open dialog box. The Open dialog box behaves just like the ones in other Macintosh applications, with a folder bar at top, a scrolling list of files, a Desktop button, and the usual file management and navigation options. You can also use standard navigational shortcuts. Press ⌘-left and right arrow to change drives, ⌘-up and down arrow to exit and enter folders, and ⌘-D to switch to the desktop view.

But Photoshop's Open dialog box goes the extra mile by offering a few options that other Open dialog boxes lack. It sports a couple of check boxes, a thumbnail preview of the selected image on the left side of the scrolling list, and two Find buttons on the right. The following sections explain how these specialized options work.

Viewing the thumbnail

Turn on the Show Thumbnail check box to display a thumbnail preview of the selected image on the left side of the dialog box, as shown in Figure 4-6. If you deselect the option, the preview disappears and the Open dialog box collapses to save screen space.

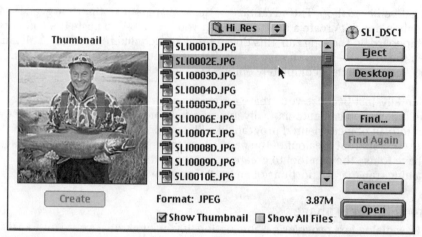

Figure 4-6: Turn on the Show Thumbnail check box to see a preview of the image in the Open dialog box.

If the thumbnail space is empty, it means the file does not contain a Photoshop-compatible preview. The file may have been created by a piece of hardware or software that doesn't support thumbnails, or the thumbnail feature may have simply been turned off. To save thumbnails from Photoshop, press ⌘-K, ⌘-2 to display the Saving Files panel of the Preferences dialog box. Then turn on the Macintosh Thumbnail check box, as discussed in Chapter 2. Alternatively, you can set the Image Previews pop-up menu to Ask When Saving, in which case Photoshop gives you the option of adding a thumbnail to the image inside the Save dialog box.

But just because you don't see a thumbnail in the Open dialog box doesn't mean all chance of previewing is gone. Under the right circumstances, you can generate a thumbnail preview on the fly by clicking on the Create button. The QuickTime system extension must be running for this button to function, and even then, the button only applies to a few file formats including PICT, GIF, JPEG, and the native Photoshop format. If the image is saved in any other file format—notably TIFF or EPS—you can generate a preview only by opening the image and resaving it.

If you've swapped images with Windows users, you might have received a request or two to start providing thumbnail previews with your images, even though you could have sworn you already were. The problem was, your Mac thumbnails weren't surviving the journey to the other side. See, Photoshop for the Mac saves thumbnails in the so-called resource fork of the file, but Windows programs can't even see the resource fork, much less translate it. Fortunately for all, both versions of Photoshop 5 can save Windows thumbnails. On the Mac, the Saving Files panel of the Preferences dialog box contains a check box called Windows Thumbnail. When turned on, a thumbnail is added to the data fork of the file, which translates to Windows fully intact.

Sadly, thumbnails don't work in the other direction. Because Windows doesn't recognize the resource fork, Photoshop for Windows can't save a Macintosh-style thumbnail. And because Photoshop on the Mac relies on Apple's QuickTime to interpret thumbnails, it can't see data-fork thumbnails. Dang.

Opening elusive files

The scrolling list in the Open dialog box contains the names of just those documents that Photoshop recognizes it can open. If you can't find a desired document, it may be because Photoshop doesn't recognize the document's four-character *type code*. The type code for a document created or last edited on a Macintosh computer corresponds to the file format under which the image was saved (as explained in the upcoming "File Format Roundup" section).

For example, TIFF is the type code for a TIFF image; JPEG is the code for a JPEG image; GIFf is the code for a GIF image, and so on. However, if you transfer a document from another platform, such as a Windows machine or Unix workstation, it probably lacks a type code. In the absence of a type code, Photoshop looks for a three-character extension at the end of the file name, such as *.tif* or *.jpg* or *.gif*. But if the extension is so much as a character off — *.tff* or *.jpe* or *.jif* — Photoshop won't know the file from Adam.

To see *all* documents regardless of type code or extension, select the Show All Files check box inside the Open dialog box. When you click on a document in the scrolling list, Photoshop displays the format that it thinks the file is saved in — if it has any thoughts to offer — in the Format option. If you disagree, click on the Format option and select the correct file format from the pop-up menu, as demonstrated in Figure 4-7. Provided that the image conforms to the selected format option, Photoshop opens the image when you press Return. If Photoshop gives you an error message instead, you need to either select a different format or try to open the document in a different application.

Tip

Normally, you can't see a file's four-character type code because it's socked away inside the resource fork. Unless, that is, you're willing to purchase a special utility such as PrairieSoft's (*www.prgrsoft.com*) DiskTop or Apple's (*www.apple.com*) ResEdit. Both are great, but DiskTop is more convenient for the simple day-to-day tasks of viewing and modifying type codes and other invisible resources.

Finding lost files

If you know the name of a file — or at least part of the name — but you can't remember where you put it, you can look for it using the Find button. Just click on the button or press ⌘-F, enter some text in the resulting option box, and press the Return key. Photoshop searches the disk in a fairly random fashion and takes you to the first file name that contains the exact characters you entered.

If the first file name isn't the one you're looking for, click on the Find Again button or press ⌘-G to find the next file name that contains your text. If you want to search for a different string of characters, press ⌘-F and enter some different text.

Figure 4-7: Select the Show All Files option to access any document regardless of its four-character type code.

Duplicating an image

Have you ever wanted to try an effect without permanently damaging an image? Photoshop 5 offers multiple undos, and you'll get a kick out of using the History palette to see before and after views of your image (as I explain in Chapter 10). But what if you want to apply a series of effects to an image independently and compare them side by side? And save the variations as separate files? Or perhaps even merge them? This is a job for image duplication.

To create a new window with an independent version of the foreground image, choose Image ⇨ Duplicate. A dialog box appears, requesting a name for the new image. Just like the Name option in the New dialog box, the option is purely an organizational tool you can use or ignore. If your image contains multiple layers, Photoshop will, by default, retain all layers in the duplicate document. Or you can merge all visible layers into a single layer by selecting the Merged Layers Only check box. (Hidden layers remain independent.) Press Return to create your new, independent image. Bear in mind that this image is unsaved; you need to choose File ⇨ Save to save any changes to disk.

If you're happy to let Photoshop automatically name your image and you don't care what it does with the layers, press Option while choosing Image ➪ Duplicate. This bypasses the Duplicate Image dialog box and immediately creates a new window.

Saving an image to disk

The first rule of storing an image on disk is to save it frequently. If the foreground image is untitled, as it is when you work on a new image, choosing File ➪ Save (⌘-S) displays the Save dialog box, enabling you to name the image, specify its location on disk, and select a file format.

In Chapter 2, I recommended that you set the Image Previews option in the Saving Files preferences panel (⌘- K, ⌘- 2) to Ask When Saving. If you followed this sage advice, then the Save dialog box offers a slew of Image Previews check boxes. For print work, I generally select both the Macintosh and Windows Thumbnail options. The previews consume extra disk space, but it's well worth it in exchange for being able to see the file before opening it. Why save a Windows thumbnail? Insurance, my friend. I know, I know, some of you think you'll die before you ever buy a PC. But if the Macintosh platform ever goes the way of hula-hoops and 8-track tapes, you want to be ready to land on your feet. As the wise fellow once said: all good things come to an end. And the Mac is a very good thing indeed.

The only reason *not* to save a thumbnail with an image is if you plan to post it on the Web. In that case, the file has to be as streamlined as possible, and that means shaving away the preview.

After you save the image once, choosing the Save command updates the file on disk without bringing up the Save dialog box. Choose File ➪ Save As or press ⌘-Shift-S to change the name, location, or format of the image stored on disk. By the way, if your only reason for choosing the Save As command is to change the file format, it's perfectly acceptable to overwrite (save over) the original document, assuming you no longer need the previous copy of the image. Granted, your computer could crash during the Save As operation, but because Photoshop actually creates a new file during any save operation, your original document should survive the accident. Besides, the chance of crashing during a Save As is extremely remote — no more likely than crashing during any other save operation.

To speed the save process, I usually save an image in Photoshop's native format until I'm finished working on it. Then, when the file is all ready to go, I choose File ➪ Save As and save the image in the compressed TIFF or JPEG format. This way, I compress each image only once during the time I work on it.

Adding an extension

The Preferences dialog box includes an option that lets you append a three-character file extension to the end of your files. (Again, this option is located in the Saving Files panel, so press ⌘-K, ⌘-2 to get to it.) Here I have two recommendations. First, leave the Use Lower Case check box turned on. It ensures fewer conflicts if and when you post your images on the Web. Second, go ahead and append extensions to your file names.

Why add PC file extensions on a Mac? Obviously, it makes life easier when sharing images with PC users. But more important, it's another form of insurance. If you ever find yourself using a PC, you're going to have tons and tons of old Macintosh image files that you'd like to open and reuse. With file extensions, you'll have no problem. Without them, good luck. The file extension is the only way a Windows application has to identify the file format. If there's no file extension, you'll have to tell the application which format to use. And while I don't question the basic record-keeping capabilities of your brain, you probably have better things to remember than what file format you used five years ago.

Tip

As I mentioned in Chapter 2, you can automatically append an extension from the Save dialog box regardless of your preference settings. Press the Option key, choose an option from the Format pop-up menu, and there it is.

Saving a copy

The final save command—File ⇨ Save a Copy (⌘-Option-S)—lets you save a copy of the current image without changing that special relationship between the image and its original on disk. This is like duplicating the image, saving it, and closing the duplicate all in one step.

The whole purpose of the Save a Copy command is to save a flattened version of a layered image or to dump the extra channels in an image that contains masks. Just select the file format you want to use and let Photoshop do the flattening and dumping automatically.

When you choose the Save a Copy command, Photoshop offers three extra check boxes at the bottom of the standard Save dialog box, as shown in Figure 4-8.

✦ **Flatten Image:** Photoshop activates this check box whenever you select a format other than the native Photoshop format. Because no other format supports layers, the check box must turn on to show that the layers will fuse together when the image is saved.

✦ **Exclude Alpha Channels:** "Alpha channel" is Photoshop's techy name for an extra channel, such as a mask (discussed in Chapter 12) or spot color (Chapter 7). But only a few formats—notably Photoshop, TIFF, and DCS 2.0—support extra channels. Most other formats abandon them. Again, Photoshop automatically activates this check box when you select a no-mask, no-spot color format.

✦ **Exclude Non-Image Data:** Select this option to jettison everything except the pixels in an attempt to get your file down to the smallest size possible. When turned on, this option excludes guides, paths, text entered into the File Info dialog box, color samples, and color profiles. It also excludes thumbnails, which is why the Image Previews check boxes dim when you select Exclude Non-Image Data. Select this check box when creating graphics for the Web.

Figure 4-8: Choose the Save a Copy command to save a separate, flattened copy of a layered image. This way, you can continue to adjust the layers in the future.

The Save a Copy command is perfect for when you want to export a layered image for use in another program. A page-layout application such as QuarkXPress doesn't support Photoshop's native format, but you don't want to flatten the image and permanently lose your layers. So here's your compromise: Keep one copy with layers in the Photoshop format and create a flattened copy for QuarkXPress.

File Format Roundup

Photoshop 5 supports more than 20 file formats from inside its Open and Save dialog boxes. It can support even more through the addition of plug-in modules, which attach commands to the File ⇨ Save As, File ⇨ Import, and File ⇨ Export submenus.

File formats represent different ways to save a file to disk. Some formats provide unique image-compression schemes, which save an image in a manner that consumes less space on disk. Other formats enable Photoshop to trade images with different applications running on the Mac or some other platform.

The native format

Like most programs, Photoshop offers its own native format — that is, a format optimized for Photoshop's particular capabilities and functions. This format saves every attribute that you can apply in Photoshop — including layers, extra channels, file info, and so on — and is compatible with Versions 3 and later of the program.

Perhaps not surprisingly, Photoshop can open and save in its native format more quickly than in any other format. The native format also offers image compression. Like TIFF's compression, the Photoshop compression scheme does not result in any loss of data. But Photoshop can compress and decompress its native format much more quickly than TIFF, and the compression scheme is better able to minimize the size of mask channels (as explained in Chapter 12).

The downside of the Photoshop format is that relatively few applications other than Photoshop support it, and those that do don't always do a great job. Some applications such as Adobe After Effects can open a layered Photoshop image and interpret each layer independently. But most of the others limit their support to flat Photoshop files. To accommodate these programs, you can either 1) use File ➪ Save a Copy to save the image in the flat Photoshop 2.0 format, or 2) activate the Include Composited Image with Layered Files check box in the Preferences dialog box.

But in point of fact, I intensely dislike either of these options. (In fact, you should be sure to turn off Include Composited Image with Layered Files, as I urged in Chapter 2.) The native format was never intended to function as an interapplication standard; it was meant for Photoshop alone. So use it that way. If you want to trade a flattened image with some other program, use TIFF, JPEG, or one of the other universal formats explained over the course of this chapter.

One exception: If you're creating a grayscale image for use with Filter ➪ Distort ➪ Displace, you have to create a 2.0-compatible file. The best bet is to save the image in the Photoshop 2.0 format. Otherwise the Displace filter won't see the grayscale image. I tell more about this filter in Chapter 17.

Special-purpose formats

With 20 file formats to choose from, you can imagine that most of them are not the kinds of things you'll be using on a regular basis. In fact, apart from the native Photoshop format, you'll probably want to stick with TIFF, JPEG, and GIF for Web images, and EPS when preparing images for placement into QuarkXPress, PageMaker, and others.

Many of the other formats are provided simply so you can open an image created on another platform, saved from some antiquated paint program, or downloaded from the Web. In the spirit of sweeping away the chaff so we can move on to the good stuff, I cover these special-purpose formats first.

You'll notice that I lump Web standards GIF and PNG in with the special-purpose formats. The reason is simple — if you don't design for the Web, you rarely need them. On the other hand, if you do design for the Web, the formats take on special significance, which is why I cover them in depth in Chapter 20.

Amiga's IFF

The Amiga was a failed experiment in desktop computers pioneered by Commodore. One of the first computers to ship with a color monitor, it never caught on with mainstream developers. But despite the fact that Commodore bowed out of the computer market more than two years ago now, Amiga fans are adamant that their systems live on — as I can attest from personal experience with several angry Amiga owners responding to previous editions of this paragraph.

Dear Mac enthusiasts: If your platform dies, suck it up and deal. I don't want to hear any whining. I'm using a Mac to write this text and I think it's a great machine. But it *is* a machine, not my little electronic buddy, and machines are replaceable. Treat them with respect, use them until they break down and you can't find parts, but don't cling to them years after their Golden Age and refuse to upgrade to anything better out of some misplaced loyalty to the past. I'm an artist, not a Macintosh user, and I'll use the computer that best suits my needs.

Still, even a sensible Amiga user of the past who has gone on to bigger and better things may have several hundred Amiga files sitting around. To this end, Photoshop lets you open and save IFF (*Interchange File Format*) files. IFF is the Amiga's all-around graphics format, serving much the same function as PICT on the Mac. IFF is even supported by a few antiquated DOS applications, most notably DeluxePaint from Electronic Arts.

Microsoft Paint's BMP

Windows Bitmap (BMP) is the native format for Microsoft Paint (included with Windows) and is supported by a variety of Windows and DOS applications. Photoshop supports BMP images with up to 16 million colors. You also can use *Run-Length Encoding* (RLE), a lossless compression scheme specifically applicable to the BMP format.

The term *lossless* refers to compression schemes such as BMP's RLE and TIFF's *Lempel-Ziv-Welch* (LZW) that conserve space on disk without sacrificing any data in the image. The only reasons not to use lossless compression are that it slows down the open and save operations and it may prevent less-sophisticated applications from opening an image. (Lossy compression routines, such as JPEG, sacrifice a user-defined amount of data to conserve even more disk space, as I explain later.)

CompuServe's GIF

In the old days, the CompuServe online service championed GIF (short for *Graphics Interchange Format*) as a means of compressing files so you could quickly transfer photographs over your modem. Like TIFF, GIF uses LZW compression; but unlike TIFF, GIF is limited to just 256 colors.

With the advent of the World Wide Web, the GIF format has grown slightly more sophisticated. Two varieties of GIF currently exist, known by the helpful codes 87a and 89a. GIF87a supports strictly opaque pixels, while GIF89a permits some pixels to be transparent. You can open either kind of image using File ➪ Open. You can save an image to the GIF87a format by choosing File ➪ Save and selecting CompuServe GIF from the Format pop-up menu. To save a GIF89a file with transparent pixels, choose File ➪ Export ➪ GIF89a Export.

Before saving a GIF image, use Image ➪ Mode ➪ Indexed Color to lower the number of colors to 256 or fewer. In fact, the GIF format doesn't appear in the Format pop-up menu if your image has more than 256 colors. For complete information about creating and saving GIF images for the Web, see Chapter 20.

PC Paintbrush's PCX

PCX doesn't stand for anything. Rather, it's the extension PC Paintbrush assigns to images saved in its native file format. Although the format is losing favor, many PCX images are still in use today, largely because PC Paintbrush is the oldest painting program for DOS. Photoshop supports PCX images with up to 16 million colors. You can find an enormous amount of art, usually clip art, in this format. But don't save files to PCX unless a client specifically demands it. Other formats are better.

Adobe's paperless PDF

The *Portable Document Format* (PDF) is a variation on the PostScript printing language that enables you to view electronically produced documents on screen. This means you can create a publication in QuarkXPress or PageMaker, export it to PDF, and distribute it without worrying about color separations, binding, and other printing costs. Using a program called Adobe Acrobat, you can open PDF documents, zoom in and out of them, and follow hypertext links by clicking highlighted words. Adobe distributes Mac, Windows, and UNIX versions of the Acrobat Reader free, so about anyone with a computer can view your stuff in full, natural color.

Where Photoshop 4 offered limited support for PDF — permitting you to open Photoshop-created PDF files only — Version 5 can open arbitrary PDF files created with any application. When you open a PDF file, Photoshop lets you browse through thumbnail page previews — provided that previews were saved with the file — and select the exact page you want to open. You can even print a contact sheet showing every page in a PDF file by choosing File ➪ Automate ➪ Multi-Page PDF to PSD. Unless you create a lot of documents with Acrobat Exchange — which limits its image support to PDF files — there's not much reason to save an image in PDF. But the enhanced opening functions are great.

Apple's PICT

PICT (*Macintosh Picture*) is the Macintosh system software's native graphics format. Based on the QuickDraw display language the system software uses to convey images on screen, PICT is one of the few file formats that handles object-oriented artwork and bitmapped images with equal aplomb. It supports images in any bit depth, size, or resolution. PICT even supports 32-bit images, so you can save a fourth masking channel when working in the RGB mode.

If you've installed QuickTime, you can subject PICT images to JPEG compression. But while PICT's compression options may look similar to JPEG's, they are actually significantly inferior. The differences become especially noticeable if you open an image, make a change, and again save it to disk, effectively reapplying the compression.

In most cases, you'll want to use the JPEG format instead of PICT when compressing images. JPEG images are compatible with the Web; PICT images are not. Also, more Windows applications recognize JPEG than PICT, and it's extremely difficult to find a Windows program that can handle PICT files with QuickTime compression.

In fact, the only reason to use PICT is low-end compatibility. If you're trying to save an image in a format that your mom can open on her Mac, PICT is a better choice than JPEG. Heck, you can open PICT files inside a word processor, including everything from SimpleText to Microsoft Word. Just be sure mom has QuickTime loaded on her machine.

When you save a PICT image, Photoshop also lets you set the bit depth. You should always stick with the default option, which is the highest setting available for the particular image. Don't mess around with these options; they apply automatic pattern dithering, which is a bad thing.

PICT resource #1, the startup screen

PICT resources are images contained in the resource fork of a file. The only reason to save a PICT resource is to create a startup screen, and the most likely reason to open one is to extract images from the Scrapbook.

The startup screen is that message that welcomes you to the great big wonderful Macintosh experience when you boot your computer. If you like to customize your system, you can create your own startup screen by saving an image in the PICT Resource file format under the name *StartupScreen* in the root directory of your System Folder. My own personal startup screen appears in Color Plate 4-1.

To save an image as a startup screen, first make sure that the image is set to exactly the same pixel dimensions as your screen (which you can check in the Monitors or Monitors & Sound control panel). And set the Resolution value in the Image Size dialog box to 72 ppi. Then choose File ➪ Save, select PICT Resource from the Format pop-up menu, name the image *StartupScreen*, and save it in your System

Folder. The PICT Resources Options dialog box appears (as in Figure 4-9), asking you to enter a four-character Name code. The secret code is *SCRN*.

Figure 4-9: Be sure to set the Resolution to 72, the Name to SCRN, and the Compression to None when saving a custom startup screen.

If you're saving a 24-bit startup screen, the PICT Resources Options dialog box offers a bunch of QuickTime compression options. *Don't select any of them!* Because QuickTime isn't built into the ROM of your computer, it won't be available when the startup screen appears, and therefore a weird-looking, stretched error message will appear on screen instead. To avoid this, select None from the Compression options.

PICT resource #2, the Scrapbook

To open a PICT resource other than the startup screen file, you bypass the Open command in favor of File ⇨ Import ⇨ PICT Resource. This command lets you open an application or other nonimage file on disk and browse through any PICT resources it may contain. Figure 4-10 shows the dialog box that appears after you select a file to open. You use the double arrow symbols to advance from one PICT image to the next. Click on the Preview button to display the image in the preview box.

Figure 4-10: Choose File ➪ Import ➪ PICT Resource
to browse through the PICT images inside the
Scrapbook.

The best use of File ➪ Import ➪ PICT Resource is to open images directly from the Scrapbook. In fact, this function becomes phenomenally practical if you use a commercial or shareware screen-capture utility (such as Mainstay's Capture) that can store screen shots in the Scrapbook. You can process your screen shots *en masse* at your leisure. In fact, this is how I created most of the screen shots in this book.

Pixar workstations

Pixar has created some of the most memorable computer-animated movies and commercials in recent memory. Examples include the desk lamps playing with a beach ball from *Luxo, Jr.,* the run-amok toddler from the Oscar-winning *Tin Toy,* and the commercial adventures of a Listerine bottle that boxes gingivitis one day and swings Tarzan-like through a spearmint forest the next. But Pixar really made the grade with the feature-length *Toy Story,* which provided Disney with enough merchandising options to last a lifetime.

Pixar works its 3D magic using mondo-expensive workstations. Photoshop enables you to open a still image created on a Pixar machine or to save an image to the Pixar format so you can integrate it into a 3D rendering. The Pixar format supports grayscale and RGB images.

PNG for the Web

Pronounced *ping*, the PNG format enables you to save 16 million color images without compression for use on the Web. As I write this, neither Netscape Navigator nor Microsoft Internet Explorer support PNG without the help of a special plug-in. But for those folks who want full-color images without the pesky visual compression artifacts you get with JPEG, PNG may well be a big player in the future. (Of course, I wrote this exact same paragraph two years ago, so there's always the chance PNG will never gain acceptance.)

PNG was invented for the Web and I've never seen anyone use it for a purpose other than the Web. So, like all things Webby, you'll find more information about PNG in Chapter 20.

Scitex image-processors

Some high-end commercial printers use Scitex printing devices to generate color separations of images and other documents. Photoshop can open images digitized with Scitex scanners and save the edited images to the *Scitex CT* (Continuous Tone) format. Because you need special hardware to transfer images from the PC to a Scitex drive, you'll probably want to consult with your local Scitex service bureau technician before saving to the CT format. The technician may prefer that you submit images in the native Photoshop, TIFF, or JPEG format. The Scitex CT format supports grayscale, RGB, and CMYK images.

TrueVision's TGA

TrueVision's Targa and NuVista video boards enable you to overlay computer graphics and animation onto live video. The effect is called *chroma keying* because, typically, a key color is set aside to let the live video show through. TrueVision designed the TGA (*Targa*) format to support 32-bit images that include 8-bit alpha channels capable of displaying the live video. Support for TGA is widely implemented among professional-level color and video applications on the PC.

Interapplication formats

In the name of interapplication harmony, Photoshop supports a few software-specific formats that permit you to trade files with popular object-oriented programs such as Illustrator and QuarkXPress. Every one of these formats is a variation on EPS (*Encapsulated PostScript*), which is based in turn on Adobe's industry-standard PostScript printing language. You can use Photoshop to edit frames from a QuickTime movie created with Adobe Premiere.

Rasterizing an Illustrator or FreeHand file

Photoshop supports object-oriented files saved in the EPS format. EPS is specifically designed to save object-oriented graphics that you intend to print to a PostScript output device. Just about every drawing and page-layout program on the planet (and a few on Mars) can save EPS documents.

Prior to Version 4, Photoshop could interpret only a small subset of EPS operations supported by Illustrator (including the native format). But then Photoshop 4 came along and offered a full-blown EPS translation engine, capable of interpreting EPS illustrations created in FreeHand, CorelDraw, Deneba's Canvas, and more. You can even open EPS drawings that contain imported images, something else Version 3 could not do.

When you open an EPS or native Illustrator document, Photoshop *rasterizes* (or *renders*) the artwork — that is, it converts the artwork from a collection of objects to a bitmapped image. During the open operation, Photoshop presents the Rasterize Generic EPS Format dialog box (see Figure 4-11), which allows you to specify the size and resolution of the image, just as you can in the New dialog box. Assuming the illustration contains no imported images, you can render it as large or as small as you want without any loss of image quality.

Figure 4-11: You can specify the size and resolution at which Photoshop renders an EPS illustration.

Tip

If the EPS illustration does contain an imported image or two, you need to know the resolution of the images and factor this information into the Rasterize Generic EPS Format dialog box. Select anything but Pixels from both the Width and Height pop-up menus, and leave the suggested values unchanged. Then enter the setting for the highest-resolution imported image into the Resolution option box. (If all the images are low-rez, you may want to double or triple the Resolution value to ensure the objects render smoothly.)

You should always select the Anti-aliased check box unless you're rendering a very large image — say, 300 ppi or higher. *Anti-aliasing* blurs pixels to soften the edges of the objects so they don't appear jagged. When you're rendering a very large image, the difference between image and printer resolution is less noticeable, so anti-aliasing is unwarranted.

Photoshop renders the illustration to a single layer against a transparent background. Before you can save the rasterized image to a format other than native

Photoshop, you must eliminate the transparency by choosing Layer ⇨ Flatten Image. Or save a flattened version of the image to a separate file by choosing File ⇨ Save a Copy.

Tip

Rendering an EPS illustration is an extremely useful technique for resolving printing problems. If you regularly work in Illustrator or FreeHand, you no doubt have encountered *limitcheck errors,* which occur when an illustration is too complex for an imagesetter or other high-end output device to print. If you're frustrated with the printer and tired of wasting your evening trying to figure out what's wrong (sound familiar?), use Photoshop to render the illustration at 300 ppi and print it. Nine times out of ten, this technique works flawlessly.

If Photoshop can't *parse* the EPS file — a techy way of saying Photoshop can't break down the individual objects — it attempts to open the PICT (Mac) or TIFF (Windows) preview. This exercise is usually futile, but occasionally you may wish to take a quick look at an illustration in order to, say, match the placement of elements in an image to those in the drawing.

Placing an EPS illustration

If you want to introduce an EPS graphic into the foreground image rather than to render it into a new image window of its own, choose File ⇨ Place. Unlike other File menu commands, Place supports only EPS illustrations.

After you import the EPS graphic, it appears inside a box with a great big X across it. Then you can move, scale, and rotate the illustration into position before rasterizing it to pixels. Drag a corner handle to resize the image, drag outside the image to rotate it. You can also nudge the graphic into position by pressing the arrow keys. When everything is the way you want it, press Return or double-click inside the box to rasterize the illustration. If the placement isn't perfect, not to worry. The graphic appears on a separate layer, so you can move it with complete freedom. To cancel the Place operation, press Escape instead of Return.

Saving an EPS image

When preparing an image for placement inside a drawing or page-layout document that you plan on printing to a PostScript output device, many artists prefer to save the image in the EPS format. First, by converting the image to PostScript up front, you prevent the drawing or page-layout program from having to do the work. The result is an image that prints more quickly and with less chance of problems. (Note that an image does not *look* any different when saved in EPS. The idea that the EPS format somehow blesses an image with better resolution is pure nonsense.)

The second point in the EPS format's favor is clipping paths. As explained graphically at the end of Chapter 11, a clipping path defines a free-form boundary around an image. When you place the image into an object-oriented program, everything outside the clipping path becomes transparent. While some programs — notably PageMaker — recognize clipping paths saved with a TIFF image, most programs—Illustrator and QuarkXPress among them—acknowledge a clipping path only when saved in the EPS format.

Third, although Illustrator 7 has remedied the problems it had importing TIFF images, it still likes EPS best, especially where screen display is concerned. Thanks to the EPS file's fixed preview, Illustrator can display an EPS image on screen very quickly compared with other file formats. And Illustrator can display an EPS image both in the preview mode and in the super-fast artwork mode.

So if you want to import an image into Illustrator, QuarkXPress, or another object-oriented program, your best bet is EPS. On the downside, EPS is an inefficient format for saving images thanks to the laborious way that it describes pixels. An EPS image may be three to four times larger than the same image saved to the TIFF format with LZW compression. But this is the price we pay for reliable printing.

Absolutely avoid the EPS format if you plan on printing your final pages to a non-PostScript printer. This defeats the entire purpose of EPS, which is meant to avoid printing problems, not cause them. When printing without PostScript, use TIFF or JPEG instead.

To save an image in the EPS format, choose Photoshop EPS from the Format pop-up menu in the Save dialog box. After you press Return, Photoshop displays the dialog box shown in Figure 4-12. The options in this dialog box work as follows:

✦ **Preview:** Technically, an EPS document comprises two parts: a pure PostScript-language description of the graphic for the printer and a bitmapped preview so you can see the graphic on screen. Select the Macintosh (8 Bits/Pixel) option from the Preview pop-up menu to save a 256-color PICT preview of the image. Or select the Macintosh (JPEG) option for a 24-bit preview (which in most cases takes up less room on disk, thanks to the JPEG compression). If you plan on passing off the image to a Windows colleague, select TIFF (8 Bits/Pixel). The 1-bit options provide black-and-white previews only, which are useful if you want to save a little room on disk. Select None to include no preview and save even more disk space.

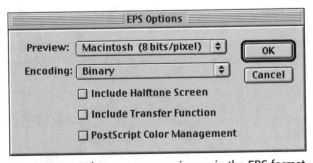

Figure 4-12: When you save an image in the EPS format, you can specify the type of preview and tack on some printing attributes.

✦ **Encoding:** If you're saving an image for import into Illustrator, QuarkXPress, or some other established program, select the Binary encoding option (also known as *Huffman encoding*), which compresses an EPS document by substituting shorter codes for frequently used characters. The letter *a*, for example, receives the 3-bit code 010, rather than its standard 8-bit ASCII code, 01100001 (the binary equivalent of what we humans call 97).

Sadly, some programs and printers don't recognize Huffman encoding, in which case you must select the less efficient ASCII option. ASCII stands for *American Standard Code for Information Interchange*, which is fancy jargon for text-only. In other words, you can open and edit an ASCII EPS document in a word processor, provided you know how to read and write PostScript.

The remaining Encoding options are JPEG settings. JPEG compression not only results in smaller files on disk, but it also degrades the quality of the image. Select JPEG (Maximum Quality) to invoke the least degradation. Better yet, avoid the JPEG settings altogether. These options work only if you plan to print your final artwork to a PostScript Level 2 or Level 3 device. Earlier PostScript printers do not support EPS artwork with JPEG compression and will choke on the code.

So, to recap, ASCII results in really big files that will work with virtually any printer or application. Binary creates smaller files which work with most mainstream applications but may choke some older-model printers. And the JPEG settings are compatible exclusively with Level 2 and later PostScript printers.

✦ **Clipping Path:** I mention this option because it no longer exists in Photoshop 5. You used to be able to specify a clipping path when saving an EPS file, now you have to specify the clipping path in advance using the Clipping Path command. To learn how, read the final section in Chapter 11.

✦ **Include Halftone Screen:** Another advantage of EPS over other formats is that it can retain printing attributes. If you specified a custom halftone screen using the Screens button inside the Page Setup dialog box, you can save this setting with the EPS document by selecting the Include Halftone Screen check box. But be careful—you can just as easily ruin your image as help it. Read Chapter 7 before you select this check box.

✦ **Include Transfer Function:** As described in Chapter 7, you can change the brightness and contrast of a printed image using the Transfer button inside the Page Setup dialog box. To save these settings with the EPS document, select the Include Transfer Function check box. Again, this option can be dangerous when used casually. See Chapter 7 for more details.

✦ **PostScript Color Management:** Like JPEG compression, this check box is compatible with Level 2 and 3 printers only. It embeds a color profile which helps the printer to massage the image during the printing cycle in order to generate more accurate colors. Unless you plan on printing to a Level 2 or later device, leave the option off. (For more information about color profiles, read Chapter 6.)

✦ **Transparent Whites:** When saving black-and-white EPS images in Photoshop, the two check boxes previously discussed drop away, replaced by Transparent Whites. Select this option to make all white pixels in the image transparent.

Although Photoshop EPS is the only format that offers the Transparent Whites option, many programs — including Illustrator — treat white pixels in black-and-white TIFF images as transparent as well.

QuarkXPress DCS

Quark developed a variation on the EPS format called *Desktop Color Separation* (DCS). When you work in QuarkXPress, PageMaker, and other programs that support the format, DCS facilitates the printing of color separations. Before you can use DCS, you have to convert your image to the CMYK color space using Image ⇨ Mode ⇨ CMYK Color. (DCS 2.0 also supports grayscale images with spot-color channels.) Then bring up the Save dialog box and select Photoshop DCS 1.0 or 2.0 from the Format pop-up menu.

Photoshop 5 introduced support for DCS 2.0 to accommodate images that contain extra spot-color channels, as explained in Chapter 7. If you add a Pantone channel to an image, DCS 2.0 is the only PostScript format you can use. If your image doesn't contain any extra channels beyond the basic four required for CMYK, then DCS 1.0 is the safer and simpler option.

After you press Return, Photoshop displays an additional pop-up menu of DCS options, which vary depending on whether you've selected DCS 1.0 or 2.0, as shown in Figure 4-13. The DCS 1.0 format invariably saves a total of five files: one master document (which is the file that you import into XPress) plus one file each for the cyan, magenta, yellow, and black color channels (which are the files that get printed). The DCS 2.0 format can be expressed as a single file (tidier) or five separate files (better compatibility).

Either way, the DCS pop-up menu gives you the option of saving a 72-ppi PostScript composite of the image inside the master document. Independent from the bitmapped preview — which you specify as usual by selecting a Preview option — the PostScript composite makes it possible to print a low-resolution version of a DCS image to a consumer-quality printer. If you're using a black-and-white printer, select the 72 pixel/inch grayscale option; if you're using a color printer, select the final option. Be forewarned, however, that the composite image significantly increases the size of the master document on disk.

Figure 4-13: The extra options for the DCS 1.0 format (top) and those for the DCS 2.0 format (bottom).

Premiere Filmstrip

Adobe Premiere is a popular QuickTime movie-editing application for both Macs and PCs. The program is a wonder when it comes to fades, frame merges, and special effects, but it offers no frame-by-frame editing capabilities. For example, you can neither draw a mustache on a person in the movie nor can you make brightly colored brush strokes swirl about in the background — at least, not inside Premiere.

You can export the movie to the Filmstrip format, though, which is a file-swapping option exclusive to Photoshop and Premiere. A Filmstrip document organizes frames in a long vertical strip, as shown on the left side of Figure 4-14. The right side of the figure shows the movie after I edited each individual frame in ways not permitted by Premiere. A boring movie of a cat stuck in a bag becomes an exciting movie of a cat-stuck-in-a-bag flying. If that doesn't sum up the miracle of digital imaging, I don't know what does.

A gray bar separates each frame. The number of each frame appears on the right; the *Society of Motion Picture and Television Engineers* (SMPTE) time code appears on the left. The structure of the three-number time code is minutes:seconds:frames, with 30 frames per second.

Caution

If you change the size of a Filmstrip document inside Photoshop in any way, you cannot save the image back to the Filmstrip format. Feel free to paint and apply effects, but stay the heck away from the Image Size and Canvas Size commands.

Figure 4-14: Four frames from a QuickTime movie as they appear in the Filmstrip format before (left) and after (right) editing the frames in Photoshop.

Tip

I don't really delve into the Filmstrip format anywhere else in this book, so I want to pass along a few quick Filmstrip tips right here and now:

✦ First, you can scroll up and down exactly one frame at a time by pressing Shift-Page Up or Shift-Page Down, respectively.

✦ Second, you can move a selection exactly one frame up or down by pressing ⌘-Shift-up arrow or ⌘-Shift-down arrow.

✦ If you want to clone the selection as you move it, press ⌘-Shift-Option-up arrow or ⌘-Shift-Option-down arrow.

And finally—here's the great one—you can select several sequential frames and edit them simultaneously by following these steps:

Steps: Selecting Sequential Frames in a Movie

1. **Select the first frame you want to edit.** Select the rectangular marquee tool by pressing the M key. Then drag around the area you want to edit in the movie. (This is the only step that takes any degree of care or coordination whatsoever.)

2. **Switch to the quick mask mode by pressing the Q key.** The areas around the selected frame are overlaid with pink.

3. **Set the magic wand Tolerance value to 0.** Double-click on the magic wand tool icon in the Toolbox to display the Magic Wand Options palette. Enter 0 for the Tolerance value and deselect the Anti-aliased check box.

4. **Click inside the selected frame (the one that's not pink) with the magic wand tool.** This selects the unmasked area inside the frame.

5. **Press ⌘-Shift-Option-down arrow to clone the unmasked area to the next frame in the movie.** When you exit the quick mask mode, both this frame and the one above it will be selected.

6. **Repeat several times.** Keep ⌘-Shift-Option-down-arrowing until you're rid of the pink stuff on all the frames you want to select.

7. **Exit the quick mask mode by pressing the Q key again.** All frames appear selected.

8. **Edit the frames to your heart's content.**

Cross-Reference

If you're new to Photoshop, half of these steps, if not all of them, probably sailed over your head like so many low-flying cats stuck in bags. If you want to learn more about selections and cloning, see Chapter 11. In Chapter 12, I explore the quick mask mode and other masking techniques. After you finish reading those chapters, return to this section to see if it doesn't make a little more sense. Or don't. It's entirely up to you.

The process of editing individual frames as just described is sometimes called *rotoscoping*, named after the traditional technique of combining live-action film with animated sequences. You also can try out some scratch-and-doodle techniques, which is where an artist scratches and draws directly on frames of film. If this isn't enough, you can emulate *xerography*, in which an animator makes Xerox copies of photographs, enhances the copies using markers or whatever else is convenient, and shoots the finished artwork, frame by frame, on film. In a nutshell, Photoshop extends Premiere's functionality by adding animation to its standard supply of video-editing capabilities.

You can save an image in the Filmstrip format only if you opened the image as a Filmstrip document and did not change the size of the image. To do so, press ⌘-S.

The mainstream formats

The formats discussed so far are mighty interesting and they all fulfill their own niche purposes. But two formats — JPEG and TIFF — are the all-stars of digital imagery. You'll use these formats the most because of their outstanding compression capabilities and almost universal support among graphics applications.

JPEG

The JPEG format is named after the folks who designed it, the Joint Photographic Experts Group. JPEG is the most efficient and essential compression format currently available and is likely to be the compression standard for years to come. JPEG is a lossy compression scheme, which means it sacrifices image quality to conserve space on disk. You can control how much data is lost during the save operation, however.

When you save an image in the JPEG format, Photoshop displays the dialog box in Figure 4-15, which offers a total of 11 compression settings. Just select an option from the Quality pop-up menu or drag the slider triangle from 0 to 10 to specify the quality setting. Of the named options, Low takes the least space on disk, but distorts the image rather severely; Maximum retains the highest amount of image quality, but consumes more disk space. Of the numbered options, 0 is the most severe compressor and 10 does the least damage.

Figure 4-15: The new JPEG Options dialog box provides a total of 11 compression settings, ranging from 0 (heaviest compression) to 10 (best quality).

Note

JPEG evaluates an image in 8 × 8-pixel blocks, using a technique called *Adaptive Discrete Cosine Transform* (or ADCT, as in "Yes, I'm an acronym ADCT"). It averages the 24-bit value of every pixel in the block (or 8-bit value of every pixel in the case of a grayscale image). ADCT then stores the average color in the upper-left pixel in the block and assigns the remaining 63 pixels smaller values relative to the average.

Next, JPEG divides the block by an 8 × 8 block of its own called the *quantization matrix,* which homogenizes the pixels' values by changing as many as possible to zero. This process saves the majority of disk space and loses data. When Photoshop opens a JPEG image, it can't recover the original distinction between the zero pixels, so the pixels become the same, or similar, colors. Finally, JPEG applies lossless Huffman encoding to translate repeating values to a single symbol.

In most instances, I recommend you use JPEG only at the Maximum quality setting (8 or higher), at least until you gain some experience with it. The smallest amount of JPEG compression saves more space on disk than any non-JPEG compression format and still retains the most essential detail from the original image. Figure 4-16 shows a grayscale image saved at each of the four compression settings.

The samples are arranged in rows from highest image quality (upper left) to lowest quality (lower right). Below each sample is the size of the compressed document on disk. Saved in the only moderately compressed native Photoshop format, the image consumes 116K on disk. From 116K to 28K—the result of the lowest-quality JPEG setting—is a remarkable savings, but it comes at a price.

I've taken the liberty of sharpening the focus of strips in each image so you can see more easily how JPEG averages neighboring pixels to achieve smaller file sizes. The first strip in each image appears in normal focus; the second strip is sharpened once by choosing Filter ⇨ Sharpen ⇨ Sharpen More, and the third strip is sharpened twice. I also adjusted the gray levels to make the differences even more pronounced. You can see that although the lower-image quality setting leads to a dramatic saving in file size, it also excessively gums up the image. The effect, incidentally, is more obvious on screen. And believe me, after you familiarize yourself with JPEG compression, you can spot other people's overly compressed JPEG images a mile away. This isn't something you want to exaggerate in your images.

Cross-Reference

To see the impact of JPEG compression on a full-color image, check out Color Plate 4-2. The original image consumes 693K in the native Photoshop format, but 116K when compressed at the JPEG module's Maximum setting. To demonstrate the differences between different settings better, I enlarged one portion of the image and oversharpened another.

Maximum   66K   High   50K

Medium   33K   Low   28K

Figure 4-16: Four JPEG settings applied to a single image, with the highest image quality setting illustrated at the upper left and the lowest at the bottom right.

Caution

JPEG is a *cumulative compression scheme,* meaning Photoshop recompresses an image every time you save it in the JPEG format. No disadvantage exists to saving an image to disk repeatedly during a single session, because JPEG always works from the on-screen version. But if you close an image, reopen it, and save it in the JPEG format, you inflict a small amount of damage. Use JPEG sparingly. In the best of all possible worlds, you should only save to the JPEG format after you finish all work on an image. Even in a pinch, you should apply all filtering effects before saving to JPEG, because these have a habit of exacerbating imperfections in image quality.

JPEG is best used when compressing continuous-tone images (images in which the distinction between immediately neighboring pixels is slight). Any image that includes gradual color transitions, as in a photograph, qualifies for JPEG compression. JPEG is not the best choice for saving screen shots, line drawings (especially those converted from EPS graphics), and other high-contrast images. These are better served by a lossless compression scheme such as TIFF with LZW. The JPEG format is available when you are saving grayscale, RGB, and CMYK images.

Occupying the bottom half of the JPEG Options dialog box are three radio buttons, designed primarily to optimize JPEG images for the Web. Progressive isn't applicable to print images, and the Baseline options don't affect print images enough to make any difference. For now, just select the first option, Baseline ("Standard"), and be done with it. If you want to learn more about the remaining options, read the "Saving JPEG Images" section of Chapter 20.

TIFF

Developed by Aldus in the early days of the Mac to standardize an ever-growing population of scanned images, *Tag Image File Format* (TIFF) is the most widely supported image printing format across both the Macintosh and PC platforms. Unlike EPS, it can't handle object-oriented artwork, and it doesn't support lossy compression like JPEG. But, otherwise, it's unrestricted. In fact, TIFF offers a few tricks of its own that make it very special.

When you save an image in the TIFF format, Photoshop displays the TIFF Options dialog box (see Figure 4-17), which offers these options:

✦ **Byte Order:** Every once in a while, Photoshop chooses to name a straightforward option in the most confusing way possible. Byte Order is a prime example. No, this option doesn't have anything to do with how you eat your food. Instead, there are two variations of TIFF, one for the PC and the other for the Mac. I'm sure this has something to do with the arrangement of 8-bit chunks of data, but who cares? You want PC or you want Mac? It's that simple.

✦ **LZW Compression:** Like Huffman encoding (previously described in the "Saving an EPS image" section), the Lempel-Ziv-Welch (LZW) compression scheme digs into the computer code that describes an image and substitutes frequently used codes with shorter equivalents. But instead of substituting characters, as Huffman does, LZW substitutes strings of data. Because LZW doesn't so much as touch a pixel in your image, it's entirely lossless. Most image editors and desktop publishing applications — including Illustrator, FreeHand, PageMaker, and QuarkXPress — import LZW-compressed TIFF images, but a few still have yet to catch on.

Figure 4-17: Photoshop enables you to save TIFF files in either the Mac or PC format and to compress the image using LZW.

Note

If names such as Huffman and LZW ring a faint bell, it may be because these are the same compression schemes used by StuffIt, Compact Pro, and other compression utilities. For this reason, using an additional utility to compress a TIFF image that you've already compressed using LZW makes no sense. Neither do you want to compress a JPEG image, because JPEG takes advantage of Huffman encoding. You may shave off a few K, but this isn't enough space to make it worth your time and effort.

In Photoshop, the TIFF format supports up to 24 channels, the maximum number permitted in any image. In fact, TIFF is the only format other than DCS 2.0, "raw," and the native Photoshop format that can save more than four channels. To save a TIFF file without extra mask channels, choose File ➪ Save a Copy and select the Don't Include Alpha Channels check box. (For an educational introduction to channels, read Chapter 6.)

Tip

If you have limited RAM, or you're working with a very large TIFF image, you can open an isolated detail of the image using File ➪ Import ➪ Quick Edit. (If this command does not appear in your menu, install the optional plug-in off your original Photoshop CD.) Photoshop displays a small preview of the image. Drag in the preview to select the area you want to open and press Enter. Photoshop opens only that isolated portion of the file. To save the detail back into the larger TIFF image, choose File ➪ Export ➪ Quick Edit.

I must admit, I have a love/hate thing going with Quick Edit. I appreciate that Quick Edit lets you open small chunks of an image at a time. But I hate that you can open uncompressed TIFF images only, and that Quick Edit doesn't support any format other than TIFF. It doesn't even support the native Photoshop format. What a drag.

The oddball formats

Can you believe it? After plowing through a half-million formats, I still haven't covered them all. The last three are the odd men out. One format has a purpose so specific that Photoshop can open files saved in the format but it can't save to the format. The second is a new format that, while moderately promising, is not implemented thoroughly enough inside Photoshop to provide much benefit. And the last is less a format than a manual can opener that may come in handy for jimmying open a file from an unknown source.

Photo CD YCC images

Photoshop can open Eastman Kodak's Photo CD and Pro Photo CD formats directly. A Photo CD contains compressed versions of every image in each of the five scan sizes provided on Photo CDs—from 128×192 pixels (72K) to $2,048 \times 3,072$ pixels (18MB).

The Pro Photo CD format can accommodate each of the five sizes included in the regular Photo CD format, plus one additional size—$4,096 \times 6,144$ pixels (72MB)—that's four times as large as the largest image on a regular Photo CD. As a result, Pro Photo CDs hold only 25 scans; standard Photo CDs hold 100. Like their standard Photo CD counterparts, Pro Photo CD scanners can accommodate 35mm film and slides. But they can also handle 70mm film and 4×5-inch negatives and transparencies. The cost might knock you out, though. While scanning an image to a standard Photo CD costs between $1 and $2, scanning it to a Pro Photo CD costs about $10. This goes to show you, once you gravitate beyond consumerland, everyone expects you to start coughing up the big bucks.

Both Photo CD and Pro Photo CD use the YCC color model, a variation on the CIE (Commission Internationale de l'Eclairage) color space, which I discuss in the next chapter. YCC provides a broader range of color—theoretically, every color your eye can see. By opening Photo CD files directly, you can translate the YCC images directly to Photoshop's Lab color mode, another variation on CIE color space that ensures no color loss.

Photoshop includes the latest Kodak Color Management Software (CMS), which tweaks colors in Photo CD images based on the kind of film from which they were scanned. When you open a Photo CD image, Photoshop displays the dialog box shown in Figure 4-18.

Note

Finding your photos on a Photo CD is a little harder than it should be. Look inside the Images folder in the Photo_CD folder. The files have friendly names like Img0017.pcd;1. The friendlier Photos folder contains PICT versions of the images generated by the operating system. While there's nothing precisely wrong with them, they don't offer the same degree of color control as the real files that are buried in the Images folder.

Figure 4-18: Use these options to select a resolution and to calibrate the colors in the Photo CD image.

The Photo CD dialog box lets you specify the image size you want to use by selecting an option from the Resolution pop-up menu. The dialog box even shows you a preview of the image. But the options that make a difference are the Source and Destination buttons:

✦ **Source:** Click on this button to select the kind of film from which the original photographs were scanned. You can select from two specific Kodak brands — Ektachrome and Kodachrome — or settle for the generic Color Negative Film option. Stock Photo CD vendors such as Digital Stock ensure a precise match by providing source profiles of their own, as I've selected in Figure 4-18. Your selection determines the method Photoshop uses to transform the colors in the image.

✦ **Destination:** After clicking this button, select an option from the Device pop-up menu to specify the color model you want to use. Select Adobe Photoshop RGB to open the image in the RGB mode; select Adobe Photoshop CIELAB to open the image in the Lab mode.

Note

A CMYK profile can be purchased separately from Kodak. Some stock photo agencies also include special color profiles. For example, Digital Stock currently provides its excellent image library on Photo CDs. The company offers a source profile for its particular drum-scanning technology, as well as CMYK destination profiles.

Photoshop cannot save to the Photo CD format. And, frankly, there's little reason you'd want to do so. Photo CD is strictly a means for transferring slides and film negatives onto the world's most ubiquitous and indestructible storage medium, the CD-ROM.

Kodak's FlashPix

Photoshop 5 supports the new FlashPix format. Developed by Kodak, Live Picture, and a few other companies eager to get into the imaging game (notice Adobe is not on this list), FlashPix is a kind of Photo CD format without the CD. And Photoshop can both open and save images in the FlashPix format. The question is, will you ever want to? The answer is, wait and see.

The purpose of FlashPix is to turn every image editor into a kind of Live Picture. In case you're not familiar with this program, Live Picture is a Macintosh image editor that processes high-resolution images very quickly by performing its edits on a screen-resolution proxy. The program records its edits as a sequence of mathematical operations, but waits until you save the image out as a TIFF file before actually applying the images to the image pixels.

In this same vein, the FlashPix format saves an image in multiple resolutions — first at full resolution, then at half resolution, then at quarter resolution, and so on. It keeps saving until it gets down to a width or height of less than 100 pixels and then it stops. With a high enough resolution file, you can end up with seven or eight iterations of the image. This kind of file structure is called a *pyramid* because each iteration of the file sits below the last. (It's really an inverted pyramid, but why spilt hairs?) FlashPix also subdivides each iteration into a bunch of 64 × 64-pixel tiles.

The point of all this iterating and subdividing is to give the image editor lots of little image chunks to work with. That way, the program can load a chunk, apply an edit to that little chunk (and thereby fool the user into thinking the entire image has been edited), record the edits to a file as it goes along, and then apply all the edits at once during the saving process while the user goes to the candy machine and gets a snack.

Luckily, Photoshop doesn't work that way. Version 5 remains the plodding pixel-by-pixel editor that we've all come to know and love. As a result, Photoshop doesn't take full advantage of the FlashPix format. (Kodak actually suggests that applications should do away with their native formats and gratefully embrace FlashPix instead. Again, count yourself lucky.)

Saving and opening FlashPix images

So, now that you understand FlashPix, what it was meant to do, and how Photoshop doesn't do that, let's see what Photoshop *does* do. When you save an image in the FlashPix format, you are greeted by the dialog box shown in Figure 4-19. Your options are to apply no compression, or apply JPEG compression. You have 10 quality settings, just like Photoshop's standard JPEG. Photoshop save the iterations and tiles in the background without bothering you with the details. What could be easier?

Opening the file is twice as easy. Photoshop simply opens the largest iteration from the pyramid. End of story. (Interestingly, early in the beat cycle, Photoshop 5 let you select the exact iteration you wanted to open, but this idea was scrapped. Too bad.)

Figure 4-19: You can save a FlashPix image with or without JPEG compression.

So when all is said and done, Photoshop's support for FlashPix serves two purposes: First, it allows Photoshop to open FlashPix images if and when you come upon them; second, it allows you to save images so that programs that rely on the FlashPix format can open them. Look for Photoshop's support for FlashPix to develop over time — particularly if the format becomes a more prominent force in the industry.

Opening a raw document

A *raw document* is a plain binary file stripped of all extraneous information. It contains no compression scheme, specifies no bit depth or image size, and offers no color mode. Each byte of data indicates a brightness value on a single color channel, and that's it. Photoshop offers this function specifically so you can open images created in undocumented formats, such as those created on mainframe computers.

To open an image of unknown origin, choose File ➪ Open and select the Show All Files check box. Then select the desired image from the scrolling list and choose Raw from the Format pop-up menu. After you press Return, the dialog box shown in Figure 4-20 appears, featuring these options:

✦ **Width, Height:** If you know the dimensions of the image in pixels, enter the values in these option boxes.

✦ **Swap:** Click on this button to swap the Width value with the Height value.

✦ **Count:** Enter the number of color channels in this option box. If the document is an RGB image, enter 3; if it is a CMYK image, enter 4.

✦ **Interleaved:** Select this value if the color values are stored sequentially by pixels. In an RGB image, the first byte represents the red value for the first pixel, the second byte represents the green value for that pixel, the third the blue value, and so on. If you turn this check box off, the first byte represents the red value for the first pixel, the second value represents the red value for the second pixel, and so on. When Photoshop finishes describing the red channel, it describes the green channel and then the blue channel.

Figure 4-20: Photoshop requires you to specify the size of an image and the number of color channels when you open an image that does not conform to a standardized file format.

✦ **Depth:** Select the number of bits per color channel. Most images contain 8 bits per channel, but scientific scans from mainframe computers may contain 16.

✦ **Byte Order:** If you specify 16 bits per channel, you must tell Photoshop whether the image comes from a Mac or a PC.

✦ **Header:** This value tells Photoshop how many bytes of data at the beginning of the file comprise header information it can ignore.

✦ **Retain Header When Saving:** If the Header value is greater than zero, you can instruct Photoshop to retain this data when you save the image in a different format.

✦ **Guess:** If you know the Width and Height values, but you don't know the number of bytes in the header — or vice versa — you can ask Photoshop for help. Fill in either the Dimensions or Header information and then click the Guess button to ask Photoshop to take a stab at the unknown value. Photoshop estimates all this information when the Raw Options dialog box first appears. Generally speaking, if it doesn't estimate correctly the first time around, you're on your own. But, hey, the Guess button is worth a shot.

Tip

If a raw document is a CMYK image, it opens as an RGB image with an extra masking channel. To display the image correctly, choose Image ➪ Mode ➪ Multichannel to free the four channels from their incorrect relationship. Then recombine them by choosing Image ➪ Mode ➪ CMYK Color.

Saving a raw document

Photoshop also enables you to save to the raw document format. This capability is useful when you create files you want to transfer to mainframe systems or output to devices that don't support other formats, such as the Kodak XL7700.

Caution

Do not save 256-color indexed images to the raw format or you lose the color lookup table and, therefore, lose all color information. Be sure to convert such images first to RGB or one of the other full-color modes before saving.

When you save an image in the raw document format, Photoshop presents the dialog box shown in Figure 4-21. The dialog box options work as follows:

✦ **File Type:** Enter the four-character file type code (TIFF, PICT, and so on) in this option box. (You should check the documentation for the application you plan to use to open the raw document.) If you plan to use this file on a computer other than a Mac, you can enter any four characters you like; only Macs use this code.

Figure 4-21: When saving a raw document, enter file type and creator codes and specify the order of data in the file.

✦ **File Creator:** Enter the four-character *creator code,* which tells the system software which application created the file. By default, the creator code is 8BIM, Photoshop's code. Ignore this option unless you have a specific reason for changing it — for example, to open the image in a particular Macintosh application. (You won't hurt anything by changing the code, but you will prevent Photoshop from opening the image when you double-click on the document icon at the Finder desktop.)

✦ **Header:** Enter the size of the header in bytes. If you enter any value but zero, you must fill in the header using a data editor such as Norton Disk Editor.

✦ **Save Channels In:** Select the Interleaved Order option to arrange data sequentially by pixels, as described earlier. To group data by color channel, select Non-interleaved Order.

Still can't get that file open?

File format specs are continually evolving. As a result, programs that provide support for a particular format may not support the specific version of the format used to save the file you're trying to open. For example, JPEG is notorious for causing problems because there were several private implementations in the early days. As a result, some JPEG files can only be read by the originating application.

If you can't open a file in Photoshop, you may have another program that can read and write the problem format. Try the problem file in every program you have — and every program your friends have. After all, what are friends for?

You may also want to try a program like DeBabelizer Toolbox or DeBabelizer Pro from Equilibrium (*www.equilibrium.com*). Absolutely the best format converter bar none, DeBabelizer handles every format Photoshop handles, as well as Dr. Halo's CUT, Fractal Design Painter's RIFF, the animation formats PICS, FLI, and ANM, as well as UNIX workstation formats for Silicon Graphics, Sun Microsystems, and others.

Still out of it? Go online and check out such forums as ADOBEAPPS on CompuServe. The Usenet newsgroups *comp.graphics.apps.photoshop* and *rec.photo.digital* are other good resources. Post a question about your problem; chances are good someone may have an answer for you.

Resampling and Cropping

After you bring up an image — whether you created it from scratch or opened an existing image stored in one of the five billion formats discussed in the preceding pages — its size and resolution are established. Neither size nor resolution is set in stone, however. Photoshop provides two methods for changing the number of pixels in an image: resampling and cropping.

Resizing versus resampling

Typically, when folks talk about *resizing* an image, they mean enlarging or reducing it without changing the number of pixels in the image, as demonstrated back in Figure 4-1. By contrast, *resampling* an image means scaling it so the image contains a larger or smaller number of pixels. With resizing, an inverse relationship exists between size and resolution — size increases when resolution decreases, and vice versa. But resampling affects either size or resolution independently. Figure 4-22 shows an image resized and resampled to 50 percent of its original dimensions. The resampled and original images have identical resolutions, while the resized image has twice the resolution of its companions.

Original

Resized   Resampled

Figure 4-22: An image (top) resized (bottom left) and resampled (bottom right) down to 50 percent. The resized image sports a higher resolution; the resampled one contains fewer pixels.

Resizing an image

To resize an image, use one of the techniques discussed in the "Changing the printing resolution" section near the beginning of this chapter. To recap briefly, the best method is to choose Image ➪ Image Size, turn off the Resample Image check box, and enter a value into the Resolution option box. See Figure 4-2 to refresh your memory.

Resampling an image

You also use Image ➪ Image Size to resample an image. The difference is you leave the Resample Image check box turned on, as shown in Figure 4-23. As its name implies, the Resample Image check box is the key to resampling.

When Resample Image is selected, the Resolution value is independent of both sets of Width and Height values. (The only difference between the two sets of options is the top options work in pixels and the bottom options work in relative units of measure like percent and inches.) You can increase the number of pixels in an image by increasing any of the five values in the dialog box; you can decrease the number of pixels by decreasing any value. Photoshop stretches or shrinks the image according to the new size specifications.

Figure 4-23: With the Resample Image check box turned on, you can modify the number of pixels in your image.

At all times, you can see the new number of pixels Photoshop will assign to the image, as well as the increased or decreased file size. In Figure 4-23, for example, I've changed the first Width value to 56 percent. The Pixel Dimensions value at the top of the dialog box reflects my change by reading *5.12M (was 16.3M),* which shows that the file size has decreased.

To calculate the pixels in the resampled image, Photoshop must use its powers of interpolation, as explained in the "General preferences" section of Chapter 2. The interpolation setting defaults to the one chosen in the Preferences dialog box. But you can also change the setting right inside the Image Size dialog box. Simply select the desired method from the Resample Image pop-up menu. Bicubic results in the smoothest effects. Bilinear is faster. And Nearest Neighbor turns off interpolation so Photoshop merely throws away the pixels it doesn't need or duplicates pixels to resample up.

Here are a few more random items you should know about resampling with the Image Size dialog box:

✦ This may sound odd, but you generally want to avoid adding pixels. When you resample up, you're asking Photoshop to make up details from thin air, and the program isn't that smart. Simply put, an enlarged image almost never looks better than the original; it merely takes up more disk space and prints slower.

✦ Resampling down, on the other hand, is a useful technique. It enables you to smooth away photo grain, halftone patterns, and other scanning artifacts. One of the most tried-and-true rules is to scan at the maximum resolution permitted by your scanner, and then resample the scan down to, say, 72 or 46 percent (with the interpolation set to Bicubic, naturally). By selecting a round value other than 50 percent, you force Photoshop to jumble the pixels into a regular, homogenous soup. You're left with fewer pixels, but these remaining pixels are better. And you have the added benefit that the image takes up less space on disk.

✦ To make an image tall and thin or short and fat, you must first turn off the Constrain Proportions check box. This enables you to edit the two Width values entirely independently of the two Height values.

✦ You can resample an image to match precisely the size and resolution of any other open image. While the Image Size dialog box is open, choose the name of the image you want to match from the Window menu.

✦ If you need help resampling an image to the proper size for a print job, choose Help ⇨ Resize Image to bring up the Resize Image Wizard. The dialog box walks you through the process of resampling step by step. It's really for rank beginners, but you might find it helpful when you want to turn the old brain off and set Photoshop to autopilot. (Note that Adobe uses the word "resize" simply because it's friendlier than "resample." Whatever it's called, this command does indeed resample.)

If you ever get confused inside the Image Size dialog box, and you want to return to the original size and resolution settings, press the Option key to change the Cancel button to Reset. Then click the Reset button to start from the beginning.

Caution

Photoshop remembers the setting of the Resample Image check box and uses this same setting the next time you open the Image Size dialog box. This can trip you up if you record a script for the Actions palette, as discussed in Chapter 3. Suppose you create a script to resize images, turning Resample Image off. If you later resample an image—turning on Resample Image—the check box stays selected when you close the dialog box. The next time you run the script, you end up resampling instead of resizing. Always check the status of the check box before you apply the Image Size command or run any scripts containing the command.

Cropping

Another way to change the number of pixels in an image is to crop it, which means to clip away pixels around the edges of an image without harming the remaining pixels. (The one exception occurs when you rotate a cropped image, in which case Photoshop has to interpolate pixels to account for the rotation.)

Cropping enables you to focus on an element in your image. For example, Figure 4-24 shows a bit of urban graffiti from a Digital Stock CD. I like this fellow's face—good chiaroscuro—but I can't quite figure out what's going on with this guy. I mean, what's with the screw? And is that a clown hat or what? That's the problem with graffiti—no art direction. Luckily, I can crop around the guy's head to delete all the extraneous image elements and hone in on his sleepy features, as shown in Figure 4-25.

Figure 4-24: This image contains too much extraneous information. Where should my eye go? I'm so confused.

Figure 4-25: Cropping enables you to clean up the background junk and focus on the essential foreground image.

Changing the canvas size

One way to crop an image is to choose Image ➪ Canvas Size, which displays the Canvas Size dialog box shown in Figure 4-26. The options in this dialog box enable you to scale the imaginary canvas on which the image rests separately from the image itself.

Figure 4-26: Choose Image ➪ Canvas Size to crop an image or to add empty space around the perimeter of an image.

If you enlarge the canvas, Photoshop surrounds the image with a white background (assuming the background color is white). If you reduce the canvas, you crop the image.

Click inside the Anchor grid to specify the placement of the image on the new canvas. For example, if you want to add space to the bottom of an image, enlarge the canvas size and then click inside the upper-middle square. If you want to crop away the upper left corner of an image, create a smaller canvas size and then click the lower-right square. The Anchor grid offers little arrows to show how the canvas will shrink or grow.

Using the crop tool

Generally speaking, the Canvas Size command is most useful for enlarging the canvas or shaving a few pixels off the edge of an image. If you want to crop away a large portion of an image, using the crop tool is a better choice.

To crop the image, select the crop tool by pressing the C key. (Selecting the tool manually is quite inconvenient thanks to the long marquee-tool pop-up menu, so get used to pressing the C key.) Then drag with the crop tool to create a rectangular marquee that surrounds the portion of the image you want to retain.

As you drag, you can press the spacebar to move the crop boundary temporarily on the fly. To stop moving the boundary and return to resizing it, release the spacebar.

If you don't get the crop marquee right the first time, you can move, scale, or rotate it at will. Here's what you do:

✦ Drag inside the crop marquee to move it.

✦ Drag one of the square handles to resize the marquee. You can Shift-drag a handle to scale the marquee proportionally (the same percentage vertically and horizontally).

✦ In Photoshop 5, you can drag a corner handle beyond the perimeter of the document boundaries. It's just the ticket for cropping layers that exceed the image dimensions.

✦ Drag outside the crop marquee to rotate it, as shown in Figure 4-27. This may strike you as weird at first, but it works wonderfully.

✦ Drag the origin point (labeled in Figure 4-27) to change the center of a rotation.

When the marquee surrounds the exact portion of the image you want to keep, press Return or double-click inside the marquee. Photoshop clips away all pixels except those that lie inside and along the border of the crop marquee.

If you change your mind about cropping, you can cancel the crop marquee by pressing Escape.

Origin point   Crop marquee   Handles   Rotate cursor

Figure 4-27: Align the crop marquee with an obvious axis in your image to determine the proper angle of rotation.

Rotating the crop marquee

As I said, you can rotate an image by dragging outside the crop marquee. Straightening out a crooked image can be a little tricky, however. I wish I had a certified check for every time I thought I had the marquee rotated properly, only to find the image was still crooked after I pressed Return. If this happens to you, choose Edit ⇨ Undo (⌘-Z) and try again. Do not try using the crop tool a second time to rotate the already rotated image. If you do, Photoshop sets about interpolating between already interpolated pixels, resulting in more lost data. Every rotation gets farther away from the original image.

A better solution is to do it right the first time. Locate a line or general axis in your image that should be straight up and down. Rotate the crop marquee so it aligns exactly with this axis. In Figure 4-27, I rotated my crop marquee so one edge bisects the graffiti guy's egg-shaped head. Don't worry because this isn't how you want to crop the image — you're just using the line as a reference. After you arrive at the correct angle for the marquee, drag the handles to size and position the boundary properly. As long as you don't drag outside the marquee, its angle remains fixed throughout.

Yet another solution is to use the new measure tool. Just drag with the tool along the axis you want to make vertical and note the angle (A:) value in the Info palette. I don't like this technique as much because it requires you to do some unnatural math—depending on how you drag, you may have to subtract 90 degrees from the A: value or subtract the A: value from 90 degrees. Then you keep an eye on the Info palette and rotate until you get an A: value that matches the answer to the previous equation. If you like math, great. If not, it's much simpler to use the technique I suggested in the previous paragraph.

Cropping an image to match another

There are two ways to crop an image so it matches the size and resolution of another:

✚ Bring the image you want to crop forward and choose Image ➪ Canvas Size. Then, while inside the Canvas Size dialog box, select the name of the image you want to match from the Window menu.

This method doesn't give you much control when cropping an image, but it's a great way to enlarge the canvas and add empty space around an image.

✚ Better yet, use the crop tool. First, bring the image you want to match to the front. Then select the crop tool and press Enter to display the Crop Options palette, pictured in Figure 4-28. Select the Fixed Target Size check box and click the Front Image button. Photoshop loads the size and resolution values into the palette's option boxes.

Now bring the image you want to crop to the front and drag with the crop tool as normal. Photoshop constrains the crop marquee to the proportions of the targeted image. After you press Return, Photoshop crops, resamples, and rotates the image as necessary.

Cropping a selection

Another way to crop an image is to create a rectangular selection and then choose Image ➪ Crop. One advantage of this technique is you needn't switch back and forth between the marquee and crop tools. One tool is all you need to select and crop. (If you're as lazy as I am, the mere act of selecting a tool can prove more effort than it's worth.) And, as with the crop tool, you can now press the spacebar while you draw a marquee to move it on the fly. It's no trick to get the placement and size exactly right—the only thing you can't do is rotate.

Another advantage of the Crop command is flexibility. You can draw a selection, switch windows, apply commands, and generally use any function you like prior to choosing Image ➪ Crop. The crop tool, by contrast, is much more limiting. After drawing a cropping marquee, you can't do anything but adjust the marquee until you press Return to accept the crop or Escape to dismiss it.

Figure 4-28: Bring the image you want to target to the front, and click each of the two options at the top of the Cropping Tool Options palette.

And finally, Image ⇨ Crop lets you crop the canvas to the boundaries of an image pasted from the Clipboard or dragged and dropped from another image window. As long as the boundaries of the pasted image are rectangular, as in the case of an image copied from a different application, you can choose Edit ⇨ Paste, ⌘-click the new layer in the Layers palette to regain the selection outline, and then choose Image ⇨ Crop. Photoshop replaces the former image and crops the window to fit the new image.

✦   ✦   ✦

Defining Colors

Selecting and Editing Colors

Occasionally, the state of computer graphics technology reminds me of television in the early 1950s. Only the upper echelon of Photoshop artists can afford to work exclusively in the wonderful world of color. The rest of us have to be prepared to print many or even most of our images in black and white.

Cross-Reference

Some of you might be thinking, "Wait a second, what about the equalizing force of the Internet? It brings color to all of us!" Well, I concur wholeheartedly. Nearly everyone owns a color monitor, so we can all share color images freely with each other. If this appeals to you, advance to Chapter 20 and learn how you can reduce color palettes and otherwise prepare your images for the bold new challenges of the Technicolor Web.

Regardless of who you are — print person or Web head — color is a prime concern. Even gray values, after all, are colors. Many folks have problems accepting this premise — I guess we're all so used to separating the worlds of grays and other colors in our minds that never the two shall meet. But gray values are only variations on what Noah Webster used to call "The sensation resulting from stimulation of the retina of the eye by light waves of certain lengths." (Give the guy a few drinks and he'd spout off 19 more definitions, not including the meanings of the transitive verb.) Just as black and white represent a subset of gray, gray is a subset of color. In fact, you'll find that using Photoshop involves a lot of navigating through these and other colorful subsets.

Specifying colors

First off, Photoshop provides four color controls in the Toolbox, as shown in Figure 5-1. These icons work as follows:

✦ **Foreground color:** The foreground color icon indicates the color you apply when you use the type, paint bucket, line, pencil, airbrush, or paintbrush tool, or if you Option-drag with the smudge tool. The foreground color also begins any gradation created with the gradient tool. You can apply the foreground color to a selection by choosing Edit ➪ Fill or Edit ➪ Stroke or by pressing Option-Delete. To change the foreground color, click the foreground color icon to display the Color Picker dialog box, select a new color in the Color palette, or click an open image window with the eyedropper tool.

Switch colors (X)
Foreground color
Background color
Default colors (D)

Figure 5-1: The color controls provided with Photoshop (along with keyboard shortcuts in parentheses, where applicable).

✦ **Background color:** The active background color indicates the color you apply with the eraser tool. The background color also ends any gradation created with the gradient tool. To change the background color, click the background color icon to display the Color Picker dialog box, use the Color palette, or Option-click any open image window with the eyedropper tool.

You can apply the background color to a selection by pressing Delete. But if the selection is floating or exists on any layer except the background layer, Delete actually deletes the selection instead of filling it. For complete safety, avoid the Delete key and use ⌘-Delete to fill a selection with the background color instead.

✦ **Switch colors:** Click this icon (or press X) to exchange the foreground and background colors.

✦ **Default colors:** Click this icon (or press D) to make the foreground color black and the background color white, according to their factory default settings. If you're editing a layer mask or adjustment layer, the default colors are reversed, as explained in Chapter 13.

Using the Color Picker

When you click the foreground or background color icon, Photoshop displays the Color Picker dialog box. (This assumes Photoshop is the active option in the Color Picker pop-up menu in the General Preferences dialog box. If you select the Apple option, the multi-paneled Apple Color Picker appears; see Chapter 2 on why you shouldn't select this option.) Figure 5-2 labels the wealth of elements and options in the Color Picker dialog box, which work as follows:

✦ **Color slider:** Use the color slider to home in on the color you want to select. Drag up or down on either of the slider triangles to select a color from a particular 8-bit range. The colors represented inside the slider correspond to the selected radio button. For example, if you select the H (Hue) radio button, which is the default setting, the slider colors represent the full 8-bit range of hues. If you select S (Saturation), the slider shows the current hue at full saturation at the top of the slider, down to no saturation — or gray — at the bottom of the slider. If you select B (Brightness), the slider shows the 8-bit range of brightness values, from solid color at the top of the slider to absolute black at the bottom. You also can select R (Red), G (Green), or B (Blue), in which case the top of the slider shows you what the current color looks like when subjected to full-intensity red, green, or blue (respectively), and the bottom of the slider shows every bit of red, green, or blue subtracted.

Cross-
Reference

For a proper introduction to the HSB and RGB color models, including definitions of specific terms such as hue, saturation, and brightness, read the "Working in Different Color Modes" section later in this chapter.

Figure 5-2: Use the elements and options in the Color Picker dialog box to specify a new foreground or background color from the 16-million-color range.

✦ **Color field:** The color field shows a 16-bit range of variations on the current slider color. Click inside it to move the color selection marker and, thereby, select a new color. The field graphs colors against the two remaining attributes not represented by the color slider. For example, if you select the H (Hue) radio button, the field graphs colors according to brightness vertically and saturation horizontally, as demonstrated in the first example of Figure 5-3. The other examples show what happens to the color field when you select the S (Saturation) and B (Brightness) radio buttons.

Likewise, Figure 5-4 shows how the field graphs colors when you select the R (Red), G (Green), and B (Blue) radio buttons. Obviously, it would help to see these images in color, but you probably couldn't afford this big, fat book if we'd printed it in full color. So I recommend you experiment with the Color Picker inside your version of Photoshop or refer to Color Plate 5-1 to see how the dialog box looks when the H (Hue), S (Saturation), and B (Brightness) options are selected.

Note

Slider and field always work together to represent the entire 16 million color range. The slider displays 256 colors, and the field displays 65,000 variations on the slider color; 256 times 65,000 is 16 million. No matter which radio button you select, you have access to the same colors; only your means of accessing them changes.

Figure 5-3: The color field graphs colors against the two attributes not represented in the slider. Here you can see how color is laid out when you select (top to bottom) the H (Hue), S (Saturation), and B (Brightness) radio buttons.

Figure 5-4: The results of selecting (top to bottom) the R (Red), G (Green), and B (Blue) radio buttons.

✦ **Current color:** The color currently selected from the color field appears in the top rectangle immediately to the right of the color slider. Click the OK button or press Return to make this the current foreground or background color (depending on which color control icon in the Toolbox you originally clicked to display the Color Picker dialog box).

✦ **Previous color:** The bottom rectangle to the right of the color slider shows how the foreground or background color—whichever one you are in the process of editing—looked before you displayed the Color Picker dialog box. Click the Cancel button or press Escape to leave this color intact.

✦ **Alert triangle:** The alert triangle appears when you select a bright color that Photoshop can't print using standard process colors. The box below the triangle shows the closest CMYK equivalent, invariably a duller version of the color. Click either the triangle or the box to bring the color into the printable range.

Entering numeric color values

In addition to selecting colors using the slider and color field, you can enter specific color values in the option boxes in the lower-right region of the Color Picker dialog box. Novices and intermediates may find these options less satisfying to use than the slider and field. These options, however, enable artists and print professionals to specify exact color values, whether to make controlled adjustments to a color already in use or to match a color used in another document. The options fall into one of four camps:

✦ **HSB:** These options stand for hue, saturation, and brightness. Hue is measured on a 360 degree circle. Saturation and brightness are measured from 0 to 100 percent. These options permit access to more than 3 million color variations.

✦ **RGB:** You can change the amount of the primary colors red, green, and blue by specifying the brightness value of each color from 0 to 255. These options enable access to more than 16 million color variations.

✦ **Lab:** This acronym stands for luminosity, measured from 0 to 100 percent, and two arbitrary color axes, a and b, whose brightness values range from 128 to 127. These options enable access to more than 6 million color variations.

✦ **CMYK:** These options display the amount of cyan, magenta, yellow, and black ink required to print the current color. In fact, when you click the alert triangle, these are the only values that don't change, because these values make up the closest CMYK equivalent.

In my opinion, the numerical range of these options is bewildering. For example, numerically speaking, the CMYK options enable you to create 100 million unique colors, whereas the RGB options enable the standard 16 million variations, and the Lab options enable a scant 6 million. Yet Lab is the largest color space, theoretically encompassing all colors from both CMYK and RGB. The printing standard CMYK provides by far the fewest colors, the opposite of what you might expect. What gives? Misleading numerical ranges. How do these weird color models work? Keep reading and you'll find out.

Working in Different Color Modes

The four sets of option boxes inside the Color Picker dialog box represent color models — or, if you prefer, color modes (one less letter, no less meaning, perfect for you folks who are trying to cut down in life). *Color models* are different ways to define colors both on screen and on the printed page.

Outside the Color Picker dialog box, you can work inside any one of these color models by choosing a command from the Image ⇨ Mode submenu. In doing so, you generally change the colors in your image by dumping a few hundred, or even a few thousand, colors with no equivalents in the new color model. The only exception is Lab, which in theory encompasses every unique color your eyes can detect.

Rather than discuss the color models in the order in which they occur in the Mode submenu, I cover them in logical order, starting with the most common and widely accepted color model, RGB. Also note, I don't discuss the duotone or multichannel modes now. Image ⇨ Mode ⇨ Duotone represents an alternative method for printing grayscale images, so it is discussed in Chapter 7. The multichannel mode, meanwhile, is not even a color model. Rather, Image ⇨ Mode ⇨ Multichannel enables you to separate an image into entirely independent channels, which you then can swap around and splice back together to create special effects. For more information, see the "Using multichannel techniques" section of Chapter 6.

RGB

RGB is the color model of light. RGB comprises three primary colors — red, green, and blue — each of which can vary between 256 levels of intensity (called brightness values, as discussed in previous chapters). The RGB model is also called the *additive primary model,* because a color becomes lighter as you add higher levels of red, green, and blue light. All monitors, projection devices, and other items that transmit or filter light, including televisions, movie projectors, colored stage lights, and even stained glass, rely on the additive primary model.

Red, green, and blue light mix as follows:

✦ **Red and green:** Full-intensity red and green mix to form yellow. Subtract some red to make chartreuse; subtract some green to make orange. All these colors assume a complete lack of blue.

✦ **Green and blue:** Full-intensity green and blue with no red mix to form cyan. If you try hard enough, you can come up with 65,000 colors in the turquoise/jade/sky blue/sea green range.

✦ **Blue and red:** Full-intensity blue and red mix to form magenta. Subtract some blue to make rose; subtract some red to make purple. All these colors assume a complete lack of green.

✦ **Red, green, and blue:** Full-intensity red, green, and blue mix to form white, the absolute brightest color in the visible spectrum.

✦ **No light:** Low intensities of red, green, and blue plunge a color into blackness.

As far as image editing is concerned, the RGB color model is ideal for editing images on screen because it provides access to the entire range of 24-bit screen colors. Furthermore, you can save an RGB image in every file format supported by Photoshop except GIF and the two DCS formats. As shown in Table 5-1, grayscale is the only other color mode compatible with a wider range of file formats.

Table 5-1
File-Format Support for Photoshop 5's Color Models

	Bitmap	Grayscale	Duotone	Indexed	RGB	Lab	CMYK
Photoshop	yes	yes	yes	yes	yes	yes	yes
BMP	yes	yes	no	yes	yes	no	no
DCS 1.0	no	no	no	no	no	no	yes
DCS 2.0	yes	yes	yes*	no	no	no	yes
EPS	yes	yes	yes	yes	yes	yes	yes
GIF	yes	yes	no	yes	no	no	no
FlashPix	no	yes	no	no	yes	no	no
JPEG	no	yes	no	no	yes	no	yes
PCX	yes	yes	no	yes	yes	no	no
PDF	yes	yes	no	yes	yes	yes	yes
PICT	yes	yes	no	yes	yes	no	no
PNG	yes	yes	no	yes	yes	no	no
Scitex CT	no	yes	no	no	yes	no	yes
TIFF	yes	yes	no	yes	yes	yes	yes

Note

Table 5-1 lists color models in the order they appear in the Image ⇨ Mode submenu. Again, I left out the multichannel mode because it is not a true color model. The one exception is with duotones. Notice how I've included an asterisk (*) with DCS 2.0 support for duotones. This is because you can save a duotone in the DCS 2.0 only after first converting the image to the multichannel mode. For more information, consult Chapter 7.

On the negative side, the RGB color model provides access to a wider range of colors than you can print. If you are designing an image for full-color printing, therefore, you can expect to lose many of the brightest and most vivid colors in your image. The only way to avoid such color loss entirely is to scan your image and edit it in the CMYK mode, which can be an exceptionally slow proposition. The better solution is to scan your images to Photo CDs and edit them in the Lab mode, as explained in the upcoming "CIE's Lab" section.

HSB

Back in Photoshop 2, the Modes menu provided access to the HSB — hue, saturation, brightness — color model, now relegated to the Color Picker dialog box and the Color palette (discussed later in this chapter). *Hue* is pure color, the stuff rainbows are made of, measured on a 360-degree circle. Red is located at 0 degrees, yellow at 60 degrees, green at 120 degrees, cyan at 180 degrees (midway around the circle), blue at 240 degrees, and magenta at 300 degrees. This is basically a pie-shaped version of the RGB model at full intensity.

Saturation represents the purity of the color. A zero saturation value equals gray. White, black, and any other colors you can express in a grayscale image have no saturation. Full saturation produces the purest version of a hue.

Brightness is the lightness or darkness of a color. A zero brightness value equals black. Full brightness combined with full saturation results in the most vivid version of any hue.

CMYK

In nature, our eyes perceive pigments according to the *subtractive color model.* Sunlight contains every visible color found on Earth. When sunlight is projected on an object, the object absorbs (subtracts) some of the light and reflects the rest. The reflected light is the color you see. For example, a fire engine is bright red because it absorbs all non-red — meaning all blue and green — from the white-light spectrum.

Pigments on a sheet of paper work the same way. You can even mix pigments to create other colors. Suppose you paint a red brush stroke, which absorbs green and blue light, over a blue brush stroke, which absorbs green and red light. You get a blackish mess with only a modicum of blue and red light left, along with a smidgen of green because the colors weren't absolutely pure.

But wait — every child knows red and blue mix to form purple. So what gives? What gives is that what you learned in elementary school is only a rude approximation of the truth. Did you ever try mixing a vivid red with a canary yellow only to produce an ugly orange-brown gloop? The reason you didn't achieve the bright orange you wanted is obvious. Red starts out darker than bright orange, which means you must add a great deal of yellow before you arrive at orange. And even then, the yellow had better be an incredibly bright lemon yellow, not some deep canary yellow with a lot of red in it.

Commercial subtractive primaries

The subtractive primary colors used by commercial printers — cyan, magenta, and yellow — are for the most part very light. Cyan absorbs only red light, magenta absorbs only green light, and yellow absorbs only blue light. On their own, these colors unfortunately don't do a good job of producing dark colors. In fact, at full intensities, cyan, magenta, and yellow all mixed together don't get much beyond a muddy brown. That's where black comes in. Black helps to accentuate shadows, deepen dark colors, and, of course, print real blacks.

In case you're wondering how colors mix in the CMYK model, it's basically the opposite of the RGB model. Because pigments are not as pure as primary colors in the additive model, though, some differences exist:

✦ **Cyan and magenta:** Full-intensity cyan and magenta mix to form a deep blue with a little violet. Subtract some cyan to make purple; subtract some magenta to make a dull medium blue. All these colors assume a complete lack of yellow.

✦ **Magenta and yellow:** Full-intensity magenta and yellow mix to form a brilliant red. Subtract some magenta to make vivid orange; subtract some yellow to make rose. All these colors assume a complete lack of cyan.

✦ **Yellow and cyan:** Full-intensity yellow and cyan mix to form a bright green with a hint of blue. Subtract some yellow to make a deep teal; subtract some cyan to make chartreuse. All these colors assume a complete lack of magenta.

✦ **Cyan, magenta, and yellow:** Full-intensity cyan, magenta, and yellow mix to form a muddy brown.

✦ **Black:** Black pigmentation added to any other pigment darkens the color.

✦ **No pigment:** No pigmentation results in white (assuming white is the paper color).

Editing in CMYK

If you're used to editing RGB images, editing in the CMYK mode can require some new approaches, especially when editing individual color channels. When you view a single color channel in the RGB mode (as discussed in the following chapter), white indicates high-intensity color, and black indicates low-intensity color. It's the opposite in CMYK. When you view an individual color channel, black means high-intensity color, and white means low-intensity color.

This doesn't mean RGB and CMYK color channels look like inverted versions of each other. In fact, because the color theory is inverted, they look much the same. But if you're trying to achieve the full-intensity colors mentioned in the preceding section, you should apply black to the individual color channels, not white as you would in the RGB mode.

Should I edit in CMYK?

RGB doesn't accurately represent the colors you get when you print an image because the RGB color space contains many colors — particularly very bright colors — that CMYK can't touch. This is why when you switch from RGB to CMYK, the colors appear duller. (If you're familiar with painting, RGB is like oils and CMYK is like acrylics. The latter lacks the depth of color provided by the former.)

For this reason, many folks advocate working exclusively in the CMYK mode, but I do not. Although working in CMYK eliminates color disappointments, it is also much slower because Photoshop has to convert CMYK values to your RGB screen on the fly.

Furthermore, your scanner and monitor are RGB devices. No matter how you work, a translation from RGB to CMYK color space must occur at some time. If you pay the extra bucks to purchase a commercial drum scan, for example, you simply make the translation at the beginning of the process — Scitex has no option but to use RGB sensors internally — rather than at the end. Every color device on Earth, in fact, is RGB except the printer.

You should wait to convert to the CMYK mode until right before you print. After your artwork is finalized, choose Image ⇨ Mode ⇨ CMYK and make whatever edits you deem necessary. For example, you might want to introduce a few color corrections, apply some sharpening, and even retouch a few details by hand. Photoshop applies your changes more slowly in the CMYK mode, but at least you're only slowed down at the end of the job, not throughout the entire process.

Before converting an image to the CMYK color space, make certain Photoshop is aware of the monitor you're using and the printer you intend to use. These two items can have a pronounced effect on how Photoshop generates a CMYK image. I discuss how to set up your personal RGB and CMYK color spaces in the "Creating Color Separations" section of Chapter 7.

Previewing the CMYK color space

This isn't to say you can't edit in the RGB mode and still get a picture of what the image will look like in CMYK. If you choose View ⇨ Preview ⇨ CMYK or press ⌘-Y, Photoshop displays colors in the CMYK color space on screen while enabling you to continue working in the larger world of RGB.

In Photoshop 5, you can also preview the individual ink plates in a CMYK image. Just choose one of the commands from the View ➪ Preview submenu. The plates will appear as grayscale unless you colorize them by selecting the Color Channels in Color option in the Preferences dialog box (⌘-K, ⌘-3). If you work with an older model color ink-jet printer, you can also choose View ➪ Preview ➪ CMY to see what the printed version of your image will look like without black ink.

View ➪ Gamut Warning (⌘-Shift-Y) is a companion to Photoshop's CMYK preview commands that covers so-called "out-of-gamut" colors — RGB colors with no CMYK equivalents — with gray. I personally find this command less useful because it demonstrates a problem without suggesting a solution. You can desaturate the grayed colors with the sponge tool (which I explain in Chapter 8), but this accomplishes little that Photoshop won't do automatically. A CMYK preview is much more serviceable and representative of the final CMYK image.

Tip

Try choosing both the Preview ➪ CMYK and Gamut Warning commands while inside Photoshop's Color Picker dialog box. CMYK Preview shows how all colors will appear in the CMYK color space, regardless of which options you use to define the color. And Gamut Warning takes on new meaning, enabling you to mask out colors that won't print. It's also an excellent way to glean a little color theory.

CIE's Lab

RGB isn't the only mode that responds quickly and provides a bountiful range of colors. Photoshop's Lab color space comprises all the colors from RGB and CMYK and is every bit as fast as RGB. Many high-end users prefer to work in this mode, and I certainly advocate this if you're brave enough.

Whereas the RGB mode is the color model of your luminescent computer screen and the CMYK mode is the color model of the reflective page, Lab is independent of light or pigment. Perhaps you've already heard the bit about how in 1931, an international color organization called the *Commission Internationale d'Eclairage* (CIE) developed a color model that, in theory, contains every single color the human eye can see. (Gnats, iguanas, fruit bats, go find your own color models; humans, you have CIE. Mutants and aliens — maybe CIE, maybe not, too early to tell.) Then, in 1976, the significant birthday of our nation, the CIE celebrated by coming up with two additional color systems. One of those systems was Lab, and the other was shrouded in secrecy. Well, at least I don't know what the other one was. Probably something that measures how the entire visible spectrum of color can bounce off your retina when using flash photography and come out looking the exact shade of red one normally associates with lab (not Lab) rabbits. But this is just a guess.

The beauty of the Lab color model is it fills in gaps in both the RGB and CMYK models. RGB, for example, provides an overabundance of colors in the blue-to-green range, but is stingy on yellows, oranges, and other colors in the green-to-red range. Meanwhile, the colors missing from CMYK are enough to fill the holes in the Albert Hall. Lab gets everything right.

Understanding Lab anatomy

The Lab mode features three color channels, one for luminosity and two others for color ranges, known simply by the initials *a* and *b*. (The Greeks would have called them alpha and beta, if that's any help.) Upon hearing luminosity, you might think, "Ah, just like HSL." Well, to make things confusing, Lab's *luminosity* is like HSB's brightness. White indicates full-intensity color.

Meanwhile, the *a* channel contains colors ranging from deep green (low-brightness values) to gray (medium-brightness values) to vivid pink (high-brightness values). The *b* channel ranges from bright blue (low-brightness values) to gray to burnt yellow (high-brightness values). As in the RGB model, these colors mix together to produce lighter colors. Only the brightness values in the luminosity channel darken the colors. So you can think of Lab as a two-channel RGB with brightness thrown on top.

To get a glimpse of how it works, try the following simple experiment.

Steps: Testing Out the Lab Mode

1. **Create a new image in the Lab mode – say, 300 × 300 pixels.**

2. **Press the D key to return the default colors to the Toolbox.** The foreground color is now black and the background color is white.

3. **Press ⌘-2. This takes you to the a channel.**

4. **Double-click on the linear gradient tool in the Toolbox.** Or press Return. Either approach displays the Linear Gradient Options palette. Make sure you see the words Normal and Foreground to Background. If these words aren't visible, select them from the first and second pop-up menus, respectively.

5. **Shift-drag with the gradient tool from the top to the bottom of the window.** This creates a vertical black-to-white gradation.

6. **Press ⌘-3. This takes you to the b channel.**

7. **Shift-drag from left to right with the gradient tool.** Photoshop paints a horizontal gradation.

8. **Press ⌘-tilde (~) to return to the composite display.** Now you can see all channels at once. If you're using a 24-bit monitor, you should be looking at a window filled with an incredible array of super bright colors. In theory, these are the brightest shades of all the colors you can see. In practice, however, the colors are limited by the display capabilities of your RGB monitor.

9. **If you really want a sobering sight, choose View ➪ CMYK Preview and watch those bright colors disappear.** Aagh, isn't it pitiful? Luckily, CMYK is capable of doing a slightly better job than this. Choose Image ➪ Adjust ➪ Auto Levels (or press ⌘-Shift-L). That's better — quite a bit better, in fact — but it's still muted compared with its Lab counterpart.

Using Lab

Because it's device independent, you can use the Lab mode to edit any image. Editing in the Lab mode is as fast as editing in the RGB mode and several times faster than editing in the CMYK mode. If you plan on printing your image to color separations, you may want to experiment with using the Lab mode instead of RGB, because Lab ensures no colors are altered when you convert the image to CMYK, except to change colors that fall outside the CMYK range. In fact, any time you convert an image from RGB to CMYK, Photoshop automatically converts the image to the Lab mode as an intermediate step.

Tip

If you work with Photo CDs often, open the scans directly from the Photo CD format as Lab images. Kodak's proprietary YCC color model is nearly identical to Lab, so you can expect an absolute minimum of data loss; some people claim no loss whatsoever occurs.

Grayscale

Grayscale is possibly my favorite color mode. Grayscale frees you from all the hassles and expense of working with color and provides access to every bit of Photoshop's power and functionality. Anyone who says you can't do as much with grayscale as you can with color, missed out on *Citizen Kane*, *Grapes of Wrath*, *Manhattan*, and *Raging Bull*. You can print grayscale images to any laser printer, reproduce them in any publication, and edit them on nearly any machine. Besides, they look great, they remind you of old movies, and they make a hefty book like this one affordable. What could be better?

Other than extolling its virtues, however, there isn't a whole lot to say about grayscale. You can convert an image to the grayscale mode regardless of its current mode, and you can convert from grayscale to any other mode just as easily. In fact, choosing Image ➪ Mode ➪ Grayscale is a necessary step in converting a color image to a duotone or black-and-white bitmap.

Search your channels before converting

When you convert an image from one of the color modes to the grayscale mode, Photoshop normally weights the values of each color channel in a way that retains the apparent brightness of the overall image. For example, when you convert an image from RGB, Photoshop weights red more heavily than blue when computing dark values. This is because red is a darker-looking color than blue (much as that might seem contrary to popular belief).

Tip

If you choose Image ➪ Mode ➪ Grayscale while viewing a single color channel, though, Photoshop retains all brightness values in that channel only and abandons the data in the other channels. This can be an especially useful technique for rescuing a grayscale image from a bad RGB scan.

So before switching to the grayscale mode, be sure to look at the individual color channels — particularly the red and green channels (the blue channel frequently contains substandard detail) — to see how each channel might look on its own. To browse the channels, press ⌘-1 for red, ⌘-2 for green, and ⌘-3 for blue. Or ⌘-1 for cyan, ⌘-2 for magenta, ⌘-3 for yellow, and ⌘-4 for black. Or even ⌘-1 for luminosity, ⌘-2 for *a*, and ⌘-3 for *b*. Chapter 6 describes color channels in more detail.

Black and white (bitmap)

Choose Image ➪ Mode ➪ Bitmap to convert a grayscale image to exclusively black-and-white pixels. This may sound like a boring option, but it can prove useful for gaining complete control over the printing of grayscale images. After all, output devices, such as laser printers and imagesetters, render grayscale images as a series of tiny dots. Using the Bitmap command, you can specify the size, shape, and angle of those dots.

When you choose Image ➪ Mode ➪ Bitmap, Photoshop displays the Bitmap dialog box, shown in Figure 5-5. Here you specify the resolution of the black-and-white image and select a conversion process. The options work as follows:

✦ **Output:** Specify the resolution of the black-and-white file. If you want control over every single pixel available to your printer, raise this value to match your printer's resolution. As a rule of thumb, try setting the Output value somewhere between 200 and 250 percent of the Input value.

✦ **50% Threshold:** Select this option to make every pixel that is darker than 50 percent gray black and every pixel that is 50 percent gray or lighter white. Unless you are working toward some special effect — for example, overlaying a black-and-white version of an image over the original grayscale image — this option most likely isn't for you. (And if you're working toward a special effect, Image ➪ Adjust ➪ Threshold is the better alternative.)

✦ **Pattern Dither:** To *dither* pixels is to mix them up to emulate different colors. In this case, Photoshop mixes up black and white pixels to produce shades of gray. The Pattern Dither option dithers an image using a geometric pattern. Unfortunately, the results are pretty ugly, as demonstrated in the top example in Figure 5-6. And the space between dots has a tendency to fill in, especially when you output to a laser printer.

Figure 5-5: The Bitmap dialog box converts images from grayscale to black and white.

Figure 5-6: The results of selecting the Pattern Dither option (top) and the much more acceptable Diffusion Dither option (bottom).

✦ **Diffusion Dither:** Select this option to create a mezzotint-like effect, as demonstrated in the second example in Figure 5-6. Again, because this option converts an image into thousands of stray pixels, you can expect your image to darken dramatically when output to a low-resolution laser printer and when reproduced. So be sure to lighten the image with something like the Levels command (as described in Chapter 18) before selecting this option.

✦ **Halftone Screen:** When you select this option and press Return, Photoshop displays the dialog box shown in Figure 5-7. These options enable you to apply a dot pattern to the image, as demonstrated in Figure 5-8. Enter the number of dots per inch in the Frequency option box and the angle of the dots in the Angle option box. Then select a dot shape from the Shape pop-up menu. Figure 5-8 shows examples of four shapes, each with a frequency of 24 lines per inch.

I cover screen patterns and frequency settings in more depth in the "Changing the halftone screen" section of Chapter 7.

Figure 5-7: This dialog box appears when you select the Halftone Screen option in the Bitmap dialog box.

✦ **Custom Pattern:** If you've defined a repeating pattern using Edit ⇨ Define Pattern, you can use it as a custom dither pattern. Figure 5-9 shows two custom examples. I created the first pattern using the Twirl Pattern file, which is stored in the Displacement Maps folder in the Plug-Ins folder. I created the second pattern manually using the Add Noise, Emboss, and Ripple filters (as discussed in the "Creating texture effects" section of Chapter 17).

For a complete guide to creating and defining patterns in Photoshop, see the "Applying Repeating Patterns" section of Chapter 10.

Figure 5-8: Four random examples of halftone cell shapes. In all cases, the Frequency value was set to 24.

Caution

Photoshop lets you edit individual pixels in the so-called bitmap mode, but that's about the extent of it. After you go to black-and-white, you can neither perform any serious editing nor expect to return to the grayscale mode and restore your original pixels. So be sure to finish your image editing before choosing Image ➪ Mode ➪ Bitmap. Even more important, make certain to save your image before converting it to black-and-white. Frankly, saving is a good idea prior to performing any color conversion.

Figure 5-9: Two examples of employing repeating patterns (created with Edit ⇨ Define Pattern) as custom halftoning patterns.

Using Photoshop's Other Color Selection Methods

In addition to the Color Picker dialog box, Photoshop provides a handful of additional techniques for selecting colors. The sections that finish out this chapter explain how to use the Custom Colors dialog box, the Colors palette, and the eyedropper tool. None of this information is terribly exciting, but it will enable you to work more efficiently and conveniently.

Predefined colors

If you click the Custom button inside the Color Picker dialog box, Photoshop displays the Custom Colors dialog box shown in Figure 5-10. In this dialog box, you can select from a variety of predefined colors by choosing the color family from the Book pop-up menu, moving the slider triangles up and down the color slider to specify a general range of colors and, ultimately, selecting a color from the color list on the left. If you own the swatchbook for a color family, you can locate a specific color by entering its number on the keyboard.

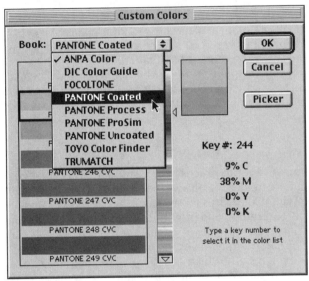

Figure 5-10: The Custom Colors dialog box enables you to select predefined colors from brand-name libraries.

The color families represented in the Book pop-up menu fall into six brands: ANPA (now NAA, as I explain shortly), DIC, Focoltone, Pantone, Toyo, and Trumatch, all of which get a big kick out of capitalizing their names in dialog boxes. I honestly think one of these companies would stand out better if its name weren't capitalized. Anyway, at the risk of offending a few of these companies, you're likely to find certain brands more useful than others. The following sections briefly introduce the brands in order of their impact on the American market — forgive me for being ethnocentric in this regard — from smallest to greatest impact.

The number-one use for predefined colors in Photoshop is in the creation of duotones, tritones, and quadtones (described in Chapter 7). You can also use predefined colors to match the colors in a logo or some other important element in an image to a commercial standard. And in Photoshop 5, you can now add an independent channel for a predefined color and print it to a separate plate, as discussed in Chapter 6.

Focoltone, DIC, and Toyo

Focoltone, Dianippon Ink and Chemical (DIC), and Toyo fall into the negligible impact category. All are foreign color standards with followings abroad. Focoltone is an English company; not English speaking — although they probably do — but English living, as in commuting-to-France-through-the-Channel England. DIC and Toyo are popular in the Japanese market, but have next to no subscribers outside Japan.

Newspaper Association of America

American Newspaper Publishers Association (ANPA) recently changed its name to NAA, which stands for Newspaper Association of America, and updated its color catalog. NAA provides a small sampling of 33 process colors (mixes of cyan, magenta, yellow, and black ink) plus 5 spot colors (colors produced by printing a single ink). The idea behind the NAA colors is to isolate the color combinations that reproduce most successfully on inexpensive newsprint and to provide advertisers with a solid range of colors from which to choose, without allowing the color choices to get out of hand. You can purchase a Pocket Tint Chart from NAA for $175. Members pay $100.

Trumatch

Trumatch remains my personal favorite process-color standard. Designed entirely using a desktop system and created especially with desktop publishers in mind, the Trumatch Colorfinder swatchbook features more than 2,000 process colors, organized according to hue, saturation, and brightness. Each hue is broken down into 40 tints and shades. Tints are created by reducing the saturation in 15 percent increments; shades are created by adding black ink in 6 percent increments. The result is a guide that shows you exactly which colors you can attain using a desktop system. If you're wondering what a CMYK blend will look like when printed, you need look no further than the Trumatch Colorfinder.

As if the Colorfinder weren't enough, Trumatch provides the ColorPrinter Software utility, which automatically prints the entire 2,000-color library to any PostScript-compatible output device. The utility integrates EfiColor and PostScript Level 2, thereby enabling design firms and commercial printers to test the entire range of capabilities available to their hardware. Companies can provide select clients with swatches of colors created on their own printers, guaranteeing what you see is darn well what you'll get.

Pantone

On the heels of Trumatch, Pantone released a 3,006-color Process Color System Guide (labeled Pantone Process in the Book pop-up menu) priced at $75, $10 less than the Trumatch Colorfinder. Pantone also produces the foremost spot color swatchbook, the Color Formula Guide 1000. Then there's the Process Color Imaging Guide, which enables you to figure out quickly if you can closely match a Pantone spot color using a process-color blend or if you ought to give it up and stick with the spot color.

Pantone spot colors are ideal for creating duotones and adding custom colors to an image for logos and the like, both discussed in Chapter 7. Furthermore, Pantone is supported by every computer application that aspires to the color prepress market. As long as the company retains the old competitive spirit, you can, most likely, expect Pantone to remain the primary color printing standard for years to come.

The Color palette

Another means of selecting colors in Photoshop is to use the Color palette, shown in Figure 5-11. The Color palette is convenient, it's always there, and it doesn't hog your screen like the Color Picker dialog box. Frankly, this is the tool that I use most often to select colors in Photoshop.

Figure 5-11: The Color and Swatches palettes let you edit colors without having to display the screen-hogging Color Picker dialog box.

To display the palette, choose Window ⇨ Show Color or press the F6 key. You then can use the elements and options inside the palette as explained in the upcoming list.

✦ **Foreground color/background color:** Click the foreground or background color icon in the Color palette to specify the color you want to edit. If you click the foreground or background color icon when it's already highlighted — as indicated by a double-line frame — Photoshop displays the Color Picker dialog box.

✦ **Slider bars:** Drag the triangles in the slider controls to edit the highlighted color. By default, the sliders represent the red, green, and blue primary colors when a color image is open. You can change the slider bars by choosing a different color model from the palette menu.

✦ **Option boxes:** Alternatively, you can enter numerical values into the option boxes to the right of the sliders. Press Tab to advance from one option box to the next; press Shift-Tab to go to the previous option.

✦ **Alert triangle:** Photoshop displays the alert triangle when a color falls outside the CMYK color gamut. The color swatch to the right of the triangle shows the closest CMYK equivalent. Click the triangle or the color swatch to replace the current color with the CMYK equivalent.

✦ **Color bar:** The bar along the bottom of the Color palette displays all colors contained in the CMYK spectrum. Click or drag inside the color bar to lift a color and make it the current foreground or background color (depending on whether the foreground or background icon is selected above). The sliders update as you drag. Option-click or drag to lift the background color if the foreground icon is selected or the foreground color if the background color is selected.

✦ **Color Bar option:** You needn't accept the CMYK spectrum in the color bar. To change to a different spectrum, select the Color Bar command from the palette menu. The resulting dialog box enables you to change to the RGB spectrum or to select a black-to-white gradation (Grayscale Slider). If you select Current Colors, the color bar is filled with a gradation from the current foreground color to the current background color. The color bar continuously updates to represent the newest foreground and background colors.

Tip

Save yourself the effort of choosing the Color Bar command by learning these nifty shortcuts. To bring up the same dialog box that Color Bar displays, ⌘-click on the color bar. Better yet, Control-click on the color bar to access a pop-up menu containing the same options found in the dialog box. Or best of all, Shift-click the bar to cycle from one color bar to the next.

The Swatches palette

As shown in Figure 5-11, the Color palette offers an additional panel called Swatches. The Swatches palette enables you to collect colors for future use, sort of like a favorite color reservoir.

Tip

Here's a list of the hidden tricks for using the swatches in the reservoir:

✦ Click a color swatch to make that color the foreground color. Option-click to set the background color.

✦ To add the current foreground color to the reservoir, Shift-click an existing color swatch to replace the old color or click an empty swatch to append the new color. In either case, your cursor temporarily changes to a paint bucket.

✦ To insert a color anywhere in the palette, Shift-Option-click a swatch. The other colors scoot over to make room.

✦ To delete a color from the panel, ⌘-click a color swatch. Your cursor changes to a pair of scissors and cuts the color away.

You can also save and load color palettes on disk using options in the pop-up menu. The Load Swatches option adds the colors in the file to the current set of swatches; Replace Swatches replaces the current swatches with the ones in the file. The Palettes folder, located inside the same folder that contains the Photoshop application, contains palettes for the major color libraries from Pantone, Trumatch, and others. When one of these palettes is loaded, positioning your cursor over a color swatch makes the name of that color appear in place of the word Swatches in the panel tab.

The eyedropper tool

The eyedropper tool — which you can select by pressing the I key — provides the most convenient and straightforward means of selecting colors in Photoshop. This is so straightforward, in fact, it's hardly worth explaining. But quickly, here's how the eyedropper tool works:

✦ **Selecting a foreground color:** To select a new foreground color, click the desired color inside any open Image window with the eyedropper tool. (This assumes the foreground icon in the Color palette is selected. If the background icon is selected, Option-click with the eyedropper tool to lift the foreground color.) You can even click inside a background window to lift a color without bringing that window to the foreground.

✦ **Selecting a background color:** To select a new background color, Option-click the desired color with the eyedropper tool. (Again, this assumes the foreground icon is selected in the Color palette. If the background icon is selected, click with the eyedropper to lift the background color.)

✦ **Skating over the color spectrum:** You can animate the foreground color control box by dragging with the eyedropper tool in the Image window. As soon as you achieve the desired color, release your mouse button. To animate the background color icon, Option-drag with the eyedropper tool. The icon color changes as you move the eyedropper tool.

✦ **Sampling multiple pixels:** Normally, the eyedropper tool selects the color from the single pixel on which you click. If you prefer to average the colors of several neighboring pixels, however, press Return or double-click the eyedropper icon in the Toolbox to display the Eyedropper Options palette. Then select a different option from the Sample Size pop-up menu. Or right-click with the eyedropper to bring up a convenient pop-up menu of sampling options.

To access the eyedropper tool temporarily when using the type, paint bucket, gradient, line, pencil, airbrush, or paintbrush tool, press Option. The eyedropper cursor remains in force for as long as the Option key is down. The eyedropper lifts whatever color is active in the Color palette (foreground or background). To lift the other color, switch to the eyedropper tool by pressing the I key and then Option-click an image window.

The color sampler tool

A new tool shares a slot in the toolbox with the eyedropper. Dubbed the color sampler, it looks like the eyedropper with a little crosshair target. But where the eyedropper lifts foreground and background colors, the color sampler merely measures the colors of pixels so you can monitor how the pixels react to various color changes.

Select the color sampler and click somewhere inside the image window. Photoshop adds a crosshair target to indicate the point you clicked. The program also brings up the Info palette (if it isn't up already) and adds a new color measurement item labeled #1. This item corresponds to the target in the image, which is likewise labeled 1. Click again and you add a second target and a corresponding item #2 in the Info palette. You can add up to four targets to an image, as demonstrated in Figure 5-12.

The color sampler is primarily intended for printers and technicians who want to monitor the effects of color corrections on specific points in an image. If you apply Image ➪ Adjust ➪ Levels, for example, Photoshop constantly updates the items in the Info palette to reflect your changes (as I explain in more detail in Chapter 18). But you can also sample points in an image to monitor the effects of filters (Chapters 15 through 17), blend modes (Chapter 19), and edit tools such as dodge and burn (Chapter 8). The color sampler is just another way to monitor changes made to an image.

Figure 5-12: The color sampler tool lets you measure the colors of four points in your image, as indicated by the black arrows. You can also measure a fifth point by merely moving the cursor around, as indicated by the white arrow.

Here are a few more techniques of interest when color sampling:

✦ Photoshop limits you to four color targets. If you try to create a fifth one, the program generates an error message. If you want to measure a different point in the image, you can either hover your cursor over the point and note the top set of color values in the Info palette (as in Figure 5-12) or move one of the targets.

✦ To move a target inside the image window, just drag it with the color sampler tool. You can also move a target by ⌘-dragging it with the eyedropper tool.

✦ To delete a target, Option-click on it.

✦ The Info palette grows to more than twice its normal size when you start clicking with the color sampler. To hide the sampler information without deleting targets, click on the Info palette's collapse box or choose Hide Color Samplers from the palette menu. Either way, you have to choose Show Color Samplers to bring the samples back.

✦ By default, the sampler items in the Info palette measure colors in the active color space. If you want to track a target in a different color space, click on the item's eyedropper icon in the Info palette. This displays a pop-up menu of color space alternatives, including Grayscale, RGB, and several others that you may recall from previous explanations in this chapter.

Tip

To select the color sampler, press Shift-I when the eyedropper is active or Option-click on the eyedropper icon. You can also temporarily access the color sampler any time the eyedropper is active by pressing the Shift key. This little trick also works when a color correction dialog box like Levels or Curves is open, as explained in Chapter 18. It's just the ticket when you're in the middle of an adjustment and you need to know how it's affecting specific portions of the image.

✦   ✦   ✦

Basic Color Management

Plunging Headlong into Color

Now that we've gotten our feet wet with some basic color theory and waded around in the Color and Swatches palettes, it's time to don scuba gear and immerse ourselves fully in the larger world of color under Photoshop 5. We'll immediately dive to 20 feet and take an elementary test run through Photoshop's color-space conversion capabilities. At 50 feet down, we'll stop and examine a school of exotic Profile Setup options. Then we'll risk nitrogen narcosis and drop to 100 feet where we'll find the Channels palette, the entryway to Photoshop's vital and mesmerizing color caverns.

I use this diving metaphor not merely to invoke a sense of wonder, but because, to most artists, color management is every bit as mysterious as the contours of the ocean floor. It's no exaggeration to say that color management is perhaps the least understood topic in all of computer imaging. From my experience with talking to Photoshop users, most folks expect to calibrate their monitors to achieve reliable if not perfect color, but in point of fact, there's no such thing. So called *device-dependent color*—that is, synthetic color produced by a piece of hardware—is a moving target. Photoshop's role is to convert from one target to the next.

For what it's worth, most consumer monitors (and video boards, for that matter) are beyond calibration, in the strict sense of the word. You can try your hand at using a hardware calibrator—one of those devices where you plop a little suction cup onto your screen, such as the cross-platform OptiCal from The Color Partnership (*www.colorpar.com*). But calibrators often have less to do with changing screen colors than identifying them, a process known as *characterization*. Even if your monitor permits prepress-quality calibration— as in the case of the $4,000 PressView 21SR from Radius (*www.radius.com*)—it's not enough to simply correct the colors on screen, you also have to tell Photoshop what you've done.

Therefore, color management is first and foremost about identifying your monitor. You have to explain your screen's foibles to Photoshop so that it can make every attempt to account for them. In the old days, Photoshop used the screen data to calculate CMYK conversions and that was it. But with Version 5, Photoshop goes two steps farther, embedding *International Color Consortium* (ICC) *profiles* that identify the source of the image and using this information to translate colors from one monitor to another. The new Color Settings commands are both wonderful and bewildering. They can just as easily mess up colors as fix them. But if you read this chapter, you and your colors should be able to ride the currents safely from one digital destination to the next.

The Color Settings Commands

In Photoshop 5, the File ➪ Color Settings pop-up menu includes the following four commands:

✦ **RGB Setup:** Your RGB environment is what you see on screen. This command lets you confirm that you've correctly identified your monitor. But its primary purpose is to specify the RGB space that you want Photoshop to simulate.

✦ **CMYK Setup:** In Version 4 and earlier, Photoshop provided three commands for setting up your final CMYK output device. Now there's just one. I touch very lightly on this command in this chapter, but because it applies only to CMYK printing, I save most of the information for Chapter 7.

✦ **Grayscale Setup:** This command defines how Photoshop displays a grayscale image. You can see either an untreated RGB version of your image, or preview it the way it will print complete with dot gain (as defined by the Dot Gain value in the CMYK Setup dialog box).

✦ **Profile Setup:** This is the command that makes it all happen. Here you specify whether you want to save source profiles with an image and how to handle color conversions when you open images created on other computers. If there is one hinge pin in Photoshop's color matching functions, Profile Setup is it (which is why it gets it's own section later in this chapter).

Like the Preferences commands, you only need to visit the Color Settings commands once and then forget about them. Photoshop even has the courtesy to save your settings in an independent file called Color Settings in the Adobe Photoshop Settings folder.

After getting everything set up the way you like, it's a good idea to copy the Color Settings file to a safe backup location. This way, if the settings file ever becomes corrupt, you can reinstate your careful color choices as easily as copying the backed up file.

A Typical Color-Matching Scenario

The easiest way to understand the Color Settings commands is to see them in action. In this basic scenario, I'll take an RGB image I've created on my Mac and open it up on my PC. The Mac is equipped with a top-of-the-line PressView 21SR and the PC is hooked up to a generic Sony Trinitron screen, so I've got both extremes pretty well covered. Yet despite the change of platforms and the even more dramatic change in monitors, Photoshop maintains a high degree of consistency so the image looks the same on both sides of the divide. While the specifics of setting up your system will obviously vary, this walk-through should give you an idea of how the strange and intricate Color Settings commands work.

Setting up the source monitor

If you own a monitor with calibration capabilities, I recommend that you start off by calibrating it. In the case of the PressView, I launch a utility called ProSense that works with the hardware calibrator to both adjust screen colors and save screen profiles in a variety of formats. For the purposes of Photoshop for the Mac, the most important format is ColorSync, which is Apple's system-wide color management extension. I also save a Photoshop Monitor File version of the profile, as shown in Figure 6-1.

Figure 6-1: When calibrating my PressView monitor, I direct the ProSense utility to save a ColorSync and Photoshop Monitor File version of the screen profile.

The next step is to open the profile in ColorSync. I choose Apple ⇨ Control Panels ⇨ ColorSync System Profile. Then I click on the Set Profile button to display the scrolling list of options shown in Figure 6-2. At the end of the list is the item PressView 21sr, which turns out to be the profile I just created with the ProSense utility. I select it and move on.

Figure 6-2: On the Mac, you use the ColorSync control panel to load monitor profiles which will automatically work with Photoshop.

The Gamma wizard

"Swell," I can hear you say, "But what do those of us with more down-to-earth monitors do?" For everyday people, Photoshop ships with a nicely improved version of the Gamma control panel. Open the Goodies folder inside the folder that contains Photoshop. Then open the Calibration folder. Inside is a utility called Adobe Gamma.

Double-click on the Adobe Gamma icon to bring up the introductory screen shown in Figure 6-3. Select the Step by Step option to walk through the setup process one step at a time. Then all you have to do is answer questions and click on the Next button to advance from one screen to another. Occasionally, you'll be asked to make some tricky choices. (The white point defines the general color cast of your screen, from 5,000 degrees for slightly red to 9,300 degrees for slightly blue; 6,500 degrees is a happy "daylight" medium.) But most of the questions are pretty cut and dry. If you aren't sure about an answer to a setting—such as Phosphors— consult your monitor's documentation or call the vendor. (If the screen bows out slightly horizontally but is absolutely flat vertically, the answer is Trinitron.)

Figure 6-3: Select the Step By Step option to advance one step at a time through the monitor setup process.

When you click on the Finish button, the Gamma utility generates a custom monitor profile and automatically alerts Photoshop to the change, even if the program is already running. You don't even have to bring up the ColorSync control panel (though you may want to just to confirm). Photoshop is now officially aware of your monitor's capabilities and limitations.

Note   Just so you know, Gamma places the monitor profile in the ColorSync Profiles folder inside the Preference folder in the System Folder.

Note   Incidentally, the term *gamma* refers to the amount of correction required to convert the color signal generated inside the monitor (let's call it *x*) to the color display that you see on screen (*y*). Imagine a simple graph with the input signal *x* along the bottom and the output *y* along the side. A gamma of 1.0 would result in a diagonal line from bottom left to upper right corner. A higher gamma value tugs at the center of that line and curves it upward. As you tug, more and more of the curve is taken up by darker values, resulting in a darker display. So a typical Mac screen with default gamma of 1.8 is lighter than a typical PC screen with a default gamma of 2.2. (For a real-time display of gamma in action, check out the discussion of the Curve dialog box included in Chapter 18.)

Inventing your ideal RGB environment

Now that I've identified my monitor, I need to explain my ideal RGB environment to Photoshop. This is the strangest step and it requires a little bit of imagination to fully understand.

I start by choosing File ➪ Color Settings ➪ RGB Setup inside Photoshop on my Mac. Photoshop displays the dialog box shown in Figure 6-4. Notice that the Monitor item is automatically set to PressView 21sr, thanks to the fact that I chose this profile with ColorSync. (If you used Adobe Gamma, your profile will appear here as well.) This shows that my monitor is recognized and accounted for.

Figure 6-4: The SMPTE-240M option provides access to a large theoretical RGB spectrum.

But I still have to specify the larger RGB environment using the RGB pop-up menu. There are two purposes to this option:

✦ First, it lets you preview how an RGB image will look on another screen when no color correction is applied. For example, to see how an image will look on a typical PC screen, you could select sRGB. This is a fantastic feature for Web designers, as I explain more in Chapter 20.

✦ Second and more important, this is Adobe's attempt to create the perfect RGB environment, one that doesn't depend on a specific piece of hardware. As I said, some imagination is in order.

My recommendation here is to select the SMPTE-240M option from the RGB pop-up menu and have done with it. Based on the new high-definition television format, SMPTE-240M includes a wide range of theoretical RGB colors, whether they can truly be displayed on a monitor or not. You may see some *clipping* on screen—that is, two distinct colors in the SMPTE-240M space may appear as one on your screen —but Photoshop has greater latitude when interpolating and calculating colors.

The RGB Setup dialog box includes two check boxes. Preview just permits you to see the results of your changes on screen. But Display Using Monitor Compensation creates a monitor-to-ideal RGB conversion on the fly. In my case, Photoshop converts all colors from the PressView 21sr gamut to the unfettered SMPTE-240M The result is that my colors brighten up considerably.

Embedding the profiles

The final step on the Mac side is to embed my profiles into a test image. (The word *embed* simply means that Photoshop adds a little bit of code to the beginning of the file stating where it was last edited.) For this, I choose File ⇨ Color Settings ⇨ Profile Setup, which displays the big dialog box in Figure 6-5. By default, all of the check boxes across the top of the dialog box are selected. This means Photoshop will embed profiles for the four main color spaces into the image. The RGB check box tells Photoshop to embed my ideal RGB setting — SMPTE-240M — into the test image. I click on the OK button to confirm that this is indeed what I want.

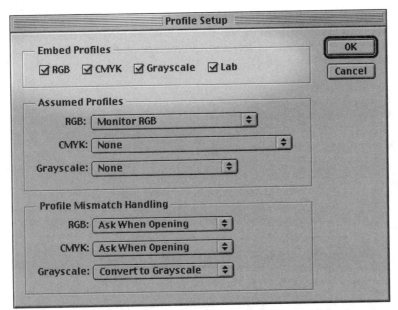

Figure 6-5: Select the check boxes across the top of this dialog box to append profiles into all saved images.

Next, I save my test image using the standard Save command. Thanks to my settings in the Profile Setup dialog box, Photoshop automatically saves my RGB environment along with the image.

Tip

If you had already saved the image before changing the RGB settings, the Save command will appear dimmed. Photoshop does not recognize RGB Setup as a significant modification to the image. You can either choose File ➪ Save As and write over the last saved version of the image, or make a minor adjustment — click on a pixel with the pencil tool — and then choose File ➪ Save.

Setting up the destination monitor

After saving the text image with RGB profile embedded, I network the test image from my Mac over to my PC (via Miramar's PC MacLAN). No translation occurs here; this is a simple file copy from one computer to another.

Now before I can open this image and have it display properly on my PC, I have to set up my RGB colors. I start by setting up my monitor. This time, I'm using a no-frills Sony Multiscan monitor, so I have to perform the calibration using the Adobe Gamma control panel, as discussed previously in the "The Gamma wizard" section.

After I finish with Adobe Gamma, I go into Photoshop and choose File ➪ Color Settings ➪ RGB Setup, just as I did on the Mac. Behold, Photoshop has automatically instated my Gamma settings, as I can see by the message Monitor: Sony Multiscan.icm (see Figure 6-6).

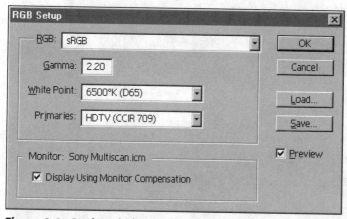

Figure 6-6: On the Windows side, I select sRGB as my ideal RGB environment to force Photoshop to make a conversion. (Nevertheless, I recommend you select SMPTE-240M, just as I did on the Mac.)

Now if I were really trying to calibrate my systems to match up, I would select SMPTE-240M from the RGB pop-up menu, just as I did on the Mac. But for purposes of this demonstration, I want to force Photoshop to perform a conversion, and a good conversion requires a little dissension. So this time around, I select sRGB —

short for *standard RGB*, the universal monitor space presently touted by Microsoft, Pantone, Hewlett-Packard, and a host of others. This just so happens to be Photoshop's default setting, the reason being that many users will never visit this dialog box and, for better or worse, sRGB is fast becoming a cross-platform standard. (For the reasons I mentioned earlier, I and most inside Adobe believe SMPTE-240M is the better solution for savvy users who dare to change their defaults.)

Converting the color space

The Profile Setup command determines not only how Photoshop embeds profiles but also how it reads embedded profiles. So I choose File ⇨ Color Settings ⇨ Profile Setup to display the dialog box shown in Figure 6-7, this time concentrating on the lower options. The three Profile Mismatch Handling pop-up menus determine how Photoshop reacts when it tries to open an image whose embedded profiles don't match the active color settings. By default, the RGB pop-up menu is set to Convert to RGB, which converts the colors in the image from the embedded RGB space to the current RGB space. But I'm not a big fan of having my images change automatically without warning or consent, so I set the RGB pop-up menu to Ask When Opening, as in Figure 6-7.

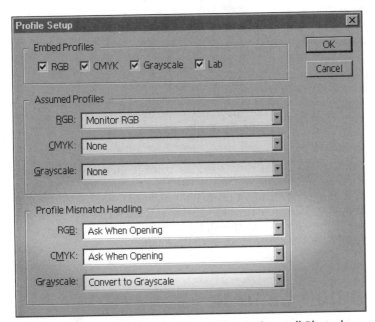

Figure 6-7: The Profile Mismatch Handling options tell Photoshop what to do when it opens an image created on a different computer.

Now I'm ready to open the test image. I choose File ⇨ Open just as I normally would. As Photoshop for Windows opens the test image, it detects that the embedded SMPTE-240M profile doesn't match the active sRGB profile. Justly troubled by this development, Photoshop displays the alert box shown in Figure 6-8. You have several conversion options — you can even choose to have an external color management system such as Kodak's ICC CMS step in and perform the conversion — but there are really just two choices that matter — Convert or Don't Convert. The Convert button converts the colors in the image from the SMPTE-240M space to the sRGB space. The Don't Convert button opens the image as is, without making any changes.

Figure 6-8: The alter box gives you the option of converting the colors from the foreign image or opening the image as is.

Obviously, I choose Convert. Photoshop spends a few seconds mulling it over and then displays the converted image on screen. The result is an almost perfect match. Granted the blues demonstrate a slight propensity toward green, as illustrated in Color Plate 6-1. And while I imagine I could address this by finessing the profile for my Sony Multiscan slightly on my PC, the match is frankly amazing, much better than the sort of results you could achieve with Photoshop 4.

Color Conversion Central

As I mentioned near the outset of this chapter, the Profile Setup command is the feature that puts Photoshop's color conversion functions in play. RGB Setup, CMYK Setup, and Grayscale Setup define the parameters, but File ⇨ Color Settings ⇨ Profile Setup makes the color conversions happen.

Now that you've seen Profile Setup in action, I'd like to take a few moments and run through the specific features according to the way they're grouped inside the Profile Setup dialog box.

Embed profiles

When you save an image using the Save or Save As commands, Photoshop 5 saves color profiles with the image according to the Embed Profiles settings in the Profile Setup dialog box:

✦ **RGB** embeds the device-independent RGB profile (for example, SMPTE-240M) defined in the RGB Setup dialog box. This is very important — it does *not* embed the monitor profile. The conversion from monitor space to RGB space is handled internally by RGB Setup without Profile Setup's help. So if we all agree on SMPTE-240M, no color conversions will ever be necessary and all our images will display consistently on any machine in this best of all possible worlds. Amen.

One exception to this rule: Images saved in Photoshop 4 and earlier use the monitor setup as the profile because this is how Adobe used to deal with color spaces in the days before the RBG Setup command.

✦ **CMYK** embeds the profile defined in the CMYK Setup dialog box (which I discuss at length in the next chapter).

✦ **Grayscale** embeds the active Grayscale Setup setting. If RGB is the active setting in the Grayscale Setup dialog box (as by default), Photoshop also embeds the Gamma setting from the RGB Setup dialog box (2.2 in the case of SMPTE-240M). If you set the Grayscale Setup option to Black Ink, Photoshop jettisons Gamma and instead embeds the Dot Gain setting from the CMYK Setup dialog box.

✦ **Lab** appends Photoshop's CIE Lab profile to the image. There's no way to change this; it's simply a way for Photoshop to identify it's native device-independent color space to the image.

Notice that you don't see Indexed Color on that list. So if you save an image as a GIF file — which is always indexed — Photoshop doesn't include any profile. The same goes for duotones and black-and-white bitmaps.

Thanks to a Macintosh file's resource fork, Photoshop can save profiles with any file format. (Actually, this goes for GIF as well — Photoshop *can* save a profile with GIF, it simply chooses not to.) If you swap files with Windows folks, the resource fork dries up. This leaves just five color-savvy file formats — native Photoshop, EPS, PDF, JPEG, and TIFF. The others don't permit extra data to be saved with the image.

For typical prepress work, there's really no reason not to embed profiles. They add very little to the size of a file. However, if you're creating a JPEG image for the Web, you might want to dump the profiles to keep the file size at its lowest. No need to visit Profile Setup and turn off all the Embed Profiles check boxes just for one file. Instead, choose File ➪ Save a Copy (⌘-Option-S) and select the Exclude Non-Image Data check box.

But don't assume that you should always bail on color profiles for Web images. There's a big push right now to build profile support into the browsers so that image colors will automatically adapt to a viewer's screen. (Pantone already distributes Netscape Navigator plug-ins that read and interpret profiles for JPEG and TIFF images.) While this technology is still in its infancy, it's very probable that it will find mainstream acceptance in the near future.

When you elect not to embed a profile, Photoshop adds a little marker that tells the program the file was saved explicitly without a profile. When you open that file in the future, Photoshop will skip the conversion profile process, regardless of any other settings selected inside the Profile Setup dialog box.

Assumed profiles

Given that this is the first version of Photoshop to embed profiles, you can imagine that most other applications don't either. So most of the files you open will be utterly profileless. Photoshop has to invent a family tree for these motherless images. You specify this ancestry using the Assumed Profiles pop-up menus.

By default, the RGB option is set to Monitor RGB and the CMYK and Grayscale options are set to None. To maintain consistent colors from no-profile images — particularly from images created in previous versions of Photoshop — it's essential that Monitor RGB be active. Photoshop then makes a conversion from the monitor space to the device-independent RGB space, thus preventing the sort of wild color shifts that might happen without conversion. For example, if the RGB space is set to SMPTE-240M, the color saturation will go through the roof without proper conversion.

Having CMYK and Grayscale set to None ensures that no conversion occurs. Again, these are very sound defaults. CMYK images are typically designed for specific printing environments and unthinkingly converting them to another space could ruin them. (That said, if you know for a fact that you want to take a CMYK image designed for a Tektronix Phaser 220i and instead print it from a SWOP proofing device, conversion can be a very good thing. It's the difference between making a deliberate choice and having the choice made for you.) Grayscale images are likewise designed to be printed, so arbitrary conversion can be hazardous.

Profile mismatch handling

The final set of pop-up menus control how Photoshop reacts when an image contains a profile (or an assumed profile) that doesn't match the parameters established by the RGB, CMYK, and Grayscale Setup commands. Personally, I set every one of them to Ask When Opening. I am not a fan of having color conversions occur without my permission — as they do by default — even when the converter is a trusted application like Photoshop. So long as Ask When Saving is active, an alter box appears and asks you permission to perform the conversion. You are always made aware of current events.

Ask When Opening also gives you the opportunity to try out different color scenarios. If you accept a color conversion and it ends up looking unusually garish, you can simply close the image and open it up again using different conversion settings or no conversion at all.

One case where I almost invariably decline conversion is when processing screen shots. Photoshop offers to convert every screen shot that I bring over from the PC, but because screen elements are designed for any monitor, they work best when I turn conversion off. I also advise that you refrain from converting CMYK and grayscale images unless you have a specific purpose in mind.

Introducing Color Channels

After a chapter and a half of me droning on about color in Photoshop, it might surprise you when I say that Photoshop is at its heart a grayscale editor. Oh sure, it offers an array of color conversion features and it displays and prints spectacular full-color images. But when it comes to editing the image, everything happens in grayscale.

This is because Photoshop approaches every full-color image not as a single collection of 24-bit pixels, but as three or four bands of 8-bit (grayscale) pixels. An RGB file contains a band of red, a band of green, and a band of blue, each of which functions as a separate grayscale image. A Lab image likewise contains three bands, one corresponding to luminosity and the others to the variables *a* and *b*. A CMYK file contains four bands, one for each of the process-color inks. These bands are known as *channels*.

Channels frequently correspond to the structure of an input or output device. Each channel in a CMYK image, for example, corresponds to a different printer's plate when the document goes to press. The cyan plate is inked with cyan, the magenta plate is inked with magenta, and so on. Each channel in an RGB image corresponds to a pass of the red, green, or blue scanner sensor over the original photograph or artwork. Only the Lab mode is device independent, so its channels don't correspond to any piece of hardware.

Why you should care

But so what, right? Who cares how many planes of color an image comprises? You want to edit the photograph, not dissect it. "Dammit, Jim, I'm an artist, not a doctor!" Well, even if you don't like to rebuild car engines or poke preserved frog entrails with sharp knives, you'll get a charge out of editing channels. The fact is, channels provide you with yet another degree of selective control over an image.

Consider this example: Your client scanned a photograph of his gap-toothed daughter that he wants you to integrate into some goofy ad campaign for his car dealership. Unfortunately, the scan is downright rotten. You don't want to offend the guy, so you praise him on his fine offspring and say something to the effect of, "No problem, boss." But after you take it back to your office and load it into Photoshop, you break out in a cold sweat. You try swabbing at it with the edit tools, applying a few filters, and even attempting some scary-looking color correction commands, but the image continues to look like the inside of a garbage disposal. (Not that I've ever seen the inside of a garbage disposal, but it can't be attractive.)

Suddenly, it occurs to you to look at the channels. What the heck, it can't hurt. With very little effort, you discover that the red and green channels look okay, but the blue channel looks like it's melting. Her mouth is sort of mixed in with her teeth, her eyes look like an experiment in expressionism, and her hair has taken on a slightly geometric appearance. (If you think that this is a big exaggeration, take a look at a few blue channels from a low-end scanner or digital camera. They're frequently rife with tattered edges, random blocks of color, stray pixels, and other so-called *digital artifacts*.)

The point is, you've located the cancer. You don't have to waste your time trying to perform surgery on the entire image; in fact, doing so may very well harm the channels that are in good shape. You merely have to fix this one channel. A wave of the Gaussian Blur filter here, an application of the Levels command there, and some selective rebuilding of missing detail borrowed from the other channels — all of which I'll get to in future sections and chapters — result in an image that resembles a living, breathing human being. Granted, she still needs braces, but you're an artist, not an orthodontist.

How channels work

Photoshop devotes 8 bits of data to each pixel in each channel, thus permitting 256 brightness values, from 0 (black) to 255 (white). Therefore, each channel is actually an independent grayscale image. At first, you may be thrown off by this. If an RGB image is made up of red, green, and blue channels, why do all the channels look gray?

Photoshop provides an option in the Display & Cursors panel of the Preferences dialog box (⌘-K, ⌘-3) called Color Channels in Color. When selected, this function displays each channel in its corresponding primary color. But although this feature can be reassuring — particularly to novices — it's equally counterproductive.

When you view an 8-bit image composed exclusively of shades of red, for example, it's easy to miss subtle variations in detail that may appear obvious when you print the image. You may have problems accurately gauging the impact of filters and tonal adjustments. I mean, face it, red isn't a friendly shade to stare at for a half hour of intense editing. So leave the Color Channels in Color option off and temporarily suspend your biological urge for on-screen color. With a little experience, you'll be able to better monitor your adjustments and predict the outcome of your edits in plain old grayscale.

Images that include 256 or fewer colors can be expressed in a single channel and therefore do not include multiple channels that you can edit independently. A grayscale image, for example, is just one channel. A black-and-white bitmap permits only one bit of data per pixel, so a single channel is more than enough to express it.

You can add channels above and beyond those required to represent a color or grayscale image for the purpose of storing masks, as described in Chapter 12. But even then, each channel is typically limited to 8 bits of data per pixel — meaning that it's just another grayscale image. Mask channels do not affect the appearance of the image on-screen or when it is printed. Rather, they serve to save selection outlines, as Chapter 12 explains.

How to switch and view channels

To access channels in Photoshop, display the Channels palette by choosing Window ➪ Show Channels. Every channel in the image appears in the palette — including any mask channels — as shown in Figure 6-9. Photoshop even shows little thumbnail views of each channel so that you can see what it looks like.

To switch to a different channel, click on a channel name in the Channels palette. The channel name becomes gray — like the Blue channel in Figure 6-9 — showing that you can now edit it independently of other channels in the image.

To edit more than one channel at a time, click on one channel name and then Shift-click on another. You can also Shift-click on an active channel to deactivate it independently of any others.

When you select a single channel, Photoshop displays just that one channel on screen. However, you can view additional channels beyond those that you want to edit. To specify which channels appear and which remain invisible, click in the far left column of the Channels palette. Click on an eyeball icon to make it disappear and hence hide that channel. Click where there is no eyeball to create one and thus display the channel.

Eyeball icon   Active channel

Figure 6-9: Photoshop displays tiny thumbnails of each color channel in the Channels palette.

When only one channel is visible, that channel appears as a grayscale picture in the image window (possibly colorized in accordance with the Color Channels in Color check box in the Preferences dialog box). However, when more than one channel is visible, you always see color. If both the blue and green channels are visible, for example, the image appears blue-green. If the red and green channels are visible, the image has a yellow cast, and so on.

In addition to the individual channels, Photoshop provides access to a *composite view* that displays all colors in an RGB, CMYK, or Lab image at once. (The composite view does not show mask channels; you have to specify their display separately.) The composite view is listed first in the Channel palette and is displayed by default. Notice that when you select the composite view, all the names of the individual color channels in the Channels palette turn gray along with the composite channel. This shows that all the channels are active. The composite view is the one in which you will perform the majority of your image editing.

Press ⌘ plus a number key to switch between color channels. Depending on the color mode you're working in, ⌘-1 takes you to the red (RGB), cyan (CMYK), or luminosity (Lab) channel; ⌘-2 takes you to the green, magenta, or *a* channel; and ⌘-3 takes you to the blue, yellow, or *b* channel. In the CMYK mode, ⌘-4 displays the black channel. Other ⌘-key equivalents — up to ⌘-9 — take you to mask or spot-color channels (if there are any). To go to the composite view, press ⌘-tilde (~). Tilde is typically the key to the left of 1, or on some keyboards, to the right of the spacebar.

Tip

When editing a single channel, you may find it helpful to monitor the results in both grayscale and full-color views. Choose View ➪ New View to create a new window for the image, automatically set to the color composite view. Then return to the first window and edit away on the individual channel. One of the amazing benefits to creating multiple views in Photoshop is that the views may show entirely different channels, layers, and other image elements.

The shortcuts are slightly different when you're working on a grayscale image. You access the image itself by pressing ⌘-1. ⌘-2 and higher take you to extra spot-color and mask channels.

Trying Channels on for Size

Feeling a little mystified? Need some examples? Fair enough. Color Plate 6-2 shows a woman in a bright yellow swim suit on a bright red floatation device set against a bright green ocean beneath a bright blue sky. These colors — yellow, red, green, and blue — cover the four corners of the color spectrum. Therefore, you can expect to see a lot of variation between the images in the independent color channels.

RGB channels

Suppose that the sunbathing woman is an RGB image. Figure 6-10 compares a grayscale composite of this same image (created by choosing Image ➪ Mode ➪ Grayscale) compared with the contents of the red, green, and blue color channels from the original color image. The green channel is quite similar to the grayscale composite because green is an ingredient in all colors in the image, except for the red of the raft. The red and blue channels differ more significantly. The pixels in the red channel are lightest in the swimsuit and raft because they contain the highest concentrations of red. The pixels in the blue channel are lightest in the sky and water because — you guessed it — the sky and water are rich with blue.

Notice how the channels in Figure 6-10 make interesting grayscale images in and of themselves? The red channel, for example, looks like the sky darkening above our bather, even though the sun is blazing down.

I mentioned this as a tip in the previous chapter, but it bears a bit of casual drumming into the old noggin. When converting a color image to grayscale, you have the option of calculating a grayscale composite or simply retaining the image exactly as it appears in one of the channels. To create a grayscale composite, choose Image ➪ Mode ➪ Grayscale when viewing all colors in the image in the composite view, as usual. To retain a single channel only, switch to that channel and then choose Image ➪ Mode ➪ Grayscale. Instead of the usual *Discard color information?* message, Photoshop displays the message *Discard other channels?* If you click on the OK button, Photoshop chucks the other channels into the electronic abyss.

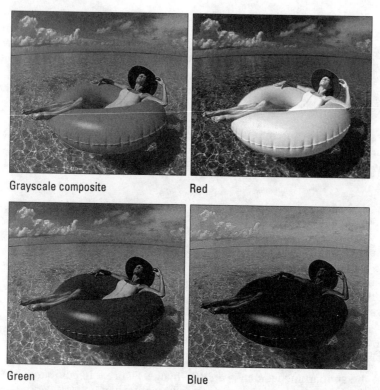

Grayscale composite

Red

Green

Blue

Figure 6-10: A grayscale composite of the image from Color Plate 6-2 followed by the contents of the red, green, and blue color channels.

CMYK channels

In the name of fair and unbiased coverage, Figures 6-11 and 6-12 show the channels from the image after it was converted to other color modes. In Figure 6-11, I converted the image to the CMYK mode and examined its channels. Here, the predominant colors are cyan (sky and water) and yellow (in the swimsuit and raft). Because this color mode relies on pigments rather than light, as explained in the "CMYK" section of Chapter 5, dark areas in the channels represent high color intensity. For that reason, the sky in the cyan channel is dark, whereas it's light in the blue channel back in Figure 6-10.

Notice how similar the cyan channel in Figure 6-11 is to its red counterpart in Figure 6-10. Same with the magenta and green channels, and the yellow and blue channels. The CMY channels have more contrast than the RGB pals, but the basic brightness distribution is the same. Here's another graphic demonstration of color theory. In a perfect world, the CMY channels would be identical to the RGB channels — one color model would simply be the other turned on its head. But because this is not a perfect world (you might have noticed that as you've traveled life's bitter highway), Photoshop has to boost the contrast of the CMY channels and throw in black to punch up those shadows.

Cyan

Magenta

Yellow

Black

Figure 6-11: The contents of the cyan, magenta, yellow, and black channels from the image shown in Color Plate 6-2.

Lab channels

To create Figure 6-12, I converted the image in Color Plate 6-2 to the Lab mode. The image in the luminosity channel looks very similar to the grayscale composite because it contains the lightness and darkness values for the image. The *a* channel maps the greens and magentas, while the *b* channel maps the yellows and blues, so both channels are working hard to provide color information for this photograph. Certainly there are differences — the *a* channel is hotter in the raft, while the *b* channel offers more cloud detail — but the two channels carry roughly equivalent amounts of color information.

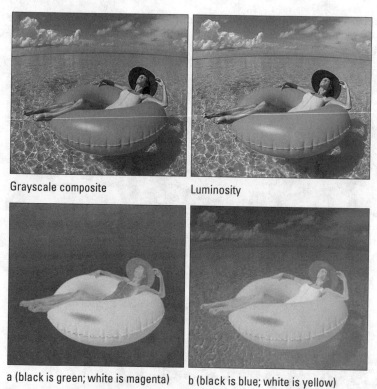

Grayscale composite   Luminosity

a (black is green; white is magenta)   b (black is blue; white is yellow)

Figure 6-12: The grayscale composite followed by the contents of the luminosity channel and the a and b color channels after converting the image shown in Color Plate 6-1 to the Lab mode.

You can achieve some entertaining effects by applying commands from the Image ➪ Adjust submenu to the *a* and *b* color channels. For example, if I go to the *a* channel in Figure 6-12 and reverse the brightness values by choosing Image ➪ Adjust ➪ Invert (⌘-I), the water turns a sort of salmon red and the raft turns green, as demonstrated in the first example of Color Plate 6-3. If I apply Image ➪ Adjust ➪ Auto Levels (⌘-Shift-L) to the *b* channel, the sky lights up with brilliant blue without altering so much as a color in the woman or her raft, as in the second example. The third example in Color Plate 6-3 shows what happens when I apply both Invert and Auto Levels to both the *a* and *b* channels. Now there's the way I want to vacation — on a different planet!

Other Channel Functions

In addition to viewing and editing channels using any of the techniques discussed in future chapters of this book, you can choose commands from the Channels palette menu and select icons along the bottom of the palette (labeled back in Figure 6-9). The following items explain how the commands and icons work.

Cross-Reference

You'll notice that I say "see Chapter 12" every so often when explaining these options, because many of them are specifically designed to accommodate masks. This list is designed to introduce you to *all* the options in the Channels palette, even if you'll need more background to use a few of them. After I introduce the options, we'll revisit the ones that have a direct affect on managing the colors in your image.

✦ **Palette Options:** Even though this is the last command in the menu, it's the easiest, so I'll start with it. When you choose Palette Options, Photoshop displays four Thumbnail Size radio buttons, enabling you to change the size of the thumbnail previews that appear along the left side of the Channels palette. Figure 6-13 shows the four thumbnail settings — nonexistent, small, medium, and large.

Figure 6-13: The Palette Options command lets you select between four thumbnail preview options and a Merlin.

Have you ever wondered what those thumbnail icons in the Palette Options dialog box are supposed to show? They're silhouettes of tiny Merlins on a painter's palette. How do I know that? Switch to the Layers palette and choose Palette Options and you'll see them in color. But how do I know they're specifically Merlins? Press Option when choosing Palette Options to see the magician up close. We're talking vintage Easter egg, here—circa Photoshop 2.5.

✦ **New Channel:** Choose this command to add a mask channel to the current image. The Channel Options dialog box appears, requesting that you name the channel. You also can specify the color and translucency that Photoshop applies to the channel when you view it with other channels. I explain how these options work in the "Changing the red coating" section of Chapter 12. An image can contain up to 24 total channels, regardless of color mode.

You can also create a new channel by clicking on the new channel icon at the bottom of the Channels palette. (It's the one that looks like a little page.) Photoshop creates the channel without displaying the dialog box. To force the dialog box to appear on-screen, Option-click on the page icon.

✦ **Duplicate Channel:** Choose this command to create a duplicate of the selected channel, either inside the same document or as part of a new document. (If the composite view is active, the Duplicate Channel command is dimmed, because you can only duplicate one channel at a time.) The most common reason to use this command is to convert a channel into a mask. Again, you can find real-life applications in Chapter 12.

You can also duplicate a channel by dragging the channel name onto the new channel icon. No dialog box appears; Photoshop merely names the channel automatically. To copy a channel to a different document, drag the channel name and drop it into an open image window. Photoshop automatically creates a new channel for the duplicate.

✦ **Delete Channel:** To delete a channel from an image, click on the channel name in the palette and choose this command. You can delete only one channel at a time. The Delete Channel command is dimmed when any essential color channel is active, or when more than one channel is selected.

If choosing a command is too much effort, just drag the channel onto the delete channel icon (which is the little trash icon in the lower right corner of the Channels palette). Or you can just click on the trash icon, in which case Photoshop asks you if you really want to delete the channel. To bypass this warning, Option-click on the trash icon.

✦ **New Spot Channel:** Photoshop 5 lets you add spot color channels to an image. Each spot color channel prints to a separate plate, just like spot colors in Illustrator or QuarkXPress. When you choose the New Spot Color command, Photoshop asks you to specify a color and a Solidity. Click on the color square to bring up the Custom Colors dialog box, from which you can select a Pantone or other spot color (see Figure 6-14). The Solidity option lets you increase the opacity of the ink, perfect for Day-Glo fluorescents and metallic inks.

Tip

To create a spot color channel without choosing a command, ⌘-click on the page icon at the bottom of the Channels palette. For more information on spot-color channels, read the "Spot-Color Separations" section at the end of Chapter 7.

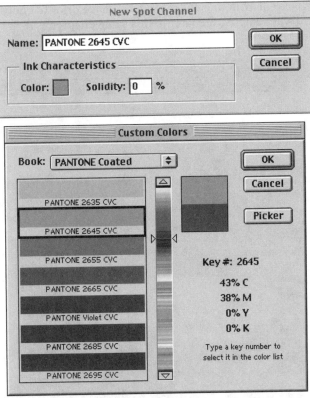

Figure 6-14: When creating a spot-color channel, Photoshop asks you to select a color and specify the degree to which the spot color will cover up other inks in the printed image.

✦ **Merge Spot Channel:** Select a spot-color channel and choose this command to merge the spot color in with the RGB, Lab, or CMYK colors in the image. Most spot colors don't have precise RGB or CMYK equivalents, so you will lose some color fidelity in the merge. Adobe includes this command to allow you to proof an image to a typical midrange color printer.

✦ **Channel Options:** Choose this command or double-click on the channel name in the palette's scrolling list to change the settings assigned to a spot-color or mask channel. The Channel Options command is dimmed when a regular, everyday color channel is active.

✦ **Split Channels:** When you choose this command, Photoshop splits off each channel in an image to its own independent grayscale image window. As demonstrated in Figure 6-15, Photoshop automatically appends the channel color to the end of the window name. The Split Channels command is useful as a first step in redistributing channels in an image prior to choosing Merge Channels, as I will demonstrate later in this same chapter.

Figure 6-15: When you choose the Split Channels command, Photoshop relocates each channel to an independent image window.

✦ **Merge Channels:** Choose this command to merge several images into a single multichannel image. The images you want to merge must be open, they must be grayscale, and they must be absolutely equal in size—the same number of pixels horizontally and vertically. When you choose Merge Channels, Photoshop displays the Merge Channels dialog box, shown in Figure 6-16. It then assigns a color mode for the new image based on the number of open grayscale images that contain the same number of pixels as the foreground image.

Figure 6-16: The two dialog boxes that appear after you choose Merge Channels enable you to select a color mode for the merged image (top) and to associate images with color channels (bottom).

You can override Photoshop's choice by selecting a different option from the Mode pop-up menu. (Generally, you won't want to change the value in the Channels option box because doing so causes Photoshop to automatically select Multichannel from the Mode pop-up menu. I explain multichannel images in the upcoming "Using multichannel techniques" section.)

After you press Return, Photoshop displays a second dialog box, which also appears in Figure 6-16. In this dialog box, you can specify which grayscale image goes with which channel by choosing options from pop-up menus. When working from an image split with the Split Channels command, Photoshop automatically organizes each window into a pop-up menu according to the color appended to the window's name. For example, Photoshop associates the window Sunbather.jpg.Cyan with the Cyan pop-up menu.

Color Channel Effects

Now that you know how to navigate among channels and apply commands, permit me to suggest a few reasons for doing so. The most pragmatic applications for channel effects involve the restoration of bad color scans. If you use a color scanner, know someone who uses a color scanner, or just have a bunch of color scans lying around, you can be sure that some of them look like dog meat. (Nothing against dog meat, mind you. I'm sure that Purina has some very lovely dog meat scans in their advertising archives.) With Photoshop's help, you can turn those scans into filet mignon — or at the very least, into an acceptable Sunday roast.

Improving the appearance of color scans

The following are a few channel editing techniques you can use to improve the appearance of poorly scanned full-color images. Keep in mind that these techniques don't work miracles, but they can retrieve an image from the brink of absolute ugliness into the realm of tolerability.

Don't forget that you can choose View ➪ New View to maintain a constant composite view. Or you can click on the eyeball icon in front of the composite view in the Channels palette to view the full-color image, even when editing a single channel.

✦ **Aligning channels:** Every so often, a scan may appear out of focus even after you use Photoshop's sharpening commands to try to correct the problem, as discussed in Chapter 15. If, on closer inspection, you can see slight shadows or halos around colored areas, one of the color channels probably is out of alignment. To remedy the problem, switch to the color channel that corresponds to the color of the halos. Then select the move tool (by pressing the V key) and use the arrow keys to nudge the contents of the channel into alignment. Use the separate composite view (created by choosing View ➪ New View) or click on the eyeball in front of the composite channel to monitor your changes.

✦ **Channel focusing:** If all channels seem to be in alignment (or, at least, as aligned as they're going to get), one of your channels may be poorly focused. Use the ⌘-key equivalents to search for the responsible channel. When and if you find it, use the Unsharp Mask filter to sharpen it as desired. You may also find it helpful to blur a channel, as when trying to eliminate moiré patterns in a scanned halftone. (For a specific application of these techniques, see the "Cleaning up Scanned Halftones" section in Chapter 15.)

✦ **Bad channels:** In your color channel tour, if you discover that a channel is not so much poorly focused as simply rotten to the core — complete with harsh transitions, jagged edges, and random brightness variations — you may be able to improve the appearance of the channel by mixing other channels with it.

Suppose that the blue channel is awful, but the red and green channels are in fairly decent shape. Photoshop 5's new Channel Mixer command lets you mix channels together, whether to repair a bad channel or achieve an interesting effect. Choose Image ➪ Adjust ➪ Channel Mixer and press ⌘-3 to switch to the blue channel. Then raise the Red and Green values and lower the Blue value to mix the three channels together to create a better blue. To maintain consistent brightness levels, it's generally a good idea to use a combination of Red, Green, and Blue values that adds up to 100 percent, as in Figure 6-17. If you can live with the inevitable color changes, the appearance of the image should improve dramatically.

Figure 6-17: Here I use the Channel Mixer command to repair the blue channel by mixing in 10 percent of the red channel and 30 percent of the green channel. The red and green channels remain unaffected.

Note that Channel Mixer is also a great command for creating custom grayscale images. Rather than choosing Image ➪ Mode ➪ Grayscale and taking what Photoshop gives you, you can choose the Channel Mixer command and select the Monochrome check box. Then adjust the Red, Green, and Blue values to mix your own grayscale variation.

Incidentally, the Constant slider simply brightens or darkens the image across the board. Usually, you'll want to leave it set to 0. But if you're having problems getting the color balance right, give it a tweak.

Although Image ➪ Adjust ➪ Channel Mixer is new to Photoshop 5, I've been including my own channel mixing filter with the Photoshop Bible for better than three years now. Created in Photoshop's Filter Factory (see Chapter 17), this filter coincidentally went by the name . . . *Channel Mixer!* I submit Figure 6-18 as Exhibit A. "But Deke," you say, "Your filter doesn't look anything like Adobe's Channel Mixer, and your sliders don't make nearly as much sense." Yes, I imagine that's precisely what they want you to think. Perhaps now you're beginning to understand how diabolically crafty these Photoshop programmers can be.

Figure 6-18: An early version of the Channel Mixer invented by yours truly. Has Adobe gone and swiped my visionary idea? You be the judge.

Using multichannel techniques

The one channel function I've so far ignored is Image ➪ Mode ➪ Multichannel. When you choose this command, Photoshop changes your image so that channels no longer have a specific relationship to one another. They don't mix to create a full-color image; instead, they exist independently within the confines of a single image. The multichannel mode is generally an intermediary step for converting between different color modes without recalculating the contents of the channels.

For example, normally when you convert between the RGB and CMYK modes, Photoshop maps RGB colors to the CMYK color model, changing the contents of each channel as demonstrated back in Figures 6-10 and 6-11. But suppose, just as an experiment, that you want to bypass the color mapping and instead transfer the exact contents of the red channel to the cyan channel, the contents of the green channel to the magenta channel, and so on. You convert from RGB to the multichannel mode and then from multichannel to CMYK as described in the following steps.

Steps: Using the Multichannel Mode as an Intermediary Step

1. **Open an RGB image.** If the image is already open, make sure that it is saved to disk.

2. **Choose Image ➪ Mode ➪ Multichannel.** This eliminates any relationship between the formerly red, green, and blue color channels.

3. **Click on the new channel icon at the bottom of the Channels palette.** Or choose the New Channel command from the palette menu and press Return to accept the default settings. Either way, you add a mask channel to the image. This empty channel will serve as the black channel in the CMYK image. (Photoshop won't let you convert from the multichannel mode to CMYK with less than four channels.)

4. **Press ⌘-I.** Unfortunately, the new channel comes up black, which would make the entire image black. To change it to white, press ⌘-I or choose Image ➪ Adjust ➪ Invert.

5. **Choose Mode ➪ CMYK.** The image looks washed out and a tad bit dark compared to its original RGB counterpart, but the overall color scheme of the image remains more or less intact. This is because the red, green, and blue color channels each have a respective opposite in the cyan, magenta, and yellow channels.

6. **Press ⌘-Shift-L.** Or choose Image ➪ Adjust ➪ Auto Levels. This punches up the color a bit by automatically correcting the brightness and contrast.

7. **Convert the image to RGB, and then back to CMYK again.** The problem with the image is that it lacks any information in the black channel. So although it may look okay on-screen, it will lose much of its definition when printed. To fill in the black channel, choose Image ➪ Mode ➪ RGB Color, then choose Image ➪ Mode ➪ CMYK Color. Photoshop automatically generates an image in the black channel in keeping with the standards of color separations (as explained in Chapter 7).

Keep in mind that these steps are by no means a recommended procedure for converting an RGB image to a CMYK image. Rather, they are merely intended to suggest one way to experiment with channel conversions to create a halfway decent image. You can likewise experiment with converting between the Lab, multichannel, and RGB modes, or Lab, multichannel, and CMYK.

Replacing and swapping color channels

If you truly want to abuse the colors in an RGB or CMYK image, there's nothing like replacing one color channel with another to produce spectacular effects. Color Plate 6-4 shows a few examples applied to an RGB image.

✦ In the first example, I used the Channel Mixer to replace the red channel with the blue. I did this by setting the Output Channel to Red, changing the Red value to 0 percent and the Blue value to 100 percent. The result is a green woman floating in a green sea under a purple sky.

✦ To achieve the next example, I again started from the original RGB image and used Channel Mixer to replace the green channel with the red. The result this time is a yellow woman against a deep blue background.

✦ To create the purple woman in a green world on the right side of Color Plate 6-4, I replaced the blue channel with the red.

You can create more interesting effects by using Color Mixer to swap the contents of color channels. For example, in the lower left example of Color Plate 6-4, I swapped the contents of the red and blue channels to create a blue woman on a green sea under an orange sky. To accomplish this, I set the Output Channel to Red, set the Red value to 0 and the Blue to 100. Then I switched to the Blue channel (⌘-3) and set the Red value to 100 and the Blue to 0.

The next two examples along the bottom of Color Plate 6-4 show the results of swapping the red and green channels (for a bright green woman) and the green and blue channels. Because the green and blue channels contain relatively similar data, this produces the most subtle effect, chiefly switching the sea and sky colors and turning the swimsuit pink.

✦   ✦   ✦

Printing Images

Welcome to Printing

On one hand, printing can be a straightforward topic. You choose the Print command, press Return, wait for something to come out of your printer, and admire yet another piece of forestry that you've destroyed. On the other hand, printing can be a ridiculously complicated subject, involving dot gain compensation, hardware calibration, under color removal, toxic processor chemicals, separation table generation, and so many infinitesimal color parameters, you're liable to spend half your life trying to figure out what's happening.

This chapter is about finding a middle ground. Although it is in no way intended to cover every possible facet of printing digitized images, this chapter walks you through the process of preparing and printing the three major categories of output: composites, color separations, and duotones. By the end of the chapter, you'll be familiar with all of Photoshop's printing options. You'll also be prepared to communicate with professionals at your service bureau or commercial printer, if need be, and to learn from their input and expertise.

Understanding Printing Terminology

I'm not a big believer in glossaries. Generally, they contain glib, jargony, out-of-context definitions — about as helpful in gaining understanding of a concept as a seminar in which all the presenters speak pig latin. But before I delve into the inner recesses of printing, I want to introduce, in a semilogical, sort of random order, a smattering of the printing terms you'll encounter. Ood-gay uck-lay:

+ **Service bureau:** A *service bureau* is a shop filled with earnest young graphic artists (at least they were young and earnest when *I* worked there), printer operators, and about a billion dollars' worth of hardware. A small service bureau is usually outfitted with a few laser printers, photocopiers, and self-service computers. Big service bureaus offer scanners, imagesetters, film recorders, and other varieties of professional-quality input and output equipment.

✦ **Commercial printer:** Generally speaking, a *commercial printer* takes up where the service bureau leaves off. Commercial printers reproduce black-and-white and color pages using offset presses, Web presses, and a whole bunch of other age-old technology I don't cover in this miniglossary (or anywhere else in this book, for that matter). The process is less expensive than photocopying when you're dealing with large quantities, say, more than 100 copies, and it delivers professional-quality reproductions.

✦ **Output device:** This is just another way to say *printer*. Rather than writing *Print your image from the printer*, which sounds repetitive and a trifle obvious, I write *Print your image from the output device*. *Output devices* also include laser printers, imagesetters, film recorders, and a whole bunch of other machines.

✦ **Laser printer:** A *laser printer* works much like a photocopier. First, it applies an electric charge to a cylinder, called a *drum*, inside the printer. The charged areas, which correspond to the black portions of the image being printed, attract fine, petroleum-based dust particles called *toner*. The drum transfers the toner to the page, and a heating mechanism fixes the toner in place. Most laser printers have resolutions of at least 300 dots (or *printer pixels*) per inch. The newer printers offer higher resolutions, such as 600 and 1,200 dots per inch (*dpi*).

✦ **Color printers:** *Color printers* fall into three categories. Generally speaking, ink-jet and thermal-wax printers are at the low end, and dye-sublimation printers occupy the high end. *Ink-jet printers* deliver colored dots from disposable ink cartridges. *Thermal-wax* printers apply wax-based pigments to a page in multiple passes. Both kinds of printers mix cyan, magenta, yellow, and, depending on the specific printer, black dots to produce full-color output. If you want photographic quality prints — the kind you'd be proud to hang on your wall — you must migrate up the price ladder to *dye-sublimation printers*. Dye-sub inks permeate the surface of the paper, literally dying it different colors. Furthermore, the cyan, magenta, yellow, and black pigments mix in varying opacities from one dot to the next, resulting in a continuous-tone image that appears nearly as smooth on the page as it does on screen.

✦ **Imagesetter:** A typesetter equipped with a graphics page-description language (most often PostScript) is called an *imagesetter*. Unlike a laser printer, an imagesetter prints photosensitive paper or film by exposing the portions of the paper or film that correspond to the black areas of the image. The process is like exposing film with a camera, but an imagesetter only knows two colors: black and white. The exposed paper or film collects in a light-proof canister. In a separate step, the printer operator develops the film in a processor. Developed paper looks like a typical glossy black-and-white page. Developed film is black where the image is white and transparent where the image is black. Imagesetters typically offer resolutions between 1,200 and 3,600 dpi.

But the real beauty of imageset pages is blacks are absolutely black (or transparent), as opposed to the irregular gray you get with laser-printed pages.

✦ **Film recorder:** The *film recorder* transfers images to full-color 35mm and 4 × 5 slides perfect for professional presentations. Slides also can be useful to provide images to publications and commercial printers. Many publications can scan from slides, and commercial printers can use slides to create color separations. So, if you're nervous a color separation printed from Photoshop won't turn out well, ask your service bureau to output the image to a 35mm slide. Then have your commercial printer reproduce the image from the slide.

✦ **PostScript:** The *PostScript* page-description language was the first project developed by Adobe—the same folks who sell Photoshop—and is now a staple of hundreds of brands of laser printers, imagesetters, and film recorders. A *page-description language* is a programming language for defining text and graphics on a page. PostScript specifies the locations of points, draws line segments between them, and fills in areas with solid blacks or *halftone cells* (dot patterns that simulate grays).

✦ **Spooling:** Printer *spooling* allows you to work on an image while another image prints. Rather than communicating directly with the output device, Photoshop describes the image to the system software. Under System 7 and OS 8, this function is performed by a program called PrintMonitor. When Photoshop finishes describing the image—a relatively quick process—you are free to resume working while the system software prints the image in the background.

✦ **Calibration:** Traditionally, *calibrating* a system means synchronizing the machinery. In the context of Photoshop, however, calibrating means to adjust or compensate for the color displays of the scanner, monitor, and printer so what you scan is what you see on screen, which in turn is what you get from the printer. Colors match from one device to the next. Empirically speaking, this is impossible; a yellow image in a photograph won't look exactly like the on-screen yellow or the yellow printed from a set of color separations. But calibrating is designed to make the images look as much alike as possible, taking into account the fundamental differences in hardware technology. Expensive hardware calibration solutions seek to change the configuration of scanner, monitor, and printer. Less expensive software solutions, including those provided by Photoshop, manipulate the image to account for the differences between devices.

✦ **Brightness values/shades:** As described in Chapter 5, a fundamental difference exists between the way your screen and printer create gray values and colors. Your monitor shows colors by lightening an otherwise black screen; the printed page shows colors by darkening an otherwise white piece of paper. On-screen colors, therefore, are measured in terms of *brightness values*. High values equate to light colors; low values equate to dark colors. On the printed page, colors are measured in percentage values called *shades* or, if you prefer, *tints*. High-percentage values result in dark colors, and low-percentage values result in light colors.

✦ **Composite:** A *composite* is a page that shows an image in its entirety. A black-and-white composite printed from a standard laser printer or imagesetter translates all colors in an image to gray values. A color composite printed from a color printer or film recorder shows the colors as they actually appear. Composites are useful any time you want to proof an image or print a final grayscale image from an imagesetter, an overhead projection from a color printer, or a full-color image from a film recorder.

✦ **Proofing:** To *proof* an image is to see how it looks on paper before the final printing. Consumer proofing devices include laser printers and color printers, which provide quality and resolution sufficient only to vaguely predict the appearance of your final output. Professional-level proofing devices include the 3M Rainbow dye-sublimation printer, which prints images of photographic quality, and the IRIS, which uses a special variety of ink-jet technology to create arguably the most accurate electronic proofs in the business.

✦ **Bleeds:** Simply put, a *bleed* is an area that can be printed outside the perimeter of a page. You use a bleed to reproduce an image all the way to the edge of a page, as in a slick magazine ad. For example, this book includes bleeds. Most of the pages — like the page you're reading — are encircled by a uniform 2-pica margin of white space. This margin keeps the text and figures from spilling off into oblivion. A few pages, however — including the parts pages and the color plates in the middle of the book — print all the way to the edges. In fact, the original artwork goes 2 picas beyond the edges of the paper. This ensures that if the paper shifts when printing — as it invariably does — you won't see any thin white edges around the artwork. This 2 picas of extra artwork is the bleed. In Photoshop, you create a bleed by clicking on the Bleed button in the Page Setup dialog box.

✦ **Color separations:** To output color reproductions, commercial printers require *color separations* (or slides, which they can convert to color separations for a fee). A color-separated image comprises four printouts, one each for the cyan, magenta, yellow, and black primary printing colors. The commercial printer transfers each printout to a *plate*, which is used in the actual reproduction process.

✦ **Duotone:** A grayscale image in Photoshop can contain as many as 256 brightness values, from white on up to black. A printer can convey significantly fewer shades. A laser printer, for example, provides anywhere from 26 to 65 shades. An imagesetter provides from 150 to 200 shades, depending on resolution and screen frequency. And this assumes perfect printing conditions. You can count on at least 30 percent of those shades to get lost in the reproduction process. A *duotone* helps to retain the depth and clarity of detail in a grayscale image by printing with two inks. The number of shades available to you suddenly jumps from 150 to a few thousand. Photoshop also lets you create *tritones* (three inks) and *quadtones* (four inks). Note, using more inks translates to higher printing costs.

Photoshop 5.0

✦ **Spot color:** Most color images are printed as a combination of four *process color* inks — cyan, magenta, yellow, and black. But Photoshop also lets you add premixed inks called *spot colors*. As I mentioned in Chapter 5, the most popular purveyor of spot-colors in the United States is Pantone, which provides a library with hundreds of mixings. But many large corporations use custom spot colors for logos and other proprietary emblems. Most spot colors fall outside the CMYK gamut and thus increase the number of colors available to you. In addition to using spot colors in duotone, Photoshop 5 lets you add a spot color channel to any image.

Printing Composites

Now that you've picked up some printer's jargon, you're ready to learn how to put it all together. This section explores the labyrinth of options available for printing composite images. Later in this chapter, I cover color separations and duotones.

Like any Macintosh application, Photoshop can print composite images to nearly any output device you can hook up to your computer. Assuming your printer is turned on, properly attached, and in working order, printing a composite image from Photoshop is a five-step process, as outlined below. The sections that follow describe each of these steps in detail.

Steps: Printing a Composite Image

1. **Choose your printer.** Use the Chooser to select the output device to which you want to print. If your computer is not part of a network, you probably rely on a single output device, in which case you can skip this step.

2. **Choose File ⇨ Page Setup (⌘-Shift-P):** This command permits you to specify the page size and the orientation of the image on the page. Depending on your printer, you may also be able to access specialized output functions via an Options button.

3. **Adjust the halftone screens, if needed.** Click on the Screens button to change the size, angle, and shape of the halftone screen dots. This step is purely optional, useful mostly for creating special effects.

4. **Adjust the transfer function again, if needed.** Click on the Transfer button to map brightness values in an image to different shades when printed. This step is also optional, though frequently useful.

5. **Choose File ⇨ Print (⌘-P).** Photoshop prints the image according to your specifications.

If you already have your printer set up to your satisfaction, you may be thinking about drag-and-drop printing, where you can drag a file and drop it onto the printer icon at the desktop. Don't. While this approach may seem more convenient, drag-and-drop printing has to launch Photoshop and access the same functions as the manual process. And in the worst-case scenario, the operating system may print your image from the wrong application. Drag-and-drop printing is great for making quick copies of text files, but when printing photographs and other artwork, don't look for shortcuts.

Choosing a printer

If you are connected to more than one network, you may need to choose the AppleTalk control panel to select the connection that you want to use. After that, select the Chooser desk accessory from the Apple menu to bring up the dialog box shown in Figure 7-1. The dialog box is split in two, with the left half devoted to a scrolling list of printer driver icons and/or network zones and the right half to specific printer options.

Figure 7-1: Use the Chooser desk accessory to select the desired output device.

Select the printer driver icon that matches your model of printer. *Printer drivers* help the Macintosh hardware, system software, and Photoshop translate the contents of an image to the printer hardware and the page-description language it uses. You'll generally want to select the driver for your specific model of printer. But you can, if necessary, prepare an image for output to a printer that isn't currently hooked up to your computer. For example, you can use this technique prior to submitting a document to be output on an imagesetter at a service bureau.

Any PostScript printer driver beyond LaserWriter 8 includes support for *PostScript printer description (PPD)* files. A single driver can't account for the myriad differences between different models of PostScript printers, so each PPD serves as a little guidance file, customizing the driver to accommodate a specific printer model. After selecting a printer from the right-hand scrolling list, you can access the proper PPD by clicking on the Setup button. (Or just double-click on the printer name in the list.) Then click on the Auto Setup button to instruct the system software to automatically select the correct PPD for your printer.

If you select a networked printer, you may see a Background Printing option in the bottom right corner of the dialog box. When on, this option lets you print an image in the background while you continue to work in Photoshop or some other application. This enables you to take advantage of spooling, as defined earlier in this chapter. Normally, spooling works fine. But if you encounter printing problems, this is the first option you want to turn off.

Tip

If you use the Macintosh control strip, you may be able to bypass the Chooser when switching printers. Just click on the printer icon in the control strip and select the desired printer from the pop-up menu. Not all printers support this function, however, so you may have to visit the Chooser whether you like it or not.

Setting up the page

The next step is to define the relationship between the current image and the page on which it prints. Choosing File ➪ Page Setup (or pressing ⌘-Shift-P) displays the Page Setup dialog box. The Page Setup dialog box varies depending on what kind of printer you use. I usually show the Page Setup dialog box for a standard PostScript printer. But this time around, I reckoned a color ink-jet printer might be more in keeping with the current state of the art. Therefore, Figure 7-2 shows the Page Setup options for Epson's Color Stylus 800.

Even though different printers offer different options, they all offer the following (or their equivalents):

✦ **Paper Size:** Select the size of the paper loaded into your printer's paper tray. The paper size you select determines the *imageable area* of a page — that is, the amount of the page that Photoshop can use to print the current image. For example, the US Letter option calls for a page that measures 8.5 × 11 inches, but only about 7.5 × 10 inches is imageable.

✦ **Orientation:** You can specify whether an image prints upright on a page (Portrait) or on its side (Landscape) by selecting the corresponding Orientation icon. Use the landscape setting when an image is wider than it is tall.

✦ **Reduce or Enlarge:** Enter a percentage value into this option box to enlarge or reduce the size of the image when printed. Usually, you want to leave this option set to 100 percent. If you change the value, just know that your new setting gets saved with the file.

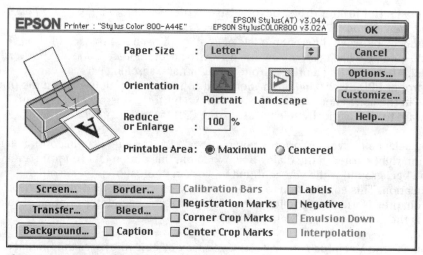

Figure 7-2: Use this dialog box to specify the relationship between the printed image and the page on which it appears.

These aren't all the options available to your printer, just the most common ones. If you want to explore other printing settings, click on the Options button or choose Options from a pop-up menu to display a dialog box of additional choices. In the case of the Color Stylus 800, for example, clicking on the Options button displays the dialog box shown in Figure 7-3. Here I can modify the print quality, select whether to print in black-and-white or color, and specify the type of paper I'm using.

Figure 7-3: Click on the Options button to access still more settings that are specific to the kind of printer you're using.

Photoshop's special printing options

All of the options I've described so far are constant regardless of what application you're using. However, it's a different story when you descend to the bottom of the Page Setup dialog box. The options from the Screen button on down are unique to Photoshop. (If you don't see a Screen button, then you should see a pop-up menu near the top of the Page Setup dialog box. Select Adobe Photoshop 5.0 from this pop-up menu to make Screen and the other options come into view.)

Here's how the buttons work:

✦ **Screens:** Click on this button to enter a dialog box that enables you to change the size, angle, and shape of the printed halftone cells, as described in the upcoming "Changing the halftone screen" section.

✦ **Transfer:** The dialog box that appears when you click on this button enables you to redistribute shades in the printed image, as explained in the upcoming section, "Specifying a transfer function."

✦ **Background:** To assign a color to the area around the printed image, click on this button and select a color from the Color Picker dialog box, described in Chapter 5. This button and the one that follows (Border) are designed specifically to accommodate slides printed from a film recorder.

✦ **Border:** To print a border around the current image, click on this button and enter the thickness of the border into the Width option box. The border automatically appears in black.

✦ **Bleed:** This button lets you print outside the imageable area of the page when outputting to an imagesetter. (Imagesetters print to huge rolls of paper or film, so you can print far outside the confines of standard page sizes. Most other printers use regular old sheets of paper; any bleed — were the printer to acknowledge it — would print off the edge of the page.) Click on the Bleed button and enter the thickness of the bleed into the Width option box. Two picas (24 points) is generally a good bet. (Bleeds are defined in the "Understanding Printing Terminology" glossary at the beginning of this chapter.)

The image-annotation check boxes

Most of the check boxes — all except Negative, Emulsion Down, and Interpolation — append special labels and printer marks to the printed version of the image. Figure 7-4 illustrates how these labels and marks look when printed.

Here's how the check boxes work:

✦ **Caption:** To print a caption beneath the image, select this option. Then press Return to exit this dialog box, choose File ⇨ File Info, and enter a caption into the File Info dialog box. The caption prints in 9-point Helvetica. This is strictly an image-annotation feature, something to help you 17 years down the road, when your brain starts to deteriorate and you can't remember why you printed the darn thing. (You might also use the caption to keep images straight in a busy office where hundreds of folks have access to the same images, but I don't like this alternative as much because I can't make fun of it.)

Label

Cranky kiddo.tiff

Corner crop marks

Modern youngster

Center crop marks

Calibration bar

Registration marks

Hey, don't mess with me, man. I'm grumpy 'cause
I can't change the font for this caption. Aargh!

Caption

Figure 7-4: An image printed with nearly all the Page Setup check boxes turned on.

✦ **Calibration Bars:** A calibration bar is a 10-step grayscale gradation beginning at 10 percent black and ending at 100 percent black. The function of the calibration bar is to ensure all shades are distinct and on target. If not, the output device isn't properly calibrated, which is a fancy way of saying the printer's colors are out of whack and need realignment by a trained professional armed with a hammer and hacksaw. When you print color separations, the Calibration Bars check box instructs Photoshop to print a gradient tint bar and progressive color bar, also useful to printing professionals.

✦ **Registration Marks:** Select this option to print eight crosshairs and two star targets near the four corners of the image. Registration marks are imperative when you print color separations; they provide the only reliable means to ensure exact registration of the cyan, magenta, yellow, and black printing plates. When printing a composite image, however, you can ignore this option.

✦ **Corner Crop Marks:** Select this option to print eight hairline crop marks — two in each of the image's four corners — which indicate how to trim the image in case you anticipate engaging in a little traditional paste-up work.

✦ **Center Crop Marks:** Select this option to print four pairs of hairlines that mark the center of the image. Each pair forms a cross. Two pairs are located on the sides of the image, the third pair is above it, and the fourth pair is below the image.

✦ **Labels:** When you select this check box, Photoshop prints the name of the image and the name of the printed color channel in 9-point Helvetica. If you process many images, you'll find this option extremely useful for associating printouts with documents on disk.

✦ **Negative:** When you select this option, Photoshop prints all blacks as white and all whites as black. In-between colors switch accordingly. For example, 20 percent black becomes 80 percent black. Imagesetter operators use this option to print composites and color separations to film negatives.

✦ **Emulsion Down:** The emulsion is the side of a piece of film on which an image is printed. When the Emulsion Down check box is turned off, film prints from an imagesetter emulsion side up; when the check box is turned on, Photoshop flips the image so the emulsion side is down. Like the Negative option, this option is useful only when you print film from an imagesetter and should be set in accordance with the preferences of your commercial printer.

✦ **Interpolation:** If you own an output device equipped with PostScript Level 2 or later, you can instruct Photoshop to antialias the printed appearance of a low-resolution image by selecting this option. The output device resamples the image up to 200 percent, and then reduces the image to its original size using bicubic interpolation (as described in the "General preferences" section of Chapter 2), thereby creating a less-jagged image. This option has no effect on older-model PostScript devices.

Note

Incidentally, Figure 7-4 shows the actual labels and marks exactly as they print. I started by printing the Photoshop image to disk as an EPS file (as I describe later in the "Printing pages" section). Then I used Illustrator to open the EPS file and assign the callouts. This may not sound like much, but in the old days this would have been impossible. Figure 7-4 represents a practical benefit to Illustrator's (and Photoshop's) ability to open just about any EPS file on the planet.

Changing the halftone screen

Before I proceed, I need to explain a bit more about how printing works. To keep costs down, commercial printers use as few inks as possible to create the appearance of a wide variety of colors. Suppose you want to print an image of a pink flamingo wearing a red bow tie. Your commercial printer could print the flamingos in one pass using pink ink, let that color dry, and then load the red ink and print all the bow ties. But why go to all this trouble? After all, pink is only a lighter shade of red. Why not imitate the pink by lightening the red ink?

Unfortunately, with the exception of dye-sublimation printers, high-end ink jets, and film recorders, output devices can't print lighter shades of colors. They recognize only solid ink and the absence of ink. So how do you print the lighter shade of red necessary to represent pink?

The answer is *halftoning*. The output device organizes printer pixels into spots called halftone cells. Because the cells are so small, your eyes cannot quite focus on them. Instead, the cells appear to blend with the white background of the page to create a lighter shade of an ink. Figure 7-5 shows a detail of an image enlarged to display the individual halftone cells.

The cells grow and shrink to emulate different shades of color. Large cells result in dark shades; small cells result in light shades. Cell size is measured in printer pixels. The maximum size of any cell is a function of the number of cells in an inch, called the screen frequency.

For example, suppose the default frequency of your printer is 60 halftone cells per linear inch and the resolution is 300 printer pixels per linear inch. Each halftone cell must, therefore, measure 5 pixels wide × 5 pixels tall ($300 \div 60 = 5$), for a total of 25 pixels per cell (5^2). When all pixels in a cell are turned off, the cell appears white; when all pixels are turned on, you get solid ink. By turning on different numbers of pixels—from 0 up to 25—the printer can create a total of 26 shades, as demonstrated in Figure 7-6.

Figure 7-5: A detail from an image (left) is enlarged so you can see the individual halftone cells (right).

Figure 7-6: 5 × 5-pixel halftone cells with different numbers of pixels activated, ranging from 25 (top left) to 0 (bottom right). Each cell represents a unique shade from 100 to 0 percent black.

Photoshop enables you to change the size, angle, and shape of the individual halftone cells used to represent an image on the printed page. To do so, click on the Screens button in the Page Setup dialog box. The Halftone Screens dialog box shown in Figure 7-7 appears.

Figure 7-7: Use the Halftone Screens dialog box to edit the size, angle, and shape of the halftone cells for any one ink.

In the dialog box, you can manipulate the following options:

✦ **Use Printer's Default Screens:** Select this check box to accept the default size, angle, and shape settings built into your printer's ROM. All other options in the Halftone Screens dialog box automatically become dimmed to show they are no longer in force.

✦ **Ink:** If the current image is in color, you can select the specific ink you want to adjust from the Ink pop-up menu. When you work with a grayscale image, no pop-up menu is available.

✦ **Frequency:** Enter a new value into this option box to change the number of halftone cells that print per linear inch. A higher value translates to a larger quantity of smaller cells; a smaller value creates fewer, larger cells. Frequency is traditionally measured in *lines-per-inch*, or *lpi* (as in lines of halftone cells), but you can change the measurement to lines per centimeter by selecting Lines/cm from the pop-up menu to the right of the option box.

Tip

Higher screen frequencies result in smoother-looking printouts. Raising the Frequency value, however, also decreases the number of shades an output device can print because it decreases the size of each halftone cell and, likewise, decreases the number of printer pixels per cell. Fewer printer pixels means fewer shades. You can calculate the precise number of printable shades using the following formula:

Number of shades = (printer resolution ÷ frequency)² + 1

✦ **Angle:** To change the orientation of the lines of halftone cells, enter a new value into the Angle option box. In the name of accuracy, Photoshop accepts any value between negative and positive 180 degrees.

When printing color composites to ink-jet and thermal-wax printers, and when printing color separations, Photoshop calculates the optimum Frequency and Angle values required to print seamless colors. In such a case, you should change these values only if you know exactly what you're doing. Otherwise, your printout may exhibit weird patterning effects. When printing grayscale images, though, you can edit these values to your heart's content.

✦ **Shape:** By default, most PostScript printers rely on roundish halftone cells. You can change the appearance of all cells for an ink by selecting one of six alternate shapes from the Shape pop-up menu. For a demonstration of four of these shapes, see Figure 5-8 in the "Black and white (bitmap)" section of Chapter 5. If you know how to write PostScript code, you can select the Custom option to display a text-entry dialog box and code away.

✦ **Use Accurate Screens:** If your output device is equipped with PostScript Level 2 or later, select this option to subscribe to the updated screen angles for full-color output. Otherwise, don't worry about this option.

✦ **Use Same Shape for All Inks:** Select this option if you want to apply a single set of size, angle, and shape options to the halftone cells for all inks used to represent the current image. Unless you want to create some sort of special effect, leave this check box deselected. The option is unavailable when you are printing a grayscale image.

✦ **Auto:** Click on this button to display the Auto Screens dialog box, which automates the halftone editing process. Enter the resolution of your output device in the Printer option box. Then enter the screen frequency you want to use in the Screen option box. After you press Return to confirm your change, Photoshop automatically calculates the optimum screen frequencies for all inks. This technique is most useful when you print full-color images — because Photoshop does the work for you, you can't make a mess of things.

✦ **Load/Save:** You can load and save settings to disk in case you want to reapply the options to other images. These buttons are useful if you find a magic combination of halftone settings that results in a really spectacular printout.

You can change the default size, angle, and shape settings Photoshop applies to all future images by Option-clicking on the Save button. When you press Option, the Save button changes to read →Default. To restore the default screen settings at any time, Option-click on the Load button (←Default).

The Halftone Screens dialog box settings don't apply only to printing images directly from Photoshop. You can export these settings along with the image for placement in QuarkXPress or some other application by saving the image in the Photoshop EPS format. Make sure you turn on the "Include Halftone Screen" check box in the EPS Format dialog box, as discussed in the "Saving an EPS image" section of Chapter 4. This also applies to transfer function settings, explained in the following section.

Caution

If you do decide to include the halftone screen information with your EPS file, be sure the settings are compatible with your intended output device. You don't want to specify a low Frequency value such as 60 lpi when printing to a state-of-the-art 3,600-dpi imagesetter, for example. If you have any questions, make certain to call your service bureau or printer before saving the image. You don't want both a last-minute surprise and a hefty bill to boot.

Specifying a transfer function

A *transfer function* enables you to change the way on-screen brightness values translate — or *map* — to printed shades. By default, brightness values print to their nearest shade percentages. A 30 percent gray pixel on screen (which equates to a brightness value of roughly 180) prints as a 30 percent gray value.

Problems arise, however, when your output device prints lighter or darker than it should. For example, in the course of using a LaserWriter NTX over the past seven years or so — I know it's going to die one day but, until then, it keeps chugging along — I've discovered all gray values print overly dark. Dark values fill in and become black; light values appear a dismal gray, muddying up any highlights. The problem increases if I try to reproduce the image on a photocopier.

To compensate for this overdarkening effect, I click on the Transfer button in the Page Setup dialog box and enter the values shown in Figure 7-8. Notice I lighten 20 percent on screen grays to 10 percent printer grays. I also lighten 90 percent screen grays to 80 percent printer grays. The result is a smooth, continuous curve that maps each gray value in an image to a lighter value on paper.

Figure 7-8: The transfer function curve enables you to map on screen brightness values to specific shades on paper.

The options in the Transfer Functions dialog box work as follows:

✦ **Transfer graph:** The *transfer graph* is where you map on screen brightness values to their printed equivalents. The horizontal axis of the graph represents on-screen brightness values; the vertical axis represents printed shades. The *transfer curve* charts the relationship between on-screen and printed colors. The lower-left corner is the origin of the graph — the point at which both on-screen brightness value and printed shade are white. Move to the right in the graph for darker on-screen values; move up for darker printed shades. Click in the graph to add points to the line. Drag up on a point to darken the output; drag down to lighten the output.

For a more comprehensive explanation of how to graph colors on a curve, read about the incredibly powerful Curves command, covered in Chapter 18.

✦ **Percentage option boxes:** The option boxes are labeled according to the on-screen brightness values. To lighten or darken the printed brightness values, enter higher or lower percentage values in the option boxes. Note: There is a direct correlation between changes made to the transfer graph and the option boxes. For example, if you enter a value in the 50 percent option box, a new point appears along the middle line of the graph.

✦ **Override Printer's Default Functions:** As an effect of printer calibration, some printers have custom transfer functions built into their ROM. If you have problems making your settings take effect, select this check box to instruct Photoshop to apply the transfer function you specify, regardless of the output device's built-in transfer function.

✦ **Load/Save:** Use these buttons to load and save settings to disk. Option-click on the buttons to retrieve and save default settings.

✦ **Ink controls:** When you print a full-color image, five options appear in the lower-right corner of the Transfer Functions dialog box. These options enable you to apply different transfer functions to different inks. Select the All Same check box to apply a single transfer function to all inks. To apply a different function to each ink, deselect the check box, and then select one of the radio buttons and edit the points in the transfer graph as desired.

Printing pages

When you finish slogging your way through the Page Setup options, you can initiate the printing process by choosing File ➪ Print (⌘-P). The Print dialog box appears, shown in its RGB and CMYK forms in Figure 7-9.

Cross-Reference

Figure 7-9: The Print dialog box as it appears when printing a color image.

Many of the options in this dialog box are a function of the Macintosh system software, but a few at the bottom of the dialog box are exclusive to Photoshop. The options work as follows:

✦ **Copies:** Enter the number of copies you want to print in this option box. You can print up to 999 copies of a single image, although why you would want to do so is beyond me.

✦ **Pages:** No such thing as a multipage document exists in Photoshop, so you can ignore the All, From, and To options.

✦ **Destination:** Exclusively applicable to PostScript printing (which is why it doesn't appear for the non-PostScript Color Stylus 800 featured in Figure 7-9), this option lets you save a PostScript-language version of the file on disk rather than printing it directly to your printer. Select the Printer option to print the image to an output device as usual. Select File to write a PostScript-language version of the image to disk.

Because Photoshop offers its own EPS option via the Save dialog box, you'll probably want to ignore this option. In fact, the only reason to select File is to capture printer's marks, as I did back in Figure 7-4. If you do, a second dialog box appears, asking where you want to save the PostScript file. You can navigate just as in the Open and Save dialog boxes. For the best results, select the Binary radio button.

✦ **Print Selected Area:** Select this option to print the portion of an image that is selected with the rectangular marquee tool. You can use this option to divide an image into pieces when it's too large to fit on a single page. (Note that some printers make you select Adobe Photoshop 5.0 from a pop-up menu to see this and the next option.)

✦ **Space:** Back in Photoshop 4 and earlier, you could select whether to print in a few rudimentary color spaces — grayscale, RGB, and CMYK — but that was it. Thanks to Version 5's improved color management scheme, now you can convert to any color space offered by either Photoshop or Apple's ColorSync, as illustrated by the pop-up menu in Figure 7-9. Ideally, you want to select the specific profile for your brand of printer. If you can't find such a profile, you'll probably want to stick with the RGB Color space (specified with File ➪ Color Settings ➪ RGB Setup). Another option is to choose CMYK Color which prints the image just as if you had converted it to the CMYK color space. Unfortunately, most consumer printers are designed to accommodate RGB images and fair pretty badly when printing artwork converted to CMYK. (This is precisely the reason I frequently select RGB Color even when printing a CMYK image — it flat out produces better results.)

But you don't have to stop there. If you own a color printer, I encourage you to take an hour out of your day and conduct a few tests with the other Space options. For example, if you select Apple RGB, your printed image will darken several shades. This might throw you. Because the Apple RGB profile features the lightest of the monitor gammas — 1.8 — you might expect the image to print lighter. But what Photoshop is really doing is converting the colors as if the printer was as naturally light as an Apple RGB monitor. In order to maintain consistent color, the conversion therefore darkens the image to account for this unusually light device. Select the Wide Gamut setting and the colors appear lighter and washed out, again accounting for this hyper-saturated Space setting. So think opposite.

Yet another alternative is to convert an RGB image to the grayscale color space during printing. But it's generally a bad alternative. Asking Photoshop to convert colors on the fly dramatically increases the output time as well as the likelihood of printing errors. It's better and much faster to simply convert the image to the grayscale mode (Image ➪ Mode ➪ Grayscale) and then print it.

✦ **Encoding:** If your network doesn't support binary encoding (highly unlikely in this day and age), select the ASCII option to transfer PostScript data in the text-only format. The printing process takes much longer to complete, but at least it's possible. If your printer supports PostScript Level 2 or later, you can also choose to use JPEG compression to reduce the amount of data sent to the printer. (This option is applicable to PostScript printers only.)

Press Return inside the Print dialog box to start the printing process on its merry way. To cancel a print in progress, click on the Cancel button or press the Escape key. If you neglect to cancel before Photoshop spools the print job, don't worry, you can still cancel. If your printer driver installed an icon on the desktop, double-click on it. Then select the print job and click on the pause button to interrupt it or click on the trash can to cancel. If there is no desktop icon, check the Extensions folder in the System Folder to see if there's a Monitor utility for your printer. It may even be running as it spools, in which case you can locate it in the Applications menu on the far right side of the screen.

Creating Color Separations

It's rare that you'll ever have to print color separations directly from Photoshop. You'll more likely import the image into QuarkXPress, PageMaker, or a similar application before printing separations. It's even more likely that you'll take the image or page-layout file to a commercial printer and have a qualified technician take care of it.

So why discuss this process? Two reasons. First, it's always a good idea to at least peripherally understand all phases of the computer imaging process, even if you have no intention of becoming directly involved. This way, if something goes wrong on the printer's end, you can decipher the crux of the problem and either propose a solution or strike a compromise that still works in your favor.

Second, before you import your image into another program or submit it to a commercial printer, you'll want to convert the RGB image to the CMYK color space. (You don't absolutely *have* to do this — with Photoshop 5's improved color matching functions, you can exchange RGB images with greater confidence — but it's always a good idea to prepare your images down to the last detail, and CMYK is invariably the final destination for printed imagery.) Accurately converting to CMYK is the trickiest part of printing color separations; the other steps require barely any effort at all.

So without further ado, here's how you convert an image to the CMYK color space and print separations. Many of the steps are the same as when printing a grayscale or color composite, others are new and different.

Steps: Printing CMYK Color Separations

1. **Calibrate your monitor and specify the desired RGB environment.** Use the Gamma utility and File ⇨ Color Settings ⇨ RGB Setup as discussed at length in Chapter 6.

2. **Identify the final output device.** Use File ⇨ Color Settings ⇨ CMYK Setup to tell Photoshop what kind of printer you intend to use. If you're lucky, your commercial printer may provide a CMYK table that you can load and avoid the hassle. Otherwise, you'll have to grapple with some weird settings. The good news is that you only need to complete this step once for each time you switch hardware. If you always use the same commercial printer, then you can set it up and forget about it.

3. **Convert the image to the CMYK color space.** Choose Image ⇨ Mode ⇨ CMYK Color to convert the image from its present color mode to CMYK.

4. **Adjust the individual color channels.** Switching color modes can dramatically affect the colors in an image. To compensate for color and focus loss, you can edit the individual color channels as described in the "Color Channel Effects" section of Chapter 6.

5. **Trap your image, if necessary.** If your image features lots of high-contrast elements and you're concerned your printer might not do the best job of registering the cyan, magenta, yellow, and black color plates, you can apply Image ⇨ Trap to prevent your final printout from looking like the color funnies. (When working with typical "continuous-tone" photographs, you can skip this step.)

6. **Choose your printer.** Select the printer you want to use, as described previously in the "Choosing a printer" section.

7. **Turn on a few essential printer marks.** Choose File ⇨ Page Setup (⌘-Shift-P) to specify the size of the pages and the size and orientation of the image on the pages, as described earlier in this chapter. Also be sure to select — at the very least — the Calibration Bars, Registration Marks, and Labels check boxes.

8. **Adjust the halftone and transfer functions as needed.** Click on the Screen and Transfer buttons to modify the halftone screen dots and map brightness values for each of the CMYK color channels, as described earlier in the "Changing the halftone screen" and "Specifying a transfer function" sections. This step is entirely optional.

9. **Choose File ⇨ Print (⌘-P).** Then choose the Separations option from the Space pop-up menu. This tells Photoshop to print each color channel to a separate piece of paper or film.

Note

You also can create color separations by importing an image into a page-layout or drawing program. Instead of choosing your printer in Step 6, you'd save the image in the DCS format, as described in the "QuarkXPress DCS" section of Chapter 4.

Steps 6 through 9 are repeats of concepts explained in previous sections of this chapter. Steps 1, 3, and 4 were covered at length in Chapters 5 and 6. This leaves Steps 2 and 5 — CMYK Setup and trapping — which I explain in the following sections.

Printer calibration

To prepare an image for reproduction on a commercial offset or web press, choose File ⇨ Color Settings ⇨ CMYK Setup. Shown in Figure 7-10, the CMYK Setup dialog box determines both how Photoshop converts images from the RGB to CMYK color spaces, and how CMYK images appear on screen (that is, the conversion from CMYK to RGB).

Figure 7-10: Use the options in the CMYK Setup dialog box to prepare an image for printing on a commercial offset or web press.

Photoshop 5.0

If you're familiar with previous versions of Photoshop, the CMYK Setup dialog box combines options from the old Printing Inks Setup, Separation Setup, and Separation Tables dialog boxes. Although this makes for a more complicated dialog box, it eliminates a lot of confusion; some of the options in the old dialog boxes overlapped and canceled each other out.

The following list explains each and every option in the CMYK Setup dialog box. If you're not a print professional, some of these descriptions may seem a little abstruse. After reading this section, you may want to talk with your commercial printer and find out what options, if any, he recommends.

✦ **Ink Colors:** This pop-up menu offers access to a handful of common press inks and paper stocks. Select the option that most closely matches your printing environment. (Your commercial printer can easily help you with this one.) The default setting, SWOP (Coated), represents the most common press type and paper stock used in the U.S. for magazine and high-end display work. Regardless of which setting you choose, Photoshop automatically changes the Dot Gain value to the most suitable setting.

✦ **Dot Gain:** Enter any value from –10 to 40 percent to specify the amount by which you can expect halftone cells to shrink or expand during the printing process, a variable known as *dot gain*. When printing to uncoated stock, for example, you can expect halftone cells to bleed into the page and expand by about 25 to 30 percent. For newsprint, it varies from 30 to 40 percent. If the dot gain varies between plates, choose Curves from the pop-up menu to display a transfer graph that works just like the one in the Transfer Functions dialog box. Whether you enter a percentage value or use the graph, Photoshop automatically adjusts the brightness of CMYK colors to compensate, lightening the image for high values and darkening it for low values.

✦ **Separation Type:** When the densities of cyan, magenta, and yellow inks reach a certain level, they mix to form a muddy brown. The GCR (*gray component replacement*) option avoids this unpleasant effect by overprinting these colors with black to the extent specified with the Black Generation option. If you select the UCR (*under color removal*) option, Photoshop removes cyan, magenta, and yellow inks where they overlap black ink. GCR is almost always the setting of choice except when printing on newsprint.

✦ **Black Generation:** Available only when the GCR option is active, the Black Generation pop-up menu determines how dark the cyan, magenta, and yellow concentrations must be before Photoshop adds black ink. Select Light to use black ink sparingly; select Heavy to apply it liberally. The None option prints no black ink whatsoever, while the Maximum option prints black ink over everything. You may want to use the UCA Amount option to restore cyan, magenta, and yellow ink if you select the Heavy or Maximum option.

✦ **Black Ink Limit:** Enter the maximum amount of black ink that can be applied to the page. By default, this value is 100 percent, which is solid ink coverage. If you raise the UCA Amount value, you'll probably want to lower this value by a similar percentage to prevent the image from overdarkening.

✦ **Total Ink Limit:** This value represents the maximum amount of all four inks permitted on the page. For example, assuming you use the default Black Ink Limit and Total Ink Limit values of 100 and 300 percent, respectively, the darkest printable color contains 100 percent black ink. The sum total of cyan, magenta, and yellow inks, therefore, is the difference between these values,

200 percent. A typical *saturated black* — a mix of inks that results in an absolute pitch-black pigment — is 70 percent cyan, 63 percent magenta, 67 percent yellow, and 100 percent black. And 70 + 63 + 67 + 100 =, you guessed it, 300.

✦ **UCA Amount:** The opposite of UCR, UCA stands for *under color addition,* which enables you to add cyan, magenta, and yellow inks to areas where the concentration of black ink is highest. For example, a value of 20 percent raises the amount of cyan, magenta, and yellow inks applied with black concentrations between 80 and 100 percent. This option is dimmed when the UCR radio button is active.

✦ **Gray Ramp:** The Gray Ramp graph shows the effects of your changes. Four lines — one in each color — represent the four inks. Although you can't edit the colored lines in this graph by clicking and dragging them, you can observe the lines to gauge the results of your settings. If you have an urge to grab a curve and yank on it, choose Custom from the Black Generation pop-up menu. The ensuing dialog box lets you edit the black curve directly while you preview its effect on the C, M, and Y curves in the background.

✦ **Preview:** Turn this option on to see how your changes affect any open CMYK images. RGB, Lab, and grayscale images remain unchanged.

If you prefer not to mess around with these complicated settings, you can rely on one of two kinds of predefined printer profiles. To load an ICC profile provided by ColorSync, select ICC from the CMYK Model radio buttons (along the top of the CMYK Setup dialog box). Then select a printer from the Profile pop-up menu. Keep in mind, however, that these represent color printers and high-end printing devices, not commercial presses.

If you have access to Photoshop separation tables — such as the ColorMatch 3.0 profiles from Radius (included with the company's PressView monitor series) — you can load the table into Photoshop without further fanfare. Just select Tables from the CMYK Model radio buttons. Then click on the Load button and open up the desired table. (If you want to use a ColorMatch file or other separation table on the Windows side, be sure to give it the extension *.ast.*)

As shown in Figure 7-11, a separation file includes two tables — the From CMYK Table and the To CMYK Table. The first describes how CMYK colors should be displayed on screen. The second determines how Photoshop converts an RGB image to the CMYK color space. You don't have to worry about this — it's all handled automatically and you load just the one file — but as always it's good to know what's going on in the background.

Photoshop 5.0

In Photoshop 5, you can create a table of CMYK instructions using the built-in CMYK Setup options and then save the settings as an ICC profile. To do so, select the Built-In radio button at the top of the dialog box and fill out the desired options for your printer. Then select Tables from the CMYK Model options and click on the Save button. Photoshop saves an ICC table which you can use with any other ICC-compliant application.

Figure 7-11: You can load a ColorMatch or other predefined separation table by selecting the Tables option and clicking on the Load button.

Color trapping

If color separations misalign slightly during the reproduction process (a problem called *misregistration*), the final image can exhibit slight gaps between colors. Suppose an image features a 100 percent cyan chicken against a 100 percent magenta background. (Pretty attractive image idea, huh? Go ahead, you can use it if you like.) If the cyan and magenta plates don't line up exactly, you're left with a chicken with a white halo around it. Yuck.

A *trap* is a little extra bit of color that fills in the gap. For example, if you choose Image ➪ Trap and enter 4 into the Width option box, Photoshop outlines the chicken with an extra 4 pixels of cyan and the background with an extra 4 pixels of magenta. Now the registration can be off a full 8 pixels without any halo occurring.

Continuous-tone images, such as photographs and natural-media painting, don't need trapping because no harsh color transitions occur. In fact, trapping will actually harm such images by thickening up the borders and edges, smudging detail, and generally dulling the focus.

One of the primary reasons to use the Trap command, therefore, is to trap rasterized drawings from Illustrator or FreeHand. Some state-of-the-art prepress systems trap documents by first rasterizing them to pixels and then modifying the pixels. Together, Photoshop and Illustrator (or FreeHand) constitute a more rudimentary but, nonetheless, functional trapping system. When you open an illustration in Photoshop, the program converts it into an image according to your size and resolution specifications, as described in the "Rasterizing an Illustrator or FreeHand file" section of Chapter 4. Once the illustration is rasterized, you can apply Image ➪ Trap to the image as a whole. Despite the command's simplicity, it handles nearly all trapping scenarios, even going so far as to reduce the width of the trap incrementally as the colors of neighboring areas grow more similar.

Caution   If you plan on having a service bureau trap your files for you, do not apply Photoshop's Trap command. You don't want to see what happens when someone traps an image that's already been trapped. If you're paying the extra bucks for professional trapping, leave it to the pros.

Printing Duotones

It's been a few pages since the "Understanding Printing Terminology" section, so here's a quick recap: A *duotone* is a grayscale image printed with two inks. This technique expands the depth of the image by allowing additional shades for highlights, shadows, and midtones. If you've seen a glossy magazine ad for perfume, designer clothing, a car, or just about any other overpriced commodity, you've seen a duotone. Words like *rich*, *luxurious*, and *palpable* come to mind.

Photoshop also enables you to add a third ink to create a tritone and a fourth ink to create a quadtone. Color Plate 7-1 shows an example of an image printed as a quadtone. Figure 7-12 shows a detail from the image printed in its original grayscale form. See the difference?

Figure 7-12: This salute to all-around athlete Jim Thorpe by artist Mark Collen looks pretty good, but if you want to see great, check out the quadtone in Color Plate 7-1.

Creating a duotone

To convert a grayscale image to a duotone, tritone, or quadtone, choose Image ⇨ Mode ⇨ Duotone. Photoshop displays the Duotone Options dialog box shown in Figure 7-13. By default, Monotone is the active Type option, and the Ink 2, Ink 3, and Ink 4 options are dimmed. To access the Ink 3 option, select Tritone from the Type pop-up menu; to access both Ink 3 and Ink 4, select Quadtone from the pop-up menu.

You specify the color of each ink you want to use by clicking on the color box associated with the desired ink option. The first time you define colors, Photoshop displays the Color Picker dialog box. You can either define colors in the Color Picker or click on Custom Colors to select a color from the Custom Colors dialog box, as described in the "Predefined colors" section of Chapter 5.

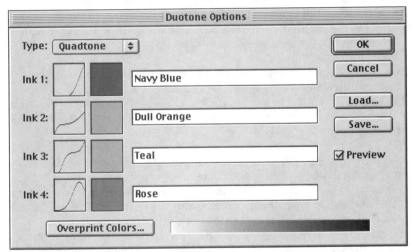

Figure 7-13: The Duotone Options dialog box enables you to apply multiple inks to a grayscale image.

Photoshop 5 takes the guesswork out of creating a duotone by previewing your settings in the image window so long as the Preview check box is turned on. Keep in mind, the preview may not exactly match your output when using certain Pantone inks. (This is a common problem when previewing Pantone inks in any program, but it's always a good idea to keep in mind, particularly since Photoshop mixes inks to create its dutone effects.)

The next time you create a duotone, Photoshop displays the same colors you defined in your last visit to the Duotone Options dialog box. If you previously defined colors in the Custom Colors dialog box, clicking on a color box brings up that same dialog box (click on Picker to get to the Color Picker dialog box).

When creating duotones, tritones, and quadtones, prioritize your inks in order — from darkest at the top to lightest at the bottom — when you specify them in the Duotone Options dialog box. Because Photoshop prints inks in the order they appear in the dialog box, the inks will print from darkest to lightest. This ensures rich highlights and shadows and a uniform color range.

After selecting a color, you can use either of two methods to specify how the differently colored inks blend. The first and more dependable way is to click on the transfer function box associated with the desired ink option. Photoshop then displays the Transfer Functions dialog box, described back in the "Specifying a transfer function" section of this chapter. This permits you to emphasize specific inks in different portions of the image according to brightness values.

For example, Figure 7-13 shows the inks and transfer functions assigned to the quadtone in Color Plate 7-1. The Navy Blue color is associated only with the darkest brightness values in the image; Rose peaks at about 80 percent gray and then descends; Teal covers the midtones in the image; Dull Orange is strongest in the light values. The four colors mix to form an image whose brightness values progress from light orange to olive green to brick red to black.

The second method for controlling the blending of colors is to click on the Overprint Colors button. An Overprint Colors dialog box appears, showing how each pair of colors will mix when printed. Other color swatches show how three and four colors mix, if applicable. To change the color swatch, click on it to display the Color Picker dialog box.

The problem with this second method is it complicates the editing process. Photoshop doesn't actually change the ink colors or transfer functions in keeping with your new specifications; it just applies the new overprint colors without any logical basis. And you lose all changes made with the Overprint Colors dialog box when you adjust any of the ink colors or any of the transfer functions.

To return and change the colors or transfer functions, choose Image ➪ Mode ➪ Duotone again. Instead of reconverting the image, the command now lets you edit the existing duotone, tritone, or quadtone.

Reproducing a duotone

If you want a commercial printer to reproduce a duotone, tritone, or quadtone, you must print the image to color separations, just like a CMYK image. Because you already specified which inks to use and how much of each ink to apply, however, you needn't mess around with all those commands in the File ➪ Color Settings submenu. Just take the following familiar steps:

Steps: Printing a Duotone, Tritone, or Quadtone

1. **Choose the printer you want to use.** Select a printer as described previously in the "Choosing a printer" section.

2. **Turn on the printer marks.** Choose File ➪ Page Setup (⌘-Shift-P) to specify the size of the pages and the size and orientation of the image on the pages, as described earlier in this chapter in the "Setting up the page" section. Be sure to select the Registration Marks option.

3. **Adjust the halftone screens, if desired.** If you're feeling inventive, click on the Screens button to change the size, angle, and shape of the halftone screen dots for the individual color plates, as described previously in the "Changing the halftone screen" section.

4. **Choose File ➪ Print (⌘-P).** Select the Separations option from the Space pop-up menu to print each ink to a separate sheet of paper or film.

To prepare a duotone to be imported into QuarkXPress, Illustrator, or some other application, save the image in the EPS format, as described in the "Saving an EPS image" section of Chapter 4. As listed back in Table 5-1 of Chapter 5, EPS is the only file format other than the native Photoshop format that supports duotones, tritones, and quadtones.

Editing individual duotone plates

If you'll be printing your duotone using CMYK colors and you can't quite get the effect you want inside the Duotone Options dialog box, you can convert the duotone to the CMYK mode by choosing Image ➪ Mode ➪ CMYK. Not only will all the duotone shades remain intact, but you'll also have the added advantage of being able to tweak colors and to add color using Photoshop's standard color-correction commands and editing tools. You can even edit individual color channels, as described in Chapter 6.

If your duotone includes Pantone or other spot colors, converting to CMYK is not an option. But you can still access and edit the individual color channels. To separate the duotone inks into channels, choose Image ➪ Mode ➪ Multichannel. Each ink appears as a separate spot color inside the Channels palette, as shown in Figure 7-14. You can experiment with different color combinations by turning eyeball icons on and off. In Color Plate 7-2, for example, I turned off one channel in the top row and two channels in the bottom. You can even switch out one spot color for another by double-clicking on the channel name and then clicking on the color swatch.

Figure 7-14: Here I chose Image ➪ Mode ➪ Multichannel to separate my quadtone into four independent spot-color channels.

To save a duotone converted to the multichannel mode, you have just two options: native Photoshop (as always) and DCS 2.0. For complete information on the latter, read the "QuarkXPress DCS" section in Chapter 4.

Spot-Color Separations

Photoshop 5 now permits you to add spot colors to your images. While it's unlikely that you'll use spot colors to widen the gamut of your photographs — after all, scanners can't scan spot colors and Photoshop can't automatically lift them out of, say, the RGB color space — you may want to toss in a spot color to highlight a logo, a line of type, and some other special element.

For example, suppose you have a full-color image of a jet ski. The logo along the side of the boat is fully visible, just as the client wants it, but the color is off. Normally, the logo appears in Pantone 265 purple. But the CMYK equivalent for this color looks about three shades darker, four shades redder, and several times muddier. The only solution is to assign the proper spot color — Pantone 265 — to the logo. The following steps tell how:

Steps: Adding a Spot Color to an Image

1. **Select the logo.** You can use the magic wand tool or some more exacting method, as described in Chapters 11 and 12.

2. **Fill the selection with white.** Press the D key to get the default foreground and background colors, then press ⌘-Delete. It's important that you erase the old logo so that it appears in pure spot color without any mixing with the CMYK inks. But do *not* deselect your selection! It must remain active for Step 5 to work.

3. **Create a new spot channel.** As explained in Chapter 6, the easiest way to do this is to ⌘-Click on the page icon at the bottom of the Channels palette. But you can also choose New Spot Channel from the Channels palette menu if you prefer.

4. **Set the color to Pantone 265.** Click on the Color swatch in the New Spot Channel dialog box. Then select Pantone 265 from the Custom Colors dialog box. (If the Color Picker comes up instead, click on the Custom button.)

5. **Press Return or click OK twice.** Photoshop adds the new spot color to the Channels palette and automatically fills the selection. Your logo automatically appears in the spot color. (Cool, huh?)

6. **Choose Image ➪ Trap.** It's a good idea to trap the spot color so that it covers up any gaps that may result from misregistration. Enter a value of 1 or 2 pixels and hit Return. Photoshop spreads the logo but leaves the CMYK image alone. Very intelligent program, that Photoshop.

7. **Save the image.** You have two choices of formats, native Photoshop or DCS 2.0. If you want to import the image into a different program, use the latter.

Naturally, you don't want to trust Photoshop's on-screen representation of the spot color any more than you would in Illustrator, QuarkXPress, or any other program. The screen version is an approximation, nothing more. So it's a good idea to have a Pantone swatch book on hand so that you know exactly what the color should look like when printed. (If the printed logo doesn't match the swatch book, it's the printer's fault, not Photoshop's.)

Printing Contact Sheets

Photoshop's final printing feature is a representative from the new Actions plug-ins. This means that the command performs a series of automated operations — much like a script created in the Actions palette — but with the interface of a filter or other plug-in.

The purpose of File ➪ Automated ➪ Contact Sheet is to print a folder-full of images as thumbnails on a contact sheet. This way, you can quickly peruse the images in that folder and decide whether or not any of them would make good candidates for editing. It's sort of a do-it-yourself cataloging feature.

This command shows off both the strengths and weaknesses of Actions plug-ins. On the up side, it lets you do something you couldn't do before without requiring the programmer to invent a completely new feature. This means Actions plug-ins are easy to create and you'll probably see lots of them in the future years. On the down side, the plug-in is limited in its capabilities and slow.

In fact, the down side is sufficiently awful that I considered ignoring this command entirely. But contact sheets are extremely useful, so what the heck? Just bear in mind, you're going to have to be patient and resourceful to get predictable results out of this sucker.

Steps: Creating a Contact Sheet

1. **Choose File ➪ Automated ➪ Contact Sheet.** This displays the dialog box shown in Figure 7-15. This is the interface for the script.

2. **Click on the Choose button.** Then locate the folder of images that you want to print on the contact sheet. Pay attention to how many images the folder contains. Photoshop will assemble only as many as will fit on a single page. The Contact Sheet plug-in is not smart enough to continue assembling images onto a second page.

3. **Enter the size and resolution of the contact sheet file.** The Contact Sheet command is unable to resample images as it brings them in — probably its greatest oversight — so be sure to make your contact sheet very large. To hold 30 digital snapshots, I had to set mine to 8 × 10 inches at 300 ppi.

4. **Specify a color mode.** This isn't something you're going to color separate, so RGB should do fine.

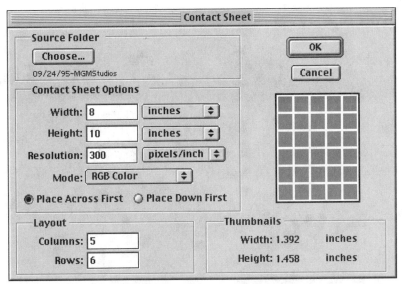

Figure 7-15: The Contact Sheet dialog box invokes a series of operations that open images from a folder and assembles them together on a single page.

5. **Set the number of Columns and Rows of thumbnails.** The total number of thumbnails should match or exceed the number of images in the folder you selected with the Choose button. Excess images will be ignored.

6. **Press Return and watch the fireworks.** Photoshop creates a new contact sheet image, opens the first image from the folder, copies and pastes it into the contact sheet image, moves it into position, flattens the file, and then moves onto the next image. It takes several minutes to open, copy, paste, and position 30 or more images, so a break is definitely in order. When the command finishes, you should get something on the order of Figure 7-16. It looks pretty hodgepodge, but then it's not supposed to be a work of art.

7. **Resample the image down to a more reasonable size.** You can skip this step if you like, but a 20MB file seems excessive for what is ostensibly a quick reference of thumbnails. I'd take the image down to 50 percent at least, maybe more.

8. **Save the contact sheet and print it.** Then repeat for all your other images. At about 10 minutes per collection of 30, it should take me, oh, about 5 days to get through my digital snapshots. Yet another project to put off until my dotage.

(continued)

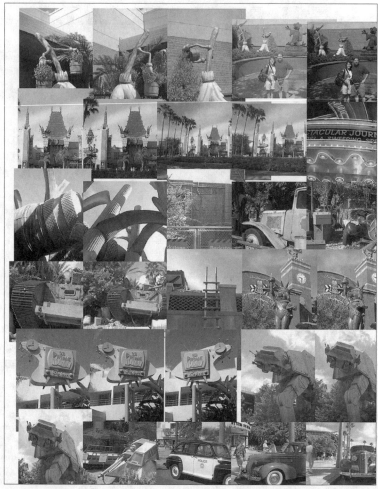

Figure 7-16: A sample contact sheet of images I shot with a Kodak DC40 at MGM Studios in Disney World. That was a couple of years ago now, so naturally I completely forget what I shot. This contact sheet should come in handy.

All in all, Contact Sheet reminds me of the kind of 75 percent-baked filters that found their way into Illustrator 5 for the Mac. (The original Create Star filter is a far cry from Illustrator 7's fully realized star tool.) It's useful in theory but clumsy in practice. Still, Contact Sheet gives you an idea of what Actions plug-ins are all about and the wonders that they hold in store. My guess (or should I say, my hope) is that we can expect better things from this command in the future.

✦   ✦   ✦

Painting and Retouching Images

Painting and Editing

Paint and Edit Tool Basics

Here it is, Chapter 8, and I'm finally getting around to explaining how to use Photoshop's painting tools. You must feel like you're attending some kind of martial arts ritual where you have to learn to run away, cry, beg, and attempt bribery before you get to start karate-chopping bricks and kicking your instructor. "The wise person journeys through the fundamentals of image editing before painting a single brushstroke, Grasshoppa." *Wang, wang, wang.* (That's a musical embellishment, in case you didn't recognize it. Man, I hate to have to explain my jokes. Especially when they're so measly.) Now that you've earned your first belt or tassel or scouting patch or whatever it is you're supposed to receive for slogging this far through the book, you're as prepared as you'll ever be to dive into the world of painting and retouching images.

You may think these tools require artistic talent. In truth, each tool provides options for about any level of proficiency or experience. Photoshop offers get-by measures for novices who want to make a quick edit and put the tool down before they make a mess of things. If you have a few hours of experience with other painting programs, you'll find Photoshop's tools provide at least as much functionality and, in many cases, more. (The one exception is Painter, which is several times more capable than Photoshop in the painting department.) And if you're a professional artist — well, come on now — you'll have no problems learning how to make Photoshop sing. No matter who you are, you'll find electronic painting and editing tools more flexible, less messy, and more forgiving than their traditional counterparts.

Cross-Reference

If you screw something up in the course of painting your image, stop and choose Edit ➪ Undo (or press ⌘-Z). If this doesn't work, press ⌘-Option-Z to step back through your paint strokes. Or you can select a previous state in the History palette, as explained in Chapter 10. The History palette lists brushstrokes and other changes according to the tool you used to create them.

Meet your tools

Photoshop provides three paint tools: the pencil, the paintbrush, and the airbrush. You also get six edit tools: smudge, blur, sharpen, burn, dodge, and sponge. Figure 8-1 shows these tools. The keyboard equivalent for each tool appears in parentheses.

Figure 8-1: The three paint tools, the two edit tools that appear in the toolbox by default, and the four alternative edit tools.

Cross-Reference

In case you're wondering about all the other tools, Figure 8-2 segregates tools by category and lists the chapter in which you can find more information.

Figure 8-2: The rest of Photoshop's tools fall into the categories listed above each toolbox. The chapter in which I discuss each category of tools appears in parentheses.

The paint tools

The paint tools apply paint in the foreground color. In this and other respects, they work like their counterparts in other painting programs, but there are a few exceptions:

✦ **Pencil:** Unlike pencil tools found in most other painting programs — which paint lines 1-pixel thick — Photoshop's pencil paints a hard-edged line of any thickness. Figure 8-3 compares the default single-pixel pencil line with a fatter pencil line, a paintbrush line, and an airbrush line.

If you're used to selecting the pencil tool by pressing the P key (as in Photoshop 3) or the Y key (as in Version 4), prepare for yet another change. You now select the pencil by pressing N, the old shortcut for the line tool.

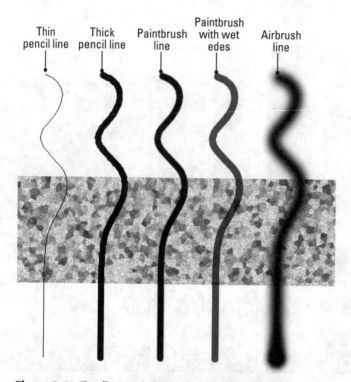

Figure 8-3: Five lines painted in black with the pencil, paintbrush, and airbrush tools. The Wet Edges option (second from right) causes the line to appear translucent. Notice I held the airbrush tool in place for a few moments at the end of the rightmost line.

✦ **Paintbrush:** The paintbrush works like the pencil tool, except it paints an antialiased line that blends in with its background.

The paintbrush offers a Wet Edges option. (Double-click on the paintbrush tool icon in the toolbox and you'll see the Wet Edges check box in the bottom left corner of the Paintbrush Options palette.) When this option is turned on, the paintbrush creates a translucent line with darkened edges, much as if you were painting with watercolors. Soft brush shapes produce more naturalistic effects. An example of this effect is shown in Figure 8-3.

✦ **Airbrush:** Dismissing Photoshop's airbrush tool as a softer version of the paintbrush is tempting because it uses a softer brush shape by default. Photoshop's default settings also call for a lighter pressure, so the airbrush paints a translucent line. But unlike the paintbrush, which applies a continuous stream of color and stops applying paint when you stop dragging, the airbrush applies a series of colored dollops and continues to apply these dollops as long as you press the mouse button. Figure 8-3 shows the dark glob of paint that results from pressing the mouse button while holding the mouse motionless at the end of the drag.

Like the pencil, the shortcut for the airbrush has changed. Now that the A key has been traded to the direct selection tool (used to edit paths), the airbrush has been assigned the one previously unused alphabetic key, J.

The edit tools

The edit tools don't apply color; rather, they influence existing colors in an image. Figure 8-4 shows each of the six edit tools applied to a randomized background. The tools work as follows:

✦ **Blur:** The first of the two focus tools, the blur tool blurs an image by lessening the amount of color contrast between neighboring pixels.

Figure 8-4: These are the effects of dragging with each of Photoshop's edit tools. The boundaries of each line are highlighted so you can clearly see the distinctions between line and background.

✦ **Sharpen:** The second focus tool selectively sharpens by increasing the contrast between neighboring pixels. Generally speaking, both the blur and sharpen tools are less useful than their command counterparts in the Filters menu. They provide less control and usually require scrubbing at an image. Maybe I've been using a computer too long, but my wrist starts to ache when I use these tools. If, unlike me, you like the basic principle behind the tools, but you want to avoid carpal tunnel syndrome, you can achieve consistent, predictable results without scrubbing by using the tools in combination with the Shift key, as described in the next section.

✦ **Smudge:** The smudge tool smears colors in an image. The effect is much like dragging your finger across wet paint. In Photoshop 5, the smudge tool has been demoted to an alternative to the focus tools. Otherwise, it's the same old tool.

✦ **Dodge:** The first of three toning tools, the dodge tool, enables you to lighten a portion of an image by dragging across it. Named after a traditional film exposure technique, the dodge tool is supposed to look like a little paddle thingie — you know, like one of those spoons you put over your eye at the optometrist's — that you wave over photographic paper to cast a shadow and thereby lighten the exposure. Thank golly we no longer have to wave little paddle thingies in our modern age.

✦ **Burn:** The burn tool lets you darken a portion of an image by dragging over it. The effect is similar to burning a film negative, which you apparently do by holding your hand in a kind of O shape in an effort to focus the light, kind of like frying a worker ant using a magnifying glass (except not quite so smelly). At least, that's what they tell me. Sadly, I've never had the pleasure of trying it.

If you're like most folks, you have difficulty remembering which tool lightens and which one darkens. So here's a little tip: That little hand icon looks like it could be holding a piece of toast, and when you burn toast, it gets darker. Hand, toast, burn, darker. That other tool, eye doctor paddle, not holding toast, must lighten. You'll never have problems again.

✦ **Sponge:** The final toning tool, the sponge tool, robs an image of both saturation and contrast. Or you can set the tool so it boosts saturation and adds contrast. For more information, stay tuned for the upcoming section "Mopping up with the sponge tool."

To access the sharpen tool temporarily when the blur tool is selected, press and hold the Option key while using the tool. The sharpen tool remains available only as long as you press the Option key. You also can press Option to access the blur tool when the sharpen tool is selected, to access the burn tool when the dodge tool is selected, and to access the dodge tool when the burn tool is selected. (If the sponge tool is active, pressing the Option key has no effect, except maybe to give your finger a cramp.)

You can replace the blur tool with the sharpen tool in the toolbox by Option-clicking on the tool's icon. Option-click again to select the smudge tool and yet again to cycle back to the blur tool. Likewise, you can Option-click on the dodge tool icon to cycle between the dodge, burn, and sponge tools.

As explained in Chapter 3, the keyboard equivalents also toggle between the tools. When the blur tool is selected, press Shift-R to toggle to the sharpen tool. Repeated pressings of Shift-R take you to the smudge tool and back to the blur tool. When the dodge tool is selected, press Shift-O to toggle to the burn tool; press Shift-O again to get the sponge.

 Tip

To modify the performance of a tool, double-click on its icon in the toolbox to display the customized Options palette. Or you can simply press Return while the tool is selected. I discuss the options inside the various Options palettes throughout the remainder of this chapter.

Basic techniques

I know several people who claim they can't paint, and yet they create beautiful work in Photoshop. Even though they don't have sufficient hand-eye coordination to write their names on screen, they have unique and powerful artistic sensibilities and they know lots of tricks that enable them to make judicious use of the paint and edit tools. I can't help you in the sensibilities department, but I can show you a few tricks to boost your ability and inclination to use the paint and edit tools.

Painting a straight line

You're probably already aware you can draw a straight line with the line tool. If not, try it. The line tool is the alternative tool for the pencil. (Press N then Shift-N to get to it quickly.) After selecting the tool, drag with it inside the image window to create a line. Pretty hot stuff, huh? Well, no, it's actually pretty dull, not to mention limited. In fact, the only reason I ever use this tool is to draw arrows, like those in Figure 8-6. (I explain how in the "Applying Strokes and Arrowheads" section of Chapter 9.) If you don't want to draw an arrow, you're better off using Photoshop's other means for creating straight lines: the Shift key.

To draw a straight line with any of the paint or edit tools, click at one point in the image and then press Shift and click at another point. Using the current tool, Photoshop draws a straight line between the two points.

To create free-form polygons, continue to Shift-click with the tool. Figure 8-5 features a photograph and a tracing I made on a separate layer (cover in Chapter 13) exclusively by Shift-clicking with the paintbrush tool. As an academic exercise, I never dragged with the tool, I never altered the brush size, and I used just two colors: black and gray.

 Tip

The Shift key makes the blur and sharpen tools halfway useful. Suppose you want to edit the perimeter of the car shown in Figure 8-6. The arrows in the figure illustrate the path your Shift-clicks should follow. Figure 8-7 shows the effect of Shift-clicking with the blur tool; Figure 8-8 demonstrates the effect of Shift-clicking with the sharpen tool.

Figure 8-5: Starting from an image by photographer Barbara Penoyar (left), I created a stylized tracing (right) by clicking and Shift-clicking with the paintbrush tool on a separate layer.

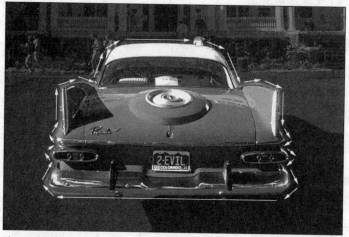

Figure 8-6: It takes one click and 24 Shift-clicks to soften or accentuate the edges around this car using the blur or sharpen tool.

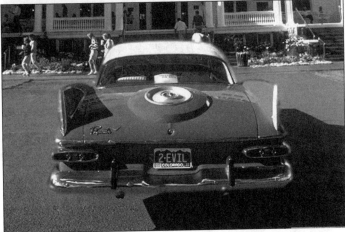

Figure 8-7: These are the results of blurring the car's perimeter with the pressure set to 50 percent (top) and 100 percent (bottom). You set the pressure using the slider bar in the Blur Options palette.

Figure 8-8: The results of sharpening the car with the pressure set to 50 percent (top) and 100 percent (bottom).

Painting a perpendicular line

To draw a perpendicular line — either a vertical or a horizontal line — with any of the paint or edit tools, press and hold the mouse button, press the Shift key, and begin dragging in a vertical or horizontal direction. Don't release the Shift key until you finish dragging or until you want to change the direction of the line, as shown in Figure 8-9. Notice, pressing the Shift key in mid-drag snaps the line back into perpendicular alignment.

Press mouse button, press Shift, begin drag

Release Shift

Press Shift again...

...to snap line back to perpendicular

Release mouse button, release Shift

Figure 8-9: Pressing the Shift key after you start to drag with a paint or edit tool results in a perpendicular line for as long as the key is pressed.

One way to exploit the Shift key's penchant to snap to the perpendicular is to draw "ribbed" structures. Being left-handed, I dragged from right to left with the paintbrush to create both of the central outlines around the skeleton that appears at the top of Figure 8-10. I painted each rib by pressing and releasing the Shift key as I dragged with the paintbrush tool. Pressing Shift snapped the line to the horizontal axis, whose location was established by the beginning of the drag.

In this figure, I represented the axis for each line in gray. After establishing the basic skeletal form, I added some free-form details with the paintbrush and pencil tools, as shown in the middle image in Figure 8-10. I then selected a general area around the image and chose Filter ➪ Stylize ➪ Emboss to create the finished fossil image. Nobody's going to confuse my painting with a bona fide fossil, but it's not bad for a cartoon.

It's no accident Figure 8-10 features a swordfish instead of your everyday round-nosed carp. To snap to the horizontal axis, I had to establish the direction of my drag as being more horizontal than vertical. If I had, instead, dragged in a fish-faced convex arc, Photoshop would have interpreted my drag as vertical and snapped to the vertical axis.

Figure 8-10: To create the basic structure for our bony pal, I periodically pressed and released the Shift key while dragging with the paintbrush (top). Then I embellished the fish using the paintbrush and pencil (middle). Finally, I applied the Emboss filter to transform fish into fossil (bottom).

Painting with the smudge tool

Many first-time Photoshop artists misuse the smudge tool to soften color transitions. In fact, softening is the purpose of the blur tool. The smudge tool *smears* colors by shoving them into each other. The process bears more resemblance to the finger painting you did in grade school than to any traditional photographic-editing technique.

In Photoshop, the performance of the smudge tool depends in part on the settings of the Pressure and Finger Painting options. Both reside in the Smudge Tool Options palette (see Figure 8-11), which you access by pressing Return when the smudge tool is active. These two options work as follows:

✦ **Pressure:** Measured as a percentage of the brush shape, this option determines the distance the smudge tool drags a color. Higher percentages and larger brush shapes drag colors farthest. A Pressure setting of 100 percent equates to infinity, meaning the smudge tool drags a color from the beginning of your drag until the end of your drag, regardless of how far you drag. Cosmic, Daddy-O.

✦ **Finger Painting:** The folks at Adobe used to call this effect *dipping*, which I think more accurately expressed how the effect works. When you select this option, the smudge tool begins by applying a smidgen of foreground color, which it eventually blends in with the colors in the image. It's as if you dipped your finger in a color and then dragged it through an oil painting. Use the Pressure setting to specify the amount of foreground color applied. If you turn on Finger Painting and set the Pressure to 100 percent, the smudge tool behaves exactly like the paintbrush tool.

Tip

You can reverse the Finger Painting setting by Option-dragging. If the option is off, Option-dragging dips the tool into the foreground color. If Finger Painting is turned on, Option-dragging smudges normally.

Figure 8-11: Combined with brush shape, the Pressure and Finger Painting options are the most important considerations when using the smudge tool.

For some examples of the smudge tool in action, see Figure 8-12. This figure shows the effects of using the smudge tool set to four different Pressure percentages and with the Finger Painting option both off and on. In each instance, the brush shape is 13 pixels in diameter and the foreground color is set to black.

The third option highlighted in Figure 8-11 — Use All Layers (previously called Sample Merged) — instructs the smudge tool to grab colors in all visible layers and smudge them into the current layer. Whether the option is on or off, only the current layer is affected; the background and other layers remain intact.

For example, suppose the inverted eyes of the woman at the top of Figure 8-13 are on a different layer than the rest of the face. If I use the smudge tools on the eyes layer with Use All Layers turned off, Photoshop ignores the face layer when smudging the eyes. As a result, details like the nose and teeth remain unsmudged, as you can see in the lower left example. If I turn Use All Layers on, Photoshop lifts colors from the face layer and mixes them in with the eyes layer, as shown in the lower right example.

Figure 8-12: Eight drags with the smudge tool subject to different Pressure and Finger Painting settings.

Note that all this activity occurs exclusively on the eyes layer. To give you a better look, the two lower examples on the eyes layer are shown independently of those on the face layer in Figure 8-14. You can now clearly see the proliferation of face details mixed into the eyes in the right example. Meanwhile, the face layer remains absolutely unaffected.

Figure 8-13: The original image (top) features inverted eyes on a layer above the rest of the face. I first smudged the eyes with Use All Layers turned off (lower left) and then with the option turned on (lower right).

Figure 8-14: The eyes layer from the previous figure shown by itself.

Mopping up with the sponge tool

The sponge tool is actually a pretty darn straightforward tool, hardly worth expending valuable space in a book as tiny as this one. But I'm a compulsive explainer, so here's the deal: Press Return when the sponge tool is active to gain access to the Sponge Options palette. In the upper left corner of the palette is a pop-up menu that offers two options: Desaturate and Saturate.

✦ When set to Desaturate, the tool reduces the saturation of the colors over which you drag. When editing a grayscale image, the tool reduces the contrast.

✦ If you select the Saturate option, the sponge tool increases the saturation of the colors over which you drag or increases contrast in a grayscale image. Higher Pressure settings produce more dramatic results.

In Photoshop 5, you can switch between the Desaturate and Saturate modes from the keyboard. Press Shift-Option-J to select the Desaturate option. Press Shift-Option-A for Saturate.

Consider Color Plate 8-1. The upper left example shows the original PhotoDisc image. The upper right example shows the result of applying the sponge tool set to Desaturate. I dragged with the tool inside the pepper and around in the corner area. The Pressure was set to 100 percent. Notice the affected colors are on the wane, sliding toward gray. In the lower right example, the effect is even more pronounced. I applied the sponge tools here with great vim and vigor two additional times. Hardly any hint of color is left in these areas now.

To create the lower left example in Color Plate 8-1, I applied the sponge tool set to Saturate. This is where things get a little tricky. If you boost saturation levels with the sponge tool in the RGB or Lab color modes, you can achieve colors of absolutely neon intensity. However, these high-saturation colors don't stand a snowball's chance in a microwave of printing in CMYK. So I recommend you choose View ⇨ Preview ⇨ CMYK (⌘-Y) before boosting saturation levels with the sponge tool. This way, you can accurately view the results of your edits. After you're finished, choose View ⇨ Preview ⇨ CMYK to turn off the CMYK preview and return to the RGB view.

Figure 8-15 shows the yellow channel from each of the images in Color Plate 8-1. Because yellow is the most prevalent primary color in the image, it is the most sensitive to saturation adjustments. When I boosted the saturation in the lower left example, the yellow brightness values deepened, adding yellow ink to the CMYK image. When I lessened the saturation in the two right examples, the amount of ink diminished.

Figure 8-15: The yellow channel from Color Plate 8-1 shows the greatest amount of variation when reducing and boosting the saturation with the sponge tool.

One of Adobe's recommended purposes of the sponge tool is to reduce the saturation levels of out-of-gamut RGB colors before converting an image to the CMYK mode. I'm not too crazy about this use of the tool because it requires a lot of scrubbing. Generally, selecting the out-of-gamut area and reducing the colors using more automated controls is easier (as discussed in Chapter 16). You might prefer, instead, to use the sponge tool when a more selective, personal touch is required, as when curbing a distracting color that seems to leap a little too vigorously off the screen or boosting the saturation of a detail in the CMYK mode.

Brush Shape and Opacity

So far, I mentioned the words *brush shape* several times and I have yet to explain what the Sam Hill I'm talking about. Luckily, it's simple. The brush shape is the size and shape of the tip of your cursor when you use a paint or edit tool. A big, round brush shape paints or edits in broad strokes. A small, elliptical brush shape is useful for performing hairline adjustments.

Although Photoshop is not set up this way by default, it is capable of displaying a cursor whose outline reflects the selected brush shape. To access this incredibly useful cursor, press ⌘-K to bring up the Preferences dialog box and press ⌘-3 for the Display & Cursors panel. Then select Brush Size from the Painting Cursors radio buttons.

Unlike previous versions of Photoshop, Version 5 is not limited to displaying brush sizes of 300 pixels. You can now fill an entire 21-inch monitor with one big huge brush. (The actual brush size limit is 2,000 pixels, which is larger than any screen currently on the market.) Granted, a 21-inch brush is a bit excessive, but the point is, all limits are gone.

When using very small brushes, as when using the single-pixel pencil to do precise retouching, the cursor includes four dots around its perimeter, making the cursor easier to locate. If you need a little more help, press the Caps Lock key to access the more obvious crosshair cursor.

The Brushes palette

You access brush shapes by choosing Window ⇨ Palettes ⇨ Show Brushes to display the Brushes palette. Or you can press the F5 key. Figure 8-16 shows the Brushes palette with its pop-up menu wide open for your viewing pleasure.

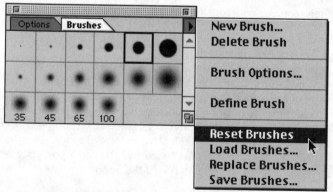

Figure 8-16: Photoshop's Brushes palette enables you to select a predefined brush shape or create one of your own.

You can switch brush shapes from the keyboard without displaying the Brushes palette. Press the left-bracket key, [, to select the previous brush shape in the palette; press the right-bracket key,], to select the next brush shape. You can also press Shift-[to select the first brush shape in the palette and Shift-] to select the last shape.

Editing a brush shape

To edit a brush shape in the Brushes palette, select the brush you want to change and choose Brush Options from the palette menu. To create a new brush shape, choose New Brush. Either way, the dialog box shown in Figure 8-17 appears. (If you choose the New Brush command, the Title bar is different, but the options are the same.)

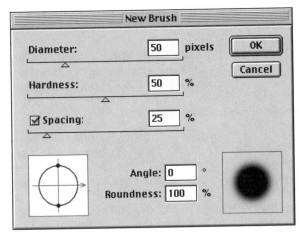

Figure 8-17: The Brush Options dialog box enables you to change the size, shape, and hardness of the brush shape.

If you hate menus — and who doesn't? — you can more conveniently edit a brush shape by simply double-clicking on it. To create a new brush shape, click once on an empty brush slot, as shown in the first example in Figure 8-18. (Incidentally, you can also delete a brush from the palette. To do so, press ⌘ to display the scissors cursor — as in the second example in Figure 8-18 — then click. It's a great little housekeeping tip.)

Figure 8-18: Clicking on an empty brush slot (left) brings up the New Brush dialog box so you can create a new brush shape. ⌘-clicking on a brush shape (right) deletes it from the palette.

Whether you're editing an existing brush or creating a new one, you have the following options at your disposal:

✦ **Diameter:** This option determines the width of the brush shape. If the brush shape is elliptical instead of circular, the Diameter value determines the longest dimension. You can enter any value from 1 to 999 pixels. Brush shapes with diameters of 30 pixels or higher are too large to display accurately in the Brushes palette and instead appear as circles with inset Diameter values.

✦ **Hardness:** Except when you use the pencil tool, brush shapes are always antialiased. You can further soften the edges of a brush, however, by dragging the Hardness slider bar away from 100 percent. The softest setting, 0 percent, gradually tapers the brush from a single solid color pixel at its center to a ring of transparent pixels around the brush's perimeter. Figure 8-19 demonstrates how low Hardness percentages expand the size of a 100-pixel brush beyond the Diameter value (as demonstrated by the examples set against black). Even a 100-percent hard brush shape expands slightly because it is antialiased. The Hardness setting is ignored when you use the pencil tool.

✦ **Spacing:** The Spacing option controls how frequently a tool affects an image as you drag, measured as a percentage of the brush shape. Suppose the Diameter of a brush shape is 12 pixels and the Spacing is set to 25 percent (the setting for all default brush shapes). For every 3 pixels (25 percent of 12 pixels) you drag with the paintbrush tool, Photoshop lays down a 12-pixel wide spot of color. A Spacing of 1 percent provides the most coverage, but may also slow down the performance of the tool. If you deselect the Spacing check box, the effect of the tool is wholly dependent on the speed at which you drag; this can be useful for creating splotchy or oscillating lines. Figure 8-20 shows examples.

✦ **Angle:** This option enables you to pivot a brush shape on its axes. Unless the brush is elliptical, though, this won't make a difference in the appearance of the brush shape.

Figure 8-19: A 100-pixel diameter brush shown as it appears when set to a variety of Hardness percentages. I changed the background pixels below from white to black, so you can see the actual diameter of each brush shape. The tick marks indicate 10-pixel increments.

✦ **Roundness:** Enter a value of less than 100 percent into the Roundness option to create an elliptical brush shape. The value measures the width of the brush as a percentage of its height, so a Roundness value of 5 percent results in a long, skinny brush shape.

You can adjust the angle of the brush dynamically by dragging the gray arrow inside the box to the left of the Angle and Roundness options. Drag the handles on either side of the black circle to make the brush shape elliptical, as demonstrated in Figure 8-21.

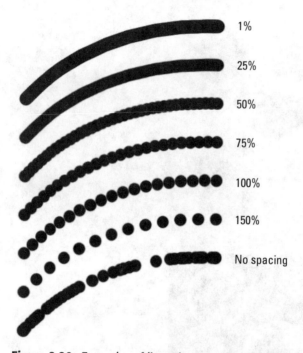

1%

25%

50%

75%

100%

150%

No spacing

Figure 8-20: Examples of lines drawn with different Spacing values in the Brush Options dialog box. Gaps or ridges generally begin to appear when the Spacing value exceeds 30 percent. The final line was created by turning off the Spacing option.

New Brush

Diameter: 40 pixels   OK

Hardness: 70 %   Cancel

☑ Spacing: 25 %

Angle: 46 °
Roundness: 48 %

Figure 8-21: Drag the gray arrow or the black handles to change the angle or roundness of a brush, respectively. The Angle and Roundness values update automatically, as does the preview of the brush in the lower right corner of the dialog box.

I heartily recommend you take a few moments soon to experiment at length with the Brush Options dialog box. By combining paint and edit tools with one or more specialized brush shapes, you can achieve artistic effects unlike anything permitted via traditional techniques. Starting with a PhotoDisc image lightened and filtered to serve as a template, I painted Figure 8-22 using the flat, 45-pixel brush shape shown in the dialog box. No other brush shape or special effect was applied. Think of what you can accomplish if you don't limit yourself as ridiculously as I did.

Figure 8-22: Just to show off, I painted over a scanned image with the paintbrush tool, using the brush shape shown in the dialog box at the top.

Creating and using custom brushes

You can define a custom brush shape by selecting a portion of your image that you want to change to a brush and choosing the Define Brush command from the Brushes palette pop-up menu.

In addition to giving you the flexibility to create a brush from some element in your image, Photoshop ships with a file called Assorted Brushes, which contains all kinds of little symbols and doodads you can assign as custom brush shapes. You can load the contents of the Assorted Brushes file into the Brushes palette by choosing the Replace Brushes command from the palette menu (or Load Brushes if you don't want to lose the brush shapes that currently occupy the palette). You'll find Assorted Brushes in the Brushes & Patterns folder, which resides in the Goodies folder inside the main Photoshop folder. Figure 8-23 shows an inspirational image I created using Photoshop's predefined custom brushes.

Figure 8-23: Yes, it's Boris, the sleeping custom-brush guy. If you suspect this image is meant to suggest custom brushes are more amusing than utilitarian, you're right. The brushes from the Assorted Brushes file appear on the right.

To return to the original default brush shapes, choose Reset Brushes from the palette menu. You then have the option of either replacing the existing brushes with the default brushes or simply adding the default brushes to the end of the palette.

In Photoshop, you can adjust the performance of a custom brush in the following ways:

✦ **Brush options:** Choose the Brush Options command from the palette menu or double-click on the custom brush in the Brushes palette to bring up the dialog box shown in Figure 8-24. Here you can adjust the spacing of the brush shape and specify whether Photoshop *anti-aliases* (softens) the edges or leaves them as is. If the brush is sufficiently large, the Anti-aliased check box appears dimmed. All custom brushes are hard-edged when you use the pencil tool.

Figure 8-24: The dialog box that appears when you double-click on a custom brush

✦ **Brush color:** The foreground color affects a custom brush just as it does a standard brush shape. To erase with the brush, select white as the foreground color. To paint in color, select a color.

✦ **Opacity and brush modes:** The setting of the Opacity slider bar and the brush modes pop-up menu also affect the application of custom brushes. For more information on these options, keep reading this chapter.

You can achieve some unusual and, sometimes, interesting effects by activating the smudge tool's Finger Painting option and painting in the image window with a custom brush. At high Pressure settings, say 80 to 90 percent, the effect is rather like applying oil paint with a hairy paintbrush, as illustrated in Figure 8-25.

Figure 8-25: I created this organic, expressive image by combining the smudge tool's dipping capability with four custom brushes. I don't know what those finger-like growths are, but they'd probably feel right at home in an aquarium.

Opacity, pressure, and exposure

Another way to change the performance of a paint or edit tool is to modify the amount of color or pressure that Photoshop applies to the canvas. You modify this behavior by entering a value into the option box in the upper right corner of the Options palette. Photoshop assigns one of three labels to this option box, as illustrated in Figure 8-26.

Figure 8-26: The option boxes in the upper right corner of the Options palette assumes one of these functions, depending on the selected paint or edit tool.

✦ **Opacity:** The Opacity value determines the translucency of colors applied with the paint bucket, gradient, line, pencil, paintbrush, eraser, or rubber stamp tool. At 100 percent, the applied colors appear opaque, completely covering the image behind them. (The one exception is the paintbrush with Wet Edges active, which is always translucent.) At lower settings, the applied colors mix with the existing colors in the image.

✦ **Pressure:** The Pressure value affects different tools in different ways. When you use the airbrush tool, the Pressure value controls the opacity of each spot of color the tool delivers. The effect appears unique because the airbrush lays each spot of color onto the previous spot, mixing them together. This results in a progressive effect. Meanwhile, the paintbrush and pencil tools are not progressive, so their spots blend to form smooth lines.

When you use the smudge tool, the Pressure value controls the distance the tool drags colors in the image. And in the case of the blur, sharpen, or sponge tool, the value determines the degree to which the tool changes the focus or saturation of the image, 1 percent being the minimum and 100 percent being the maximum.

✦ **Exposure:** If you select the dodge or burn tool, the title of this particular option box changes to Exposure. A setting of 100 percent applies the maximum amount of lightening or darkening to an image, which is still far short of either absolute white or black.

The factory default setting for all Exposure and Pressure values is 50 percent; the default setting for all Opacity values is 100 percent.

Tip

As long as one of the tools listed in this section is selected, you can change the Opacity, Pressure, or Exposure setting in 10 percent increments by pressing a number key on the keyboard or keypad. Press 1 to change the setting to 10 percent, press 2 for 20 percent, and so on, all the way up to 0 for 100 percent.

Want to change the Opacity, Pressure, or Exposure setting in 1 percent increments? No problem — just press two keys in a row. Press 4 twice for 44 percent, 0 and 7 for 7 percent, and so on. This tip and the previous one work whether or not the Options palette is visible. Get in the habit of using the number keys and you'll thank yourself later.

Tapered Lines

Photoshop provides two ways to create tapering lines reminiscent of brushstrokes created using traditional techniques. You can specify the length over which a line fades by entering a value into the Fade option box, as described in the next section. Or, if you own a pressure-sensitive drawing tablet, you can draw brushstrokes that fade in and out automatically according to the amount of pressure you apply to the stylus. Both techniques enable you to introduce an element of spontaneity into what, otherwise, seems at times like an absolute world of computer graphics.

Fading the paint

All three paint tools offer Fade check boxes in their respective Options palettes, which enable you to create lines that gradually fade away as you drag. Figure 8-27 shows the Fade option as it appears in the Paintbrush Options palette, along with some examples of the effect.

After selecting the Fade check box, enter a value into the option box to specify the distance over which the color fading should occur. The fading begins at the start of your drag and is measured in brush shapes.

For example, assume the foreground color is black. If you enter 40 into the Fade option box — as in Figure 8-27 — Photoshop paints 40 brush shapes, the first in black and the remaining 39 in increasingly lighter shades of gray.

Figure 8-27: This is the Fade check box as it appears in the Paintbrush Options palette, along with four examples.

Cross-Reference

In Photoshop, you can paint gradient lines by selecting the To Background radio button. Photoshop fades the line from the foreground color to the background color, much the same way the gradient tool fades the interior of a selection. For more information on the gradient tool, see the "Applying Gradient Fills" section of Chapter 9.

Fading and spacing

The physical length of a fading line is dependent both on the Fade value and on the value entered into the Spacing option box in the Brush Options dialog box, discussed back in the "Editing a brush shape" section earlier in this chapter.

To recap, the Spacing value determines the frequency with which Photoshop lays down brush shapes, and the Fade value determines the number of brush shapes laid down. Therefore, as demonstrated in Figure 8-28, a high Fade value combined with a high Spacing value creates the longest line.

Creating sparkles and comets

Fading lines may strike you as pretty ho-hum, but they enable you to create some no-brainer, cool-mandoo effects, especially when combined with the Shift key techniques discussed earlier, in the "Painting a straight line" section.

1%

12%

25%

37%

50%

Figure 8-28: Here are five fading lines drawn with the paintbrush tool. In each case, the Fade option is set to 36 brush shapes. I changed the Spacing value incrementally from 1 to 50 percent, as labeled.

Figures 8-29 and 8-30 demonstrate two of the most obvious uses for fading straight lines: creating sparkles and comets. The top image in Figure 8-29 features two sets of sparkles, each made up of 16 straight lines emanating from the sparkle's center. To create the smaller sparkle on the right, I set the Fade value to 60 and drew each of the four perpendicular lines with the paintbrush tool. I changed the Fade value to 36 before drawing the four 45-degree diagonal lines. The eight very short lines that occur between the perpendicular and diagonal lines were drawn with a Fade value of 20. I, likewise, created the larger sparkle on the left by periodically adjusting the Fade value, this time from 90 to 60 to 42.

For comparison's sake, I used different techniques to add a few more sparkles to the bottom image in Figure 8-29. To achieve the reflection in the upper left corner of the image, I chose Filter ➪ Render ➪ Lens Flare and selected 50-300mm Zoom from the Lens Type options. (Lens Flare works exclusively in the RGB mode, so I had to switch to RGB to apply the filter, even though Figure 8-29 is a grayscale image.)

I created the two tiny sparkles on the right edge of the bumper using a custom brush shape. I merely selected the custom brush, set the foreground color to white, and clicked once with the paintbrush tool in each location. So many sparkles make for a tremendously shiny image.

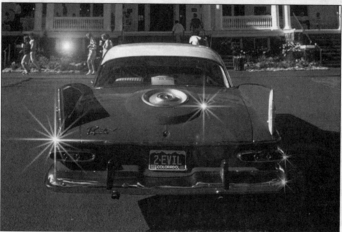

Figure 8-29: I drew the sparkles in the top image using the paintbrush tool. The second image features a reflection applied with the Lens Flare filter (upper left corner) and two dabs of a custom brush shape (right edge of the bumper).

In Figure 8-30—a nostalgic tribute to the days when gas was cheap and the whole family would pile in the Plymouth for a Sunday drive through space—I copied the car and pasted it on top of a NASA photograph of Jupiter. I then went nuts clicking and Shift-clicking with the paintbrush tool to create the comets—well, if you must know, they're actually cosmic rays—you see shooting through and around the car. It's so real, you can practically hear the in-dash servo unit warning, "Duck and cover!"

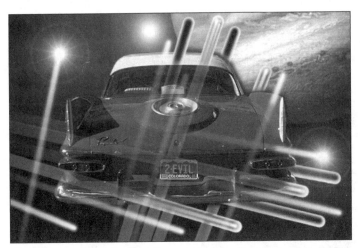

Figure 8-30: To create the threatening cosmic rays, I set the Fade option to 110 and then clicked and Shift-clicked on opposite sides of the image with the paintbrush tool.

After masking portions of the image (a process described at length in Chapter 12), I drew rays behind the car and even one ray that shoots up through the car and out the spare tire. The three bright lights in the image — above the left fin, above the roof, and next to the right-turn signal — are more products of the Lens Flare filter in the RGB mode.

Note

I drew all the fading lines in Figures 8-29 and 8-30 with the paintbrush tool, using a variety of default brush shapes. Because I didn't edit any brush shape, the Spacing value for all lines was a constant 25 percent.

Setting up pressure-sensitive tablets

The pressure-sensitive tablet may be the single most useful piece of optional hardware available to computer artists. Not only can you draw with a pen-like *stylus* instead of a clunky mouse, you also can dynamically adjust the thickness of lines and the opacity of colors by changing the amount of pressure you apply to the stylus. Several vendors currently manufacture pressure-sensitive tablets, but the most dynamic vendor — and the one with the best products — continues to be Wacom (*www.wacom.com*).

Of these, the best introductory all-purpose tablet is Wacom's $200 ArtPad II. Measuring a diminutive 7 × 7.25 inches (with an active area of 4 × 5 inches), this thing is smaller than a standard mouse pad. The tablet offers 256 levels of pressure and a resolution of thousands of lines per inch. (Like any digital tracking device, a tablet uses pixels to communicate the location of your stylus. The higher the resolution, the smoother your mouse movements.)

Wacom's cordless stylus comes in several different varieties — illustrated in Figure 8-31 — each of which weighs less than an ounce. All of them feature both a pressure-sensitive nib and at least one side switch for double-clicking or choosing macros. Many offer erasers at the opposite end from the nib. When you use the eraser, Photoshop automatically switches to the eraser tool. Then there's the WideBody series, where the nib includes real pencil lead or ink. This way, you can see what you're drawing both on paper and on screen. Oh, what miracles the modern age brings!

Figure 8-31: Wacom boasts the largest pressure-sensitive stylus library of any tablet vendor. You can customize the settings for your particular stylus from a pop-up menu in the central control panel.

Wacom's most recent miracle is the PL-300. Pictured in Figure 8-32, this tablet combines a drawing tablet with a fully functioning color LCD screen. If your computer includes an extra monitor port or video card, you can connect the PL-300 as a second screen. Then you can paint directly on the screen, just as you used to back in those ancient days when you used pencil and paper. It's nothing short of a computerized canvas. As I write this, the price ($2,700) is high enough to dissuade all but the most serious few. But it certainly fires the imagination — the day they combine a PressView and tablet all into one, I'm all over it.

If you're an artist and you've never experimented with a pressure-sensitive tablet — whether LCD-equipped or not — I recommend you do so soon. You'll be amazed at how much it increases your range of artistic options. Thirty minutes after I installed my first tablet back in 1990, I had executed the cartoon you see in Figure 8-33. Whether you like the image or not — I'll admit there's a certain troglodyte quality to the slope of his forehead, and that jaw could bust a coconut — it shows off the tablet's capability to paint tapering lines and accommodate artistic expression.

Figure 8-32: The PL-300 includes an LCD monitor so that you can draw directly on the screen.

If you do own a Wacom tablet, you're in luck. Wacom offers a collection of pressure-sensitive painting and editing filters called PenTools. The filters are fun, easy to use, and best of all, free. You can check them out on the CD at the back of this book. The only caveat is that you need a Wacom-brand tablet to use them.

Undoing pressure-sensitive lines

In the old days, pressure-sensitive lines were a pain to undo. Because a stylus is so sensitive to gradual pressure, you can unwittingly let up and repress the stylus during what you perceive as a single drag. If, after doing so, you decide you don't like the line and press ⌘-Z (Edit ➪ Undo), Photoshop deletes only the last portion of the line, because it detected a release midway.

This is why it's a good idea to get in the habit of using ⌘-Option-Z, if you haven't already. Each time you press this shortcut, you take another step back in the history of your image, permitting you to eliminate every bit of a line regardless of how many times you let up on the stylus. (See Chapter 10 for more information on Photoshop 5's multiple undos.)

Figure 8-33: Although I painted this caricature years ago, it still demonstrates the range of artistic freedom provided by a pressure-sensitive tablet.

Tip

Better yet, create a new layer before you paint with or without a stylus. Then you can refine your lines and erase them without harming the original appearance of your image. (You can do this without layers using the history brush, again explained in Chapter 10, but a relatively old-fashioned layer tends to be less hassle.)

Pressure-sensitive options

All paint and edit tools, as well as the eraser and rubber stamp, provide three check boxes for controlling Photoshop's reaction to stylus pressure (see Figure 8-34). Available from the Options palette only when a pressure-sensitive tablet is hooked up to your computer, these options include the following:

✦ **Size:** If you select the Size check box, Photoshop varies the thickness of the line. The more pressure you apply, the thicker the line. The Size check box is selected by default. Figure 8-35 shows three paintbrush lines drawn with the Size option selected. I drew the first line using a hard brush, the second with a soft brush, and the third with a hard brush and with the Wet Edges check box selected.

Figure 8-34: Photoshop provides three check boxes for interpreting the signals from a pressure-sensitive tablet.

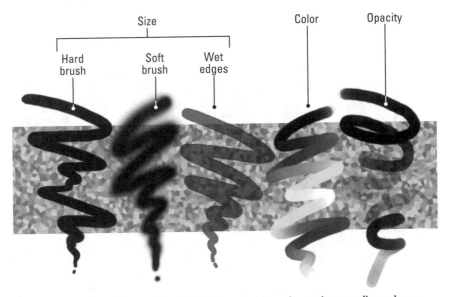

Figure 8-35: The effects of the Size, Color, and Opacity options on lines drawn with the paintbrush tool and a pressure-sensitive tablet.

✦ **Color:** Select this option to create custom gradient lines. Full pressure paints in the foreground color, slight pressure paints in the background color, medium pressure paints a mix of the two.

✦ **Opacity:** This option paints an opaque coat of foreground color at full pressure that dwindles to transparency at slight pressure.

Because Photoshop presents its pressure options as check boxes, you can select more than one option at a time. For example, you can select both Size and Color to instruct Photoshop to change both the thickness and color of a line as you bear down or lift up on the stylus.

Brush Modes

When a painting or editing tool is active, the pop-up menu in the Options palettes provides access to Photoshop's brush modes, which control how the colors applied by the tools affect existing colors in the image. Figure 8-36 shows which brush modes are available when you select various tools.

With the exception of the specialized brush modes provided for the dodge, burn, and sponge tools, brush modes are merely variations on the blend modes described in Chapter 19. Read this section to get a brief glimpse of brush modes; read Chapter 19 for a more detailed account that should appeal to brush-mode aficionados.

Figure 8-36: The number of options in the brush modes pop-up menu varies depending on whether you select a paint tool (left), an edit tool (top right), the dodge or burn tool (middle right), or the sponge tool (bottom right).

You can now change brush modes from the keyboard by pressing Shift-plus (+) or Shift-minus (−). Shift-plus takes you to the next brush mode listed in the pop-up menu, Shift-minus selects the previous blend mode. It's a great way to cycle through the brush modes without losing your place in the image.

The 19 paint tool modes

Photoshop offers 19 possible brush modes when you use the pencil, paintbrush, airbrush, or any of the other tools shown along the left side of Figure 8-36. (The one mode missing from the figure is Threshold, which is an alternative to Normal in certain color modes.) To show you what these brush modes look like when applied to an image, Color Plates 8-2, 8-3, and 8-4 illustrate all 19. In each case, I used the paintbrush tool to apply a bit of green graffiti to a work of fourteenth-century religious iconography. Who among us hasn't been tempted with the primal urge to paint "Kilroy" on something old and priceless? Now, thanks to the miracle of digital imagery, you need resist this temptation no longer.

Just as you can cycle from one brush mode to the next from the keyboard, you can jump directly to a specific brush mode as well. Just press Shift-Option and a letter key. For example, Shift-Option-N selects the Normal mode, Shift-Option-C selects the Color mode. I list the letter key for each brush mode in parentheses along with its description below:

Photoshop 5.0

> ✦ **Normal (N):** Choose this mode to paint or edit an image normally. A paint tool coats the image with the foreground color, and an edit tool manipulates the existing colors in an image according to the Opacity or Pressure value.

> ✦ **Threshold (L):** Two color modes prevent Photoshop from rendering soft or translucent edges. The black-and-white and indexed modes (Image ⇨ Mode ⇨ Bitmap and Image ⇨ Mode ⇨ Indexed Color) simply don't have enough colors to go around. When painting in such a low-color image, Photoshop replaces the Normal brush mode with Threshold, which results in harsh, jagged edges, just like a stroke painted with the pencil tool. You can alternatively dither the soft edges by selecting the Dissolve mode, as described next.

> ✦ **Dissolve (I):** This mode and the six that follow are not applicable to the edit tools (though I wonder why—the Dissolve mode would be especially useful with the smudge tool). Dissolve scatters colors along the edge of a brushstroke randomly throughout the course of your drag. The Dissolve mode produces the most pronounced effects when used with soft brushes and the airbrush tool.

> ✦ **Behind (Q):** This one is applicable exclusively to layers with transparent backgrounds. When Behind is selected, the paint tool applies color behind the image on the active layer, showing through only in the transparent and translucent areas. In Color Plate 8-2, for example, I painted over the Madonna's head, and yet the brushstroke appears behind her head because she is positioned on an independent layer. When you're working on an image without layers or on the background layer of a multilayered image, the Behind mode is dimmed.

> ✦ **Multiply (M):** The Multiply mode combines the foreground color with an existing color in an image to create a third color, darker than the other two. Using the multiply analogy, red times white is red, red times yellow is orange, red times green is brown, red times blue is violet, and so on. As discussed in Chapter 5, this is subtractive (CMYK) color theory at work. The effect is

almost exactly like drawing with felt-tipped markers, except the colors don't bleed. Check out the first Kilroy in Color Plate 8-3 to see the Multiply mode in action.

The multiply mode has no effect on the paintbrush when it's set to Wet Edges; the Wet Edges brush already multiplies.

✦ **Screen (S):** The inverse of the Multiply mode, Screen combines the foreground color with each colored pixel you paint over to create a third color, lighter than the other two. Red on white is white, red on yellow is off-white, red on green is yellow, and red on blue is pink. The Screen mode uses additive (RGB) color theory. If the effect has a traditional counterpart, it's like some impossibly bright, radioactive Uranium-238 highlighter, hitherto used only by G-Men to mark the pants' cuffs of Communist sympathizers.

Because the Wet Edges option always multiplies, combining it with the Screen mode must render the brush invisible. If the paintbrush tool isn't working, this could be your problem.

✦ **Overlay (O):** Overlay, Soft Light, and Hard Light are cousins. Each mode multiplies the dark pixels in an image and screens the light pixels as you lay down color with a paint tool. But although related, the three modes are not variations on an identical theme. In other words, you can't emulate the Soft Light mode by simply applying the Hard Light mode at 70 percent or some similar opacity.

Of the three modes, Overlay is the kindest. Overlay always enhances contrast and boosts the saturation of colors in an image. In fact, Overlay works rather like a colored version of the sponge tool set to Saturate. It mixes the colors in the image with the foreground color to come up with a vivid blend that is almost always visually pleasing. Overlay may be the most interesting and downright useful brush mode of the bunch.

✦ **Soft Light (F):** This mode applies a subtle glazing of color to an image. In fact, Soft Light is remarkably similar to painting a diluted acrylic wash to a canvas. Soft Light never completely covers the underlying detail — even black or white applied at 100 percent Opacity does no more than darken or lighten the image — but it does slightly diminish contrast.

✦ **Hard Light (H):** This mode might better be named *Obfuscate*. It's as if you were applying a thicker, more opaque wash to the image. You might think of Hard Light as Normal with a whisper of underlying detail mixed in.

For examples of Overlay, Soft Light, and Hard Light, check out the middle brushstrokes in Color Plate 8-3.

✦ **Color Dodge (D):** This brush mode lightens the pixels in an image according to the lightness or darkness of the foreground color. Color Dodge produces a harsher, chalkier effect than the Screen mode and is designed to act like a dodge tool that also adds color. At 100 percent Opacity, even painting with black has a lightening effect.

✦ **Color Burn (B):** If Color Dodge is like drawing with chalk, Color Burn is like drawing with coal. It darkens pixels according to the lightness or darkness of the foreground color and is designed to simulate a colored version of the burn tool. For examples of Color Dodge and Color Burn, look to the last two Kilroys in Color Plate 8-3.

✦ **Darken (K):** Ah, back to the old familiars. If you choose the Darken mode, Photoshop applies a new color to a pixel only if that color is darker than the present color of the pixel. Otherwise, the pixel is left unchanged. The mode works on a channel-by-channel basis, so it might change a pixel in the green channel, for example, without changing the pixel in the red or blue channel. I used this mode to create the first brushstroke of Color Plate 8-4.

✦ **Lighten (G):** The opposite of the previous mode, Lighten ensures that Photoshop applies a new color to a pixel only if the color is lighter than the present color of the pixel. Otherwise, the pixel is left unchanged. On or off — either you see the color or you don't.

✦ **Difference (E):** When a paint tool is set to the Difference mode, Photoshop subtracts the brightness value of the foreground color from the brightness value of the pixels in the image. If the result is a negative number, Photoshop simply makes it positive. The result of this complex-sounding operation is an inverted effect. Black has no effect on an image; white inverts it completely. Colors in between create psychedelic effects. In the third example of Color Plate 8-4, for example, the Difference mode inverts the green paint to create a red brushstroke.

Tip

Because the Difference mode inverts an image, it results in an outline around the brushstroke. You can make this outline thicker by using a softer brush shape. For a really trippy effect, select the paintbrush tool, turn on Wet Edges, and apply the Difference mode with a soft brush shape.

✦ **Exclusion (X):** When I first asked Mark Hamburg, lead programmer for Photoshop, for his definition of Exclusion, he kindly explained, "Exclusion applies a probabilistic, fuzzy-set-theoretic, symmetric difference to each channel." Don't think about it too long — your frontal lobe will turn to boiled squash. After Mark remembered he was communicating with a lower life form, he told me (very slowly) that Exclusion inverts an image in much the same way as Difference, except colors in the middle of the spectrum mix to form medium gray. Exclusion typically results in high-contrast effects with less color saturation than Difference. My suggestion is you try the Difference mode first. If you're looking for something a little different, press ⌘-Z and try Exclusion instead. (Both Difference and Exclusion brushstrokes appear in Color Plate 8-4.)

✦ **Hue (U):** Understanding the next few modes requires a color theory recap. Remember how the HSL color model calls for three color channels? One is for hue, the value that explains the colors in an image; the second is for saturation, which represents the intensity of the colors; and the third is for luminosity, which explains the lightness and darkness of colors. If you choose the Hue brush mode, therefore, Photoshop applies the hue from the foreground color without changing any saturation or luminosity values in the existing image.

None of the HSL brush modes — Hue, Saturation, Color, or Luminosity — is available when painting within grayscale images.

✦ **Saturation (T):** If you choose this mode, Photoshop changes the intensity of the colors in an image without changing the colors themselves or the lightness and darkness of individual pixels. In Color Plate 8-4, Saturation has the effect of breathing new life into those ancient egg-tempura colors.

✦ **Color (C):** Color mode might be more appropriately titled *Hue and Saturation*. Color enables you to change the colors in an image and the intensity of those colors without changing the lightness and darkness of individual pixels.

The Color mode is most often used to colorize grayscale photographs. Open a grayscale image and then choose Image ⇨ Mode ⇨ RGB Color to convert the image to the RGB mode. Then select the colors you want to use and start painting. The Color mode ensures the details in the image remain completely intact.

✦ **Luminosity (Y):** The opposite of the Color mode, Luminosity changes the lightness and darkness of pixels, but leaves the hue and saturation values unaffected. Frankly, this mode is rarely useful. But its counterpart — the Luminosity blend mode — is exceptionally useful when applied to layers. Read Chapter 19 to find out more.

The three dodge and burn modes

Phew, that takes care of the brush modes available to the paint tools, the smudge tool, and the two focus tools. I already explained the Desaturate and Saturate modes available to the sponge tool (in the "Mopping up with the sponge tool" section of this chapter). That leaves us with the three brush modes available to the dodge and burn tools.

As with other brush modes, you can select the dodge and burn modes from the keyboard. Just press Shift-Option and the letter in parentheses below.

✦ **Shadows (W):** Along with the Midtones and Highlights modes (described next), Shadows is unique to the dodge and burn tools. When you select this mode, the dodge and burn tools affect dark pixels in an image more dramatically than they affect light pixels and shades in between.

✦ **Midtones (V):** Select this mode to apply the dodge or burn tools equally to all but the very lightest or darkest pixels in an image.

✦ **Highlights (Z):** When you select this option, the dodge and burn tools affect light pixels in an image more dramatically than they affect dark pixels and shades in between.

Selecting Shadows when using the dodge tool or selecting Highlights when using the burn tool has an equalizing effect on an image. Figure 8-37 shows how using either of these functions and setting the Exposure slider bar to 100 percent lightens or darkens pixels in an image to nearly identical brightness values.

Figure 8-37: The dodge and burn tool applied at 100 percent Exposure settings subject to each of the three applicable brush modes.

✦   ✦   ✦

Filling and Stroking

Filling Portions of an Image

No explanation of filling and stroking would be complete without a definition, so here goes: To *fill* a selection or layer is to put color inside it; to *stroke* a selection or layer is to put color around it. Some folks prefer the term "outline" to "stroke," but I defer to PostScript terminology because that's where this whole desktop graphics thing started. Besides, when I think outline, I think perimeter, boundary, enclosure, prison, let me out of here. Stroke is more like brush, caress, pet, puppy, warm fire, glad heart. I'm a joker, I'm a smoker, I'm a midnight stroker. I'd rather be stroking. Stop me before I stroke again. And, that timeless favorite, keep on strokin'. So you see, people who prefer the word "outline" have no soul.

But whatever you call them, Photoshop's fill and stroke functions are so straightforward that you may have long since dismissed them as wimpy little tools with remarkably limited potential. But the truth is, you can do a world of stuff with them. In this chapter, for example, I'll show you how to fill selections using nifty keyboard shortcuts, how to create an antique framing effect, how to make the most of Photoshop's new gradient tools, and how to add an arrowhead to a curving line, all in addition to the really basic stuff every Photoshop user needs to know.

As the poet said, "Teacher don't you *fill* me up with your rules, I know *strokin's* not allowed in school." I'd love to share the entire transcript from "Strokin' in the Boy's Room," but this is, after all, a family book.

Filling an Area with Color

You can fill an area of an image with color in four ways:

✦ **The paint bucket tool:** You can apply the foreground color or a repeating pattern to areas of related color in an image by clicking in the image window with the paint bucket tool (known in some circles as the fill tool). For example, if you want to turn all midnight blue pixels in an image into red pixels, set the foreground color to red and then click on one of the blue pixels.

✦ **The Fill command:** Select the portion of the image you want to color and then fill the entire selection with the foreground color or a repeating pattern by choosing Edit ➪ Fill.

Tip

To choose the Fill command without so much as moving the mouse, press Shift-Delete.

✦ **Delete key techniques:** After selecting part of a single-layer image — or part of the Background layer in a multilayered image — you can fill the selection with the background color by pressing the Delete key. On any other layer, press ⌘-Delete. To fill the selection with the foreground color, press Option-Delete.

✦ **The gradient tool:** Drag across a selection with a gradient tool to fill it with a multicolor gradation. in Photoshop 5, you can choose between five styles of gradation by pressing Shift-G to cycle between gradient tools.

The following sections discuss each of these options in depth.

The paint bucket tool

Unlike remedial paint bucket tools in other painting programs, which apply paint exclusively within outlined areas or areas of solid color, the Photoshop paint bucket tool offers several useful adjustment options. To explore them, double-click on the paint bucket icon in the toolbox to display the Paint Bucket Options palette, shown in Figure 9-1. (Or you can press the K key to select the paint bucket tool and then press Return to display the Options palette.)

Figure 9-1: The Paint Bucket Options palette governs the performance of the paint bucket tool.

The brush mode pop-up menu and the Opacity value work like their counterparts in the Paintbrush Options palette, which I covered at length in Chapter 8. But in case you need a recap, here's how these and other options work, in the order they appear in the palette:

✦ **Brush modes:** Select an option from the brush mode pop-up menu to specify how and when color is applied. For example, if you select Darken (Shift-Option-K), the paint bucket tool affects a pixel in the image only if the foreground color is darker than that pixel. If you select Color (Shift-Option-C), the paint bucket colorizes the image without changing the brightness value of the pixels.

In Color Plate 9-1, for example, I used the Color mode to change a few oranges to blue and the background to green, all by clicking on five different spots with the paint bucket tool. I then touched up the stray pixels the paint bucket didn't catch with the paintbrush and airbrush tools.

✦ **Opacity:** Enter a new value or press a number key to change the translucency of a color applied with the paint bucket.

✦ **Tolerance:** You can raise or lower the Tolerance value to increase or decrease the number of pixels affected by the paint bucket tool. The Tolerance value represents a range in brightness values, as measured from the pixel which you click on with the paint bucket.

Immediately after you click on a pixel, Photoshop reads the brightness value of that pixel from each color channel. Next, the program calculates a color range based on the Tolerance value — which can vary from 0 to 255. The program adds the Tolerance to the brightness value of the pixel on which you clicked to determine the top of the range, and subtracts the Tolerance from the pixel's brightness value to determine the bottom of the range. For example, if the pixel's brightness value is 100 and the Tolerance value is 32, the top of the range is 132, and the bottom is 68.

After establishing a Tolerance range, Photoshop applies the foreground color to any pixel that both falls inside the range and touches some other affected pixel. (This way, the paint bucket fills an isolated area, rather than seeping out into every similarly colored pixel in the image.)

Figure 9-2 shows the result of clicking on the same pixel three separate times, each time using a different Tolerance value. In Color Plate 9-1, I raised the Tolerance to 120. But even with this high setting, I had to click several times to recolor all the nooks and crannies of the oranges. The moral is, don't get too hung up on getting the Tolerance exactly right — no matter how you paint it, the bucket is not a precise tool.

Figure 9-2: The results of applying the paint bucket tool to the exact pixel after setting the Tolerance value to 16 (top), 32 (middle), and 64 (bottom). In each case, the foreground color is light gray.

✦ **Anti-aliased:** Select this option to soften the effect of the paint bucket tool. As demonstrated in the left-hand example of Figure 9-3, Photoshop creates a border of translucent color between the filled pixels and their unaffected neighbors. If you don't want to soften the transition, turn off the Anti-aliased check box. Photoshop then fills only those pixels that fall inside the Tolerance range, as demonstrated in the right example of the figure.

Figure 9-3: The results of turning on (left) and off (right) the Anti-aliased check box prior to using the paint bucket tool. It all depends on whether you want cottage cheese or little spiky coral edges.

✦ **Contents:** In this pop-up menu, you can choose whether you want to apply the foreground color or a repeating pattern created using Edit ⇨ Define Pattern. The Define Pattern command is covered in the "Applying Repeating Patterns" section of Chapter 10.

✦ **Use All Layers:** Select this option to make the paint bucket see beyond the current layer. When the option is selected, the tool takes all visible layers into account when calculating the area to fill. Mind you, it only fills the active layer, but the way it fills an area is dictated by all layers.

For an example of Use All Layers, look no further than Figure 9-4. The dog sits on one layer and the fire hydrant rests on another layer directly below it. If I were to click on the fire hydrant when the dog layer was active and the Use All Layers check box was turned off, I'd fill everything around the dog. The paint bucket couldn't see the hydrant; all the paint bucket could see would be the transparent area of the dog layer, so it would try to fill that area. To avoid this, I selected Use All Layers and then clicked on the hydrant. With Use All Layers on, the paint bucket could see all layers, so it contained its fill within the hydrant, as in the second example of the figure.

Figure 9-4: Although dog and hydrant are on separate layers (top), I can mix them together with Use All Layers. This option enables me to fill an area of the hydrant (middle), even though the dog layer is active. Then I paint in front of and behind the fill without harming the hydrant (bottom).

Because the fill and hydrant were on separate layers, I could edit the two independently of each other. I used the airbrush to paint inside and behind the fill alternatively (using the Behind brush mode, discussed in the previous chapter). I painted the teeth and eyes with the paintbrush and used the smudge tool to mix colors around the white fill. (Naturally, I had to turn on the Use All Layers check box inside the Smudge Tool Options palette as well.) As a result, all the bizarre alterations you see in the bottom example of Figure 9-4 were applied to the dog layer. I didn't change a single pixel in the hydrant layer (which is a good thing— in light of my changes, I might like to get that hydrant back).

Tip

To limit the area affected by the paint bucket, select a portion of the image before using the tool. As when using a paint or edit tool, the region outside the selection outline is protected from the paint bucket. To see an interesting application of this, skip ahead to the "Using the paint bucket inside a selection" section later in this chapter.

When working on a layer, you can, likewise, protect pixels by turning on the Preserve Transparency check box in the Layers palette. Like all layering issues, I cover Preserve Transparency in Chapter 13.

Tip

Here's one more paint bucket tip for good measure: You can use the paint bucket to color the empty window area around your image. First, make your image window larger than your image, so you can see some gray canvas area around the image. Now Shift-click with the paint bucket to fill the canvas area with the foreground color. This technique can come in handy if you're creating a presentation or you simply don't care for the default shade of gray.

The Fill command

The one problem with the paint bucket tool is its lack of precision. Although undeniably convenient, the effects of the Tolerance value are so difficult to predict, you typically have to click with the tool, choose Edit ➪ Undo when you don't like the result, adjust the Tolerance value, and reclick with the tool several times more before you fill the image as desired. For my part, I rarely use the paint bucket for any purpose other than filling same-colored areas. On my machine, the Tolerance option is nearly always set to 0 and Anti-alias is generally off, which puts me right back in the all-the-subtlety-of-dumping-paint-out-of-a-bucket camp.

A better option is to select the area you want to fill and choose Edit ➪ Fill or press Shift-Delete. (If you prefer function keys, try Shift-F5.) In this way, you can define the exact area of the image you want to color using the entire range of Photoshop's selection tools, which are so extensive they consume all four chapters in Part IV. For example, instead of putting your faith in the paint bucket tool's Anti-aliased option, you can draw a selection outline that features hard edges in one area, antialiased edges elsewhere, and downright blurry edges in between.

When you press Shift-Delete, Photoshop displays the Fill dialog box shown in Figure 9-5. In this dialog box, you can apply a translucent color or pattern by entering a value into the Opacity option box. You can also choose a brush mode option from the Mode pop-up menu. In addition to its inherent precision, the Fill command maintains all the functionality of the paint bucket tool — and then some.

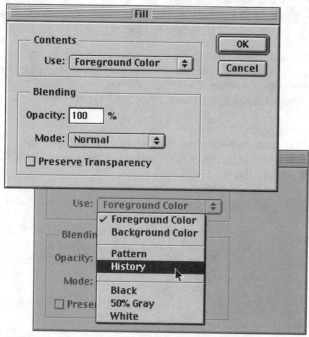

Figure 9-5: The Fill dialog box combines the Opacity and brush mode options from the Paint Bucket Options palette with an expanded collection of Contents options.

If you display the Contents pop-up menu, as shown in the lower example in Figure 9-5, you'll see a collection of things you can use to fill the selected area. Foreground Color and Pattern perform the same functions they do with the paint bucket tool. You can also fill a selection with the Background Color and such monochrome options as Black, White, and 50% Gray. Black and White are useful if the foreground and background colors have been changed from their defaults; 50% Gray fills the selection with the absolute medium color without having to mess around with the Color palette. History enables you to revert the selected area to a previous appearance, as I discuss at length in Chapter 10.

The Preserve Transparency check box works exactly like the identically named option in the Layers palette (discussed in Chapter 13). When the option is turned on, you can't fill the transparent pixels in the active layer. When Preserve

Transparency is turned off, you can fill the selection outline uniformly. (The option is dimmed when you're working on the background layer or when the Preserve Transparency check box in the Layers palette is already turned on.)

Delete-key techniques

Of all the fill techniques, the Delete key is by far the most convenient and, in most respects, every bit as capable as the others. The key's only failing is that it can neither fill a selection with a repeating pattern nor revert a selection to a previous state. But with the exception of those two items, you can rely on the Delete key for the overwhelming majority of your fill needs.

Here's how to get a ton of functionality out of Delete:

✦ **Background color, method 1:** To fill a selection on the background layer with solid background color, press Delete. The selection outline remains intact.

✦ **Background color, method 2:** The problem with pressing Delete is it's unreliable. If the selection is floating, as I explain in Chapter 11, the Delete key deletes it. The Delete key also erases pixels on a layer. So there's no time like the present to get into a new habit — press ⌘-Delete instead. ⌘-Delete fills the selection with the background color, no matter where it is.

✦ **Foreground color:** To fill a selection or layer with solid foreground color, press Option-Delete. This works when filling floating and nonfloating selections alike.

✦ **Black or white:** To fill an area with black, press D to get the default foreground and background colors and then press Option-Delete. To fill it with white, press D for the defaults and then ⌘-Delete.

✦ **Preserve transparency:** Add the Shift key and you get two more key tricks that will make more sense when you read Chapter 13. (Don't worry, I'll repeat the tricks then.) You can fill only the opaque pixels in a layer — whether or not Preserve Transparency is turned on — by pressing Shift. Press Shift-Option-Delete to fill a selection with the foreground color while preserving transparency. Press ⌘-Shift-Delete to fill the opaque pixels with the background color.

Using the paint bucket inside a selection

So far, I've come up with two astounding generalizations: The paint bucket tool is mostly useless, and you can fill anything with the Delete key. Well, just to prove you shouldn't believe everything I say — some might even suggest you dismiss everything I say — the following steps explain how to create an effect you can perform only with the paint bucket tool. Doubtless, it's the only such example you'll ever discover using Photoshop — after all, the paint bucket is mostly useless and you can fill anything with the Delete key — but I'm man enough to eat my rules this once.

The following steps explain how to create an antique photographic frame effect like the one shown in Figure 9-6.

Steps: Creating an Antique Framing Effect

1. **Use the rectangular marquee tool to select the portion of the image you want to frame.** Make certain the image extends at least 20 pixels outside the boundaries of the selection outline. And be sure to use a photo—this effect won't look right against a plain white background.

2. **Choose Select ⇨ Feather (⌘-Option-D).** Then specify a Radius value somewhere in the neighborhood of 6 to 12 pixels. I've found these values work for nearly any resolution of image. (If you enter too high a value, the color you'll add in a moment with the paint bucket will run out into the image.)

Figure 9-6: I created this antique frame effect by filling a feathered selection with the paint bucket tool.

3. **Choose Select ⇨ Inverse (⌘-Shift-I).** This exchanges the selected and deselected portions of the image.

4. **Press the D key to make certain the background color is white.** Then press ⌘-Delete to fill the selected area with the background color.

5. **Select the paint bucket tool and press Return to display the Paint Bucket Options palette.** Enter 20 to 30 in the Tolerance option box and turn on the Anti-aliased check box. (You can also experiment with turning off this option.)

6. **Click inside the feathered selection to fill it with black.** The result is an image fading into white and then into black, like the edges of a worn slide or photograph, as shown in Figure 9-6.

Figure 9-7 shows a variation on this effect you can create using the Dissolve brush mode. Rather than setting the Tolerance value to 20, raise it to around 60. Then select the Dissolve option from the brush mode pop-up menu in the Paint Bucket Options palette. When you click inside the feathered selection with the paint bucket tool, you create a frame of random pixels, as illustrated in the figure.

Figure 9-7: Select Dissolve from the Brushes palette pop-up menu to achieve a speckled frame effect.

Applying Gradient Fills

The last two versions of Photoshop have witnessed great strides in the gradation department. Version 4 introduced the Edit button into the Gradient Options palette. This one button made it possible to create a gradient with as many as 32 colors, name gradients and save them to disk, and adjust the transparency of colors so they fade in and out over the course of the fill.

Version 5 goes a step better, widening the range of gradient styles to include angled (conical), reflected, and diamond patterns. You can also reverse the foreground and background colors from within the Gradient Options palette, a nice convenience feature when applying radial and diamond fills. You still can't apply a gradation along a path, but that seems to be the only remaining omission.

If you're used to using gradients in a drawing program — such as Illustrator or FreeHand — Photoshop is better. Because Photoshop is a pixel editor, it lets you blur and mix colors in a gradation if they start *banding* — banding being when you can see a hard edge between one color and the next when you print the image. And Photoshop's gradations will never choke the printer or slow it down, no matter how many colors you add. While each band of color in an object-oriented gradation is expressed as a separate shape — so one gradation can contain hundreds, or even thousands, of objects — gradations in Photoshop are plain old colored pixels, the kind we've been editing for eight and a half chapters.

Using the gradient tools

First, the basics. A *gradation* (also called a *gradient fill*) is a progression of colors that fade gradually into one another, as demonstrated in Figure 9-8. You specify a few key colors in the gradation, and Photoshop automatically generates the hundred or so colors in between to create a smooth transition.

You apply gradations using one of the five gradient tools, located just above the eyedropper in the toolbox. Unlike the paint bucket, which fills areas of similar color according to the Tolerance setting, the gradient tool affects all colors within a selection. If you don't select a portion of your image, Photoshop applies the gradation to the entire layer.

To select the default linear gradient tool, press the G key. To use the tool, drag inside the selection, as shown in the left example of Figure 9-8. The point at which you begin dragging (upper-left corner in the figure) defines the location of the first color in the gradation. The point at which you release (lower-right corner) defines the location of the last color. If multiple portions of the image are selected, the gradation fills all selections continuously, as demonstrated by the right example of Figure 9-8.

Figure 9-8: Dragging with the gradient tool within a single selection (left) and across multiple selections (right) the gradation.

Gradient styles

In Photoshop 5, switching to a different gradient tool changes the style of gradation. In previous versions, you could select between two styles — linear and radial — by selecting a Type option from the Gradient Options palette. Now, you switch styles either by Option-clicking on the gradient tool icon in the toolbox or by pressing Shift-G.

Shown in Figure 9-9, the five styles are as follows:

✦ **Linear:** A linear gradation progresses in bands of color in a straight line between the beginning and end of your drag. The top two examples in Figure 9-9 show linear gradations created from black to white, and from white to black. The point labeled B marks the beginning of the drag; E marks the end.

✦ **Radial:** A radial gradation progresses outward from a central point in concentric circles, as in the second row of examples in Figure 9-9. The point at which you begin dragging defines the center of the gradation, and the point at which you release defines the outermost circle. This means the first color in the gradation appears in the center of the fill. So to create the gradation on the right side of Figure 9-9, you must set white to the foreground color and black to the background color (or select the Reverse check box in the Gradient Options palette).

Figure 9-9: Examples of each of the five gradient styles created using the default foreground and background colors (left column) and with the foreground and background colors reversed (right column). B marks the beginning of the drag, E marks the end.

✦ **Angle:** The angle gradient tool creates a fountain of colors flowing in a counterclockwise direction with respect to your drag, as demonstrated by the middle two examples of Figure 9-9. This type of gradient is known more commonly as a conical gradation, because it looks like the bird's eye view of the top of a cone.

Of course, a real cone doesn't have the sharp edge between black and white that you see in Photoshop's angle gradient. To eliminate this edge, create a custom gradation from black to white to black again, as I explain in the "Adding and deleting color stops" section later in this chapter. (Take a peek at Figure 9-16 if you're not sure what I'm talking about.)

✦ **Reflected:** Drag with the fourth gradient tool to create a linear gradation that reflects back on itself. Photoshop positions the foreground color at the beginning of your drag and the background color at the end, as when using the linear gradient tool. But it also repeats the gradient in the opposite direction of your drag, as demonstrated in Figure 9-9. It's great for creating natural shadows or highlights that fade in two directions.

✦ **Diamond:** The last gradient tool creates a series of concentric diamonds (if you drag at a 90-degree angle) or squares (if you drag at a 45-degree angle, as in Figure 9-9). Otherwise, it works exactly like the radial gradient tool.

Gradient options

To master any of the gradient tools, you must understand how to modify its performance. Press Return when a gradient tool is active to display the Gradient Options palette, shown in Figure 9-10. (This happens to be the Linear Gradient Options palette, but they all look the same.) This palette lets you specify the colors in a gradation, as well as the arrangement of those colors, using the following options:

✦ **Brush mode and Opacity:** These options work the same way they do in the paint and edit tool Options palettes, in the Paint Bucket Options palette, in the Fill dialog box, and everywhere else they pop up. Select a different brush mode to change how colors are applied; lower the Opacity value to make a gradation translucent. In both cases — as with all the other options in this palette — you must adjust the options before using the gradient tool. They do not affect existing gradations.

✦ **Gradient:** The Gradient pop-up menu provides access to gobs of factory-predefined gradations. When you select a gradation, Photoshop displays it in the gradient preview (labeled in Figure 9-10). The first three factory gradations are dependent on the current foreground and background colors. The others contain specific colors bearing no relationship to the colors in the toolbox. If you create and name your own custom gradations, they will also show up in this menu.

Figure 9-10: The Gradient Options palette provides access to the all-important Edit button, which enables you to create custom gradations.

✦ **Transparency:** You can specify different levels of opacity throughout a gradation. For example, the Transparent Stripes effect (available from the Gradient pop-up menu) lays down a series of alternately black and transparent stripes. But you needn't use this transparency information. If you prefer to apply a series of black and white stripes instead, you can make all portions of the gradation equally opaque by turning off the Transparency check box.

For example, in Figure 9-11, I applied Transparent Stripes as a radial gradation in two separate swipes, at top and bottom. Both times, I changed the Opacity setting to 50 percent, so dog and hydrant would never be obscured. (The Opacity setting works independently of the gradation's built-in transparency, providing you with additional flexibility.) In the top gradation, the Transparency check box is on, so the white stripes are completely transparent. In the bottom gradation, Transparency is turned off, so the white stripes become 50 percent opaque (as prescribed by the Opacity setting).

✦ **Dither:** In the old days, Photoshop drew its gradients one band at a time. Each band was filled with an incrementally different shade of color. The potential result was banding, in which you could clearly distinguish the transition between two or more bands of color. The Dither check box helps to eliminate this problem by mixing up the pixels between bands (much as Photoshop dithers pixels when converting a grayscale image to black and white). You should leave this option turned on unless you want to use the banding to create a special effect.

✦ **Reverse:** When active, this simple check box begins the gradation with the background color and ends it with the foreground color. Use this option when you want to start a radial or other style of gradation with white, but you want to keep the foreground and background colors set to their defaults.

Photoshop **5.0**

Transparency on

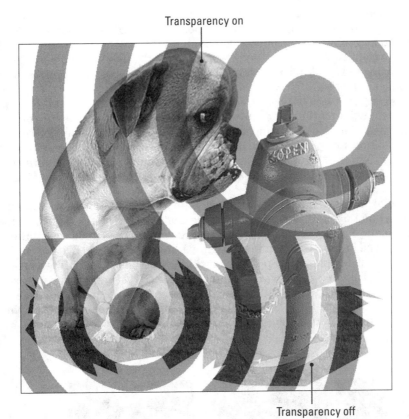

Transparency off

Figure 9-11: With the Opacity value set to 50 percent, I applied the Transparent Stripes gradation with Transparency on (top) and off (bottom). When Transparency is off, the white stripes obscure the view of the underlying image.

Eliminating gradient banding

Adobe assures me that banding problems have been all but eliminated in Photoshop 5. And while gradations are certainly smoother in the new version, I'm not sure I'd go so far as to assure you that banding is altogether a thing of the past. After all, banding has as much to do with the capabilities of your printer as with Photoshop's ability to generate properly colored pixels. If you never once see any banding in your output, excellent. Skip this section and have a nice day. But if you do experience banding, this section describes how to eliminate it.

As explained in Chapter 15, the Add Noise filter randomizes pixels in a selection. So when you apply Filter ➪ Noise ➪ Add Noise to a gradation, it randomly mixes the bands of color, very much like a variable dithering function. In fact, it enables you to outdither the Dither check box.

The first column in Figure 9-12 shows linear and radial gradations. In the second column, I applied the Add Noise filter three times in a row to both gradations. To make the effect as subtle as possible — you don't want the noise to be obvious — I specified an Amount value of 8 and selected the Uniform radio button inside the Add Noise dialog box. Multiple repetitions of a subtle noise effect are preferable to a single application of a more radical effect.

If noise isn't enough or if the noise appears a little too obvious, you can further mix the colors in a gradation by applying a directional blur filter. To blur a linear or reflected gradation, apply the Motion Blur filter in the direction of the gradation. In the top-right example of Figure 9-12, I applied Filter ➪ Blur ➪ Motion Blur with an Angle value of 90 degrees (straight up and down) and a Distance value of 3 pixels.

To blur a radial, angle, or diamond gradation, apply the Radial Blur filter (Filter ➪ Blur ➪ Radial Blur). To mix the noise around the center of the gradation, select the Spin option in the Radial Blur dialog box. To blend color in the bands, select the Zoom option. The lower right example in Figure 9-12 is divided into two halves. To create the top half, I applied the Spin option with an Amount value of 10; to create the bottom half, I applied Zoom with an Amount value of 20. (If you can barely see any difference between the two — that's the idea when it comes to gradations — look closely at the perimeter of the gradients. The top one, created with the Spin option, is smooth; the bottom one, created with the Zoom option, is rougher.)

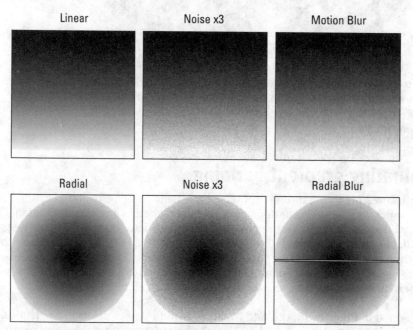

Figure 9-12: The results of applying noise (middle column) and directional blur effects (right column) to linear and radial gradations.

You can get a sense of what the Add Noise, Motion Blur, and Radial Blur filters do by experimenting with them for a few minutes. If you want to learn even more, I discuss all four in Chapter 15.

Creating custom gradations

The only remaining option in the Gradient Options palette is the Edit button. Click on this button to create your own custom gradation or to edit one of the factory presets. Photoshop answers your request with the Gradient Editor dialog box, pictured in Figure 9-13. Because this dialog box has so much going on in it, I've lifted the most essential options and labeled them in Figure 9-14.

Figure 9-13: Click on the Edit button in the Gradient Options palette to bring up this dialog box, which allows you to design your own custom gradations.

Select a named gradation that interests you from the scrolling list. Then click on the Duplicate button to design a new gradation based on the selected one. Photoshop asks you to name the new gradient. Do so and then press Return.

Figure 9-14: These few small options are quite powerful. Despite the array of buttons available in the Gradient Editor dialog box, these controls are where it's happening.

Positioning colors and midpoint markers

Below the scrolling list is the *fade bar* (labeled in Figure 9-14). The starting color appears as a house-shaped *color stop* on the left; the ending color appears on the far right. Positioned between each pair of color stops along the top of the fade bar is a diamond-shaped *midpoint marker*, which represents the spot where the two colors mix in exactly equal amounts. You can change the location of any stop or marker by dragging it. Or you can click on a stop or marker to select it and then enter a value into the Location option box below the fade bar. The selected stop or marker appears black.

    ✦ When numerically positioning a selected color stop, a value of 0 percent indicates the left end of the fade bar; 100 percent indicates the right end. Even if you add more color stops to the gradation, the values represent absolute positions along the fade bar.

    ✦ When repositioning a midpoint marker, the initial setting of 50 percent is smack dab between the two color stops; 0 percent is all the way over to the left stop; and 100 percent is all the way over to the right. Midpoint values are, therefore, measured relative to color stop positions. In fact, when you move a color stop, Photoshop moves the midpoint marker along with it to maintain the same relative positioning. Figure 9-15 shows four radial gradations subjected to different midpoint settings.

Tip

Pressing Return after you enter a value into the Location option box is tempting, but don't do it. If you do, Photoshop will dump you out of the Gradient Editor dialog box. Instead, press the Tab key. Tab advances you from one marker to the next — from color stop to midpoint marker to the next color stop and so on. Press Shift-Tab to move to the previous marker.

Color Plate 4-1
An example of a custom 1024×768-pixel startup screen saved as a PICT resource file.

Color Plate 4-2
This little warlock shows off the differences between the four different JPEG compression settings, from maximum quality, minimum compression (upper left) to minimum quality, maximum compression (lower right). Inspect the enlarged eye and sharpened staff for subtle erosions in detail.

Maximum   116K

High   66K

Medium   50K

Low   46K

Color Plate 5-1

The colors inside the field and slider in the Color Picker dialog box change to reflect the selection of the H (Hue), S (Saturation), and B (Brightness) radio buttons.

Color Plate 6-1

An image created on the Mac in the SMPTE-240M space (left) and then opened on the PC and converted to sRGB (right). If you look closely in the medium blue areas, you'll see a slight shift toward green on the right. Even so, Photoshop has done a terrific job of converting the colors.

Color Plate 6-2
This colorful image is the basis for an awful lot of channel discussions in Chapter 6. Right about now, I'm wishing I was in that inner tube instead of editing it.

Color Plate 6-3
One of the wonderful things about the Lab mode is that it allows you to edit the colors in an image independently of the brightness values. Here I've inverted and boosted the contrast of the *a* and *b* color channels to produce some startling effects, all without harming a smidgen of detail.

Invert a   Auto Levels b   Invert and Auto Levels a and b

Replace red with blue   Replace green with red   Replace blue with red

Swap red and blue   Swap red and green   Swap green and blue

Color Plate 7-1
I converted this grayscale piece by Seattle-based artist Mark Collen to a quadtone using the colors navy blue, rose, teal, and dull orange. All colors were defined and printed using CMYK pigments.

Color Plate 7-2
After converting Mark's quadtone to a multichannel image, I experimented with hiding different channels. In the top row, I hide one spot color and left the other three visible. In the bottom row, I hid two channels per image.

Navy, Orange, Teal   Orange, Teal, Rose   Navy, Orange, Rose

Navy, Orange   Teal, Rose   Orange, Rose

Color Plate 8-1
Starting with an image of typical saturation (upper left), I applied the sponge tool set to Desaturate to the inside of the pepper and the corn in the background (upper right). I then repeated the effect twice more to make the areas almost gray (lower right). Returning to the original image, I then selected the Saturate icon and again scrubbed inside the pepper and in the corn to boost the colors (lower left).

Behind

Dissolve

Normal

Color Plate 8-2
Here I've gone and desecrated a pivotal work of European iconography by scribbling the name of America's patron saint of graffiti. Reading up from the bottom, the Normal brush mode applies paint normally. The Dissolve mode scattered pixels along the fuzzy edge of the brushstroke. And the Behind mode paints behind the current layer, in this case, a layer containing the Madonna's head.

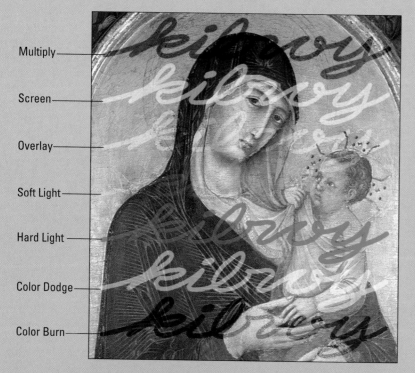

Multiply

Screen

Overlay

Soft Light

Hard Light

Color Dodge

Color Burn

Color Plate 8-3
Here I've painted green lines using the seven brush modes in the middle of the Options palette pop-up menu. Multiply darkens uniformly and Screen lightens uniformly. (In fact, Multiply and Screen are direct opposites.) Overlay, Soft Light, and Hard Light all multiply the darkest pixels and screen the lightest ones to produce different contrast-enhancing effects. Color Dodge and Color Burn work like dodge and burn tools that also add color to an image.

Color Plate 8-4

Here are the effects of the final eight entries in Photoshop's enormous arsenal of brush modes. Darken and Lighten are opposites, Difference and Exclusion are very closely related, and the last four apply different bits and pieces of the HSL color model. Because many of these modes produce slight effects—particularly the Saturation and Luminosity modes—I have added dark halos around the brushstrokes to offset them slightly from the background. Naturally, the halos feel right at home.

- Darken
- Lighten
- Difference
- Exclusion
- Hue
- Saturation
- Color
- Luminosity

Color Plate 9-1

Here I've used the paint bucket to colorize two oranges (top) with bright blue. First, I set the Tolerance value in the Paint Bucket Options palette to 120 and changed the brush mode to Color. Then I clicked at each of the four points marked with blue arrows (middle). Then I changed the foreground color to green and clicked just once in the lower right corner of the image (marked with the green arrow). Unfortunately, the paint bucket isn't very precise, so I had to touch up the dimples and edges with the paintbrush, also set to the Color mode. Finally, I used the airbrush—set to the Color Burn mode—to deepen some of the blue shadows inside the fruit.

Color Plate 9-2
I started by designing a three-color gradient that fades twice into transparency, as demonstrated by the checkerboard background (left). Such a gradation is meant to be blended with an image, such as the piano keys (middle). So I selected the Overlay brush mode from the Gradient Tool Options palette and tickled my gradation across the ivories (right).

Color Plate 10-1
To see how I scanned this 90-year-old photograph (left) and cloned away its considerable supply of tears, creases, stains, and flaking (right), read the "Restoring an old photograph" section of Chapter 10.

Color Plate 11-1

If you attempt to select this whimsical sign with the magic wand tool, you end up selecting old little fragments of the yellow areas at a time. However, by switching to the blue channel—in which both sign and Sasquatch appear black against a relatively light background—you can easily select both portions of the sign in two easy clicks. I then inverted the sign (right) by pressing ⌘-I. The effect isn't perfect, but it's as good as it gets with the magic wand.

Color Plate 12-1

At top, we see two selection outlines (both from Figure 12-1) expressed as masks. The masks appear as transparent red overlays, permitting you to see mask and image at the same time. Red-tinted areas are masked, representing deselected areas in the image; untinted areas are unmasked, and represent selected areas. In the bottom examples, I inverted the selected areas to demonstrate the full extent of the selection outlines.

Color Plate 12-2
In the left example, I drew a black to white gradation in the quick mask mode, extending from the base of the top row of pillars to the top of the flagpole. Then I applied the Add Noise filter to jumble up the pixels a little. Finally, I exited the quick mask mode to convert the mask to a selection, and ⌘-dragged the Capitol into the lava image (right).

Color Plate 12-3
Which twin has the Toni? With the help of a very precise mask, I dragged this girl in from her old environment into this new one. But despite the mask's accuracy, I managed to bring in some blue from her prior background (left). To fix this problem, I brushed in some color from the new background, and erased a few of the overly dark hairs (right).

Color Plate 13-1
Photoshop lets you copy layer effects from one layer and paste them onto another. After applying the Outer Glow command to some bananas and Pillow Emboss to a pineapple (left), I decided the pillow emboss is all wrong. So I copied the pillow emboss effect from the pineapple and applied it to the new thought-balloon layer. Then I copied the outer glow from the bananas and pasted it onto the pineapple (right).

Color Plate 13-2
Here I've used a clipping group to fill some characters of type with a water pattern. I started by adding a couple of pool images that I shot with a digital camera to a layer above my text—which is itself on an independent layer—as demonstrated on the left. Then I just Option-clicked on the horizontal line between the two layers in the Layers palette. Photoshop automatically assigned the type layer's transparency mask to the pool layer, filling the letters.

Unsharp Mask

Dust & Scratches

Smart Blur

High Pass

Color Plate 15-1
Shown here are the results of four corrective filters, including representatives from the Filter ⇨ Sharpen, Blur, Noise, and Other submenus. Normally, the High Pass filter takes the saturation out of an image, leaving many areas gray, like an old, sun-bleached slide. To restore the colors, I chose Filter ⇨ Fade High Pass (⌘-Shift-F) and selected Luminosity from the Mode pop-up menu in the Fade dialog box.

Zig Zag

Difference
Clouds

Mezzotint

Find Edges

Color Plate 15-2
Here are the effects of four destructive filters from the Filter ⇨ Distort, Pixelate, Render, and Stylize submenus. Every one of these filters has a dramatic impact on the color and detail of an image. From a pixel's perspective, destructive filters are dynamite, so use with care and moderation.

Color Plate 15-3
The results of applying the Unsharp Mask filter to independent color channels in an RGB image. In each case, the Amount value was 500, the Radius value was 4.0, and the Threshold was 0.

Red

Green

Blue

Red & green

Green & blue

Blue & red

Color Plate 15-4
Again, I applied Unsharp Mask to the independent color channels, but this time with an exaggerated Radius value, 20.0, a more moderate Amount value, 250, and the default Threshold, 0. Rather than pinpointing the sharpening effect, as in Color Plate 15-3, the high Radius value allows the colors to bleed as they are strengthened by the Amount value.

Red

Green

Blue

Red & green

Green & blue

Blue & red

Color Plate 15-5
The results of applying Filter ⇨ Other ⇨ High Pass with a Radius value of 5.0 to each channel and pair of channels in an RGB image. To boost the color values in the images slightly, I applied the Auto Levels command (⌘-Shift-L) after each application of High Pass.

Red

Green

Blue

Red & green

Green & blue

Blue & red

Color Plate 15-6
After applying the Gaussian Blur filter with a Radius of 8.0, I used the Fade Gaussian Blur command to mix the filtered image with the original. The labels tell the blend mode and Opacity setting applied to each image.

Normal, 60%

Luminosity, 50%

Darken, 80%

Lighten, 80%

Color Plate 15-7
An image scanned from an ancient issue of *Macworld* magazine shown as it appears in the normal RGB mode (top right) and when each channel is viewed separately (top left). The middle images show the affects of the Dust & Scratches filter set to a Radius of 2 and a Threshold of 20. The bottom images show how the channels look after suppressing the moiré patterns with the Gaussian Blur, Median, and Unsharp Mask filters.

Color Plate 16-1
The result of applying the Extrude filter to a red rose. If you select the Blocks and Solid Front Faces options, the filter transforms the image into mosaic tiles and shoves the tiles out at you in 3D space.

Color Plate 16-2
Here I applied Filter ➪ Sketch ➪ Charcoal with the foreground color set to dark green and the background color light blue (as demonstrated in the upper left inset). Then I used the Fade Charcoal command to change the blend mode to Overlay.

Color Plate 16-3
I applied the Mezzotint filter set to the Long Strokes effect in each of the RGB, Lab, and CMYK color modes (top row). After each application of the filter, I pressed ⌘-Shift-F and faded the filtered image into the original using the Overlay mode and an Opacity setting of 40 percent (bottom row).

RGB Lab CMYK

Color Plate 16-4
In both examples, I applied the Emboss filter armed with an Angle of 135 degrees, a Height value of 2, and an Amount of 300 percent. To create the left image, I used the Fade command to mix embossed and original images together using the Luminosity blend mode and an Opacity setting of 80 percent. To get the psychedelic effect on right, I selected the Difference mode and reduced the Opacity value to 40 percent.

Original

Blur and Find Edges

Overlay

Color Plate 16-5
After selecting an image from the PhotoDisc library (top left), I layered the image, blurred it, applied the Find Edges filter, and darkened it with the Levels command (top middle). I then composited the image using the Overlay mode and an Opacity setting of 80 percent (top right). The bottom row shows the results of applying three effects filters set to the Luminosity mode and 80 percent Opacity settings.

Bas Relief

Plastic Wrap

Chrome

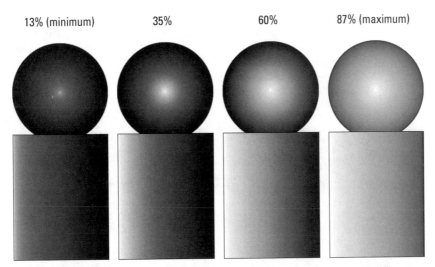

13% (minimum)   35%   60%   87% (maximum)

Figure 9-15: Four sets of white-to-black gradations — radial on top and linear at bottom — subject to different midpoint settings.

Adjusting the colors in a gradation

You can change the colors in a gradation by selecting a color stop and clicking on the active stop swatch (immediately to the left of the Location option box). Photoshop displays the familiar Color Picker dialog box. Select the desired color and press Return.

Tip

That's the hard way. The easy way is to lift a color from the image window. When you move the cursor outside the dialog box into the image window, it changes to an eyedropper. Just click on the color in the image you want to use. You can also click on the Color palette's color bar or in the Swatches palette.

If you want a color stop to vary with the active foreground color, select the color stop and click on the little F icon in the stop types area (on the left side of the dialog box, labeled back in Figure 9-14). To use the background color, select a stop and click on the little B icon.

Adding and deleting color stops

Here are three last items you should know about color stops:

✦ Photoshop 4 was limited to 32 colors per gradient, but Version 5 lets you add as many colors as you like. To add a color stop, click anywhere along the bottom of the fade bar. A new stop appears right where you click. Photoshop also adds a midpoint marker between the new color stop and its neighbor.

✦ To duplicate a color stop, Option-drag it to a new location along the fade bar. One great use for this to create a reflecting gradation.

For example, select Foreground to Background from the scrolling list of gradients and click on the Duplicate button. After naming your new gradient — something like Fore to Back to Fore — click on the B stop and change the Location value to 50. Then Option-drag the F stop all the way to the right. This new gradient is perfect for making true conical gradations with the angle gradient tool, as demonstrated in Figure 9-16.

Foreground to Background   Fore to Back to Fore

Figure 9-16: Two gradations created with the angle gradient tool, one using the standard Foreground to Background gradient (left) and the other with my reflected Fore to Back to Fore style (right). Which looks better to you?

✦ To remove a color stop, drag the stop away from the fade bar. The stop icon vanishes and the fade bar automatically adjusts as defined by the remaining color stops.

Adjusting the transparency mask

If you like, you can include a *transparency mask* with each gradation. The mask determines where the colors are opaque and where they fade into translucency or even transparency. You create and edit this mask independently of the colors in the gradation, and you can turn it on and off using the Transparency check box in the Gradient Options palette (as explained earlier).

To create a transparency mask, click on the Transparency radio button in the Gradient Editor dialog box. The fade bar changes to reflect the transparency settings (if any), as shown in Figure 9-17. As when editing colors, you click under the fade bar to add *transparency stops*, drag the stops to move them, and to edit the Location value to position a selected stop numerically.

Figure 9-17: Click on the Transparency radio button to switch to a different fade bar that controls how the gradation fades in and out of sight.

The difference is, instead of changing the color of the stops, you modify their opacity. By default, each new stop is 100 percent opaque. You can modify the transparency by selecting a stop and changing the Opacity value. The preview along the bottom of the dialog box updates to reflect your changes. A checkerboard pattern represents the underlying image.

Color Plate 9-2 demonstrates the effect of applying a three-color gradation to a photograph. The gradation fades from red to transparency to green to transparency and, finally, to blue. In the first example in the color plate, I dragged over a standard checkerboard pattern with the gradient tool, from the lower-left corner to the upper-right corner. The second example shows the photograph prior to applying the gradation. In the last example, I applied the gradient — again from lower left to upper right — using the Overlay brush mode.

Saving gradients

Photoshop automatically saves your custom gradients to the Adobe Photoshop 5 Prefs file. But as we all know, Prefs can go bad. Clicking on the Save button in the Gradient Editor dialog box gives you the option of saving the selected gradients to a more secure, less volatile location.

Note that Photoshop 5 saves only those gradients that you select from the list. (Version 4 saved all gradients, whether selected or not.) This gives you more control, so you don't go saving the same gradient to multiple files — unless, of course, you want to.

Tip

To save a range of gradients, click on one and then Shift-click on another before clicking on the Save button. To select multiple non-sequential gradients, ⌘-click on them.

Gradations and brush modes

Overlay isn't the only brush mode you can use with gradations. All 19 of the standard brush modes are available and they make a tremendous impression on the performance of the gradient tool. This section examines yet another way to apply a brush mode in conjunction with the tool. Naturally, it barely scrapes the surface of what's possible, but it may inspire you to experiment and discover additional effects on your own.

The following steps tell you how to use the Dissolve mode in combination with a radial gradation to create a supernova explosion. (At least, it looks like a supernova to me — not that I've ever seen one up close, mind you.) Figures 9-18 through 9-20 show the nova in progress. The steps offer you the opportunity to experiment with a brush mode setting and some general insight into creating radial gradations.

Cross-Reference

These steps involve the use of the elliptical marquee tool. Generally speaking, it's an easy tool to use. But if you find you have problems making it work according to my instructions, you may want to read the "Geometric selection outlines" section of Chapter 11. It's only a few pages long.

Steps: Creating a Gradient Supernova

1. **Create a new image window.** Make it 500 × 500 pixels. A grayscale image is fine for this exercise.

2. **Click with the pencil tool at the apparent center of the image.** Don't worry if it's not the exact center. This point is merely intended to serve as a guide. If a single point is not large enough for you to identify easily, draw a small cross.

3. **Option-drag from the point with the elliptical marquee tool to draw the marquee outward from the center.** You can select the elliptical marquee tool by pressing the M key twice in a row. While dragging with the tool, press and hold the Shift key to constrain the marquee to a circle. Release Shift after you release the mouse button. Draw a marquee that fills about ¾ of the window.

4. **Choose Image ⇨ Adjust ⇨ Invert (⌘-I).** This fills the marquee with black and makes the center point white.

5. **Choose Select ⇨ Deselect (⌘-D).** As the command name suggests, this deselects the circle.

6. **Again, Option-drag from the center point with the elliptical marquee tool.** And, again, press Shift to constrain the shape to a circle. Create a marquee roughly 20 pixels larger than the black circle.

7. **Option-drag from the center point with the elliptical marquee tool.** This subtracts a hole from the selection. After you begin dragging, release the Option key (but keep that mouse button down). Then press and hold both Shift and Option together and keep them down. Draw a marquee roughly 20 pixels smaller than the black circle. Release the mouse button and finally release the keys. The result is a doughnut-shaped selection — a large circle with a smaller circular hole — as shown in Figure 9-18.

Figure 9-18: The result of creating a black circle and two circular marquees, all centered about a single point.

8. **Choose Select ⇨ Feather (⌘-Option-D) and enter 10 for the Radius value.** Then press Enter to feather the section outline.

9. **Press the D key, and then press X.** This makes the foreground color white and the background color black.

10. **Select the radial gradient tool.** Assuming default settings, you can get to it by pressing G and then Shift-G. Otherwise, just keep pressing Shift-G until it comes up.

11. **Press Return to display the Options palette.** Then select Foreground to Background from the Gradient pop-up menu.

12. **Select Dissolve from the brush mode pop-up menu.** It's the one on the left side of the Gradient Options palette.

13. **Drag from the center point in the image window to anywhere along the outer rim of the largest marquee.** The result is the fuzzy gradation shown in Figure 9-19.

(continued)

Figure 9-19: The Dissolve brush mode option randomizes the pixels around the feathered edges of the selection outlines.

14. **Choose Select ➪ Deselect (⌘-D) to deselect the image.**

15. **Choose Image ➪ Adjust ➪ Invert (⌘-I) to invert the entire image.**

16. **Press the D key to restore black and white as foreground and background colors, respectively.** Then use the eraser tool to erase the center point. The finished supernova appears in Figure 9-20.

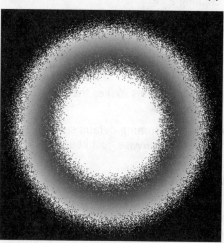

Figure 9-20: By inverting the image from the previous figure and erasing the center point, you create an expanding series of progressively lighter rings dissolving into the black void of space, an effect better known to its friends as a supernova.

Chapter 9 ✦ Filling and Stroking

Applying Strokes and Arrowheads

Photoshop is nearly as adept at drawing lines and outlines as it is at filling selections. The following sections discuss how to apply a border around a selection outline — which is practical, if not terribly exciting — and how to create arrowheads — which can yield more interesting results than you might think.

Stroking a selection outline

Stroking is useful for creating frames and outlines. Generally speaking, you can stroke an image in Photoshop in three ways:

✦ **The Stroke command:** Select the portion of the image you want to stroke and choose Edit ➪ Stroke to display the Stroke dialog box shown in Figure 9-21. Enter the thickness of the stroke in pixels into the Width option box. Select a Location radio button to specify the position of the stroke with respect to the selection outline. The Stroke dialog box also includes Opacity, Mode, and Preserve Transparency options that work like those in the Fill dialog box.

Figure 9-21: Use the options in the Stroke dialog box to specify the thickness of a stroke and its location with respect to the selection outline.

Tip

When in doubt, select Inside from the Location radio buttons. This setting ensures the stroke is entirely inside the selection outline in case you decide to move the selection. If you select Center or Outside, Photoshop may apply part or all of the stroke to the deselected area around the selection outline.

✦ **The Border command:** Select a portion of the image and choose Select ➪ Modify ➪ Border to retain only the outline of the selection. Specify the size of the border by entering a value in pixels into the Width option box and press Enter. To fill the border with the background color, press ⌘-Delete. To fill the border with the foreground color, press Option-Delete. To apply a repeating pattern to the border, choose Edit ➪ Fill and select the Pattern option from the Use pop-up menu. You can even apply a command under the Filter menu or some other special effect.

✦ **The Canvas Size trick:** Okay, so this one is a throwaway, but I use it all the time. To create an outline around the entire image, change the background color (yes, the background color) to the color you want to apply to the outline. Then choose Image ➪ Canvas Size and add twice the desired border thickness to the Width and Height options in pixels.

For example, to create a 1-pixel border all the way around, add 2 pixels to the Width value (1 for the left side and 1 for the right) and 2 pixels to the Height value (1 for the top and 1 for the bottom). Leave the Anchor option set to the center tile. When you press Return, Photoshop enlarges the canvas size according to your specifications and fills the new pixels around the perimeter of the image with the background color. Simplicity at its best.

Applying arrowheads

The one function missing from all the operations in the previous list is applying arrowheads. The fact is, in Photoshop, you can apply arrowheads only to straight lines drawn with the line tool.

Photoshop 5.0

To get to the line tool in Photoshop 5, you have to Option-click on the pencil tool icon in the toolbox. Or press N to select the pencil tool slot then Shift-N to switch to the line tool.

Double-click on the line tool icon in the toolbox (or press Return when the line tool is active) to display the Line Options palette shown in Figure 9-22. Enter a value into the Weight option box to specify the thickness of the line and then use the Arrowheads options as follows:

✦ **Start:** Select this check box to append an arrowhead to the beginning of a line drawn with the line tool.

✦ **End:** Select this check box to append an arrowhead to the end of a line. (Like you needed me to tell you this.)

✦ **Shape:** Click on the Shape button to display the Arrowhead Shape dialog box, which also appears in Figure 9-22.

Figure 9-22: Click on the Shape button in the Line Options palette (top) to display the Arrowhead Shape dialog box (bottom). The line tool remains the only way to create arrowheads in Photoshop.

The Arrowhead Shape dialog box contains three options, which enable you to specify the size and shape of the arrowhead as a function of the line weight:

✦ **Width:** Enter the width of the arrowhead into this option box. The width is measured as a percentage of the line weight, so if the Weight is set to 6 pixels and the Width value is 500 percent, then the width of the arrowhead will be 30 pixels. Math in action.

✦ **Length:** Enter the length of the arrowhead, measured from the base of the arrowhead to its tip, again as a percentage of the line weight.

✦ **Concavity:** You can specify the shape of the arrowhead by entering a value between negative and positive 50 percent into the Concavity option box. Figure 9-23 shows examples of a few Concavity settings applied to an arrowhead 50 pixels wide and 100 pixels long.

Figure 9-23: Examples of a 50 × 100-pixel arrowhead subject to five different Concavity values.

Appending arrowheads to curved lines

Applying arrowheads to straight lines is a simple matter. Double-click on the line tool icon, select a few choice options, and draw a line. Applying an arrowhead to a stroked selection outline is a little trickier, but still possible. The following steps explain the process.

Steps: Adding an Arrowhead to a Free-form Stroke

1. **Create a new layer.** Display the Layers palette by pressing the F7 key. Then click on the little page icon at the bottom of the palette to create a new layer.

2. **Draw and stroke a selection.** Draw any selection outline you like. Stroke it by choosing Edit ⇨ Stroke and applying whatever settings strike your fancy. Remember the value you enter into the Width option. In Figure 9-24, I drew a wiggly line with the lasso tool and applied a 4-pixel black stroke set to 30 percent Opacity.

Figure 9-24: Here, I created a new layer, drew a free-form shape with the lasso tool, and stroked it with a 4-pixel black outline at 30 percent Opacity.

3. **Press ⌘-D.** This deselects all portions of the image.

4. **Erase the portions of the stroke you don't need.** Select the eraser tool by pressing the E key. Then drag to erase through the stroke layer without harming the layer below. Erase away the areas of the stroke at which you

want to add arrowheads. I wanted to add an arrowhead behind the fly, so I erased around the fly.

5. **Select the line tool and press Return.** Up comes the Line Options palette.

6. **Specify the arrowhead settings.** Enter the line weight you used when stroking the selection outline into the Weight option box (in my case, 4 pixels). Then select the End check box and deselect the Start check box. Click on the Shape button and specify the width, length, and concavity of the arrowhead as desired.

7. **Set the foreground color as needed.** I applied a black stroke at 30 percent Opacity, so I set the foreground color to 30 percent gray. (Click on the stroke with the eyedropper to change the foreground color to the stroke color.)

8. **Zoom in on the point in the image at which you want to add the arrowhead.** You have to get in close enough to see what you're doing, as in Figure 9-25.

9. **Draw a very short line exactly the length of the arrowhead at the tip of the stroke.** Figure 9-25 illustrates what I mean. This may take some practice to accomplish. Start the line a few pixels in from the end of the stroke to make sure the base of the arrowhead fits snugly. If you mess up the first time, choose Edit ➪ Undo (⌘-Z) and try again.

Figure 9-25: Use the line tool to draw a line no longer than the arrowhead. This appends the arrow to the end of the stroke. The view size of this image is magnified to 300 percent.

That's all there is to it. From there on, you can continue to edit the stroke as you see fit. In Figure 9-26, for example, I erased a series of scratches across the stroke to create a dashed-line effect, all the rage for representing cartoon fly trails. I then set the eraser brush size to the largest, fuzziest setting and erased the end of the stroke (above the dog's head) to create a gradual trailing off. That crazy fly is now officially distracting our hero from his appointed rounds.

Figure 9-26: I finished by erasing dashes into the line and softening the end of the trail with a large, fuzzy eraser.

✦   ✦   ✦

Retouching, Repeating, and Restoring

Three of the Best

So far in Part III, we've looked at more than a dozen tools covering a host of editing disciplines — smearing and sponging, focus and color adjustment, filling and stroking, and plain old painting. But while most of these tools perform as well as can be expected, they don't add up to a hill of beans compared with Photoshop's foremost retouchers — the rubber stamp, the eraser, and the history brush. These remarkable three permit you to repair damaged images, create and apply repeating patterns, erase away mistakes, and restore operations from your recent past. Together, they permit you to perform the sorts of miracles that simply weren't possible in the days before computer imaging, all without the slightest fear of damaging your image in the slightest.

Very briefly, here's how each tool works:

✦ **Rubber stamp:** Use the rubber stamp to replicate pixels from one area in an image to another. This one feature makes the rubber stamp the perfect tool for removing dust and scratches, repairing defects, and eliminating distracting background elements. Option-click on the rubber stamp icon in the toolbox or press Shift-S to switch to the pattern stamp tool, which paints with a repeating image fragment defined using Edit ⇨ Define Pattern.

If you're wondering what happened to the rubber stamp's From Saved, From Snapshot, and Impressionist functions, they've been transferred to the history brush.

Photoshop **5.0**

Eraser: When used in a single-layer image or on the Background layer, the eraser paints in the background color. When applied to a layer, it erases pixels to reveal the layers below. You can change the performance of the eraser either by Option-clicking on the eraser icon in the toolbox or by pressing Shift-E. This cycles through the four brush settings shown in Figure 10-1.

✦ **History brush:** The new history brush selectively reverts to any of several previous states listed in the History palette. To select the "source state" that you want to paint with, click in the first column of the History palette. A brush icon identifies the source state, as illustrated by the Duplicate item in Figure 10-1.

(If Photoshop displays a little not-allowed cursor when you try to use the history brush, it means you can't paint from the selected state. Click on another state in the History palette and try again.)

Figure 10-1: The three image restoration tools shown with the primary options for modifying their performance.

Obviously, these are but the skimpiest of all possible introductions, every bit as stingy with information as a nineteenth-century headmaster might have been with his Christmas gruel and treacle. But fear not, my hungry one. This chapter doles out so many courses of meaty facts, fibrous techniques, and sweet, buttery insights that you'll need a whole box of toothpicks to dislodge the excess tips from your incisors.

Cloning Image Elements

Photoshop 5.0

In previous versions of Photoshop, the rubber stamp tools did everything but mop the floor, iron your socks, and call the kids for dinner. It had become a clearing house for every misfit function that didn't seem to fit anywhere else. Thankfully, the new history brush has appropriated and improved upon the most extreme of the superfluous functions, leaving the rubber stamp to do what it does best — clone image elements.

Personally, I've always found the name "rubber stamp" misleading. First, no tree sap is involved — let's get that sticky issue resolved right off the bat. Second, you don't use the tool to stamp an image. When I think of rubber stamps, I think of those things you see in stationery stores that plunk down smiley faces and Pooh bears. Elementary school teachers and little girls use rubber stamps. I've never seen a professional image editor walking around with a rubber stamp in my life.

A better name for the rubber stamp is the clone tool, because that's precisely what it does — it duplicates portions of an image. After selecting the tool (by pressing the S key), Option-click in the image window to specify the portion of the image you want to clone. Then paint with the tool to clone the Option-clicked area of the image.

If this is your first experience with a clone tool, it might sound peculiar. Sheep, cows, dinosaurs — these are things you might want to clone. Pixels, never. But as any dyed-in-the-wool Photoshop user will tell you, the rubber stamp is nothing short of invaluable for touching up images. You can remove dust fragments, hairs, and other impurities; rebuild creased or torn photographs, and even eliminate elements that wandered into your picture when you weren't looking. So get set for what is undoubtedly the best retouching tool of them all.

Note

You also can use the rubber stamp to duplicate specific elements in an image, such as petals in a flower or umbrellas on a beach (actual suggestions from previous editions of Photoshop's manual). But this is rarely an efficient use of the tool. If you want to duplicate an element, you'll have better luck if you select it and clone it, as explained in Chapter 11. Selection tools let you specify the exact boundaries of the element, the softness of the edges, and the precise location of the clone. Because of its reliance on a brush metaphor — that is, you drag across the image window to paint with it — the rubber stamp is better suited to buffing away defeats and filling in missing details.

The cloning process

To clone part of an image, Option-click in the image window to specify a point of reference in the portion of the image you want to clone. Then click or drag with the tool in some other region of the image to paint a cloned spot or line.

In Figure 10-2, for example, I Option-clicked above and to the right of the bird's head, as demonstrated by the appearance of the stamp pickup cursor. I then painted the line shown inside the white rectangle. The rubber stamp cursor shows the end of my drag; the clone reference crosshair shows the corresponding point in the original image.

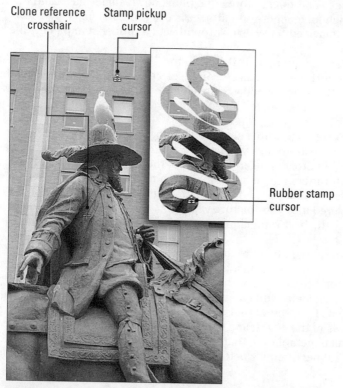

Clone reference
crosshair

Stamp pickup
cursor

Rubber stamp
cursor

Figure 10-2: After Option-clicking at the point indicated by the stamp pickup cursor, I dragged with the rubber stamp tool to paint with the image. (The only reason I painted inside the white rectangle was to set off the line so you can see it better.)

Tip

Photoshop lets you clone not only from within the image you're working on, but also from an entirely separate image window. This technique makes it possible to merge two different images together, as demonstrated in Figure 10-3. To achieve this effect, Option-click in one image, bring a second image to the foreground, and then drag with the rubber stamp tool to clone from the first image. You can also clone between layers. Option-click on one layer, then switch to a different layer and drag.

Figure 10-3: I merged the area around the horse and rider with a water image from another open window (see the upcoming Figure 10-6). The translucent effects were created by periodically adjusting the Opacity value to settings ranging from 50 to 80 percent.

Aligned and not-aligned cloning

The Rubber Stamp Options palette features the standard brush mode, Opacity, and Use All Layers options that I covered in Chapter 8. The only unique item is the Aligned check box. To understand how this option works, think of the locations where you Option-click and begin dragging with the rubber stamp tool as opposite ends of an imaginary straight line, as illustrated in the top half of Figure 10-4. When Aligned is turn on, the length and angle of this imaginary line remains fixed until the next time you Option-click. As you drag, Photoshop moves the line, cloning pixels from one end of the line and laying them down at the other. The upshot is that regardless of how many times you start and stop dragging with the stamp tool, all brushstrokes match up as seamlessly as pieces in a puzzle.

Aligned

Not aligned

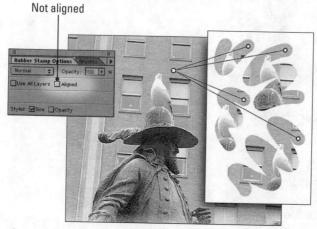

Figure 10-4: Turn on the Aligned check box to instruct Photoshop to clone an image continuously, no matter how many lines you paint (top). If you turn the option off, Photoshop clones each new line from the point at which you Option-click.

If you want to clone from a single portion of an image repeatedly, turn off the Aligned check box. The second example in Figure 10-4 shows how Photoshop clones from the same point every time you paint a new line with the rubber stamp tool. As a result, each of the four brushstrokes features part of the bird and none line up with each other.

Stamp differences

After nearly five years of incessant complaining from yours truly, Photoshop 5 reinstates the performance of the original rubber stamp tool. As in Version 2 and earlier, the rubber stamp clones the image as it existed before you began using the tool. Even when you drag over an area containing a clone, the tool references the original appearance of the image. This prevents you from creating more than one clone during a single drag and produces the entirely predictable effect pictured in the first example of Figure 10-5.

Single replication (Photoshops 1, 2, and 5)

Hall of mirrors (Photoshops 3 and 4)

Figure 10-5: Photoshop 5 reinstates the behavior of the rubber stamp tool from the good old days, when it cloned the image as it existed before you started using the tool (top). In Version 4, the tool cloned and recloned images during a single drag (bottom).

In the dim days from Photoshop 2.5 to 4.0, the rubber stamp tool suffered from what at least one programmer at Adobe characterized as the "hall of mirrors" syndrome. Any changes you made to the image affected the tool as you used it, which resulted in the repeating patterns such as those shown in the second example in Figure 10-5. Although you could achieve some interesting effects, the hall of mirrors was a real pain in the neck when retouching, frequently creating obvious patterns that betrayed your adjustments.

Not everyone is in agreement with this vintage setup, so you never know what the future will bring. One day we might get a Hall of Mirrors check box in the Rubber Stamp Options palette. But for now, the stamp clones from one and only one source, just as God intended it. Life is good again.

Touching up blemishes

One of the best uses of the rubber stamp tool is to touch up a scanned photo. Figure 10-6 shows a Photo CD image desperately in need of the stamp tool's attention. Normally, Kodak's Photo CD process delivers some of the best consumer-quality scans money can buy. But this particular medium-resolution image looks like the folks at the lab got together and blew their respective noses on it. It's too late to return to the service bureau and demand they rescan the photo, so my only choice is to touch it up myself.

Figure 10-6: This appallingly bad Photo CD image is riddled with blotches and big hurky wads of dust that didn't exist on the original 35mm slide.

The best way to fix this image — or any image like it — is to use the rubber stamp over and over again, repeatedly Option-clicking at one location and then clicking at another. Begin by selecting a brush shape slightly larger than the largest blotch. Of the default brushes, the hard-edged varieties with diameters of 5 and 9 pixels generally work best. (The soft-edged brush shapes have a tendency to only partially hide the blemishes and leave ghosted versions behind.)

Option-click with the stamp tool at a location that features similarly colored pixels to the blemished area. Be sure to Option-click far enough away from the blemish that you don't run the risk of duplicating the blemish as you clone. Then click — do not drag — directly on the blemish to clone over it. The idea is to change as few pixels as possible.

If the retouched area doesn't look quite right, press ⌘-Z to undo it, Option-click at a different location, and try again. If your touchup appears seamless — *absolutely* seamless, there's no reason to settle for less — move on to the next blemish. Repeat the Option-click and click routine for every dust mark on the photo.

This process isn't necessarily time-consuming, but it does require patience. For example, although it took more than 40 Option-click and click combinations (not counting 10 or so undos) to arrive at the image shown in Figure 10-7, the process itself took less than 15 minutes. Boring, but fast.

Figure 10-7: The result of Option-clicking and clicking more than 40 times on the photo shown in Figure 10-6. Notice I also cropped the image and added a border.

Retouching hairs is a little trickier than dust and other blobs. This is because a hair, although very thin, can be surprisingly long. The retouching process is the same, though. Rather than dragging over the entire length of the hair, Option-click and click your way through it, bit by little bit. The one difference is brush shape. Because you'll be clicking so many times in succession, and because the hair is so thin, you'll probably achieve the least-conspicuous effects if you use a soft brush shape, such as the default 9-pixel model in the second row of the Brushes palette.

At this point you might wonder, "Why go to all this work to remove dust and scratches when Photoshop provides the automated feature Filter ⇨ Noise ⇨ Dust & Scratches?" The reason is — and I'm going to be painfully blunt here — the Dust & Scratches filter stinks. No offense to the designers of this filter: They're wonderful people, every one of them, but the filter simply doesn't produce the effect it advertises. It mucks up the detail in your image by averaging neighboring pixels, and this simply isn't an acceptable solution. Do your photograph a favor — fix its flaws manually (not to mention lovingly) with the rubber stamp tool.

Restoring an old photograph

Dust, hairs, gloops, and other blemishes are introduced during the scanning process. But what about more severe problems that trace back to the original image? Figure 10-8 is a prime example. This photograph of my wife's grandmother was shot sometime prior to 1910. It's a wonderful photo, but 90 years is a long time for something as fragile and transient as a scrap of paper. It's torn, faded, stained, creased, and flaking. The normally simple act of extracting it from its photo album took every bit as long as scanning it.

But despite it's rough condition, it was quite possible to restore the image in Photoshop, as evidenced by Figure 10-9. (For a full-color view of the before and after images, see Color Plate 10-1.) As in the case of the pool image (Figure 10-7), I used the rubber stamp to do most of the work. And as before, the process was tedious but straightforward. After about an hour and a few hundred brushstrokes, I had the image well in hand.

If an hour sounds like a long time to fix a few rips and scrapes, then wake up and smell the coffee. This is not one-button editing. Photographic restoration is a labor-intensive activity that depends heavily on your talents and your mastery of Photoshop. The rubber stamp tool goes a long way toward making your edits believable, but it does little to automate the process. Retouching calls for a human touch, and that's where you come in.

Figure 10-8: This photo's seen better days. Then again, I hope to look so good when I'm 90 years old.

I considered documenting every single one of my brushstrokes, but I value your time (yes, and my own) too highly. Suffice it to say that the general approach was the same as it was for the pool image. Option-click in an area that looks like it'd do a good job of covering up the blemish, then drag over the blemish. And repeat about 250 times.

Figure 10-9: The same image after about an hour of work with the rubber stamp tool.

That said, I do have some advice to offer that specifically addresses the art of photo restoration:

✦ Most images in this kind of condition are black-and-white. Scan them in color and then peruse the color channels to see which grayscale version of the image looks best. As you can see in Color Plate 10-1, the original image had lots of yellow stains around the tears. So when I viewed at the individual color channels (Figure 10-10), I was hardly surprised to see dark blotches in the blue channel. (Blue is the opposite of yellow, so where yellow is prominent, the blue channel was dark.) In my case, the red channel was in the best shape, so I switched to the red channel and disposed of the other two by choosing Image ➪ Mode ➪ Grayscale. The simple act of trashing the green and blue channels went a long way toward getting rid of the splotches.

Red   Green   Blue

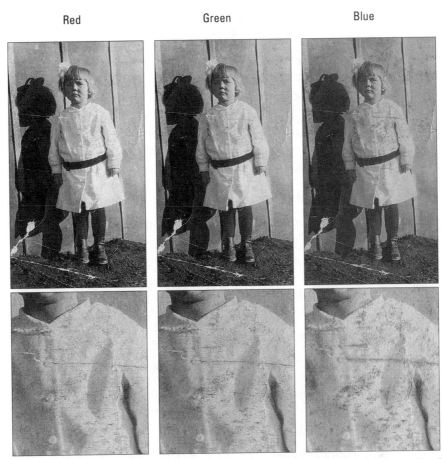

Figure 10-10: A quick peek through the color channels shows the red channel to be my best choice. The blotches are most evident in the girl's blouse, enlarged along the bottom.

✦ Work at 100 percent view size (⌘-Option-0) or larger. It's impossible to judge scratches and other defects accurately at smaller zoom ratios.

✦ Keep the original photo next to you as you work. What looks like a scratch on screen may actually be a photographic element, and what looks like an element may be a scratch. Only by referring to the original image can you be sure.

✦ Don't crop until you're finished retouching the image. You'd be surprised how useful that extra garbage around the perimeter is when it comes to covering up really big tears.

✦ Use hard brush shapes against sharp edges. But when working in general areas like the shadow, the ground, and the wall, mix it up between hard and soft brushes. Staying random is the best way to avoid harsh transitions, repeating patterns, and other digital giveaways.

✦ Paint in short strokes. This helps keep things random, but it also means you don't have to redraw a big long brushstroke if you make a mistake.

✦ When you *do* make a mistake, don't press ⌘-Z. Instead, use the history brush to paint back the image as it appeared before the last rubber stamp operation. (I explain more about the history brush later in this chapter.)

✦ Another way to stay random is to change the source of your clone frequently. That means Option-clicking after every second or third brushstroke. And keep the Aligned check box turned off—an aligned clone is not a random one.

✦ Feel free to experiment with the brush modes and the Opacity setting. For example, as shown magnified in Figure 10-11, the girl has a scratch over the left eye (her right). I corrected this by cloning the right eye, but the cloned eye was so much lighter that it gave the girl a possessed look. To fix this, I set the brush mode to Multiply and changed the Opacity to 30 percent. Then I cloned a bit of the shadowed flesh over the eye to get the finished effect.

Figure 10-11: The left eye in the original image is scratched (top). I clone the right eye (middle), but it's too bright. So I set the brush mode to Multiply, lower the Opacity to 30 percent, and clone a little flesh over the eye (bottom).

✦ Don't attempt to smooth out the general appearance of grain in the image. Grain is integral to an old photo and hiding it usually makes the image look faked. If things get too smooth, or if your cloning results in irregular patterns, select the problem area and apply Filter ➪ Noise ➪ Add Noise. Enter very small Amount values (4 to 8); if necessary, press ⌘-F to reapply the filter one or more times. Remember, grain is good.

With Photoshop's history brush at your side, there's really no way to permanently harm an image. You can even let four or five little mistakes go and then correct them *en masse* with the history brush. Just click to the left of the state in the History palette that directly precedes your first screw-up, and then drag with the history brush. It's easy, satisfying, and incredibly freeing. To paint back to the original scanned image, click in front of the very top item in the History palette. For more information, check out "An Entirely New Reversion Metaphor" later in this chapter.

Eliminating distracting background elements

Another way to apply the stamp tool's cloning capabilities is to eliminate background action that competes with the central elements in an image. For example, Figure 10-12 shows a nifty news photo shot by Michael Probst for the Reuters image library. Although the image is well photographed and historic and all that good stuff, that rear workman doesn't contribute anything to the scene; in fact, he draws your attention away from the foreground drama. I mean, hail to the worker and everything, but the image would be better off without him. The following steps explain how I eradicated the offending workman from the scene.

Note

Remember as you read the following steps that deleting an image element with the rubber stamp tool is something of an inexact science; it requires considerable patience and a dash of trial and error. So regard the following steps as an example of how to approach the process of editing your image rather than as a specific procedure that works for all images. You may need to adapt the process slightly depending upon your image.

On the other hand, any approach that eliminates an element as big as the workman can also correct the most egregious of photographic flaws, including mold, holes, and fire damage. You can even restore photos that have been ripped into pieces, a particular problem for pictures of ex-boyfriends and the like. These steps qualify as major reconstructive surgery.

Figure 10-12: You have to love that old Soviet state-endorsed art. So bold, so angular, so politically intolerant. But you also have to lose that rear workman.

Steps: Eliminating Distracting Elements from an Image

1. **I began by cloning the area around the neck of the statue with a soft brush shape.** Abandoning the controlled clicks I recommended in the last section, I allowed myself to drag with the tool because I needed to cover relatively large portions of the image. The apartment building (or whatever that structure is) behind the floating head is magnificently out of focus, just the thing for hiding any incongruous transitions I might create with the rubber stamp. So I warmed up to the image by retouching this area first. Figure 10-13 shows my progress.

Notice, I covered the workman's body by cloning pixels from both his left and right sides. I also added a vertical bar where the workman's right arm used to be to maintain the rhythm of the building. Remember, variety is the key to using the rubber stamp tool: If you consistently clone from one portion of the image, you create an obvious repetition the viewer can't help but notice.

Figure 10-13: Cloning over the background worker's upper torso was fairly easy because the background building is so regular and out of focus, it provides a wealth of material from which to clone.

2. **The next step was to eliminate the workman's head.** This was a little tricky because it involved rubbing up against the focused perimeter of Lenin's neck. I had to clone some of the more intricate areas using a hard-edged brush. I also ended up duplicating some of the neck edges to maintain continuity. In addition, I touched up the left side of the neck (your left, not Lenin's) and removed a few of the white spots from his face. You see my progress in Figure 10-14.

Figure 10-14: I eliminated the workman's head and touched up details around the perimeter of his neck.

3. **Now for the hard part: eliminating the worker's legs and lower torso.** See that fragment of metal that the foreground worker is holding? What a pain. Its edges were so irregular, there was no way I could restore it with the rubber stamp tool on the off chance that I messed up while trying to eradicate the background worker's limbs. So I lassoed around the fragment to select it and chose Select ⇨ Inverse (⌘-Shift-I) to protect it. I also chose Select ⇨ Feather (⌘-Option-D) and gave it a Radius value of 1 to soften its edges slightly. This prevented me from messing up the metal no matter what edits I made to the background worker's remaining body parts.

4. **From here on, it was just more cloning.** Unfortunately, I barely had anything from which to clone. See the little bit of black edging between the two "legs" of the metal fragment? That's it. This was all I had to draw the strip of edging to the right of the fragment that eventually appears in Figure 10-15. To pull off this feat, I made sure that the Aligned check box was turned off in the Rubber Stamp Options palette. Then I Option-clicked on the tiny bit of edging and click, click, clicked my way down the street.

Figure 10-15: After about 45 minutes of monkeying around with the rubber stamp tool — a practice declared illegal during Stalin's reign — the rear workman is gone, leaving us with an unfettered view of the dubious V. I. Lenin himself.

5. **Unfortunately, the strip I laid down in Step 4 appeared noticeably blobular — it looked for all the world like I clicked a bunch of times.** Darn. To fix this problem, I clicked and Shift-clicked with the smudge tool set to about 30 percent pressure. This smeared the blobs into a continuous strip but, again, the effect was noticeable. It looked as if I had smeared the strip. So I went back and cloned some more, this time with the Opacity value set to 50 percent.

6. **To polish the image off, I chose Select ⇨ Deselect (⌘-D) and ran the sharpen tool along the edges of the metal fragment.** This helped to hide that I'd retouched around it and further distinguished the fragment from the unfocused background. I also cropped away 20 or so pixels from the right side of the image to correct the balance of the image.

What I hope I demonstrated in these steps is this: Cloning with the rubber stamp tool requires you to alternate between patching and whittling away. There are no rights and wrongs, no hard and fast rules. Anything you can find to clone is fair game. As long as you avoid mucking up the foreground image, you can't go wrong (so I guess there is *one* hard and fast rule). If you're careful and diligent, no one but you is going to notice your alterations.

Caution

Any time you edit the contents of a photograph, you tread on sensitive ground. Although some have convincingly argued that electronically retouching an image is, theoretically, no different than cropping a photograph — a technique available and in use since the first daguerreotype — photographers have certain rights under copyright law that cannot be ignored. A photographer may have a reason for including an element you wish to eliminate. So, before you edit any photograph, be sure to get permission either from the original photographer or from the copyright holder (as I did for this photo).

Applying Repeating Patterns

The rubber stamp tool's alternate is the pattern stamp tool, which paints with a rectangular pattern tile. You can use the pattern stamp to create frames, paint wallpaper-type patterns, or retouch textured patches of grass, dirt, or sky. To switch to the pattern stamp tool, press Shift-S or Option-click on the stamp tool icon in the toolbox.

The pattern stamp doesn't require you to Option-click to set a source. Instead, you must first define a pattern by selecting a portion of the image with the rectangular marquee tool and choosing Edit ⇨ Define Pattern. Note that you have to use the rectangular marquee — no other selection tool will do. Also, the selection cannot be feathered, smoothed, expanded, or in any other way altered. If the selection is anything but rectangular, the command is dimmed.

Figure 10-16 shows an example of how you can apply repeating patterns. I selected the single apartment window (labeled in the figure) and chose Edit ⇨ Define Pattern. I then painted with the pattern stamp tool at 80 percent opacity over the horse and rider statue.

Pattern tile

Figure 10-16: After marqueeing a single window (top) and choosing Edit ⇨ Define Pattern, I painted a translucent coat of the pattern over the statue with the pattern stamp tool (bottom).

Caution   As with an image in the Clipboard, Photoshop can retain only one pattern at a time and it remembers the pattern throughout a single session. Any time you choose Edit ⇨ Define Pattern, you delete the previous pattern as you create a new one. Photoshop also deletes the pattern when you choose Edit ⇨ Purge ⇨ Pattern or quit the program.

Aligning patterns (or not)

Like the Rubber Stamp Options palette, the Pattern Stamp Options palette provides an Aligned check box. When active, Photoshop aligns all patterns you apply with the stamp tool, regardless of how many times you start and stop dragging. The two left examples in Figure 10-17 show the effects of selecting this option. The elements in the pattern remain exactly aligned throughout all the brushstrokes. I painted the top image with the Opacity value set to 50 percent, which is why the strokes darken when they meet.

Figure 10-17: Select the Aligned check box to align the patterns in all brushstrokes so that they match up perfectly (left). If you turn the option off, Photoshop starts each pattern with the beginning of the brushstroke (right).

To allow patterns in different brushstrokes to start and end at different locations, turn the Aligned option off. The position of the pattern within each stroke is determined by the point at which you begin dragging. I dragged from right to left to paint the horizontal strokes and from top to bottom to paint the vertical strokes. The two right examples in Figure 10-17 show how nonaligned patterns overlap.

Note

As discussed in Chapter 9, you can also apply a pattern to a selected portion of an image by choosing Edit ➪ Fill and selecting the Pattern option from the Use pop-up menu. If you have an old grayscale image saved in the Photoshop 2 format sitting around, you can alternatively choose Filter ➪ Render ➪ Texture Fill to open the image and repeat it as many times as it takes to fill the selection. (Texture Fill is intended primarily for preparing textures and bump maps for a three-dimensional drawing program, so most folks never touch this filter.)

Creating patterns and textures

The biggest difficulty with painting patterns is not figuring out the pattern stamp tool, but creating the patterns in the first place. Ideally, your pattern should repeat continuously, without vertical and horizontal seams. Here are some ways to create repeating, continuous patterns:

✦ **Load a displacement map:** Photoshop offers a Displacement Maps folder inside the Plug-Ins folder. This folder contains several images, each of which represents a different repeating pattern, as illustrated in Figure 10-18. To use one of these patterns, open the image, choose Select ➪ All (⌘-A), and choose Edit ➪ Define Pattern. (For more information on displacement maps, see Chapter 17.)

12-sided   Cees   Crumbles   Fragment layers

Honeycomb   Mezzo effect   Pentagons   Random strokes

Rectangular tiles   Schnable effect   Streaks pattern   Twirl pattern

Figure 10-18: The 12 patterns contained in the Displacement Maps folder included with Photoshop.

✦ **Illustrator patterns:** Inside the Photoshop/Patterns folder are Illustrator EPS files that contain repeating object patterns. The patterns, some of which appear in Figure 10-19, are all seamless repeaters. You can open them and rasterize them to any size you like. Then press ⌘-A, choose Edit ➪ Define Pattern, and you have your pattern.

Figure 10-19: A random sampling of the illustrations contained in the PostScript Patterns folder inside the Patterns folder.

✦ **Using filters:** As luck would have it, you can create your own custom textures without painting a single line. In fact, you can create a nearly infinite variety of textures by applying several filters to a blank document. To create the texture shown in the top row of Figure 10-20, for example, I created a new 200 × 200-pixel image. I then chose Filter ⇨ Noise ⇨ Add Noise, entered a value of 64, and selected the Gaussian radio button. I pressed ⌘-F twice to apply the noise filter two more times. Finally, I chose Filter ⇨ Stylize ⇨ Emboss and entered 45 into the Angle option box, 2 into the Height option box, and 100 percent into the Amount option box. The result is a bumpy surface that looks like stucco.

To get the second row effects in Figure 10-20, I started with the noise pattern and applied Filter ⇨ Pixelate ⇨ Crystallize with a Cell Size of 10 pixels. Then I again applied the Emboss filter with the same settings as before. To create the third row of textures, I started with a blank image and chose Filter ⇨ Render ⇨ Clouds. Then I applied the Emboss filter with an Amount value of 500 percent. To punch up the contrast, I choose Image ⇨ Adjust ⇨ Auto Levels (⌘-Shift-L).

Naturally, I could go on like this for days. To learn more about filters so you can make up your own textures, read Chapters 15 and 16. Chapter 15 covers Add Noise; Chapter 16 explains Emboss, Crystallize, and Clouds.

Noise x3

Emboss, 100%

Crystallize

Emboss, 100%

Clouds

Emboss, 500%

Figure 10-20: Three examples of filtered effects before (left) and after (right) applying the Emboss command.

✦ **Marquee and clone:** You can use the rectangular marquee and pattern stamp tools to transform a scanned image into a custom pattern. Because this technique is more complicated as well as more rewarding than the others, I explain it in the following section.

Building your own seamless pattern

The following steps describe how to change a scanned image into a seamless, repeating pattern. To illustrate how this process works, Figures 10-21 through 10-24 show various stages in a project I completed. You need only two tools to carry out these steps: the rectangular marquee tool and the rubber stamp tool.

Cross-Reference

Even so, those of you reading sequentially will notice that these steps involve a few selection and layering techniques I haven't yet discussed. If you become confused, you can find out more about selecting, moving, and cloning images in Chapter 11.

Steps: Building a Repeating Pattern from a Scanned Image

1. **Open the image that you want to convert into a pattern.** I started with an image from the PhotoDisc image library.

2. **Select the rectangular marquee tool, then press Return/Enter.** Photoshop displays the Marquee Options palette. Select Fixed Size from the Style pop-up menu and enter specific values into the Width and Height option boxes. This way, you can easily reselect a portion of the pattern in the steps that follow, as well as use the fixed-size marquee to define the pattern when you finish. To create the patterns shown in the figures, I set the marquee to 128 × 128 pixels.

3. **Select the portion of the image you want to feature in the pattern.** Because you've specified an exact marquee size, Photoshop selects a fixed area whenever you click. You can also drag to move the marquee around in the window.

4. **Press ⌘-C.** This copies the image to the Clipboard.

5. **Choose File ⇨ New (⌘-N) and triple the Width and Height values.** In my case, Photoshop suggested a new image size of 128 × 128 pixels, which matches the size of the image I copied to the Clipboard. By tripling these values, I arrived at a new image size of 384 × 384 pixels.

6. **Press ⌘-V.** Photoshop pastes the copied image smack dab in the center of the window, which is exactly where you want it. This image will serve as the central tile of your repeating pattern.

7. **⌘-click on the item labeled Layer 1 in the Layers palette.** Photoshop pastes the image on a new layer. But in order to duplicate the image and convert it into a pattern, you need to select the image and flatten it. ⌘-clicking on the layer name does the selecting.

8. **Press ⌘-E.** This merges the layer with the background, thereby flattening it. Or you can choose Layer ⇨ Flatten Image. Either way, the selection outline remains intact.

9. **Choose Edit ⇨ Define Pattern.** This establishes the selected image as a pattern tile.

10. **Press ⌘-D to deselect the image.** You neither need nor want the selection outline any more. You'll need to be able to fill and clone freely without a selection outline getting in the way.

11. **Press Shift-Delete or choose Edit ⇨ Fill.** Then select Pattern from the Use pop-up menu and press Return. This fills the window with a 3 × 3-tile grid, as shown in Figure 10-21.

Figure 10-21: To build the repeating pattern shown in Figure 10-24, I started by creating a grid of nine image tiles. As you can see, the seams between the tiles in this grid are harsh and unacceptable.

12. **Drag the title bar of the new image window to position it so you can see the portion of the image you copied in the original image window.** If necessary, drag the title bar of the original image window to reposition it, as well. After you have your windows arranged, click on the title bar of the new image to make it the active window.

13. **Select the rubber stamp.** Press the S key.

14. **Turn off the Aligned check box in the Rubber Stamp Options palette.** Ironic as it may sound, it's easier to get the alignment between clone-from and clone-to points established with Aligned turned off.

15. **Specify the image you want to clone by Option-clicking in the original image window.** No need to switch out of the new window. Option-click on an easily identifiable pixel that belongs to the portion of the image you copied. The exact pixel you click on is very important. If you press the Caps Lock key, you get the crosshair cursor, which makes it easier to narrow in on a pixel. In my case, I clicked on the corner of the Buddha's mouth. (At least, I assume that's Buddha. Then again, I'm a Western-bred ignoramus, so what do I know?)

16. **Now click with the stamp tool on the matching pixel in the central tile of the new window.** If you clicked the correct pixel, the tile should not change one iota. If it shifts at all, press ⌘-Z and try again. Because Aligned is turned off, you can keep undoing and clicking over and over again without resetting the clone-from point in the original image.

17. **Turn the Aligned check box on.** Once you click in the image without seeing any shift, select the Aligned option in the Rubber Stamp Options palette to lock in the alignment between the clone-from and clone-to points.

(continued)

18. **Use the stamp tool to fill in portions of the central tile.** For example, in Figure 10-22, I extended the Buddha's cheek and neck down into the lower row of tiles. I also extended the central forehead to meet the Buddha on the left.

Figure 10-22: I used the rubber stamp's cloning capability to extend the features in the central face toward the left and downward.

19. **Select a portion of the modified image.** After you establish one continuous transition between two tiles in any direction — up, down, left, or right — click with the rectangular marquee tool select an area that includes the transition. In my case, I managed to create a smooth transition between the central and bottom tiles. Therefore, I selected a region that includes half the central tile and half the tile below it.

20. **Repeat Steps 9 through 11.** That is, choose Edit ➪ Define Pattern, press ⌘-D, choose Edit ➪ Fill, and press Return. This fills the image with your new transition. Don't worry if the tiles shift around a bit — that's to be expected.

Tip

If you plan on creating a lot of patterns, you might want to record Steps 9 through 11 as a script in the Actions palette. Then you can replay the script after each time you clone away a seam.

21. **If you started by creating a horizontal transition, use the rubber stamp tool to create a vertical transition.** Likewise, if you started vertically, now go horizontally. You may need to turn off the Aligned check box again to establish the proper alignment between clone-from and clone-to points. In my case, I shifted the clone-to point several times — alternatively building on the central Buddha, the right-hand one, and the

Note

middle one in the bottom row. Each time you get the clone-to point properly positioned, turn the Aligned check box back on to lock in the alignment. Then clone away.

As long as you get the clone-from and clone-to points properly aligned, you can't make a mistake. If you change your mind, realign the clone points and try again. In my case, I cloned the long droopy earlobe down into the face of the Buddha below. (I guess our young Buddha didn't stop to think that once the droopy-ear fad passed, he would be stuck with it for the rest of his life.) I also cloned the god's chin onto the forehead of the one to the right, ultimately achieving the effect shown in Figure 10-23.

Figure 10-23: After completing a smooth transition between the central tile and the tiles below and to the right of it, I selected a portion of the image and chose Edit ➪ Define Pattern.

22. **After you build up one set of both horizontal and vertical transitions, click with the rectangular marquee tool to select the transitions.** Figure 10-23 shows where I positioned my 128 × 128-pixel selection boundary. This includes parts of each of four neighboring heads, including the all-important droopy ear. Don't worry if the image doesn't appear centered inside the selection outline. What counts is that the image flows seamlessly inside the selection outline.

23. **Repeat Steps 9 through 11.** Or play that script I suggested in Step 20 if you bothered to record it. If the tiles blend together seamlessly, as in Figure 10-24, then you're finished. If not, clone some more with the rubber stamp tool and try again.

(continued)

Figure 10-24: This Eastern montage is the result of applying the Buddha pattern. Buddha sure looks serene and comfortable, especially considering he's resting on his own head.

An Entirely New Reversion Metaphor

Since roughly the dawn of recorded time, folks have been begging, pleading, and screaming at the top of their lungs for multiple undos in Photoshop. But every time I witnessed an Adobe representative respond on the subject, the company line seemed to be the same: Multiple undos and pixels just don't mix. Photoshop is already caching enough data in RAM without asking it to keep track of 10 or 20 previous operations. If you want to backstep through editing history, buy a time machine.

In fact, my expectations had been sufficiently whittled down that I held out little hope of anything productive on the undo front. *If* Photoshop ever got around to adding multiple undos to its feature list, it'd be a partial implementation that would require the user to tag significant operations, or it would turn out to be smoke and mirrors *a la* Live Picture, xRes, and a host of others. The entire population of Roswell stood a better chance of being beamed aboard the Heaven's Gate spaceship than you and I stood of being able to undo the second-to-last operation in Photoshop.

Photoshop **5.0**

Well, I just hope there's room on Hale-Bopp's tail for 40,000 New Mexicans, because Photoshop 5 has multiple undos. You can revisit as many as 100 consecutive operations from your past, just as in Illustrator, FreeHand, and virtually every other program that doesn't involve pixels.

But it gets better than that. Rather than settling for simple backstepping, Version 5 invents the best implementation of multiple undos that I've ever seen. The History palette takes the whole reversion metaphor into *Slaughterhouse Five* territory. If you've never read the novel (or you've somehow forgotten), Kurt Vonnegut, Jr. suggested that humans live from one moment to the next like a person strapped to a boxcar, unable to change the speed or direction of the train as it hurtles through time. With multiple undos, you can make the train stop and back up, but you're still strapped to it. The History palette is the first tool that lets you get off the train and transport to any point on the track — instantaneously. In short, we now have a digital version of time travel.

Here are just a few of the marvelous innovations of the History palette:

✦ **Undo-independent stepping.** Step backward by pressing ⌘-Option-Z; step forward by pressing ⌘-Shift-Z. Every program with multiple undos does this, but Photoshop's keyboard equivalents are different. Why? Because you can backstep independent of the Undo command, so that even backstepping is undoable.

✦ **Before and after.** Revert to a point in history to see a "before" view of your image, then fly forward to see the "after" view. From then on, ⌘-Z becomes a super-undo, toggling between the before and after views. The opportunities for comparing states and changing your mind are truly colossal.

✦ **Dynamic time travel.** If before and after isn't enough, how about animated history? You can drag a control to slide dynamically forward and backward through operations. It's like you recorded the operations to videotape, and now you're rewinding and fast-forwarding through them.

✦ **Sweeping away the mistakes.** Select a point in the history of your image and paint back to it using the history brush. You can let the mistakes pile up and then brush them away. This brush isn't a paintbrush, it's a hand broom.

✦ **Take a picture, it'll last longer.** You can save any point in the History palette as a snapshot. That way, even several hundred operations after that point in history is long gone, you can revisit the snapshot.

✦ **This is your life, Image A.** Each and every image has its own history. So after performing a few hundred operations on Image A, you can still go back to Image B and backstep through operations you performed hours ago. The caveat is that the history remains available only so long as an image is open. Close the image, and its history goes away.

The only thing you can't do is travel forward into the future—say, to about three days from now when you've finished your grueling project, submitted it to your client, and received your big fat paycheck. Believe it or not, that's actually good news. The day Adobe can figure out how to do your work for you, your clients will hire Photoshop and stop hiring you.

So I ask you—Photoshop 5, *Slaughterhouse Five*, just a coincidence? Well, yes, I suppose it is. But the fact remains, you now have the option of getting off the boxcar. How you make use of your newfound freedom is up to you.

Using the traditional undo functions

Before I dive into the History palette, I should take a moment to summarize Photoshop's more traditional reversion functions. (If you already know about this stuff, skip to the next section.)

✦ **Undo:** To restore an image to the way it looked before the last operation, choose Edit ➪ Undo (⌘-Z). You can undo the effect of a paint or edit tool, a change made to a selection outline, or a special-effect or color-correction command. You can't undo disk operations, such as opening or saving. Photoshop does enable you to undo an edit after printing an image, though. You can test out an effect, print it, and then undo it if you think the effect looks awful.

✦ **Revert:** Choose File ➪ Revert (or press the F12 key) to reload an image from disk. This is generally the last-resort function, the command you choose after everything else has failed.

To restore the image back to the way it looked when you originally opened it — which may precede the last-saved state — scroll to the top of the History palette and click on the topmost item. (This assumes that you haven't gone and turned off the Automatically Create First Snapshot check box in the History Options dialog box.)

✦ **Selective reversion:** To revert a selected area to the way it appeared when it was first opened — or some other source state identified in the History palette — choose Edit ➪ Fill (Shift-Delete). Then select History from the Use pop-up menu and press Return.

Better yet, just press ⌘-Option-Delete. This one keystroke fills the selection with the source state in a jiffy. (You set the source state by clicking in the left column of the History palette, as I explain in the very next section.)

✦ **The eraser tool:** Drag in the Background layer with the eraser tool to paint in white or some other background color. You're essentially erasing the image back to bare canvas. Or apply the eraser to a layer to delete pixels and expose underlying layers.

You can also Option-drag with the eraser to revert back to the targeted state in the History palette. But you're better off using the history brush for this purpose. The history brush offers more capabilities—notably brush modes—and you don't have to press Option.

Where warranted, I explain these functions in greater detail in the following sections. But first, let's look at the central headquarters for the new reversion metaphor . . .

The History palette

Choose Window ➪ Show History to view the History palette, annotated with the palette menu in full view in Figure 10-25. The History palette records each significant operation — everything other than settings and preferences (for example, selecting a new foreground color) — and adds it to a list. The oldest operations appear at the top of the list with the most recent operations at the bottom.

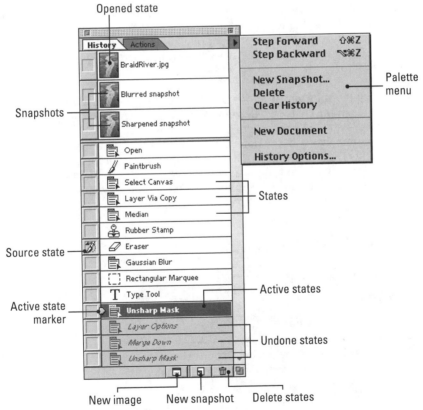

Figure 10-25: The History palette records each significant event as an independent state. To return to a state, just click on it.

Each item in the list is called a *state*. That's not my word, it's Adobe's, and several have voiced the opinion that the term is too stiff and formal. But I think it's dead on. Each item in the palette represents a stepping stone in the progression of the image, a condition at a moment in time — in other words, a state.

Photoshop automatically names each item according to the tool, command, or operation used to arrive at the state. The icon next to the name helps to identify the state further. But the best way to find out what a state is like is to click on it. Photoshop instantaneously undoes all operations performed after that state and returns you to the state so that you can inspect it in detail. To redo all the operations you just did in one fell swoop, press ⌘-Z or choose Edit ➪ Undo State Change.

That one action — clicking on a state — is the gist of what you need to know to travel forward and backward through time in Photoshop. If that's all you ever learn, you'll find yourself working with greater speed, freedom, and security than is possible in virtually any other graphics application. But this represents only the first in a long list of the History palette's capabilities. Here's the rest of what you might want to know:

✦ **Changing the number of undos:** By default, Photoshop records the last 20 operations in the History palette. When you perform the 21st operation, the first state is shoved off the list. To change this behavior, choose the History Option command from the palette menu and enter a new Maximum History Items value (see Figure 10-26). If your computer is equipped with 32MB or less of RAM, you might want to lower the value to 5 or 10 to maintain greater efficiency. On the other hand, if you become a time-traveling freak (like me) and you have plenty of RAM, then turn it up, baby, all the way up!

Figure 10-26: Choose the History Options command to change the number of undos and permit Photoshop to record states out of order.

✦ **Undone states:** When you revert to a state by clicking on it, every subsequent state turns gray to show that it's been undone. You can redo a grayed state simply by clicking on it. But if you perform a new operation, all grayed states disappear. You have one opportunity to bring them back by pressing ⌘-Z, but if you perform another new operation, the once grayed states are gone for good.

✦ **Working with non-sequential states:** If you don't like the idea of losing your undone states—every state is sacred, after all—then choose the History Options command and select the Allow Non-Linear History check box (see Figure 10-26). Undone states no longer drop off the list when you perform a new operation. They remain available on the off chance that you might want to revisit them. It's like having multiple possible time trails.

The Allow Non-Linear History check box does not permit you to undo a single state without affecting the subsequent states. For example, let's say you paint with the airbrush, smear with the smudge tool, and then clone with the rubber stamp. You can revert back to the airbrush state and then apply other operations without losing the option of restoring the smudge and clone. But you can't undo the smudge and leave the clone intact. Operations can only occur in the sequence they were applied.

✦ **Stepping through states:** As I mentioned earlier, you can press ⌘-Option-Z to undo the active step or ⌘-Shift-Z to redo the next step in the list. Backstepping goes up the list of states in the History palette, forward stepping goes down. Keep in mind that if the Allow Non-Linear History check box is active, backstepping may take you to a state that was previously inactive.

✦ **Flying through states:** Drag the right-pointing active step marker (labeled in Figure 10-25) up and down the list to rewind and fast-forward through time. If the screen image doesn't appear to change as you fly by certain states, it most likely means those states involve small brushstrokes or changes to selection outlines. Otherwise, the changes are quite apparent.

✦ **Taking a snapshot:** Every once in a while, a state comes along that's so great, you don't want it to fall by the wayside 20 operations from now. To set a state aside, choose New Snapshot or click on the little page icon at the bottom of the History palette. Photoshop asks you if you want to save all layers (as by default), flatten the image, or retain just the active layer. The new *snapshot*—as it's called—then appears in the top portion of the palette.

To create a snapshot without going through the New Snapshot dialog box, Option-click on the page icon. (The state has to be active to convert it to a snapshot, so you can't drag a state and drop it onto the page icon, as you can drag-and-drop elements in other palettes.)

Photoshop 5 lets you store as many snapshots as your computer's RAM will permit. Also worth noting, the program automatically creates a snapshot of the image as it appears when it's first opened. If you don't like this opening snapshot, you can turn it off using the History Options command.

✦ **Saving the state permanently:** The problem with snapshots is that they only last as long as the current session. If you quit Photoshop or the program crashes, you lose the entire history list, snapshots included. To save a state so you can refer to it several days from now, choose the New Document command or click on the leftmost icon at the bottom of the History palette. You can also drag and drop a state onto the icon. Either way, Photoshop duplicates the state to a new image window. Then you can save the state to the format of your choice.

✦ **Setting the source:** Click to the left of a state to identify it as the *source state*. The history brush icon appears where you click. The source state affects the performance of the history brush, the magic eraser, and the Fill command. The keystroke ⌘-Option-Delete fills the selection with the source state.

✦ **Trashing states:** If your machine is equipped with little RAM or you're working on a particularly large image, Photoshop may slow down as the states accumulate. If things get too slow, you may want to purge. You can delete every state from the active state forward by clicking on the trash can icon at the bottom of the palette. (Option-click the icon to bypass the warning.) If the Allow Non-Linear History check box is on, clicking on the trash can deletes just the active state.

To clear all states from the History palette, choose the Clear History command from the palette menu. (You can also choose Edit ➪ Purge ➪ Histories, but the advantage of Clear Histories is that you can undo it if you change your mind.)

Painting away the past

The History palette represents the regimental way to revert images inside Photoshop. You can retreat, march forward, proceed in linear or non-linear formation, capture states, and retire them. Every state plays backward in the same way it played forward. It's precise, predictable, and positively by the book.

But what if you want to get free-form? What if you want to brush away the present and paint in the past? In that case, a palette isn't going to do you any good. What you need is a pliable, emancipated, free-wheeling tool.

As luck would have it, Photoshop offers two candidates — the eraser and the history brush. The eraser washes away pixels to reveal underlying pixels or exposed canvas. The history brush takes you back to a kinder, simpler state. Although the two overlap slightly, they each have a very specific purpose, as will become clear in the following sections.

The eraser tool

Select the eraser tool by pressing the E key. Then press Return to display the Eraser Options palette, shown in Figure 10-27. The palette offers a pop-up menu of four eraser styles: Paintbrush, Airbrush, Pencil, and Block. *Block* is the old 16 × 16-pixel square eraser that's great for hard-edged touch-ups. The other options work exactly like the tools for which they're named.

Tip

You needn't go to the trouble of selecting the options from the pop-up menu. When the eraser tool is active, press Shift-E to cycle through the different styles.

Figure 10-27: The eraser tool can paint like the paintbrush, the airbrush, the pencil, or the vintage Photoshop 2.5 eraser (Block).

As if this weren't enough, the eraser is pressure sensitive, it responds to Opacity settings, and you can create fading eraser strokes. When the Paintbrush option is active, you even have access to the Wet Edges check box described in Chapter 8. The only thing missing is the brush modes menu.

While the eraser tool is pretty straightforward, there's no sense in leaving any stone unturned. So here's everything you ever wanted to know about the art of erasing:

✦ **Erasing on a layer:** When working on the Background layer, the eraser merely paints in the background color. Big whoop. What distinguishes the eraser tool from the other brushes is layers. When working on a layer (with the Preserve Transparency check box turned off), the eraser tool actually removes paint and exposes portions of the underlying image. The eraser tool suddenly performs like a real eraser.

If the Layer palette's Preserve Transparency check box is turned on, Photoshop won't let the eraser bore holes in the layer. Instead, it paints in the background color. For more information on Preserve Transparency and its other pals in the Layers palette, read Chapter 13.

✦ **Erasing lightly:** Change the Opacity setting in the Eraser Options palette to make portions of a layer translucent in inverse proportion to the Opacity value. For example, if you set the Opacity to 90 percent, you remove 90 percent of the opacity from the layer and, therefore, leave 10 percent of the opacity behind. The result is a nearly transparent stroke through the layer.

✦ **The eraser compared with layer masks:** As described in the "Creating layer-specific masks" section of Chapter 13, you can also erase holes in a layer using a layer mask. But unlike the eraser — which eliminates pixels for good — a layer mask doesn't do any permanent damage. On the other hand, using the eraser tool doesn't increase the size of your image as much as a layer mask does. (One can argue *any* operation—even a deletion—increases the size of the image in RAM because the History palette has to track it. But the eraser is still more memory-efficient than a layer mask.) So it's a trade-off.

✦ **Erasing with the pencil:** If you double-click on the pencil icon in the toolbox and select the Auto Erase check box in the Pencil Options palette, the pencil draws in the background color any time you click or drag on a pixel colored in the foreground color. This can be useful when you're drawing a line against a plain background. Set the foreground color to the color of the line; set the background color to the color of the background. Then use the pencil tool to draw and erase the line until you get it just right. I use this feature all the time when preparing screen shots. Adobe engineers call the Auto Erase check box their "ode to Fatbits," from the ancient MacPaint zoom function.

Note

Unlike the eraser, the pencil always draws either in the foreground or background color, even when used on a layer.

✦ **The magic eraser:** Press the Option key to access the "magic" eraser. Option-dragging paints with the source state identified by the history brush icon in the History palette. (By default, Photoshop sets the source state to the image as it appeared when first opened.) It's like scraping away the paint laid down by the operations following the source state, as demonstrated quite graphically in Figure 10-28.

Or, you can also select the Erase to History check box in the Eraser Options palette. In this case, dragging with the eraser reverts and Option-dragging paints in the background color.

Figure 10-28: After making a dreadful mistake (left), I Option-dragged with the eraser tool to restore the image to the way it looked in the source state (right).

The history brush

Photoshop 5.0

The history brush tool works like the magic eraser, except without the Option key. Just drag with the tool to paint down to the source state targeted in the History palette.

But the history brush offers three advantages over the magic eraser:

✦ **Brush modes:** First, you can take advantage of brush modes. By choosing a different brush mode from the pop-up menu in the upper left corner of the History Brush Options palette, you can mix pixels from the changed and saved images to achieve interesting and, sometimes, surprising effects.

✦ **Impressionist:** The other advantage is the Impressionist check box, highlighted in Figure 10-29. This option retrieves the source state and sort of smears it around to create a gooey, unfocused effect. You can achieve some mildly interesting effects by combining Impressionist with the Overlay, Hard Light, or Soft Light brush modes, but it's clearly a special effects function.

✦ **Fewer keystrokes:** You don't have to cycle through brush styles as with the eraser tool. Just press the Y key to select the history brush and start painting.

Figure 10-29: The history brush offers two advantages over the magic eraser — the brush modes pop-up menu and the Impressionist check box — both highlighted here.

Personally, I advise you to get in the habit of using the history brush instead of the magic eraser. Granted, the eraser gives you different cursors — pencil style and block — but when weighed against brush modes, this hardly seems much of an advantage at all. All things considered, the history brush is superior and it doesn't require you to press Option. The history brush is also more intuitive, because its icon matches the source state icon in the History palette.

Merging alternative realities

The history brush is a great tool for erasing away mistakes. But you don't have to limit yourself to painting into the past. Just as the History palette lets you skip back and forth along the train track of time, the history brush lets you paint to any point in time.

The following steps provide an example of how you can use the History palette to establish an alternative reality and then follow up with the history brush to merge that reality with the present. It's trippy stuff, I realize, but I'm confident that with a little effort, you can give that post-modern brain of yours a half twist and wrap it around these steps like a big, mushy Mobius Strip.

Steps: Brushing to a Parallel Time Line

1. **Open the image you want to warp into the fourth dimension.** I begin with a map of Japan (Figure 10-30). Japan is a wacky combination of seventeenth-century cultural uniformity, 1950's innocence, and twenty-first century corporate imperialism, so it strikes me as a perfect subject for my compound-time experiment.

Figure 10-30: This map of Japan comes from the Digital Stock image library.

2. **Apply a couple of filters.** I choose Filter ⇨ Pixelate ⇨ Mosaic and set the Cell Size value to 20 pixels. Then I apply Filter ⇨ Stylize ⇨ Emboss with a Height of 5 pixels and an Amount of 200 percent. Figure 10-31 shows the results.

3. **Choose the History Options command from the History palette menu.** Then turn on the Allow Non-Linear History check box and press Return.

4. **Click on the Open item in the History palette.** This reverts the image to the state at which it existed when you first opened it. But thanks to non-linear history, Photoshop retains the alternate filtered versions of the image just in case you'd like to revisit this timeline in the future.

Figure 10-31: The results of applying the Mosaic (left) and Emboss (right) filters. Both of these effects are overstated, so I'll undo them and then paint them back in with the history brush.

5. **Click in front of the first filter effect in the History palette to make it the source state.** In my case, I click in front of the Mosaic item.

6. **Select the history brush and start painting.** As you do, you'll paint with the filtered version of the image. For my part, I set the blend mode to Darken and painted around the island country to give it a digital edge, as in the first example of Figure 10-32.

Figure 10-32: I set the brush mode to Darken and painted in the Mosaic effect with the history brush (left). Then I changed the brush mode to Overlay and brushed in the Emboss effect (right).

(continued)

7. **Switch the source state by clicking in front of the second filter effect.** Naturally, I clicked in front of the Emboss item.

8. **Paint again with the history brush.** This time, I changed the brush mode to Overlay and painted randomly over Japan and the surrounding ocean. The result appears in the second example of Figure 10-32.

Once you finish, you can toss the filtered states. This alternate timeline has served its purpose. Or keep it around as a snapshot to come back to later.

Source state limitations

Sadly, there are some minor limitations to history brushing. Photoshop won't let you paint with either the history brush or magic eraser if the source state is a different width or height than the current image. One pixel different and the source state is a moot point. (This also goes for Edit ➪ Fill and ⌘-Option-Delete.)

If Photoshop displays the not-allowed cursor (the circle with a slash through it) when you try to use the history brush, then move the source state icon in the History palette to a point after you modified the width or the height of the image. Commands that can mix up the history brush include Image ➪ Image Size, Canvas Size, Rotate Canvas, and Crop, as well as the crop tool. If you applied one of these operations in the very last state, then you either have to backstep before that operation or find some alternative to the history brush.

It's not a big deal, though. Give it some time and you'll learn to anticipate this problem. In the case of my experiment with Japan, for example, I made sure to resample and crop the image before I began my experiment. Get the dimensions ironed out, and then start laying down your time trails.

✦   ✦   ✦

Selections, Layers, and Text

Selections and Paths

Selection Fundamentals

Selections direct and protect. If it weren't for Photoshop's selection capabilities, you and I would be flinging paint on the canvas for all we're worth, like so many Jackson Pollock and Vasily Kandinsky wannabes without any means to constrain, discriminate, or otherwise regulate the effects of our actions. Without selections, there'd be no filters, no color corrections, and no layers. In fact, we'd all be dangerously close to real life, that dreaded environment we've spent so much time and money to avoid.

No other program gives you so much control over the size and shape of selections. You can finesse selection outlines with unparalleled control, alternatively adding to selected areas, subtracting from them, and moving and rotating selections independent of the pixels inside them. You can even mix masks and selection outlines together, as covered in Chapter 12.

That's why this chapter and the one that follows are the most important chapters in this book.

Note

Pretty cool, huh? You put a provocative sentence like that on a line by itself and it resonates with authority. Granted, it's a little overstated, but can you blame me? I mean, I can't have a sentence like, "If you want my opinion, I think these are some pretty dog-gone important chapters — at least, that's the way it seems to me; certainly, you might have a different opinion," on a line by itself. The other paragraphs would laugh at it.

At any rate, I invite you to pay close attention to the fundamental concepts and approaches documented throughout this chapter. While I wouldn't characterize each and every technique as essential — lots of artists get by without paying much attention to paths, for example, while other artists swear by them — a working knowledge of selection outlines is key to using Photoshop successfully.

How selections work

Before you can edit a portion of an image, you must first *select* it, which is computerese for indicating the boundaries of the area you want to edit. To select part of an image in a painting program, you must surround it with a selection outline or marquee; this tells Photoshop where to apply your editing instructions. The selection outline appears as a moving pattern of dash marks, lovingly termed *marching ants* by doughheads who've been using computers too long. (See Figure 11-1 for the inside story.)

Figure 11-1: A magnified view of a dash mark in a selection outline reveals a startling discovery.

Photoshop 5 provides 11 tools for drawing selection outlines — up three from Version 4 — all of which I describe briefly in the following list. You can access most of the tools from the keyboard, as noted in the parentheses:

✦ **Rectangular marquee (M):** The rectangular marquee tool has long been a staple of painting programs. This tool enables you to select rectangular or square portions of an image.

✦ **Elliptical marquee (Shift-M):** The elliptical marquee tool works like the rectangular marquee except it selects elliptical or circular portions of an image. (Pressing the M key switches between the rectangular and elliptical marquee tools.)

✦ **Single-row/single-column:** The single-row and single-column tools enable you to select a single row or column of pixels that stretches the entire width or height of the image. These are the only tools in all of Photoshop you can't access from the keyboard.

✦ **Lasso (L):** The lasso tool enables you to select a free-form portion of an image. You simply drag with the lasso tool around the area you want to edit. Unlike the lasso tools in most painting programs, which shrink selection outlines to disqualify pixels in the background color, Photoshop's lasso tool selects the exact portion of the image you enclose in your drag.

✦ **Polygonal lasso (Shift-L):** Click on different points in your image to set corners in a straight-sided selection outline. This is a great way to select free-form areas if you're not good at wielding the mouse or your wrists are a tad sore. (You can achieve this same effect by Option- clicking with the lasso tool, but I'll explain this more in the "Free-form outlines" section later in this chapter.)

✦ **Magnetic lasso (Shift-L again):** Click with the magnetic lasso along the edge of an image element that you want to select independently from its background. Then move the magnetic lasso (you don't have to drag) around the edge of the element. It's a tricky tool to use, so you can be sure I describe it in excruciating detail in the coming pages.

✦ **Magic wand (W):** First introduced by Photoshop, the Magic wand tool lets you select a contiguous region of similarly colored pixels by clicking inside it. For example, you might click inside the boundaries of a face to isolate it from the hair and background elements. Novices tend to gravitate toward the magic wand because it seems like such a miracle tool but, in fact, it's the least predictable and ultimately the least useful of the bunch.

✦ **Pen (P):** Now available in the main toolbox, the pen tool is both the most difficult to master and the most accurate and versatile of the selection tools. You use the pen tool to create a *path*, which is an object-oriented breed of selection outline. You click and drag to create individual points in the path. You can edit the path after the fact by moving, adding, and deleting points. You can even transfer a path by dragging and dropping between Photoshop and either Illustrator 7 or FreeHand 8. For a discussion of the pen tool, read the "How to Draw and Edit Paths" section later in this chapter.

✦ **Magnetic pen (Shift-P):** The magnetic pen is basically an object-oriented version of the magnetic lasso tool. Click to set the first point, then move your mouse and watch Photoshop create the other points automatically. It's not a great tool, but it can prove handy when selecting image elements that stand out very clearly from their backgrounds.

✦ **Freeform pen (Shift-P again):** If you hate setting points but you need to create a clipping path, this is the tool for you. You just drag with the tool as if you were selecting with the lasso tool and let Photoshop define the points automatically. Obviously, you can expect the same level of accuracy that you get from the standard pen tool, but it's child's play to use.

Cross-Reference Photoshop's two type mask tools (press Shift-T to get to them) are also technically selection tools because Photoshop converts each character of type to a selection outline. But type involves other issues that would merely confuse the contents of this chapter. So I've awarded type its own chapter (Chapter 14).

If this were all you needed to know to use the selection tools in Photoshop, the application would be on par with the average paint program. Part of what makes Photoshop exceptional, however, is that it provides literally hundreds of little tricks to increase the functionality of every selection tool.

Furthermore, all of Photoshop's selection tools work together in perfect harmony. You can exploit the specialized capabilities of all 11 tools (and the type mask tools) to create a single selection boundary. After you understand which tool best serves which purpose, you can isolate any element in an image, no matter how complex or how delicate its outline.

Geometric selection outlines

The default tool in the upper left corner of the toolbox is the rectangular marquee tool. You can access the elliptical marquee tool by Option-clicking on the marquee tool icon or by pressing Shift-M when the rectangular marquee tool is already selected. Pressing Shift-M again returns you to the rectangular marquee tool. Option-clicking cycles through the single-row and single-column tools, as well.

The marquee tools are more versatile than they may appear at first glance. You can adjust the performance of each tool as follows:

✦ **Constraining to a square or circle:** Press and hold Shift *after* beginning your drag to draw a perfect square with the rectangular marquee tool or a perfect circle with the elliptical marquee tool. (Pressing Shift *before* dragging also works if no other selection is active; otherwise, this adds to a selection, as I explain later in the "Ways to Change Selection Outlines" section.)

✦ **Drawing a circular marquee:** When perusing an online forum a while back, someone asked how to create a perfect circular marquee. Despite more than a month of helpful suggestions — some highly imaginative — no one offered the easiest suggestion of all (well, I ultimately did, but I'm a know-it-all). So remember to press Shift after you begin to drag and you'll be one step ahead of the game.

✦ **Drawing out from the center:** Press and hold the Option key after you begin dragging to draw the marquee from the center outward instead of from corner to corner. (Again, pressing Option before dragging works if no selection outline is active; otherwise, this subtracts from the selection.) This technique is especially useful when you draw an elliptical marquee. Locating the center of the area you want to select is frequently easier than locating one of its corners — particularly because ellipses don't have corners.

Tip

✦ **Moving the marquee on the fly:** While drawing a marquee, press and hold the spacebar to move the marquee rather than resize it. When you get the marquee in place, release the spacebar and keep dragging to modify the size. The spacebar is most helpful when drawing elliptical selections or when drawing a marquee out from the center — this eliminates the guesswork, so you can position your marquees exactly on target.

✦ **Selecting a single-pixel line:** Use the single-row and single-column tools to select a single row or column of pixels. I use these tools to fix screw-ups such as a missing line of pixels in a screen shot, to delete random pixels around the perimeter of an image, or to create perpendicular lines within a fixed space.

✦ **Constraining the aspect ratio:** If you know you want to create an image that conforms to a certain height/width ratio — called an *aspect ratio* — you can constrain either a rectangular or an elliptical marquee so the ratio between height and width remains fixed, no matter how large or small a marquee you create. To accomplish this, press Return when the marquee tool is active to display the Marquee Options palette, shown in Figure 11-2. Then select Constrained Aspect Ratio from the Style pop-up menu. Enter the desired ratio values into the Width and Height option boxes.

For example, if you want to crop an image to the ratio of a 13-inch (640 × 480-pixel) screen, enter 4 and 3, respectively, into the Width and Height option boxes and press Return to confirm your changes. Then select the area of the image you want to retain and choose Image ⇨ Crop.

Figure 11-2: Select the Constrained Aspect Ratio option in the Marquee Options palette to constrain the width and height of a marquee.

✦ **Sizing the marquee numerically:** If you're editing a screen shot or some other form of regular or schematic image, you may find specifying the size of a marquee numerically helpful. To do so, select the Fixed Size option from the Style pop-up menu and enter size values into the Width and Height option boxes. To match the selection to a 640 × 480-pixel screen, for example, just change the Width and Height values to 640 and 480.

✦ **Drawing feathered selections:** A Feather option box is available when you use either of the marquee tools. To feather a selection is to blur its edges beyond the automatic antialiasing afforded to most tools. For more information on feathering, refer to the "Softening selection outlines" section later in this chapter.

✦ **Creating jagged ellipses:** By default, elliptical selection outlines are antialiased. If you don't want antialiasing — you might prefer harsh edges when editing screen shots or designing screen interfaces — deselect the Anti-aliased check box. (This option is dimmed when you use the rectangular marquee because antialiasing is always on for this tool.)

Frequently, Photoshop's lack of geometric shape tools throws novices for a loop. In fact, such tools do exist—you simply don't recognize them. To draw a rectangle or ellipse in Photoshop, draw the shape as desired using the rectangular or elliptical marquee tool. Then choose Edit ➪ Fill or Edit ➪ Stroke, respectively, to color the interior or outline of the selection. You can also fill the selection using the Delete-key techniques discussed in Chapter 9. It's that easy.

Freeform outlines

In comparison to the rectangular and elliptical marquee tools, the lasso tool provides a rather limited range of options. Generally speaking, you drag in a free-form path around the image you want to select. The few special considerations are as follows:

✦ **Feathering and antialiasing:** To adjust the performance of the lasso tool, press Return while the lasso tool is selected to display the Lasso Options palette. The palette contains just two options, a Feather option box and an Anti-aliased check box. Just as you can feather rectangular and elliptical marquees, you can feather selections drawn with the lasso tool. You can also soften the edges of a lasso outline by selecting the Anti-aliased check box.

Be aware that, although you can adjust the feathering of any selection after you draw it by choosing Select ➪ Feather, you must specify antialiasing before you draw a selection. Unless you have a specific reason for doing otherwise, leave the Anti-aliased check box turned on (as it is by default).

✦ **Drawing polygons:** If you press and hold the Option key, the lasso tool works like a free-form polygon tool. (*Polygon*, incidentally, means a shape with multiple straight sides.) With the Option key down, click to specify corners in a free-form polygon, as shown in Figure 11-3. If you want to add curves to the selection outline, drag with the tool while still pressing the Option key. Photoshop closes the selection outline the moment you release both the Option key and the mouse button.

You can extend a polygon selection outline to the absolute top, right, or bottom edges of an image. Just Option-click with the lasso tool outside the image window or, if the image window is larger than the image, on the background canvas surrounding the image. You can even click on the scroll bars. Figure 11-3 illustrates the idea.

✦ **The polygonal lasso tool:** If you don't want to bother with pressing the Option key, you can use the polygonal lasso tool. Press Shift-L when the lasso is active to switch to the polygonal lasso tool. Then click inside the image to set corners in the selection. Click on the first point in the selection or double-click with the tool to complete the selection outline.

Option-click on scroll bar

End drag

Option-click   Begin drag

Figure 11-3: Option-click with the lasso tool to create corners in a selection outline, shown as black squares in the bottom image. Drag to create free-form curves. Surprisingly, you can Option-click outside the image to add corners outside the boundaries of the image window.

Tip

If you make a mistake while creating a selection outline with the polygonal lasso, you can press Delete to eliminate the last segment you drew. Keep pressing Delete to eliminate more segments in the selection outline. This technique works until you close the selection outline and it turns into marching ants.

To create free-form curves with the polygonal lasso tool, press the Option key and drag.

Adobe added the polygonal lasso for those times when Option-clicking isn't convenient. If no portion of the image is selected, it's no trick to Option-click with the standard lasso to draw a straight-sided selection. But if some area in the image is selected, pressing Option tells Photoshop that you want to subtract from the selection outline. For this reason, it's often easier to use the polygonal lasso (although you still can make it work by pressing Option *after* you click with the lasso tool, as I explain in the "Using Shift and Option like a pro" section later in this chapter).

Magnetic selections

In the old days of black-and-white painting programs — most notably MacPaint — black pixels were considered foreground elements and white pixels were the background. To select a black element, you have only to vaguely drag around it with the lasso tool and the program would automatically omit the white pixels and "shrink" the selection around the black ones.

The magnetic lasso tool is Adobe's attempt to transfer shrinking into the world of color. Under ideal conditions — very ideal conditions, I might add — a selection drawn with the magnetic lasso automatically shrinks around the foreground element and omits the background. Naturally, it rarely works this miraculously, but it does produce halfway decent selection outlines with very little effort — provided that you know what you're doing.

Using the magnetic lasso tool

Typically, when people have a problem using the magnetic lasso tool, it's because they're trying to make the process too complex. Work less and it works smarter. Here are the basic steps for using this unusual tool:

Steps: Making Sense of the Magnetic Lasso Tool

1. **Select an image with very definite contrast between the foreground image and its background.** The skull in Figure 11-4 is a good example. A light gray skull against a dark gray background. Here's something that Photoshop can really sink its teeth into.

2. **Select the magnetic lasso.** Press the L key to select the lasso tool, then press Shift-L a couple of times to cycle to the magnetic setting.

3. **Click anywhere along the edge of the foreground element.** I clicked at the top of the skull, as labeled in Figure 11-4.

4. **Move the cursor around the edge of the foreground element.** Move the mouse, don't drag it — that is, there's no need to press the mouse button. Dragging is more difficult to control, it's harder on our wrists, and it doesn't do any good. Move the cursor around the image and Photoshop will do the rest of the work for you.

Click to
begin selection . . .

. . . then move cursor
along edge

Figure 11-4: After clicking to set the start point (top), I moved
the magnetic lasso cursor along the edge of the skull. Then I
reversed the completed selection (⌘-Shift-I) and pressed
Delete to fill it with white (bottom).

Tip

As you move, the magnetic lasso lays down a line along the edge of the
element, as Figure 11-4 shows. If you don't like where it puts a line, just
back up the cursor and try moving along the edge again. The magnetic
lasso also lays down anchor points at significant locations around the
image. If you don't like where it puts a point, press the Delete key. Each
time you press Delete, Photoshop gets rid of the most recent point along
the line. To set your own anchor points, just click.

5. **When you make it all the way around to the beginning of the shape,
click on the first point in the outline to close the selection.** Or just
double-click to close with a straight edge.

As I mentioned before, the magnetic lasso does not perform miracles. It will almost never select an image exactly the way you would like it to. After moving the cursor around the skull, I reversed the selection by choosing Select ➪ Inverse (⌘-Shift-I); then I pressed the Delete key to fill the background with white. The result appears in the second example in Figure 11-4. As you can see, the magnetic lasso did a very nice job of isolating the skull — much better than I could have done with the lasso alone — but the selection isn't perfect. Notice the gap on the right side of the skull and the clumsy treatment of the tip of the pointy lower jaw on left. Okay, no automated selection tool is perfect, but the magnetic lasso makes as few mistakes as any I've seen.

To create a straight segment while working with the magnetic lasso tool, press the Option key and click. Release the option key and drag momentarily to reset the tool to its normal magnetic self.

Modifying the magnetic lasso options

You can modify the performance of the magnetic lasso tool by adjusting the values in the Magnetic Lasso Options palette, shown in Figure 11-5. The first two options — Feather and Anti-aliased — define the softness of the final selection outline, just as they do for the standard lasso tool. The others control how the magnetic lasso positions lines and lays down points:

✦ **Lasso Width:** I might have named this option Sloppiness Factor. It determines how close to an edge you have to move the cursor in order for Photoshop to accurately see the image element. Large values are great for smooth elements that stand out clearly from their backgrounds. If I raise the Lasso Width to 20 when selecting the top of the skull, for example, I can move the cursor 20 pixels away from the skull and Photoshop still shrinks the selection tight around the skull's edge. That's a lot of wiggle room and it makes my life quite a bit easier. But when selecting narrow passageways, the value needs to be low to keep Photoshop from veering off to the wrong edge. The location at which the pointy jaw meets with the snout is a good example of a place where I need to set a small Lasso Width and move very carefully around the edge.

The great thing about the Lasso Width value is that you can change it on the fly by pressing a bracket key as you work with the magnetic lasso. Press the [key to lower the Lasso Width value; press the] key to raise the value. Shift-[lowers the value to its minimum, 1, and Shift-] raises it to the maximum, 40.

If you have a pressure-sensitive tablet, you can control the sloppiness factor dynamically according to how hard you press on the pen. Bear down to be careful, let up to be sloppy. Because this is the way you probably work naturally, the tool accommodates your movements pretty much without you even thinking about it.

Figure 11-5: These options determine how the magnetic lasso tool draws lines and places points inside the image window.

✦ **Frequency:** This option tells the magnetic lasso when to lay down points. As you drag with the tool, the line around the image changes to keep up with your movements. When some point in the line stays still for a few moments, Photoshop decides it must be on target and anchors it down with a point. If you want Photoshop to anchor points more frequently, raise the value. For less frequent anchoring, lower the option. High values tend to do better for rough edges, lower values do better for smooth edges.

✦ **Edge Contrast:** This is the simplest of the options. It tells Photoshop how much contrast there has to be between the element you're trying to select and it's background in order to even be recognized. If the foreground element stands out clearly, you might want to raise the Edge Contrast value to avoid selecting random flack around the edges. If the contrast between foreground and background is subtle, lower the value.

Most of the time, you can rely on the bracket keys to adjust the Lasso Width and leave the Frequency and Edge Contrast values set to their defaults. When dealing with a low-contrast image, lower the Edge Contrast value to 5 percent or so. And when selecting unusually rough edges, raise the Frequency to 70 or more. But careful movements with the magnetic lasso tool will go farther than adjusting any of these settings.

The world of the wand

Using the magic wand tool is a no-brainer, right? You just click with the tool and it selects all the neighboring colors that fall within a selected range. The problem is getting the wand to recognize the same range of colors you see on screen. For example, if you're editing a photo of a red plate against a pink tablecloth, how do you tell the magic wand to select the plate and leave the tablecloth alone?

Sadly, adjusting the performance of the wand is pretty tricky and frequently unsatisfying. If you press Return when the magic wand is active, you'll see three options inside the Magic Wand Options palette:

✦ **Anti-aliased** softens the selection, just as it does for the lasso tool.

✦ **Tolerance** determines the range of colors the tool selects when you click with it in the image window.

✦ **Use All Layers** allows you to take all visible layers into account when defining a selection.

Adjusting the tolerance

By now you already understand what's up with the Anti-aliased option, so I'll start with Tolerance. You may have heard the standard explanation for adjusting the Tolerance value: You can enter any number from 0 to 255 in the Tolerance option box. Enter a low number to select a small range of colors; increase the value to select a wider range of colors.

Nothing is wrong with this explanation — in its own small way, the explanation is accurate — but it doesn't provide one iota of information you couldn't glean on your own. If you really want to understand this option, you have to dig a little deeper.

When you click on a pixel with the magic wand tool, Photoshop first reads the brightness value assigned to that pixel by each of the color channels. If you're working with a grayscale image, Photoshop reads a single brightness value from the one channel only; if you're working with an RGB image, it reads three brightness values, one each from the red, green, and blue channels; and so on. Because each color channel permits 8 bits of data, brightness values range from 0 to 255.

Next, Photoshop applies the Tolerance value, or simply *tolerance*, to the pixel. The tolerance describes a range that extends in both directions — lighter and darker — from each brightness value.

Suppose you're editing a standard RGB image. The tolerance is set to 32 (as it is by default); you click with the magic wand on a turquoise pixel, whose brightness values are 40 red, 210 green, and 170 blue. Photoshop adds and subtracts 32 from each brightness value to calculate the magic wand range that, in this case, is 8 to 72 red, 178 to 242 green, and 138 to 202 blue. Photoshop selects any pixel that both falls inside this range and can be traced back to the original pixel via an uninterrupted line of other pixels, which also fall within the range.

From this information, you can draw the following basic conclusions about the magic wand tool:

✦ **Creating a contiguous selection:** The magic wand selects a contiguous region of pixels emanating from the pixel on which you click. If you're trying to select land masses on a globe, for example, clicking on St. Louis selects everything from Juneau to Mexico City. It doesn't select London, though, because the cities are separated by an ocean of water that doesn't fall within the tolerance range.

✦ **Clicking on midtones maintains a higher range:** Because the tolerance range extends in two directions, you cut off the range when you click on a light or dark pixel, as demonstrated in Figure 11-6. Consider the two middle gradations: In both cases, the tolerance is set to 60. In the top gradation, I clicked on a pixel with a brightness of 140, so Photoshop calculated a range from 80 to 200. But when I clicked on a pixel with a brightness value of 10, as in the bottom gradation, the range shrank to 0 to 70. Clicking on a medium-brightness pixel, therefore, permits the most generous range.

Figure 11-6: Note the results of clicking on a pixel with a brightness value of 140 (top row) and a brightness value of 10 (bottom row) with the tolerance set to three different values.

✦ **Selecting brightness ranges:** Many people have the impression the magic wand selects color ranges. The magic wand, in fact, selects brightness ranges within color channels. So if you want to select a flesh-colored region — regardless of shade — set against an orange or red background, roughly equivalent in terms of brightness values, you probably should use a different tool.

✦ **Selecting from a single channel:** If the magic wand repeatedly fails to select a region of color that appears unique from its background, try isolating that region inside a single-color channel. You'll probably have the most luck isolating a color on the channel that least resembles it. For example, to select the yellow Sasquatch Xing sign shown in Color Plate 11-1, I switched to the blue channel (⌘-3). Because yellow contains no blue, and the brambly background contains quite a bit of blue — as demonstrated in the last example of Figure 11-7 — the magic wand can distinguish the two relatively easily. Experiment with this technique and it will prove even more useful over time.

Figure 11-7: Because the yellow Sasquatch sign contains almost no blue, it appears most clearly distinguished from its background in the blue channel. So the blue channel is the easiest channel in which to select the sign with the magic wand.

Making the wand see beyond a single layer

The final option in the Magic Wand Options palette, the Use All Layers option, enables you to create a selection based on pixels from different layers (see Chapter 13). For example, returning to my previous land mass example, suppose you set Europe on one layer and North America on the layer behind it. The two continents overlap. Normally, if you clicked inside Europe with the magic wand tool, the wand would select an area inside Europe without extending out into the area occupied by North America. This is because the wand doesn't even see the contents of other layers; anything outside Europe is an empty void. We're talking pre-Columbus Europe here.

If you select the Use All Layers option, though, things change. Suddenly, the wand can see all the layers you can see. If you click on Europe, and if North America and Europe contain similar colors, the wand selects across both shapes.

Mind you, the Use All Layers option does not permit the wand to select images on two separate layers. Strange as this may sound, no selection tool can pull off this feat. Every one of the techniques explained in this chapter is applicable to only a single layer at a time. Use All Layers merely allows the wand to draw selection outlines that appear to encompass colors on many layers.

What good is this? Well, suppose you want to apply an effect to both Europe and North America. With the help of Use All Layers, you can draw a selection outline that encompasses both continents. After you apply the effect to Europe, you can switch to the North America layer — the selection outline remains intact — and then reapply the effect.

Ways to Change Selection Outlines

If you don't draw a selection outline correctly the first time, you have two options. You can either draw it again from scratch, which is a real bore, or you can change your botched selection outline, which is likely to prove the more efficient solution. You can deselect a selection, add to a selection, subtract from a selection, and even select the stuff that's not selected and deselect the stuff that is. (If this sounds like a load of nonsense, keep reading.)

Quick changes

Some methods of adjusting a selection outline are automatic: You choose a command and you're done. The following list explains how a few commands — all members of the Select menu — work:

✦ **Hide Edges (⌘-H):** Get those marching ants out of my face! We're all grown-ups, right? Do we really need constant streams of marching ants to tell us what we've selected? We were there; we remember. My point is, although visible selection outlines can be helpful sometimes, they can as readily impede your view of an image. When they annoy you, press ⌘-H. Press ⌘-H again if you later need to see the selection outline.

✦ **Deselect (⌘-D):** You can deselect the selected portion of an image in three ways. You can select a different portion of the image; click anywhere in the image window with the rectangular marquee tool, the elliptical marquee tool, or the lasso tool; or choose Select ➪ Deselect. Remember, though, when no part of an image is selected, the entire image is susceptible to your changes. If you apply a filter, choose a color-correction command, or use a paint tool, you affect every pixel of the foreground image.

✦ **Reselect (⌘-Shift-D):** If you accidentally deselect an image, you can retrieve the most recent selection outline by choosing Select ➪ Reselect. It's a great function that operates entirely independently of the Undo command and History palette, and it works even after performing a long string of selection-unrelated operations. (You can restore older selections from the History palette, but that usually means undoing operations along the way.)

✦ **Inverse (⌘-Shift-I):** Choose Select ➪ Inverse to reverse the selection. Photoshop deselects the portion of the image that was previously selected and selects the portion of the image that was not selected. This way, you can begin a selection by outlining the portion of the image you want to protect, rather than the portion you want to affect.

Manually adding and subtracting

Ready for some riddles? When editing a portrait, how do you select both eyes without affecting any other portion of the face? Answer: By drawing one selection and then tacking on a second selection. How do you select a doughnut and leave the hole behind? Answer: Encircle the doughnut with the elliptical marquee tool, and then use the same tool to subtract the center.

Photoshop enables you to whittle away at a selection, add pieces on again, whittle away some more, ad infinitum, until you get it exactly right. Short of sheer laziness or frustration, no reason exists why you can't eventually create the selection outline of your dreams:

✦ **Adding to a selection outline:** To increase the area enclosed in an existing selection outline, Shift-drag with one of the marquee or lasso tools. You also can Shift-click with the magic wand tool or Shift-click with one of the marquee tools when the Fixed Size option is active (as described back in the "Geometric selection outlines" section earlier in this chapter).

✦ **Subtracting from a selection outline:** To take a bite from an existing selection outline, press the Option key while using one of the selection tools.

✦ **Intersecting one selection outline with another:** Another way to subtract from an existing selection outline is to Shift-Option-drag around the selection with the rectangular marquee, elliptical marquee, or lasso tool. You also can Shift-Option-click with the magic wand tool. Shift-Option-dragging instructs Photoshop to retain only the portion of an existing selection that also falls inside the new selection outline. I frequently use this technique to confine a selection within a rectangular or elliptical border.

To help you keep the various techniques straight, Photoshop presents you with special cursors that help explain what you're doing. Say that you've selected part of an image and the lasso tool is active. When you press the Shift key, Photoshop appends a little plus sign to the lasso cursor to show you're about to add. When you press Option, you see a little minus sign. Press Shift-Option to get an × for intersect. Watching your cursors will make the transition easier.

Using Shift and Option like a pro

The roles of the Shift and Option keys in adding, subtracting, and intersecting selection outlines can interfere with your ability to take advantage of other functions of the selection tools. For example, when no portion of an image is selected, you can Shift-drag with the rectangular marquee tool to draw a square. But after a selection is active, Shift-dragging adds a rectangle — not a square — to the selection outline.

The trick is to learn when to press the Shift and Option keys. Sometimes you have to press the key before you begin your drag; other times you must press the key after you begin the drag, but before you release. For example, to add a square to a selection outline, Shift-drag, release Shift while keeping the mouse button pressed, and press Shift again to snap the rectangle to a square. The same goes for adding a circle with the elliptical marquee tool.

A few other techniques follow that you'll do well to master. They sound pretty elaborate, I admit, but with a little practice, they become second nature (so does tightrope walking, but don't let that worry you):

✦ To subtract a square or circle from a selection, Option-drag, release Option, press Shift, drag until you get it right, release the mouse button, and then release Shift.

✦ To add a rectangle or ellipse and draw from the center outward, Shift-drag, release Shift, press the Option key, and hold Option until after you release the mouse button. You can even press the spacebar during the drag to move the marquee around, if you like.

✦ To subtract a marquee drawn from the center outward, Option-drag, release Option, press Option again, and hold the key down until after you release.

✦ What about drawing a straight-sided selection with the lasso tool? To add a straight-sided area to an existing selection, Shift-drag with the tool for a short distance. With the mouse button still down, release Shift and press the Option key. Then click around as you normally would, while keeping the Option key down.

✦ To subtract a straight-sided area, Option-drag with the lasso, release Option, press Option again, and click around with the tool.

If you can't manage the last two lasso-tool techniques, then switch to the polygonal lasso instead. In fact, the reason Adobe provided the polygonal lasso tool was to accommodate folks who don't want to deal with pressing the Option key seven times during a single drag (which I strangely quite enjoy).

Adding and subtracting by command

Photoshop provides several commands under the Select menu that automatically increase or decrease the number of selected pixels in an image according to numerical specifications. The commands in the Select ➪ Modify submenu work as follows:

✦ **Border:** This command selects an area of a specified thickness around the perimeter of the current selection outline and deselects the rest of the selection. For example, to select a 6-point-thick border around the current selection, choose Select ➪ Modify ➪ Border, enter 6 into the Width option box, and press Return. But what's the point? After all, if you want to create an outline around a selection, you can accomplish this in fewer steps by choosing Edit ➪ Stroke. The Border command, however, broadens your range of options. You can apply a special effect to the border, move the border to a new location, or even create a double-outline effect by first applying Select ➪ Modify ➪ Border and then Edit ➪ Stroke.

✦ **Smooth:** This command rounds off the sharp corners and weird anomalies in the outline of a selection. When you choose Select ➪ Modify ➪ Smooth, the program asks you to enter a Sample Radius value. Photoshop smoothes out corners by drawing little circles around them, and the Sample Radius value determines the radius of these circles. Larger values result in smoother corners.

The Smooth command is especially useful in combination with the magic wand. After you draw one of those weird, scraggly selection outlines with the wand tool, use Select ➪ Modify ➪ Smooth to smooth out the rough edges.

✦ **Expand and Contract:** Both of these commands do exactly what they say, either expanding or contracting the selected area by 1 to 16 pixels. For example, if you want an elliptical selection to grow by 8 pixels, choose Select ➪ Modify ➪ Expand, enter 8, and call it a day. These are extremely useful commands I'll refer to several times throughout the book.

Both Expand and Contract have a flattening effect on a selection. To round things off, apply the Smooth command with a Sample Radius value equal to the number you just entered into the Expand Selection or Contract Selection dialog box. You'll end up with a pretty vague selection outline, but what do you expect from automated commands?

In addition to the Expand command, Photoshop provides two older commands — Grow and Similar — that increase the area covered by a selection outline. Both commands resemble the magic wand tool because they measure the range of eligible pixels by way of a Tolerance value. In fact, the commands rely on the same Tolerance value found inside the Magic Wand Options palette. So if you want to adjust the impact of either command, you must first select the magic wand icon in the toolbox:

✦ **Grow:** Choose Select ➪ Grow to select all pixels that both neighbor an existing selection and resemble the colors included in the selection, in accordance with the Tolerance value. In other words, Select ➪ Grow is the command equivalent of the magic wand tool. If you feel constrained because you can only click on one pixel at a time with the magic wand tool, you may prefer to select a small group of representative pixels with a marquee tool, and then choose Select ➪ Grow to initiate the wand's magic.

✦ **Similar:** Another member of the Select menu, the Similar command works like the Grow command, except the pixels needn't be adjacent to one another. When you choose Select ➪ Similar, Photoshop selects any pixel that falls within the tolerance range, regardless of the location of the pixel in the foreground image.

One of the best applications for the Similar command is to isolate a complicated image set against a consistent background whose colors are significantly lighter or darker than the image. Consider Figure 11-8, which features a dark and ridiculously complex foreground image set against a continuous background of medium-to-light brightness values. Although the image features sufficient contrast to make it a candidate for the magic wand tool, I would never in a million years recommend using this tool; too many of the colors in the foreground image are discontinuous. The following steps explain how to separate this image using the Similar command in combination with a few other techniques I've described thus far.

Steps: Isolating a Complex Image Set Against a Plain Background

1. **Use the rectangular marquee tool to select some representative portions of the background.** In Figure 11-8, I selected the lightest and darkest portions of the background along with some representative shades in between. Remember, you make multiple selections by Shift-dragging with the tool.

Figure 11-8: Before choosing Select ⇨ Similar, select a few sample portions of the background, so Photoshop has something on which to base its selection range.

(continued)

2. **Double-click on the magic wand tool icon to display the Tolerance option box.** For my image, I entered a Tolerance value of 16, a relatively low value, in keeping with the consistency of the background. If your background is less homogenous, you may want to enter a higher value. Make certain you turn on the Anti-aliased check box.

3. **Choose Select ➪ Similar.** Photoshop should select the entire background. If Photoshop fails to select all the background, choose Edit ➪ Undo (⌘-Z) and use the rectangular marquee tool to select more portions of the background. You may also want to increase the Tolerance value in the Magic Wand Options palette. If Photoshop's selection bleeds into the foreground image, try reducing the Tolerance value.

4. **Choose Select ➪ Inverse.** Or press ⌘-Shift-I. Photoshop selects the foreground image and deselects the background.

5. **Modify the selection as desired.** If the detail you want to select represents only a fraction of the entire image, Shift-Option-drag around the portion of the image you want to retain using the lasso tool. In Figure 11-9, I Shift-Option-dragged with the polygonal lasso tool to draw a straight-sided outline around the selection.

Figure 11-9: Shift-Option-drag with the polygonal lasso tool to intersect the area you want to select with a straight-sided outline.

6. **Congratulations, you've isolated your complex image.** Now you can filter your image, colorize it, or perform whatever operation inspired you to select this image in the first place. For myself, I wanted to super-impose the image onto a different background. To do so, I copied the image to the Clipboard (⌘-C), opened the desired background image, and then pasted the first image into place (⌘-V). The result, shown in Figure 11-10, still needs some touching up with the paint and edit tools, but it's not half bad for an automated selection process.

Figure 11-10: The completed selection superimposed onto a new background.

Whenever you introduce a selection into another image—by copying and pasting or by dragging the selection and dropping it into another image window— Photoshop automatically assigns the selection to a new layer. This is a great safety mechanism that prevents you from permanently affixing the selection to its new background. But it also means you can't save the image in a file format other than the native Photoshop format without first flattening the image. For the big story on layers, read Chapter 13.

Softening selection outlines

You can soften a selection in two ways. The first method is antialiasing, introduced in the "Rasterizing an Illustrator or FreeHand file" section of Chapter 4. Antialiasing is an intelligent and automatic softening algorithm, which mimics the appearance of edges you'd expect to see in a sharply focused photograph.

Note

Where did the term *anti-alias* originate? Anytime you try to fit the digital equivalent of a square peg into a round hole—say, by printing a high-resolution image to a low-resolution printer—the data gets revised during the process. This revised data, called an *alias*, is frequently inaccurate and undesirable. Anti-aliasing is the act of revising the data ahead of time, essentially rounding off the square peg so it looks nice as it goes into the hole. According to a reader who spent time at MIT's Architecture Machine Group, "We did the first work with displaying smooth lines. We called the harsh transitions *jaggies* and the display process *dejaggying*. Somehow, this easy-to-understand term slid sideways into 'alias' (which it isn't, really, but it's too late to change)." Now you know.

When you draw an anti-aliased selection outline in Photoshop, the program calculates the hard-edged selection at twice its actual size. The program then shrinks the selection in half using bicubic interpolation (described in the "General preferences" section of Chapter 2). The result is a crisp image with no visible jagged edges.

The second softening method, *feathering*, is more dramatic. Feathering gradually dissipates the selection outline, giving it a blurry edge. Photoshop accommodates partially selected pixels; feathering fades the selection both inward and outward from the original edge.

You can specify the number of pixels affected either before or after drawing a selection. To feather a selection before you draw it, double-click on the marquee or lasso tool icon and enter a value into the Feather option box in the Options palette. To feather a selection after drawing it, choose Select ➪ Feather. Or press the new keyboard shortcut, ⌘-Option-D. (The old shortcut, ⌘-Shift-D, was reassigned to the Reselect command.)

The Feather Radius value determines the approximate distance over which Photoshop fades a selection, measured in pixels in both directions from the original selection outline. Figure 11-11 shows three selections lifted from the image at the bottom of the figure. The first selection is antialiased only. I feathered the second and third selections, assigning Feather Radius values of 4 and 12, respectively. As you can see, a small feather radius makes a selection appear fuzzy; a larger radius makes it fade into view.

The math behind the feather

A few eagle-eyed readers have written to ask me why feathering blurs a selection outline more than the number of pixels stated in the Feather Radius value. A radius of 4 pixels actually affects a total of 20 pixels: 10 inward and 10 outward. The reason revolves around Photoshop's use of a mathematical routine called the *Gaussian bell curve*, which exaggerates the distance over which the selection outline is blurred.

Figure 11-11: Three clones selected with the elliptical marquee tool. The top image is antialiased and not feathered, the next is feathered with a radius of 4 pixels, and the third is feathered with a radius of 12 pixels.

Figure 11-12 demonstrates the math visually. The top-left image shows a hard-edged elliptical selection filled with white against a black background. To its right is a side view of the ellipse, in which black pixels are short and white pixels are tall. (Okay, so it's a really a graph, but I didn't want to scare you.) Because no gray pixels are in the ellipse, the side view has sharp vertical walls.

The bottom-left image shows what happens if I first feather the selection with a radius of 4 pixels and then fill it with white. The side view now graphs a range of gray values, which taper gradually from black to white. See those gray areas on the sides (each labeled *Diameter*)? Those are the pixels that fall into the 8-pixel diameter, measured 4 pixels in and out from the original selection outline. These gray areas slope in straight lines.

Figure 11-12: Here are some graphic demonstrations of what happens when you feather a selection. Photoshop tapers the ends of the feathered selections (shown by the black areas, bottom right) to prevent your eye from easily detecting where the feathering starts and stops.

The rounded areas of the side view—painted black—are the Gaussian bell curves. These are appended onto the radius of the feather to ensure smooth transitions between the blurry edges and the selected and deselected pixels. Programs that do not include these extra Gaussian curves, such as Corel Photo-Paint for Windows, end up producing ugly feathered selections that appear to have sharp, incongruous edges.

Tip

If exact space is an issue, you can count on the Feather command affecting about 2.7 times as many pixels as you enter into the Feather Radius option box, both in and out from the selection. That's a total of 5.4 times as many pixels as the radius in all.

If this is more than you wanted to know, cast it from your mind. Feathering makes the edges of a selection fuzzy — 'nuff said.

Putting feathering to use

You can use feathering to remove an element from an image while leaving the background intact, a process described in the following steps. The image described in these steps, shown in Figure 11-13, is a NASA photo of a satellite with Earth in the background. I wanted to use this background with another image, but to do so I first had to eliminate that satellite. By feathering and cloning a selection outline, I covered the satellite with a patch so seamless you'd swear the satellite was never there.

Steps: Removing an Element from an Image

1. **Draw a selection around the element using the lasso tool.** The selection needn't be an exact fit; in fact, you want it rather loose, so allow a buffer zone of at least six pixels between the edges of the image and the selection outline.

Figure 11-13: Your mission, if you choose to accept it, is to remove the satellite by covering it with selections cloned from the background.

(continued)

2. **Drag the selection outline over a patch in the image.** Now that you've specified the element you want to remove, you must find a patch, that is, some portion of the image to cover the element in a manner that matches the surrounding background. In Figure 11-14, the best match seemed an area just below and to the right of the satellite. To select this area, move the selection outline independently of the image merely by dragging it with the lasso tool. (Dragging a selection with a selection tool moves the outline without affecting the pixels.) Make certain you allow some space between the selection outline and the element you're trying to cover.

Figure 11-14: After drawing a loose outline around the satellite with the lasso tool, I dragged the outline to select a portion of the background.

3. **Choose Select ⇨ Feather.** Or press ⌘-Option-D. Enter a small value (8 or less) in the Feather Radius option box—just enough to make the edges fuzzy. (I entered 3.) Then press Enter to initiate the operation.

4. **Clone the patch onto the area you want to cover.** Select the move tool by pressing the V key. Then Option-drag the feathered selection to clone the patch and position it over the element you want to cover, as shown in Figure 11-15. To align the patch correctly, choose Select ⇨ Hide Edges (⌘-H) to hide the marching ants and then nudge the patch into position with the arrow keys.

5. **Repeat as desired.** My patch was only partially successful. The upper-left corner of the selection matches clouds in the background, but the lower-right corner is dark and cloudless, an obvious rift in the visual continuity of the image. The solution: try again. With the lasso tool, I drew a loose outline around the dark portion of the image and dragged it up and to the left as shown in Figure 11-16.

Figure 11-15: Next, I used the move tool to Option-drag the feathered selection over the satellite. Sadly, the patch was imperfect and required further adjustments.

Figure 11-16: I used the lasso tool to draw a new outline around the dark, cloudless portion of the patch. Then I dragged the outline to a different spot in the background.

(continued)

6. **It's all déjà vu from here.** I chose Select ➪ Feather, entered 6 into the Feather Radius option box—thus allowing the clouds a sufficient range to taper off—and pressed Return. I then selected the move tool and Option-dragged the feathered patch over the dark, cloudless rift. Finally, I nudged, nudged, nudged with the arrow keys, and voilà, no more satellite. Figure 11-17 shows $200 million worth of hardware vaporized in less than five minutes.

Figure 11-17: I selected a new bit of cloudy sky and placed it over the formerly cloudless portion of the patch. Satellite? What satellite?

Moving and Duplicating Selections

The previous steps showed how you can move either the selected pixels or the empty selection outline to a new location. Now it's time to examine these techniques in greater depth.

The role of the move tool

To move the selected pixels, you have to use the move tool. No longer is it acceptable merely to drag inside the selection with the marquee, lasso, or wand tool, as it was in Photoshop 3 and earlier. If you haven't gotten used to it yet, then now is as good a time as any. The move tool is here to stay.

You can select the move tool at any time by pressing the V key (for *mooV*). The advantage of the move tool is no chance exists of deselecting an image or harming the selection outline. Drag inside the selected area to move the selection; drag outside the selection to move the entire layer, selection included. I explain layers in more detail in Chapter 13.

Tip

To access the move tool on a temporary basis, press and hold the ⌘ key. The move tool remains active as long as ⌘ is pressed. This shortcut works when any tool except the hand or pen tool is active. Assign this shortcut to memory at your earliest convenience. Believe me, you spend a lot of time ⌘-dragging in Photoshop.

Making precise movements

Photoshop provides three methods for moving selections in prescribed increments. In each case, the move tool is active, unless otherwise indicated:

Tip

✦ First, you can nudge a selection in 1-pixel increments by pressing an arrow key on the keyboard or nudge in 10-pixel increments by pressing Shift with an arrow key. This technique is useful for making precise adjustments to the position of an image.

To nudge a selected area when the move tool is not active, press ⌘ with an arrow key. Press ⌘ and Shift with an arrow key to move in 10-pixel increments. Once the selection is floating — that is, after your first nudge — you can let up on the ⌘ key and use only the arrows (assuming a selection tool is active).

✦ Second, you can press Shift during a drag to constrain a move to some 45-degree direction — that is, horizontally, vertically, or diagonally.

✦ And third, you can use the Info palette to track your movements and to help locate a precise position in the image.

To display the Info palette, choose Window ➪ Show Info or press F8. Figure 11-18 shows the Info palette as it appears in Photoshop. The first section of the Info palette displays the color values of the image area beneath your cursor. When you move a selection, the other eight items in the palette monitor movement, as follows:

✦ **X, Y:** These values show the coordinate position of your cursor. The distance is measured from the upper-left corner of the image in the current unit of measure. The unit of measure in Figure 11-19 is pixels.

✦ **ΔX, ΔY:** These values indicate the distance of your move as measured horizontally and vertically.

✦ **A, D:** The A and D values reflect the angle and direct distance of your drag.

✦ **W, H:** These values reflect the width and height of your selection.

Figure 11-18: The Info palette provides a world of numerical feedback when you move a selection.

Cloning a selection

When you move a selection, you leave a hole in your image in the background color, as shown in the top half of Figure 11-19. If you prefer, instead, to leave the original in place during a move, you have to *clone* the selection — that is, create a copy of the selection without upsetting the contents of the Clipboard. Photoshop offers several different ways to clone a selection:

✦ **Option-dragging:** When the move tool is active, press the Option key and drag a selection to clone it. The bottom half of Figure 11-19 shows a selection I Option-dragged three times. (Between clonings, I changed the gray level of each selection to set them apart a little more clearly.)

✦ **⌘-Option-dragging:** If some tool other than the move tool is active, ⌘-Option-drag the selection to clone it. This is probably the technique you'll end up using most often.

✦ **Option-arrowing:** When the move tool is active, press Option in combination with one of the arrow keys to clone the selection and nudge it one pixel away from the original. If you want to move the image multiple pixels, press Option-arrow the first time only. Then nudge the clone using the arrow key alone. Otherwise, you'll create a bunch of clones which can be a pain in the neck to undo.

✦ **⌘-Option-arrowing:** If some other tool is active, press ⌘ and Option with an arrow key. Again, press only the Option key the first time, unless you want to create a string of clones.

✦ **Drag-and-drop:** Like about every other program on the planet, Photoshop lets you clone a selection between documents by dragging it with the move tool from one open window and dropping it in another, as demonstrated in Figure 11-20. As long as you manage to drop it into the second window, the original image remains intact and selected in the first window. My advice: Don't worry about exact positioning during a drag-and-drop; first get it into the second window and then worry about placement.

Cross-Reference

You can drag-and-drop multiple layers if you link the layers first. For more information on this subject, see "Linking layers" in Chapter 13.

Figure 11-19: When you move a selection, you leave a gaping hole in the selection's wake (top). When you clone an image, you leave a copy of the selection behind. To make a point, I cloned the selection in the bottom image three times.

✦ **Shift-drop:** If the two images are exactly the same size — pixel for pixel — press the Shift key when dropping the selection to position it in the same spot from which it came in the original image. This is called *registering* the selection.

If an area is selected in the destination image, Shift-dropping positions the selection you're moving in the center of the selection in the destination image. This tip works regardless of whether or not the two images are the same size.

✦ **⌘-drag-and-drop:** Again, if some other tool than the move tool is selected, you must press the ⌘ key when you drag to move the selected pixels from one window to the other.

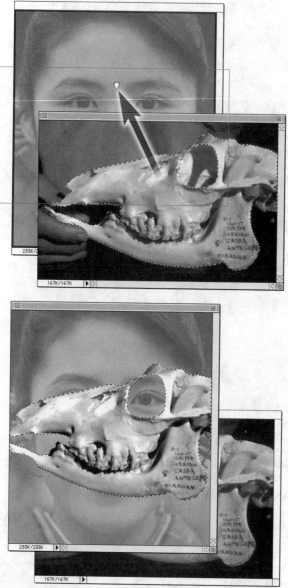

Figure 11-20: Use the move tool to drag a selection from one open window and drop it into another (top). This creates a clone of the selection in the receiving window (bottom).

Moving a selection outline independently of its contents

After all this talk about the move tool and the ⌘ key, you may wonder what happens if you drag a selection with the marquee, lasso, or wand. The answer is, you move the selection outline independently of the image. This technique serves as yet another means to manipulate inaccurate selection outlines. It also enables you to mimic one portion of an image inside another portion of the image or inside a completely different image window.

In the top image in Figure 11-21, I used the marquee tool to drag the skull outline down and to the right, so it only partially overlapped the skull. Note, the image itself remains unaltered. I then lightened the new selection, applied a few strokes to set it off from its background, and gave it stripes, as shown in the bottom image. For all I know, this is exactly what a female Russian Saiga antelope looks like.

Tip

You can nudge a selection outline independently of its contents by pressing an arrow key when a selection tool is active. Press Shift with an arrow key to move the outline in 10-pixel increments.

The great news about the revised role of the selection tools is you can drag-and-drop empty selection outlines between images. Just drag the selection from one image and drop it into another, as demonstrated in the first example of Figure 11-20. The only difference is just the selection outline gets cloned; the pixels remain behind. This is a great way to copy pixels back and forth between images. You can set up an exact selection in Image A, drag it into Image B with the marquee tool, move it over the pixels you want to clone, and ⌘-drag-and-drop the selection back into Image A. This is slick as hair grease, I'm telling you.

So remember, the selection tools now affect only the selection outline. The selection tools never affect the pixels themselves; that's the move tool's job.

Scaling or rotating a selection outline

In Photoshop 5, you can also scale, rotate, skew, and otherwise transform selection outlines independently of the image. To transform a selection outline, choose Select ⇨ Transform Selection. Photoshop displays a transformation boundary framed by eight handles. Here are the basic ways to use it:

- ✦ **Scale:** Drag any of the handles to scale the selection. Shift-drag to scale proportionally, Option-drag to scale with respect to the origin (labeled in Figure 11-22). You can move the origin just by dragging it.

- ✦ **Rotate:** Drag outside the transformation boundary to rotate the selection, as in the second example in Figure 11-22. The rotation always occurs with respect to the origin.

Figure 11-21: Drag a selection with a selection tool to move the outline independently of its image (top). Wherever you drag the selection outline becomes the new selection (bottom).

✦ **Flip:** You can flip a selection outline by dragging one handle past its opposite handle. But this is a lot of work. The easier way is to Control-click inside the image window and choose Flip Horizontal or Flip Vertical from the pop-up menu.

✦ **Skew and distort:** To skew the selection outline, ⌘-drag a side, top, or bottom handle. To distort the selection, ⌘-drag a corner handle.

✦ **Do it by the numbers:** Control-click in the image window and choose Numeric to display the Numeric Transform dialog box. Here you can move, scale, rotate, and skew the selection by a specific numerical amount.

When you get the selection outline the way you want it, press Return or double-click inside the boundary. To cancel the transformation, press the Escape key.

Drag a handle to scale   Transformation origin

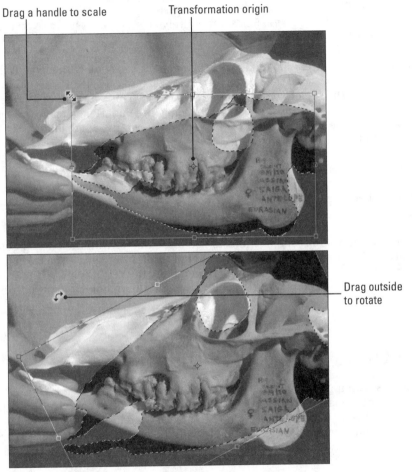

Drag outside
to rotate

Figure 11-22: After choosing Select ➪ Transform Selection,
you can scale the selection outline (top) and rotate it (bottom),
all without harming the image in the slightest.

Cross-Reference

If that felt like an awfully fast explanation of the Transform Selection command, that's because it's virtually identical to Edit ➪ Free Transform which I discuss at length elsewhere in the book. To check out this more detailed explanation, read the "Transforming layers and selections" section of Chapter 13.

The untimely demise of floating selections

One brief note before I move on to my long and glorious explanation of paths: It is with sad heart that I announce the near death of floating selections. As you may (or may not) recall, Photoshop 4 bludgeoned floating selections into a state of unconsciousness. While Version 5 has not entirely killed them, it has moved them to the critical list.

In case you're unsure what I'm talking about, a *floating selection* is an element that hovers above the surface of the image. Any time you move a selection or clone it, Photoshop floats the selection onto a temporary layer. This way, you can move the selection or nudge it into position without harming the underlying image. And if you press the Delete key, Photoshop deletes the floater rather than filling the selection with the background color.

But that's all there is to floating selections in Photoshop 5. The *Floating Selection* item that used to appear in the Layers palette is a thing of the past, so you don't even know when a selection is floating or not. And the only way to defloat a floater is to deselect it.

Quite unexpectedly, Photoshop 5 still lets you mix a floater with the image behind it by modifying the opacity and blend mode settings. After dragging a selection to float it, choose Filter ➪ Fade (⌘-Shift-F). Then modify the settings inside the Fade dialog box to mix the floater with the background. It's incredibly nonintuitive, but it works.

How to Draw and Edit Paths

Photoshop's path tools provide the most flexible and precise ways to define a selection short of masking. However, while a godsend to the experienced user, the path tools represent something of a chore to novices and intermediates. Most people take some time to grow comfortable with the pen tool because it requires you to draw a selection outline one point at a time.

If you're familiar with Illustrator's pen tool and other path-editing functions, you'll find Photoshop's tools are nearly identical. Photoshop doesn't provide the breadth of options available in Illustrator — you can't join paths or apply sophisticated path operations in Photoshop, for example — but the basic techniques are the same.

Photoshop 5 includes two additional pen tools designed to help smooth out the learning curve for inexperienced users. The freeform pen and magnetic pen work just like the lasso and magnetic lasso tools, automatically generating points as you drag. Neither tool is as precise as the traditional point-by-point pen tool, but nor are they as difficult to use.

The following pages are designed to get you up and running with paths. I'll explain how you approach drawing a path, how you edit it, how you convert it to a selection outline, and how you stroke it with a paint or edit tool. All in all, you'll learn more about paths than you ever wanted to know.

Paths overview

Photoshop makes the path tools available in the toolbox. Meanwhile, the path management options — which enable you to convert paths to selections, fill and stroke paths, and save and delete them — reside in the Paths palette, as labeled in Figure 11-23. Together, tools and palette options make up a fully functioning path-drawing environment, which rivals (though does not equal) similar features provided by Illustrator or FreeHand.

Figure 11-23: The toolbox provides access to every one of Photoshop's path-drawing tools. To save and organize your paths, display the Paths palette by choosing Window ⇨ Show Paths.

How paths work

Paths differ from normal selections because they exist on the equivalent of a distinct, object-oriented layer, which sits in front of the bitmapped image. After you draw a path, this setup enables you to edit it with point-by-point precision to make sure the path meets the exact requirements of your artwork. This also prevents you from accidentally messing up the image, as you can when you edit ordinary selection outlines. After you create the path, you convert it into a standard selection outline before you use it to edit the contents of the image, as explained in the section "Converting and saving paths," later in this chapter.

The following steps explain the basic process of drawing a selection outline with the path tools. I explain each step in more detail throughout the remainder of this chapter.

Steps: Create a Selection with the Path Tools

1. **Draw the path.** Use the pen tool to draw the outline of your prospective selection. You can select the pen tool by pressing the P key. Or cycle to the magnetic or freeform pen by pressing Shift-P.

2. **Edit the path.** If the outline of the path requires some adjustment, reshape it using the other path tools. These tools have their own keyboard shortcuts, such as A for the arrow, + for the insert point tool, and − for the remove point tool.

3. **Save the path.** When you get the path exactly as you want it, save the path in Photoshop by choosing the Save Path command from the Paths palette menu. Or you can double-click on the *Work Path* item in the scrolling list.

4. **Convert the path to a selection.** You can make the path a selection outline by choosing the Make Selection command. Or press the Enter key on the numeric keypad when a path or selection tool is active.

That's it. After you convert the path to a selection, it works like any of the selection outlines described earlier. You can feather a selection, move it, copy it, clone it, or apply one of the special effects described in future chapters. The path remains intact in case you want to do further editing or to use it again.

Using the Paths palette tools

Before I get into my long-winded description of how you draw and edit paths, here is a quick introduction to the seven path tools:

Pen: Use the pen tool to draw paths in Photoshop one point at a time. Click to create a corner in a path, drag to make a smooth point which results in a continuous arc. (Never fear, I explain this tool *ad nauseum* in the "Drawing with the pen tools" section.) Press the P key to select the pen.

Magnetic pen: Click on the edge of the foreground element you want to select, then move the cursor along the edge of the shape. Photoshop automatically assigns points as it deems appropriate.

Freeform pen: Drag with this tool to create a path that automatically follows the twists and turns of your drag. Simplicity at its best, control at its lowest. Luckily, you can turn around and edit the path with any of the following tools.

Insert point: Click on an existing path to add a point to it. To select the insert point tool from the keyboard, press the plus (+) key.

Remove point: Click on an existing point in a path to delete the point without creating a break in the path's outline. Press the minus key (-) to select this tool.

Arrow: The arrow (or direct selection) tool permits you to drag points and handles to reshape a path. You can access the arrow tool when any other path tool is active by pressing and holding the ⌘ key. Or press the A key to make the tool permanently active.

Convert point: Click or drag on a point to convert it to a corner or smooth point. You also can drag on a handle to convert the point. Press Option to access the convert point tool when the pen is active. Press ⌘ and Option when the arrow tool is active.

Note

The terms *anchor point*, *smooth point*, and others associated with drawing paths are explained in the upcoming section.

Drawing with the pen tools

When drawing with the default point-by-point pen tool, you build a path by creating individual points. Photoshop automatically connects the points with segments, which are simply straight or curved lines.

Note

Adobe prefers the term *anchor points* because the points anchor the path into place. But most folks just call 'em *points*. I mean, *all* points associated with paths are anchor points, so it's not like there's some potential for confusion.

All paths in Photoshop are *Bézier* (pronounced bay-zee-ay) paths, meaning they rely on the same mathematical curve definitions that make up the core of the PostScript printer language. The Bézier curve model allows for zero, one, or two levers to be associated with each point in a path. These levers, labeled in Figure 11-24, are called *Bézier control handles* or simply *handles*. You can move each handle in relation to a point, enabling you to bend and tug at a curved segment like a piece of soft wire.

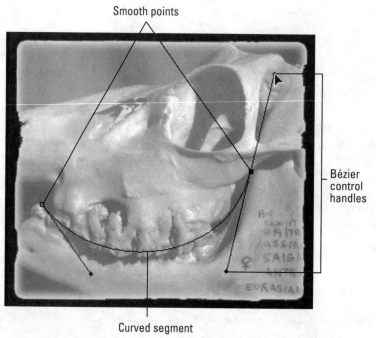

Smooth points

Bézier
control
handles

Curved segment

Figure 11-24: Drag with the pen tool to create a smooth
point flanked by two Bézier control handles.

The following list summarizes how you can use the pen tool to build paths in
Photoshop:

✦ **Adding segments:** To build a path, create one point after another until the
  path is the desired length and shape. Photoshop automatically draws a
  segment between each new point and its predecessor.

✦ **Closing the path:** If you eventually plan to convert the path to a selection
  outline, you need to complete the outline by clicking again on the first point in
  the path. Every point will then have one segment entering it and another
  segment exiting it. Such a path is called a *closed path* because it forms one
  continuous outline.

✦ **Leaving the path open:** If you plan to apply the Stroke Path command
  (explained later), you may not want to close a path. To leave the path open,
  so it has a specific beginning and ending, deactivate the path by saving it
  (choose the Save Paths command from the Paths palette menu). After you
  complete the save operation, you can click in the image window to begin a
  new path.

✦ **Extending an open path:** To reactivate an open path, click or drag one of its
  endpoints. Photoshop draws a segment between the endpoint and the next
  point you create.

✦ **Joining two open paths:** To join one open path with another open path, click or drag an endpoint in the first path, and then click or drag an endpoint in the second.

Tip

To get a better sense of how the pen tool works, press Return when the pen is active and turn on the Rubber Band check box in the Pen Options palette. This tells Photoshop to draw an animated segment between the last point drawn and the cursor. Unless you're an old pro and the connecting segment gets in your face, there's no reason not to select Rubber Band. (Besides, what with the '70s being so hot with the teenies, the Rubber Band check box makes the pen tool seem, well, kind of funky. Consider it another chance to bond with today's youth.)

The anatomy of points and segments

Points in a Bézier path act as little road signs. Each point steers the path by specifying how a segment enters it and how another segment exits it. You specify the identity of each little road sign by clicking, dragging, or Option-dragging with the pen tool. The following items explain the specific kinds of points and segments you can create in Photoshop. See Figure 11-25 for examples.

✦ **Corner point:** Click with the pen tool to create a *corner point*, which represents the corner between two straight segments in a path.

✦ **Straight segment:** Click at two different locations to create a straight segment between two corner points. Shift-click to draw a 45-degree-angle segment between the new corner point and its predecessor.

✦ **Smooth point:** Drag to create a *smooth point* with two symmetrical Bézier control handles. A smooth point ensures that one segment meets with another in a continuous arc.

✦ **Curved segment:** Drag at two different locations to create a curved segment between two smooth points.

✦ **Curved segment followed by straight:** After drawing a curved segment, Option-click on the smooth point you just created to delete the forward Bézier control handle. This converts the smooth point to a corner point with one handle. Then click at a different location to append a straight segment to the end of the curved segment.

✦ **Straight segment followed by curved:** After drawing a straight segment, drag from the corner point you just created to add a Bézier control handle. Then drag again at a different location to append a curved segment to the end of the straight segment.

✦ **Cusp point:** After drawing a curved segment, Option-drag from the smooth point you just created to redirect the forward Bézier control handle, converting the smooth point to a corner point with two independent handles, sometimes known as a *cusp point*. Then drag again at a new location to append a curved segment that proceeds in a different direction than the previous curved segment.

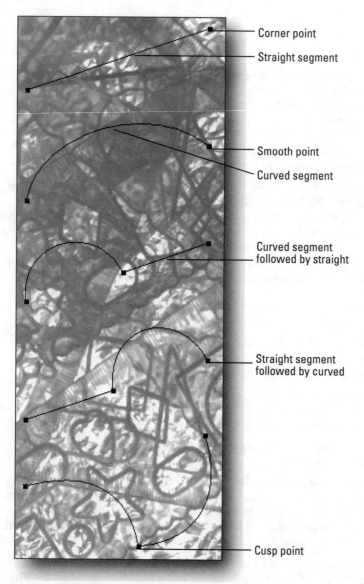

Corner point

Straight segment

Smooth point

Curved segment

Curved segment followed by straight

Straight segment followed by curved

Cusp point

Figure 11-25: The different kinds of points and segments you can draw with the pen tool.

Going freeform

If the pen tool is too much work, then try the freeform pen tool (two Shift-Ps over from the standard pen). As you drag with the tool, Photoshop tracks the motion of the cursor with a continuous line. After you release the mouse button, the program automatically assigns and positions the points and segments needed to create the Bézier path.

Tip

You can draw straight segments with the freeform pen by pressing Option. As you're dragging with the freeform pen, press and hold the Option key. Then click around to create points. When you're finished drawing straight segments, again drag with the freeform pen and release Option. (If you release Option when the mouse button is not pressed, Photoshop completes the path.)

Alas, automation is rarely perfect. (If it were, what need would these machines have for us?) When the program finishes its calculations, a path may appear riddled with far too many points or equipped with too few.

Fortunately, you can adjust the performance of the freeform pen to accommodate your personal drawing style using the Curve Fit option in the Freeform Pen Options palette. When the freeform pen is active, just press Return to highlight the Curve Fit value. You can enter any new value between 0.5 and 10, which Photoshop interprets in screen pixels. The default value of 2, for example, instructs the program to ignore any jags in your mouse movements that do not exceed 2 pixels in length or width. Setting the value to 0.5 makes the freeform pen extremely sensitive; setting the value to 10 smoothes the roughest of gestures.

A Curve Fit from 2 to 4 is generally adequate for most folks, but you should experiment to determine the best setting. Like the magic wand's Tolerance setting, you can't alter the Curve Fit value for a path after you've drawn it. Photoshop calculates the points for a path only once, after you release the mouse button.

Going magnetic

The magnetic pen works like a combination of the magnetic lasso and the freeform pen. Like the magnetic lasso, you begin by clicking anywhere along the edge of the image element you want to select. (For a pertinent blast from the past, see Figure 11-4.) Then move the cursor — no need to drag — around the perimeter of the element and watch Photoshop do its work. To set an anchor point, click. When you come full circle, click on the point where you started to complete the path.

As with the freeform pen, you can Option-click to create straight segments. And you have access to a Curve Fit option (in the Magnetic Pen Options palette) that controls the smoothness of the path. Lower values trace the edges more carefully, higher values result in fewer points and smoother edges.

The remaining options in the Magnetic Pen Options palette — Lasso Width, Frequency, Edge Contrast, and Stylus — are lifted right out of the magnetic lasso playbook. Read "Modifying the magnetic lasso options" near the beginning of this chapter for complete information.

Reshaping and transforming paths

If you take time to master the default pen tool, you'll find yourself drawing accurate paths more and more frequently. But you'll never get it right 100 percent of the time — or even 50 percent of the time. And when you rely on the freeform or magnetic pen tools, the results are never dead on. From your first timid steps until you develop into a seasoned pro, you'll rely heavily on Photoshop's ability to *reshape* paths by moving points and handles, adding and deleting points, and converting points to change the curvature of segments. So don't worry too much if your path looks like an erratic stitch on the forehead of Frankenstein's monster. The path-edit tools provide all the second chances you'll ever need.

Using the arrow tool

The arrow tool (which you get by pressing the A key) represents the foremost path-reshaping function in Photoshop. After selecting this tool, you can perform any of the following functions:

✦ **Selecting points:** Click on a point to select it independently of other points in a path. Shift-click to select an additional point, even if the point belongs to a different path than other selected points. Option-click on a path to select all its points in one fell swoop. You can even marquee points by dragging in a rectangle around them. You cannot, however, apply commands from the Select menu, such as All or None, to the selection of paths.

✦ **Drag selected points:** To move one or more points in a path, select the points you want to move and then drag one of the selected points. All selected points move the same distance and direction. When you move a point while a neighboring point remains stationary, the segment between the two points shrinks, stretches, and bends to accommodate the change in distance. Segments located between two selected or deselected points remain unchanged during a move.

You can move selected points in 1-pixel increments by pressing arrow keys. If both a portion of the image and points in a path are selected, the arrow keys move the point only. Because paths reside on a higher layer, they take precedence in all functions that might concern them.

✦ **Drag a straight segment:** You also can reshape a path by dragging its segments. When you drag a straight segment, the two corner points on either side of the segment move, as well. As illustrated in Figure 11-26, the neighboring segments stretch, shrink, or bend to accommodate the drag.

This technique works best with straight segments drawn with the default pen tool. Segments created by Option-clicking with the freeform or magnetic pens may include trace control handles that make Photoshop think the segment is actually curved.

Figure 11-26: Drag a straight segment to move the segment and change the length, direction, and curvature of the neighboring segments.

Tip

✦ **Drag a curved segment:** When you drag a curved segment, you stretch, shrink, or bend that segment, as demonstrated in Figure 11-27.

When you drag a curved segment, drag from the middle of the segment, approximately equidistant from both its points. This method provides the best leverage and ensures the segment doesn't go flying off in some weird direction you hadn't anticipated.

Figure 11-27: Drag a curved segment to change the curvature of that segment only and leave the neighboring segments unchanged.

✦ **Drag a Bézier control handle:** Select a point and drag either of its Bézier control handles to change the curvature of the corresponding segment without moving any of the points in the path. If the point is a smooth point, moving one handle moves both handles in the path. If you want to move a smooth handle independently of its partner, you must use the convert point tool, as discussed in the "Converting points" section later in this chapter.

✦ **Clone a path:** To make a duplicate of a selected path, Option-drag it to a new location in the image window. Photoshop automatically stores the new path under the same name as the original.

✦ **Deselect a path:** Click with the arrow tool outside any path to deselect all active paths. Because many options affect the selected path only, deselecting the paths before choosing a command you want to apply to all visible paths is often a good idea.

Tip

Press and hold the ⌘ key to access the arrow tool temporarily when one of the pen or path-edit tools are selected. When you release the ⌘ key, the cursor returns to the selected tool. This is a great way to edit the path while you're still drawing it.

Adding and deleting points

The quantity of points and segments in a path is forever subject to change. Whether a path is closed or open, you can reshape it by adding and deleting points, which, in turn, forces the addition or deletion of a segment:

✦ **Appending a point to the end of an open path:** If an existing path is open, you can activate one of its endpoints by either clicking or dragging it with the pen tool, depending on the identity of the endpoint and whether you want the next segment to be straight or curved. Photoshop is then prepared to draw a segment between the endpoint and the next point you create.

✦ **Closing an open path:** You also can use the technique I just described to close an open path. Just select one endpoint, click or drag on it with the pen tool to activate it, and then click or drag on the opposite endpoint. Photoshop draws a segment between the two endpoints, closing the path and eliminating both endpoints by converting them to *interior points*, which simply means the points are bound on both sides by segments.

✦ **Joining two open paths:** You can join two open paths to create one longer open path. To do so, activate an endpoint of the first path, then click or drag with the pen tool on an endpoint of the second path.

✦ **Inserting a point in a segment:** Select the insert point tool (by pressing the + key) and click anywhere along an open or closed path to insert a point and divide the segment on which you click into two segments. Photoshop automatically inserts a corner or smooth point, depending on its reading of the path. If the point does not exactly meet your needs, use the convert point tool to change it.

Tip

Any of the three pen tools changes to the insert point cursor when you hover it over a segment in an existing path. Just click on the segment, and Photoshop inserts a point. You can also insert points with the remove point tool by Option-clicking.

✦ **Deleting a point and breaking the path:** The simplest way to delete a point is to select it with the arrow tool and press either the Delete or Clear key. (You also can choose Edit ➪ Clear, though why you would want to expend so much effort is beyond me.) When you delete an interior point, you delete both segments associated with that point, resulting in a break in the path. If you delete an endpoint from an open path, you delete the single segment associated with the point.

✦ **Removing a point without breaking the path:** Select the remove point tool (by pressing the – key) and click on a point in an open or closed path to delete the point and draw a new segment between the two points that neighbor it. The remove point tool ensures no break occurs in a path.

Tip

To access the remove point tool when using one of the pen tools, hover your cursor over a selected interior point in an existing path. Click on the point and it goes away. Alternately, you can remove a point when the insert point tool is active by Option-clicking.

✦ **Deleting a segment:** You can delete a single interior segment from a path without affecting any point. To do so, first click outside the path with the arrow tool to deselect the path. Then click on the segment you want to delete and press the Delete key. When you delete an interior segment, you create a break in your path.

✦ **Deleting a whole path:** To delete an entire path, select any portion of it and press the Delete key twice. The first time you press Delete, Photoshop deletes the selected point or segment and automatically selects all other points in the path. The second time you press Delete, Photoshop eliminates everything it missed the first time around.

Converting points

Photoshop lets you change the identity of an interior point. You can convert a corner point to a smooth point and vice versa. You perform all point conversions using the convert point tool as follows:

✦ **Smooth to corner:** Click on an existing smooth point to convert it to a corner point with no Bézier control handle.

✦ **Smooth to cusp:** Drag one of the handles of a smooth point to move it independently of the other, thus converting the smooth point to a cusp.

✦ **Corner to smooth:** Drag from a corner point to convert it to a smooth point with two symmetrical Bézier control handles.

✦ **Cusp to smooth:** Drag one of the handles of a cusp point to lock both handles back into alignment, thus converting the cusp to a smooth point.

Tip

Press the Option key to temporarily access the convert point tool when one of the three pen tools is active and positioned over a selected point. To do the same when the arrow tool is active, press ⌘ and Option.

Transforming paths

Photoshop 5 broadens your range of path editing options by permitting you to scale, rotate, skew, and otherwise transform paths independently of the image. First, select the arrow key (by pressing the A key) to enter path editing mode. Then do one of the following:

✦ To transform all paths in a group — such as both the eye and skull outline in the first example of Figure 11-28 — select the arrow tool and click off a path to make sure all paths are deselected. Then choose Edit ➪ Free Transform Path.

✦ To transform a single path independently of others in a group, Option-click on it with the arrow tool. Then choose Edit ➪ Free Transform Points.

✦ Photoshop even lets you transform some points independently of others inside a single path, as demonstrated in the second example of Figure 11-28. Just select the points you want to modify and choose Edit ➪ Free Transform Points.

Tip

The keyboard shortcut for all of these operations is ⌘-T. If you select an independent path — or specific points inside a path — press ⌘-Option-T to transform a duplicate of the path and leave the original unaffected.

In an attempt to conserve tree matter — which is being wasted liberally enough in this tome — I explain the larger topic of transformation in one central location, the "Applying Transformations" section of Chapter 13. Even so, here's a brief rundown of your transformation options after you press ⌘-T:

✦ **Scale:** To scale a path, drag one of the eight square handles that adorn the transformation boundary. Option-drag a handle to scale with respect to the origin point. (You can move the origin by dragging it.)

✦ **Rotate:** Drag outside the boundary to rotate the paths or points, as demonstrated in Figure 11-28.

✦ **Flip:** Control-click in the transformation mode to access a pop-up menu of transformation options. Choose Flip Horizontal or Flip Vertical to create a mirror image of the path.

✦ **Skew:** ⌘-drag one of the side handles to slant the paths. Press the Shift key along with ⌘ to constrain the slant along a consistent axis.

✦ **Distort:** ⌘-drag one of the corner handles to distort the paths — a feat, incidentally, that you can't pull off even half as elegantly in Illustrator 7. (I can't speak for later versions. As I write this, Version 7 is the most recent incarnation.)

Rotate cursor   Transformation origin

Figure 11-28: To transform multiple paths at once (top), deselect all paths and press ⌘-T. You can alternatively transform independent paths or points by selecting them with the arrow tool and pressing ⌘-T (bottom).

✦ **Perspective:** ⌘-Shift-Option-drag a corner handle to achieve a perspective effect. Again, this is not handled even a tenth as well in Illustrator. For shame, Illustrator, for shame.

Caution

Note that you can't take advantage of the distortion or perspective feature when individual points are selected. They only apply to whole paths.

✦ **Numerical transformations:** If you need to transform a path by a very specific amount, Control-click in the image window and choose the Numeric command. The Numeric Transform dialog box tracks the changes you've made so far. Modify the values as desired and press Return.

When you finishing stretching and distorting your paths, press Return or double-click inside the boundary to apply the transformation. You can undo the last transformation inside the transform mode by pressing ⌘-Z or bag the whole thing by pressing the Escape key.

Tip

To repeat the last transformation on another path, press ⌘-Shift-T. Again, this is not possible in Illustrator. At this rate, we'll be using Photoshop to do our drawing in a few years!

Filling paths

After you finish drawing a path and getting it exactly the way you want it, you can convert it to a selection outline — as described in the upcoming "Converting paths to selections" section — or you can paint it. You can either paint the interior of the path by choosing the Fill Path command from the Paths palette menu, or you can paint the outline of the path by choosing Stroke Path.

The Fill Path command works much like Edit ⇨ Fill. After drawing a path, choose the Fill Path command or Option-click on the fill path icon in the lower-left corner of the palette (the one that looks like a filled circle). Photoshop displays a slight variation of the Fill dialog box discussed in Chapter 9, the only difference being the inclusion of two Rendering options. Enter a value into the Feather Radius option box to blur the edges of the fill, as if the path were a selection with a feathered outline. Select the Anti-aliased check box to soften slightly the outline of the filled area.

If one path falls inside another, Photoshop leaves the intersection of the two paths unfilled. Suppose you draw two round paths, one fully inside the other. If you deselect both paths and then choose the Fill Path command, Photoshop fills only the area between the two paths, resulting in the letter *O*.

Caution

If the Fill Path command fills only part or none of the path, the path probably falls outside the selection outline. Choose Select ⇨ Deselect (⌘-D) to deselect the image and then choose the Fill Path command again.

Note

If you select one or more paths with the arrow tool, the Fill Path command changes to Fill Subpaths, enabling you to fill the selected paths only. The fill path icon also affects only the selected paths.

Painting along a path

Unlike the Fill Path command, which bears a strong resemblance to Edit ⇨ Fill, the Stroke Path command is altogether different than Edit ⇨ Stroke. Where Edit ⇨ Stroke creates outlines and arrowheads, the Stroke Path command enables you to paint a brush stroke along the contours of a path. This may not sound like a big deal at first, but this feature enables you to combine the spontaneity of the paint and edit tools with the structure and precision of a path.

To paint a path, choose the Stroke Path command from the Paths palette menu to display the Stroke Path dialog box shown in Figure 11-29. In this dialog box, you can choose the paint or edit tool with which you want to stroke the path (which only means to paint a brush stroke along a path). Photoshop drags the chosen tool along the exact route of the path, retaining any tool or brush shape settings that were in force when you chose the tool.

Figure 11-29: Photoshop displays this dialog box when you choose the Stroke Path command while a tool other than a paint or edit tool is selected.

Tip

You can also display the Stroke Path dialog box by Option-clicking on the stroke path icon, the second icon at the bottom of the Paths palette (labeled back in Figure 11-23). If you prefer to bypass the dialog box, select a paint or edit tool and then either click on the stroke path icon or simply press the key on the numeric keypad. Instead of displaying the dialog box, Photoshop assumes you want to use the selected tool and strokes away.

Note

If the path is selected, the Stroke Path command becomes a Stroke Subpath command. Photoshop then only strokes the selected path, rather than all paths saved under the current name.

The following steps walk you through a little project I created by stroking paths with the paintbrush and smudge tools. Figures 11-30 through 11-32 show the progression and eventual outcome of the image.

Steps: Stroking Paths with Paint and Edit Tools

1. **After opening a low-resolution version of a hurricane image, I drew the zigzag path shown in Figure 11-30.** As you can see, the path emits from the eye of the hurricane. I drew the path starting at the eye and working upward, which is important because Photoshop strokes a path in the same direction in which you draw it.

Figure 11-30: I drew this path starting at the eye of the hurricane and working my way upward.

2. **I next saved the path.** I double-clicked on the *Work Path* item in the Paths palette, entered a name for my path, and pressed Return.

3. **I used the Brushes palette to specify three brush shapes.** Each one had a Roundness value of 40. The largest brush had a diameter of 16, the next largest had a diameter of 10, and the smallest had a diameter of 4.

4. **I double-clicked on the paintbrush tool to bring up the Paintbrush Options palette.** Then I set the Fade-out value to 400. Next, I selected the To Background radio button, so Photoshop would draw gradient strokes between the foreground and background colors.

5. **I stroked the path with the paintbrush three times using the Stroke Path command.** I changed the foreground and background colors for each stroke. The first time, I used the largest brush shape and stroked the path from gray to white; the second time, I changed to the middle brush shape and stroked the path from black to white, and the final time I used the smallest brush shape and stroked the path from white to black. The result of all this stroking is shown in Figure 11-31.

6. **Next, I created two clones of the zigzag path by Option-dragging the path with the arrow tool.** I pressed the Shift key while dragging to ensure the paths aligned horizontally. I then clicked in an empty portion of the image window to deselect all paths, so they appeared as shown in Figure 11-31. This enabled me to stroke them all simultaneously in Step 9.

Figure 11-31: After stroking the path three times with the paintbrush tool, I cloned the path twice.

7. **I created a 60-pixel version of my brush shape and reduced its Hardness value to 0 percent.** I then painted a single white spot at the bottom of each of the new paths. I painted a black spot at the bottom of the original path.

8. **I selected the smudge tool by pressing Shift-R three times.** To get a strong effect, I changed the Pressure value in the Smudge Options palette to 98 percent and selected a brush shape with a radius of 16 pixels. At this setting, the tool has a tremendous range, but it eventually fades out.

9. **I pressed Enter on the numeric keypad to apply the smudge tool to all three paths at once.** The finished image appears in Figure 11-32.

Figure 11-32: I stroked all three paths with the smudge tool set to 98 percent pressure to achieve this unusual extraterrestrial-departure effect. At least, I guess that's what it is. It could also be giant space slinkies probing the planet's surface. Hard to say.

Tip

If you're really feeling precise—I think they have a clinical term for that—you can specify the location of every single blob of paint laid down in an image. When the Spacing option in the Brush Options dialog box is deselected, Photoshop applies a single blob of paint for each point in a path. If this isn't sufficient control, I'm a monkey's uncle. (What a terrible thing to say about one's nephew!)

Converting and saving paths

Photoshop provides two commands to switch between paths and selections, both of which are located in the Paths palette menu. The Make Selection command converts a path to a selection outline; the Make Path command converts a selection to a path. And regardless of how you create a path, you can save it with the current image, which enables you not only to reuse the path but also to hide and display it at will.

Converting paths to selections

When you choose the Make Selection command or Option-click on the make selection icon (which looks like a dotted circle, as labeled back in Figure 11-23), Photoshop displays the dialog box shown in Figure 11-33. You can specify whether to antialias or feather the selection and to what degree. You can also instruct Photoshop to combine the prospective selection outline with any existing selection in the image. The Operation options correspond to the keyboard functions discussed in the "Manually adding and subtracting" section earlier in this chapter.

Figure 11-33: When you choose the Make Selection command, you have the option of combining the path with an existing selection.

Photoshop offers several alternative ways to convert a path to a selection outline, all of which are more convenient than the Make Selection command:

✦ **Press the Enter key on the numeric keypad:** As long as a path or selection tool is active, the Enter key converts the path to a selection.

✦ **⌘-click on the path name:** If some other tool is selected, you can ⌘-click on the name of a path in the Paths palette. The path needn't be active.

✦ **Shift-Enter or ⌘-Shift-click:** To add the path to an existing selection, press Shift with one of the above techniques. You can press Shift-Enter. Or ⌘-Shift-click on a path name in the palette.

✦ **Option-Enter or ⌘-Option-click:** Naturally, if you can add, you can subtract. Just press the Option key with Enter or ⌘-clicking to subtract the path from the selection.

✦ **Shift-Option-Enter or ⌘-Shift-Option-click:** Now we're starting to get into some obscure stuff, but what's possible is possible. You select the intersection of a path and a selection outline by pressing a whole mess of keys.

All of these wonderful techniques have the added advantage of hiding the path when converting the path to a selection. This way, you have full, unobstructed access to your selection outline.

By contrast, the Make Selection command leaves the path on screen in front of the converted selection. If you try to copy, cut, delete, or nudge the selection, you perform the operation on the path instead.

Converting selections to paths

When you choose the Make Paths command, Photoshop produces a single Tolerance option. Unlike the Tolerance options you've encountered so far, this one is accurate to $\frac{1}{10}$ pixel and has nothing to do with colors or brightness values. Rather, it works like the Curve Fit option in the Freeform Pen Options palette — that is, it permits you to specify Photoshop's sensitivity to twists and turns in a selection outline. The value you enter determines how far the path can vary from the original selection. The lowest possible value, 0.5, not only ensures Photoshop retains every nuance of the selection, but it can also result in overly complicated paths with an abundance of points. If you enter the highest value, 10, Photoshop rounds out the path and uses few points. If you plan on editing the path, you probably won't want to venture any lower than 2.0, the default setting.

To bypass the Make Work Path dialog box and turn your selection into a path using the current Tolerance settings, click on the make path icon.

Saving paths with an image

As mentioned at the beginning of the paths discussion, saving a path is an integral step in the path-creation process. You can store every path you draw and keep it handy in case you decide later to select an area again. Because Photoshop defines paths as compact mathematical equations, they take up virtually no room when you save an image to disk.

You save one or more paths by choosing the Save Path command from the Paths palette menu or by simply double-clicking on the italicized *Work Path* item in the scrolling list. After you perform the save operation, the path name appears in upright characters. A path name can include any number of separate paths. In fact, if you save a path and then set about drawing another one, Photoshop automatically adds that path in with the saved path. To start a new path under a new name, you first must hide the existing path. Or click on the new path icon — the little page at the bottom of the Paths palette — to establish an independent path.

To hide all paths, click on the empty portion of the scrolling list below the last saved path name. You can even hide unsaved paths in this way. If you hide an unsaved path and then begin drawing a new one, however, the unsaved path is deleted, never to return again.

To hide all paths when the Paths palette is all full up and there is no empty area at the bottom of the scrolling list, choose Turn Off Path from the Paths palette menu. If you typically create five or six paths in a single image, you're going to love this command.

Swapping Paths with Illustrator

Photoshop can swap paths directly with the most recent versions of Illustrator and FreeHand. All you must do is copy a path to the Clipboard and paste it into the other program. This special cross-application compatibility feature expands and simplifies a variety of path-editing functions. For example, suppose you want to scale and rotate a path:

If you own Illustrator, select the path in Photoshop with the arrow tool and copy it to the Clipboard (⌘-C). Then switch to Illustrator, paste the path, and edit as desired. About 95 percent of Illustrator's capabilities are devoted to the task of editing paths, so despite my ongoing complaints about Illustrator, you have many more options at your disposal than in Photoshop. When you finish modifying the path, copy it again, switch to Photoshop, and paste.

When you paste an Illustrator path into Photoshop, the dialog box shown in Figure 11-34 offers you the option of rendering the path to pixels — just as you can render an Illustrator EPS document using File ➪ Open — or keeping the path information intact. Select the Paste as Paths option to add the copied paths to the selected item in the Paths palette. (If no item is selected, Photoshop creates a new *Work Path* item.) You can then use the path to create a selection outline or whatever.

Figure 11-34: When pasting a path copied from Illustrator, Photoshop greets you with this dialog box.

Tip

Things can get pretty muddled in the Clipboard, especially when you're switching applications. If you copy something from Illustrator, but the Paste command is dimmed inside Photoshop, you may be able to force the issue a little. Inside Illustrator, press the Option key and choose Edit ➪ Copy. This is intended to copy a PICT version of the path, but it sometimes has the added benefit of waking up the Clipboard to the fact that, yes indeed, there is something in here that Photoshop can use.(Computers are kind of slow sometimes. Every once in a while, you must give them a kick in the pants.)

Note

You can copy paths from Photoshop and paste them into Illustrator or some other drawing program regardless of the setting of the Export Clipboard check box in the Preferences dialog box. That option affects pixels only. Paths are so tiny, Photoshop always exports them.

Exporting to Illustrator

If you don't have enough memory to run both Illustrator and Photoshop at the same time, you can export Photoshop paths to disk and then open them in Illustrator. To export all paths in the current image, choose File ➪ Export ➪ Paths to Illustrator. Photoshop saves the paths as a fully editable Illustrator document. This scheme enables you to trace images exactly with paths in Photoshop and then combine these paths as objects with the exported EPS version of the image inside Illustrator. Whereas tracing an image in Illustrator can prove a little tricky because of resolution differences and other previewing limitations, you can trace images in Photoshop as accurately as you like.

Note

Unfortunately, Illustrator provides no equivalent function to export paths for use in Photoshop; nor can Photoshop open Illustrator documents from disk and interpret them as paths. This means the Clipboard is the only way to take a path created or edited in Illustrator and use it in Photoshop.

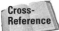
Cross-Reference

Only about half of Photoshop users own Illustrator. Meanwhile, close to 90 percent of Illustrator users own Photoshop. This is why I cover the special relationship between Illustrator and Photoshop in-depth in Chapter 13 of my Illustrator book, *Real World Illustrator 7*. You'll find out more about using Photoshop with FreeHand in the *FreeHand 8 Bible* (IDG Books Worldwide, 1998).

Retaining transparent areas in an image

When you import an image into Illustrator, FreeHand, CorelDraw, QuarkXPress, PageMaker, or some other object-oriented program, the image comes in as a rectangle with opaque pixels. Even if the image appeared partially transparent in Photoshop—on a layer, for example—the pixels are filled with white or some other color in the receiving application. These same object-oriented applications, however, do enable you to mask portions of an image you want to appear transparent by establishing a clipping path. Elements that lie inside the clipping path are opaque; elements outside the clipping path are transparent. Photoshop enables you to export an image in the EPS format with an object-oriented clipping path intact. When you import the image into the object-oriented program, it appears premasked with a perfectly smooth perimeter, as illustrated by the clipped image in Figure 11-35.

Figure 11-35: I drew one path around the perimeter of the skull and another around the eye socket. After defining the paths as clipping paths, I exported the image in the EPS format, imported it into Illustrator, and set it against a black background for contrast.

The following steps explain how to assign a set of saved paths as clipping paths.

Steps: Saving an Image with Clipping Paths

1. **Draw one or more paths around the portions of the image you want to appear opaque.** Areas outside the paths will be transparent.

2. **Save the paths.** Double-click on the *Work Path* item in the Paths palette, enter a name, and press Return. (Try to use a name that will make sense

three years from now when you have to revisit this document and determine what the heck you did.)

3. **Choose the Clipping Path command from the Paths palette menu.** Photoshop displays the dialog box shown in Figure 11-36, which asks you to select the saved paths you want to assign as the clipping path.

Note

If you like, enter a value into the Flatness option box. This option enables you to simplify the clipping paths by printing otherwise fluid curves as polygons. The Flatness value represents the distance — between 0.2 and 100, in printer pixels — the polygon may vary from the true mathematical curve. A higher value leads to a polygon with fewer sides. This means it looks chunkier, but it also prints more quickly. I recommend a value of 3. Many experts say you can go as high as 7 when printing to an imagesetter without seeing the straight edges. But I strongly suspect it depends on how much of a perfectionist you are. Me? I like 3.

After you set a path to a clipping path, Photoshop identifies it in the Paths palette by displaying its name in outline type, as illustrated in Figure 11-36.

Figure 11-36: After you choose the Clipping Path command (top), Photoshop identifies the clipping path name in the Paths palette with outline type (bottom).

4. **Choose File ⇨ Save As and select Photoshop EPS from the Format pop-up menu.** Select the desired Preview and Encoding settings, and press the Return key. Photoshop saves the EPS image with masked transparencies to disk.

Note

PageMaker is unique in that it supports clipping paths saved in the TIFF format. So if you plan on placing the image in PageMaker, you can save the image in TIFF instead of EPS in Step 4.

Figure 11-37 shows an enhanced version of the clipped skull from Figure 11-35. In addition to exporting the image with clipping paths in the EPS format, I saved the paths to disk by choosing File ➪ Export ➪ Paths to Illustrator. Inside Illustrator, I used the exported paths to create the outline around the clipped image. I also used them to create the shadow behind the image. The white of the eyeball is a reduced version of the eye socket, as are the iris and pupil. The background features a bunch of flipped and reduced versions of the paths. This may look like a lot of work, but the only drawing required was to create the two initial Photoshop paths.

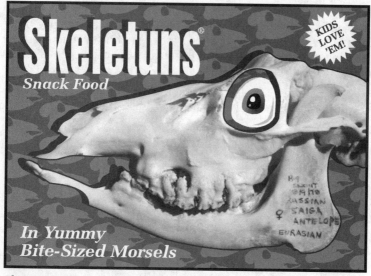

Figure 11-37: It's amazing what you can accomplish by combining scans edited in a painting program with smooth lines created in a drawing program.

Be prepared for your images to grow by leaps and bounds when imported into Illustrator. The EPS illustration shown in Figure 11-37 consumes six times as much space on disk as the original Photoshop image saved in the TIFF format.

Caution

When used in excess, clipping paths presents problems for the most sophisticated printing devices. You should use a clipping path only when it's absolutely necessary and can't be avoided. If you want to place an image against a bitmapped background, for example, do it in Photoshop, not in Illustrator, QuarkXPress, or any other application. This will invariably speed printing and may mean the difference between whether or not a file prints successfully.

✦   ✦   ✦

Creating Masks

Selecting Via Masks

Most Photoshop users don't use masks. If my personal experience is any indication, it's not only because masks seem complicated, it's because they strike most folks as being more trouble than they're worth. Like nearly everyone, when I first started using Photoshop, I couldn't even imagine a possible application for a mask. I have my lasso tool and my magic wand. If I'm really in a rut, I can pull out my pen tool. What more could I possibly want?

Quite a bit, as it turns out. Every one of the tools I just mentioned is only moderately suited to the task of selecting images. The lasso tools let you create free-form selections, but none of them — not even the magnetic lasso — can account for differences in focus levels. The magic wand selects areas of color, but it usually leaves important colors behind and the edges of its selection outlines often appear ragged and ugly. The pen tool is extremely precise, but it results in mechanical outlines that may appear incongruous with the natural imagery they contain.

Masks offer all the benefits of the other tools. With masks, you can create free-form selections, select areas of color, and generate amazingly precise selections. Masks also address all the deficiencies associated with the selection tools. They can account for different levels of focus, they give you absolute control over the look of the edges, and they create selections every bit as natural as the image itself.

In fact, a mask *is* the image itself. Masks use pixels to select pixels. Masks are your way to make Photoshop see what you see using the data inherent in the photograph. Masks enable you to devote every one of Photoshop's powerful capabilities to the task of creating a selection outline. Masks are, without a doubt, the most accurate selection mechanism available in Photoshop.

Masking defined

For those folks who aren't clear on what a mask is, I'll tell you: A *mask* is a selection outline expressed as a grayscale image.

✦ Selected areas appear white.

✦ Deselected areas appear black.

✦ Partially selected parts of the image appear in gray. Feathered edges are also expressed in shades of gray, from light gray near the selected area to dark gray near the deselected area.

Figure 12-1 shows two selection outlines and their equivalent masks. The top-left example shows a rectangular selection that has been inverted (using Image ➪ Adjust ➪ Invert, ⌘-I). Below this example is the same selection expressed as a mask. Because the selection is hard-edged with no anti-aliasing or feathering, the mask appears hard-edged, as well. The selected area is white and is said to be *unmasked;* the deselected area is black, or *masked.*

The top-right example in Figure 12-1 shows a feathered selection outline. Again, I've inverted the selection so you can better see the extent of the selection outline. (Marching ants can't accurately express softened edges, so the inversion helps show things off more.) The bottom-right image is the equivalent mask. Here, the feathering effect is completely visible.

When you look at the masks along the bottom of Figure 12-1, you may wonder where the heck the image went. One of the wonderful things about masks is they can be viewed independently of an image, as in Figure 12-1, or with an image, as in Figure 12-2. In the second figure, the mask is expressed as a color overlay. By default, the color of the overlay is a translucent red, like a conventional rubylith. (To see the overlay in its full, natural color, see Color Plate 12-1.) Areas covered with the rubylith are masked (deselected); areas that appear normal — without any red tint — are unmasked (selected). When you return to the standard marching ants mode, any changes you make to your image will affect only the unmasked areas.

Now that you know roughly what masks are (the definition will become progressively clearer throughout this chapter), the question remains, what good are they? Because a mask is essentially an independent grayscale image, you can edit the mask using any of the paint and edit tools discussed in Chapters 8 through 10, any of the filters discussed in Chapters 15 through 17, any of the color correction options discussed in Chapter 18, and virtually any of the functions described in the other chapters. You can even use the selection tools, as discussed in the previous chapter. With all these features at your disposal, you can't help but create a more accurate selection outline in a shorter amount of time.

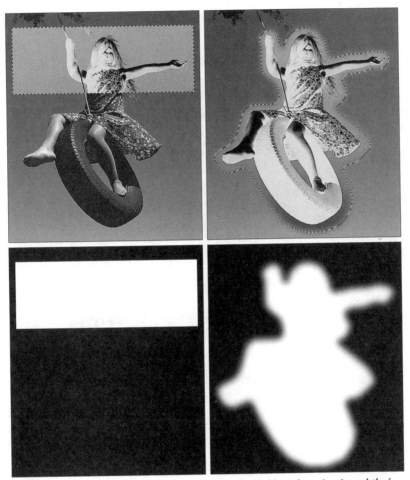

Figure 12-1: Two selection outlines with inverted interiors (top) and their equivalent masks (bottom)

Figure 12-2: Here are the masks from Figure 12-1, shown as they appear when viewed along with an image.

Painting and Editing Inside Selections

Before we immerse ourselves in masking techniques, let's start with a warm-up topic, *selection masking*. When you were in grade school, you might have had a teacher who nagged you to color within the lines. (I didn't. My teachers were more concerned about preventing me from writing on the walls and coloring on the other kids, or so I'm told.) If so, he or she would have been pleased by this incredibly straightforward feature. If you dread to paint inside an image because you're afraid you'll screw it up, selection masking is the answer. Regardless of which tool you use to create the selection—marquee, lasso, magic wand, or pen—Photoshop permits you to paint or edit only the selected area. The paint can't enter the deselected (or protected) portions of the image, so you can't help but paint inside the lines. As a result, all selection outlines act as masks, hence the term *selection masking*. (And you thought this chapter was going to be hard.)

Figures 12-3 through 12-6 show the familiar skull image subject to some pretty free-and-easy use of the paint and edit tools. (You think I ought to lay off the heavy metal or what?) The following steps describe how I created these images using a selection mask.

Steps: Painting and Editing inside a Selection Mask

1. **I selected the slightly rotting skull of the enchanting Russian Saiga antelope.** You can see the selection outline in such golden oldies as Figures 11-19 and 11-21. If those figures are too remote, just look at the top example in Figure 12-3. For the record, I drew this selection outline using the pen tool.

Figure 12-3: After drawing a selection outline around the antelope skull (top), I inversed the selection and deleted the background (bottom).

(continued)

2. **I reversed the selection with the Inverse command.** I wanted to edit the area surrounding the skull, so I chose Select ⇨ Inverse (⌘-Shift-I) to reverse which areas were selected and which were not.

3. **I pressed ⌘-Delete to fill the selected area with the background color.** In this case, the background color was white — as shown in the bottom half of Figure 12-3.

4. **I painted inside the selection mask.** But before I began, I chose Select ⇨ Hide Edges (⌘-H). This enabled me to paint without being distracted by those infernal marching ants. (In fact, this is one of the most essential uses for the Hide Edges command.)

5. **I selected the paintbrush tool and expressed myself.** I selected the 21-pixel soft brush shape in the Brushes palette. With the foreground color set to black, I dragged the paintbrush around the perimeter of the skull to set it apart from its white background, as shown in Figure 12-4. No matter how sloppily I painted, the skull remained unscathed.

Figure 12-4: I painted inside the selection mask with a 21-pixel soft brush shape.

6. **I next selected and used the smudge tool.** I set the Pressure slider bar inside the Smudge Options palette to 80 percent by pressing the 8 key. I dragged from inside the skull outward 20 or so times to create a series of curlicues. I also dragged from outside the skull inward to create white gaps between the curlicues. As shown in Figure 12-5, the smudge tool can smear colors from inside the protected area, but it does not apply these colors until you go inside the selection. This is an important point to remember, because it demonstrates that although the protected area is safe from all changes, the selected area may be influenced by colors from protected pixels.

Figure 12-5: Dragging with the smudge tool here smeared colors from pixels outside the selection mask without changing the appearance of those pixels.

7. **I double-click on the airbrush tool icon in the toolbox to display the Airbrush Options palette.** Then I selected the Fade check box and set the Fade value to 20, leaving the Transparent option selected in the pop-up menu. I then selected a 60-pixel soft brush shape and, again, dragged outward from various points along the perimeter of the skull. As demonstrated in Figure 12-6, combining airbrush and mask is as useful in Photoshop as it is in the real world.

Figure 12-6: I dragged around the skull with the airbrush to distinguish it further from its background. Pretty cool effect, huh? Well, if this is not your cup of tea, maybe you can track down a teenager who will appreciate it.

Working in Quick Mask Mode

Selection masks give you an idea of what masks are all about, but they only scrape the surface. The rest of the discussions in this chapter revolve around using masks to define complex selection outlines.

The most straightforward environment for creating a mask is the *quick mask mode*. In the quick mask mode, a selection is expressed as a rubylith overlay. All the deselected areas in your image appear coated with red and the selected areas appear without red coating, as shown in the middle examples of Color Plate 12-1. You can then edit the mask as desired and exit the mode to return to the standard selection outline. The quick mask mode is — as its name implies — expeditious and convenient, with none of the trappings or permanence of more conventional masks. It's kind of like a fast food restaurant — you use it when you aren't overly concerned about quality and you aim to get in and out in a hurry.

How the quick mask mode works

Typically, you'll at least want to rough out a selection with the standard selection tools before entering the quick mask mode. Then you can concentrate on refining and modifying your selection inside the quick mask, rather than having to create the selection from scratch. (Naturally, this is only a rule of thumb. I violate the rule several times throughout this chapter, but only because the quick mask mode and I are such tight friends.)

To enter the quick mask mode, click on the quick mask mode icon, as I've done in Figure 12-7. Or press the Q key. When I pressed *Q* after wreaking my most recent havoc on the extinct antelope skull, I got the image shown in Figure 12-7. The skull receives the mask because it is not selected. (In Figure 12-7, the mask appears as a light gray coating; on your color screen, the mask appears in red.) The area outside the skull looks the same as it always did because it's selected and, therefore, not masked.

Notice the selection outline disappears when you enter the quick mask mode. This is because it temporarily ceases to exist. Any operations you apply affect the mask itself and leave the underlying image untouched. When you click on the marching ants mode icon (to the left of the quick mask mode icon) or again press the Q key, Photoshop converts the mask back into a selection outline and again enables you to edit the image.

Figure 12-7: Click on the quick mask mode icon (highlighted in the toolbox) to instruct Photoshop to express the selection temporarily as a grayscale image.

Note

If you click on the quick mask mode icon without seeing anything change on screen, your computer isn't broken, it simply means you didn't select anything before you entered the mode. When nothing is selected, Photoshop makes the whole image open for editing; in other words, everything's selected. (Only a smattering of commands under the Edit, Layer, and Select menus require something to be selected before they work.) If everything is selected, the mask is white; therefore, the quick mask overlay is transparent and you don't see any difference on screen. This is another reason it's better to select something before you enter the quick mask mode — you get an immediate sense you're accomplishing something.

Also, Photoshop enables you to specify whether you want the red mask coating to cover selected areas or deselected areas. For information on how to change this setting, see "Changing the red coating," later in this chapter.

Once in the quick mask mode, you can edit the mask in the following ways:

✦ **Subtracting from a selection:** Paint with black to add red coating and, thus, deselect areas of the image, as demonstrated in the top half of Figure 12-8. This means you can selectively protect portions of your image by merely painting over them.

✦ **Adding to a selection:** Paint with white to remove red coating and, thus, add to the selection outline. You can use the eraser tool to whittle away at the masked area (assuming the background color is set to white). Or you can swap the foreground and background colors so you can paint in white with one of the painting tools.

Figure 12-8: After subtracting some of the selected area inside the eye socket by painting in black with the paintbrush tool (top), I feathered the outline by painting with white, using a soft 45-pixel brush shape (bottom).

✦ **Adding feathered selections:** If you paint with a shade of gray, you add feathered selections. You also can feather an outline by painting with black or white with a soft brush shape, as shown in the bottom image in Figure 12-8.

✦ **Clone selection outlines:** If you have a selection outline that you want to repeat in several locations throughout the image, the quick mask is your friend. Select the transparent area with one of the standard selection tools and ⌘-Option-drag it to a new location in the image, as shown in Figure 12-9. Although I use the lasso tool in the figure, the magic wand tool also works well for this purpose. To select an anti-aliased selection outline with the wand tool, set the tolerance to about 10 and be sure the Anti-aliased check box is active. Then click inside the selection. It's that easy.

Figure 12-9: To clone the eye socket selection, I lassoed around it (top) and ⌘-Option-dragged it (bottom).

✦ **Transform selection outlines:** You can scale or rotate a selection independently of the image, just as you can with the Transform Selection command (covered in Chapter 11). Enter the quick mask mode, select the mask using one of the standard selection tools, and choose Edit ➪ Free Transform or press ⌘-T. (See Chapter 13 for more information on Free Transform and related commands.)

These are only a few of the unique effects you can achieve by editing a selection in the quick mask mode. Others involve tools and capabilities I haven't yet discussed, such as filters and color corrections.

When you finish editing your selection outlines, click on the marching ants mode icon (to the left of the quick mask mode icon) or press the Q key again to return to the marching ants mode. Your selection outlines again appear flanked by marching ants, and all tools and commands return to their normal image-editing functions. Figure 12-10 shows the results of switching to the marching ants mode and deleting the contents of the selection outlines created in the last examples of the previous two figures.

As demonstrated in the top example of Figure 12-10, the quick mask mode offers a splendid environment for feathering one selection outline, while leaving another hard-edged or anti-aliased. Granted, because most selection tools offer built-in feathering options, you can accomplish this task without resorting to the quick mask mode. But the quick mask mode enables you to change feathering selectively after drawing selection outlines, something you can't accomplish with Select ➪ Feather. The quick mask mode also enables you to see exactly what you're doing. Kind of makes those marching ants look piddly and insignificant, huh?

Changing the red coating

By default, the protected region of an image appears in translucent red in the quick mask mode, but if your image contains a lot of red, the mask can be difficult to see. Luckily, you can change it to any color and any degree of opacity that you like. To do so, double-click on the quick mask icon in the toolbox (or double-click on the *Quick Mask* item in the Channels palette) to display the dialog box shown in Figure 12-11.

✦ **Color Indicates:** Select the Selected Areas option to reverse the color coating, that is, to cover the selected areas in a translucent coat of red and view the deselected areas normally. Select the Masked Areas option (the default setting) to cover the deselected areas in color.

You can reverse the color coating without ever entering the Quick Mask Options dialog box. Simply Option-click on the quick mask icon in the toolbox to toggle between coating the masked or selected portions of the image. The icon itself changes to reflect your choice.

Figure 12-10: The results of deleting the regions selected in the final examples of Figures 12-8 (top) and 12-9 (bottom). Kind of makes me want to rent *It's the Great Pumpkin, Charlie Brown.* I mean, who wouldn't give this antelope a rock?

Figure 12-11: Double-click on the quick mask mode icon to access the Quick Mask Options dialog box. You then can change the color and opacity of the protected or selected areas when viewed in the quick mask mode.

✦ **Color:** Click on the Color icon to display the Color Picker dialog box and select a different color coating. (If you don't know how to use this dialog box, see the "Using the Color Picker" section of Chapter 5.) You can lift a color from the image with the eyedropper after the Color Picker dialog box comes up, but you probably want to use a color that isn't in the image so you can better see the mask.

✦ **Opacity:** Enter a value to change the opacity of the translucent color that coats the image. A value of 100 percent is absolutely opaque.

Change the color coating to achieve the most acceptable balance between being able to view and edit your selection and being able to view your image. For example, the default red coating shows up badly on my grayscale screen shots, so I changed the color coating to light blue and the Opacity value to 65 percent before shooting the screens featured in Figures 12-7 through 12-9.

Gradations as masks

If you think the Feather command is a hot tool for creating softened selection outlines, wait until you get a load of gradations in the quick mask mode. No better way exists to create fading effects than selecting an image with the one of the gradient tools.

Fading an image

Consider the U.S. Capitol building shown in Figure 12-12. Whether you care for the folks who reside inside — personally, I'm sick of all this cynicism about the government, but I'm happy to exploit it for a few cheap laughs — you must admit, this is one beautiful building. Still, you might reckon the structure would be even more impressive if it were to fade into view out of a river of hot Hawaiian lava, like the one to the Capitol's immediate right. Well, you're in luck, because this is one of the easiest effects to pull off in Photoshop.

Switch to the quick mask mode by pressing the Q key. Then use the linear gradient tool to draw a gradation from black to white. (You can set the gradient style in the Linear Gradient Options palette to either Foreground to Background or Black, White.) The white portion of the gradation represents the area you want to select. I decided to select the top portion of the Capitol, so I drew the gradation from the top of the second tier to the top of the flag, as shown in the first example of Figure 12-13. Because the gradient line is a little hard to see, I've added a little arrow to show the direction of the drag. (To see the mask in full color, check out the first image in Color Plate 12-2.)

Figure 12-12: You can use the linear gradient tool in the quick mask mode to make the Capitol (left) fade out of the lava (right).

Banding can be a problem when you use a gradation as a mask. To eliminate the banding effect, therefore, apply the Add Noise filter at a low setting several times. To create the right example in Figure 12-13, I applied Add Noise using an Amount value of 24 and the Uniform distribution option.

Tip Notice in the right example of Figure 12-13, I've hidden the image so only the mask is visible. As the figure shows, the Channels palette lists the *Quick Mask* in italics. This is because Photoshop regards the quick mask as a temporary channel. You can hide the image and view the mask in black and white by clicking on the eyeball in front of the color composite view, in this case RGB. Or just press the tilde key (~) to hide the image. Press tilde again to view mask and image together.

To apply the gradation as a selection, I returned to the marching ants mode by again pressing Q. I then ⌘-dragged the selected portion of the Capitol and dropped it into the lava image to achieve the effect shown in Figure 12-14. I could say something about Congress rising up from the ashes, but I have no idea what I'd mean by this. For the color version of this splendid image, see Color Plate 12-2.

Figure 12-13: After drawing a linear gradation in the quick mask mode near the center of the image (left), I hid the image and applied the Add Noise filter with an Amount of 24 (right).

Applying special effects gradually

You also can use gradations in the quick mask mode to fade the outcomes of filters and other automated special effects. For example, I wanted to apply a filter around the edges of the Lincoln colossus that appears in Figure 12-15. I began by deselecting everything in the image (⌘-D) and switching to the quick mask mode. Then I brought up the Linear Gradient Options palette and selected the Foreground to Transparent option from the Gradient pop-up menu.

I pressed the D key to make the foreground color black and the background color white. Then I dragged with the linear gradient tool from each of the four edges of the image inward to create a series of short gradations that trace around the boundaries of the image, as shown in Figure 12-16. (As you can see, I've hidden the image so you see the mask in black and white.) Because I've selected the Foreground to Transparent option, Photoshop adds each gradation to the last one.

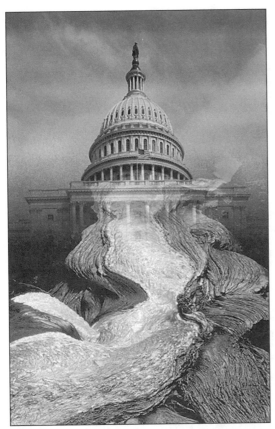

Figure 12-14: The result of selecting the top portion of the Capitol using a gradient mask and then ⌘-dragging and dropping the selection into the lava image.

To jumble the pixels in the mask, I applied Filter ⇨ Noise ⇨ Add Noise with an Amount value of 24. This is the effect that appears in Figure 12-16.

Tip

The only problem is I want to select the outside of the image, not the inside. So I need the edges to appear black and the inside to appear white, the opposite of what you see in Figure 12-16. No problem. All I do is press ⌘-I (Image ⇨ Adjust ⇨ Invert) to invert the image. Inverting inside the quick mask mode produces the same effect as applying Select ⇨ Inverse to a selection.

Figure 12-15: This time around, my intention is to surround Lincoln with a gradual filtering effect.

Figure 12-16: Inside the quick mask mode, I dragged from each of the four edges with the gradient tool (as indicated by the arrows).

Finally, I switched back to the marching ants mode by again pressing Q. Then I applied Filter ⇨ Render ⇨ Clouds to get the atmospheric effect you see in Figure 12-17. Yes, he's Abe the Illusionist — Lincoln as you've never seen him before! Once he gets to Vegas, he'll wipe the floor with David Copperfield.

Figure 12-17: After switching back to the marching ants mode, I chose Filter ⇨ Render ⇨ Clouds to create the foggy effect shown here.

Tip

Notice the corners in the mask in Figure 12-16? These corners are rounded, but you can achieve all kinds of corner effects with the linear gradient tool. For harsher corners, select the Foreground to Background option and set the brush mode to Lighten. For some *really* unusual corner treatments, try out the Difference and Exclusion brush modes. Wild stuff.

Creating gradient arrows

A few sections ago, Figure 12-13 featured an upward-pointing arrow that faded into view with a dark halo around it. I could have created this arrowhead in a drawing program to get nice sharp points and smooth outlines. But I chose to create it in Photoshop, so I could take advantage of two options drawing programs don't offer: gradient lines and halos. Naturally, you can create both in the quick mask mode.

The following steps explain how to add cool fading arrows to any image, as demonstrated in Figures 12-18 and 12-19. The steps involve the quick mask mode, the gradient tool, the Fill command, and good old Delete.

Steps: Creating Fading Arrows with Halos

1. **Choose the New Snapshot command from the History palette menu.** Photoshop adds a new snapshot thumbnail at the top of the palette. Click in front of it to make it the source state. Now you're ready to revert to this state if need be, as called for in Step 15.

2. **Deselect everything (⌘-D) and switch to the quick mask mode (Q).** The image should appear absolutely normal.

3. **Select the line tool (Shift-N twice) and press Return.** Adjust the line weight and arrowhead settings in the Line Options palette to fit your needs. To create my first arrows (the ones that come inward from the corners in Figure 12-19), I set the Weight value to 20 and the Width, Length, and Concavity values in the Arrowhead Shape dialog box to 400, 600, and 20, respectively.

4. **Press D to switch to the default colors.**

5. **Draw your line, which will show up in red.** If you don't get it right the first time — as is often the case with this tool — press ⌘-Z and try again. The beauty of drawing a line in the quick mask mode is you can edit it after the fact without damaging the image. (You could also do the same on a separate layer, but the quick mask mode affords you a little more flexibility in this specific exercise.)

6. **Select the linear gradient tool (G) and press Return.** Make sure the Gradient pop-up menu in the Options palette is set to Foreground to Background. Also set the Opacity value to 100 percent. Then choose Lighten from the brush mode pop-up menu.

7. **Use the gradient tool to fade the base of the line.** Drag with the linear gradient tool from the point at which you want the line to begin to fade, down to the base of the line. Try to make the direction of your drag parallel to the line itself, thus ensuring a smooth fade. The first example in Figure 12-18 shows me in the progress of dragging along one of my arrows with the gradient tool. The small white arrow shows the direction of my drag. (The black line shows the actual cursor you see on screen.) The second image shows the result of the drag.

8. **Choose Image ⇨ Adjust ⇨ Invert (⌘-I).** This inverts the quick mask, thus making the arrow the selected area.

Figure 12-18: Drag from the point at which you want the arrow to begin fading to the base of the line (left) parallel to the line itself (indicated here by the white arrow) to fade the line out (right).

9. **Copy the quick mask to a separate channel.** Drag the *Quick Mask* item in the Channels palette onto the little page icon at the bottom of the palette to copy the quick mask to a permanent mask channel. You'll need it again.

10. **Press Q to switch back to the marching ants mode.** Your arrow appears as a selection outline.

11. **Expand the selection to create the halo.** Choose Select ⇨ Modify ⇨ Expand and enter the desired value, based on the size and resolution of your image. I entered 6 to expand the selection outline 6 pixels.

12. **Choose Select ⇨ Feather (⌘-Option-D).** Enter the same value and press Return.

13. **Fill the selection with white for a light halo, or black for a dark one.** I wanted a white halo, so I pressed the D key to restore the default foreground and background colors. Then I pressed ⌘-Delete to fill the selection with white.

14. **⌘-click on the Quick Mask Copy item in the Channels palette.** This regains your original arrow-shaped selection outline. (I explain channel masks in detail later in this chapter, but for now, just ⌘-click.)

(continued)

15. **Press ⌘-Option-Delete.** If you set the source state properly in Step 1, this shortcut reverts the portion of the image inside the arrows to its original appearance.

16. **Copy the selection to an independent layer.** Press ⌘-J or choose Layer ➪ New ➪ Layer via Copy.

17. **Fill the layered arrow with a color.** Change the foreground color to anything you like and press Shift-Option-Delete to fill the arrow (and only the arrow).

18. **Choose Multiply from the blend mode pop-up menu in the upper-left corner of the Layers palette.** This burns the colored arrow into the image. Then set the Opacity value to the desired level. I pressed the 4 key to change the Opacity to 40 percent.

After that, I simply kept adding more and more arrows by repeating the process. I saved occasional snapshot states so I could create arrows on top of arrows. Most notably, I made a snapshot of the image before adding the last, big arrow that shoots up from the bottom. Then I filled the arrow with the snapshot to bring back bits and pieces of a few of the other arrows. (Had I not filled back in time via the History palette, the arrow fragments behind the big arrow would have disappeared.)

Generating Masks Automatically

Another convenient method for creating a mask is the Color Range command under the Select menu. This command enables you to generate selections based on color ranges. You use the familiar eyedropper cursor to specify colors that should be considered for selection, and other colors you want to rule out. The Color Range command is a lot like the magic wand tool, except it enables you to select colors with more precision and to change the tolerance of the selection on the fly.

Using the Color Range command

When you choose Select ➪ Color Range, Photoshop displays the Color Range dialog box shown in Figure 12-20. Like the magic wand combined with the Similar command, Color Range selects areas of related color all across the image, whether or not the colors are immediate neighbors. You click in the image window to select and deselect colors, as you do with the wand. But rather than adjusting a Tolerance value before you use the tool, you adjust a Fuzziness option any old time you like. Photoshop dynamically updates the selection according to the new value. Think of Color Range as the magic wand on steroids.

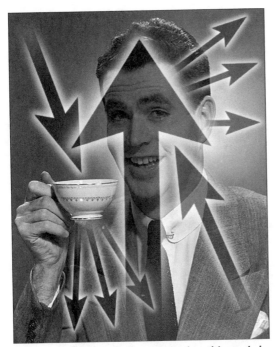

Figure 12-19: I don't know whether this guy's in store for a cold front or what, but if you ever need to annotate an image with arrows, this gradient-arrowhead trick is certainly the way to do it.

Note

So why didn't the folks at Adobe merely enhance the functionality of the magic wand rather than adding this strange command? The Color Range dialog box offers a preview of the mask — something a tool can't do — which is pretty essential for gauging the accuracy of your selection. And the magic wand is convenient, if nothing else. If Adobe were to combine the two functions, you would lose functionality.

Notice, when you move your cursor outside the Color Range dialog box, it changes to an eyedropper. Click with the eyedropper to specify the color on which you want to base the selection — I call this the base color — as if you were using the magic wand. Or you can click inside the preview area, labeled in Figure 12-20. In either case, the preview area updates to show the resulting mask.

Preview

Figure 12-20: The Color Range dialog box enables you to generate a mask by dragging with the eyedropper tool and adjusting the Fuzziness option.

You can also do the following:

✦ **Add colors to the selection:** To add base colors to the selection, select the add color tool inside the Color Range dialog box and click inside the image window or preview area. You can also access the tool while the standard eyedropper is selected by Shift-clicking (just as you Shift-click with the magic wand to add colors to a selection). You can even Shift-drag with the eyedropper to add multiple colors in a single pass, something you can't do with the wand tool.

✦ **Remove colors from the selection:** To remove base colors from the selection, click with the remove color tool or Option-click with the eyedropper. You can also drag or Option-drag to remove many colors at a time.

Tip

If adding or removing a color sends your selection careening in the wrong direction, press ⌘-Z. Yes, the Undo command works inside the Color Range dialog box as well as out of it.

✦ **Adjust the Fuzziness value:** This option resembles the Tolerance value in the Magic Wand Options palette because it determines the range of colors to be selected beyond the ones on which you click. Raise the Fuzziness value to expand the selected area; lower the value to contract the selection. A value of 0 selects the clicked color only. Unlike changes to Tolerance, however, changing the Fuzziness value adjusts the selection on the fly; no repeat clicking is required, as it is with the wand tool.

Fuzziness and Tolerance also differ in the kind of selection outlines they generate. Tolerance entirely selects all colors within the specified range and adds anti-aliased edges. If the selection were a mask, most of it would be white with a few gray pixels around the perimeter. By contrast, Fuzziness entirely selects only the colors on which you click and Shift-click, and partially selects the other colors in the range. That's why most of the mask is expressed in shades of gray. The light grays in the mask represent the most similar colors; the dark grays represent the least similar pixels that still fall within the Fuzziness range. The result is a tapering, gradual selection, much more likely to produce natural results.

✦ **Reverse the selection:** Select the Invert check box to reverse the selection, changing black to white and white to black. As when using the magic wand, it may be easier to isolate the area you don't want to select than the area you do want to select. When you encounter such a situation, select Invert.

✦ **Toggle the preview area:** Use the two radio buttons below the preview area to control the preview's contents. If you select the first option, Selection, you see the mask that will be generated when you press Return. If you select the Image option, the preview shows a reduced version of the image.

Tip

You can toggle between the two previews by pressing and holding the ⌘ key. My advice is to leave the option set to Selection and press the ⌘ key when you want to view the image.

✦ **Control the contents of the image window:** The Selection Preview pop-up menu at the bottom of the dialog box enables you to change what you see in the image window. Leave the option set to None — the default setting — to view the image normally in the image window. Select Grayscale to see the mask on its own. Select Quick Mask to see the mask and image together. Select Black Matte or White Matte to see what the selection would look like against a black or white background.

Although they may sound weird, the Matte options enable you to get an accurate picture of how the selected image will mesh with a different background. Figure 12-21 shows Lincoln's head at the top with the grayscale mask on the right. The mask calls for the shadows in Lincoln's face to be selected, with the highlights deselected. The two Matte views help you see how this particular selection looks against two backgrounds as different as night and day. Use the Fuzziness option in combination with Black Matte or White Matte to come up with a softness setting that will ensure a smooth transition.

✦ **Select by predefined colors:** Choose an option from the Select pop-up menu at the top of the dialog box to specify the means of selecting a base color. If you choose any option besides Sampled Colors, the Fuzziness option and eyedropper tools become dimmed to show they are no longer operable. Rather, Photoshop selects colors based on their relationship to a predefined color. For example, if you select Red, the program entirely selects red and partially selects other colors based on the amount of red they contain. Colors composed exclusively of blue and green are not selected.

None   Grayscale

Black Matte   White Matte

Figure 12-21: Selecting an option from the Selection Preview pop-up menu changes the way the Color Range command previews the selection in the image window.

The most useful option in this pop-up menu is Out of Gamut, which selects all the colors in an RGB or Lab image that fall outside the CMYK color space. You can use this option to select and modify the out-of-gamut colors before converting an image to CMYK.

✦ **Load and save settings:** Click on the Save button to save the current settings to disk. Click on Load to open a saved settings file.

When you define the mask to your satisfaction, click on the OK button or press Return to generate the selection outline. Although the Color Range command is more flexible than the magic wand, you can no more expect it to generate perfect selections than any other automated tool. After Photoshop draws the selection outline, therefore, you'll probably want to switch to the quick mask mode and paint and edit the mask to taste.

If you learn nothing else about the Color Range dialog box, at least learn to use the Fuzziness option and the eyedropper tools. Basically there are two ways to approach these options. If you want to create a diffused selection with gradual edges, set the Fuzziness option to a high value—60 or more—and click and Shift-click two or three times with the eyedropper. To create a more precise selection, enter a Fuzziness of 40 or lower and Shift-drag and Option-drag with the eyedropper until you get the exact colors you want.

Figure 12-22 shows some sample results. To create the left images, I clicked with the eyedropper tool once in Lincoln's face and set the Fuzziness to 160. To create the right images, I lowered the Fuzziness value to 20; then I clicked, Shift-clicked, and Option-clicked with the eyedropper to lift exactly the colors I wanted. The top examples show the effects of stroking the selections, first with 6-pixel white strokes, and then with 2-pixel black ones. In the two bottom examples, I copied the selections and pasted them against an identical background of—what else?—the Lincoln Memorial. In all four cases, the higher Fuzziness value yields more generalized and softer results; the lower value results in a more exact but harsher selection.

A few helpful Color Range hints

Tip

You can limit the portion of an image that Select ➪ Color Range affects by selecting part of the image before choosing the command. When a selection exists, the Color Range command masks only those pixels that fall inside it. Even the preview area reflects your selection. Try it and see.

You can also add or subtract from an existing selection using the Color Range command. Press Shift when choosing Select ➪ Color Range to add to a selection. Press Option when choosing Color Range to subtract from a selection.

If you get hopelessly lost when creating your selection and you can't figure out what to select and what to deselect, click with the eyedropper tool to start over. This clears all the colors from the selection except the one you click. Or you can press Option to change the Cancel button to a Reset button. Option-click on the button to return the settings inside the dialog box to those in force when you first chose Select ➪ Color Range.

Fuzziness: 160   Fuzziness: 20

Figure 12-22: After creating two selections with the Color Range command — one with a high Fuzziness value (left) and one with a low one (right) — I alternately stroked the selections (top) and pasted them against a different background (bottom).

Creating an Independent Mask Channel

The problem with masks generated via the quick mask mode and Color Range command is that they're here one day and gone the next. Photoshop is no more prepared to remember them than it is a lasso or wand selection.

Most of the time, that's okay. You'll only use the selection once, so there's no reason to sweat it. But what if the selection takes you a long time to create? What if, after a quarter hour of Shift-clicking here and Option-dragging there, adding a few strokes in the quick mask mode, and getting the selection outline exactly right, your boss calls a sudden meeting or the dinner bell rings? You can't just drop everything; you're in the middle of a selection. But nor can you convey your predicament to non-Photoshop users because they'll have no idea what you're talking about and no sympathy for your plight.

The simplest solution is to back up your selection, save your file, and move on to the next phase of your life. In fact, anytime that you spend 15 minutes or more on a selection, I'd save it. After all, you never know when all heck is going to break loose and 15 minutes is just too big a chunk of your life to repeat it. (The average person racks up a mere 2.5 million quarter hours, so use them wisely!) You wouldn't let 15 minutes of image-editing go by without saving, and the rules don't change just because you're working on a selection.

Saving a selection outline to a mask channel

The following steps describe how to back up a selection to an independent mask channel, which is any channel above and beyond those required to represent a grayscale or color image. Mask channels are saved along with the image itself, making it a safe and sturdy solution.

Steps: Transferring a Selection to an Independent Channel

1. **Convert the selection to a mask channel.** One way to do this is to choose Select ➪ Save Selection (or Control-click in the image window and choose Save Selection from the pop-up menu), which saves the selection as a mask. The dialog box shown in Figure 12-23 appears, asking you where you want to put the mask. In most cases, you'll want to save the mask to a separate channel inside the current image. To do so, make sure the name of the current image appears in the Document pop-up menu. Then select New from the Channel pop-up menu, enter any name for the channel that you like, and press Return.

   If you have an old channel you want to replace, select the channel's name from the Channel pop-up menu. The radio buttons at the bottom of the dialog box become available, permitting you to add the mask to the channel, subtract it, or intersect it. These radio buttons work like the equivalent options that appear when you make a path into a selection outline (as discussed in the previous chapter) but, instead, they blend the masks together. The result is the same as if you were adding, subtracting, or intersecting selection outlines, except it's expressed as a mask.

(continued)

Tip

Or you can save the mask to a new multichannel document all its own. To do this, choose New from the Document pop-up menu and press Return.

Man, what a lot of options! If you only want to save the selection to a new channel and be done with it, you needn't bother with the Save Selection command or dialog box. Just click on the make channel icon at the bottom of the Channels palette (labeled in Figure 12-23). Photoshop automatically creates a new channel, converts the selection to a mask, and places the mask in the channel.

Figure 12-23

Make selection   Make channel   Delete channel
                           New channel

Figure 12-23: The Save Selection dialog box enables you to convert your selection outline to a mask and save it to a new or existing channel.

Regardless of which of these many methods you choose, your selection outline remains intact.

2. **View the mask in the Channels palette.** To do so, click on the appropriate channel name in the Channels palette — automatically named *Alpha 1* unless you assigned a name of your own. In Figure 12-23, I replaced the contents of a channel called Existing Mask, so this is where my mask now resides.

This step isn't the least bit mandatory. It just lets you see your mask and generally familiarize yourself with how masks look. Remember, white represents selection, black is deselected, and gray is partial selection.

If you didn't name your mask in Step 1 and you want to name it now, double-click on the Alpha 1 item in the Channels palette and enter a name in the active option box.

3. **Return to the standard image-editing mode by clicking on the first channel name in the Channels palette.** Better yet, press ⌘-1 if you're editing a grayscale image or ⌘-tilde (~) if the image is in color.

4. **Save the image to disk to store the selection permanently as part of the file.** A handful of formats — FlashPix, PICT, Pixar, PNG, TIFF, Targa, and native Photoshop — accommodate RGB images with an extra mask channel. But only the TIFF and native format can handle more than four channels, both saving up to 24 channels in all. I generally use the TIFF format with LZW compression when saving images with masks — unless the image contains layers, in which case you have no choice but to save in the Photoshop format.

Both the native Photoshop format and TIFF are capable of compressing the sizes of masks so that they take up substantially less room on disk. The Photoshop format does this automatically. When saving a TIFF image, be sure to turn on the LZW Compression check box. In both cases, this run-line compression is entirely safe. It does not change a single pixel in the image; it merely writes the code in a more efficient manner.

Photoshop also permits you to save a mask with a GIF file. But if you do, all pixels in the masked area are saved as gray, indicating transparency. This means that all detail in the masked areas goes away, and you cannot access the mask independent of the image.

If you performed the steps in the "Creating gradient arrows" section earlier in this chapter, you know that you can also save a quick mask to its own channel for later use. But in case you missed those steps, or you're saving them for a special occasion, here's how it works. When you enter the quick mask mode, the Channels palette displays an item called *Quick Mask*. The italic letters show the channel is temporary and will not be saved with the image. (To clone it to a permanent channel, drag the *Quick Mask* item onto the page icon at the bottom of the Channels palette). Now save the image to the TIFF or Photoshop format and you're backed up.

Converting a mask to a selection

To retrieve your selection later, choose Select ⇨ Load Selection. A dialog box nearly identical to the one shown in Figure 12-23 appears except for the addition of an Invert check box. Select the document and channel that contain the mask you want to use. You can add it to a current selection, subtract it, or intersect it. Select the Invert option if you want to reverse the selected and deselected portions of the mask.

Want to avoid the Load Selection command? ⌘-click on the channel name in the Channels palette that contains the mask you want to use. For example, if I ⌘-clicked on the Existing Mask item in Figure 12-23, Photoshop would load the equivalent selection outline into the image window.

Tip

But wait, there's more:

✦ You can press ⌘-Option plus the channel number to convert the channel to a selection. For example, ⌘-Option-4 would convert the Existing Mask channel shown in the figure.

✦ You can also select the channel and click on the far-left mask selection icon at the bottom of the Channels palette. But for my money, this takes too much effort.

✦ To add a mask to the current selection outline, ⌘-Shift-click on the channel name in the Channels palette.

✦ ⌘-Option-click on a channel name to subtract the mask from the selection.

✦ And ⌘-Shift-Option-click to find the intersection.

You can convert color channels to selections as well as mask channels. For example, if you want to select the black pixels in a piece of scanned line art in grayscale mode, ⌘-click on the first item in the Channels palette. This selects the white pixels; press ⌘-Shift-I (or choose Select ⇨ Inverse) to reverse the selection to the black pixels.

Viewing mask and image

Photoshop lets you view any mask channel along with an image, just as you can view mask and image together in the quick mask mode. To do so, click in the first column of the Channels palette to toggle the display of the eyeball icon. An eyeball in front of a channel name indicates you can see that channel. If you are currently viewing the image, for example, click in front of the mask channel name to view the mask as a translucent color coating, again as in the quick mask mode. Or, if the contents of the mask channel appear by themselves on screen, click in front of the image name to display it as well.

When the mask is active, you can likewise toggle the display of the image by pressing the tilde (~) key. Few folks know about this shortcut, but it's a good one to assign to memory. It works whether the Channels palette is open or not, and it permits you to focus on the mask without moving your mouse all over the screen.

Using a mask channel is different from using the quick mask mode in that you can edit either the image or the mask channel when viewing the two together. You can even edit two or more masks at once. To decide which channel you want to edit, click on the channel name in the palette. To edit two channels at once, click on one and Shift-click on another. All active channel names appear highlighted.

You can change the color and opacity of each mask independent of other mask channels and the quick mask mode. Double-click on the mask channel name or choose the Channel Options command from the Channels palette menu. (This command is dimmed when editing a standard color channel, such as Red, Green, Blue, Cyan, Magenta, Yellow, or Black.) A dialog box similar to the one shown back in Figure 12-11 appears, but this one contains a Name option box so you can change the name of the mask channel. You can then edit the color overlay as described in the "Changing the red coating" section earlier in this chapter.

If you ever need to edit a selection outline inside the mask channel using paint and edit tools, click on the quick mask mode icon in the toolbox. It may sound a little incestuous — like a play within a play, perhaps — but you can access the quick mask mode even when working within a mask channel. Make sure the mask channel color is different from the quick mask color so you can tell what's happening.

Building a Mask from an Image

So far, everything I've discussed in this chapter has been pretty straightforward. Now it's time to see how the professionals do things. This final section in the chapter explains every step required to create a mask for a complex image — updated especially for this edition of the book. Here's how to select the image you never thought you could select, complete with wispy little details like hair.

Take a gander at Figure 12-24 and you'll see what I mean. I chose this subject not for her good looks or her generous supply of freckles, but for that hair. I mean, look at all that hair. Have you ever seen such a frightening image-editing subject in your life? Not only is this particular girl blessed with roughly 15 googol strands of hair, but every one of them is leaping out of her head in a different direction and at a different level of focus. Can you imagine selecting any one of them with the magnetic lasso or magic wand? No way. As demonstrated by the second example of Figure 12-24, these tools lack sufficient accuracy to do any good. Furthermore, you'd be fit for an asylum by the time you finished selecting the hairs with the pen tools, and the edges aren't definite enough for Select ➪ Color Range to latch onto.

Figure 12-24: Have you ever wanted to select wispy details, like the hair shown on left? You certainly aren't going to make it with the magnetic lasso (right) or other selection tools. But with masks, it's a piece of cake.

So what's the solution? Manual masking. Although masking styles vary as widely as artistic style, a few tried-and-true formulas work for everyone. First, you peruse the channels in an image to find the channel that will lend itself best to a mask. You're looking for high degrees of contrast, especially around the edges. Next, you copy the channel and boost the level of contrast using Image ➪ Adjust ➪ Levels. (Some folks prefer Image ➪ Adjust ➪ Curves, but Levels is more straightforward.) Then you paint inside the lines until you get the mask the way you want it.

The only way to get a feel for masking is to try it out for yourself. The following steps explain exactly how I masked this girl and pasted her against a different background. The final result is so realistic, you'd think she was born there.

Steps: Selecting a Monstrously Complicated Image Using a Mask

1. **Browse the color channels.** Press ⌘-1 to see the red channel, ⌘-2 for green, and ⌘-3 for blue. (This assumes you're working inside an RGB image. You can also peruse CMYK and Lab images. If you're editing a grayscale image, you have only one channel from which to choose—Black.)

Figure 12-25 shows the three channels in my RGB image. Of the three, the red channel offers the most contrast between the hair, which appears very light, and the background, which appears quite dark.

Figure 12-25: Of the three color channels, the red channel offers the best contrast between hair and background.

2. **Copy the channel.** Drag the channel onto the little page icon at the bottom of the Channels palette. (I naturally copy the red channel.) Now you can work on the channel to your heart's content without harming the image itself.

3. **Choose Filter ⇨ Other ⇨ High Pass.** The next thing you want to do is to force Photoshop to bring out the edges in the image so you don't have to hunt for them manually. And when you think edges, you should think filters. All of Photoshop's edge-detection prowess is packed into the Filter menu. Several edge-detection filters are available to you — Unsharp Mask, Find Edges, and many others that I discuss in Chapter 15. But the best filter for finding edges inside a mask is Filter ⇨ Other ⇨ High Pass.

High Pass selectively turns an image gray. High Pass may sound strange, but it's quite useful. The filter turns the non-edges completely gray while leaving the edges mostly intact, thus dividing edges and non-edges into different brightness camps, based on the Radius value in the High Pass dialog box. Unlike in most filters, a low Radius value produces a more pronounced effect than a high one, in effect locating more edges.

(continued)

Figure 12-26 shows the original red channel on left with the result of the High Pass filter on right. I used a Radius of 10, which is a nice, moderate value. The lower you go, the more edges you find and the more work you make for yourself. A Radius of 3 is accurate, but it'll take you an hour to fill in the mask. Granted, 10 is less accurate, but if you value your time, it's more sensible.

Figure 12-26: After copying the red channel (left), I apply the High Pass filter with a Radius value of 10 to highlight the edges in the image (right).

4. **Choose Image ➪ Adjust ➪ Levels (⌘-L).** After adding all that gray to the image, follow it up by increasing the contrast. And the best command for enhancing contrast is Levels. Although I discuss this command in-depth in Chapter 18, here's the short version: Inside the Levels dialog box, raise the first Input Levels value to make the dark colors darker, and lower the third Input Levels value to make the light colors lighter. (For now you can ignore the middle value.)

Figure 12-27 shows the result of raising the first Input Levels value to 110 and lowering the third value to 155. As you can see in the left-hand image, this gives me some excellent contrast between the white hairs and black background.

To demonstrate the importance of the High Pass command in these steps, I've shown what would happen if I had skipped Step 3 in the right-hand image in Figure 12-27. Here I've applied the same Levels values as the left image, and yet the image is washed out and quite lacking in edges. Look at that wimpy hair. It simply is unacceptable.

Figure 12-27: Here are the results of applying the Levels command to the mask after the High Pass step (left) and without High Pass (right). As you can see, High Pass has a pronounced effect on the edge detail.

5. **Use the lasso tool to remove the big stuff you don't need.** By way of High Pass and Levels, Photoshop has presented you with a complex coloring book. From here on, it's a matter of coloring inside the lines. To simplify things, get rid of the stuff you know you don't need. All you care about is the area where the girl meets her background — mostly hair and arms. Everything else goes to white or black.

   For example, in Figure 12-28, I selected a general area inside the girl by Option-clicking with the lasso tool. Then I filled it with white by pressing ⌘-Delete. I also selected around the outside of the hair and filled it with black. At all times, I was careful to stay about 10 to 20 pixels away from the hair and other edges; these I need to brush in carefully with the eraser. (Be sure to press ⌘-D to eliminate the selection before continuing to the next step.)

(continued)

Figure 12-28: To tidy things up a bit, I selected the general areas inside and outside the girl with the lasso tool and filled them with white or black (left). Then I painted inside the lines with the block eraser (right).

6. **Erase inside the lines with the block eraser.** This is the most time-consuming part. You now have to paint inside the lines to make the edge pixels white (selected) or black (not). I like to use the block eraser because it's a hard-edged block. See, Photoshop has already presented me with these lovely and accurate edges. I don't want to gum things up by introducing new edges with a soft paintbrush or airbrush. The block eraser is hard, you can easily see its exact boundaries, and it automatically adjusts as you zoom in and out — affecting fewer pixels at higher levels of magnification, which is what you need. When working in a mask, the eraser always paints in the background color. So use the X key to toggle the background color between white and black.

The second example in Figure 12-28 shows the fruits of my erasing. As you can see, I make a few judgment calls and decide — sometimes arbitrarily — where the hair gets so thick that background imagery won't show through. You may even disagree with some of my eraser strokes. But you know what? It doesn't matter. Despite whatever flaws I may have introduced, my mask is more than accurate enough to select the girl and her unruly hair, as I'll soon demonstrate.

7. **Switch to the color composite view.** Press ⌘-tilde (~). Or if you're working in a grayscale image, press ⌘-1. By the way, now is a good time to save the image if you haven't already done so.

8. **⌘-click on the mask channel to convert it to a selection.** This mask is ready to go prime time.

9. **⌘-drag the selection and drop it into a different image.** Figure 12-29 shows the result of dropping the girl into a background of rolling California hills. Thanks to my mask, she looks as natural in her new environment as she did in her previous one. In fact, an uninitiated viewer might have difficulty believing this isn't how she was originally photographed. But if you take a peek at Figure 12-24, you can confirm that Figure 12-29 is indeed an artificial composite. I lost a few strands of hair in the transition, but she can afford it.

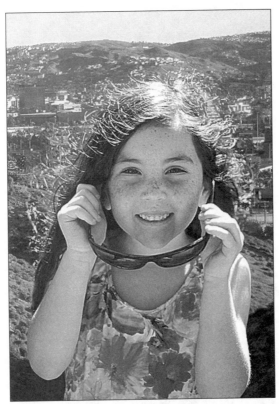

Figure 12-29: Thanks to masking, our girl has found a new life in southern California. Now she's ready to finally put on those sunglasses.

The grayscale Figure 12-29 looks great but, in all honesty, your compositions may not fare quite so well in color, as illustrated by the first girl in Color Plate 12-3. Her hair is fringed with blue, an unavoidable holdover from her original blue background. The solution is to brush in the color from her new background. Using the paintbrush tool set to the Color brush mode, you can Option-click in the Background layer to lift colors from the new background and then paint them into the hair. I also took the liberty of erasing a few of the more disorderly hairs, especially the dark ones above her head. (I used a soft paintbrush-style eraser, incidentally, not the block.) After a minute or two of painting and erasing, I arrived at the second girl in the color plate. Now if that isn't compositing perfection, I don't know what is.

✦   ✦   ✦

Layers and Transformations

Layers, Layers Everywhere

Layers are at once Photoshop's most overrated and most underused feature. On one hand — and let's be perfectly clear about this — they add absolutely no functionality to Photoshop. Anything you can accomplish with layers, you can also accomplish without layers. Photoshop artists have been devising fantastic compositions, applying all varieties of selections, and masking and blending images since the program was first released. Very wisely, in my opinion, Adobe has yet to make any feature exclusive to layers.

What layers add is flexibility. Because each layer in a composition is altogether independent of other layers, you can change your mind on a moment's notice. Consider Figure 13-1. Here I've compiled the ingredients for a very bad day at the doctor's office. (By golly, this may explain the reason for my chronic heartburn.) Each of the bits and pieces of hardware are located on a separate layer, all of which float above the surface of the background X-ray. Even though the pixels from the hardware blend with the X-ray and with each other, I can easily reposition and modify them as the mood strikes me. Photoshop automatically reblends the pixels on the fly.

To show what I mean, I've repositioned and transformed every single layer in the second example in Figure 13-1. The MO cartridge is smaller and rotated, the mess of cords hangs up instead of down, and the lock and key are just plain skewed. I can also exchange the order of the layers, merge layers together, and adjust their translucency until I keel over from sheer alternative overload.

Figure 13-1: So that's what I did with my SCSI cable! Thanks to the flexibility of layers, you can arrange a bunch of images one way one moment (top) and quite differently the next (bottom). Layers enable you to modify a composition without sacrificing quality.

Layers are also uniquely versatile. You can apply three levels of masking to layers — all of which can be in force simultaneously, if you like. You can move and transform multiple layers at a time. You can create a special kind of layer that adjusts the colors in the layers below it (as I explain in Chapter 18), and mix layers together using predefined mathematical calculations (Chapter 19). Again, you can do it all without layers if you want, but with layers, the world becomes an infinitely editable place.

Thanks to the further demise of floating selections, Photoshop 5 forces you to use layers in many situations. Whether you like this ironhanded approach or not — I happen to think Adobe went a tad overboard — you can't argue with the logic. We should all use layers more often. Layers make it harder to make mistakes, they make it easier to make changes, and they expand your range of options. If a layer might help, there's very little reason not to add one. You may not appreciate having to use layers, but at least they're for your own good.

Sending a Selection to a Layer

To its credit, Photoshop lets you establish a new layer in roughly a billion different ways. If you want to add a selected portion of one image to another image, the easiest method is to ⌘-drag the selection and drop it into its new home, as demonstrated in Figure 13-2. Photoshop makes you a new layer, lickety-split.

Dropped selection becomes new layer

Figure 13-2: ⌘-drag a selection and drop it into a different image window to introduce the selection as a new layer. As you can see in the Layers palette, the camera becomes a new layer in front of the television.

Caution

Be sure to ⌘-drag or use the move tool. If you merely drag the selection with the marquee, lasso, or wand, you drop an empty selection outline into the new image window.

When you drop the selection, your selection outline disappears. Not to worry, though. Now that the image resides on an independent layer, the selection outline is no longer needed. You can move the layer using the move tool — as you would move a selection. You can even paint inside what was once the selection by selecting the Preserve Transparency check box in the Layers palette. I explain both the move tool and Preserve Transparency in greater detail throughout this chapter.

If you want to clone a selection to a new layer inside the same image window — useful when performing complex filter routines and color corrections — choose Layer ➪ New ➪ Layer Via Copy. Or press ⌘-J, as in Jump.

Other ways to make a layer

Those are only two of many different ways to create a new layer in Photoshop. Here are a few others:

✦ Copy a selection (⌘-C) and paste it into another image (⌘-V). Photoshop pastes the selection as a new layer.

✦ If you want to relegate a selection exclusively to a new layer, choose Layer ➪ New ➪ Layer Via Cut or press ⌘-Shift-J. Rather than cloning the selection, Layer Via Cut removes the selection from the background image and places it on its own layer.

✦ To convert a floating selection — one which you've moved or cloned — to a new layer, press ⌘-Shift-J. The Shift key is very important. If you press ⌘-J without Shift, Photoshop clones the selection and leaves an imprint of the image on the layer below.

✦ To create an empty layer — as when you want to paint a few brushstrokes without harming the original image — choose Layer ➪ New ➪ Layer or press ⌘-Shift-N. Or click on the new layer icon at the bottom of the Layers palette (labeled in Figure 13-3).

Incidentally, you can also create a new layer by choosing New Layer from the Layers palette menu. But as you can see in the wonderfully easy-to-follow Figure 13-3 — can you imagine a more illuminating piece of info art? — nearly all the palette commands are duplicated in the Layer menu. The only unique palette command is Palette Options (circled in the figure), which lets you change the size of the thumbnails in front of the layer names.

Figure 13-3: All but one of the commands in the Layers palette menu are duplicated in the Layer menu.

Tip

When you choose the Layer Via Copy or Layer Via Cut command or click on the new layer icon, Photoshop automatically names the new layer for you. Unfortunately, the automatic names—Layer 1, Layer 2, and so on—are fairly meaningless and don't help to convey the contents of the layer. (Dammit, Photoshop, don't you know a camera when you see one?) If you want to specify your own name, add the Option key. Press ⌘-Option-J to clone the selection to a layer, press ⌘-Shift-Option-J to cut the selection, or Option-click on the new layer icon to create a blank layer. In any case, you'll see the dialog box shown in Figure 13-4. Enter a name for the layer and press Return. (You can ignore the other options in this dialog box for now.)

When creating a new layer from the keyboard, press ⌘-Shift-Option-N to bypass the dialog box. So Option works both ways, forcing the dialog box sometimes and suppressing it others. The only time it produces no effect is when pasting or dropping an image. Too bad—I for one would get a lot of use out of it.

Tip

To rename a layer, double-click on its name in the Layers palette. (You can also choose Layer ➪ Layer Options, but what sane human being would go to all that effort?) Then enter a new name and whack that Return key.

Figure 13-4: Press Option to force the display of the New Layer dialog box, which lets you name the new layer.

Duplicating a layer

To clone the active layer, you can choose Layer ⇨ Duplicate Layer. But that's the sucker's way. The more convenient way is to drag the layer name you want to clone onto the new layer icon at the bottom of the Layers palette.

To specify a name for the cloned layer or to copy the layer into another image, Option-drag the layer onto the new layer icon. Always the thoughtful program, Photoshop displays the dialog box shown in Figure 13-5. You can name the cloned layer by entering something into the As option box. To jettison the layer to some other open image, choose the image name from the Document pop-up menu. Or choose New and enter the name for an entirely different image in the Name option box, as the figure shows.

Figure 13-5: You can duplicate the layer into an entirely different image by Option-dragging the layer onto the new layer icon in the Layers palette.

In Photoshop 5, you can also clone a layer simply by ⌘-Option-dragging it. This way, you clone the layer and reposition it in one operation. Just be sure no portion of the image is selected; otherwise, you create a floating selection.

Working with Layers

Regardless of how you create a new layer, Photoshop lists the layer along with a little thumbnail of its contents in the Layers palette. The new layer's name appears highlighted to show it's active. The little paintbrush icon in front of the layer name also indicates an active layer.

To the left of the paintbrush icon is a column of eyeballs, which invite you to hide and display layers temporarily. Click on an eyeball to hide the layer. Click where the eyeball previously was to bring it back and redisplay the layer. Whether hidden or displayed, all layers remain intact and ready for action.

Tip

To view a single layer by itself, Option-click on the eyeball icon before the layer name to hide all other layers. Option-click in front of the layer again to bring all the layers back into view.

Switching between layers

You can select a different layer by clicking on its name in the Layers palette. This layer becomes active, enabling you to edit it. Only one layer may be active at a time in Photoshop — you can't Shift-click to select and edit multiple layers, I'm sorry to say.

If your image contains several layers — like the one back in Figure 13-1 — it might prove inconvenient, or even confusing, to switch from one layer to another in the Layers palette. Luckily, Photoshop offers a better way. With any tool, ⌘-Control-Option-click on an element in your composition to go directly to the layer containing the element. For example, ⌘-Control-Option-clicking on the SCSI cable in Figure 13-1 would take me to the SCSI Cable layer.

Why ⌘-Control-Option-clicking? Here's how it breaks down:

✦ ⌘ gets you the move tool. (If the move tool is already selected, you don't have to press ⌘; Control-Option-clicking works just fine.)

✦ Control-clicking alone brings up a context-sensitive pop-up menu. When you Control-click with the move tool — or ⌘-Control-click with any other tool — Photoshop displays a pop-up menu that lists the layer the image is on and any other layers in the image, as in Figure 13-6. (If a layer is completely transparent at the spot where you Control-click, that layer name doesn't appear in the pop-up menu.) Select the desired layer to go there.

✦ The Option key bypasses the pop-up menu and goes straight to the clicked layer.

Add them all together, and you get ⌘-Control-Option-click. It's a lot to remember, but believe me, it's a great trick once you get the hang of it.

Figure 13-6: ⌘-Control-Option-click on an image to view a pop-up menu. The menu lists the location of the image on which you've clicked and the background layer.

If you'd prefer Photoshop *always* go directly to the layer on which you click and avoid all these messy keyboard tricks, then press the V key to select the move tool and press Return. Inside the Move Options dialog box, you'll find the Auto Select Layer check box. Turn it on. Now whenever you click on a layer with the move tool — or ⌘-click with some other tool — Photoshop goes right to that layer.

Switching layers from the keyboard

You can also ascend and descend the layer stack from the keyboard:

✦ **Option-]:** Press Option-right bracket to go to the next layer up in the stack. If you're already at the top layer, Photoshop takes you back around to the lowest one.

✦ **Option-[:** Press Option-left bracket to go down a layer. If the background layer is active, Option-[takes you to the top layer.

✦ **Shift-Option-]:** This takes you to the top layer in the image.

✦ **Shift-Option-[:** This activates the background layer (or the lowest layer if no background exists).

Understanding transparency

Although the selection outline disappears when you convert a selection to a layer, no information is lost. Photoshop retains every little nuance of the original selection outline — whether it's a jagged border, a little bit of anti-aliasing, or a feathered edge. Anything that wasn't selected is now transparent. The data that defines the opacity and transparency of a layer is called the *transparency mask*.

To see this transparency in action, click on the eyeball icon in front of the Background item in the Layers palette. This hides the background layer and enables you to view the new layer by itself. In Figure 13-7, I hid the background TV from Figure 13-6 to view the camera on its own. The transparent areas are covered in a checkerboard pattern. Opaque areas look like the standard image, and translucent areas — where they exist — appear as a mix of image and checkerboard.

Figure 13-7: When you hide the background layer, you see a checkerboard pattern that represents the transparent portions of the layer.

Tip

If the checkerboard pattern is hard to distinguish from the image, you can change the appearance of the pattern. Press ⌘-K and then ⌘-4 to go to the Transparency & Gamut panel of the Preferences dialog box. Then edit away (as explained back in Chapter 2).

If you apply an effect to the layer while no portion of the layer is selected, Photoshop changes the opaque and translucent portions of the image, but leaves the transparent region intact. For example, if you press ⌘-I (or choose Image ➪ Adjust ➪ Invert), Photoshop inverts the image but doesn't change a single pixel in the checkerboard area. If you click in the left column in front of the Background item to bring back the eyeball icon, you may notice a slight halo around the inverted image, but the edge pixels blend with the background image as well as they ever did. In fact, it's exactly as if you applied the effect to a selection, as demonstrated in Figure 13-8. The only difference is this selection is altogether independent of its background. You can do anything you want to it without running the risk of harming the underlying background.

Figure 13-8: Applying the Invert command to the camera layer inverts only the camera without affecting any of the transparent pixels. The TV remains every bit as visible as ever.

Only a few operations affect the transparent areas of a layer, and most of these are limited to tools. You can paint on transparent pixels to make them opaque. You can clone with the rubber stamp, or smear pixels with the edit tools. But you can send pixels back to transparency using the eraser, as well. All these operations change both the contents of the layer and the composition of the transparency mask.

Tip

You can also fill all pixels by pressing Option-Delete for the foreground color and ⌘-Delete for the background color. To fill the pixels in a layer without altering the transparency mask, toss in the Shift key. Shift-Option-Delete fills the opaque pixels with the foreground color, while ⌘-Shift-Delete fills them with the background color.

In both cases, the transparent pixels remain every bit as transparent as they ever were.

When a portion of the layer is selected, pressing plain old Delete eliminates the selected pixels and makes them transparent, revealing the layers below.

Note

Transparent pixels take up next to no space in memory, but opaque and translucent pixels do. Thus, a layer containing 25 percent as many pixels as the background layer takes up roughly 25 percent as much space. I wouldn't let this influence how you work in Photoshop, but it is something to keep in mind.

Modifying the background layer

At the bottom of the layer stack is the *background layer*, the fully opaque layer that represents the base image. The background image is as low as you go. Nothing can be slipped under the background layer and pixels in the background layer cannot be made transparent, unless you first convert the background to a "normal" layer.

To make the conversion, double-click on the background item in the Layers palette. Then enter a name for the new layer — Photoshop suggests Layer 0 — and press Return. You can now change the order of the layer or erase down to transparency.

In Figure 13-9, I converted the background television to a layer. This particular image (from the PhotoDisc Object Series) included a predrawn path that encircled the TV. I ⌘-clicked on the path to convert it to a selection outline, then I pressed ⌘-Shift-I to reverse the selection. Finally, I pressed the Delete key to erase the pixels outside the TV, as the figure demonstrates.

From this point, I can reorder the camera and television layers or add layers in back of the TV. I can also introduce a new background layer. (A program like QuarkXPress or PageMaker doesn't recognize Photoshop's transparency, so there's no point in leaving the background transparent. As I mentioned in Chapter 11, if you want to export transparency, you must use a clipping path.)

To add a new background layer, choose Layer ⇨ New ⇨ Background. This is also a step in converting the lowest layer in the stack to the background. Choose Layer ⇨ New ⇨ Background, then press Option-] to select the next layer up, and press ⌘-E to merge it with the background.

In Figure 13-10, I added a new background layer. I used the Add Noise and Emboss filters to create a paper texture pattern (as I explained back in Chapter 10). Then I used Layer ⇨ Effects ⇨ Drop Shadow to add a drop shadow that matched the contours of the TV. (To learn all about the Layer ⇨ Effects commands, read the "Automatic Shadows, Glows, and Bevels" section later in this chapter.)

Figure 13-9: After converting the TV image to a layer, I
⌘-clicked on the path, inversed the selection, and pressed
the Delete key to reveal the transparent void below.

Figure 13-10: I added a background layer behind the television
and applied a paper texture and drop shadow to give my
composition a little false depth.

Reordering layers

What good would layers be if you couldn't periodically change what's on the top and what's on the bottom? There are two ways to reorder layers. First, you can drag a layer name up or down in the scrolling list to move it forward or backward in layering order. The only trick is to make sure that the black bar appears at the point where you want to move the layer before you release the mouse button, as illustrated in Figure 13-11.

Figure 13-11: Drag a layer between two other layers to make the all-important black bar appear (left). Then release to change the hierarchy of the layer (right).

The second way to reorder layers is to choose a command from the Layer ➪ Arrange submenu. For example, choose Layer ➪ Arrange ➪ Bring Forward to move the active layer up one level; choose Layer ➪ Arrange ➪ Send to Back to move the layer to above the background layer.

You can move faster if you remember the following keyboard shortcuts:

✦ **⌘-Shift-]:** Press ⌘-right bracket to move the active layer to the top of the stack.

✦ **⌘-Shift-[:** This shortcut moves the active layer to the bottom of the stack, just above the background layer.

✦ **⌘-]:** This nudges the layer up one level.

✦ **⌘-[:** This nudges the layer down.

Note You can neither reorder the background layer nor move any other layer below the background until you first convert the background to a normal layer, as explained in the preceding section.

Automated matting techniques

When you convert an anti-aliased selection to a layer, you sometimes take with you a few pixels from the selection's previous background. These *fringe pixels* can result in an unrealistic outline around your layer that cries out, "This image was edited by a hack." For example, Figure 13-12 shows a magnified detail from one of my original attempts to add a drop shadow to the TV. Although the selection outline was accurate, I managed to retain a few white pixels around the edges, as you can see around the outline of the picture tube and arm that holds the tube.

Figure 13-12: This enlarged detail of the TV layer against the textured background shows the fringe pixels left over from the TV's original white background.

You can instruct Photoshop to replace the fringe pixels with colors from neighboring pixels by choosing Layer ➪ Matting ➪ Defringe. Enter the thickness of the perceived fringe in the Width option box to tell Photoshop which pixels you want to replace. To create the image shown in Figure 13-13, I entered a Width value of 1. But even at this low value, the effect is pretty significant, leaving gummy edges in its wake.

Figure 13-13: Here I used the Defringe command set to a Width value of 1 to replace the pixels around the perimeter of the layer with colors borrowed from neighboring pixels.

Photoshop provides two additional commands under the Layer ➪ Matting submenu: Remove Black Matte and Remove White Matte. Frankly, it's unlikely you'll have much call to use them, but here's the scoop:

✦ **Remove Black Matte:** This command removes the residue around the perimeter of a layer that was lifted from a black background.

✦ **Remove White Matte:** This command removes a white ring around a layer.

Adobe tells me these commands were designed specifically for compositing a scene rendered in a 3-D drawing program against a black or white background. But for other purposes, they almost never work. For example, my television is a prime candidate for Remove White Matte — it originated from a white background — and yet it leaves behind more white pixels than the Defringe command set to its lowest setting.

Tip

If you encounter unrealistic edge pixels and the automatic matting commands don't solve your problem, you may be able to achieve better results by fixing the edges manually. First, switch to the layer that's giving you fits and ⌘-click on its name in the Layers palette. This creates a tight selection around the contents of the layer. Then choose Select ⇨ Modify ⇨ Contract and enter the width of the fringe in the Contract By option box. Next, choose Select ⇨ Feather (⌘-Shift-D) and enter this same value into the Feather Radius option box. Finally, press ⌘-Shift-I to inverse the selection and press Delete to eliminate the edge pixels.

Figure 13-14 shows the results of applying this technique to my television. By setting the Contract and Feather commands to 1 pixel, I managed to remove the edges without harming the layer itself. And the effect looks better than that produced by the Defringe command (as you can compare for yourself with Figure 13-13).

Figure 13-14: Here I removed the edges manually using the Contract, Feather, and Inverse commands. This looks way better than anything Photoshop can do automatically.

Blending layers

Photoshop lets you blend layers like no other program in the business. In fact, Photoshop does such a great job that it takes me an entire chapter — Chapter 19 — to explain these options in detail. I offer this section only by way of introduction, so you're at least aware of the basics. If you have bigger questions, then Chapter 19 is ready to tell all.

The Layers palette provides three basic ways to blend pixels between layers. None of these techniques changes as much as a pixel in any layer, so you can always return and reblend the layers at a later date (see Figure 13-15).

✦ **The Opacity value:** Enter a value into the Opacity option box near the top of the Layers palette to change the opacity of the active layer or floating selection. If you reduce the Opacity value to 50 percent, for example, Photoshop makes the pixels on the active layer translucent, so the colors in the active layer mix evenly with the colors in the layers below.

If any tool other than a paint or edit tool is active—including the selection and navigation tools—you can press a number key to change the Opacity value. Press 1 for 10 percent, 2 for 20 percent, up to 0 for 100 percent. Or you can enter a specific Opacity value by pressing two number keys in a row. For example, press 3 and then 7 for 37 percent.

✦ **The blend mode pop-up menu:** Choose an option from the blend mode pop-up menu—open in Figure 13-15—to mix every pixel in the active layer with the pixels below it, according to one of several mathematical equations. For example, when you choose Multiply, Photoshop really does multiply the brightness values of the pixels and then divides the result by 255, the maximum brightness value. Blend modes use the exact same math as the brush modes covered in Chapter 8. But you can accomplish a lot more with blend modes, which is why I spend so much time examining them in Chapter 19.

In Photoshop 5, you can select a blend mode from the keyboard when a selection or navigation tool is active. Press Shift-plus to advance incrementally down the list; press Shift-minus to inch back up. You can also press Shift-Option plus a letter key to select a specific mode. For example, Shift-Option-M selects the Multiply mode. Shift-Option-N restores the mode to Normal.

Figure 13-15: The blend mode pop-up menu and the Opacity option box enable you to mix layers together without making any permanent changes to the pixels.

✦ **Layer Options:** Choose Layer ➪ Layer Options or double-click on a layer name to display the Layer Options dialog box. This dialog box provides access to an Opacity value and a Mode pop-up menu, but it also offers a few unique functions. Using the Blend If slider bars, you can specify which colors are visible in the active layer and which colors show through from the layers behind it. You can also mix the colors using special fuzziness controls and change the slider bar settings for an individual color channel.

This is enough to prepare you for anything I might throw at you between now and Chapter 19. But as I've mentioned four times now, Chapter 19 contains the whole story. (Oops, make that five.)

Fusing several layers into one

Although layers are wonderful and marvelous creatures, they have their price. Layers expand the size of an image in RAM and ultimately lead to slower performance. And as explained in Chapter 4, you can save layered images in only one format, the native Photoshop format.

In the name of slimming down the size of your image, Photoshop provides the following methods for merging layers together:

✦ **Merge Down (⌘-E):** Choose Layer ➪ Merge Down to merge a layer with the layer immediately below it. When generating screen shots, I use this command 50 or 60 times a day. I paste the screen shot into the image window, edit the layer as desired, and then press ⌘-E to set it down. Then I can save the screen shot in any format I like.

Note

If the active layer is linked to other layers or part of a clipping group — two conditions I discuss later in this chapter — the Merge Down command changes to Merge Linked or Merge Group, respectively. Again, these commands use ⌘-E as a shortcut. Merge Down is forever changing to suit the situation.

✦ **Merge Visible (⌘-Shift-E):** Choose the Merge Visible command to merge all visible layers into a single layer. If the layer is not visible — that is, if no eyeball icon appears in front of the layer name — Photoshop doesn't eliminate it; the layer simply remains independent.

Tip

To create a merged clone, press the Option key when applying either Layer ➪ Merge Down or Layer ➪ Merge Visible. Option-choosing Merge Down (or pressing ⌘-Option-E) clones the contents of the active layer into the layer below it. Option-choosing Merge Visible (or pressing ⌘-Shift-Option-E) copies the contents of all visible layers to the active layer.

To copy the merged contents of a selected area, choose Edit ➪ Copy Merged or press ⌘-Shift-C. You can then paste the selection into a layer or make it part of a different image.

✦ **Flatten Image:** This command, on the other hand, merges all visible layers and throws away the invisible ones. The result is a single, opaque background layer. Photoshop does not give this command a keyboard shortcut because it's so dangerous. More often than not, you'll want to flatten an image incrementally using the two Merge commands.

Note that Photoshop suggests that you flatten an image when converting from one color mode to another by choosing a command from the Image ⇨ Mode submenu. You can choose not to flatten the image (by pressing the D key) but this may come at the expense of some of the brighter colors in your image.

Dumping layers

You can also merely throw a layer away: Drag the layer name onto the trash can icon at the bottom of the Layers palette. Or click on the trash can icon to delete the active layer.

When you click on the trash can icon, Photoshop displays a message asking whether you really want to toss the layer. To give this message the slip in the future, Option-click on the trash can icon.

Saving a flattened version of an image

Only one file format, the native Photoshop format, saves images with layers. If you want to save a flattened version of your image — that is, with all layers fused together into a single image — in some other file format, choose File ⇨ Save a Copy (⌘-Option-S) and select the desired format from the Format pop-up menu. If you select any format other than Photoshop, the program selects and dims the Flatten Image check box in the lower-left corner of the dialog box.

The Save a Copy command neither affects the image on screen — all layers remain intact — nor changes the name of the image in the title bar. It merely creates a flattened duplicate of the image on disk.

Selecting the Contents of Layers

A few sections back, I mentioned that every layer (except the background) includes a *transparency mask*. This mask tells Photoshop which pixels are opaque, which are translucent, and which are transparent. Like any mask, Photoshop lets you convert the transparency mask for any layer — active or not — to a selection outline. In fact, you use the same keyboard techniques you use to convert paths to selections (as explained in Chapter 11) and channels to selections (Chapter 12):

✦ ⌘-click on an item in the Layers palette to convert the transparency mask for that layer to a selection outline.

✦ To add the transparency mask to an existing selection outline, ⌘-Shift-click on the layer name. The little selection cursor includes a plus sign to show you that you're about to add.

✦ To subtract the transparency mask, ⌘-Option-click on the layer name.

✦ And to find the intersection of the transparency mask and the current selection outline, ⌘-Shift-Option-click on the layer name.

If you're uncertain you'll remember all these keyboard shortcuts, you can use Select ⇨ Load Selection instead. After choosing the command, select the Transparency item from the Channel pop-up menu. (You can even load a transparency mask from another open image if the image is exactly the same size as the one in which you're working.) Then use the Operation radio buttons to merge the mask with an existing selection, as described in the "Converting a mask to a selection" section of Chapter 12.

Selection outlines exist independently of layers, so you can use the transparency mask from one layer to select part of another layer. For example, to select part of the background layer that exactly matches the contents of another layer, you press Shift-Option-[to descend to the background layer and then ⌘-click on the name of the layer you want to match.

The most common reason to borrow a selection from one layer and apply it to another is to create manual shadow and lighting effects. After ⌘-clicking on a layer, you can use this selection to create a drop shadow that precisely matches the contours of the layer itself. No messing with the airbrush or the lasso tool — Photoshop does the tough work for you.

Now, you might think that with Photoshop 5's new automated effects (found in the Layer ⇨ Effects submenu), manual drop shadows and the like would be a thing of the past. After all, you have only to choose Layer ⇨ Effects ⇨ Drop Shadow and, bang, the program adds a drop shadow. But the old, manual methods still have their advantages. You don't have to visit a dialog box to edit a manual drop shadow, you can reposition a manual shadow from the keyboard, and you can expand and contract a manual shadow with more precision than an automatic one.

On the other hand, this is not to say the old ways are always better. A shadow created with the Drop Shadow command takes up less room in memory, it moves and rotates with a layer, and you can edit the softness of the shadow long after creating it.

What we have is two equally powerful solutions, each with its own characteristic pros and cons. Therefore, the wise electronic artist will develop a working knowledge of both. This way, you're ready and able to apply the technique that makes the most sense for the job at hand.

Cross-Reference

The following sections explore the manual drop shadows, highlights, and spotlights. For everything you ever wanted to know about the Layer ⇨ Effects commands, read the section "Automatic Shadows, Glows, and Bevels" a few pages from now in this same chapter.

Drop shadows

In these first steps, I'll take the dolphin from Figure 13-16 and insert a drop shadow behind it. This might not be the exact subject to which you'll apply drop shadows — sea critters so rarely cast such shadows onto the water's surface — but it accurately demonstrates how the effect works.

Figure 13-16: A dolphin in dire need of a drop shadow.

Steps: Creating a Drop Shadow

1. **Select the subject you want to cast the shadow.** In my case, I selected the dolphin by painting the mask shown in Figure 13-17 inside a separate mask channel. These days, I add a mask to nearly every image I create to distinguish the foreground image from its background. I converted the mask to a selection outline by ⌘-clicking on the mask name in the Channels palette and then pressing ⌘-tilde (~) to switch back to the composite view.

(continued)

Figure 13-17: This mask separates the dolphin from its watery home.

2. **Send the image to a separate layer by pressing ⌘-J.** Now that the selection is elevated, you can slip in the drop shadow beneath it.

3. **Retrieve the selection outline for your new layer and apply it to the background layer.** To do this, ⌘-click on the new layer name (presumably Layer 1), then press Shift-Option-[to switch to the background layer. (Because I saved the mask to a separate channel, I could have instead ⌘-clicked on the Mask item in the Channels panel to retrieve the selection. Or I could have pressed ⌘-Option-4.)

4. **To create a softened drop shadow – indicative of a diffused light source – choose Select ➪ Feather (⌘-Option-D).** The Radius value you enter depends on the resolution of your image. I recommend dividing the resolution of your image by 20. When working on a 200 ppi image, for example, enter a Radius value of 10. My image is a mere 140 ppi, so I entered 7. Then press Return to soften the image.

5. **Press ⌘-J to send the feathered selection to a new layer.**

6. **Fill the feathered area with black.** If necessary, press the D key to make the foreground color black. Then press Shift-Option-Delete to fill only the area inside the transparency mask. A slight halo of dark pixels forms around the edges of the image.

7. Press ⌘ with the arrow keys to nudge the shadow to the desired location.
In Figure 13-18, I nudged the shadow 12 pixels to the right. (Press ⌘-Shift-arrow key to nudge the shadow 10 pixels.)

Figure 13-18: A drop shadow is nudged 12 pixels due right from the dolphin head, which is situated on the layer above it.

8. Lower the Opacity setting. If the shadow is too dark — black lacks a little subtlety — change the Opacity value in the Layers palette to change the opacity of the shadow. Or press M to make sure a selection tool is active and then press a number key to change the opacity. I typically press 7 for 70 percent, but I'm probably in a rut.

Tip

If you don't like a black drop shadow, you can make a colored one with only slightly more effort. Instead of filling the shadow with black in Step 6, select a different foreground color and press Shift-Option-Delete. For the best result, select a color that is the complementary opposite of your background color. (In Color Plate 13-1, for example, the background is blue, so I selected a reddish orange as the foreground color.) Next, choose Multiply from the blend mode pop-up menu in the Layers palette (or press Shift-Option-M). This burns the colors in the shadow into those in the lower layers to create a darkened mix. Finally, press a number key to specify the opacity. (In the color plate, I again used 70 percent. I'm definitely in a rut.)

Halos

Creating a halo is similar to creating a drop shadow. The only differences are, you must expand the selection outline and fill the halo with white (or some other light color) instead of black. The following steps tell all.

Steps: Creating a Downright Angelic Halo

1. **Follow Steps 1 through 3 of the previous instructions.** You'll end up with a version of the selected image on an independent layer and a matching selection outline applied to the background image. (See, I told you this was like creating a drop shadow.)

2. **Expand the selection outline.** Unlike a drop shadow, which is offset slightly from an image, a halo fringes the perimeter of an image pretty evenly. You need to expand the selection outline beyond the edges of the image so you can see the halo clearly. To do this, choose Select ➪ Modify ➪ Expand. You'll be greeted by an Expand By option box. Generally speaking, you want the expansion to match the size of your feathering, so the softening occurs outward. Therefore, I entered 7. (The maximum permissible value is 16; if you want to expand more than 16 pixels, you must apply the command twice.)

3. **Choose Select ➪ Feather and enter the same value you entered in the Expand By option box.** Again, you decide this value by dividing the resolution of your image by 20 (or thereabouts).

4. **Send the selection to a new layer.** Press ⌘-J.

5. **Fill the halo with white.** Assuming the background color is white, press ⌘-Shift-Delete.

That's it. Figure 13-19 shows an enlightened-looking dolphin set against a halo effect. I also drew a conventional halo above its head, added some sparklies, and even changed my finned friend's eye using the eyeball brush shape included in the Assorted Brushes document. I mean, if this aquatic mammal's not bound for glory, I don't know who is.

Tip

Incidentally, you needn't create a white halo any more than you must create a black drop shadow. In Step 5, set the background color to something other than white. Then select the Screen option from the blend mode pop-up menu in the Layers palette (Shift-Option-S), thus mixing the colors and lightening them at the same time. If you don't like the effect, select a different background color and press ⌘-Shift-Delete again. With the halo on a separate layer, you can do just about anything to it without running a risk of harming the underlying original.

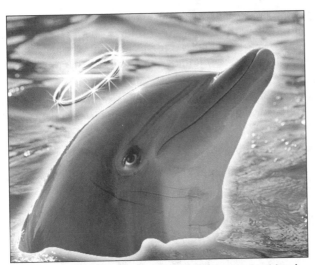

Figure 13-19: Few dolphins reach this level of spiritual awareness, even if you do set them off from their backgrounds using the halo effect. He kind of looks like one of the cast members from *Cocoon,* don't you think?

Spotlights

Now, finally, for the spotlight effect. I use spotlights about a billion times in this book to highlight some special option I want you to look at in a palette or dialog box. I've received so many questions (from fellow authors mostly) on how to perform this effect, I've decided to write the information in this book and be done with it. So here goes.

Steps: Shining a Spotlight on Something Inside an Image

1. **Draw an oval selection inside your image.** Obviously, the best tool for this purpose is the elliptical marquee tool. The selection represents the area where the spotlight will shine. If you don't like where the oval is located, but you like its basic size and shape, drag the outline to a more satisfactory location.

(continued)

2. **Choose Select ⇨ Feather and enter whatever Radius value you please.** Again, you may want to follow the divide-the-resolution-by-20 rule, but use whatever value you like. (There's no such thing as a wrong Radius value.) To create Figure 13-20, I doubled my Radius value to 14 pixels to create a soft effect.

3. **Press ⌘-Shift-I.** Most likely, you really want to darken the area outside the spotlight, not lighten the spotlight itself. So choose Select ⇨ Inverse (⌘-Shift-I) to swap what's selected and what's not.

4. **Send the selection to a new layer.** That's ⌘-J, of course.

5. **Fill the transparency mask with black.** With the foreground color set to black, press Shift-Option-Delete.

6. **Lower the Opacity setting by pressing a number key.** To get the effect in Figure 13-20, I pressed 6 for 60 percent.

Figure 13-20: Create an elliptical selection, feather it, inverse it, layer it, fill it with black, and lower the opacity to create a spotlight effect like this one.

Actually, the image in Figure 13-20 isn't all that convincing. Although the preceding steps are fine for spotlighting flat images such as screen shots, they tend to rob photographs of some of their depth. After all, in real life, the spotlight wouldn't hit the water in the same way it hits the dolphin.

Tip

But there is a way around this. You can combine the oval selection outline with the mask used to select the foreground image, thereby eliminating the background from the equation entirely. First establish the selection and feather it (Steps 1 and 2). Assuming your image has a mask saved in a separate channel, ⌘-Shift-Option-click on the mask name in the Channels palette. This retains just the intersection of the mask and the spotlight selection. Then perform the preceding Steps 3 through 6 — that is, inverse the selection (⌘-Shift-I), send it to a layer (⌘-J), fill the transparency mask with black (Shift-Option-Delete), and change the opacity. For my part, I first rotated the oval selection using Select ➪ Transform Selection. Then I found the intersection of the mask and rotated the oval to achieve the more natural spotlight shown in Figure 13-21.

Figure 13-21: You can mix the feathered selection with the contents of a mask channel to limit the spotlighting effect to the foreground character only.

Cross-Reference

Sometimes, the darkness of the area around the spotlight appears sufficiently dark that it starts bringing the spotlighted area down with it. To brighten the spotlight, inverse the selection (⌘-Shift-I) so the spotlight is selected again. Then apply the Levels command (⌘-L) to brighten the spotlighted area. The Levels command is explained at length in Chapter 18.

Just for fun — what other possible reason would there be? — Color Plate 13-2 shows one result of combining the spotlight effect with the halo effect. After selecting the oval area, feathering it, and rotating it with the Transform Selection command, I inversed the selection (⌘-Shift-I). Then I ⌘-Shift-Option-clicked on the dolphin mask in the Channels palette to retain the area outside the oval and inside the dolphin. (The background was therefore deselected.) I cloned this area to a separate layer, filled it with a deep blue, and applied the Multiply blend mode. Then, using my original dolphin mask, I sent the dolphin to a separate layer and created a yellowish, pinkish halo behind it. Finally, I returned to the background layer and inverted it by pressing ⌘-I. An interestingly lit dolphin in a radioactive bath is the result.

Automatic Shadows, Glows, and Bevels

Photoshop 5 adds a series of so-called *layer effects* that automate the application of shadows, glows, and beveled edges. To apply a layer effect, select a foreground element in your image, press ⌘-J to copy it to an independent layer, and choose one of the first five commands from the Layer ➭ Effects submenu:

✦ **Drop Shadow:** The Drop Shadow command applies a common, everyday drop shadow. You specify the color, opacity, blend mode, position, and softness of the shadow. Photoshop does the rest.

✦ **Inner Shadow:** This command applies a drop shadow inside the layer, as demonstrated by the second example in Figure 13-22. The command simulates the kind of shadow you'd get if the layer were punched out of the background — that is, the background looks like it's in front, casting a shadow onto the layer. Inner Shadow is especially effective with type, as I explain in Chapter 14.

✦ **Outer Glow:** The Outer Glow command creates a traditional halo, like the one I applied to our aquatic friend back in the "Halos" section. You specify color, opacity, blend mode, and softness.

✦ **Inner Glow:** This command applies the effect inside the layer rather than outside, as demonstrated in the second row of Figure 13-22.

To create a neon strip around the perimeter of a layer, apply both the Outer Glow and Inner Glow commands. For an example of a neon edge, see the bottom-right image in Figure 13-22.

✦ **Bevel and Emboss:** Layer ➭ Effects ➭ Bevel and Emboss produces four distinct edge effects, each of which appears in Figure 13-23. You can add a three-dimensional beveled edge around the outside of the layer, as in the first example in the figure. The Inner Bevel effect produces a beveled edge inside the layer. The Emboss effect combines inner and outer bevels. And the Pillow Emboss reverses the inner bevel so the image appears to sink in and then rise back up along the edge of the layer.

Drop shadow

Inner shadow

Outer glow

Inner glow

Drop + inner shadow

Outer + inner glow

Figure 13-22: The first four examples above illustrate the effects of the first four commands under the Layer ⇨ Effects submenu. You can also combine multiple effects on a single layer, as demonstrated by the two images at bottom.

Outer Bevel

Inner Bevel

Emboss

Pillow emboss

Outer bevel + inner glow

Inner bevel + outer glow

Figure 13-23: Layer ➪ Effects ➪ Bevel and Emboss permits you to apply one of four effects, demonstrated in the first four examples above. The last row of images show what happens when you combine beveled edges with glows.

Layer effects are a godsend to beginners, but experienced users might be tempted to dismiss them. After all, you can create every one of these effects manually using layers, selection outlines, and blends modes. But there is much to like about the Layer ➪ Effects commands.

✦ First, they stick to the layer. Move or transform the layer and the effect tags along with it.

✦ Second, the effect is temporary. So long as you save the image in the native Photoshop format, you can edit the shadows, glows, and bevels long into the future.

✦ Third, layer effects are applicable equally to both standard layers and editable text layers. (As explained in Chapter 14, editable text resides on a special kind of layer that prohibits certain kinds of edits.)

✦ Fourth, you can combine multiple effects on a single layer.
Fifth, you can copy an effect from one layer and paste it onto another.
Sixth, you can temporarily disable and enable using simple keyboard tricks.
Seventh — why the heck do you need a seventh advantage? Isn't six enough?

Now that you're chomping at the bit — or as the dolphins say, "bonkin' at the beach ball" — to get your flippers on these effects, the following sections tell you how, why, and what for.

Working inside the Effects dialog box

When you choose one of the first five commands from the Layer ⇨ Effects submenu, Photoshop displays the Effects dialog box, featured in Figure 13-24. This one dialog box provides access to all five effects. Just select the desired effect from the first pop-up menu (labeled in the figure), then select the Apply check box to apply the effect, or deselect the check box to turn it off.

Most of the options in the Effects dialog box are self-explanatory. You select a blend mode from the Mode pop-up menu. You change the opacity by entering a value in the Opacity option box. (Everybody say, "Duh!") Still, not every option is so transparent. Here's how the more unusual features work:

✦ **Switching effects:** To switch between effects from the keyboard, press ⌘-1 for Drop Shadow, ⌘-2 for Inner Shadow, and on up to ⌘-5 for Bevel and Emboss.

✦ **Color swatch:** To change the color of the shadow, glow, or beveled edge, click on the color swatch. (Okay, you could have figured that out, but you're smarter than most.)

✦ **Mode:** The Mode pop-up menu controls the blend mode. That much is obvious. But did you know that you can use the Mode menu to turn an effect upside-down? Select a light color and apply the Screen mode to change a drop shadow into a directional halo. Or use a dark color with Multiply to change an outer glow into a shadow that evenly traces the edge of the layer. Don't be constrained by pedestrian notions of shadows and glows. Layer effects can be anything.

✦ **Angle and Distance:** The Drop Shadow and Inner Shadow panels feature Angle and Distance values that determine the distance between the farthest edge of the effect and the corresponding edge of the layer.

Effects pop-up menu   Color swatch   Drag shadow to move it

Figure 13-24: To position a shadow when the Effects dialog box is up on screen, just drag inside the image window.

Tip

Again, fairly obvious. But what you may not know is that you can avoid these numerical options and simply drag the shadow to the desired location. When the Effects dialog box is visible, move your cursor into the image window and drag away. Photoshop gives you the standard move cursor, as illustrated in Figure 13-24.

✦ **Use Global Angle:** In the real world, the sun casts all shadows in the same direction. Oh, sure, the shadows change minutely from one object to the next, but what with the sun being 90 million miles away and all, the changes are astronomically subtle. I doubt if a single-celled organism, upon admiring its shadow compared with that of its neighbor, could perceive the slightest difference. (The fact that single-celled organisms lack eyes, brains, and other perceptual organs does not in any way lessen the truth of this powerful argument.)

As I was saying, one sun means one lightness and one darkness. By turning on the Use Global Angle check box, you tell Photoshop to cast *all* direction-dependent effects — drop shadows, inner shadows, and the four kinds of bevels — in the same direction. If you change the angle of a drop shadow applied to Layer 1, Photoshop rotates the sun in its heaven and so changes the angle of the pillow emboss applied to Layer 9, thus proving that even a computer program may subscribe to the immutable laws of nature.

Conversely, if you turn the check box off, you tell nature to take a hike. You can change an Angle value in any which way you like and none of the other layers will care.

Tip

If you have established a consistent universe, you can edit the angle of the sun by choosing Layer ⇨ Effects ⇨ Global Angle. Enter a new angle and all shadows and bevels created with Use Global Angle turned on will move in unison. "Sun rise, sun set," as the Yiddish fiddlers say. That doesn't shed any light on the topic, of course, but when in doubt, I like to quote a great musical to class up the joint.

✦ **Blur:** This option works like the Feather command, softening the boundary of the effect.

✦ **Intensity:** By itself, the Intensity option does nothing. But combined with the Blur value, it permits you to spread the effect. Figure 13-25 shows how raising the Intensity value from 0 percent to its maximum setting, 600 percent, gradually grows the shadow outward from its layer. Raising the Blur value creates more pronounced effects.

Intensity = 0

Intensity = 50

Intensity = 150

Intensity = 600

Figure 13-25: Several Intensity values combined with an Opacity value of 50 percent and a Blur of 20 pixels. As you can see, higher Intensity values spread the drop shadow out from the layer.

✦ **Up, Down:** When working in the Bevel and Emboss panel, you'll notice two radio buttons named Up and Down (spotlighted in Figure 13-26). If the Angle value denotes the direction of the sun (or other light source), then Up positions the highlight along the edge near the sun and the shadow along the opposite edge. Down swaps things around, positioning the shadow near the light source. Presumably, this means the layer sinks into its background rather than protrudes out from it. But in practice, the layer typically appears merely as though it's lit differently.

Figure 13-26: The Up and Down options specify whether an embossed layer swells outward from its background or sinks into it.

Modifying and resolving effects

After you apply a layer effect, Photoshop stamps the layer with a small florin symbol (cursive *f*), as shown in Figure 13-27. From that point on, you can edit the effect by double-clicking on the florin. Be sure to double-click inside the florin circle; if you double-click anywhere else on the layer, Photoshop brings up the Layer Options dialog box.

Disabling effects

To temporarily disable all effects applied to a layer, choose Layer ➪ Effects ➪ Hide All Effects. To turn the effects back on, choose the Show All Effects command.

To permanently disable an effect, Option-double-click on the florin symbol in the Layers palette. If many effects are applied to the layer, Option-choose the specific effect you want to turn off from the Layer ➪ Effects submenu.

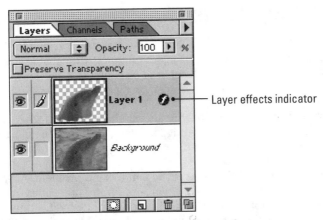

Figure 13-27: The florin symbol indicates that one or more layer effects have been applied to the layer.

Duplicating effects

Once you apply a layer effect to any layer, the effect becomes an element that you can copy and apply to other layers. Select the layer with the effect you want to duplicate and choose Layer ⇨ Effects ⇨ Copy Effects. Then select another layer and choose Layer ⇨ Effects ⇨ Paste Effects. To repeat a copied effect onto multiple layers at a time, link them together (as explained in the upcoming "Linking layers" section) and then choose the Paste Effects to Linked command.

The Copy and Paste Effects commands bypass the Clipboard. This means you can copy an image and then copy an effect without displacing the image.

If you spend a lot of time copying and pasting effects, you'll quickly tire of burrowing your way into the inconvenient Layer ⇨ Effects submenu. The better way to bring up the Effects commands is to Control-click on the florin symbol in the Layers palette.

Scattering effects to the four winds

When you apply an effect, Photoshop is actually doing all the manual layer work for you in the background. This means if Photoshop doesn't seem to be generating the precise effect you want, you can take over and edit the layers to your satisfaction. Choose Layer ⇨ Effects ⇨ Create Layers to resolve the automated effect into a series of layers and clipping groups. Then edit at will.

After choosing Create Layers, you're on your own. From that point on, you lose the ability to edit the effects using the Layer ⇨ Effects commands (unless, of course, you decide to go back in time via the History palette).

Moving and Aligning Layers

You can move an entire layer or the selected portion of a layer by dragging in the image window with the move tool. If you have a selection going, drag inside the marching-ants outline to move only the selection; drag outside the selection to move the entire layer.

As I mentioned in Chapter 11, you can temporarily access the move tool when some other tool is active by pressing the ⌘ key. To nudge a layer, press ⌘ with an arrow key. Press ⌘ and Shift together to nudge in 10-pixel increments.

If part of the layer disappears beyond the edge of the window, no problem. As long as you don't move your cursor outside the image window, Photoshop saves even the hidden pixels in the layer, enabling you to drag it into view later. (This only works when moving all of a layer. If you move a selection beyond the edge of the image window using the move tool, Photoshop clips the selection at the window's edge the moment you deselect it.) If you move your cursor outside the image window, however, Photoshop thinks you are trying to drag-and-drop pixels from one image to another and responds accordingly.

If you ⌘-drag the background image — either when no portion of the image is selected or by dragging outside the selection outline — Photoshop automatically converts the background to a new layer (called Layer 0). The area revealed by the move appears as checkerboard transparency. Photoshop saves the hidden portions of the background image in case you ever decide to move the background back into its original position.

Note

If you regularly work on huge images or your machine is old and kind of slow, Photoshop lets you speed up the display of whole layers on the move. Press the V key to select the move tool, press Return to display the Move Options palette, and select the Pixel Doubling check box. From now on, Photoshop will show you a low-resolution proxy of the layer as you drag it (or ⌘-drag it) across the screen.

Pixel Doubling has no effect when you ⌘-drag selections. It only works when you move entire layers.

Linking layers

Photoshop lets you move multiple layers at a time. To do so, you have to establish a *link* between the layers you want to move and the active layer. Begin by selecting the first layer in the Layers palette you want to link. Then click in the second column to the left of the other layer you want to link. A chain link icon appears in front of each linked layer, as in Figure 13-28. This icon shows the linked layers will move in unison when you ⌘-drag the active layer. To break the link, click on a link icon, which hides it.

Note

Dragging inside a selection outline moves the selection independently of any linked layers. Dragging outside the selection moves all linked layers at once.

Link column

Link icons

Figure 13-28: Click in the second column in the Layers palette to display or hide link icons. Here I've linked all layers except the background, so I can ⌘-drag them in unison.

To link many layers at a time, drag up and down the link column. To unlink the active layer from all others, Option-click on the paintbrush icon in the link column.

In Photoshop 5, you can also link layers via the context-sensitive pop-up menu. As you may recall from the "Switching between layers" section earlier in this chapter, you can bring up a pop-up menu listing the layers in an image by ⌘-Control-clicking on an image element with any tool. Add Shift while selecting a layer from the pop-up menu to link or unlink the layer rather than switch to it. But that's not all. If you're plum crazy for shortcuts, you can change the link state without visiting the pop-up menu by — drum roll please — ⌘-Shift-Option-Control-clicking on an element in the image window. Okay, I love shortcuts, but even *I* have to admit this one is gratuitous!

When you drag-and-drop linked layers into another document, all linked layers move together and the layers retain their original order. If you hold down Shift when dropping, Photoshop centers the layers in the document. If the document is exactly the same size as the one from which you dragged the layers, then Shift-dropping lands the image elements in the same position they held in the original document. And finally, if something is selected in the document, the Shift-dropped layers are centered inside that selection.

Using guides

Photoshop grids and guides allow you to move selections and layers into alignment. Together with the move tool, grids and guides enable you to create rows and columns of image elements, and even align layers by their centers.

To create a guide, press ⌘-R (View ➪ Show Rulers) to display the horizontal and vertical rulers. Then drag a guideline from the ruler. At the top of Figure 13-29, you can see me dragging a horizontal guide down from the top ruler. Then ⌘-drag layers and selections in alignment with the guide. In the bottom portion of the figure, I've dragged the MO disk, film reel, and tape — each on different layers — so they snap into alignment at their centers. (The reel has some film hanging from it, which Photoshop considers in calculating the center.) You'll know when the layer snaps into alignment because the move cursor becomes hollow, like the labeled cursor in Figure 13-29.

Text layers snap to guides a little differently than other kinds of layers. Rather than snapping by the top or bottom edge of the layer, Photoshop snaps a text guide by its baseline. It's just what you need when aligning type.

Guides are pretty straightforward creatures. I mean, you don't have to study them rigorously for years to understand them — a few minutes are all you need to master them. But there are a few hidden treats:

✦ You can show and hide all guides by pressing ⌘-semicolon (;) or by choosing the Hide (or Show) Guides command from the View menu. When the guides are hidden, layers and selections do not snap into alignment.

✦ You can turn on and off guide snappiness while the guides remain visible by pressing ⌘-Shift-semicolon (or choosing View ➪ Snap to Guides).

✦ As with all image elements in Photoshop, you can move a guide with the move tool. If some other tool is active, ⌘-dragging also works.

✦ To lock all guides so you can't accidentally move them while you're trying to ⌘-drag something else, press ⌘-Option-semicolon or choose View ➪ Lock Guides. Press ⌘-Option-semicolon again to unlock all guides.

✦ When moving a guide, press the Shift key to snap the guide to the nearest ruler tick mark.

✦ To convert a horizontal guide to a vertical guide, or vice versa, press the Option key while moving the guide.

Figure 13-29: Drag from one of the rulers to create a guide (top), and then ⌘-drag each layer or selection into alignment (bottom).

✦ If you rotate your document in exact multiples of 90 degrees or flip the image horizontally or vertically, your guides also rotate unless they are locked.

✦ You can position a guide outside the image if you want. To do so, make the image window larger than the image. Now you can drag a guide into the empty canvas surrounding the image. You can then snap a layer or selection into alignment with the guide.

✦ To edit the color of the guides, ⌘-double-click on a guide to display the Guides & Grid panel of the Preferences dialog box. You can also change the guides from solid lines to dashed. (This is for screen purposes, by the way. Guides don't print.)

✦ Like paths, Photoshop saves guides with any file format. If you export the image into another program, the guides are invisible. However, the only formats that support guides on a cross-format basis — so you can use your Photoshop guides on a Mac — are Photoshop, JPEG, TIFF, and EPS.

✦ If you don't need your guides anymore, choose View ➪ Clear Guides to delete them all in one housekeeping operation. (I wish I had a command like this built into my office — I'd choose Maid ➪ Clear Dust and be done with it.)

Automatic alignment and distribution

Photoshop 5 also lets you align and distribute layers by choosing a command from the Layer ➪ Align Linked or Distribute Linked submenu. The commands are pretty straightforward — quite familiar if you've ever used a drawing or page-layout program — but applying them is a little unusual.

Here's how to align two or more layers:

Steps: Aligning Layers

1. **Select the layer that will serve as the anchor.** Whenever you align layers, one layer remains still and the others align to it. The still layer is the one you select.

2. **Link the layers you want to align.** Click in front of the layers you want to align to display the link icon. (And be sure to unlink any layers you *don't* want to align.) You have to link at least two layers — after all, there's no point in aligning a layer to itself.

3. **Choose a command from the Layer ➪ Align Linked submenu.** If you don't like the result, press ⌘-Z and try a different command.

The Distribute Linked commands will space linked layers apart evenly. So it doesn't matter which of the linked layers is selected — the command distributes all linked layers with respect to the two horizontal or vertical extremes. Naturally, it's meaningless to space apart one or two layers, so the Distribute Linked commands require three or more layers to be linked together.

Setting up the grid

Photoshop also offers a grid, which is a regular series of snapping increments. You view the grid — and turn it on — by pressing ⌘-quote (") or choosing View ➪ Show Grid. Turn the snapping forces of the grid on and off by pressing ⌘-Shift-quote or choosing View ➪ Snap to Grid.

You edit the grid in the Guides & Grid panel of the Preferences dialog box (which you can get to by pressing ⌘-K and ⌘-6 or by ⌘-double-clicking on a guide). I explain how to use these options in the "Guides & Grid" section of Chapter 2. But, for the record, you enter the major grid increments in the Gridline Every option box and enter the minor increments in the Subdivisions option box. For example, in Figure 13-30, I set the Gridline Every value to 50 pixels and the Subdivisions value to 5. This means a moved layer will snap in 10-pixel (50 pixels divided by 5) increments. Figure 13-30 also demonstrates each of the three Style settings.

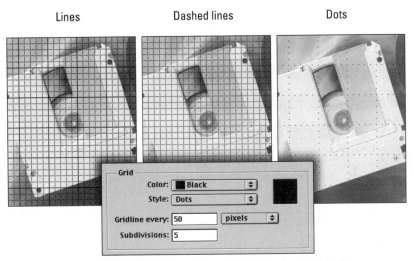

Figure 13-30: Here are the three styles of grid with the Grid Preferences options shown at the bottom.

Using the measure tool

The final method for controlling movements in Photoshop 5 is the measure tool. Press the U key to select the tool. Then drag from one point to another point in the image window. Photoshop itemizes the distance and angle between the two points in the Info palette. The measure tool is even smart enough to automatically display the Info palette if it's hidden.

From that point on, any time you select the measure tool, Photoshop displays the original measurement line. This way, you can measure a distance, edit the image, and press U at any time to refer back to the measurement.

To measure the distance and angle between two other points, you can draw a new line with the measure tool. Or drag the endpoints of the existing measurement line.

Photoshop accommodates only one measurement line per document. But you can break the line in two using what Adobe calls the "protractor" feature. Option-drag on one of the endpoints to draw forth a second segment. The Info palette then measures the angle between the two segments. As demonstrated in Figure 13-31, the D1 item in the Info palette lists the length of the first segment, D2 lists the length of the second segment, and A tells the angle between the segments.

Measure cursor

Protractor data

D2
A
D1

Figure 13-31: Here I measured the angle of the key, and then Option-dragged from the top endpoint to measure the angle between the key and lock.

Tip

The measure tool is great for straightening crooked layers. After drawing a line with the measure tool, choose Edit ⇨ Transform ⇨ Numeric. The Rotate value automatically conforms to the A (angle) value listed in the Info palette. If you look closely, the two values may not exactly match. That's because Photoshop intelligently translates the value to between –45 and +45 degrees, which happens to be the simplest way to express any rotation. If you're unclear what I'm talking about, just trust in Photoshop. It does the math so you don't have to.

Applying Transformations

Photoshop and other graphics programs treat some kinds of edits differently than others. Edits that affect the geometry of a selection or layer are known collectively as *transformations*. These transformations include scaling, rotating, flipping, slanting, and distorting. (Technically, moving is a transformation as well.) Transformations are special because they can affect a selection, a layer, multiple layers, or an entire image at a time.

Transforming the entire image

There are two varieties of transformations in Photoshop. Transformation commands that affect the entire image—including all layers, paths, guides, and so on—are listed in the Image menu. Those that affect layers and selected portions of layers are found in the Edit menu.

The following list explains how to apply transformations to every pixel in an image, regardless of whether the image is selected or not:

✦ **Scale:** To resize the image, use Image ⇨ Image Size. Because this command is one of the most essential low-level functions in the program, I covered it way back in Chapter 4.

✦ **Rotate:** To rotate the entire image, choose a command from the Image ⇨ Rotate Canvas submenu. To rotate an image scanned on its side, choose the 90° CW or 90° CCW command. (That's clockwise and counterclockwise, respectively.) Choose 180° to spin the image on its head. To enter some other specific value, choose Image ⇨ Rotate Canvas ⇨ Arbitrary.

Tip

To fix a slightly crooked scanned image, for example, select the measure tool by pressing the U key. Then drag along the edge of the image and note the A value in the Info palette. When you figure out the proper angle, choose Image ⇨ Rotate Canvas ⇨ Arbitrary and enter it into the Angle option box.

Whenever you apply the Arbitrary command, Photoshop has to expand the canvas size to avoid clipping any of your image. This results in background-colored wedges at each of the four corners of the image. You'll need to either clone with the rubber stamp tool to fill in the wedges or to clip them away with the crop tool.

✦ **Flip:** Choose Image ⇨ Rotate Canvas ⇨ Flip Horizontal to flip the image so left is right and right is left. To flip the image upside-down, choose Image ⇨ Rotate Canvas ⇨ Flip Vertical.

No command is specifically designed to slant or distort the entire image. In the unlikely event you're keen to do this, you'll have to link all layers and apply one of the commands under the Edit ⇨ Transform submenu, as explained in the next section.

Transforming layers and selected pixels

To transform a layer or selection, you can apply one of the commands in the Edit ⇨ Transform submenu. Nearly a dozen commands are here, all of which you can explore on your own. I'm not copping out; it's unlikely you'll use any of these commands on a regular basis. (The notable exception is Numeric, which I discuss in the following section.) These commands aren't bad, but one command—Free Transform—is infinitely better.

With Free Transform, you can scale, flip, rotate, slant, distort, and move a selection or layer in one continuous operation. This one command lets you get all your transformations exactly right before pressing Return to apply the final changes.

To initiate the command, press ⌘-T or choose Edit ➪ Free Transform. Photoshop surrounds the layer or selection with an eight-handle marquee. You are now in the Free Transform mode, which prevents you from doing anything except transform the image until you apply the operation or cancel it.

Here's how to work in the Free Transform mode:

✦ **Scale:** Drag one of the eight square handles to scale the image inside the marquee. To scale proportionally, Shift-drag a corner handle. To scale about the central *transformation origin* (labeled in Figure 13-32), Option-drag a corner handle.

By default, the origin is located in the center of the layer or selection. But you can move it to any place inside the image by dragging it. The origin snaps to the grid and guides, as well as the center or any corner of the layer.

✦ **Flip:** You can flip the image by dragging one handle past its opposite handle. For example, dragging the left side handle past the right handle flips the image horizontally.

If you want to perform a simple flip, it's generally easier to choose Edit ➪ Transform ➪ Flip Horizontal or Flip Vertical. Better yet, Control-click in the image window and choose one of the Flip commands from the pop-up menu. Quite surprisingly, you can choose either command while working in the Free Transform mode.

✦ **Rotate:** To rotate the image, drag outside the marquee, as demonstrated in the first example in Figure 13-32. Shift-drag to rotate in 15-degree increments.

✦ **Distort:** You can distort the image by ⌘-dragging a corner handle. You can tug the image to stretch it in any of four directions.

To tug two opposite corner handles in symmetrical directions, ⌘-Option-drag either of the handles. I show this technique in the second example in Figure 13-32.

✦ **Perspective:** For a one-point perspective effect, ⌘-Shift-drag a corner handle. To move two points in unison, ⌘-Shift-Option-drag a corner handle.

✦ **Move:** Drag inside the marquee to move the image. This is useful when you're trying to align the selection or layer with a background image and you want to make sure the transformations match up properly.

✦ **Undo:** To undo the last modification without leaving the Free Transform mode altogether, press ⌘-Z.

✦ **Zoom:** You can change the view size by choosing one of the commands in the View menu. You can also use the keyboard zoom shortcuts (⌘-spacebar-click, Option-spacebar-click, ⌘-plus, ⌘-minus).

Figure 13-32: After pressing ⌘-T to initiate the Free Transform command, drag outside the marquee to rotate the layer (top). You can also ⌘-Option-drag a corner handle to move the opposite corner handle symmetrically.

✦ **Apply:** Press Return to apply the final transformation and interpolate the new pixels. You can also double-click inside the marquee.

   If the finished effect looks jagged, it's probably because you selected Nearest Neighbor from the Interpolation pop-up menu in the Preferences dialog box. To fix this problem, press ⌘-Z to undo the transformation, and then press ⌘-K and select the Bicubic option from the General panel of the Preferences dialog box. Then press ⌘-Shift-T to reapply the transformation.

   ✦ **Skew:** ⌘-drag a side handle (including the top or bottom handle) to slant the image. To constrain the slant, useful for producing perspective effects, ⌘-Shift-drag a side handle.

   ✦ **Cancel:** To cancel the Free Transform operation, press the Escape key.

To transform a clone of a selected area, press Option when choosing the Free Transform command, or press ⌘-Option-T. This only works with selected areas — you can't clone an entire layer this way any more than you can by Option-dragging with the move tool.

If no part of the image is selected, you can transform multiple layers at a time by linking them, as described in the "Linking layers" section earlier in this chapter. For example, I could have linked the TV and camera layers to transform the two in unison back in Figure 13-32.

To replay the last transformation on any layer or selection, press ⌘-Shift-T. This is a great technique to use if you forgot to link all the layers that you want to transform. You can even transform a path or selection outline to match a transformed layer. It's a handy feature.

Numerical transformations

To track your transformations numerically, display the Info palette (F8) *before* you apply the Free Transform command. After you initiate Free Transform, you can't change the visible palettes until you complete or cancel the operation.

Alternatively, choose Edit ➪ Transform ➪ Numeric. You can apply this command while working in the Free Transform mode, or apply the entire transformation numerically by choosing the Numeric command at the outset. In any case, you get the dialog box shown in Figure 13-33. If you're in the middle of a Free Transform operation, the dialog box reflects the changes you've made so far (minus the distortions). Otherwise, Photoshop displays the last settings applied.

For the most part, this dialog box is pretty straightforward. Use the check boxes to decide which kinds of transformations you want to apply. The Relative check box controls whether a move is measured relative to the previous position of the element or with respect to the absolute 0,0 coordinate (generally in the upper-left corner of the image).

I imagine most folks will use this dialog box strictly for scaling and rotating. You'd need the spatial awareness of a NASA navigation system to predict a numerical slant.

Figure 13-33: Press ⌘-Shift-T to transform a selection or layer numerically.

Masking and Layers

Layers offer special masking options unto themselves. You can paint inside the confines of a layer as if it were a selection mask; you can add a special mask for a single layer; or you can group multiple layers together and have the bottom layer in the group serve as the mask. Quite honestly, these are the kinds of thoughtful and useful functions I've come to expect from Photoshop. Although they're fairly complicated to use — you must be on your toes once you start juggling layer masks — these functions provide new realms of opportunities.

Preserving transparency

You may have already noticed a little check box called Preserve Transparency near the top of the Layers palette. If not, the option appears spotlighted in Figure 13-34. When checked, it prevents you from painting inside the transparent portions of the layer.

Suppose I want to paint inside the girl shown in Figure 13-34. If this were a flat, nonlayered image, I'd have to draw a selection outline carefully around her hair and arms, as I did back in Chapter 12. But there's no need to do this when using layers. Because the girl lies on a different layer than her background, a permanent selection outline tells Photoshop which pixels are transparent and which are opaque. This is the transparency mask.

Figure 13-34: The Preserve Transparency check box (upper right) enables you to paint inside the layer's transparency mask without harming the transparent pixels.

The first example in Figure 13-35 shows the girl on her own with the background hidden. The transparent areas outside the mask appear in the checkerboard pattern. When the Preserve Transparency option is turned off, you can paint anywhere you want inside the layer. Selecting Preserve Transparency activates the transparency mask and places the checkerboard area off limits.

The right image in Figure 13-35 shows what happens after I select Preserve Transparency and paint around the girl with the airbrush. (The foreground color is set to white.) Notice, no matter how much paint I may apply, none of it leaks out onto the background.

Although this enlightening discussion pretty well covers it, I feel compelled to share a few additional words about Preserve Transparency:

Tip

✦ You can turn Preserve Transparency on and off from the keyboard by pressing the standard slash character, /, right there on the same key with the question mark.

Figure 13-35: The layered girl as she appears on her own (left) and when airbrushed with the Preserve Transparency check box turned on (right).

✦ Remember, you can fill only the opaque pixels in a layer, whether Preserve Transparency is on or off. Use ⌘-Shift-Delete to fill with the background color, and Shift-Option-Delete to fill with the foreground color.

✦ The Preserve Transparency check box is dimmed when the background layer is active because this layer is entirely opaque. There's no transparency to preserve, eh? (That's my impression of a Canadian explaining layer theory. It needs a little work, but I think I'm getting close.)

And finally, here's a question for all you folks who think you may have Photoshop mastered. Which of the brush modes (explained in Chapter 8) is the exact opposite of Preserve Transparency? The answer is Behind. If you turn off Preserve Transparency and select the Behind brush mode in, say, the Paintbrush Options palette, you paint exclusively outside the transparency mask, thus protecting the opaque pixels. So it follows, when Preserve Transparency is turned on, the Behind brush mode is dimmed.

The moral? Behind is not a true brush mode and should not be grouped with the brush modes. The better solution would be a Preserve Opacity check box. Alas, Adobe's engineers have so far ignored my advice, but after they were so kind as to implement a dozen or so suggestions from the previous edition, I remain optimistic for the future.

Creating layer-specific masks

In addition to the transparency mask that accompanies every layer (except the background), you can add a mask to a layer to make certain pixels in the layer transparent. Now, you might ask, "Won't simply erasing portions of a layer make those portions transparent?" (I just love these little chats we have.) The answer is yes, but when you erase, you delete pixels permanently. By creating a layer mask, you instead make pixels temporarily transparent. You can return several months later and bring those pixels back to life again simply by adjusting the mask. So layer masks add yet another level of flexibility to a program that's already a veritable image-editing contortionist.

To create a layer mask, select the layer you want to mask and choose Layer ⇨ Add Layer Mask ⇨ Reveal All. Or more simply, click on the layer mask icon at the bottom of the Layers palette, as labeled in Figure 13-36. A second thumbnail preview appears to the left of the layer name, also labeled in the figure. A heavy outline around the preview shows the layer mask is active.

Tip

If the heavy outline is hard to see, keep your eye on the icon directly to the left of the layer name. If the icon is a paintbrush, the layer and not the mask is active. If the icon is a little dotted circle, the mask is active.

To edit the mask, simply paint in the image window. Paint with black to make pixels transparent. Because black represents deselected pixels in an image, it makes these pixels transparent in a layer. Paint with white to make pixels opaque.

Thankfully, Photoshop is smart enough to make the default foreground color in a layer mask white and the default background color black. This ensures painting with the paintbrush or airbrush makes pixels opaque, where painting with the eraser makes them transparent, just as you would expect.

In Figure 13-36, I created a feathered oval, inversed it, and filled it with black by pressing ⌘-Delete. This results in a soft vignette around the layer. If I decide I eliminated too much of the hair, not to worry. I merely paint with white to bring it back again.

Photoshop goes nuts in the layer mask department, adding lots of bells and whistles to make the function both convenient and powerful. Here's everything you need to know:

✦ **Reveal Selection:** If you select some portion of your layer, Photoshop automatically converts the selection to a layer mask when you click on the layer mask icon at the bottom of the palette. The area outside the selection becomes transparent. (The corresponding command is Layer ➪ Add Layer Mask ➪ Reveal Selection.)

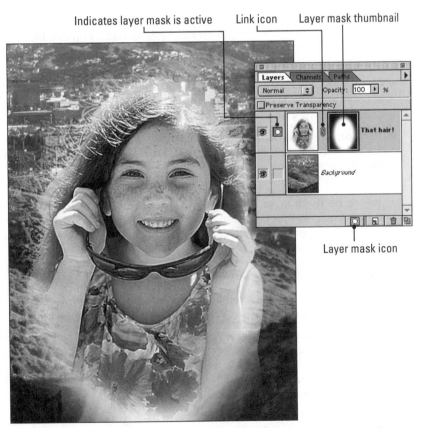

Figure 13-36: The black area in the layer mask (which you can see in the thumbnail view, top right) translates to transparent pixels in the layer itself.

✦ **Hide Selection:** You can also choose to reverse the prospective mask, making the area inside the selection transparent and the area outside opaque. To do this, choose Layer ➪ Add Layer Mask ➪ Hide Selection. Or, better yet, Option-click on the layer mask icon in the Layers palette.

✦ **Hide everything:** To begin with a black mask that hides everything, choose Layer ➪ Add Layer Mask ➪ Hide All. Or press ⌘-D to deselect everything and Option-click on the layer mask icon.

✦ **View the mask:** Photoshop regards a layer mask as a layer-specific channel. You can actually see it listed in italics in the Channels palette. To view the mask on its own — as a black-and-white image — Option-click on the layer mask thumbnail in the Layers palette. Option-click again to view the image instead.

✦ **Layer mask rubylith:** To view the mask as a red overlay, Shift-Option-click on the layer mask icon. Or simply press the backslash key, \, above Return.

After you have both layer and mask visible at once, you can hide the mask by pressing \, or hide the layer and view only the mask by pressing the tilde key (~). So many alternatives!

✦ **Change the overlay color:** Double-click on the layer mask thumbnail to access the Layer Mask Display Options dialog box, which enables you to change the color and opacity of the rubylith.

✦ **Turn off the mask:** You can temporarily disable the mask by Shift-clicking on the mask thumbnail. A red *X* covers the thumbnail when it's disabled, and all masked pixels in the layer appear opaque. Shift-click again to put the mask in working order again.

✦ **Switch between layer and mask:** As you become more familiar with layer masks, you'll switch back and forth between layer and mask quite frequently, editing the layer one minute, editing the mask the next. You can switch between layer and mask by clicking on their respective thumbnails. As I mentioned before, look to the icon to the left of the layer name to see whether the layer or the mask is active.

You can also switch between layer and mask from the keyboard. Press ⌘-tilde (~) to make the layer active. Press ⌘-\ to switch to the mask.

✦ **Link layer and mask:** A little link icon appears between the layer and mask thumbnails in the Layers palette. When the link icon is visible, you can move or transform the mask and layer as one. If you click on the link icon to turn it off, layer and mask move independently. (You can always move a selected region of the mask or layer independently of the other.)

✦ **Convert mask to selection:** As with all masks, you can convert a layer mask to a selection. To do so, ⌘-click on the layer mask icon. Throw in the Shift and Option keys if you want to add or subtract the layer mask with an existing selection outline.

When and if you finish using the mask—you can leave it in force as long as you like—you can choose Layer ⇨ Remove Layer Mask. Or just drag the layer mask thumbnail to the trash can icon. Either way, an alert box asks you if you want to discard the mask or permanently apply it to the layer. Click on the button that corresponds to your innermost desires.

Pasting inside a selection outline

One command, Edit ⇨ Paste Into (⌘-Shift-V), creates a layer mask automatically. Choose Paste Into command to paste the contents of the Clipboard into the current selection, so the selection acts as a mask. Because Photoshop pastes to a new layer, it converts the selection into a layer mask. But here's the interesting part: By default, Photoshop turns off the link between layer and mask. This way, you can ⌘-drag the layer inside a fixed mask to position the pasted image.

Once upon a time in Photoshop, a command existed named Edit ⇨ Paste Behind. (Or something like that. It might have been Paste in Back. My memory's a little hazy.) The command (whatever its name) pasted a copied image in back of a selection. But while the command is gone, its spirit still lives. Now you press the Option key when choosing Edit ⇨ Paste Into. Or just press ⌘-Shift-Option-V. Photoshop creates a new layer with an inverted layer mask, masking away the selected area.

Masking groups of layers

About now, you may be growing fatigued with the topic of layering masking. But one more option requires your immediate attention. You can group multiple layers into something called a *clipping group,* in which the lowest layer in the group masks the others. Where the lowest layer is transparent, the other layers are hidden; where the lowest layer is opaque, the contents of the other layers are visible.

Despite the similarities in name, a clipping group bears no relation to a clipping path. That is, a clipping group doesn't allow you to prepare transparent areas for import into QuarkXPress and the like.

There are two ways to create a clipping group:

✦ Option-click on the horizontal line between any two layers to group them into a single unit. Your cursor changes to the group cursor labeled in Figure 13-37 when you press Option; the horizontal line becomes dotted after you click. To break the layers apart again, Option-click on the dotted line to make it solid.

✦ Select the higher of the two layers you want to combine into a clipping group. Then choose Layer ⇨ Group with Previous, or press ⌘-G. To make the layers independent again, choose Layer ⇨ Ungroup (⌘-Shift-G).

Figures 13-37 and 13-38 demonstrate two steps in a piece of artwork I created for *Macworld* magazine. I had already created some text on an independent layer using the type tool (the subject of the next chapter), and I wanted to fill the text with water. So I added some photographs I shot of a swimming pool to a layer above the text, as shown in Figure 13-37. Then I combined text and pool images into a clipping group. Because the text was beneath the water, Photoshop masked the pool images according to the transparency mask assigned to the text. The result is a water pattern that exactly fills the type, as in Figure 13-38. (For a full-color version of these figures, see Color Plate 13-3.)

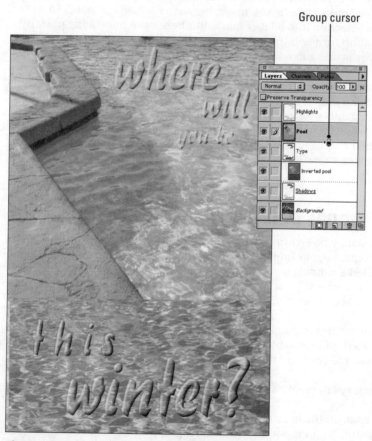

Figure 13-37: Option-click on the horizontal line between two layers to group them together.

Figure 13-38: After combining pool water and type layers into a single clipping group, Photoshop applies the type layer's transparency mask to the pool layer.

Note

If you're familiar with Illustrator, you may recognize this clipping group metaphor as a relative to Illustrator's clipping path. One object in the illustration acts as a mask for a collection of additional objects. In Illustrator, however, the topmost object in the group is the mask, not the bottom one. So much for consistency.

✦   ✦   ✦

Amazing Text Stuff

The State of Type in Photoshop 5

Photoshop 5.0

Photoshop 5 has given us something you don't see very often — editable bitmapped type. Long after you create a line or two of text, you have the option of changing the words, typeface, size, leading, kerning, and so on, just as you can in other graphics and electronic publishing programs. You can also mix and match formatting attributes inside a single text block, something you couldn't do in Version 4 and earlier. In only one upgrade cycle, Photoshop has made a quantum leap from grim Stone Age letter wrangling to something that might actually pass for contemporary typesetting.

Now, the astute reader might discern that my tone — while generally enthusiastic — falls short of effusive. Although undeniably improved, Photoshop's type capabilities suffer two enduring flaws. First, you still have to work inside a dialog box. This means that you can't edit and format type directly in the image window. And second, as with all things in Photoshop, type is made of pixels. Each character invariably conforms to the exact same resolution as the rest of the image. So if you want to add super-smooth object-oriented type, you'll have to import the image into a program like Illustrator or QuarkXPress, just as you have in the past.

But don't let these shortcomings make you bitter and resentful. You can rest assured that Photoshop 5's brave new type tool runs circles around the old one. Even if it only does 75 percent of what you'd like it to do, that's a tremendous improvement.

The limitation of bitmapped type

When you come right down to it, type is just another kind of graphic. A typeface is nothing more than a library of clip art that you can access from the keyboard. So it's little surprise that Photoshop treats type like any other collection of pixels.

The legibility of your type is therefore dependent upon the size and resolution of your image.

For example, Figure 14-1 shows four lines of type printed at equal sizes but different resolutions. (If these lines were printed at the same resolution, each line would be twice as large as the line that precedes it.) As you can see, the low-resolution type at top is jagged, and high-resolution type at bottom is smooth. Hence, big type printed at a high resolution yields smooth, legible output, just as a big image printed at a high resolution yields smooth, detailed output. In fact, everything that you can say about an image is true of bitmapped type.

Figure 14-1: Four lines of type set in the PostScript font Tekton. Each line is printed at twice the resolution of the line that precedes it, starting at 37.5 ppi (top) and working up to 300 ppi (bottom).

The disadvantage of working with pixel-based type is painfully obvious. Rather than matching the resolution of your printer — a function provided by virtually every program from word processors on up — Photoshop prints type at the same resolution it prints the rest of the image. A pixel is a pixel.

The benefits of bitmapped type

What Photoshop gives you in exchange is a whole lot of flexibility. Simply put, you can do all kinds of things with pixel-based type that you could never hope to accomplish in Illustrator, FreeHand, or a host of other programs. Here are a few examples:

✦ **Create translucent type:** Because Photoshop automatically creates type on a new layer, you can change the translucency of type as easily as adjusting the Opacity value in the Layers palette. Using this simple technique, you can merge type and images to create subtle overlay effects, as illustrated in Figure 14-2.

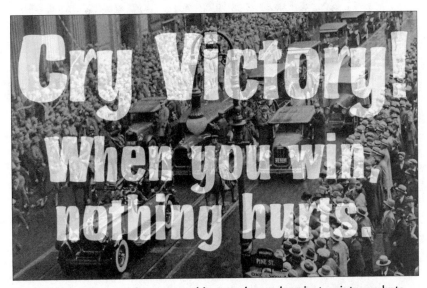

Figure 14-2: After creating some white type layered against a vintage photo, I lowered the opacity setting to 70 percent. Though child's play in Photoshop, this effect is virtually impossible in most drawing programs.

✦ **Use type as a selection:** Photoshop provides two type tools that create letter-shaped selection outlines. This means you can use type to select a portion of an image and then move, copy, or transform it. To create Figure 14-3, for example, I used my text to select the vintage photo. Then I dragged it into a different stock photo background and applied the Multiply blend mode from the Layers palette. Naturally, you'd be hard-pressed to tell that there's a parade inside those letters, but it serves as an interesting texture.

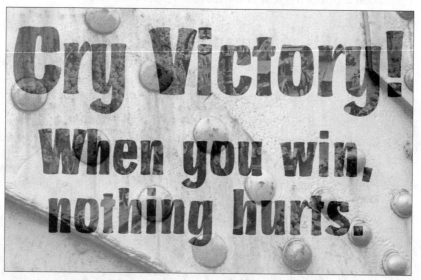

Figure 14-3: Photoshop is virtually unique in permitting you to select an image using type. Here I selected the image from Figure 14-2 and dragged the selection into a different background.

✦ **Apply layer effects:** Photoshop 5's new layer effects are fully applicable to type. In Figure 14-4, I replaced the industrial background from Figure 14-3 with a background texture created with the Clouds and Emboss filters (see Chapter 10). Then I applied a pillow emboss effect to the text layer using Layer ➪ Effects ➪ Bevel and Emboss.

✦ **Edit type as part of the image:** Once converted to a standard layer using the Render Layer command, you can paint type, erase it, smear it, fill it with a gradation, apply a filter or two, or do anything else that you can do to pixels. In Figure 14-5, I embossed the type, flattened it against its background, applied a few effects filters, and made it sway with the Wave filter. Don't even think about trying to accomplish this without pixels.

✦ **Trade images freely:** If you've ever shared a document created in a word processor, you know what a nightmare fonts can be. If your associate's machine isn't equipped with the fonts you used, then your document comes up all wrong. When you work with images, your font worries are over. The other guy doesn't need special screen or printer fonts to view your image exactly as you created it. He won't be able to edit the image using your font, but that's to be expected.

Figure 14-4: I used the Bevel and Emboss command to apply a pillow emboss effect. Again, an effect that takes a minute or two in Photoshop would be absolutely impossible in an object-oriented program.

Figure 14-5: This images is the result of going nuts for 15 minutes or so using the commands under the Filter menu. Emboss, Radial Blur, Colored Pencil, Craquelure, and Wave are all represented.

Using the Type Tool

In a drawing or desktop publishing program, the type tool typically serves two purposes: you can create text with the tool or you can edit existing text by highlighting characters and either replacing them or applying formatting commands. In Photoshop, the primary purpose of the type tool is to create text. As a convenience, you can click on an existing text layer to edit it, but this is just a sideline. First and foremost, the type tool creates.

To create a new layer of text, select the type tool—the one that looks like a solid T—and click in the image window. (Not coincidentally, you can select the type tool from the keyboard by pressing the T key.) Instead of producing a blinking insertion marker in the window, as in other graphics programs, Photoshop displays the Type Tool dialog box shown in Figure 14-6.

The lower portion of the Type Tool dialog box is taken up by the text-entry area. This is where you enter and edit the text that you want to add to your image. As you enter the text, Photoshop gives you two simultaneous previews. You can monitor the type in black-and-white in the text-entry area and in color in the background image window. You can also zoom either preview to get a better look. To zoom the preview inside the text-entry area, use the zoom controls in the bottom left corner of the dialog box. Zoom outside the dialog box by ⌘-spacebar-clicking and Option-spacebar-clicking, or by pressing ⌘-plus and ⌘-minus.

Photoshop
5.0

But the image window isn't just for previewing. If you don't like the placement of the type inside the image, you can move the text simply by dragging it, as demonstrated in Figure 14-6. So while Photoshop 5 technically doesn't let you edit text directly in the image window, it comes awfully darn close. What we have here is a special blend of the best and worst worlds, which I like to call Direct Text Editing with a Big Fat Dialog Box in Your Way.

As you enter text, it's bound to reach the right edge of the text-entry area. But instead of knocking the text to a new line, as in the old days, Photoshop scrolls your view in the dialog box. If you want to see the entire line from start to finish, drag the resize box in the lower right corner to scale the dialog box. Photoshop 5 has made significant strides in making the Type Tool dialog box present an accurate picture of your text.

Photoshop has no concept of column width, so it never breaks a line of text automatically, no matter how long it gets. You have to add a manual break by pressing the Return key. It's like using a typewriter, but without the little bell. (Dang, I miss that bell.)

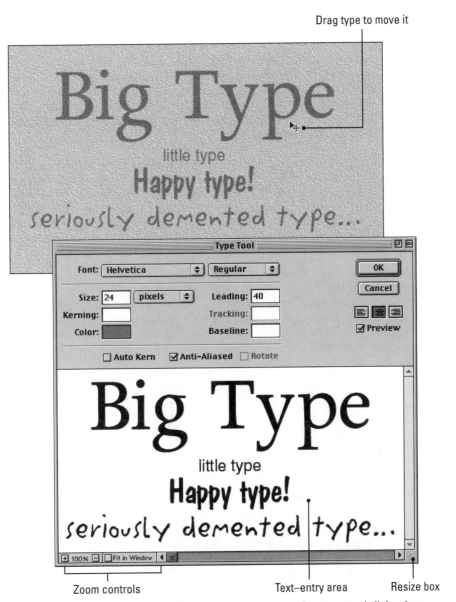

Figure 14-6: To create type in Photoshop, enter it into the Type Tool dialog box, which appears after you click with the type tool. You can now drag in the background window to move type, as shown at top.

Accepting and editing

Tip

To accept the text and return to the image window, press the Enter key on the keypad. If one of the option boxes is active — Size, Leading, Kerning, Tracking, or Baseline — you can alternatively press Return. But it's a good idea to get in the habit of pressing Enter, because otherwise you run the risk of inserting a line break in the text-entry area. Train yourself and avoid irritation; that's my motto. (My other motto is "Click softly and carry a big Nerf gun." But in this particular case, that advice seems counterproductive.)

Upon pressing Enter (or clicking on the OK button if you're a conventionalist), Photoshop creates your text as a new layer. But not just any layer — a special type layer. As you can see in Figure 14-7, Photoshop even adds a little T to the right of the layer name to show what a special layer it is. This T indicates two things:

✦ First, the text is fully editable. You can revisit it time and time again and make any changes you like.

✦ Second, many pixel-level edits are prohibited. You can change the color of the type, modify the blend mode or Opacity value, press ⌘-T to transform it, and apply as many layer effects as you like. But before you can paint on the text or apply filters, you have to convert the type to a standard layer by choosing Layer ➪ Type ➪ Render Layer. The trade-off is that after that point, the type is no longer editable.

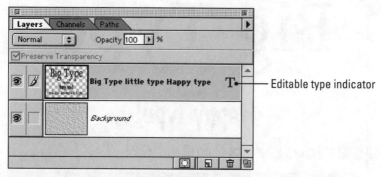

Figure 14-7: When you see the telltale T next to a layer, you know it's editable type.

To give you an idea, the text back in Figures 14-2 and 14-4 was 100 percent editable. (Figure 14-3 shows the effect of creating selection outlines in the shapes of letters, which is never editable.) But before going off the deep end into Figure 14-5, I had to choose the Render Layer command and forsake future editing. There is a perfectly good reason for this — pixel-level edits fundamentally change the composition of the text so it has nothing to do with its original character forms. But if that doesn't do it for you, then just remember, such is the way of Photoshop.

To revisit the Type Tool dialog box and edit a text block, you have two options:

✦ Double-click on the layer name or the T icon in the Layers palette. (Don't double-click on the thumbnail preview — that brings up the Layer Options dialog box.)

✦ When the text layer is active, use the type tool to click on a letter inside the image window. The cursor appears as a plain I-beam (no dotted outline) to show that Photoshop is ready to edit the type.

Tip

If you want to create a new text block when an editable type layer is active, Shift-click with the type tool. When a standard layer is active, just click with the type tool. Either way, the Type Tool dialog box brings up the last text you created.

By now, you may have noticed that Photoshop 5 automatically names text layers after the first 31 characters. This is a handy feature, but you can change the layer name to anything you like without affecting the editability of the text. Double-click on the thumbnail preview for the layer in the Layers palette to bring up the Layer Options dialog box, then enter a name more to your liking.

Selecting type

Prior to Version 5, Photoshop formatted all type entered into the text-entry area identically according to a global set of specifications. The fact that Photoshop 5 lets you mix and match formatting attributes is at once helpful and confusing. The benefits are obvious — now you have more control and flexibility. But if you're used to entering a bit of text, applying some formatting settings, and hitting Enter, then prepare for some extra steps.

Before you can modify so much as a word of type, you have to select it. Fortunately, selecting has improved a bit in Photoshop 5. You can still drag over characters to highlight them, but you also have access to a wider range of keyboard tricks, as outlined in Table 14-1.

Table 14-1
Selecting Text from the Keyboard

Text Selection	Keystrokes
Select character to left or right	Shift-left or right arrow
Select whole word	Double-click on word
Move left or right one word	⌘-left or right arrow
Select word to left or right	⌘-Shift-left or right arrow
Select one line up or down	Shift-up or down arrow
Select range of characters	Click at one point, Shift-click at another
Select all text	⌘-A

After selecting type, you can replace it by entering new text from the keyboard. You can likewise cut, copy, or paste text by pressing the standard keyboard shortcuts (⌘-X, C, and V) or by choosing commands from the Edit menu. You can undo a text modification by pressing ⌘-Z or choosing Edit ➪ Undo. And if things go terribly wrong, press the Option key to change the Cancel button to Reset. Option-click on this button to reset the type to its appearance when you first opened the dialog box.

Formatting type

Now that you know the basics of creating, selecting, and mucking about with type, it's time to cover the specific formatting attributes that do so much to make your type readable and alluring. The following sections explain the formatting options in the order they appear at the top of the Type Tool dialog box.

Font

Select the typeface and type style you want to use from the side-by-side Font pop-up menus. Rather than offering lowest-common-denominator Bold and Italic check boxes (as was the case for Photoshop 4), Version 5 is smart enough to present a full list of designer-style options. For example, though Times is limited to Bold and Italic, the Helvetica family may yield such stylistic variations as Oblique, Light, Black, Condensed, Inserat, and Ultra Compressed.

The old Underline, Outline, and Shadow check boxes are gone, and I say good riddance. Few folks want or need underlined type in Photoshop — if you do, you can easily draw one. And the outline and shadow styles were truly awful. The colloquial contraction "b'ugly" comes to mind, and b'ugly is something we can all do without.

Size

Type size is measured either in points or pixels. You can select the desired measurement from the pop-up menu to the right of the Size option box. If the resolution of your image is 72 ppi, points and pixels are equal. (There are 72 points in an inch, so 72 ppi means one pixel per point.) If the resolution is higher, however, a single point may include many pixels. The moral is to select the points option when you want to scale text according to the image resolution; select pixels when you want to map text to an exact number of pixels in an image.

Type is measured from the top of its *ascenders*—letters like *b, d,* and *h* that rise above the level of most lowercase characters—to the bottom of its *descenders*— letters like *g, p,* and *q* that sink below the baseline. That's the way it's supposed to work, anyway. But throughout history, designers have played pretty loose and free with type size. To illustrate, Figure 14-8 shows the two standards Times and Helvetica along with a typical display font and a typical script. Each line is set to a type size of 180 pixels and then placed inside a 180-pixel box. The dotted horizontal lines indicate the baselines. As you can see, the only font that comes close to measuring the full 180 pixels is Tekton. The Brush Script sample is relatively minuscule (and Brush Script is husky compared with most scripts). So if you're looking to fill a specific space, be prepared to experiment. The only thing you can be sure of is that the type *won't* measure the precise dimensions you enter into the Size option box.

Figure 14-8: Four samples of 180-pixel type set inside 180-pixel boxes. As you can see, type size is an art, not a science.

In Photoshop 5, you can change every numerical formatting attribute from the keyboard. To increase the type size in 2-point (or pixel) increments, press ⌘-Shift-greater than (>). To similarly decrease the size, press ⌘-Shift-less than (<). Add the Option key to raise or lower the type size in 10-point (or pixel) increments.

Leading

Also called line spacing, *leading* is the vertical distance between the baseline of one line of type and the baseline of the next line of type, as illustrated in Figure 14-9. Leading is measured in the unit you selected from the Size pop-up menu. If you leave the Leading value blank, Photoshop automatically applies a leading equal to 125 percent of the type size.

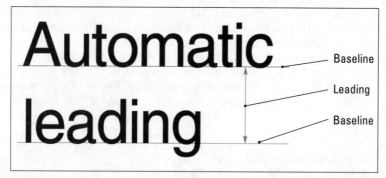

Figure 14-9: Leading is the distance between any two baselines in a single paragraph of text. Here, the type size is 120 pixels and the leading is 150 pixels.

The easiest way to change the distance between one line and another is like so: First, when adjusting the space between a pair of lines, select the bottom of the two. Then press Option-up arrow to decrease the leading in 2-point (or pixel) increments and move the lines closer together. Press Option-down arrow to increase the leading and spread the lines apart. To work in 10-point (or pixel) increments, press ⌘-Option-up or down arrow.

Kerning and Auto Kern

Technically, *kern* is the predetermined amount of space that surrounds each character of type and separates it from its immediate neighbors. (Some type-heads also call it *side bearing*.) But as is so frequently the case with our molten magma of a language, kern has found new popularity in recent years as a verb. So if a friend says, "Let's kern!" don't reach for your rowing oars. Get psyched to adjust the amount of room between characters of type. (Yes, there are people who love to kern and, yes, it is sad.)

The first line of defense in the battle against ugly character spacing is the Auto Kern check box. When turned off, Photoshop applies the default amount of side bearing to each character, as prescribed by the specifications included in the individual font files on your hard drive. But some character combinations don't look right when subjected to the default bearing. The spacing that separates a *T* and an *h* doesn't look so good when you scrap the *h* and insert an *r*. Therefore, the character combination *T* and *r* is a special-needs pair, a typographic marriage that requires kern counseling.

When you turn on the Auto Kern check box, Photoshop digs farther into the font specifications and pulls out a list of special-needs letter pairs. Then it applies a prescribed amount of spacing compensation, as illustrated by the second line in Figure 14-10.

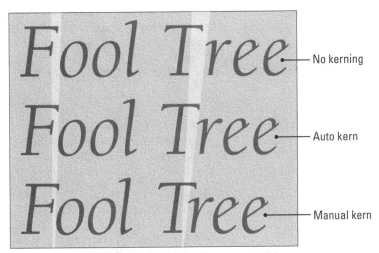

— No kerning

— Auto kern

— Manual kern

Figure 14-10: Three examples of the kerning options in Photoshop 5. I've added wedges to track the ever-decreasing space between the difficult pairs *Fo* and *Tr*.

Photoshop 5.0

In most cases, you'll want to leave Auto Kern turned on and trust in the designers' pair-kerning expertise. But there may be times when the prescribed kerning isn't to your liking. In this case, Photoshop 5 lets you kern manually. Inside the Type Tool dialog box, click between two badly spaced characters of type. Then turn off the Auto Kern check box to enable the Kerning option box. Enter a negative value to shift the letters closer together. Enter a positive value to kern them farther apart. The last line in Figure 14-10 shows examples of my tighter manual kerns.

To decrease the Kerning value (and thereby tighten the spacing) in increments of 20, press Option-left arrow. To increase the Kerning value by 20, press Option-right arrow. You can also modify the kerning in increments of 100 by pressing ⌘-Option-left or right arrow.

Incidentally, the Kerning and Tracking values are measured in ⅟₁₀₀₀ em, where an *em* (or *em space*) is the width of the letter *m* in the current font at the current size. This may sound weird, but it's actually very helpful. Working in ems ensures that your character spacing automatically updates to accommodate changes in font and type size.

Tracking

The Tracking value is virtually identical to Kerning. It affects character spacing, as measured in em spaces. It even reacts to the same keyboard shortcuts. The only differences are that you can apply Tracking to multiple characters at a time. And Photoshop permits you to apply a Tracking value on top of either automatic or manual kerning. (For folks experienced with Photoshop 4 and earlier, Tracking is more or less the equivalent of the old Spacing option, but measured in ems.)

Color

Click on the Color swatch to display the Color Picker dialog box. This is the one attribute that Photoshop applies to all text in the dialog box, whether selected or not. Personally, I find it more convenient to apply color outside the Type Tool dialog box by selecting a color from the Color palette and pressing Option-Delete. The effect is the same.

Baseline

The Baseline value raises or lowers the selected text with respect to the baseline, as measured in pixels or points depending on the Size pop-up menu setting. In type parlance, this is called *baseline shift*. Raising type results in a superscript. Lowering type results in a subscript. An example of each appears in Figure 14-11.

You can also raise type to create a built fraction. To access the special fraction slash, press Shift-Option-1. Then select the number before the slash (the *numerator*) and enter a positive value into the Baseline option box. Reduce the size of the value after the slash (the *denominator*) but leave the Baseline blank. That's all I did to get the fraction at the bottom of Figure 14-11.

Press Shift-Option-up arrow to raise the Baseline value by 2 or Shift-Option-down arrow to lower the value by 2. To change the value in increments of 10, add in the ⌘ key.

+60

-30

+40

Figure 14-11: Baseline shift frequently finds its way into the worlds of math and science. The labels show the Baseline values.

Alignment

The three nameless icons below the Cancel button control how lines of type align with one another. By default, the alignment is measured from the point at which you originally clicked with the type tool. But as I mentioned earlier, you can move this alignment point by dragging in the image window even when the Type Tool dialog box is open. Photoshop lets you align text left, center, or right. Because it has no concept of column width, there is no justification setting.

Old timers will notice the loss of vertical alignment options. To create vertical text, exit the Type Tool dialog box and choose Layer ⇨ Type ⇨ Vertical. Or create the type from the outset with the vertical type tool, as I explain later in this chapter.

You can change the alignment using standard keyboard tricks. Press ⌘-Shift-L to align selected lines to the left. ⌘-Shift-C centers text, and ⌘-Shift-R aligns it to the right.

Anti-Aliased

When you select the Anti-Aliased check box, Photoshop softens characters by slightly blurring pixels around the perimeter. Unless you want to create very small type or you intend to match the resolution of your output device — printing a 300 ppi image to a 300 dpi printer, for example — you should turn this option on. Unless otherwise indicated, I created all figures in this chapter with the Anti-Aliased check box selected. In fact, the only exception I can think of is the second example in Figure 14-12.

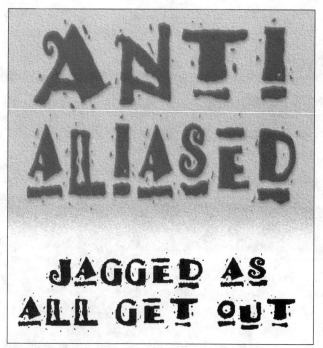

Figure 14-12: I created the top example with the Anti-Aliased check box turn on and the bottom with the option turned off. Unless you're looking for a harsh, exacting effect, leave Anti-Aliased on.

Creating vertical type

For westerners, Photoshop 5 offers a new vertical type tool for aligning type from top to bottom instead of left to right. To get to this tool, press Shift-T twice when the type tool is active. In truth, the vertical type tool is nothing more than the standard type tool lifted from the Japanese version of Photoshop. As shown in the first example of Figure 14-13, it creates vertical columns of type that read right to left, as in Japan. If you want to make columns of type that read left to right, you'll have to create each column as an independent text block.

When editing vertical type, the Type Tool dialog box presents you with a Rotate check box. Select this check box to rotate each character 90 degrees and achieve the effect illustrated in the second example of Figure 14-13.

You can convert vertical text to horizontal by choosing Layer ⇨ Type ⇨ Horizontal. To go the other way, choose Layer ⇨ Type ⇨ Vertical.

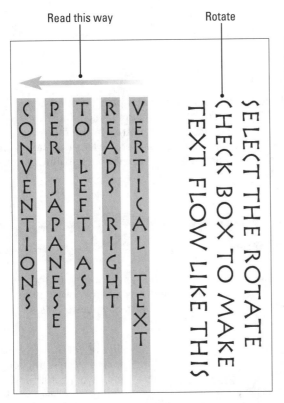

Figure 14-13: By default, vertical type reads right to left, as shown in the first example. If you select the Rotate check box in the Type Tool dialog box, Photoshop creates the effect on right.

Character Masks and Layer Effects

Photoshop offers two more type tools. Known as the type mask tools (regular and vertical), they create character-shaped selection outlines. You can switch to the type mask tool by pressing Shift-T when the standard type tool is active. Or select the T with the dotted outline in the pop-up in the toolbox. If you want to select the vertical type mask tool (unlikely, but you never know), press Shift-T twice more.

Generally speaking, the type mask tool works like any other type tool, the one exception being that you can't edit the type in the same way as in a self-contained type layer. If you misspell a word or you change your mind about the type size, press ⌘-D to deselect the image and click again with the type mask tool to bring up your last settings.

The type mask tools are ultimately selection tools, so they work a lot like the magic wand, lasso, and others:

- ✦ Click with a type mask tool to create a new selection outline.
- ✦ Shift-click to add the character outlines to an existing selection.

✦ Option-click to subtract from a selection.

✦ And Shift-Option-click to find the intersection.

Type masks on the march

The most obvious use for the type mask tool is to select a portion of an image. In a matter of seconds, you get type filled with photographic imagery. While nifty in theory, finding a use for photographic type is another matter. In the following steps, I use the type mask tool to select a portion of an image, send it to a new layer, and then modify brightness values to distinguish the text from its background. Though very easy, it yields some interesting results.

Steps: Selecting Part of an Image Using Character Outlines

1. **Assemble the image you want to mask.** In my case, I start with the classic eel erupting from a clock pictured in Figure 14-14. I know, you're thinking, "Deke, how do you come up with such attractive stuff?" It's a knack, I guess. Try not to be jealous.

Figure 14-14: I created this image by selecting an eel, layering it against a clock, and using a layer mask to blend the two images. Then I flattened the image and saved it.

2. **Create your text.** Select the type mask tool and click in the image window. Enter the text you want to use into the Type Tool dialog box, format it as desired, and press the Enter key on the keypad to display the type outlines in the image window. Bear in mind, Photoshop does not preview type masks in the image window, so you'll have to rely on the preview inside the Type Tool dialog box.

3. **Modify the selection outlines an needed.** I chose Select ⇨ Transform Selection and then ⌘-dragged the corner handles to distort my character outlines, as in Figure 14-15. (The character outlines are hard to see, so I've added a translucent white fill to make the text more legible. The fill is there merely for the purpose of the screen shot.)

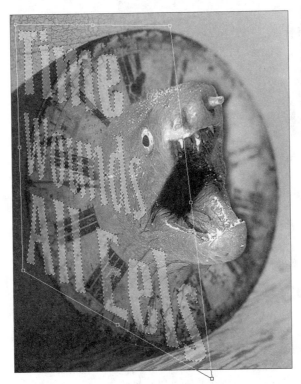

Figure 14-15: The Transform Selection command enabled me to apply a perspective effect to my character outlines before using them to select the image.

4. **Send the selected text to a separate layer by pressing ⌘-J.** The selection outlines disappear, so the image looks like it did before you started. But rest assured, you have characters filled with imagery on a separate layer.

(continued)

5. **Return to the background layer and create a new layer by clicking on the page icon at the bottom of the Layers palette.** The easiest way to distinguish text from background image is to darken the background image and lighten the text (or vice versa). This new layer is just the ticket.

6. **Fill the layer with a dark color.** Then choose the Multiply mode (Shift-Option-M) and lower the Opacity value. For my part, I added a black-to-white gradation starting from the lower left and ending in the upper right portion of the image. Thanks to the Multiply mode, just the area behind the text was darkened, as shown in Figure 14-16. I also lowered the Opacity to 40 percent.

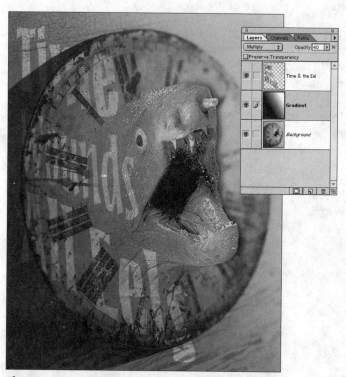

Figure 14-16: To darken the area behind the type, I added a black-to-white gradation on a new layer and set the layer to the Multiply mode.

7. **Switch to the type layer.** Now to make the type a lighter color.

8. **Create a new layer and fill it with a light color.** Set the blend mode to Screen (Shift-Option-S) and adjust the Opacity value as desired. I filled my layer with white and set the Opacity to 80 percent.

9. **Press ⌘-G.** This groups the light layer with the type below it, as demonstrated in Figure 14-17. The light area outside the type goes away. Now the type stands out clearly from its background, even though you can see the image both inside and outside the letters.

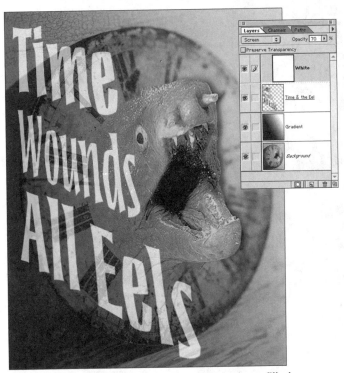

Figure 14-17: To lighten the text, I added a layer filled entirely with white and grouped it with the type layer.

(continued)

10. **Apply whatever additional effects strike your fancy.** I returned to the type layer and chose Layer ➪ Effects ➪ Bevel and Emboss. Then I selected the Outer Bevel setting to create the letters shown in Figure 14-18. I also applied the Drop Shadow effect to the text in the upper-right corner and the Pillow Emboss effect to the Jelly-Vision logo.

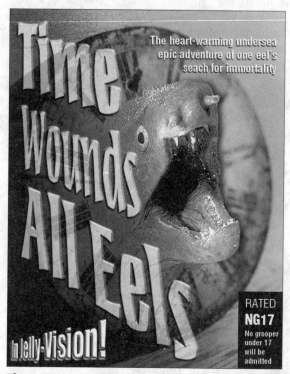

Figure 14-18: Using nothing but text, I managed to transform a strange, drab composition into this mighty attractive poster art.

As the enlarged view of the Jelly-Vision logo in Figure 14-19 shows, Photoshop's layer effects can work super-fast miracles on type. In a matter of seconds, I was able to transform the top example in the figure into the bottom one. (Note that in order to distort the type to achieve the perspective effect, I had to first convert it to a standard layer using Layer ➪ Type ➪ Render Layer.)

Figure 14-19: Creating the Jelly-Vision logo was as simple as distorting the text and applying a Pillow Emboss layer effect.

Layer effects bonanza

You'll have a blast experimenting with layer effects and type. Layer effects are fast, flexible, easy to use, and they were designed largely with editable type in mind. I have no doubt that they'll get *waaaay* overused. But as with any cool feature, you can stay ahead of the curve by applying your effects creatively.

Figure 14-20 shows three very simple but unusual implementations of layer effects. All three effects rely on character masks, but I created these selection outlines using the standard type tool. I clicked with the type tool; entered the words *Shake*, *Murder*, and *Imprint*; formatted them; and hit Enter to create a new type layer. Then I ⌘-clicked on the layer to draw out the selection outlines as I needed them.

Tip

Why use the standard type tool to create selection outlines instead of the type mask tool? Two reasons. First, the type tool shows you what it's up to in the image window, which is invaluable when formatting type to fit in a confined space. Second, I can always go back and edit my type when it's on an independent layer. (These edits won't affect my existing character masks, but I can ⌘-click to generate new masks any time I like.) The wonderful thing about the standard type tool is that it permits you to create both editable text and type masks. This one tool does everything you need, which is why I for one never change type tools; I always work with the upright black T.

Figure 14-20: Three example of childishly simple layer effects applied creatively to character masks.

That's really the key to creating cool effects. The rest is just "scribbling and bibbling," as a dramatized Mozart once said. But because the scribbles and bibbles may prove of minor interest to you, here's how I made each effect:

✦ **Shake:** First, the boring stuff. I extracted the layer mask for the word Shake by ⌘-clicking on my type layer and Shift-Option-dragging around the word Shake with the rectangular marquee tool to deselect Murder and Imprint. Then I switched to the background layer and pressed ⌘-J to send Shake to an independent layer. Finally I pressed the / key to turn on Preserve Transparency, so I could edit the type and only the type.

Now for the fun stuff. Using Edit ➪ Define Pattern, I created a pattern from the embossed texture back in Figure 14-5. Then I used Edit ➪ Fill to fill Shake with the pattern. Last, I brought up the Effects dialog box and applied a drop shadow set to black and Multiply, and an Inner Shadow set to white and Screen. The upshot is that the drop shadow darkens the background and the inner shadow lightens the characters. Figure 4-21 shows my settings.

Figure 14-21: The Drop Shadow and Inner Shadow settings used to create the word Shake in Figure 14-20.

✦ **Murder:** I filled the background layer behind the word Murder with black. Then I did all the boring stuff that I mentioned two paragraphs ago — ⌘-clicked the type layer, intersected Murder with the marquee tool, pressed ⌘-J to send Murder to its own layer, and selected Preserve Transparency.

I set the foreground color to white and brushed across the Murder layer with the paintbrush set to 40 percent opacity. Because Preserve Transparency was on, I painted inside the letters only. Finally, I chose Layer ➪ Effects ➪ Drop Shadow and applied a white halo set to Screen according to the settings in Figure 14-22. The result is a directional glow.

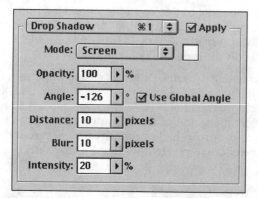

Figure 14-22: I used the Drop Shadow effect to add a halo behind the word Murder.

✦ **Imprint:** I filled the area behind Imprint with the same pattern I defined for Shake, then I mushed the pattern together using the filters Noise ⇨ Median and Blur ⇨ Gaussian Blur (both explained in Chapter 15). Then, as usual, I did the boring stuff — ⌘-clicked on the original type layer, intersected Imprint with the marquee tool, and pressed ⌘-J and the / key.

With Imprint on its own layer, I chose Layer ⇨ Effects ⇨ Bevel and Emboss, and applied the fairly typical settings shown in Figure 14-23. The subsequent effect was a bit disappointing. Muted and dark, it didn't have the punch I wanted. To brighten it up, I duplicated the Imprint layer by dragging it onto the page icon at the bottom of the Layers palette. Then I pressed Shift-Option-S to apply the Screen mode. The final result is the much sharper effect you see in Figure 14-20.

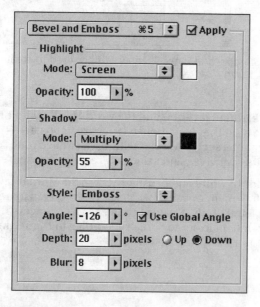

Figure 14-23: After applying these settings to the word Imprint, I duplicated the layer and selected the Screen blend mode.

Other Type Options

Version 5's type capabilities have changed pretty radically, but Photoshop still has its limitations. Take type on a curve, for example. While you can rest assured Adobe intends to add type on a curve to a future version of Photoshop, the feature isn't available yet.

One option is to align your type to a curve in a drawing program such as Illustrator or FreeHand, and then drag and drop it into Photoshop. If you don't own a drawing program — or if you're looking for an integrated solution that doesn't require you to leave Photoshop — then you might want to purchase a good third-party plug-in. The one that looks most promising is PhotoText, part of the PhotoDraw suite that should be available in fall of 1998 from Extensis (*www.extensis.com*). As the screen shot from Figure 14-24 shows, PhotoText will let you bind text to primitive shapes like ellipses and regular polygons, as well as free-form Bézier paths. PhotoText will also support justified paragraphs, tabs, and custom styles, all advantages over Photoshop 5.

Figure 14-24: PhotoText from Extensis serves as a fully functioning text-editing environment, complete with type on a curve. Bear in mind, this is an early alpha screen shot sneaked to me months before PhotoText is to ship. The final interface may look different.

If you want to create three-dimensional type effects inside Photoshop, you have two third-party plug-ins to choose from. The first is the $200 TypeCaster from Xaos Tools (*www.xaostools.com*). To use the plug-in, you simply open a dialog box, enter some text, select a font, and modify the type in 3D space. You can rotate, scale, and adjust the depth of the extrusion. You can also apply and modify surface textures to the face, bevel, and extruded sides of the type, as demonstrated in Figure 14-25. Finally, you can assign and position light sources inside a separate dialog box. TypeCaster isn't perfect — live previews, manual kerning, and letter warping would all go a long way — but it's an excellent addition to Photoshop.

Figure 14-25: TypeCaster lets you create 3-D type inside Photoshop. But because it doesn't permit you to hand-kern letters, you'll probably need to adjust the type manually on a separate layer.

The second 3-D type product is HotText from Vertigo (*www.vertigo3d.com*). Priced $50 cheaper than TypeCaster, HotText shares TypeCaster's inability to kern and lacks the option to create beveled edges. But in exchange, HotText lets you align your text to a free-form path so that the characters dip, pivot, and spin in 3-D space. It's just the thing for making type that rushes toward the viewer. Naturally, all of the products mentioned here — PhotoDraw, TypeCaster, and HotText — are available for the Mac.

✦   ✦   ✦

Filters and Effects

Corrective Filtering

Filter Basics

In Photoshop, *filters* enable you to apply automated effects to an image. Although named after photographers' filters, which typically correct lighting and perspective fluctuations, Photoshop's filters can accomplish a great deal more. You can slightly increase the focus of an image, introduce random pixels, add depth to an image, or completely rip it apart and reassemble it into a hurky pile of goo. Any number of special effects are made available via filters.

At this point, a little bell should be ringing in your head, telling you to beware of standardized special effects. Why? Because everyone has access to the same filters that you do. If you rely on filters to edit your images for you, your audience will quickly recognize your work as poor or at least unremarkable art.

Imagine this scenario: You're wasting away in front of your TV, flipping aimlessly through the channels. Just as your brain is about to shrivel and implode, you stumble across the classic "Sledgehammer" video. Outrageous effects, right? Peter Gabriel rides an imaginary roller coaster, bumper cars crash playfully into his face, fish leap over his head. You couldn't be more amused or impressed.

As the video fades, you're so busy basking in the glow that you neglect for a split second to whack the channel-changer. Before you know it, you're midway through an advertisement for a monster truck rally. Like the video, the ad is riddled with special effects — spinning letters, a reverberating voice-over slowed down to an octave below the narrator's normal pitch, and lots of big machines filled with little men filled with single brain cells working overtime.

In and of themselves, these special effects aren't bad. There was probably even a time when you thought that spinning letters and reverberating voice-overs were hot stuff. But sometime after you passed beyond preadolescence, you managed to grow tired of these particular effects. You've come to associate them with raunchy, local car-oriented commercials. Certainly, these effects are devoid of substance, but more importantly, they're devoid of creativity.

This chapter and the two that follow, therefore, are about the creative application of special effects. Rather than trying to show an image subjected to every single filter — a service already performed quite adequately by the manual included with your software — these chapters explain exactly how the most important filters work and offer some concrete ways to use them.

You'll also learn how to apply several filters in tandem and how to use filters to edit images and selection outlines. My goal is not so much to teach you what filters are available — you can find that out by tugging on the Filter menu — but how and when to use filters.

A first look at filters

You access Photoshop's special effects filters by choosing commands from the Filter menu. These commands fall into two general camps — *corrective* and *destructive*.

Corrective filters

Corrective filters are workaday tools used to modify scanned images and prepare an image for printing or screen display. In many cases, the effects are subtle enough that the viewer won't even notice that you applied a corrective filter. As demonstrated in Figure 15-1 and Color Plate 15-1, these filters change the focus of an image, enhance color transitions, and average the colors of neighboring pixels, among other effects. You'll find these filters in the Filter ➪ Blur, Noise, Sharpen, and Other submenus.

Many corrective filters have direct opposites. Blur is the opposite of Sharpen, Add Noise is the opposite of Median, and so forth. This is not to say that one filter entirely removes the effect of the other; only reversion functions such as the History palette provide that capability. Instead, two opposite filters produce contrasting effects.

Corrective filters are the subject of this chapter. Although they number fewer than their destructive counterparts, I spend more time on them because they represent the functions you're most likely to use on a day-to-day basis.

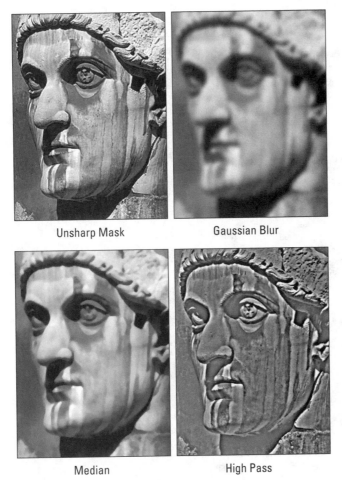

Unsharp Mask   Gaussian Blur

Median   High Pass

Figure 15-1: The gigantic head of fourth-century Roman emperor Constantine subject to four corrective filters, including one each from the Sharpen, Blur, Other, and Noise submenus (reading clockwise from upper left).

Destructive filters

The destructive filters produce effects so dramatic that they can, if used improperly, completely overwhelm your artwork, making the filter more important than the image itself. For the most part, destructive filters reside in the Filter ➪ Distort, Pixelate, Render, and Stylize submenus. A few examples of overwhelmed images appear in Figure 15-2 and Color Plate 15-2.

Wave   Crystallize

Emboss   Lens Flare

Figure 15-2: The effects of applying four destructive filters, one each from the Distort, Pixelate, Render, and Stylize submenus (clockwise from upper left). Note that Lens Flare is applicable to color images only, so I had to convert Constantine to the RGB mode before applying the filter.

Destructive filters produce way-cool effects, and many people gravitate toward them when first experimenting with Photoshop. But the filters invariably destroy the original clarity and composition of the image. Granted, every Photoshop function is destructive to a certain extent, but destructive filters change your image so extensively that you can't easily disguise the changes later by applying other filters or editing techniques.

Destructive filters are the subject of Chapter 16. Rather than explaining every one of these filters in detail, I try to provide a general overview.

Effects filters

Photoshop also provides a subset of destructive filters called the "effects" filters. These 47 filters originate from the Gallery Effects collection developed by Silicon Beach, which got gobbled up by Aldus (of PageMaker fame) and was finally acquired by Adobe Systems. Not knowing what exactly to do with this grab bag of plug-ins, Adobe integrated them into Photoshop.

Little about these filters has changed since Gallery Effects 1.5 came out in 1993. A couple of filters have been renamed—the old GE Ripple filter is now Ocean Ripple to avoid confusion with Photoshop's own Ripple filter. One filter, GE Emboss, is gone, presumably because it detracted from the popular Filter ➪ Stylize ➪ Emboss. But Adobe hasn't bothered with any meaningful retooling. You can't raise or lower a GE dialog box value using the arrow keys, you can't preview the effect in the image window, you can't switch applications when an effects dialog box is visible, and a few are dreadfully slow.

As a result, I devote only passing attention to the effects filters, explaining those few that fulfill a real need. Of course, I encourage you to experiment and derive your own conclusions. After all, as Figure 15-3 illustrates, these filters do produce intriguing special effects. I mean, that Plaster effect is just plain cool. For the record, most of the effects filters reside in the Filter ➪ Artistic, Brush Strokes, Sketch, and Texture submenus. A few have trickled out into other submenus, including Filter ➪ Distort ➪ Diffuse Glow, Glass, and Ocean Ripple; and Filter ➪ Stylize ➪ Glowing Edges.

Tip

If your experimentation leads you to my conclusion—you can live through most days without the effects filters—you can turn them off to save a whole lot of space in RAM better devoted to storing pixels. All the effects filters are stored in the Effects folder inside the Plug-Ins folder on your hard drive. Move the Effects folder out of the Plug-Ins folder, and all 47 filters will be turned off.

How filters work

When you choose a command from the Filter menu, Photoshop applies the filter to the selected portion of the image. If no portion of the image is selected, Photoshop applies the filter to the entire image. Therefore, if you want to filter every nook and cranny of an image, press ⌘-D and then choose the desired command.

External plug-ins

Some filters are built into the Photoshop application. Others are external modules that reside in the Plug-Ins folder. This enables you to add functionality to Photoshop by purchasing additional filters from third-party collections. Gallery Effects used to be such a collection. Others include PhotoTools from Extensis, Eye Candy from Alien Skin, the Series collections from Andromeda, Paint Alchemy from Xaos Tools, and Kai's Power Tools from MetaCreations.

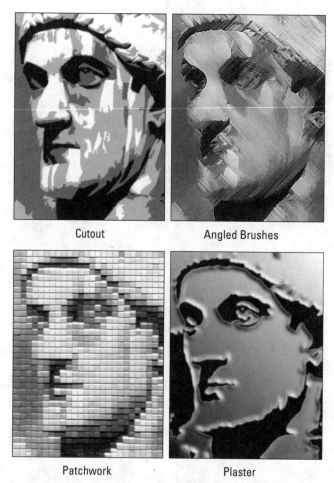

Cutout   Angled Brushes

Patchwork   Plaster

Figure 15-3: The "effects" filters come from Gallery Effects, a little toy surprise that Adobe accidentally acquired when it purchased Aldus Corporation. Here we see the impact of one filter each from the Filter ⇨ Artistic, Brush Strokes, Sketch, and Texture submenus (clockwise from upper left).

If you open the Plug-Ins folder inside the Photoshop folder, you'll see that it contains several subfolders. By default, Photoshop places the filters in the Filters and Effects subfolders, but you can place additional filters anywhere inside the Plug-Ins folder. Even if you create a new folder inside the Plug-Ins folder and call it *No Filters Here,* create another folder inside that called *Honest, Fresh Out of Filters,* toss in one more folder called *Carpet Beetles Only,* and put every plug-in you own inside this latest folder, Photoshop sees through your clever ruse and displays the exact same filters you always see under their same submenus in the Filter menu. The only purpose of the subfolders is to keep things tidy, so that you don't have to look through a list of 6,000 files.

Previewing filters

For years, the biggest problem with Photoshop's filters was that they did not offer previews to help you predict the outcome of an effect. You just had to tweak your 15,000 meaningless settings and hope for the best. But today, life is much better. Photoshop 3 introduced previews, Version 4 made them commonly available to all but the most gnarly filters, and Version 5 had the good sense to leave well enough alone.

Photoshop offers two previewing capabilities:

✦ **Dialog box previews:** Labeled in Figure 15-4, the 100×100-pixel preview box is now a common feature to all filter dialog boxes. Drag inside the preview box to scroll the portion of the image you want to preview. Move the cursor outside the dialog box to get the square preview cursor (labeled in the figure). Click with the cursor to center the contents of the preview box at the clicked position in the image.

Click on the zoom buttons (+ and –) to reduce the image inside the preview box. You can even take advantage of the standard zoom tool by pressing ⌘-spacebar or Option-spacebar, depending on whether you want to zoom in or out.

✦ **Image window previews:** Most corrective filters — as well as a couple of destructives like Mosaic and Emboss — also preview effects in the full image window. Just select the Preview check box to activate this function. While the effect is previewing, a blinking progress line appears under the check box. In Figure 15-4, for example, you can see that the bottom of the image still hasn't finished previewing, so the progress line strobes away. If you're working on a relatively poky computer, you'll probably want to turn this check box off to speed up the pace at which the filter functions.

Note

Incidentally, the Preview check box has no effect on the contents of the preview box. The latter continually monitors the effects of your settings, whether you like it or not.

Tip

Use the Preview check box to compare the before and after effects of a corrective filter in the image window. Turn it on to see the effect; turn it off to see the original image. You can also compare the image in the preview box by clicking in the box. Mouse down to see the old image; release to see the filtered image. It's like an electronic, high-priced, adult version of peek-a-boo. But not nearly as likely to induce giggles.

Even though a dialog box is on-screen and active, you can zoom and scroll the contents of the image window. ⌘-spacebar-click to zoom in, Option-spacebar-click to zoom out, and spacebar-drag to scroll. You can also choose commands from the View and Window menus. Feel free to switch applications.

Image window   Preview box

Preview cursor

Figure 15-4: Most filter dialog boxes let you preview the effects of the filter both inside the dialog box and in the image window.

One more tip: When you press the Option key, the Cancel button changes to a Reset button. Option-click on this button to restore the settings that appeared when you first opened the dialog box. (These are not necessarily the factory default settings; they are the settings you last applied to an image.)

Most destructive filters make no attempt to preview effects in the image window. Seven filters continue to offer no previews whatsoever: Radial Blur, Displace, Color Halftone, Extrude, Tiles, De-Interlace, and Offset. Of course, single-shot filters — the ones that don't bring up dialog boxes — don't need previews because there aren't any settings to adjust.

Reapplying the last filter

To reapply the last filter used in the current Photoshop session, choose the first command from the Filter menu or simply press ⌘-F. If you want to reapply the filter subject to different settings, Option-choose the first Filter command or press ⌘-Option-F to redisplay that filter's dialog box.

Both techniques work even if you undo the last application of a filter. If you cancel a filter while in progress, however, pressing ⌘-F or ⌘-Option-F applies the last uncanceled filter.

Nudging numerical values

In addition to entering specific numerical values inside filter dialog boxes, you can nudge the values using the up and down arrow keys. When working with percentage values, press an arrow key to raise or lower the value by 1. Press Shift-up or down arrow to change the value in increments of 10.

If the value accommodates decimal values, it's probably more sensitive to the arrow key. Press an arrow for a 0.1 change; press Shift-arrow for 1.0.

As I mentioned earlier, these tricks don't work in some of the destructive filters dialog boxes, most notably those associated with old Gallery Effects filters.

Fading a filter

In many cases, you apply filters to a selection or image at full intensity — meaning that you marquee an area using a selection tool, choose a filter command, enter whatever settings you deem appropriate if a dialog box appears, and sit back and watch the fireworks.

What's so "full intensity" about that? Sounds normal, right? Well, the fact is, you can reduce the intensity of the last filter applied by choosing the Filter ⇨ Fade command or pressing ⌘-Shift-F. This command permits you to mix the filtered image with the original, unfiltered one.

As shown in Figure 15-5, the Fade dialog box provides you with the basic tools of image mixing — an Opacity value and a blend mode pop-up menu. To demonstrate the wonders of Filter ⇨ Fade, I've applied two particularly destructive Gallery Effects filters to the colossal marble head — Filter ⇨ Stylize ⇨ Glowing Edges and Filter ⇨ Sketch ⇨ Note Paper. In the second column of heads, I pressed ⌘-Shift-F and lowered the Opacity of the two effects to 30 percent. The right-hand images show the effects of two blend modes, Lighten and Overlay, with the Opacity value restored to 100 percent.

Glowing Edges

Lighten

Note Paper

30% Opacity

Overlay

Figure 15-5: Press ⌘-Shift-F to mix the filtered image with the unfiltered original. Now, is it me, or is Constantine on Note Paper the spitting image of Rambo? That's got to be keeping some art historian awake at night.

Despite its placement in the Filter menu, the Fade command also affects the opacity of floating selections, as explained in Chapter 11. You can likewise choose Filter ➪ Fade to change the intensity of the last color correction command, as explained in Chapter 18.

Creating layered effects

The drawback of the Fade command is that it's only available immediately after you apply a filter (or color correction). If you so much as modify a selection outline after applying the filter, the Fade command dims, only to return when you apply the next filter.

Therefore, you may find it more helpful to copy a selection to a separate layer (⌘-J) before applying a filter. This way, you can perform other operations, and even apply many filters in a row, before mixing the filtered image with the underlying original.

Filtering inside a border

Here's another reason to layer before you filter: If your image has a border around it — like the ones shown in Figure 15-6 — you don't want Photoshop to factor the border into the filtering operation. To avoid this, select the image inside the border and press ⌘-J to layer it prior to applying the filter. The reason is that most filters take neighboring pixels into consideration even if they are not selected. By contrast, when a selection floats, it has no neighboring pixels, and therefore the filter affects the selected pixels only.

Figure 15-6 shows the results of applying two filters discussed in this chapter — Unsharp Mask and Motion Blur — when the image is anchored in place and when it's layered. In all cases, the 2-pixel border was not selected. In the left examples, the Unsharp Mask filter leaves a high-contrast residue around the edge of the image, while Motion Blur duplicates the left and right edges of the border. Both problems vanish when the filters are applied to layered images, as seen on the right.

Even if the area outside the selection is not a border per se — perhaps it's just a comparatively dark or light area that serves as a visual frame — layering comes in handy. You should always layer the selection unless you specifically want edge pixels to be calculated by the filter.

Undoing a sequence of filters

Okay, here's one last reason to layer before you filter. Copying an image to a layer protects the underlying image. If you just want to experiment a little, pressing ⌘-J is often more convenient than restoring a state in the History palette. After applying four or five effects to a floating image, you can undo all that automated abuse by Option-clicking on the trash icon at the bottom of the Layers palette. The underlying original remains unharmed.

Heightening Focus and Contrast

If you've experimented at all with Photoshop, you've no doubt had your way with many of the commands in the Filter ➪ Sharpen submenu. By increasing the contrast between neighboring pixels, the sharpening filters enable you to compensate for image elements that were photographed or scanned slightly out of focus.

The Sharpen, Sharpen More, and Sharpen Edges commands are easy to use and immediate in their effect. You can achieve better results and widen your range of sharpening options, however, if you learn how to use the Unsharp Mask and High Pass commands, which I discuss at length in the following pages.

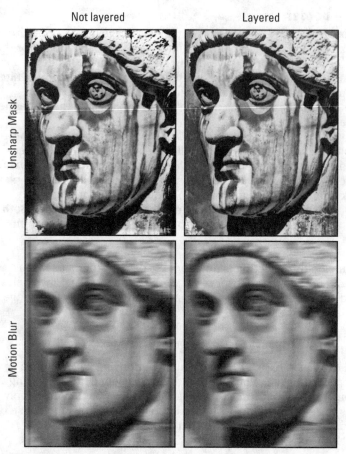

Figure 15-6: The results of applying two sample filters to images surrounded by borders. In each case, only the image was selected; the border was not. Layering the right examples prevented the borders from affecting the performance of the filters.

Using the Unsharp Mask filter

The first thing you need to know about the Unsharp Mask filter is that it has a weird name. The filter has nothing to do with "unsharpening" — whatever that is — nor is it tied into Photoshop's masking capabilities. Unsharp Mask is named after a traditional film compositing technique (which is also oddly named) that highlights the edges in an image by combining a blurred film negative with the original film positive.

That's all very well and good, but most Photoshop artists have never touched a stat camera (an expensive piece of machinery, roughly twice the size of a washing machine, used by image editors of the late Jurassic, pre-Photoshop epoch). Even folks like me who used to operate stat cameras professionally never had the time to delve into the world of unsharp masking. In addition — and much to the filter's credit — Unsharp Mask goes beyond traditional camera techniques.

To understand Unsharp Mask — or Photoshop's other sharpening filters, for that matter — you first need to understand some basic terminology. When you apply one of the sharpening filters, Photoshop increases the contrast between neighboring pixels. The effect is similar to what you see when you adjust a camera to bring a scene into sharper focus.

Two of Photoshop's sharpening filters, Sharpen and Sharpen More, affect whatever area of your image is selected. The Sharpen Edges filter, however, performs its sharpening operations only on the *edges* in the image — those areas that feature the highest amount of contrast.

Unsharp Mask gives you both sharpening options. It can sharpen only the edges in an image or it can sharpen any portion of an image according to your exact specifications, whether it finds an edge or not. It fulfills the exact same purposes as the Sharpen, Sharpen Edges, and Sharpen More commands, but it's much more versatile. Simply put, the Unsharp Mask tool is the only sharpening filter you'll ever need.

When you choose Filter ⇨ Sharpen ⇨ Unsharp Mask, Photoshop displays the Unsharp Mask dialog box, shown in Figure 15-7, which offers the following options:

✦ **Amount:** Enter a value between 1 and 500 percent to specify the degree to which you want to sharpen the selected image. Higher values produce more pronounced effects.

Figure 15-7: Despite any conclusions you may glean from its bizarre name, the Unsharp Mask filter sharpens images according to your specifications in this dialog box.

✦ **Radius:** This option determines the thickness of the sharpened edge. Low values produce crisp edges. High values produce thicker edges with more contrast throughout the image.

✦ **Threshold:** Enter a value between 0 and 255 to control how Photoshop recognizes edges in an image. The value indicates the numerical difference between the brightness values of two neighboring pixels that must occur if Photoshop is to sharpen those pixels. A low value sharpens lots of pixels; a high value excludes most pixels from the running.

The preview options offered by the Unsharp Mask dialog box are absolutely essential visual aids that you're likely to find tremendously useful throughout your Photoshop career. Just the same, you'll be better prepared to experiment with the Amount, Radius, and Threshold options and less surprised by the results if you read the following sections, which explain and demonstrate the effects of these options in detail.

Specifying the amount of sharpening

If Amount were the only Unsharp Mask option, no one would have any problems understanding this filter. If you want to sharpen an image ever so slightly, enter a low percentage value. Values between 25 and 50 percent are ideal for producing subtle effects. If you want to sharpen an image beyond the point of good taste, enter a value somewhere in the 300 to 500 percent range. And if you're looking for moderate sharpening, try out some value between 50 and 300 percent. Figure 15-8 shows the results of applying different Amount values while leaving the Radius and Threshold values at their default settings of 1.0 and 0, respectively.

If you're not sure how much you want to sharpen an image, try out a small value, in the 25 to 50 percent range. Then reapply that setting repeatedly by pressing ⌘-F. As you can see in Figure 15-9, repeatedly applying the filter at a low setting produces a nearly identical result to applying the filter once at a higher setting. For example, you can achieve the effect shown in the middle image in the figure by applying the Unsharp Mask filter three times at 50 percent or once at 250 percent. I created the top-row results in Figure 15-9 using a constant Radius value of 1.0. In the second row, I lowered the Radius progressively from 1.0 (left) to 0.8 (middle) to 0.6 (right).

The benefit of using small values is that they enable you to experiment with sharpening incrementally. As the figure demonstrates, you can add sharpening bit by bit to increase the focus of an image. You can't, however, reduce sharpening incrementally if you apply too high a value; you must press ⌘-Z and start again.

Just for fun, Color Plate 15-3 shows the results of applying the Unsharp Mask filter to each of the color channels in an RGB image independently. In each case, I maxed out the Amount value to 500 percent and set the Radius and Threshold to 4.0 and 0 respectively. The top row shows the results of applying the filter to a single channel; in the second row, I applied the filter to two of the three channels (leaving only one channel unfiltered). You can see how the filter creates a crisp halo of color around the chess pieces. Sharpening the red channel creates a red halo, sharpening the red and green channels together creates a yellow halo, and so forth. Applying the filter to the red and green channels produced the most noticeable effects because these channels contain the lion's share of the image detail. The blue channel contained the least detail — as is typical — so sharpening this channel produced the least dramatic results.

Figure 15-8: The results of sharpening an image with the Unsharp Mask filter using eight different Amount values. The Radius and Threshold values used for all images were 1.0 and 0, respectively (the default settings).

50% twice   50% times three   50% times four

100%   250%   500%

Figure 15-9: Repeatedly applying the Unsharp Mask filter at 50 percent (top row) is nearly equivalent on a pixel-by-pixel basis to applying the filter once at higher settings (bottom row).

Cross-Reference   If you're a little foggy on how to access individual color channels, read Chapter 6. Incidentally, you can achieve similar effects by sharpening the individual channels in a Lab or CMYK image.

Tip   As I mentioned in Chapter 6, Photoshop is ultimately a grayscale editor, so when you apply the Unsharp Mask command to a full-color image, Photoshop actually applies the command in a separate pass to each of the color channels. Therefore, the command always results in the color halos shown in Color Plate 15-3 — it's just that the halos get mixed together, minimizing the effect. To avoid any haloing whatsoever, convert the image to the Lab mode (Image ➪ Mode ➪ Lab Color) and apply Unsharp Mask to only the Lightness channel in the Channels palette. (Do not filter the *a* and *b* channels.) This sharpens the brightness values in the image and leaves the colors 100 percent untouched.

Setting the thickness of the edges

The Unsharp Mask filter works by identifying edges and increasing the contrast around those edges. The Radius value tells Photoshop how thick you want your edges. Large values produce thicker edges than small values.

The ideal Radius value depends on the resolution of your image and the quality of its edges:

✦ When creating screen images — such as Web graphics — use a very low Radius value such as 0.5. This results in terrific hair-line edges that look so crisp, you'll think you washed your bifocals.

✦ If a low Radius value brings out weird little imperfections — such as grain, scan lines, or JPEG compression artifacts — raise the value to 1.0 or higher. If that doesn't help, don't fret. I include two different sure-fire image fixing techniques later in this chapter, one designed to sharpen grainy old photos, and another that accommodates compressed images.

✦ When printing an image at a moderate resolution — anywhere from 120 to 180 ppi — use a Radius value of 1.0. The edges will look a little thick on-screen, but they'll print fine.

✦ For high-resolution images — around 300 ppi — try a Radius of 2.0. Because Photoshop prints more pixels per inch, the edges have to be thicker to remain nice and visible.

If you're looking for a simple formula, I'd recommend 0.1 of Radius for every 15 ppi of final image resolution. That means 75 ppi warrants a Radius of 0.5, 120 ppi warrants 0.8, 180 ppi warrants 1.2, and so on. If you have a calculator, just divide the intended resolution by 150 to get the ideal Radius value.

You can of course enter higher Radius values — as high as 250, in fact. Higher values produce heightened contrast, almost as if the image had been photocopied too many times, which is generally useful for producing special effects.

But don't take my word for it; you be the judge. Figure 15-10 demonstrates the results of specific Radius values. In each case, the Amount and Threshold values remain constant at 100 percent and 0, respectively.

Figure 15-11 shows the results of combining different Amount and Radius values. You can see that a large Amount value helps to offset the softening of a high Radius value. For example, when the Amount is set to 200 percent, as in the first row, the Radius value appears to mainly enhance contrast when raised from 0.5 to 2.0. When the Amount value is lowered to 50 percent, however, the higher Radius value does more to distribute the effect than boost contrast.

Figure 15-10: The results of applying eight different Radius values, ranging from precise edges to very gooey.

200%, 0.5   200%, 2.0   200%, 10.0

100%, 0.5   100%, 2.0   100%, 10.0

50%, 0.5   50%, 2.0   50%, 10.0

Figure 15-11: The effects of combining different Amount and Radius settings. The Threshold value for each image was set to 0, the default setting.

For those few folks who are thinking, "By gum, I wonder what would happen if you applied an unusually high Radius value to each color channel independently," you have only to consult Color Plate 15-4. In this figure, I again applied the Unsharp Mask filter to each channel and each pair of channels in the RGB chess image independently. But I changed the Amount value to 250 percent, raised the Radius value to a whopping 20.0 pixels, and left the Threshold at 0. To make the splash more apparent, I applied the filter twice to each image. The colors now bound out from the king, queen, and knight, bleeding into the gray background by as much as 20 pixels, the Radius value. Notice how the color fades away from the pieces, almost as if I had selected and feathered them? A high Radius value spreads the sharpening effect and, in doing so, allows colors to bleed. Because you normally apply the filter to all channels simultaneously, the colors bleed uniformly to create thick edges and high contrast.

Recognizing edges

By default, the Unsharp Mask filter sharpens every pixel in a selection. You can instruct the filter to sharpen only the edges in an image by raising the Threshold value from zero to some other number, however. The Threshold value represents the difference between two neighboring pixels — as measured in brightness levels — that must occur for Photoshop to recognize them as an edge.

Suppose that the brightness values of neighboring pixels are 10 and 20. If you set the Threshold value to 5, Photoshop reads both pixels, notes that the difference between their brightness values is more than 5, and treats them as an edge. If you set the Threshold value to 20, however, Photoshop passes them by. A low Threshold value, therefore, causes the Unsharp Mask Filter to affect a high number of pixels, and vice versa.

In the top row of images in Figure 15-12, the high Threshold values result in tiny slivers of sharpness that outline only the most substantial edges in the woman's face. As I lower the Threshold value incrementally in the second and third rows, the sharpening effect takes over more and more of the face, ultimately sharpening all details uniformly in the lower right example.

Using the preset sharpening filters

So how do the Sharpen, Sharpen Edges, and Sharpen More commands compare with the Unsharp Mask filter? First of all, none of the preset commands permits you to vary the thickness of your edges, a function provided by Unsharp Mask's Radius option. Secondly, only the Sharpen Edges command can recognize high-contrast areas in an image. Finally, all three commands are set in stone — you can't adjust their effects in any way. Figure 15-13 shows the effect of each preset command and the nearly equivalent effect created with the Unsharp Mask filter.

Figure 15-12: The results of applying nine different Threshold values. To best show off the differences between each image, I set the Amount and Radius values to 500 percent and 2.0, respectively.

Figure 15-13: The effects of the three preset sharpening filters (top row) compared with the Unsharp Mask equivalents (bottom row). Unsharp Mask values are listed in the following order: Amount, Radius, Threshold.

Sharpening grainy photographs

Having completed my neutral discussion of Unsharp Mask, king of the Sharpen filters, I hasten to interject a little bit of commentary, along with a helpful solution to a common sharpening problem.

First, the commentary: While Amount and Radius are the kinds of superior options that will serve you well throughout the foreseeable future, I urge young and old to observe Threshold with the utmost scorn and rancor. The idea is fine — we can all agree that you need some way to draw a dividing line between those pixels that you want to sharpen and those that you want to leave unchanged. But the Threshold setting is nothing more than a glorified on/off switch that results in harsh transitions between sharpened and unsharpened pixels.

Consider the picture of pre-presidential Eisenhower in Figure 15-14. Like so many vintage photographs, this particular image of Ike is a little softer than we're used to seeing these days. But if I apply a heaping helping of Unsharp Mask — as in the second example in the figure — I bring out as much film grain as image detail. The official Photoshop solution is to raise the Threshold value, but the option's intrinsic harshness results in a pock-marked effect, as shown on the right. Photoshop has simply replaced one kind of grain with another.

Soft

Figure 15-14: The original Ike is a bit soft (left), a condition I can remedy with Unsharp Mask. Leaving the Threshold value set to 0 brings out the film grain (middle), but raising the value results in equally unattractive artifacts (right).

These abrupt transitions are quite out of keeping with Photoshop's normal approach. Paintbrushes have antialiased edges, selections can be feathered, the Color Range command offers Fuzziness — in short, everything mimics the softness found in real life. Yet right here, inside what is indisputably Photoshop's most essential filter, we find no mechanism for softness whatsoever.

While we wait for Photoshop to give us a better Threshold — one with a Fuzziness slider or similar control — you can create a better Threshold using a simple masking technique. Using a few filters that I explore at greater length throughout this chapter and the next, you can devise a selection outline that traces the essential edges in the image — complete with fuzzy transitions — and leaves the non-edges unmolested. So get out your favorite old vintage photograph and follow along with these steps.

Steps: Creating and Using an Edge Mask

1. **Duplicate one of the color channels.** Bring up the Channels palette and drag one of the color channels onto the little page icon. Ike is a grayscale image, so I duplicate the one and only channel.

2. **Choose Filter ➪ Stylize ➪ Find Edges.** As I explain in Chapter 16, the Find Edges filter automatically traces the edges of your image with thick, gooey outlines that are ideal for creating edge masks.

3. **Press ⌘-I or choose Image ➪ Adjust ➪ Invert.** Find Edges produces black lines against a white background, but to select your edges, you need white lines against a black background. The Invert command reverses the lights and darks in the mask, as in the first example in Figure 15-15.

Find Edges, Invert

Find edge mask

Sharpened edges

Figure 15-15: I copy a channel, find the edges, and invert (left). I then apply a string of filters to expand and soften the edges (middle). After converting the mask to a selection outline, I reapply Unsharp Mask with winning results (right).

4. **Choose Filter ➪ Noise ➪ Median.** You need fat, gooey edges, and the current ones are a bit tenuous. To firm up the edges, choose the Median filter, enter a value of 2 (or thereabouts), and press Return.

5. **Choose Filter ➪ Other ➪ Maximum.** The next step is to thicken up the edges. The Maximum filter expands the white areas in the image, serving much the same function in a mask as Select ➪ Modify ➪ Expand serves when editing a selection outline. Enter 4 for the Radius value and press Return.

6. **Choose Filter ⇨ Blur ⇨ Gaussian Blur.** Unfortunately, the Maximum filter results in a bunch of little squares that don't do much for our cause. You can merge the squares into a seamless line by choosing the Gaussian Blur command and entering 4, the same radius you entered for Maximum. Then press Return.

   The completed mask is pictured in the second example of Figure 15-15. Although hardly an impressive sight to the uninitiated eye, you're looking at the perfect edge mask — soft, natural, and extremely accurate.

7. **Return to the standard composite view.** Press ⌘-tilde (~) in a color image. Since I'm working in a grayscale image, I press ⌘-1.

8. **Convert the mask to a selection outline.** ⌘-click on the mask name in the Channels palette. Photoshop selects the most essential edges in the image without selecting the grain.

9. **Choose Filter ⇨ Sharpen ⇨ Unsharp Mask.** In the last example in Figure 15-15, I applied the highest permitted Amount value, 500 percent, and a Radius of 2.0.

10. **Whatever values you use, make sure the Threshold is set to 0.** Always leave it at 0 from this day forward.

In case Figures 15-14 and 15-15 are a little too subtle, I include enlarged views of the great general's eyes in Figure 15-16. The top eyes show the result of using the Threshold value, the bottom eyes were created using the edge mask. Which ones appear sharper and less grainy to you?

Figure 15-16: Enlarged views of the last examples from Figures 15-14 (top) and 15-15 (bottom). A good edge mask beats the Threshold value every time.

Using the High Pass filter

The High Pass filter falls more or less in the same camp as the sharpening filters but is not located under the Filter ⇨ Sharpen submenu. This frequently overlooked gem enables you to isolate high-contrast image areas from their low-contrast counterparts.

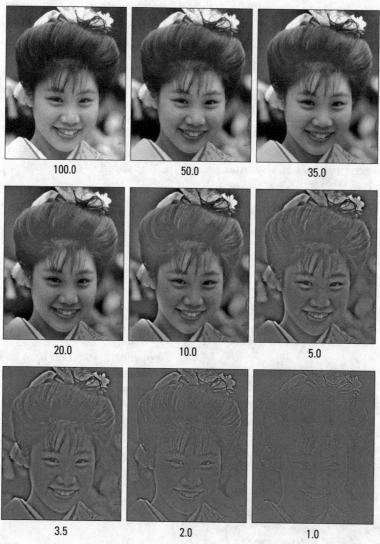

Figure 15-17: The results of separating high- and low-contrast areas in an image with the High Pass filter set at eight different Radius values.

When you choose Filter ⇨ Other ⇨ High Pass, Photoshop offers a single option: the familiar Radius value, which can vary from 0.1 to 250.0. As demonstrated in Figure 15-17, high Radius values distinguish areas of high and low contrast only slightly. Low values change all high-contrast areas to dark gray and low-contrast areas to a slightly lighter gray. A value of 0.1 (not shown) changes all pixels in an image to a single gray value and is therefore useless.

Applying High Pass to individual color channels

In my continuing series of color plates devoted to adding a bit of digital color to the ages-old chess, Color Plate 15-5 shows the results of applying the High Pass filter set to a Radius value of 5.0 to the various color channels. This application is actually a pretty interesting use for this filter. When applied to all channels at once, High Pass has an irritating habit of robbing the image of color in the low-contrast areas, just where the color is needed most. But when applied to a single channel, there's no color to steal. In fact, the filter adds color. For example, because there is almost no contrast in the dark shadows, High Pass elevates the black to gray in each of the affected color channels. The gray in the red channel appears red, the gray in the red channel mixed with the gray in the green channel appears yellow, and so forth. As a result, the filter imbues each image with a chalky glow.

Note

I enhanced the High Pass effect slightly in Color Plate 15-5 by increasing the contrast of each affected color channel using the Levels command. Using the three Input option boxes at the top of the Levels dialog box, I changed the first value to 65 and the third value to 190, thereby compressing the color space equally on both the black and white sides. Had I not done this, the images would appear a little more washed out. (Not a lot, but I figure that you deserve the best color I can deliver.) For detailed information on the Levels command, read Chapter 18.

Converting an image into a line drawing

The High Pass filter is especially useful as a precursor to Image ⇨ Adjust ⇨ Threshold, which converts all pixels in an image to black and white (again, covered in Chapter 18). As illustrated in Figure 15-18, the Threshold command produces entirely different effects on images before and after you alter them with the High Pass filter. In fact, applying the High Pass filter with a low Radius value and then issuing the Threshold command converts your image into a line drawing.

In the second row of examples in the figure, I followed Threshold with Filter ⇨ Blur ⇨ Gaussian Blur (the subject of the next section). I set the Gaussian Blur Radius value to 1.0. Like the Threshold option in the Unsharp Mask dialog box, the Threshold command results in harsh transitions; Gaussian Blur softens them to produce a more natural effect.

Why change your image to a bunch of slightly different gray values and then apply a command such as Threshold? One reason is to create a mask, as discussed at length in the "Building a Mask from an Image" section of Chapter 12. (In Chapter 12, I used Levels instead of Threshold, but both are variations on the same theme.)

5.0   2.5   1.0

Threshold and Gaussian Blur

Opacity: 45%, Overlay mode

Figure 15-18: Several applications of the High Pass filter with low Radius values (top row), followed by the same images subject to Image ⇨ Adjust ⇨ Threshold and Filter ⇨ Blur ⇨ Gaussian Blur (middle). I then layered the second row onto the first and modified the Opacity and blend mode settings.

You might also want to bolster the edges in an image. For example, to achieve the last row of examples in Figure 15-18, I layered the images prior to applying High Pass, Threshold, and Gaussian Blur. Then I monkeyed around with the Opacity setting and the blend mode to achieve an edge-tracing effect.

Note

I should mention that Photoshop provides several automated edge-tracing filters—including Find Edges, Trace Contour, and the Gallery Effects acquisition, Glowing Edges. But High Pass affords more control than any of these commands and permits you to explore a wider range of alternatives. Also worth noting, several Gallery Effects filters—most obviously Filter ➪ Sketch ➪ Photocopy—lift much of their code directly from High Pass. Although it may seem at first glance a strange effect, High Pass is one of the seminal filters in Photoshop.

Blurring an Image

The commands under the Filter ➪ Blur submenu produce the opposite effects of their counterparts under the Filter ➪ Sharpen submenu. Rather than enhancing the amount of contrast between neighboring pixels, the Blur filters diminish contrast to create softening effects.

Applying the Gaussian Blur filter

The preeminent Blur filter, Gaussian Blur, blends a specified number of pixels incrementally, following the bell-shaped Gaussian distribution curve I touched on earlier. When you choose Filter ➪ Blur ➪ Gaussian Blur, Photoshop produces a single Radius option box, in which you can enter any value from 0.1 to 250.0. (Beginning to sound familiar?) As demonstrated in Figure 15-19, Radius values of 1.0 and smaller blur an image slightly; moderate values, between 1.0 and 5.0, turn an image into a rude approximation of life without my glasses on; and higher values blur the image beyond recognition.

Moderate to high Radius values can be especially useful for creating that hugely amusing *Star Trek* Iridescent Female effect. This is the old *Star Trek,* of course. Captain Kirk meets some bewitching ambassador or scientist who has just beamed on board. He takes her hand in sincere welcome as he gives out with a lecherous grin and explains how truly honored he is to have such a renowned guest in his transporter room, and so charming to boot. Then we see it—the close-up of the fetching actress shrouded in a kind of gleaming halo that prevents us from discerning if her lips are chapped or perhaps she's hiding an old acne scar, because some cockeyed cinematographer smeared Vaseline all over the camera lens. I mean, what *wouldn't* you give to be able to re-create this effect in Photoshop?

Unfortunately, I don't have any images of actresses adorned in futuristic go-go boots, so Constantine cum Rambo will have to do in a pinch. The following steps explain how to make the colossal head glow as demonstrated in Figure 15-20.

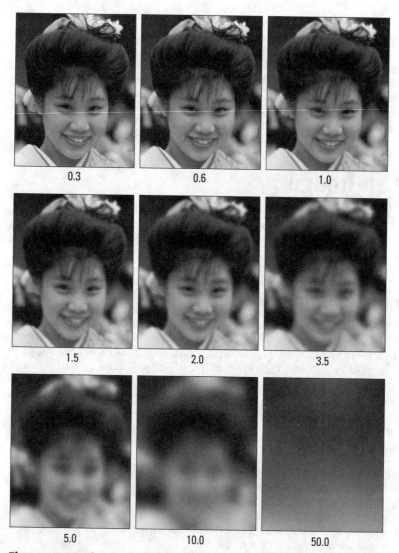

Figure 15-19: The results of blurring an image with the Gaussian Blur filter using eight different Radius values, ranging from slightly out of focus to Bad Day at the Ophthalmologist's Office.

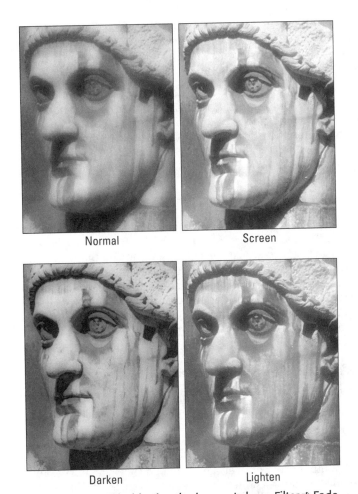

Normal   Screen

Darken   Lighten

Figure 15-20: After blurring the image, I chose Filter ➪ Fade Gaussian Blur and changed the Opacity value to 70 percent. Then I applied the labeled blend modes to alter the image further.

Steps: The Captain Kirk Myopia Effect

1. **Press ⌘-A to select the entire image.** If you only want to apply the effect to a portion of the image, be sure to feather the selection with a radius in the neighborhood of 5 to 8 pixels.

2. **Choose Filter ➪ Blur ➪ Gaussian Blur.** Enter some unusually large value into the Radius option box — say, 8.0 — and press Return.

(continued)

3. **Press ⌘-Shift-F to bring up the Fade dialog box.** To achieve the effects shown in Figure 15-20, I reduced the Opacity value to 70 percent, making the blurred image slightly translucent. This way, you can see the hard edges of the original image through the filtered one.

4. **You can achieve additional effects by selecting options from the Mode pop-up menu.** For example, I created the upper right example in the figure by selecting the Screen option, which uses the colors in the filtered image to lighten the original. I created the two bottom examples in the figure by applying the Darken and Lighten options.

Color Plate 15-6 shows an image that's more likely to interest Captain Kirk. It shows a young agrarian woman subject to most of the same settings I applied earlier to Constantine. Again, I applied the Gaussian Blur filter with a Radius of 8.0. Then I used Filter ⇨ Fade Gaussian Blur to adjust the Opacity value and blend mode. The upper left image shows the Normal mode, but the upper right image shows the Luminosity mode. In this case, the Screen mode resulted in a washed-out effect, whereas Luminosity yielded an image with crisp color detail and fuzzy brightness values. As a result, there are some interesting places where the colors leap off her checkered dress. As in Figure 15-20, the bottom two images show the effects of the Darken and Lighten modes.

You know, though, as I look at this woman, I'm beginning to have my doubts about her and Captain Kirk. I mean, she has Scotty written all over her.

The preset blurring filters

Neither of the two preset commands in the Filter ⇨ Blur submenu, Blur and Blur More, can distribute its blurring effect over a bell-shaped Gaussian curve. For that reason, these two commands are less functional than the Gaussian Blur filter. Just so you know where they stand in the grand Photoshop focusing scheme, Figure 15-21 shows the effect of each preset command and the nearly equivalent effect created with the Gaussian Blur filter.

Antialiasing an image

If you have a particularly jagged image, such as a 256-color GIF file, there's a better way to soften the rough edges than applying the Gaussian Blur filter. The best solution is to antialias the image. How? After all, Photoshop doesn't offer an Antialias filter. Well, think about it. Back in the "Softening selection outlines" section of Chapter 11, I described how Photoshop antialiases a brushstroke or selection outline at twice its normal size and then reduces it by 50 percent and applies bicubic interpolation. You can do the same thing with an image.

Blur   Blur More

0.3   0.7

Figure 15-21: The effects of the two preset blurring filters (top row) compared with their Gaussian Blur equivalents (bottom row), which are labeled according to Radius values.

Choose Image ➪ Image Size and enlarge the image to 200 percent of its present size. Make sure that the Resample Image check box is turned on and set to Bicubic. (You can also experiment with Bilinear for a slightly different effect, but don't use Nearest Neighbor.) Next, turn right around and choose Image ➪ Image Size again, but this time shrink the image by 50 percent.

The top left example in Figure 15-22 shows a jagged image subject to this effect. I used Image ➪ Adjust ➪ Posterize to reduce Moses to four colors. It's ugly, but it's not unlike the kind of images you may encounter, particularly if you have access to an aging image library. To the right is the same image subject to Gaussian Blur with a very low Radius value of 0.5. Rather than appearing softened, the result is just plain fuzzy.

Figure 15-22: A particularly jagged image (top left) followed by the image blurred using a filter (top right). By enlarging and reducing the image one or more times (bottom left and right), I soften the pixels without making them appear blurry. The enlarged details show each operation's effect on the individual pixels.

If I instead enlarge and reduce the image with the Image Size command, however, I achieve a true softening effect, as shown in the lower left example in the figure, commensurate with Photoshop's antialiasing options. Even after enlarging and reducing the image four times in a row—as in the bottom right example—I don't make the image blurry, I simply make it softer.

Directional blurring

In addition to its everyday blurring functions, Photoshop provides two *directional blurring* filters, Motion Blur and Radial Blur. Instead of blurring pixels in feathered clusters like the Gaussian Blur filter, the Motion Blur filter blurs pixels in straight lines over a specified distance. The Radial Blur filter blurs pixels in varying degrees depending on their distance from the center of the blur. The following pages explain both of these filters in detail.

Motion blurring

The Motion Blur filter makes an image appear as if either the image or camera was moving when you shot the photo. When you choose Filter ➪ Blur ➪ Motion Blur, Photoshop displays the dialog box shown in Figure 15-23. You enter the angle of movement into the Angle option box. Alternatively, you can indicate the angle by dragging the straight line inside the circle on the right side of the dialog box, as shown in the figure. (You'll notice that the arrow cursor actually appears outside the circle. Once you begin dragging on the line, you can move the cursor anywhere you want and still affect the angle.)

Figure 15-23: Drag the line inside the circle to change the angle of the blur.

You then enter the distance of the movement in the Distance option box. Photoshop permits any value between 1 and 999 pixels. The filter distributes the effect of the blur over the course of the Distance value, as illustrated by the examples in Figure 15-24.

Original

50 pixels

100 pixels

200 pixels

300 pixels

500 pixels

Figure 15-24: A single black rectangle followed by five different applications of the Motion Blur filter. Only the Distance value varied, as labeled. A 0-degree Angle value was used in all five examples.

Note

Mathematically speaking, Motion Blur is one of Photoshop's simpler filters. Rather than distributing the effect over a Gaussian curve — which one might argue would produce a more believable effect — Photoshop creates a simple linear distribution, peaking in the center and fading at either end. It's as if the program took the value you specified in the Distance option, created that many clones of the image, offset half the clones in one direction and half the clones in the other — all spaced 1 pixel apart — and then varied the opacity of each.

Using the Wind filter

The problem with the Motion Blur filter is that it blurs pixels in two directions. If you want to distribute pixels in one absolute direction or the other, try out the Wind filter, which you can use either on its own or in tandem with Motion Blur.

When you choose Filter ➪ Stylize ➪ Wind, Photoshop displays the Wind dialog box shown in Figure 15-25. You can select from three methods and two directions to distribute the selected pixels. Figure 15-26 compares the effect of the Motion Blur filter to each of the three methods offered by the Wind filter. Notice that the Wind filter does not blur pixels. Rather, it evaluates a selection in 1-pixel-tall horizontal strips and offsets the strips randomly inside the image.

Figure 15-25: Use the Wind filter to randomly distribute a selection in 1-pixel horizontal strips in one of two directions.

To get the best results, try combining the Motion Blur and Wind filters with a translucent selection. For example, to create Figure 15-27, I cloned the entire image to a new layer and applied the Wind command twice, first selecting the Stagger option and then selecting Blast. Next, I applied the Motion Blur command with a 0-degree angle and a Distance value of 30. I then set the Opacity option in the Layers palette to 80 percent and selected Lighten from the blend mode pop-up menu.

The result is a perfect blend between two worlds. The motion effect in Figure 15-27 doesn't obliterate the image detail, as the Wind filter does in Figure 15-26. The motion also appears to run in a single direction — to the right — something you can't accomplish using Motion Blur on its own.

Motion Blur   Wind

Blast   Stagger

Figure 15-26: Here is the difference between the effects of the Motion Blur filter (upper left) and the Wind filter (other three). In each case, I selected From the Right from the Direction radio buttons.

Figure 15-27: Here is the result of combining the Wind and Motion Blur filters with a translucent selection.

Radial blurring

Choosing Filter ➪ Blur ➪ Radial Blur displays the Radial Blur dialog box shown in Figure 15-28. The dialog box offers two Blur Method options: Spin and Zoom.

Figure 15-28: Drag inside the Blur Center grid to change the point about which the Radial Blur filter spins or zooms the image.

If you select Spin, the image appears to be rotating about a central point. You specify that point by dragging in the grid inside the Blur Center box (as demonstrated in the figure). If you select Zoom, the image appears to rush away from you, as if you were zooming the camera while shooting the photograph. Again, you specify the central point of the Zoom by dragging in the Blur Center box. Figure 15-29 features examples of both settings.

Spin, Draft   Spin, Best

Zoom, Draft   Zoom, Best

Figure 15-29: Four examples of the Radial Blur filter set to both Spin and Zoom, subject to different Quality settings (left and right). I specified Amount values of 10 pixels for the Spin examples and 30 for the Zooms. Each effect is centered about the right eye (your right, that is).

After selecting a Blur Method option, you can enter any value between 1 and 100 in the Amount option box to specify the maximum distance over which the filter blurs pixels. (You can enter a value of 0, but doing so merely causes the filter to waste time without producing an effect.) Pixels farthest away from the center point move the most; pixels close to the center point barely move at all. Keep in mind that large values take more time to apply than small values. The Radial Blur filter, incidentally, qualifies as one of Photoshop's most time-consuming operations.

Select a Quality option to specify your favorite time/quality compromise. The Good and Best Quality options ensure smooth results by respectively applying bilinear and bicubic interpolation (as explained in the "General preferences" section of Chapter 2). They also prolong the amount of time the filter spends calculating pixels in your image, however.

The Draft option *diffuses* an image, which leaves a trail of loose and randomized pixels but takes less time to complete. I used the Draft setting to create the left-hand images in Figure 15-29; I selected the Best option to create the images on the right.

Blurring with a threshold

The purpose of the new Filter ⇨ Blur ⇨ Smart Blur is to blur the low-contrast portions of an image while retaining the edges. This way, you can downplay photo grain, blemishes, and artifacts without harming the real edges in the image. (If you're familiar with Filter ⇨ Pixelate ⇨ Facet, then it may help to know Smart Blur is essentially a customizable version of that filter.)

The two key options inside the Smart Blur dialog box (see Figure 15-30) are the Radius and Threshold slider bars. As with all Radius options, this one expands the number of pixels calculated at a time as you increase the value. Meanwhile, the Threshold value works just like the one in the Unsharp Mask dialog box, specifying how different two neighboring pixels must be to be considered an edge.

But the Threshold value has a peculiar and unexpected effect on the Radius. The Radius value actually produces more subtle effects if you raise the value beyond the Threshold. For example, take a look at Figure 15-31. Here we have a grid of images subject to different Radius and Threshold values. (The first value below each image is the radius.) In the top row of the figure, the 5.0 radius actually produces a more pronounced effect than its 20.0 and 60.0 cousins. This is because 5.0 is less than the 10.0 threshold, while 20.0 and 60.0 are more.

Figure 15-30: The Smart Blur filter lets you blur the low-contrast areas of an image without harming the edges.

The Quality settings control the smoothness of the edges. The High setting takes more time than Medium and Low, but it looks smoother as well. (All of the effects in Figure 15-31 were set to High.) The two additional Mode options enable you to trace the edges defined by the Threshold value with white lines. Overlay Edges shows image and lines, while Edges Only shows just the traced lines. About the only practical purpose for these options is to monitor the precise effect of the Threshold setting in the preview box. Otherwise, the Edges options are clearly relegated to special effects.

Frankly, I'm not convinced that Smart Blur is quite ready for prime time. You already know what I think of the Threshold option, and it hasn't gotten any better here. Without control over the transitions between focused and unfocused areas, things are going to look pretty strange.

Tip

The better way to blur low-contrast areas is to create an edge mask, as I explained back in the "Sharpening grainy photographs" section. Just reverse the selection by choosing Select ⇨ Inverse and apply the Gaussian Blur filter.

Figure 15-32 shows how the masking technique compares with Smart Blur. In the first image, I applied Unsharp Mask with a Threshold of 20. Then I turned around and applied Smart Blur with a Radius of 2.0 and a Threshold of 20.0, matching the Unsharp Mask value. The result makes Ike look like he has dandruff coming out of every pore in his face.

Figure 15-31: Combinations of different Radius (first number) and Threshold (second) values. Notice that the most dramatic effects occur when the radius is equal to about half the threshold.

In the second image, I created an edge mask — as explained in the "Creating and Using an Edge Mask" steps — and applied Unsharp Mask with a Threshold of 0. Then I pressed ⌘-Shift-I to reverse the selection and applied Gaussian Blur with a Radius of 2.0. The result is a smooth image with sharp edges that any president would be proud to hang in the Oval Office.

Figure 15-32: The difference between relying on Photoshop's automated Threshold capabilities (left) and sharpening and blurring with the aid of an edge mask (right). Despite the advent of computers, a little manual labor still wins out over automation.

Softening a selection outline

Gaussian Blur and other Blur filters are equally as useful when editing masks as they are when editing image pixels. As I mentioned earlier, applying Gaussian Blur to a mask has the same effect as applying Select ⇨ Feather to a selection outline. But Gaussian Blur affords more control. Where the Feather command affects all portions of a selection outline uniformly, you can apply Gaussian Blur selectively to a mask, permitting you to mix soft and hard edges within a single selection outline easily.

Another advantage to blurring a mask is that you can see the results of your adjustments on-screen, instead of relying on the seldom-helpful marching ants. For example, suppose that you want to establish a buffer zone between a foreground image and its background. You've managed to select the foreground image accurately — how do you now feather the selection exclusively outward, so that no portion of the foreground image becomes selected? Although you can pull off this feat using selection commands like Expand and Feather, it's much easier to apply filters such as Maximum and Gaussian Blur inside a mask. But before I go any further, I need to back up and explain how Maximum and its pal Minimum work.

Maximum and Minimum

Filter ⇨ Other ⇨ Maximum expands the light portions of an image, spreading them outward into other pixels. Its opposite, Filter ⇨ Other ⇨ Minimum, expands the dark portions of an image. In traditional stat photography, these techniques are known as *spreading* and *choking.*

When you are working in the quick mask mode or an independent mask channel, applying the Maximum filter has the effect of incrementally expanding the selected area, adding pixels uniformly around the edges of the selection outline. The Maximum dialog box presents you with a single Radius value, which tells Photoshop how many edge pixels to expand. Just the opposite, the Minimum filter incrementally decreases the size of white areas, which subtracts pixels uniformly around the edges of a selection.

Feathering outward from a selection outline

The following steps describe how to use the Maximum and Gaussian Blur filters to feather an existing selection outline outward so that it doesn't encroach on the foreground image.

Steps: Adding a Soft Edge in the Quick Mask Mode

1. **Select the foreground image.** As shown in Figure 15-33, my foreground image is the layered television that figured so heavily into Chapter 13. I convert the layer's transparency mask to a selection outline by ⌘-clicking on the layer's name in the Layers palette.

2. **If you're working on a layer, switch to the background image.** The quickest route is Shift-Option-[.

3. **Press Q to enter the quick mask mode.** You can create a new mask channel if you prefer, but the quick mask mode is more convenient.

4. **Choose Filter ⇨ Other ⇨ Maximum.** Enter a Radius value to expand the transparent area into the rubylith. In Figure 15-33, I've entered the highest Radius value permitted, 10 pixels. After pressing Return, I decided this wasn't enough, so I pressed ⌘-Option-F to bring up the filter again, and further expanded the selection by 4 pixels.

5. **Choose Filter ⇨ Blur ⇨ Gaussian Blur.** To ensure that you don't blur into the foreground image, enter a Radius value that's no more than half the value you entered into the Maximum dialog box. Altogether, I expanded the selection by 14 pixels, so I entered 7 into the Gaussian Blur dialog box. Photoshop blurs the transparent area, as shown in Figure 15-34.

(continued)

Figure 15-33: The Maximum filter increases the size of the transparent area inside the quick mask mode, thereby expanding the selection outline.

Figure 15-34: Use the Gaussian Blur filter to soften the transparent area, thus feathering the selection outline.

Color Plate 16-6

These two rows of images show a step-by-step experiment in abstract imagery. Starting with a two-color gradation, I convert it to a spiral with Filter⇨Distort⇨Twirl. Then I copy the spiral to a layer, flip it, and rotate it (top right), apply the Difference mode to achieve the orange image (bottom left). I clone the layer again and rotate it, then I clone a third time and rotate and flip the layer. The final image is the result of tweaking each layer with another distortion filter, including Twirl, Spherize, and ZigZag.

Gradation　　Twirl x3　　Flip Horizontal　　Rotate 90° CW

Difference　　Rotate 90° CW　　Rotate and Flip　　and more . . .

Color Plate 16-7

In this piece, titled Knowing Risk, distortion expert Mark Collen combines a variety of distortion filtering effects to create a surrealistic landscape. The cat, the book, the mongoose, and the twigs are the only scanned images.

Color Plate 16-8
You can force 3D Transform to generate a 3D shape on an independent layer, as I did when creating this goblet. But 3D Transform provides no control over lighting. The easiest workaround is to apply layer effects. In my case, I used the Drop Shadow and Inner Bevel options. The result is hardly true three-dimensional rendering, but the goblet definitely leaps off the page.

Color Plate 16-9
This time, I took my 3D goblet and set it against a different background. To achieve the more realistic lighting, I applied manual shadow and highlight techniques in combination with a few swipes of the airbrush tool. It took more than 90 minutes to put this image together, but the finished effect is well worth the effort.

Color Plate 16-10
The top row shows the results of Shift-choosing the Clouds filter (left), Shift-choosing Difference Clouds (middle), and pressing ⌘-F ten times in a row (right). I then took each of the images from the top row and mixed it with the rose using one of three blend modes (labeled above bottom row). You can create clouds, haze, and imaginative fill patterns with the Clouds filters.

Clouds   Difference Clouds   x10

Overlay   Screen   Hue

Color Plate 16-11
Here I used the Lighting Effects filter to assign a total of five white spotlights, two pointing down from above and three pointing up from below. The bumpy surfaces of the second and third images are the results of texture maps. To create the right image, I used the green channel as the texture. In the bottom image, I used a pattern created with the Pointillize filter.

Color Plate 17-1
Color versions of four Custom filter effects, including (clockwise from upper left) mild sharpening, offset sharpening, edge-detection, and full-color embossing.

Color Plate 17-2
Examples of applying four patterns from the Displacement Maps folder with the Displace filter, including (clockwise from upper left) Crumbles, Streaks pattern, Mezzo effect, and Twirl pattern.

Color Plate 17-3

The top rows shows three different applications of the Rotator filters with the Red, Green, and Blue slider bars set to various positions. The Distorto option was set to 0. In the bottom examples, I added a cranked up Distorto value to each of the rotations above. That's gotta hurt.

R:1, G:2, B:3 | R:80, G:85, B: 90 | R:240, G:230, B:250

Distort=10 | Distort=40 | Distort=140

Color Plate 17-4

Applications of six Tormentia filters I created in Filter Factory, which you'll find on the CD. Each filter has between 3 and 6 sliders, so there are all sorts of variations you can create.

Color Group | Crisscross | Full Channel Press

Noise Blaster | Ripping Pixels | Super Invert

RGB   Lab   CMYK

Color Plate 18-1
The results of applying the Invert command to a single image in each of the three color modes. I inverted all channels in the RGB and Lab images and all but the black channel in the CMYK channel.

RGB   Lab   CMYK

Color Plate 18-2
Here I administered the High Pass filter with a Radius of 3.0, and then applied Threshold separately to each color channel within the three color modes. To smooth the jagged edges, I resampled each image up to 200 percent and then back down to 50 percent using the Image Size command. Then I repeated the process.

Luminosity   Hard Light   Hue

Color Plate 18-3
After cloning the image to a new layer, I applied the High Pass filter and the Posterize command. Then I mixed the layer and the underlying original by choosing each of three overlay modes from the Layers palette. All effects were created with Opacity settings of 100 percent. To make things more colorful, I gave the saturation a healthy boost using the Hue/Saturation command.

Color Plate 18-4

You can downplay the colors in selected portions of an image by applying Desaturate to covert the pixels to gray values (top left). You can then use Filter⇨Fade to reduce the Opacity setting and bring back some colors (top right). Alternatively, you can Invert the selection, choose Filter⇨Fade, select the Color blend mode, and lower the Opacity value to 50 percent (bottom left). Raising the Opacity increases the presence of inverted colors (bottom right).

Desaturate

Fade to 50%

Invert and fade to 50%

Invert and fade to 70%

Color Plate 18-5

Starting with the uncorrected pumpkin image (top left), I applied Image⇨Adjust⇨ Auto Levels to its in each of the three color modes. The command is really designed for RGB images and tends to mess up CMYK images (lower right). As you folks who live outside Love Canal are probably aware, few pumpkins are fire-engine red.

Uncorrected

RGB

Lab

CMYK

Master, -40°

Master, +20°

Master, +60°

Color Plate 18-6
The results of choosing
Image⇨Adjust⇨
Hue/Saturation and
applying various Hue
values to an entire image
(top row) and to only the
cyan portions of the
image (bottom row).

Cyan only, -40°

Cyan only, +20°

Cyan only, +60°

Master, -50°

Master, +50°

Color Plate 18-7
The results of applying various Saturation
values to an entire image (top row) and to
certain colors—namely cyan and blue—
independently of others (bottom row).
Without creating a selection or mask,
you can isolate colored areas using the
Hue/Saturation command.

All but cyan and blue, -100

Cyan and blue, -100
All others, +50

Master, -90°

Master, +90°

Color Plate 18-8
The results of applying various Hue values
to an image when the Colorize option is
turned off (top row) and on (bottom row).
In the bottom images, I selected the blue
areas of the horse with the Color Range
command and then colorized the blue and
non-blue areas as indicated by the labels.
Notice that while the top two images
continue to possess a variety of differently
colored pixels, the bottom images contain
only two apiece—pink and green.

Blue areas, 120°
Other, -50°

Blue areas, -60°
Other, 110°

Color Plate 18-9

These images show the results of correcting images with two of Photoshop's more specialized color commands, Replace Color (top row) and Selective Color (bottom row). The Replace Color command lets you adjust colors while at the same time modifying which pixels are affected and which are not with the help of a Fuzziness option. The Selective Color command adjusts the amount of CMYK ink assigned to predefined color ranges.

Fuzziness, 40   Fuzziness, 200

Red to violet, Relative   Red to violet and
                                 black to white, Absolute

Color Plate 18-10

The effects of applying each of the thumbnails offered in the Variations dialog box to the familiar pumpkin. In each case, the slider bar was set to its default setting of midway between Fine and Coarse with the Midtones radio button selected.

More Green   Lighter   More Yellow

More Cyan   Original   More Red

More Blue   Darker   More Magenta

Original digital photo

Increase saturation to +80

Median, Gaussian Blur, and Color mode

Final sharpened image

Color Plate 18-11
Starting with a rather typically washed out image that I shot with a Kodak DC50 (top), I copied the image to a new layer and boosted the saturation with Hue/Saturation command (second). Then I applied the Median and Gaussian Blur commands and mixed the layer with the underlying original using the Color blend mode and an Opacity value of 70 percent (third). Finally, I used Median, Gaussian Blur, and Unsharp Mask to sharpen the image (bottom).

Color Plate 18-12
The celebrated Virginia statesman before (left) and after (right) I corrected him with the Levels command. The white histograms superimposed on Jefferson's chest show the original and corrected distribution of brightness values. The colored histograms illustrate the corrections made to the individual red, green, and blue channels.

Color Plate 18-13
You can use the Curves dialog box to apply gradations as color maps. In the top row, I copied the famous Roman to a new layer, blurred him silly, and applied each of three gradients (saved to disk by ⌘-clicking on the Save button in the Gradient Editor dialog box). Then I mixed the images with their underlying originals using the Color blend mode (Shift-Option-C).

Chrome   Blue, Red, Yellow   Spectrum

Color blend mode

Color Plate 18-14
The results of using the Curves command to lighten the colors in the red channel (left), increase the level of contrast in the green channel (middle), and apply an arbitrary color map to the blue channel (right).

Color Plate 18-15
These images illustrate one way to use adjustment layers to correct the colors in a flat image. After observing that my original image was way too dark (left), I created a new adjustment layer and used the Curves command to lighten the image (middle). I then added two additional layers to increase the saturation levels with Hue/Saturation and correct the brightness levels of the topiary animal with Levels (right).

Color Plate 19-1

Examples of the 17 blend mode options applied to a bright blue Saturn set against the fiery backdrop of Jupiter. I also inserted an 18th Saturn set to the Normal mode and 50 percent Opacity (second down, middle column) just for the sake of comparison. That, and to take up space.

Color Plate 19-2

Blend modes change their meaning depending on which layer is in front and which is in back. Here I've taken images of a woman and a leaf and placed them on separate layers. In the top row, the leaf layer is in front, and in the bottom row, the woman is in front. The irony is that every one of these blend modes favors the layer on bottom. Only a few—Normal, Hard Light, and Luminosity—favor the image on top.

Charcoal

Hard Light

Color

Difference

Original

Soft Light

Color Dodge

Luminosity

Color Plate 19-3
Each column of images shows a progression in which I sandwiched an image filtered with the Charcoal effect (top left) between two originals (bottom left). Each image in the top row shows the filtered image interacting with the original background layered according to the labeled blend mode. The bottom images show the results of adding the top layer of the sandwich and applying another blend mode. For example, applying Difference to the filtered layer and Luminosity to the top layer creates the bottom right effect.

Unsharp Mask

Motion Blur

Lens Flare

Find Edges

Difference Sandwich

Color Plate 19-4
The top rows the results of a series of corrective and destructive filters, each of which go a long way toward destroying the detail in my image. But when I insert the filter effect in between two copies of the original image, and then apply the Difference blend mode to the middle and top layers, I bring back much of the detail, as shown in the bottom row. No other technique restores detail quite like a tasty Difference sandwich.

Color Plate 19-5
For the sake of comparison, the first image shows the result of compositing an RGB image onto itself using the Hard Light mode. Other examples show the different effects you can achieve by duplicating the image, converting it to the Lab mode, and then mixing the RGB and Lab images together using the Apply Image command, again set to Hard Light.

RGB on RGB

Lightness on RGB

Inverted *b* on RGB

Blue on RGB

Color Plate 19-6
After creating a separate mask channel using the Color Range command (shown as a rubylith, top left), I used the mask to protect the background from my Apply Image manipulations. Although I applied some heavy duty blend modes, the blue gray background remained altogether unharmed.

RGB on RGB

Lightness on RGB

Inverted *b* on RGB

Blue on Lab

Original

System (Macintosh)

System (Windows)

Adapative, 8 bits/pixel

Adaptive, 6 bits/pixel

Adaptive, 4 bits/pixel

None, 94K

Pattern, 105K

Diffusion, 118K

Color Plate 20-2
Here I reduced the image from Color Plate 20-1 using each of three different Dither options—None, Pattern, and Diffusion. Beside each option name is the size of the file when saved in the GIF format. As you can see, GIF is better suited to compressing an image when no dithering is involved.

6. **Invert the mask by pressing ⌘-I.** So far, I've managed to select the TV, but I really want to edit the background. So I press ⌘-I to invert the mask and inverse the prospective selection.

7. **Press Q to exit the quick mask mode.** Ah, back in the workaday world of marching ants.

8. **Apply the desired effect.** I copied a zebra-skin pattern from another image. Then I chose Edit ⇨ Paste Into (⌘-Shift-V) to paste the pattern inside the selection. Photoshop created a new layer with layer mask. After ⌘-dragging the pattern into position, I applied the Overlay blend mode to achieve the effect shown in Figure 15-35.

Thanks to my expanded and softened selection outline, the stripes fade toward the television without ever quite touching it. As I said, you can achieve this effect using Select ⇨ Modify ⇨ Expand and Feather, but unless you have a special aversion to the quick mask mode, it's easier to be sure of your results when you can see exactly what you're doing.

Figure 15-35: I copied some zebra skin from one image window and pressed ⌘-Shift-V to paste it into my new selection.

Noise Factors

Photoshop offers four loosely associated filters in its Filter ➩ Noise submenu. One filter adds random pixels — known as *noise* — to an image. The other three, Despeckle, Dust & Scratches, and Median, average the colors of neighboring pixels in ways that theoretically remove noise from poorly scanned images. But in fact, they function nearly as well at removing essential detail as they do at removing extraneous noise. In the following sections, I show you how the Noise filters work, demonstrate a few of my favorite applications, and leave you to draw your own conclusions.

Adding noise

Noise adds grit and texture to an image. Noise makes an image look like you shot it in New York on the Lower East Side and were lucky to get the photo at all because someone was throwing sand in your face as you sped away in your chauffeur-driven, jet-black Maserati Bora, hammering away at the shutter release. In reality, of course, a guy over at Sears shot the photo while you toodled around in your minivan trying to find a store that sold day-old bread. But that's the beauty of Noise. It makes you look cool, even when you aren't.

You add noise by choosing Filter ➩ Noise ➩ Add Noise. Shown in Figure 15-36, the Add Noise dialog box features the following options:

✦ **Amount:** Enter any value between 1 and 999 to specify the amount that pixels in the image can stray from their current colors. The value itself represents a color range rather than a brightness range. For example, if you enter a value of 10, Photoshop can apply any color that is 10 shades more or less green, more or less blue, *and* more or less red than the current color. Any value over 255 allows Photoshop to select random colors from the entire 16-million color spectrum. The higher you go above 255, the more likely Photoshop is to pick colors at opposite ends of the spectrum — that is, white and black.

✦ **Uniform:** Select this option to apply colors absolutely randomly within the specified range. Photoshop is no more likely to apply one color within the range than another, thus resulting in an even color distribution.

✦ **Gaussian:** When you select this option, you instruct Photoshop to prioritize colors along the Gaussian distribution curve. The effect is that most colors added by the filter either closely resemble the original colors or push the boundaries of the specified range. In other words, this option results in more light and dark pixels, thus producing a more pronounced effect.

✦ **Monochromatic:** When working on a full-color image, the Add Noise filter distributes pixels randomly throughout the different color channels. When you select the Monochrome check box, however, Photoshop distributes the noise in the same manner in all channels. The result is grayscale noise. (This option does not affect grayscale images; the noise can't get any more grayscale than it already is.)

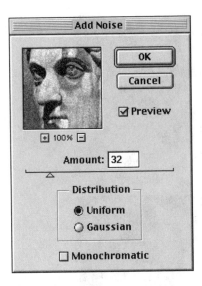

Figure 15-36: The Add Noise dialog box asks you to specify the amount and variety of noise you want to add to the selection.

Figure 15-37 compares three applications of Gaussian noise to identical amounts of Uniform noise. Figure 15-38 features magnified views of the noise so that you can compare the colors of individual pixels.

Noise variations

Normally, the Add Noise filter adds both lighter and darker pixels to an image. If you prefer, however, you can limit the effect of the filter to strictly lighter or darker pixels. To do so, apply the Add Noise filter, then choose Filter ➪ Fade Add Noise and select the Lighten or Darken blend mode. You can also copy the image to a new layer, apply the filter, and merge the filtered image with the underlying original.

Figure 15-39 shows sample applications of lighter and darker noise. After copying the image to a separate layer, I applied the Add Noise filter with an Amount value of 100, and selected Gaussian. To create the upper left example in the figure, I selected Lighten from the blend mode pop-up menu. To create the right example, I selected the Darken mode. In each case, I added a layer of strictly lighter or darker noise while at the same time retaining the clarity of the original image.

To achieve the streaked noise effects in the bottom example of Figure 15-39, I applied Motion Blur and Unsharp Mask to the layered images. Inside the Motion Blur dialog box, I set the Angle value to –30 degrees and the Distance to 30 pixels. Then I applied Unsharp Mask with an Amount value of 200 percent and a Radius of 1. Naturally, the Threshold value was 0.

Gaussian, 16 Gaussian, 32 Gaussian, 48

Uniform, 16 Uniform, 32 Uniform, 48

Figure 15-37: The Gaussian option produces more pronounced effects than the Uniform option at identical Amount values.

Gaussian, 16 Gaussian, 32 Gaussian, 48

Uniform, 16 Uniform, 32 Uniform, 48

Figure 15-38: The upper left corners of the examples from Figure 15-37 enlarged to four times their original size.

Lighten   Darken

Motion Blur, Lighten   Motion Blur, Darken

Figure 15-39: You can limit the Add Noise filter to strictly lighter (left) or darker (right) noise by applying the filter to a layered clone. To create the rainy and scraped effects (bottom examples), I applied Motion Blur and Unsharp Mask to the noise layers.

Chunky noise

My biggest frustration with the Add Noise filter is that you can't specify the size of individual specks of noise. No matter how you cut it, noise only comes in 1-pixel squares. It may occur to you that you can enlarge the noise dots in a layer by applying the Maximum or Minimum filter. But in practice, doing so simply fills in the image, because there isn't sufficient space between the noise pixels to accommodate the larger dot sizes.

Luckily, Photoshop provides several alternatives. One is the Pointillize filter, which adds variable-sized dots and then colors those dots in keeping with the original colors in the image. Although Pointillize lacks the random quality of the Add Noise filter, you can use it to add texture to an image.

To create the top left image in Figure 15-40, I chose Filter ⇨ Pixelate ⇨ Pointillize and entered 5 into the Cell Size option box. After pressing Return to apply the filter, I pressed ⌘-Shift-F and changed the Opacity value to 50 percent. The effect is rather like applying chunky bits of noise.

Pointillize, 50%   Halftone Pattern

Grain, Clumped   Speckled, 50%

Figure 15-40: The results of applying several different Add Noise-like filters, including Pointillize, Halftone Pattern, and Grain. A percentage value indicates that I modified the Opacity setting in the Fade dialog box.

The Gallery Effects filters provide a few noise alternatives. Filter ⇨ Sketch ⇨ Halftone Pattern adds your choice of dot patterns, as shown in the upper right example in Figure 15-40. But like all filters in the Sketch submenu, it replaces the colors in your image with the foreground and background colors. Filter ⇨ Texture ⇨ Grain is a regular noise smorgasbord, permitting you to select from 10 different Grain Type options, each of which produces a different kind of noise. The bottom examples in Figure 15-40 show off two of the Grain options, Clumped and Speckled. I used Filter ⇨ Fade Grain to reduce the Opacity value for the Speckled effect to 50 percent.

Removing noise with Despeckle

Now for the noise removal filters. Strictly speaking, the Despeckle command probably belongs in the Filter ⇨ Blur submenu. It blurs a selection while at the same time preserving its edges — the idea being that unwanted noise is most noticeable in the continuous regions of an image. In practice, this filter is nearly the exact opposite of the Sharpen Edges filter.

The Despeckle command searches an image for edges using the equivalent of an Unsharp Mask Threshold value of 5. It then ignores the edges in the image and blurs everything else with the force of the Blur More filter, as shown in the upper left image in Figure 15-41.

Averaging pixels with Median

Another command in the Filter ⇨ Noise submenu, Median removes noise by averaging the colors in an image, one pixel at a time. When you choose Filter ⇨ Noise ⇨ Median, Photoshop produces a Radius option box, into which you can enter any value between 1 and 16. For every pixel in a selection, the filter averages the colors of the neighboring pixels that fall inside the specified radius — ignoring any pixels that are so different that they might skew the average — and applies the average color to the central pixel. As verified by Figure 15-41, large values produce the most destructive effects.

As with Gaussian Blur, you can achieve some very interesting and useful effects by backing off the Median filter with the Fade command. But rather than creating a *Star Trek* glow, Median clumps up details, giving an image a plastic, molded quality, as demonstrated by the examples in Figure 15-42. To create every one of these images, I applied the Median Filter with a Radius of 5 pixels. Then I pressed ⌘-Shift-F to display the Fade dialog box and lowered the Opacity value to 70 percent. The only difference between one image and the next is the blend mode.

Another difference between Gaussian Blur and Median is that Gaussian Blur destroys edges and Median invents new ones. This means you can follow up the Median filter with Unsharp Mask to achieve even more pronounced sculptural effects. I sharpened every one of the examples in Figure 15-42 using an Amount value of 150 percent and a Radius of 1.5

Despeckle   Median, 1   3

5   10   16

Figure 15-41: The effects of the Despeckle filter (upper left) and Median filter. The numbers indicate Median filter Radius values.

Sharpening a compressed image

Digital cameras are the hottest thing in electronic imaging. You can take as many images as you like, download them to your computer immediately, and place them into a printed document literally minutes after snapping the picture. In the next five years, I have little doubt that you—yes, *you*—will purchase a digital camera (if you haven't already).

Unfortunately, the technology is still very young. Many brands take exceptional pictures, but most of these high-end devices cost $10,000 or more. Even midrange "mega-pixel" cameras like the Kodak DC210 and Olympus D-600L cost $1,000 or more. If you're hoping for a camera under $500, you'll have to make do with a consumer model like the Fuji DX-9 or the Minolta Dimage V. Even if you pick up this book two years after I write it, and every one of these models has been discontinued, you can expect to pay $200 to $500 for a low-end model.

If you've ever used one of these cameras—it's only a matter of time, I assure you— you know how difficult it is to sharpen the photographs. Thanks to the stingy supply of pixels and the heavy-handed compression schemes (all based on JPEG), even the daintiest application of the Unsharp Mask filter can reveal a world of ragged edges and unsightly artifacts.

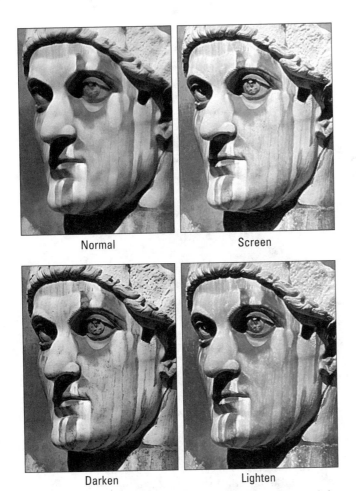

Normal   Screen

Darken   Lighten

Figure 15-42: After applying the Median filter, I reversed the effect slightly using Filter ⇨ Fade Median. Although I varied the blend mode — as labeled beneath the images — the Opacity value remained a constant 70 percent.

The solution is to firm up the detail and smooth out the color transitions by applying a combination of filters — Median, Gaussian Blur, and Unsharp Mask — to a layered version of the image. The following steps tell all.

Note

If you own a digital camera, I encourage you to record these steps with the Actions palette, as explained in Chapter 3. This way, you can set Photoshop to open squads of images, batch process them, and save them in a separate folder, leaving you free to do something fun, like read more of this book.

Steps: Adjusting the Focus of Digital Photos

1. **Select the entire image and copy it to a new layer.** That's ⌘-A, ⌘-J. Figure 15-43 shows the image that I intend to sharpen, a picture of a friend's child that I snapped with a DC40 (the predecessor to the earlier-mentioned DC50). His name, in case you're interested, is Cooper.

Figure 15-43: I captured this youthful fellow with a low-end digital camera equipped with a removable fish-eye lens. How innocent and happy he looks—obviously not a computer user.

2. **Choose Filter ⇨ Noise ⇨ Median.** After processing several thousands of these images, I've found that a Radius value of 2 is almost always the optimal choice. But if the image is particularly bad, 3 may be warranted.

3. **Choose Filter ⇨ Blur ⇨ Gaussian Blur.** Now that you've gummed up the detail a bit and rubbed out most of the compression, use the Gaussian Blur filter with a Radius of 1.0 to blur the gummy detail slightly. This softens the edges that the Median filter creates. (You don't want any fake edges, after all.)

4. **Choose Filter ⇨ Sharpen ⇨ Unsharp Mask.** All this blurring demands some intense sharpening. So apply Unsharp Mask with a maximum Amount value of 500 percent and a Radius of 1.0 (to match the Gaussian Blur radius). This restores most of the definition to the edges, as shown in Figure 15-44.

Figure 15-44: Thanks to Median, Gaussian Blur, and Unsharp Mask, Cooper is a much smoother customer. In fact, he's beyond smooth—he's a gummy kid.

5. **Lower the layer's Opacity value.** By itself, the filtered layer is a bit too smooth. So mix the filtered floater with the underlying original with an Opacity value between 30 and 50 percent. I found that I could go pretty high—45 percent—with Cooper. Kids have clearly defined details that survive filtering quite nicely.

6. **Merge the image.** Press ⌘-E to send the layer down.

7. **Continue to correct the image as you normally would.** The examples in Figure 15-45 show the difference between applying the Unsharp Mask filter to the original image (top) and the filtered mixture (bottom). In both cases, I applied an Amount value of 200 percent and a Radius of 1.0. The top photo displays an unfortunate wealth of artifacts—particularly visible in the magnified eye—while the bottom one appears smooth and crisp.

These steps work well for sharpening other kinds of compressed imagery, including old photographs that you over-compressed without creating backups, and images that you've downloaded from the Internet. If applying the Unsharp Mask filter brings out the goobers, try these steps instead.

Figure 15-45: Here you can see the difference between sharpening a digital photograph right off the bat (top) and waiting to sharpen until after you've prepared the image with Median, Gaussian Blur, and Unsharp Mask (bottom).

Cleaning up scanned halftones

Photoshop offers one additional filter in the Filter ➪ Noise submenu called Dust & Scratches. The purpose of this filter is to remove dust particles, hairs, scratches, and other imperfections that may accompany a scan. The filter offers two options, Radius and Threshold. As long as the offending imperfection is smaller or thinner than the Radius value and different enough from its neighbors to satisfy the Threshold value, the filter deletes the spot or line and interpolates between the pixels around the perimeter.

But like so many automated tools, this one works only when conditions are favorable. I'm not saying that you shouldn't ever use it — in fact, you may always want to give this filter the first crack at a dusty image. But if it doesn't work (as it probably won't), don't get your nose out of joint. Just hunker down and eliminate the imperfections manually using the rubber stamp tool, as explained in the "Touching up blemishes" section of Chapter 10.

Now, as I say, Dust & Scratches was designed to get rid of gunk on a dirty scanner. But another problem that the filter may be able to eliminate is moiré patterns. These patterns appear when scanning halftoned images from books and magazines. See, any time you scan a printed image, you're actually scanning a collection of halftone dots rather than a continuous-tone photograph. In most cases, the halftone pattern clashes with the resolution of the scanned image to produce rhythmic and distracting moirés.

Caution

When scanning published photographs or artwork, take a moment to find out if what you're doing is legal. It's up to you to make sure that the image you scan is no longer protected by copyright — most, but not all, works over 75 years old are considered free game — or that your noncommercial application of the image falls under the fair-use umbrella of commentary or criticism.

The Dust & Scratches filter can be pretty useful for eliminating moirés, particularly if you reduce the Threshold value below 40. But this also goes a long way toward eliminating the actual image detail, as shown in Color Plate 15-7. This figure features an image scanned from a previous issue of *Macworld* magazine. (Because I created the original image, *Macworld* probably won't sue me, but you shouldn't try it.)

The left half of Color Plate 15-7 shows the individual color channels in the image; the right half shows the full-color image. I've blown up a detail in each image so that you can better see the pixels in the moiré pattern.

The top example in the color plate shows the original scanned image with its awful moirés. (Actually, I've slightly exaggerated the moirés to account for any printing anomalies; but believe me, with or without enhancement, the image is a mess on-screen.) The middle example shows the same image subject to the Dust & Scratches filter with a Radius of 2 and a Threshold value of 20. The moirés are gone, but the edges have all but disappeared as well. I'm tempted to describe this artwork using adjectives like "soft" and "doughy," and them are fightin' words in the world of image-editing.

But what about that bottom example? How did I manage to eliminate the moirés *and* preserve the detail that is shown here? Why, by applying the Gaussian Blur, Median, and Unsharp Mask filters to individual color channels.

The first step is to examine the channels independently (by pressing ⌘-1, ⌘-2, and ⌘-3). You'll likely find that each one is affected by the moiré pattern to a different extent. In the case of this scan, all three channels need work, but the blue channel—the usual culprit—is the worst. The trick, therefore, is to eliminate the patterns in the blue channel and draw detail from the red and green channels.

To fix the blue channel, I applied both the Gaussian Blur and Median commands in fairly hefty doses. I chose Filter ➪ Blur ➪ Gaussian Blur and specified a Radius value of 1.5 pixels, rather high considering that the image measures only about 300 pixels tall. Then I chose Filter ➪ Noise ➪ Median and specified a Radius of 2.

The result was a thickly modeled image with no moirés but little detail. To firm things up a bit, I chose Filter ➪ Sharpen ➪ Unsharp Mask and entered 200 percent for the Amount option and 1.5 for the Radius. I opted for this Radius value because it matches the Radius that I used to blur the image. When correcting moirés, a Threshold value of 0 is almost always the best choice. A higher Threshold value not only prevents the sharpening of moiré pattern edges but also ignores real edges, which are already fragile enough as it is.

The green and red channels required incrementally less attention. After switching to the green channel, I applied the Gaussian Blur filter with a Radius of 1.0. Then I sharpened the image with the Unsharp Mask filter set to 200 percent and a Radius value of 0.5. In the red channel (⌘-1), I applied Gaussian Blur with a Radius value of 0.5. The gradual effect wasn't enough to warrant sharpening.

When you're finished, switch back to the RGB view (⌘-0) to see the combined result of your labors. (Or keep an RGB view of the image up on-screen by choosing Window ➪ New Window.) The focus of the image will undoubtedly be softer than it was when you started. You can cure this to a limited extent by applying very discreet passes of the Unsharp Mask filter, say, with an Amount value of 100 percent and a low Radius value. Keep in mind that oversharpening may bring the patterns back to life or even uncover new ones.

Tip

One last tip: Always scan halftoned images at the highest resolution available to your scanner. Then resample the scan down to the desired resolution using Image ➪ Image Size, as covered in Chapter 4. This step by itself goes a long way toward eliminating moirés.

✦   ✦   ✦

Full-Court Filtering

CHAPTER

16

Destructive Filters

Corrective filters allow you to both eliminate flaws in an image and apply special effects. Destructive filters, on the other hand, are devoted solely to special effects. That's why this chapter is actually shorter than its predecessor, even though Photoshop offers nearly twice as many destructive filters as corrective counterparts. Quite simply, destructive filters are less frequently used and ultimately less useful.

Don't get me wrong—these filters are a superb bunch. But because of their more limited appeal, I don't explain each and every one of them. Rather, I concentrate on the ones that I think you'll use most often, breeze over a handful of others, and let you discover on your own the ones that I ignore.

A million wacky effects

Oh heck, I guess I can't just go and ignore half of the commands under the Filter menu—they're not completely useless, after all. It's just that you aren't likely to use them more than once every lunar eclipse. So here are the briefest of all possible descriptions of these filters:

✦ **Color Halftone:** Located under the Filter ➪ Pixelate submenu, this command turns an image into a piece of Roy Lichtenstein artwork, with big, comic-book halftone dots. While scads of fun, the filter is ultimately a novelty that takes about a year and a half to apply.

✦ **Fragment:** Ooh, it's an earthquake! This lame filter repeats an image four times in a square formation and lowers the opacity of each to create a sort of jiggly effect. You don't even have any options to control it. It's quite possible I'm somehow missing the genius behind Filter ➪ Pixelate ➪ Fragment. Then again, maybe it just sucks.

✦ ✦ ✦ ✦

In This Chapter

Capsule descriptions of Photoshop's special effects filters

Clever ways to use the Pixelate filters

Putting the Mezzotint filter to good use

Applying the edge-enhancement filters, including Emboss and Find Edges

Creating metallic effects

Exploring new worlds with the help of the distortion filters

Designing specialized gradations and other abstractions

Transforming images in 3-D space

How to change a picture's atmosphere using Clouds

The complete inner workings of Lighting Effects

✦ ✦ ✦ ✦

✦ **Lens Flare:** Found in the Render submenu, this filter adds sparkles and halos to an image to suggest light bouncing off the camera lens. Even though photographers work their behinds off trying to make sure that these sorts of reflections don't occur, you can go and add them after the fact. You can select from three Lens Type options, adjust the Brightness slider between 10 and 300 percent (though somewhere around 100 is bound to deliver the best results), and move the center of the reflection by dragging a point around inside the Flare Center box. You can also Option-click inside the preview to position the center point numerically.

If you want to add a flare to a grayscale image, first convert it to the RGB mode. Then apply the filter and convert back to grayscale (like I did back in Figure 15-2). The Lens Flare filter is applicable to RGB images only.

Here's another great tip for using Lens Flare. Prior to choosing the filter, create a new layer, fill it with black, and apply the Screen blend mode (Shift-Option-S). Now apply Lens Flare. You get the same effect as you would otherwise, but the effect floats above the background image, protecting your original image from harm. You can even move the lens flare around and vary the Opacity value, giving you more control over the final effect.

✦ **Diffuse:** Located in the Stylize submenu — as are the next three filters — Diffuse dithers the edges of color, much as the Dissolve brush mode dithers the edges of a soft brush. Diffuse is moderately useful, but not likely to gain a place among your treasured few.

✦ **Solarize:** This single-shot command is easily Photoshop's worst filter. It's really just a color-correction effect that changes all medium grays in the image to 50 percent gray, switches all blacks and whites to black, and remaps the other colors to shades in between. (If you're familiar with the Curves command, the map for Solarize looks like a pyramid.) It really belongs in the Image ➪ Adjust submenu, or better yet, on the cutting room floor.

✦ **Tiles:** This filter breaks an image up into a bunch of regularly sized but randomly spaced rectangular tiles. You specify how many tiles fit across the width and height of the image — a value of 10, for example, creates 100 tiles — and the maximum distance each tile can shift. You can fill the gaps between tiles with foreground color, background color, or an inverted or normal version of the original image. A highly intrusive and not particularly stimulating effect.

✦ **Extrude:** The more capable cousin of the Tiles filter, Extrude breaks an image into tiles and forces them toward the viewer in three-dimensional space. The Pyramid option is a lot of fun, devolving an image into a collection of spikes. When using the Blocks option, you can select a Solid Front Faces option that renders the image as a true 3-D mosaic. The Mask Incomplete Blocks option simply leaves the image untouched around the perimeter of the selection where the filter can't draw complete tiles.

Actually, I kind of like Extrude. For the sheer heck of it, Color Plate 16-1 shows an example of Extrude applied to what was once a red rose. I set the Type to Blocks, the Size to 10, the Depth to 30 and Random, with both the Solid Front Faces and Mask Incomplete Blocks radio buttons selected. Pretty great, huh? I only wish that the filter would generate a selection outline around the masked areas of the image so that I could get rid of anything that hadn't been extruded. It's a wonderful effect, but it's not one that lends itself to many occasions.

✦ **Diffuse Glow:** The first of the Gallery Effects that I mostly ignore, Filter ➪ Distort ➪ Diffuse Glow sprays a coat of dithered, background-colored pixels onto your image. Yowsa, let me at it.

✦ **The Artistic filters:** As a rule, the effects under the Filter ➪ Artistic submenu add a painterly quality to your image. Colored Pencil, Rough Pastels, and Watercolor are examples of filters that successfully emulate traditional mediums. Other filters — Fresco, Smudge Stick, and Palette Knife — couldn't pass for their intended mediums in a dim room filled with dry ice.

✦ **The Brush Strokes filters:** I could argue that the Brush Strokes submenu contains filters that create strokes of color. This is true of some of the filters — including Angled Strokes, Crosshatch, and Sprayed Stroke. Others — Dark Strokes and Ink Outlines — generally smear colors, while still others — Accented Edges and Sumi-e — belong in the Artistic submenu. Whatever.

✦ **The Sketch filters:** In Gallery Effects parlance, Sketch means color sucker. Beware, every one of these filters replaces the colors in your image with the current foreground and background colors. If the foreground and background colors are black and white, the Sketch filter results in a grayscale image. Charcoal and Conté Crayon create artistic effects, Bas Relief and Note Paper add texture, and Photocopy and Stamp are stupid effects you could produce better and with more flexibility using High Pass.

Tip

To retrieve some of the original colors from your image after applying a Sketch filter, press ⌘-Shift-F to bring up the Fade dialog box and try out a few different Mode settings. Overlay and Luminosity are particularly good choices. In Color Plate 16-2, I applied the Charcoal filter with the foreground and background colors set to light blue and dark green. Then I used the Fade command to select the Overlay mode.

✦ **The Texture filters:** As a group, the commands in the Filter ➪ Texture submenu are my favorite effects filters. Craquelure, Mosaic Tiles, and Patchwork apply interesting depth textures to the image. And Texturizer provides access to several scaleable textures and permits you to load your own (so long as the pattern is saved in the Photoshop format), as demonstrated in Figure 16-1. The one dud is Stained Glass, which creates polygon tiles like Photoshop's own Crystallize filter, only with black lines around the tiles.

Burlap

Canvas

Sandstone

Random Strokes

Figure 16-1: Filter ➪ Texture ➪ Texturizer lets you select from four built-in patterns — including the first three shown here — and load your own. In the last example, I loaded the Random Strokes pattern included with Photoshop.

Certainly, there is room for disagreement about which filters are good and which are awful. After I wrote a two-star *Macworld* review about the first Gallery Effects collection back in 1992 — I must admit, I've never been a big fan — a gentleman showed me page after page of excellent artwork he had created with them. Recently, a woman showed me her collection of amazing Lens Flare imagery. I mean, here's a filter that just creates a bunch of bright spots, and yet this talented person was able to go absolutely nuts with it.

The moral is that just because I consider a filter or other piece of software to be a squalid pile of unspeakably bad code doesn't mean that a creative artist can't come along and put it to remarkable use. But that's because *you* are good, not the filter.

So if you're feeling particularly creative today, give the above filters a try. Otherwise, skip them with a clear conscience.

What about the others?

Some filters don't really belong in either the corrective or destructive camp. Take Filter ➪ Video ➪ NTSC Colors and Filter ➪ Other ➪ Offset, for example. Both are examples of commands that have no business being under the filter menu, and both could have been handled much better than they are.

The NTSC Colors filter modifies the colors in your RGB or Lab image for transfer to videotape. Vivid reds and blues that might otherwise prove very unstable and bleed into their neighbors are curtailed. The problem with this function is that it's not an independent color space; it's a single-shot filter that changes your colors and is done with it. If you edit the colors after choosing the command, you may very well reintroduce colors that are incompatible with NTSC devices and therefore warrant a second application of the filter. Conversion to NTSC — another light-based system — isn't as fraught with potential disaster as conversion to CMYK pigments, but it still deserves better treatment than this.

The Offset command moves an image a specified number of pixels. Why didn't I cover it in Chapter 11 with the other movement options? Because the command actually moves the image inside the selection outline while keeping the selection outline itself stationary. It's as if you had pasted the entire image into the selection outline and were now moving it around. The command is a favorite among fans of channel operations, a topic I cover in Chapter 19. You can duplicate an image, offset the entire thing a few pixels, and then mix the duplicate and original to create highlight or shadow effects. But I much prefer the more interactive control of layering and nudging with the arrow keys. I imagine the Offset filter might find favor with folks who want to automate movements from the Actions palette, but now that Photoshop 5 records movements made with the move tool, I'm not even sure about that. Okay, I admit it; the Offset command is a primitive feature with no purpose in our high-tech modern world.

Cross-Reference

Among the filters I've omitted from this chapter is Filter ➪ Stylize ➪ Wind, which is technically a destructive filter but is covered along with the blur and noise filters in Chapter 15. I discussed Filter ➪ Render ➪ Texture Fill in Chapter 10. And finally, for complete information on the Custom, Displace, and Filter Factory filters, stay tuned for Chapter 17.

As for the other filters in the Filter ➪ Distort, Pixelate, Render, and Stylize submenus, stay tuned to this chapter to discover all the latest and greatest details.

Third-party filters

In addition to the filters provided by Photoshop, you can purchase all sorts of plug-in filters from other companies. In fact, Photoshop supports its own flourishing cottage industry of third-party solutions from wonderful companies like Extensis, Alien Skin, Andromeda, and others.

Cross-Reference

The CD-ROM at the back of this book includes sample versions of some of my favorite filters. For complete information on the specific filters and the companies that provide them, read Appendix C. Many of the filters are demo versions of the shipping products, which means that you can see what they do but you can't actually apply the effects or they only work for a limited period of time. I know, it's a drag, but these folks claim that they like to make money every once in a while, and I can't say that I blame them.

One final note about RAM

Memory — that is, real RAM — is a precious commodity when applying destructive filters. As I mentioned in Chapter 2, the scratch disk space typically allows you to edit larger images than your computer's RAM might permit. But all the filters in the Distort submenu and most of the commands in the Render submenu operate exclusively in memory. If they run out of physical RAM, they choke.

Tip

Fortunately, there is one potential workaround: When editing a color image, try applying the filter to each of the color channels independently. One color channel requires just a third to a fourth as much RAM as the full-color composite. Sadly, this technique does not help either Lighting Effects or Lens Flare. These delicate flowers of the filter world are compatible only with full-color images; when editing a single channel, they appear dimmed.

The Pixelate Filters

The new Filter ➪ Pixelate submenu features a handful of commands that rearrange your image into clumps of solid color:

✦ **Crystallize:** This filter organizes an image into irregularly shaped nuggets. You specify the size of the nuggets by entering a value from 3 to 300 pixels in the Cell Size option.

✦ **Facet:** Facet fuses areas of similarly colored pixels to create a sort of hand-painted effect.

✦ **Mosaic:** The Mosaic filter blends pixels together into larger squares. You specify the height and width of the squares by entering a value into the Cell Size option box.

✦ **Pointillize:** This filter is similar to Crystallize, except that it separates an image into disconnected nuggets set against the background color. As usual, you specify the size of the nuggets by changing the Cell Size value.

The Crystal Halo effect

By applying one of these filters to a feathered selection, you can create what I call a Crystal Halo effect, named after the Crystallize filter, which tends to deliver the most successful results. (For a preview of these effects, sneak a peek at Figure 16-2.) The following steps explain how to create a Crystal Halo, using the images in Figures 16-2 and 16-3 as examples.

Steps: Creating the Crystal Halo Effect

1. **Select the foreground element around which you want to create the halo.** Then choose Select ➪ Inverse to deselect the foreground element and select the background.

2. **Press Q to switch to the quick mask mode.**

3. **Choose Filter ➪ Other ➪ Minimum.** As I explained in Chapter 15, this filter allows you to increase the size of the deselected area around the foreground element. The size of the Radius value depends on the size of the halo you want to create. For my part, I wanted a 15-pixel halo. Unfortunately, the Radius option box in the Minimum dialog box can't accommodate a value larger than 10. So I entered 10 the first time. When Photoshop finished applying the filter, I pressed ⌘-Option-F to bring up the Minimum dialog box again, and entered 5.

4. **Choose Filter ➪ Blur ➪ Gaussian Blur.** Then enter a Radius value 0.1 less than the amount by which you increased the size of the deselected area. In my case, I entered 14.9. This will cut into the image slightly, but hardly enough to be visible, as you can see in the left image in Figure 16-2.

(continued)

Figure 16-2: Create a heavily feathered selection outline (left) and then apply the Crystallize filter to refract the feathered edges (right).

5. **Choose Filter ⇨ Pixelate ⇨ Crystallize.** Enter a moderate value into the Cell Size option box. I opted for the value 12, just slightly larger than the default value. After pressing Return, you get something along the lines of the selection outline shown in the right image in Figure 16-2. The filter refracts the softened edges, as if you were viewing them through textured glass.

6. **Switch back to the marching ants mode.** Then use the selection as desired. I merely pressed ⌘-Delete to fill the selection with white, as shown in the top left image in Figure 16-3.

You may find this technique particularly useful for combining images. You can copy the selection and paste it against a different background or copy a background from a different image and choose Edit ⇨ Paste Into to paste it inside the crystal halo's selection outline.

Figure 16-3 shows several variations on the Crystal Halo effect. To create the upper right image, I substituted Filter ⇨ Pixelate ⇨ Facet for Filter ⇨ Pixelate ⇨ Crystallize in Step 5. I also sharpened the result to increase the effect of the filter (which nevertheless remains subtle). To create the lower right image, I applied the Mosaic filter in place of Crystallize, using a Cell Size value of 8. Finally, to create the lower left image, I applied the Pointillize filter. Because Pointillize creates gaps in a selection, I had to paint inside Moses to fill in the gaps and isolate the halo effect to the background before returning to the marching ants mode.

Crystallize

Facet

Pointillize

Mosaic

Figure 16-3: Which aura will Moses don today? The images illustrate the effects of applying each of four filters to a heavily feathered selection in the quick mask mode and pressing ⌘-Delete.

Creating a mezzotint

A *mezzotint* is a special halftone pattern that replaces dots with a random pattern of swirling lines and worm holes. Photoshop's Mezzotint filter is an attempt to emulate this effect. Although not entirely successful — true mezzotinting options can only be properly implemented as PostScript printing functions, not as filtering functions — it does lend itself to some pretty interesting interpretations.

The filter itself is straightforward. You choose Filter ➪ Pixelate ➪ Mezzotint, select an effect from the Type submenu, and press the Return key. A preview box allows you to see what each of the ten Type options looks like. Figure 16-4 shows off four of the effects at 230 ppi.

To create Figure 16-5, I applied the Mezzotint filter set to the Long Lines effect. Then I used the Filter ➪ Fade Mezzotint command to mix filtered and original images. I selected Overlay from the Mode pop-up menu and set the Opacity value to 40 percent. The result is a scraped image. (I've decreased the resolution of the image to 180 ppi so that you can see the effect a little more clearly.)

When applied to grayscale artwork, the Mezzotint filter always results in a black-and-white image. When applied to a color image, the filter automatically applies the selected effect independently to each of the color channels. Though all pixels in each channel are changed to either black or white, you can see a total of eight colors — black, red, green, blue, yellow, cyan, magenta, and white — in the RGB composite view. The upper left example of Color Plate 16-3 shows an image subject to the Mezzotint filter in the RGB mode.

If the Mezzotint filter affects each channel independently, then it follows that the color mode in which you work directly, and dramatically, affects the performance of the filter. For example, if you apply Mezzotint in the Lab mode, you again whittle the colors down to eight, but a very different eight — black, cyan, magenta, green, red, two muddy blues and a muddy rose — as shown in the top middle example of Color Plate 16-3. If you're looking for bright happy colors, don't apply Mezzotint in the Lab mode.

In CMYK, the filter produces roughly the same eight colors that you get in RGB — white, cyan, magenta, yellow, violet-blue, red, deep green, and black. However, as shown in the top right example of the color plate, the distribution of the colors is much different. The image appears much lighter and more colorful than its RGB counterpart. This happens because the filter has a lot of black to work with in the RGB mode but very little — just that in the black channel — in the CMYK mode.

Medium dots

Coarse dots

Short lines

Long strokes

Figure 16-4: The results of applying the Mezzotint filter set to each of four representative effects. These line patterns are on par with the halftoning options offered when you select Mode ⇨ Bitmap, as discussed back in Chapter 5.

The bottom row of Color Plate 16-3 shows the effects of the Mezzotint filter after using the Fade command to mix it with the original image. As in Figure 16-4, I chose Overlay from the Mode pop-up menu and set the Opacity value to 40 percent. These three very different images were all created using the same filter set to the same effect. Absolutely the only difference is color mode.

Figure 16-5: To get this effect, I chose Filter ➪ Fade after applying the Mezzotint filter. Then I selected the Overlay mode and set the Opacity value to 40 percent.

Edge-Enhancement Filters

The Filter ➪ Stylize submenu offers access to a triad of filters that enhance the edges in an image. The most popular of these is undoubtedly Emboss, which adds dimension to an image by making it look as if it were carved in relief. The other two, Find Edges and Trace Contour, are less commonly applied, but every bit as capable and deserving of your attention.

Embossing an image

The Emboss filter works by searching for high-contrast edges (just like the Sharpen Edge and High Pass filters), highlighting the edges with black or white pixels, and then coloring the low-contrast portions with medium gray. When you choose Filter ➪ Stylize ➪ Emboss, Photoshop displays the Emboss dialog box shown in Figure 16-6. The dialog box offers three options:

> ✦ **Angle:** The value in this option box determines the angle at which Photoshop lights the image in relief. For example, if you enter a value of 90 degrees, you light the relief from the bottom straight upward. The white pixels therefore appear on the bottom sides of the edges, and the black pixels appear on the top sides. Figure 16-7 shows eight reliefs lit from different angles. I positioned the images so that they appear lit from a single source.

Figure 16-6: The Emboss dialog box lets you control the depth of the filtered image and the angle from which it is lit.

✦ **Height:** The Emboss filter accomplishes its highlighting effect by displacing one copy of an image relative to another. You specify the distance between the copies using the Height option, which can vary from 1 to 10 pixels. Lower values produce crisp effects, as demonstrated in Figure 16-8. Values above 3 goop up things pretty good unless you also enter a high Amount value. Together, the Height and Amount values determine the depth of the image in relief.

Tip

The Height value is analogous to the Radius value in the Unsharp Mask dialog box. You should therefore set the value according to the resolution of your image — 1 for 150 ppi, 2 for 300 ppi, and so on.

✦ **Amount:** Enter a value between 1 and 500 percent to determine the amount of black and white assigned to pixels along the edges. Values of 50 percent and lower produce almost entirely gray images, as you can see in the top row of Figure 16-8. Higher values produce sharper edges, as if the relief were carved more deeply.

As a stand-alone effect, Emboss is only okey-dokey. It's one of those filters that makes you gasp with delight the first time you see it but never quite lends itself to any practical application after you become acquainted with Photoshop. But if you think of Emboss as an extension of the High Pass filter, it takes on new meaning. You can use it to edit selection outlines in the quick mask mode, just as you might use the High Pass filter. You also can use it to draw out detail in an image.

Figure 16-7: Reliefs lighted from eight different angles, in 45-degree increments. In all cases, the central sun image indicates the location of the light source. Height and Amount values of 1 pixel and 250 percent were used for all images.

Figure 16-9 shows the result of using the Fade command immediately after applying the Emboss filter. First, I applied the Emboss filter at an Angle of 135 degrees, a Height of 2 pixels, and an Amount of 250 percent. Then I pressed ⌘-Shift-F to display the Fade dialog box. To create the left example, I selected Darken from the Mode pop-up menu. This added shadows to the edges of the image, thus boosting the texture without unduly upsetting the original brightness values. I selected the Lighten blend mode to create the right example. In both cases, I set the Opacity value to 70 percent.

Figure 16-8: Examples of different Height settings (first value) and Amount settings (second value). The Angle value used for each image was 135 degrees.

Tip

To create a color relief effect, apply the Emboss filter and then select the Luminosity option in the Fade dialog box. This retains the colors from the original image while applying the lightness and darkness of the pixels from the filtered selection. The effect looks something like an inked lithographic plate, with steel grays and vivid colors mixing together. An example of this effect at 80 percent Opacity appears in the first example of Color Plate 16-4.

Figure 16-9: After applying the Emboss filter, I used my old friend the Fade command to darken (left) and lighten (right) the image.

The second example in that same color plate shows a more impressive — if less practical — technique. Rather than applying Luminosity, I chose the Difference mode inside the Fade dialog box. With its hard edges and vivid colors, this image looks like some impossible frame from an educational film on genetic engineering. I can just hear the narrator commenting, "Prom dates have changed dramatically since scientists discovered how to splice the red rose with the poppy."

Tracing around edges

Photoshop provides three filters that trace around pixels in your image and accentuate the edges, all located in the Filter ➪ Stylize submenu:

✦ **Find Edges:** This filter detects edges similarly to High Pass. Low-contrast areas become white, medium-contrast edges become gray, and high-contrast edges become black, as in the labeled image in Figure 16-10. Hard edges become thin lines; soft edges become fat ones. The result is a thick, organic outline that you can overlay onto an image to give it a waxy appearance. To achieve the bottom left effect in the figure, I chose the Fade ➪ Find Edges command and applied the Overlay mode and an 80 percent Opacity setting. She'll never get her hand off that canning jar as long as she lives.

✦ **Glowing Edges:** This Gallery Effects filter is a variation on Find Edges with two important differences: Glowing Edges produces an inverted effect, changing low-contrast areas to black and edges to white, as in the labeled image in Figure 16-10. It also displays a dialog box that lets you adjust the width, brightness, and smoothness of the traced edges. Glowing Edges is a great backup command. If you aren't satisfied with the effect produced by the Find Edges filter, choose the Glowing Edges command instead and adjust the options as desired. If you want black lines against a white background, press ⌘-I to invert the effect.

✦ **Trace Contour:** Illustrated on the right side of Figure 16-10, Trace Contour is a little more involved than the others and slightly less interesting. The filter traces a series of single-pixel lines along the border between light and dark pixels. Choosing the filter displays a dialog box containing three options: Level, Upper, and Lower. The Level value indicates the lightness value above which pixels are considered to be light and below which they are dark. For example, if you enter 128 — medium gray, as by default — Trace Contour draws a line at every spot where an area of color lighter than medium gray meets an area of color darker than medium gray. The Upper and Lower options tell the filter where to position the line — inside the lighter color's territory (Upper) or inside the space occupied by the darker color (Lower).

| Find Edges | Glowing Edges | Trace Contour |

| Overlay, 80% | Overlay, 60% | Multiply, 100% |

Figure 16-10: The top row of images demonstrates the effect of the three edge-tracing commands available from the Filter ⇨ Stylize submenu. After applying each command, I used the Fade command to apply the blend modes and Opacity values demonstrated in the bottom row.

Like Mezzotint, Trace Contour applies itself to each color channel independently and renders each channel as a 1-bit image. A collection of black lines surrounds the areas of color in each channel; the RGB, Lab, or CMYK composite view shows these lines in the colors associated with the channels. When you work in RGB, a cyan line indicates a black line in the red channel (no red plus full intensity green and blue becomes cyan). A yellow line indicates a black line in the blue channel, and so on. You get a single black line when working in the grayscale mode.

Creating a metallic coating

The edge-tracing filters are especially fun to use in combination with Filter ⇨ Fade. I first got interested in playing with these filters after trying out the Chrome filter included with the first Gallery Effects collection. Now included with Photoshop as Filter ⇨ Sketch ⇨ Chrome, this filter turns an image into a melted pile of metallic goo. No matter how you apply Chrome, it completely wipes out your image and leaves a ton of jagged color transitions in its wake. It's really only useful with color images, and then only if you follow up with the Fade command and the Luminosity mode. Even then, I've never been particularly satisfied with the results.

But it got me thinking: How can you create a metallic coating, with gleaming highlights and crisp shadows, without resorting to Chrome? Find Edges offers a way. First, copy your image to a separate layer (⌘-J). Then apply the Gaussian Blur filter. A Radius value between 1.0 and 4.0 produces the best results, depending on how gooey you want the edges to be. Next, apply the Find Edges filter. Because the edges are blurry, the resulting image is light; so I recommend you darken it using Image ⇨ Adjust ⇨ Levels (raise the first Input Levels value to 100 or so, as explained in Chapter 18). The blurry edges appear in the top left example in Figure 16-11.

To produce the bottom left image, I mixed the layer with the underlying original using the Overlay blend mode (Shift-Option-O) and an Opacity of 80 percent. The result is a shiny effect that produces a metallic finish without altogether destroying the detail in the image.

If you decide you like this effect, there's more where that came from. The second and third columns of Figure 16-11 show the results of applying Filter ⇨ Sketch ⇨ Bas Relief and Filter ⇨ Artistic ⇨ Plastic Wrap. After applying each filter, I chose Filter ⇨ Fade, selected the Overlay mode, and set the Opacity value to 80 percent, repeating the effect I applied to the Gaussian Blur and Find Edges layer.

Color Plate 16-5 shows the same effects in color. Starting with an unedited construction worker, I went through the usual calisthenics of selecting and layering the image. Next, I applied Gaussian Blur (3.0 Radius) and Find Edges. The effect was too light, so I chose Image ⇨ Adjust ⇨ Levels and entered 128 into the first option box. Everything darker than medium gray went to black, uniformly strengthening the effect. The result is the full-color metallic coating shown in the second example in the top row of the color plate. To get the top right image, I merely selected Overlay from the pop-up menu in the Layers palette (Shift-Option-O) and changed the Opacity value to 80 percent.

Blur & Find Edges   Bas Relief   Plastic Wrap

Overlay, 80%

Figure 16-11: After applying Gaussian Blur and Find Edges to a layered version of the image (top left), I composited the filtered image with the original using the Overlay mode (bottom left). The second and third columns show similar effects achieved using the effects filters Bas Relief and Plastic Wrap.

In the bottom row of Color Plate 16-5, I really went nuts. In each case, I applied one of three effects filters — Bas Relief, Plastic Wrap, and the infamous Filter ➪ Sketch ➪ Chrome. And each time, I chose Filter ➪ Fade, selected the Luminosity mode, and reduced the Opacity value to 80 percent.

Okay, okay, so Chrome still looks more metallic than the other effects, but it also plays havoc with the detail. I'm willing to settle for a more subtle effect if it means I can still recognize my subject when I'm finished.

Distortion Filters

For the most part, commands in the Distort submenu are related by the fact that they move colors in an image to achieve unusual stretching, swirling, and vibrating effects. They're rather like the transformation commands from the Layer menu in that they perform their magic by relocating and interpolating colors rather than by altering brightness and color values.

The distinction, of course, is that while the transformation commands let you scale and distort images by manipulating four control points, the Distort filters provide the equivalent of hundreds of control points, all of which you can use to affect different portions of an image. In some cases, you're projecting an image into a funhouse mirror; other times, it's a reflective pool. You can fan images, wiggle them, and change them in ways that have no correlation to real life, as illustrated in Figure 16-12.

Figure 16-12: This is your image (left); this is your image on distortion filters (right). Three filters, in fact: Spherize, Ripple, and Polar Coordinates.

Distortion filters are very powerful tools. Although they are easy to apply, they are extremely difficult to use well. Here are some rules to keep in mind:

✦ **Practice makes practical:** Distortion filters are like complex vocabulary words. You don't want to use them without practicing a little first. Experiment with a distortion filter several times before trying to use it in a real project. You may even want to write down the steps you take so that you can remember how you created an effect.

✦ **Use caution during tight deadlines:** Distortion filters are enormous time-wasters. Unless you know exactly how you want to proceed, you may want to avoid using them when time is short. The last thing you need when you're working under the gun is to get trapped trying to pull off a weird effect.

✦ **Apply selectively:** The effects of distortion filters are too severe to inflict all at once. You can achieve marvelous, subtle effects by distorting feathered and layered selections. Although I wouldn't call the image in Figure 16-12 subtle, no single effect was applied to the entire image. I applied the Spherize filter to a feathered elliptical marquee that included most of the image. I then reapplied Spherize to the eye. I selected the hair and beard and applied the Ripple filter twice. Finally, after establishing two heavily feathered vertical columns on either side of the image in the quick mask mode, I applied the Polar Coordinates filter, which reflected the front and back of the head. Turn the book upside down and you'll see a second face.

✦ **Combine creatively:** Don't expect a single distortion to achieve the desired effect. If one application isn't enough, apply the filter again. Experiment with combining different distortions.

Distortion filters interpolate between pixels to create their fantastic effects. This means that the quality of your filtered images is dependent on the setting of the Interpolation option in the General Preferences dialog box. If a filter produces jagged effects, the Nearest Neighbor option is probably selected. Try selecting the Bicubic or Bilinear option instead.

Reflecting an image in a spoon

Most folks take their first ventures into distortion filters by using Pinch and Spherize. Pinch maps an image onto the inside of a sphere or similarly curved surface; Spherize maps it onto the outside of a sphere. It's sort of like looking at your reflection on the inside or outside of a spoon.

You can apply Pinch to a scanned face to squish the features toward the center or apply Spherize to accentuate the girth of the nose. Figure 16-13 illustrates both effects. It's a laugh, and you pretty much feel as though you're onto something that no one else ever thought of before. (At least that's how I felt—but I'm easily amazed.)

Figure 16-13: Constantine does the popular throbbing facial dance — well, it was popular back in 300 AD — thanks to the Pinch (left) and Spherize (right) filters.

You can pinch or spherize an image using either the Pinch or Spherize command. As shown in Figure 16-14, a positive value in the Pinch dialog box produces a similar effect to a negative value in the Spherize dialog box. There is a slight difference between the spatial curvature of the 3-D calculations: Pinch pokes the image inward or outward using a rounded cone — we're talking bell-shaped, much like a Gaussian model. Spherize wraps the image on the outside or inside of a true sphere. As a result, the two filters yield subtly different results. Pinch produces a soft transition around the perimeter of a selection; Spherize produces an abrupt transition. If this doesn't quite make sense to you, just play with one, try out the same effect with the other, and see which you like better.

Another difference between the two filters is that Spherize provides the additional options of allowing you to wrap an image onto the inside or outside of a horizontal or vertical cylinder. To try out these effects, select the Horizontal Only or Vertical Only options from the Mode pop-up menu at the bottom of the Spherize dialog box.

Tip

Both the Pinch and Spherize filters are applicable only to elliptical regions of an image. If a selection outline is not elliptical in shape, Photoshop applies the filter to the largest ellipse that fits inside the selection. As a result, the filter may leave behind a noticeable elliptical boundary between the affected and unaffected portions of the selection. To avoid this effect, select the region you want to edit with the elliptical marquee tool and then feather the selection before filtering it. This softens the effect of the filter and provides a more gradual transition (even more so than Pinch already affords).

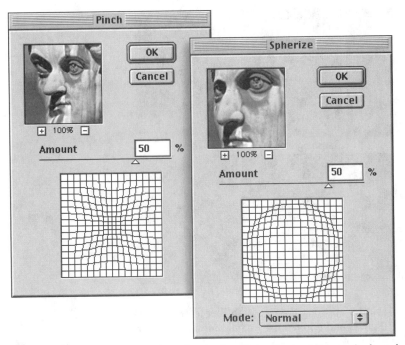

Figure 16-14: Both the Pinch and Spherize dialog boxes let you pinch and spherize images. Pinch wraps an image on a rounded cone; Spherize wraps onto a sphere.

One of the more remarkable properties of the Pinch filter is that it lets you turn any image into a conical gradation. Figure 16-15 illustrates how the process works. First, blur the image to eliminate any harsh edges between color transitions. Then apply the Pinch filter at full strength (100 percent). Reapply the filter several more times. Each time you press ⌘-F, the center portion of the image recedes farther and farther into the distance, as shown in Figure 16-15. After 10 repetitions, the face in the example all but disappeared.

Next, apply the Radial Blur filter set to Spin 10 pixels or so to mix the color boundaries a bit. The result is a type of gradation that you can't create using Photoshop's gradient tool.

Original   Gaussian blur, 5.0   Pinch, 100%

Pinch x 3   Pinch x 5   Pinch x 10, Radial Blur

Figure 16-15: After applying the Gaussian Blur filter, I pinched the image 10 times and applied the Radial Blur filter to create a conical gradation.

Twirling spirals

The Twirl filter rotates the center of a selection while leaving the sides fixed in place. The result is a spiral of colors that looks for all the world as if you poured the image into a blender set to a very slow speed.

When you choose Filter ⇨ Distort ⇨ Twirl, Photoshop displays the Twirl dialog box, shown in Figure 16-16. Enter a positive value from 1 to 999 degrees to spiral the image in a clockwise direction. Enter a negative value to spiral the image in a counterclockwise direction. As you are probably already aware, 360 degrees make a full circle, so the maximum 999-degree value equates to a spiral that circles around approximately three times, as shown in the bottom right example in Figure 16-17.

Tip

The Twirl filter produces smoother effects when you use lower Angle values. Therefore, you're better off applying a 100-degree spiral 10 times rather than applying a 999-degree spiral once, as verified by Figure 16-17.

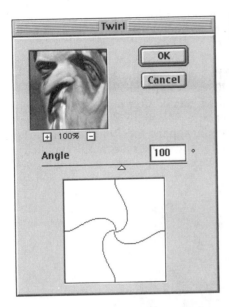

Figure 16-16: The Twirl dialog box lets you create spiraling images.

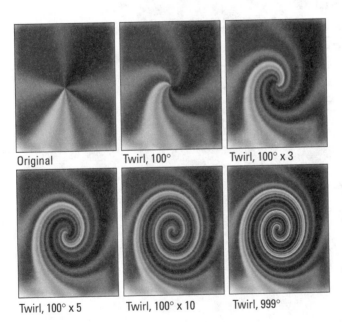

Original   Twirl, 100°   Twirl, 100° x 3

Twirl, 100° x 5   Twirl, 100° x 10   Twirl, 999°

Figure 16-17: The effects of applying the Twirl filter. Repeatedly applying the Twirl filter at a moderate value (bottom middle) produces a smoother effect than applying the filter once at a high value (bottom right).

In addition to creating ice-cream swirls like those shown in Figure 16-17, you can use the Twirl filter to create organic images virtually from scratch, as witnessed by Figures 16-18 and 16-19.

To create the images shown in Figure 16-18, I used the Spherize filter to flex the conical gradation vertically by entering 100 percent in the Amount option box and selecting Vertical Only from the Mode pop-up menu. After repeating this filter several times, I eventually achieved a stalactite-stalagmite effect, as shown in the center example of the figure. I then repeatedly applied the Twirl filter to curl the flexed gradations like two symmetrical hairs. The result merges the simplicity of pure math with the beauty of bitmapped imagery.

Original   Spherize, 100%, Vertical   Spherize x 3

Spherize x 5   Spherize x 7   Twirl, 100°

Twirl x 3   Twirl x 5   Twirl x 10

Figure 16-18: You can create surprisingly naturalistic effects using distortion filters exclusively.

Figure 16-19 illustrates a droplet technique designed by Mark Collen. I took the liberty of breaking down the technique into the following steps.

Steps: Creating a Thick-Liquid Droplet

1. **Press the D key.** As it has so many times in the past, the D key again restores the default foreground and background colors.

2. **Select a square portion of an image.** Drag with the rectangular marquee tool while pressing the Shift key.

3. **Drag inside the selection outline with the linear gradient tool.** Drag a short distance near the center of the selection from upper left to lower right, creating the gradation shown in the top-left box in Figure 16-19.

Figure 16-19: Though they appear as if they might be the result of the ZigZag filter, these images were created entirely by using the gradient tool, the Twirl filter, and a couple of transformations.

4. **Choose the Twirl filter and apply it at –360 degrees so that the spiral moves counterclockwise.** To create the top right image in the figure, I applied the Twirl filter three times. Each repetition of the filter adds another ring of ripples.

5. **Press ⌘-J to copy the selection to a layer.**

6. **Choose Edit ➪ Transform ➪ Flip Horizontal.**

(continued)

7. **Lower the Opacity value to 50 percent.** Select the rectangular marquee tool, then press the 5 key. The result appears in the lower left example in Figure 16-19.

8. **Choose Edit ⇨ Transform ⇨ Rotate 90° CW.** This rotates the layer a quarter turn, thus creating the last image in the figure. You can achieve other interesting effects by choosing Lighten, Darken, and others from the brush modes pop-up menu.

Now, if a few twirls and transformations can produce an effect this entertaining in black and white, just imagine what you can do in color. On second thought, don't imagine; check out Color Plate 16-6 instead. The first row in this eight-part color plate is nothing more than a color version of Figure 16-19, intended merely to set the scene. As you can see, I've created a gradation using two complementary colors, blue and yellow. In the fifth example (lower left), I apply the Difference blend mode to the layer (Shift-Option-E) and return the Opacity setting to 100 percent. Next, I clone that layer and rotate it another 90 degrees clockwise to produce the sixth example. The Difference blend mode remains in effect for this cloned layer as well. Not satisfied, I clone that layer, rotate it another 90 degrees, and flip it horizontally. The result, also subject to Difference, is the seventh example. Then for the *coup de grâce*, I randomly apply the Twirl, Spherize, and ZigZag filters to the layers to mutate the concentric rings into something a little more interesting.

If that went a little fast for you, not to worry. More important than the specific effect is this general category of "distortion drawings." A filter such as Pinch or Twirl enables you to create wild imagery without ever drawing a brushstroke or scanning a photograph. If you can do this much with a simple two-color gradation, just think of what you can do if you throw in a few more colors. Pixels are little more than fodder for these very powerful functions.

Creating concentric pond ripples

I don't know about you, but when I think of zigzags, I think of cartoon lightning bolts, wriggling snakes, scribbles — anything that alternately changes directions along an axis, like the letter *Z*. The ZigZag filter does arrange colors into zigzag patterns, but it does so in a radial fashion, meaning that the zigzags emanate from the center of the image like spokes in a wheel. The result is a series of concentric ripples. If you want parallel zigzags, check out the Ripple and Wave filters, described in the next section. (The ZigZag filter creates ripples and the Ripple filter creates zigzags. Go figure.)

When you choose Filter ⇨ Distort ⇨ ZigZag, Photoshop displays the ZigZag dialog box shown in Figure 16-20. The dialog box offers the following options:

✦ **Amount:** Enter an amount between negative and positive 100 in whole-number increments to specify the depth of the ripples. If you enter a negative value, the ripples descend below the surface. If you enter a positive value, the ripples protrude upward. Examples of three representative Amount values appear in Figure 16-21.

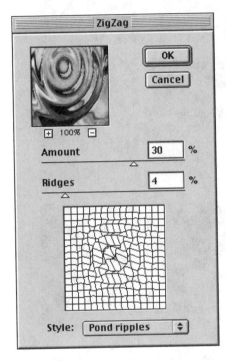

Figure 16-20: The ZigZag dialog box lets you add concentric ripples to an image, as if the image were reflected in a pond into which you dropped a pebble.

✦ **Ridges:** This option box controls the number of ripples in the selected area and accepts any value from 1 to 20. Figure 16-22 demonstrates the effect of three Ridges values.

✦ **Pond Ripples:** This option is really a cross between the two that follow. It moves pixels outward and rotates them around the center of the selection to create circular patterns. As demonstrated in the top rows of Figures 16-21 and 16-22, this option truly results in a pond ripple effect.

✦ **Out From Center:** When you select this option, Photoshop moves pixels outward in rhythmic bursts according to the value in the Ridges option box. Because the gradation image I created in Figure 16-14 was already arranged in a radial pattern, I brought in Moses to demonstrate the effect of the Out From Center option, as shown in the second rows of Figures 16-21 and 16-22.

Pond Ripples

Amount = 10   50   100

Out From Center

10   50   100

Around Center

10   50   100

Figure 16-21: The effects of the ZigZag filter subject to three Amount values and the Pond Ripples, Out From Center, and Around Center settings. In all cases, the Ridges value was 5.

✦ **Around Center:** Select this option to rotate pixels in alternating directions around the circle without moving them outward. This is the only option that produces what I would term a zigzag effect. The last rows of Figures 16-21 and 16-22 show the effects of the Around Center option.

Figure 16-22: The effects of the ZigZag filter using three Ridges values and each of the three Style pop-up menu settings. In all cases, the Amount value was 20.

Creating parallel ripples and waves

Photoshop provides four means to distort an image in parallel waves, as if the image were lying on the bottom of a shimmering or undulating pool. Of the four, the ripple filters — which include Ripple, Ocean Ripple, and Glass — are only moderately sophisticated, but they're also relatively easy to apply. The fourth filter, Wave, affords you greater control, but its options are among the most complex Photoshop has to offer.

The Ripple filter

To use the Ripple filter, choose Filter ⇨ Distort ⇨ Ripple. Photoshop displays the Ripple dialog box shown in Figure 16-23. You have the following options:

✦ **Amount:** Enter an amount between negative and positive 999 in whole-number increments to specify the width of the ripples from side to side. Negative and positive values change the direction of the ripples, but visually speaking, they produce identical effects. The ripples are measured as a ratio of the Size value and the dimensions of the selection — all of which translates to, "Experiment and see what happens." You can count on getting ragged effects from any value over 300, as illustrated in Figure 16-24.

Figure 16-23: The Ripple filter makes an image appear as if it were refracted through flowing water.

✦ **Size:** Select one of the three options in the Size drop-down menu to change the length of the ripples. The Small option results in the shortest ripples and therefore the most ripples. As shown in the upper right corner of Figure 16-24, you can create a textured glass effect by combining the Small option with a high Amount value. The Large option results in the longest and fewest ripples.

Tip

You can create a blistered effect by overlaying a negative ripple onto a positive ripple. Try this: First, copy the selection. Then apply the Ripple filter with a positive Amount value — say, 300. Next, paste the copied selection and apply the Ripple filter at the exact opposite Amount value, in this case, −300. Press 5 to change the Opacity value to 50 percent. The result is a series of diametrically opposed ripples that cross each other to create teardrop blisters.

Small, 100   300   999

Medium, 100   300   999

Large, 100   300   999

Figure 16-24: The effects of combining three different Ripple filter Amount values with three different Size settings.

Ocean Ripple and Glass

The Ocean Ripple and Glass filters are gifts from Gallery Effects. Both filters emulate the effect of looking at an image through textured glass. These two distorters so closely resemble each other that they would be better merged into one. But where the effects filters are concerned, interface design is as fickle and transitory as the face on the cover of *Tiger Beat* magazine.

The Ocean Ripple and Glass dialog boxes appear joined at the hip in Figure 16-25. While the names and effects of the specific slider bars vary, the only real difference between the two filters is that Ocean Blur subscribes to a fixed ripple texture, and Glass lets you switch out the texture by selecting from a pop-up menu.

Figure 16-25: The Ocean Ripple and Glass effects filters are two birds of a feather, ultimately born from the same yolk.

To guide you in your experimentations, Figure 16-26 shows the Pinch gradation subject to several Ocean Blur settings. The first number represents the Ripple Size value (listed first in the dialog box); the second number in the figure represents the Ripple Magnitude value. As you can see, you can vary the Size value with impunity. But raise the Magnitude value, and you're looking through sculpted glass.

3, 5   8, 5   15, 5

3, 20   8, 20   15, 20

Figure 16-26: Raising the Ripple Size value (first number in each pair) spreads out the effect, while raising the Ripple Magnitude (second number) adds more depth and contrast to the ripples.

The Wave filter

Now that you've met the ripple family, it's time to ride the Wave. I've come to love this filter — I use it all the time — but it's complex enough to warrant its own book. It wouldn't be a very big book and nobody would buy it, but you never know what a freelancer like me will do next. Keep an eye out for *Macworld Wave Filter Bible* at your local bookstore.

In the meantime, choose Filter ⇨ Distort ⇨ Wave (that's the easy part) to display the Wave dialog box shown in Figure 16-27. Photoshop presents you with the following options, which make applying a distortion every bit as easy as operating an oscilloscope:

✦ **Number of Generators:** Right off the bat, the Wave dialog box boggles the brain. A friend of mine likened this option to the number of rocks you throw in the water to start it rippling. One generator means that you throw in one rock to create one set of waves, as demonstrated in Figure 16-28. You can throw in two rocks to create two sets of waves (see Figure 16-29), three rocks to create three sets of waves, and all the way up to a quarryfull of 999 rocks to create, well, you get the idea. If you enter a high value, however, be prepared to wait a few years for the preview to update. If you can't wait, press the Escape key, which turns off the preview until the next time you enter the dialog box.

Figure 16-27: The Wave dialog box lets you wreak scientific havoc on an image. Put on your pocket protector, take out your slide rule, and give it a whirl.

✦ **Wavelength and Amplitude:** Beginning to feel like you're playing with a HAM radio? The Wave filter produces random results by varying the number and length of waves (Wavelength) as well as the height of the waves (Amplitude) between minimum and maximum values, which can range anywhere from 1 to 999. (The Wavelength and Amplitude options, therefore, correspond in theory to the Size and Amount options in the Ripple dialog box.) Figures 16-28 and 16-29 show examples of representative Wavelength and Amplitude values.

Figure 16-28: The effects of three sets of Maximum Wavelength (first value) and Amplitude (second value) settings when combined with each of the three Type settings. The Number of Generators value was 1 in all cases.

✦ **Scale:** You can scale the effects of the Wave filter between 1 and 100 percent horizontally and vertically. All the effects featured in Figures 16-28 and 16-29 were created by setting both Scale options to 15 percent.

✦ **Undefined Areas:** The Wave filter distorts a selection to the extent that gaps may appear around the edges. You can either fill those gaps by repeating pixels along the edge of the selection, as in the figures, or by wrapping pixels from the left side of the selection onto the right side and pixels from the top edge of the selection onto the bottom.

Sine

20, 50   50, 100   100, 200

Triangle

20, 50   50, 100   100, 200

Square

20, 50   50, 100   100, 200

Figure 16-29: The only difference between these images and their counterparts in Figure 16-28 is that the Number of Generators value used for all images was 2.

✦ **Type:** You can select from three kinds of waves. The Sine option produces standard sine waves that rise and fall smoothly in bell-shaped curves, just like real waves. The Triangle option creates zigzags that rise and fall in straight lines, like the edge of a piece of fabric cut with pinking shears. The Square option has nothing to do with waves at all, but rather organizes an image into a series of rectangular groupings, reminiscent of Cubism. You might think of this option as an extension of the Mosaic filter. Figures 16-28 and 16-29 demonstrate all three options.

✦ **Randomize:** The Wave filter is random by nature. If you don't like the effect you see in the preview box, click on the Randomize button to stir things up a bit. You can keep clicking on the button until you get an effect you like.

Distorting an image along a curve

The Distort command, which isn't discussed elsewhere in this book, creates four corner handles around an image. You drag each corner handle to distort the selected image in that direction. Unfortunately, you can't add other points around the edges to create additional distortions, which can be very frustrating if you're trying to achieve a specific effect. If you can't achieve a certain kind of distortion using Edit ⇨ Free Transform, the Shear filter may be your answer.

Shear distorts an image along a path. When you choose Filter ⇨ Distort ⇨ Shear, you get the dialog box shown in Figure 16-30. Initially, a single line that has two points at either end appears in the grid at the top of the box. When you drag the points, you slant the image in the preview. This plus the fact that the filter is named Shear — Adobe's strange term for skewing (it appears in Illustrator as well) — leads many users to dismiss the filter as nothing more than a slanting tool. But in truth, it's more versatile than that.

Figure 16-30: Click on the grid line in the left corner of the Shear dialog box to add points to the line. Drag these points to distort the image along the curve.

You can add points to the grid line simply by clicking on it. A point springs up every time you click on an empty space in the line. Drag the point to change the curvature of the line and distort the image along the new curve. To delete a point, drag it off the left or right side of the grid. To delete all points and return the line to its original vertical orientation, click on the Defaults button.

The Undefined Areas options work just as they do in the Wave dialog box (described in the preceding section). You can either fill the gaps on one side of the image with pixels shoved off the opposite side by selecting Wrap Around; or you can repeat pixels along the edge of the selection by selecting Repeat Edge Pixels.

Changing to polar coordinates

The Polar Coordinates filter is another one of those gems that a lot of folks shy away from because it doesn't make much sense at first glance. When you choose Filter ➪ Distort ➪ Polar Coordinates, Photoshop presents two radio buttons, as shown in Figure 16-31. You can either map an image from rectangular to polar coordinates or from polar to rectangular coordinates.

Figure 16-31: In effect, the Polar Coordinates dialog box lets you map an image onto a globe and view the globe from above.

All right, time for some global theory. The first image in Figure 16-32 shows a stretched detail of the world map from the Digital Stock library. This map falls under the heading of a *Mercator projection*, meaning that Greenland is all stretched out of proportion, looking as big as the United States and Mexico combined.

Figure 16-32: The world from the equator up, expressed in rectangular (left) and polar (right) coordinates.

The reason for this has to do with the way different mapping systems handle longitude and latitude lines. On a spherical globe, lines of latitude converge at the poles. On a Mercator map, they run absolutely parallel. Because the Mercator map exaggerates the distance between longitude lines as you progress away from the equator, it likewise exaggerates the distance between lines of latitude. The result is a map that becomes infinitely enormous at each of the poles.

When you convert the map to polar coordinates (by selecting the Rectangular to Polar radio button in the Polar Coordinates dialog box), you look down on it from the extreme north or south pole. This means that the entire length of the top edge of the Mercator map becomes a single dot in the exact center of the polar projection. The length of the bottom edge of the map wraps around the entire perimeter of the circle. The second example in Figure 16-32 shows the result. As you can see, the Rectangular to Polar option is just the thing for wrapping text around a circle.

If you select the Polar to Rectangular option, the Polar Coordinates filter produces the opposite effect. Imagine for a moment that the conical gradation shown in the upper left corner of Figure 16-33 is a fan spread out into a full circle. Now imagine closing the fan, breaking the hinge at the top, and spreading out the rectangular fabric of the fan. The center of the fan unfolds to form the top edge of the fabric, and what was once the perimeter of the circle is now the bottom edge of the fabric. Figure 16-33 shows two examples of what happens when you convert circular images from polar to rectangular coordinates.

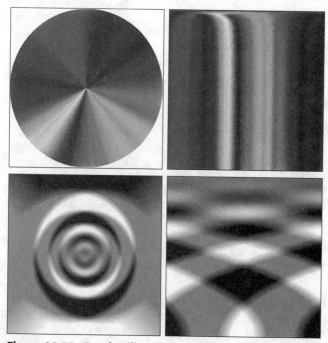

Figure 16-33: Two familiar circular images (left) converted from polar to rectangular coordinates (right). The top example is simple enough that you can probably predict the results of

the conversion in your head. The lower example looks cool, but you'd need a brain extension to predict the outcome.

Tip

The Polar Coordinates filter is a great way to edit gradations. After drawing a linear gradation with the gradient tool (as discussed in Chapter 9), try applying Filter ⇨ Distort ⇨ Polar Coordinates with the Polar to Rectangular option selected. (Rectangular to Polar just turns it into a radial gradation, sometimes with pretty undesirable results.) You get a redrawn gradation with highlights at the bottom of the selection. Press ⌘-F to reapply the filter to achieve another effect. You can keep repeating this technique until jagged edges start to appear. Then press ⌘-Z to go back to the last smooth effect.

Distorting an image inside out

The following exercise describes how to achieve a sizzling Parting-of-the-Red-Sea effect. Though it incorporates several distortion filters, the star of the effect is the Polar Coordinates filter, which is used to turn the image inside out and then convert it back to polar coordinates after flipping it upside down. No scanned image or artistic talent is required. Rumor has it that Moses puts in a guest appearance in the final image.

This effect is the brainchild of Mark Collen, easily the most imaginative distortion expert I've had the pleasure of knowing. I already mentioned his name in this chapter, in connection with the "Creating a Thick-Liquid Droplet" steps. To be perfectly honest, I probably should have mentioned him more than that, because many of the ideas conveyed in this chapter were based on long, expensive telephone conversations with the guy.

At any rate, Figures 16-34 through 16-39 show the progression of the image through the following steps, starting with a simplistic throwback to Dada (the art movement, not the family member) and continuing to the fabled sea rising in billowing streams. Color Plate 16-7 shows one of Mark's most vivid images, which was created in part using many of the techniques from the steps below. Obviously, Mark used a couple of other filtering and nonfiltering techniques to create his image, but gee whiz folks, you can't expect the guy to share everything he knows in one fell swoop. He has to make a living, after all.

Steps: The Parting-of-the-Red-Sea Effect

1. **Draw some random shapes in whatever colors you like.** My shapes appear against a black background in Figure 16-34, but you can use any shapes and colors you like. To create each shape, I used the lasso tool to draw the outline of the shape and pressed Option-Delete to fill the lassoed selection with the foreground color. The effect works best if there's a lot of contrast between your colors.

Figure 16-34: Draw several meaningless shapes with the lasso tool and fill each with a different color.

2. **Choose Image ⇨ Rotate Canvas ⇨ 90° CCW.** In Step 3, you apply the Wind Filter to add streaks to the shapes you just created, as shown in Figure 16-35. Because the Wind filter creates horizontal streaks only, and your goal is to add vertical streaks, you must temporarily reorient your image before applying the filter.

3. **Choose Filter ⇨ Stylize ⇨ Wind.** Select Blast and From the Left and press Return. To randomize the image in both directions, choose the Wind filter again and select Blast and From the Right.

4. **Choose Image ⇨ Rotate ⇨ 90° CW.** This returns the image to its original orientation.

5. **Choose Filter ⇨ Blur ⇨ Motion Blur.** Enter 90 degrees into the Angle option and use 20 pixels for the Distance option. This blurs the image vertically to soften the blast lines, as in Figure 16-35.

Figure 16-35: The result of rotating the image a quarter turn, blasting it in both directions with the Wind filter, rotating it back into place, and applying the Motion Blur filter vertically.

6. **Choose Filter ⇨ Distort ⇨ Wave.** Enter the values shown in Figure 16-36 into the Wave option box. Most of these values are approximate. You experiment with other settings if you like. The only essential value is 0 percent in the Vert. option box, which ensures that the filter waves the image in a horizontal direction only.

Figure 16-36: Apply these settings from the Wave dialog box to wave the image in a vertical direction only.

(continued)

7. **Choose Filter ➪ Distort ➪ Ocean Ripple.** I entered 15 for the Ripple Size and 5 for the Ripple Magnitude to get the effect shown in Figure 16-37.

8. **Expand the canvas size.** To perform Step 9, the Polar Coordinates filter needs lots of empty room in which to maneuver. If you filled up your canvas like I did, choose Image ➪ Canvas Size and add 200 pixels both vertically and horizontally. The new canvas size, with generous borders, appears in Figure 16-37.

Figure 16-37: After applying the Ripple filter, use the Canvas Size command to add a generous amount of empty space around the image.

9. **Choose Filter ➪ Distort ➪ Polar Coordinates.** So far, you've probably been a little disappointed by your image. I mean, it's just this disgusting little hairy thing that looks like a bad rug or something. Well, now's your chance to turn it into something special. Choose Filter ➪ Distort ➪ Polar Coordinates and select the Polar to Rectangular radio button. Photoshop in effect turns the image inside out, sending all the hairy edges to the bottom of the screen. Finally, an image worth waiting for.

10. **Choose Image ➪ Rotate Canvas ➪ Flip Vertical.** This turns the image upside down. As I believe Hemingway said, the hair also rises, as shown in Figure 16-38. This step prepares the image for the next major polar conversion, due in the year 2096.

Figure 16-38: Convert the image from polar to rectangular coordinates to turn it inside out. Then flip it vertically to prepare it for the next polar conversion.

11. **Use the rectangular marquee tool to select the central portion of the image.** Leave about 50 pixels along the top and bottom of the image deselected, as well as 100 pixels along both sides. Then feather the selection with a 15-pixel radius.

12. **Press ⌘-F to reapply the Polar Coordinates filter using the same settings as before.** Okay, so it happened before 2096. How could I have known? The pixels inside the selection now billow into a fountain.

13. **Add Moses to taste.** The finished image appears in Figure 16-39.

(continued)

Figure 16-39: Marquee the central portion of the image with a heavily feathered selection outline, convert the selection from rectangular to polar coordinates, and put Moses into the scene. My, doesn't he look natural in his new environment?

Wrapping an Image onto a 3-D Shape

I've long maintained that three-dimensional drawing programs would catch on better if they were sold as plug-in utilities for Photoshop. Imagine being able to import DXF objects, add a line or two of text, move the objects around in 3-D space, apply surface textures, and then render the piece directly to independent Photoshop layers. After that, you could change the stacking order of the layers, edit the pixels right there on the spot, maybe even double-click on a layer to edit it in 3-D space. Virtually every digital artist working in 3-D visits Photoshop somewhere during the process, so why not do the whole thing in Photoshop and save everyone a few steps? Experienced artists would love it and novices would take to 3-D in droves.

Frankly, my little fantasy isn't likely to take form any time in the near future. Photoshop would have to modify its plug-in specifications, and some brave programming team would have to spend a lot of time and money producing an aggressive suite of plug-ins. Even so, Adobe seems to share my dream. Filter ⇨ Render ⇨ 3D Transform lets you wrap an image around a three-dimensional shape. Although the drawing tools are rudimentary, the spatial controls are barely adequate, and the filter lacks any kind of lighting controls, 3D Transform is a first tentative step in the right direction.

Figure 16-40 shows exactly what 3D Transform can do. In each case, I started with the brick image shown in the upper left corner of the figure. Then I wrapped the image around the three basic kinds of *primitives* permitted by the 3D Transform filter — a cube, a sphere, and a cylinder. 3D Transform lets you add points to the side of a cylinder, as I did to get the hourglass shape. You can also mix and match primitives, as the final example in Figure 16-40 illustrates.

Notice that in each case, 3D Transform merely distorts the image. It has no effect on the brightness values of the pixels, nor does it make any attempt to light the shapes (which is why I'd prefer to see it under the Distort submenu as opposed to Render). I added the shadows using Layer ⇨ Effects ⇨ Drop Shadow.

To be perfectly fair, 3D Transform is not the first three-dimensional plug-in for Photoshop. That honor went out years ago to the Series 2: 3-D Filter from Andromeda (*www.andromeda.com*). Even now, Series 2 offers features that Photoshop's 3D Transform plug-in lacks, including a wider range of numerical controls and lighting functions. But 3D Transform is easier to use.

Using the 3D Transform filter

Choose Filter ⇨ Render ⇨ 3D Transform to bring up the window shown in Figure 16-41. Less a dialog box than a separate editing environment, the 3D Transform window contains a wealth of tools and a preview area in which you can draw and evaluate your effect. There are a dozen tools in all, but they make a bit more sense if you regard them as members of five basic categories, itemized in the following sections. Like Photoshop's standard tools, you can select the 3D Transform tools from the keyboard (assuming that you have any head room left to memorize the shortcuts). Shortcut keys are listed in parentheses.

Original image   Cylinder

Cube   Hourglass

Sphere   Mixed primitives

Figure 16-40: The 3D Transform filter lets you wrap an image (upper left) around each of three basic primitives (cube, sphere, and cylinder), a modified cylinder (hourglass), or several shapes mixed together.

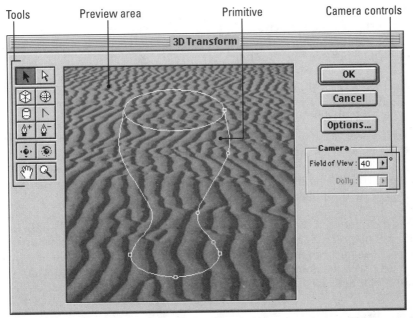

Figure 16-41: The 3D Transform dialog box contains a dozen tools that permit you to draw and edit three-dimensional shapes.

Primitive shape tools

Use one of the primitive shape tools to draw a basic 3-D shape in the preview area. This is the shape around which 3D Transform will wrap the selected image.

Cube (M): Use this tool to draw a six-sided box. Adobe selected M as the shortcut to match Illustrator, which uses M for its rectangle tool. And that M is based in turn on Photoshop's marquee tool.

Sphere (N): This tool creates a perfect sphere. Again, the shortcut comes from Illustrator, this time from the ellipse tool. Just remember, N follows M. (Ironically, S goes unused. Ain't cross-application consistency a pain in the neck?)

Cylinder (C): This cylinder tool draws your basic, everyday, dowel-like cylinders. But you can edit them to make lots of other shapes, as I explain in the upcoming "Cylinder editors." Thankfully, Illustrator offers no equivalent for the cylinder tool, so we get a sensible shortcut, C.

Basic edit tools

The two arrow tools — the black select tool and the white direct select — let you change a shape by dragging it around or moving the points. Both tools work just like their counterparts in Illustrator.

Select (V): Drag a shape with the black arrow tool to move the whole shape. If you know Illustrator, then you already know about the weird V-key shortcut. If not, think of Photoshop's own move tool.

Direct select (A): Use the white arrow to move individual points. Dragging a point in a sphere resizes it. Dragging a point in a cube or cylinder stretches or rotates the shape. Experiment and you'll quickly see how it works. (Unlike paths, there are no control handles. All you have to work with are anchor points.)

You can switch between the black and white arrow tools by pressing ⌘-Tab. But really, there's no point. The white arrow does everything the black arrow does — just drag on a segment to move the entire shape. In fact, there's just one keyboard trick you need to remember: press ⌘ to temporarily get the white arrow tool when any other tool is active. If you know that, the other keys are redundant.

Cylinder editors

The three path-edit tools are applicable exclusively to cylinders. Why? Because cylinders can be modified to create a whole family of tubular shapes. Throw the cylinder on the lathe and you can make an hourglass, a goblet, a cone — in short, any shape with radial symmetry and a flat top or bottom. To make these shapes, you use the following tools:

Insert point (+): Click on the right side of the cylinder — unless you turn it upside-down, then click on the left side — to add a point. Then drag the point with the white arrow tool to move both sides symmetrically. It's a virtual potter's wheel.

Remove point (–): Click on a point you've added with the insert point tool to remove it. Don't click on any of the square points that Photoshop put in there or the program will whine at you.

Convert point: The insert point tool adds circular smooth points which create continuous arcs in the side of the cylinder. To change the point to a sharp corner, click on it with the convert point tool. Click again to change it back to a smooth point.

Moving in 3-D space

The next two tools are the most powerful and the hardest to use. They permit you to move the object in 3-D space. When you switch to one of these tools, Photoshop renders the preview so you can see the image wrapped on the shape, as in Figure 16-42.

Pan camera (E): Drag the image to move it up, down, left, or right. How is this different from moving the primitive with the arrow tool? This time, you're moving the image in 3-D space across your field of vision. (To be more precise, you're moving the camera—which is your window into the image—while the object remains still.) As you move the image to the left, you see more of its right side. Move it up, and you see its bottom.

Trackball (R): The trackball rotates the image in 3-D space. Meanwhile, it's ultimately a 2-D control—you can't move your cursor into or out of the screen; just up, down, and side to side—making it difficult to predict the outcome of a drag.

Tip

Inevitably, you'll end up exposing the back, empty side of a shape. When this happens, spin the shape by dragging against the grain. To spin the shape head over heels, for example, drag directly up or down. To spin the shape sideways, drag horizontally. Don't fret too much about moving through the 3-D world, just watch how the program behaves when you move your mouse from one location to another. In time, you'll see some very simple patterns that you can exploit to your advantage.

Rendered preview

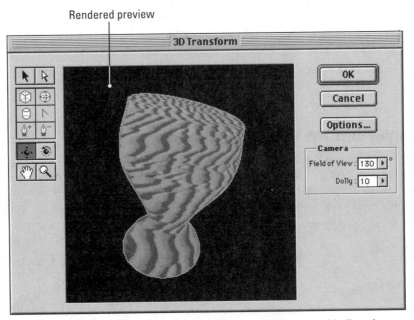

Figure 16-42: When you select either the pan camera or trackball tool, Photoshop renders the image inside the preview area.

In case you're wondering "What is with the shortcuts for these tools?" permit me to explain. The R key selects the rotate tool in Illustrator; because the trackball rotates, it was likewise assigned R. As for the pan camera tool, is has no equivalent in Illustrator 7, so it gets — one of the few keys that was never assigned in Illustrator 7. Crawl inside the mind of an Adobe engineer and it all makes perfect sense.

The camera controls

When you select the pan camera or trackball tool, Photoshop offers two Camera options on the right side of the dialog box. At first, the two options seem to do the same thing. A low value moves you in; a high value takes you out. But in truth they produce subtly different effects. Think of the Field of View option as a wide-angle lens and the Dolly option as a zoom lens, both operating at the same time. A low Field of View with a high Dolly results in shallow shapes. A high Field of View with a low Dolly shrinks you down to the size of a bug so that the depth is really coming at you.

Basic navigation

The last two tools in the 3D Transform dialog box are the standard hand and magnifying glass. They work just like their counterparts outside the 3D Transform dialog box, which is to say:

Hand (H): Drag the image to move it around inside the preview area. You can press either the H key or the spacebar to get this tool.

Zoom (Z): Click with this tool to zoom in, Option-click to zoom out. ⌘-spacebar and Option-spacebar work as well.

Layer before you apply

When you press Return, Photoshop merges your new 3-D shape with the original image. Because the 3D Transform filter provides no lighting controls, the shape may be virtually indistinguishable from its background, as Figure 16-43 makes abundantly clear. And that, dear friends, is a giant drag.

Figure 16-43: By default, the 3D Transform filter merges the 3-D image into the original image, making for an extraordinarily subtle effect.

Tip

Luckily, you can force Photoshop to deliver the 3-D shape on a separate layer. Here's what you do. First copy the image to a separate layer by dragging it onto the page icon at the bottom of the Layers palette. Then choose Filter ➪ Render ➪ 3D Transform and click on the Options button inside the dialog box. Turn off the Display Background check box, spotlighted in Figure 16-44, and press Return.

Figure 16-44: Copy the image to a separate layer and turn off the Display Background check box to make the area outside the 3-D shape transparent.

Not only will the 3D Transform filter restrict its efforts to the active layer, it will also make the area outside the 3-D shape transparent, as in the first example of Figure 16-45. Then you can apply layer effects or other lighting techniques to distinguish the 3-D shape from its background, as in the second example.

Figure 16-45: After applying the 3-D shape to a separate layer (shown by itself at left), I used the Drop Shadow and Inner Bevel effects to add some fake volumetric lighting to my goblet (right).

Color Plates 16-8 and 16-9 demonstrate some of the fun you can have with 3D Transform. In Color Plate 16-8, I relied entirely on the Drop Shadow and Inner Bevel layer effects to light the layered 3-D goblet. I also added a bit of red to the goblet using Image ➪. Adjust ➪ Hue/Saturation to distinguish the layer from its sandy background.

Color Plate 16-9 illustrates the merits of manual lighting techniques. After setting the goblet against a different background, I applied the drop shadow and haloing techniques that I discussed back in the "Selecting the Contents of Layers" section of Chapter 13. I also applied the airbrush tool set alternatively to the Multiply and Screen brush modes to hand-brush some natural tinting. Finally, I darkened the top of the goblet with the help of the elliptical marquee tool. After drawing my initial marquee, I chose Select ➪ Transform to rotate and scale it into position, pressed ⌘-J to send the selection to a separate layer, and applied the Multiply blend mode set to a low opacity. Admittedly, the finished effect involved a lot of effort, but it looks significantly more realistic than anything Photoshop can approximate automatically.

Adding Clouds and Spotlights

The remaining five filters in the Render submenu produce lighting effects. You can use Clouds and Difference Clouds to create a layer of haze over an image. Lens Flare creates light flashes and reflections (as I mentioned earlier). Lighting Effects lights an image as if it were hanging on a gallery wall. You can even use the unremarkable Texture Fill command to add an embossed texture to a piece embellished with the Lighting Effects filter.

Creating clouds

The Clouds filter creates an abstract and random haze between the foreground and background colors. Difference Clouds works exactly like layering the image, applying the Clouds filter, and selecting the Difference blend mode in the Layers palette.

Why on earth should Difference Clouds make special provisions for a single blend mode? Because you can create cumulative effects. Try this: Select blue as the foreground color and then choose Filter ⇨ Render ⇨ Clouds. Ah, just like a real sky, huh? Now choose Filter ⇨ Render ⇨ Difference Clouds. It's like some kind of weird Halloween motif, all blacks and oranges. Press ⌘-F to repeat the filter. Back to the blue sky. Keep pressing ⌘-F over and over and notice the results. A pink cancer starts invading the blue sky; a green cancer invades the orange one. Multiple applications of the Difference Clouds filter generate organic oil-on-water effects.

Tip

To strengthen the colors created by the Clouds filter, press Shift when choosing the command. This same technique works when using the Difference Clouds filter as well. In fact, I don't know of any reason *not* to Shift-choose these commands, unless you have some specific need for washed-out effects.

Color Plate 16-10 shows some pretty entertaining applications of the Clouds filters. With the foreground and background colors set to blue and orange respectively, I applied the Clouds filter to a layered copy of the rose image. For maximum effect, I Shift-chose the filter to create the top left image in the color plate. I then Shift-chose the Difference Clouds filter to create the purple montage in the figure, and pressed ⌘-F ten times to achieve the top right image. Looks to me like I definitely have something growing in my Petri dish.

Yeah, so really groovy stuff, right? Shades of "Purple Haze" and all that. But now that I've created this murky mess, what the heck do I do with it? Composite it, of course. The bottom row of Color Plate 16-10 shows examples of mixing each of the images from the top row with the original rose. In the left example, I chose the Overlay option from the Layers palette (Shift-Option-O). In the middle example, I chose the Screen mode (Shift-Option-S). And in the last example, I chose Hue (Shift-Option-U). This last one is particularly exciting, completely transforming the colors in the rose while leaving the gray (and therefore unsaturated) background untouched. Without a mask, without anything but a rectangular marquee, I've managed to precisely color the interior of the rose.

Lighting an image

Photoshop ventures farther into 3-D drawing territory with the Lighting Effects filter. This very complex function allows you to shine lights on an image, color the lights, position them, focus them, specify the reflectivity of the surface, and even create a surface map. In many ways, it's a direct lift from MetaCreations' Painter. But whereas Painter provides predefined paper textures and light refraction effects that bolster the capabilities of its excellent tool, Photoshop offers better controls and more lighting options.

The Lighting Effects filter is applicable exclusively to RGB images. Also, don't expect to be able to apply 3-D lighting to shapes created with the 3D Transform filter. Sadly, the two filters share no common elements that would permit them to work directly with each other.

When you choose Filter ⇨ Render ⇨ Lighting Effects, Photoshop displays what is easily its most complex dialog box, as shown in Figure 16-46. The dialog box has two halves: One in which you actually position light with respect to a thumbnail of the selected image, and one that contains about a billion intimidating options. Between you and me, I think Adobe could have done a better job, but the dialog box is functional.

No bones about it, this dialog box is a bear. The easiest way to apply the filter is to choose one of the predefined lighting effects from the Style pop-up menu at the top of the right side of the dialog box, see how it looks in the preview area, and — if you like it — press Return to apply the effect.

But if you want to create your own effects, you'll have to work a little harder. Here are the basic steps involved in creating a custom effect.

Footprint   Focus spot

Preview area   Hotspot

Color swatches

Handles   Light icon   Trash icon

Figure 16-46: The Lighting Effects dialog box enables you to light an image as if it were hanging in a gallery, or lying on a floor, or perhaps resting too near a hot flame.

Steps: Lighting an Image

1. **Drag from the light icon at the bottom of the dialog box into the preview area to create a new light source.** I call this area the *stage* because it's as if the image is painted on the floor of a stage and the lights are hanging above it.

2. **Select the kind of light you want from the Light Type pop-up menu.** It's just below the Style pop-up menu. You can select from Directional, Omni, and Spotlight:

   • Directional works like the sun, being a general, unfocused light that hits a target from an angle.

(continued)

- Omni is a bare light bulb hanging in the middle of the room, shining in all directions from a center point.

- And Spotlight is a focused beam that is brightest at the source and tapers off gradually.

3. **Specify the color of the light by clicking on the top color swatch.** You can also muck about with the Intensity slider bar to control the brightness of the light. If Spotlight is selected, the Focus slider becomes available. Drag the slider toward Narrow to create a bright laser of light; drag toward Wide to diffuse the light and spread it over a larger area.

4. **Move the light source by dragging at the *focus point* (the colored circle in the stage).** When Directional or Spotlight is selected, the focus point represents the spot at which the light is pointing. When Omni is active, the focus point is the actual bulb. (Don't burn yourself.)

5. **If Directional or Spotlight is active, you can change the angle of the light by dragging the *hot spot.*** The hot spot represents the location in the image that's liable to receive the most light. When you use a Directional light, the hot spot appears as a black square at the end of a line joined to the focus point. The same holds true when you edit a Spotlight; the confusing thing is that there are four black squares altogether. The light source is joined to the focus point by a line, the three *handles* are not.

To make the light brighter, drag the hot spot closer to the focus point. Dragging the hot spot away from the focus point dims the light by increasing the distance that it has to travel. It's like putting a flashlight in the living room when you're in the garage — the light gets dimmer as you move farther away from it.

6. **With Omni or Spotlight in force, you can edit the elliptical footprint of the light.** When Omni is in force, a circle surrounds the focus point. When editing a Spotlight, you see an ellipse. Either way, this shape represents the *footprint* of the light, which is the approximate area of the image affected by the light. You can change the size of the light by dragging the handles around the footprint. Enlarging the shape is like raising the light source. When the footprint is small, the light is close to the image, so it's concentrated and very bright. When the footprint is large, the light is high above the image, so it's more generalized.

When editing the footprint of a Spotlight, Shift-drag a handle to adjust the width or height of the ellipse without affecting the angle. To change the angle without affecting the size, ⌘-drag a handle.

7. Introduce more lights as you see fit.

There are a bunch of different techniques you can use to add and subtract lights on the stage. Press the Tab key to switch from one light to the next. You can duplicate a light in the stage by Option-dragging its focus point. To delete the active light, just press the Delete key. Or if you prefer, you can drag the focus point onto the trash can icon at the bottom of the dialog box.

8. **Change the Properties and Texture Channel options as you see fit.** I explain these in detail after the steps.

9. **If you want to save your settings for future use, click on the Save button.** Photoshop invites you to name the setup, which then appears as an option in the Style pop-up menu. If you want to get rid of one of the presets, select it from the pop-up menu and click on the Delete button.

10. **Press Return to apply your settings to the image.**

That's almost everything. The only parts I left out are the Properties and Texture Channel options. The Properties slider bars control how light reflects off the surface of your image:

✦ **Gloss:** Is the surface dull or shiny? Drag the slider toward Matte to make the surface flat and nonreflective, like dull enamel paint. Drag the slider toward Shiny to make it glossy, as if you had slapped on a coat of lacquer.

✦ **Material:** This option determines the color of the light that reflects back off the image. According to the logic employed by this option, Plastic reflects back the color of the light; Metallic reflects the color of the object itself. If only I had a bright, shiny plastic thing and a bright, shiny metal thing, I could check to see if this logic holds true in real life (like maybe that matters).

✦ **Exposure:** I'd like this option better if you could vary it between Sun Block 65 and Melanoma. Unfortunately, the more prosaic titles are Under and Over — exposed, that is. This option controls the brightness of all lights like a big dimmer switch. You can control a single selected light using the Intensity slider, but the Exposure slider offers the added control of changing all lights in the stage area and the ambient light (described next) together.

✦ **Ambience:** The last slider allows you to add *ambient light,* which is a general, diffused light that hits all surfaces evenly. First, select the color of the light by clicking on the color swatch to the right. Then drag the slider to cast a subtle hue over the stage. Drag toward Positive to tint the image with the color in the swatch; drag toward Negative to tint the stage with the swatch's opposite. Keep the slider set to 0 — dead in the center — to cast no hue.

The Texture Channel options let you treat one channel in the image as a *texture map,* which is a grayscale surface in which white indicates peaks and black indicates valleys. (As long as White is High is selected, that is. If you deselect that option, everything flips, and black becomes the peak.) It's as if one channel has a surface to it. By selecting a channel from the pop-up menu, you create an emboss effect, much like that created with the Emboss filter, except much better because you can light the surface from many angles at once, and it's in color to boot.

Choose a channel to serve as the embossed surface from the pop-up menu. Then change the Height slider to indicate more or less Flat terrain or huge Mountainous cliffs of surface texture.

Color Plate 16-11 shows an image lit with a total of five spotlights, two from above and three from below. In the first example, I left the Texture Channel option set to None. In the second example, I selected the green channel as the surface map. And in the third example, I filled a separate mask channel with a bunch of white and black dollops using Filter ➪ Pixelate ➪ Pointillize, then I selected the mask from the Texture Channel pop-up menu in the Lighting Effects dialog box. The result is a wonderfully rough paper texture.

✦   ✦   ✦

Constructing Homemade Effects

Creating a Custom Effect

If my wife were here right now, she might be tempted to say
something diplomatic like, "Deke, dear, I think that our guests
are growing a teeny bit tired of the subject of filters." To which
I would respond, "Nonsense, folks love this stuff! Besides, I
haven't shown everyone my home movies of all the filters
when they were babies." Whether you share my fascination
with filters or not, don't get up and go home just yet. This last-
of-the-filters chapter covers three very important entries —
Custom, Displace, and the Filter Factory — that permit you to
create your own, custom-tailored special effects.

Fully understanding the Custom and Displace filters requires
some mathematical reasoning skills — even if you're a math
whiz, you'll probably have occasional difficulty predicting the
outcomes of these filters. Using the Filter Factory requires flat-
out programming skills. If math isn't your bag, if number
theory clogs up your synapses to the extent that you feel like
a worthless math wimp, by all means don't put yourself
through the torture. Skip all the mathematical background in
this chapter and read the "Applying Custom Values" and
"Using Displacement Maps" sections to try out some specific,
no-brainer effects.

Cross-Reference

If you have no desire to learn the Filter Factory, you can
experiment with some filters that I programmed using this
plug-in. On the CD-ROM at the back of this book, you'll find
several fully-functioning filters, all of which include interactive
slider bars and previews. If you copy the filters to your Plug-
Ins folder and launch Photoshop, you'll see my filters in the

Filter ➭ Tormentia submenu. (These filters torment your image in a demented way, hence *Tormentia*. I also considered *Tormento*, but that sounds like something you'd put on your pizza.) I explain what the filters do and how they work in the `Torment.txt` file on the CD-ROM.

On the other hand, if you're not scared silly of math and you eventually want to understand how to create effects of your own, read on, you hearty soul.

The Custom filter

The Custom command enables you to design your own *convolution kernel,* which is a variety of filter in which neighboring pixels get mixed together. The kernel can be a variation on sharpening, blurring, embossing, or a half dozen other effects. You create your filter by entering numerical values into a matrix of options.

When you choose Filter ➭ Other ➭ Custom, Photoshop displays the dialog box shown in Figure 17-1. It sports a 5 × 5 matrix of option boxes followed by two additional options, Scale and Offset. The matrix options can accept values from negative to positive 999. The Scale value can range from 1 to 9,999, and the Offset value can range from negative to positive 9,999. The dialog box includes Load and Save buttons so that you can load settings from disk and save the current settings for future use.

Like most of Photoshop's filters, the Custom filter also includes a constantly updating preview box, which you'll have lots of time to appreciate if you decide to try your hand at designing your own effects. Select the Preview check box to view the effect of the kernel in the image window as well.

Figure 17-1: The Custom dialog box lets you design your own convolution kernel by multiplying the brightness values of pixels.

Here's how the filter works: When you press the Return key to apply the values in the Custom dialog box to a selection, the filter passes over every pixel in the selection, one at a time. For each pixel being evaluated—which I'll call the PBE, for short—the filter multiplies the PBE's current brightness value by the number in the center option box (the one that contains a 5 in Figure 17-1). To help keep things straight, I'll call this value the CMV, for *central matrix value*.

The filter then multiplies the brightness values of the surrounding pixels by the surrounding values in the matrix. For example, Photoshop multiplies the value in the option box just above the CMV by the brightness value of the pixel just above the PBE. It ignores any empty matrix option boxes and the pixels they represent.

Finally, the filter totals the products of the multiplied pixels, divides the sum by the value in the Scale option, and adds the Offset value to calculate the new brightness of the PBE. It then moves on to the next pixel in the selection and performs the calculation all over again. Figure 17-2 shows a schematic drawing of the process.

Perhaps seeing all of this spelled out in an equation will help you understand the process. Then again, perhaps not—but here it comes anyway. In the following equation, NP stands for *neighboring pixel* and MV stands for the corresponding matrix value in the Custom dialog box.

New brightness value = (((PBE × CMV) + (NP1 × MV1) + (NP2 × MV2) + . . .) ÷ Scale) + Offset

Luckily, Photoshop calculates the equation without any help from you. All you have to do is punch in the values and see what happens.

Custom filter advice

Now obviously, if you go around multiplying the brightness value of a pixel too much, you end up making it white. And a filter that turns an image white is pretty darn useless. The key, then, is to filter an image and at the same time maintain the original balance of brightness values. To achieve this, just be sure that the sum of all values in the matrix is 1. For example, the default values in the matrix shown back in Figure 17-1 are 5, –1, –1, –1, and –1, which add up to 1.

If the sum is greater than 1, use the Scale value to divide the sum down to 1. Figures 17-3 and 17-4 show the results of increasing the CMV from 5 to 6 and then to 7. This raises the sum of the values in the matrix from 1 to 2 and then to 3.

In Figure 17-3, I entered the sum into the Scale option to divide the sum back down to 1 (any value divided by itself is 1, after all). The result is that Photoshop maintains the original color balance of the image while at the same time filtering it slightly differently. When I did not raise the Scale value, the image became progressively lighter, as illustrated in Figure 17-4.

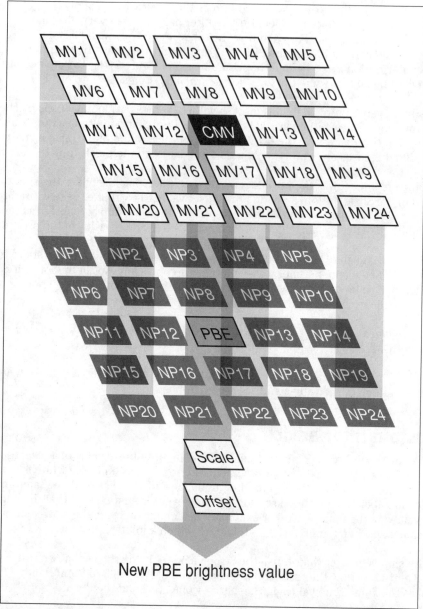

Figure 17-2: The Custom filter multiplies each matrix value by the brightness value of the corresponding pixel, adds the products together, divides the sum by the Scale value, adds the Offset value, and applies the result to the pixel being evaluated.

Figure 17-3: Raising the Scale value to reflect the sum of the values in the matrix maintains the color balance of the image.

Figure 17-4: Raising the sum of the matrix values without counterbalancing it in the Scale option lightens the image.

If the sum is less than 1, increase the CMV until the sum reaches the magic number. For example, in Figure 17-5, I lowered the values to the left of the CMV and then above the CMV by 1 apiece to increase the sharpening effect. To ensure that the image did not darken, I also raised the CMV to compensate. When I did not raise the CMV, the image turned black, as shown in Figure 17-6.

Figure 17-5: Raising the CMV to compensate for the lowered values in the matrix maintains the color balance of the image.

Figure 17-6: Lowering the sum of the matrix values without counterbalancing them with the CMV darkens the image.

Tip

Although a sum of 1 provides the safest and most predictable filtering effects, you can use different sums, such as 0 and 2, to try out more destructive filtering effects. If you do, be sure to raise or lower the Offset value to compensate. For some examples, see the "Non-1 variations" section.

Applying Custom Values

The following sections show you ways to sharpen, blur, and otherwise filter an image using specific matrix, Scale, and Offset values. It is my sincere hope that by the end of the Custom filter discussions, you not only will know how to repeat my examples, but also how to apply what you've learned to design special effects of your own.

Symmetrical effects

Values that are symmetrical both horizontally and vertically about the central matrix value produce sharpen and blur effects:

✦ **Sharpening:** A positive CMV surrounded by symmetrical negative values sharpens an image, as demonstrated in the first example of Figure 17-7. Figures 17-3 through 17-6 also demonstrate varying degrees of sharpening effects.

✦ **Blurring:** A positive CMV surrounded by symmetrical positive numbers — balanced, of course, by a Scale value as explained in the preceding section — blurs an image, as demonstrated in the second example of Figure 17-7.

✦ **Blurring with edge-detection:** A negative CMV surrounded by symmetrical positive values blurs an image and adds an element of edge-detection, as illustrated in the last example of the figure. These effects are unlike anything provided by Photoshop's standard collection of filters.

Figure 17-7: Symmetrical values can result in sharpening (left), blurring (middle), and edge-detection (right) effects.

Sharpening

The Custom command provides as many variations on the sharpening theme as the Unsharp Mask filter. In a sense, it provides even more, for whereas the Unsharp Mask filter requires you to sharpen an image inside a Gaussian radius, you get to specify exactly which pixels are taken into account when you use the Custom filter.

To create Unsharp Mask-like effects, enter a large number in the CMV and small values in the surrounding option boxes, as demonstrated in Figure 17-8. To go beyond Unsharp Mask, you can violate the radius of the filter by entering values around the perimeter of the matrix and ignoring options closer to the CMV, as demonstrated in Figure 17-9.

Figure 17-8: To create severe sharpening effects, enter a CMV just large enough to compensate for the negative values in the matrix.

You can sharpen an image using the Custom dialog box in two basic ways. First, you can enter lots of negative values into the neighboring options in the matrix and then enter a CMV just large enough to yield a sum of 1. This results in radical sharpening effects, as demonstrated throughout the examples in Figures 17-8 and 17-9.

Second, you can tone down the sharpening by raising the CMV and using the Scale value to divide the sum down to 1. Figures 17-10 and 17-11 show the results of raising the CMV to lessen the impact of the sharpening effects performed in Figures 17-8 and 17-9.

Figure 17-9: To heighten the sharpening effect even further, enter negative values around the perimeter of the matrix.

Figure 17-10: To sharpen more subtly, increase the central matrix value and then enter the sum into the Scale value.

Figure 17-11: When you soften the effect of radical sharpening, you create a thicker, higher contrast effect, much as when raising the Radius value in the Unsharp Mask dialog box.

Blurring

The philosophy behind blurring is very much the same as that behind sharpening. To produce extreme blurring effects, enter lots of values or high values into the neighboring options in the matrix, enter 1 into the CMV, and then enter the sum into the Scale option. Examples appear in Figure 17-12. To downplay the blurring, raise the CMV and the Scale value by equal amounts. In Figure 17-13, I used the same neighboring values as in Figure 17-12, but I increased the CMV and the Scale value by 3 apiece.

Figure 17-12: To create severe blurring effects, enter 1 for the CMV and fill the neighboring options with 1s and 2s.

Figure 17-13: To blur more subtly, increase the central matrix value and the Scale value by equal amounts.

Edge-detection

Many of you are probably beginning to get the idea by now, but just in case you're the kind of person who believes that friends don't let friends do math, I'll breeze through it one more time in the venue of edge-detection. If you really want to see those edges, enter 1s and 2s into the neighboring options in the matrix and then enter a CMV just *small* enough — it's a negative value, after all — to make the sum 1. Examples appear in Figure 17-14 for your viewing pleasure.

Figure 17-14: To create severe edge-detection effects, enter a negative CMV just small enough to compensate for the positive values in the matrix.

To lighten the edges and bring out the blur, raise the CMV and enter the resulting sum into the Scale option box. The first example in Figure 17-15 pushes the boundaries between edge-detection and a straight blur.

Non-1 variations

Every image shown in Figures 17-7 through 17-15 is the result of manipulating matrix values and using the Scale option to produce a sum total of 1. Earlier in this chapter, I showed you what can happen if you go below 1 (black images) or above 1 (white images). But I haven't shown you how you can use non-1 totals to produce interesting, if somewhat washed out, effects.

The key is to raise the Offset value, thereby adding a specified brightness value to each pixel in the image. By doing this, you can offset the lightening or darkening caused by the matrix values to create an image that has half a chance of printing.

Figure 17-15: To blur the edges, increase the central matrix value and then enter the sum into the Scale value.

Lightening overly dark effects

The first image in Figure 17-16 uses nearly the exact same values used to create the extreme sharpening effect in the last image of Figure 17-8. The only difference is that the CMV is 1 lower (8, down from 9), which in turn lowers the sum total from 1 to 0.

The result is an extremely dark image with hints of brightness at points of high contrast. The image looks okay on-screen—actually, it looks pretty cool because of all those little star-like sprinkles in it—but it's likely to fill in during the printing process. If the first image in Figure 17-16 looks like anything but a vague blob of blackness, it's a credit to the printer of this book. Most printers who didn't have a giant publisher breathing down their necks would have kissed this image good-bye, and rightly so. It's too darn dark.

To prevent the image from filling in and to help head off any disputes with your printer, lighten the image using the Offset value. Photoshop adds the value to the brightness level of each selected pixel. A brightness value of 255 equals solid white, so you don't need to go too high. As illustrated by the last example in Figure 17-16, an Offset value of 100 is enough to raise most pixels in the image to a medium gray. Figure 17-17 shows the results of lightening an overly dark edge-detection effect using the Offset value.

Figure 17-16: Three examples of sharpening effects with sum totals of 0. I lightened the images incrementally by entering positive values into the Offset option box.

Figure 17-17: Three examples of edge-detection effects with sum totals of 0, lightened incrementally by using progressively higher Offset values.

Darkening overly light effects

You can also use the Offset value to darken filtering effects with sum totals greater than 1. The images in Figures 17-18 and 17-19 show sharpening and edge-detection effects whose matrix totals amount to 2. On their own, these filters produce effects that are too light. As demonstrated in the middle and right examples in the figures, however, you can darken the effects of the Custom filter to create high-contrast images by entering a negative value into the Offset option box.

Figure 17-18: Three examples of sharpening effects with sum totals of 2. I darkened the images incrementally by entering negative values into the Offset option box.

Figure 17-19: Three examples of edge-detection effects with sum totals of 2, darkened incrementally with progressively lower Offset values.

Using extreme offsets

If a brightness value of 255 produces solid white and a brightness value of 0 is solid black, why in blue blazes does the Offset value permit any number between negative and positive 9,999, a number 40 times greater than solid white? The answer lies in the fact that the matrix options can force the Custom filter to calculate brightness values much darker than black and much lighter than white. Therefore, you can use a very high or very low Offset value to boost the brightness of an image in which all pixels are well below black or diminish the brightness when all pixels are way beyond white.

Figure 17-20 shows exaggerated versions of the sharpening, blurring, and edge-detection effects. The sum totals of the matrixes are −42, 54, and 42, respectively. Without some help from the Offset value, each of these filters would turn every pixel in the image black (in the case of the sharpening effect) or white (blurring and edge-detection). But as demonstrated in the figure, using enormous Offset numbers brings out those few brightness values that remain. The images are so polarized that there's hardly any difference between the three effects, except that the first image is an inverted version of the other two. The difference is even less noticeable if you lower the opacity of the effect using Filter ⇨ Fade, as demonstrated in the second row of examples in Figure 17-20.

Other custom effects

By now, I hope that you understand what an absolute trip the Custom filter can be, provided that you immerse yourself in the old adventurous spirit. Quite honestly, I could keep showing you ways to use the Custom filter for another 20 or 30 pages. But then my publisher would come unglued because I'd never finish the book, and you'd miss the pleasure of discovering variations on your own.

Nonetheless, you're probably wondering what happens if you just go absolutely berserk, in a computer-geek sort of way, and start entering matrix values in unusual or even arbitrary arrangements. The answer is that as long as you maintain a sum total of 1, you achieve some pretty interesting and even usable effects. Many of these effects will be simple variations on sharpening, blurring, and edge-detection.

Figure 17-20: You can create high-contrast effects by exaggerating all values in the matrix and then compensating by entering a very high or very low Offset value (top row). When you back off the effect using Filter ➪ Fade (bottom row), these dramatic effects are barely discernible.

Directional blurs

Figure 17-21 shows examples of entering positive matrix values all in one row, all in a column, or in opposite quadrants. As you can see, as long as you maintain uniformly positive values, you get a blurring effect. By keeping the values lowest in the center and highest toward the edges and corners, however, you can create directional blurs. The first example resembles a slight horizontal motion blur, the second looks like a slight vertical motion blur, and the last example looks like it's vibrating horizontally and vertically.

Figure 17-21: Enter positive matrix values in a horizontal formation (left) or vertical formation (middle) to create slight motion blurs. By positioning positive values in opposite corners of the matrix, you create a vibrating effect (right).

Directional sharpening

To selectively sharpen edges in an image based on the angles of the edges, you can organize negative and positive matrix values into rows or columns. For example, to sharpen only the horizontal edges in an image, fill the middle row of matrix options with positive values and the rows immediately above and below with negative values, as demonstrated in the left example in Figure 17-22. Similarly, you can sharpen only the vertical edges by entering positive values in the middle column and flanking the column on left and right with negative values, as shown in the middle example in the figure. In the last example, I arranged the positive values along a diagonal axis to sharpen only the diagonal edges.

You even can combine directional sharpening with directional blurring. Figure 17-23 shows the first example from Figure 17-22 blurred both horizontally and vertically. To blur the image horizontally, as in the middle example of Figure 17-23, I added positive values to the extreme ends of the middle row, thereby extending the range of the filter and creating a sort of horizontal jumbling effect. To blur the image vertically, as in the final example of the figure, I added positive values to the ends of the middle column.

Figure 17-22: Arrange positive values in a row (left), column (middle), or along a diagonal axis (right) to sharpen horizontal, vertical, and diagonal edges exclusively.

Figure 17-23: The image from Figure 17-22 (left) blurred horizontally (middle) and vertically (right).

Embossing

So far, we aren't going very nuts, are we? Despite their unusual formations, the matrix values in Figures 17-21 through 17-23 still manage to maintain symmetry. Well, now it's time to lose the symmetry, which typically results in an embossing effect.

Figure 17-24 shows three variations on embossing, all of which involve positive and negative matrix values positioned on opposite sides of the CMV. (The CMV happens to be positive merely to maintain a sum total of 1.)

Figure 17-24: You can create embossing effects by distributing positive and negative values on opposite sides of the central matrix value.

This type of embossing has no hard and fast light source, but you might imagine that the light comes from the general direction of the positive values. Therefore, when I swapped the positive and negative values throughout the matrix (all except the CMV), I approximated an underlighting effect, as demonstrated by the images in Figure 17-25.

Figure 17-25: Change the location of positive and negative matrix values to change the general direction of the light source.

In truth, it's not so much a lighting difference as a difference in edge enhancement. White pixels collect on the side of an edge represented by positive values in the matrix; black pixels collect on the negative-value side. So when I swapped the locations of positive and negative values between Figures 17-24 and 17-25, I changed the distribution of white and black pixels in the filtered images.

Embossing is the loosest of the Custom filter effects. As long as you position positive and negative values on opposite sides of the CMV, you can distribute the values in almost any way you see fit. Figure 17-26 demonstrates three entirely arbitrary arrangements of values in the Custom matrix. Figure 17-27 shows those same effects downplayed by raising the CMV and entering the sum of the matrix values into the Scale option box.

Incidentally, the main advantage of using the Custom filter rather than using Filter ➪ Stylize ➪ Emboss to produce embossing effects is that Custom preserves the colors in an image while Emboss sacrifices color and changes low-contrast portions of an image to gray. Color Plate 17-1 shows the matrix values from the first example of Figure 17-26 applied to a color image. It also shows examples of other Custom effects, including variations on sharpening and edge-detection.

Figure 17-26: You can create whole libraries of embossing effects by experimenting with different combinations of positive and negative values.

Figure 17-27: To emboss more subtly, increase the central matrix value and the Scale values by equal amounts.

If you become enthralled with convolution kernels and you feel compelled to explore them in more detail, you may want to check out a $200 plug-in called KPT Convolver from MetaCreations. Although steeply priced, it permits you to explore convolutions using a more intuitive interface and without using any math. Convolver doesn't do anything that you can't already do with the Custom filter, but it can simultaneously apply different convolutions to separate color channels, and it permits you to investigate filtering possibilities that you aren't likely to discover on your own.

Displacing Pixels in an Image

Photoshop's second custom effects filter is Filter ➪ Distort ➪ Displace, which enables you to distort and add texture to an image by moving the colors of certain pixels in a selection. You specify the direction and distance that the Displace filter moves colors by creating a second image called a *displacement map,* or *dmap* (pronounced *dee-map*) for short. The brightness values in the displacement map tell Photoshop which pixels to affect and how far to move the colors of those pixels:

✦ **Black:** The black areas of the displacement map move the colors of corresponding pixels in the selection a maximum prescribed distance to the right and/or down. Lighter values between black and medium gray move colors a shorter distance in the same direction.

✦ **White:** The white areas move the colors of corresponding pixels a maximum distance to the left and/or up. Darker values between white and medium gray move colors a shorter distance in the same direction.

✦ **Medium gray:** A 50 percent brightness value, such as medium gray, ensures that the colors of corresponding pixels remain unmoved.

Suppose that I create a new image window the same size as the scan of the Egyptian temple carving that I've used about 60 times now in this chapter. This new image will serve as the displacement map. I divide the image into four quadrants. As shown in the middle example of Figure 17-28, I fill the upper left quadrant with black, the lower right quadrant with white, and the other two quadrants with medium gray. (The arrows indicate the direction in which the quadrants will move colors in the affected image. They do not actually appear in the dmap.)

When finished, I save the dmap to disk in the native Photoshop format so that the Displace filter can access it. I then return to the Egyptian carving image, choose Filter ➪ Distort ➪ Displace, edit the settings as desired, and open the dmap from disk. The result is the image shown in the last example of Figure 17-28. In keeping with the distribution of brightness values in the dmap, the colors of the pixels in the upper left quadrant of the carving image move rightward, the colors of the pixels in the lower right quadrant move to the left, and the colors in the upper right and lower left quadrant remain intact.

Note

A dmap must be a color or grayscale image, and you must save the dmap as a flattened image in the native Photoshop file format. (If you want to be absolutely sure there are no layers, use the Photoshop 2.0 format.) The Displace command does not recognize PICT, TIFF, or any of the other non-native file formats. Who knows why? Those programmers move in mysterious ways.

Figure 17-28: The Displace filter moves colors in an image (left) according to the brightness values in a separate image, called the displacement map (middle). The arrows indicate the direction that the map moves colors in the image (right).

At this point, you likely have two questions: How do you use the Displace filter, and why in the name of all that is good would you possibly want to? The hows of the Displace filter are covered in the following section. To discover some whys — which should in turn help you dream up some whys of your own — read the "Using Displacement Maps" section later in this chapter.

Displacement theory

Like any custom filtering effect worth its weight in table salt — an asset that has taken something of a nose dive in the recent millennium — you need a certain degree of mathematical reasoning skills to predict the outcome of the Displace filter. Although I was a math major in college (well, actually, I double-majored in math and fine arts, and I must admit to paying the lion's share of attention to the latter), I frankly was befuddled by the results of my first few experiments with the Displace command. Don't be surprised if you are, as well. With some time and a modicum of effort, however, you can learn to anticipate the approximate effects of this filter.

Direction of displacement

Earlier, I mentioned — and I quote — "The black areas of the displacement map move . . . colors . . . to the right and/or down . . . the white areas move . . . colors . . . to the left and/or up." Yikes, talk about your fragmented quotations. I think I'll sue! Anyway, the point is, you may have wondered to yourself what all this "and/or" guff was all about. "Is it right or is it down?" you may have puzzled, and rightly so.

The truth is that the direction of a displacement can go either way. It's up to you. If you like right, go with it. If you like down, don't let me stop you. If you like both together, by all means, have at it.

Beginning to understand? No? Well, it works like this: A dmap can contain one or more color channels. If the dmap is a grayscale image with one color channel only, the Displace filter moves colors that correspond to black areas in the dmap both to the right *and* down, depending on your specifications in the Displace dialog box. The filter moves colors that correspond to white areas in the dmap both to the left and up.

Figure 17-29 shows two examples of an image displaced using a single-channel dmap, which appears on the left side of the figure. (Again, the arrows illustrate the directions in which different brightness values move colors in the affected image. They are not part of the dmap file.) I displaced the middle image at 10 percent and the right image at 20 percent. Therefore, the colors in the right image travel twice the distance as those in the middle image, but all colors travel the same direction. (The upcoming section "The Displace dialog box" explains exactly how the percentage values work.)

Figure 17-29: The results of applying a single-channel displacement map (left) to an image at 10 percent (middle) and 20 percent (right).

However, if the dmap contains more than one channel — whether it's a color image or a grayscale image with an independent mask channel — the first channel indicates horizontal displacement, and the second channel indicates vertical displacement. All other channels are ignored. Therefore, the Displace filter moves colors that correspond to black areas in the first channel of the dmap to the right and colors that correspond to white areas to the left. (Again, this depends on your specifications in the Displace dialog box.) The filter then moves colors that correspond to the black areas in the second channel downward and colors that correspond to white areas upward.

Figure 17-30 shows the effect of a two-channel dmap on our friend the pharaoh. The top row shows the appearance and effect of the first channel on the image at 10 percent and 20 percent. The bottom row shows the appearance and effect of the second channel.

Figure 17-30: The horizontal (top row) and vertical (bottom row) results of applying a two-channel displacement map (left column) to an image at 10 percent (middle) and 20 percent (right).

Brightness value transitions

If you study Figure 17-30 for any length of time, you'll notice a marked stretching effect around the edges of the image, particularly around the two right images. This is an effect you want to avoid.

The cause of the effect is twofold: First, the transition from gray to black and gray to white pixels around the perimeter of the dmap is relatively quick, especially compared with the gradual transitions in the central portion of the image. Second, transitions — reading from left to right, or top to bottom — produce a more noticeable effect when they progress from light to dark than from dark to light. The reason for this is that these transitions follow the direction of Photoshop's displacement algorithm. (I know, when I throw in a word like *algorithm,* everybody's eyes glaze over, but try to stick with me.)

For example, in the light-to-dark transition on the left side of the first-channel dmap in Figure 17-30, one gray value nudges selected colors slightly to the right, the next darker value nudges them an extra pixel, the next darker value another pixel, and so on, resulting in a machine-gun displacement effect that creates a continuous stream of the same colors over and over again. Hence, the big stretch.

Get it? Well, if not, the important part is this: To avoid stretching an image, make your dmap transitions slow when progressing from light to dark, and quick when progressing from dark to light. For example, in the revised dmap channels shown in the left column of Figure 17-31, the gray values progress slowly from gray to black, abruptly from black to gray to white, and then slowly again from white to gray. Slow light to dark, fast dark to light. The results are smoother image distortions, as demonstrated in the middle and right columns of the figure.

Figure 17-31: Changing the speeds of color transitions in the two-channel displacement map (left column) created smoother image distortions at both the 10 percent (middle) and 20 percent (right) settings.

The Displace dialog box

When you choose Filter ➪ Distort ➪ Displace, Photoshop displays the Displace dialog box. ("Displays the Displace" is the modern equivalent of "Begin the Beguine," don't you know.) As shown in Figure 17-32, the Displace dialog box provides the following options:

✦ **Scale:** You can specify the degree to which the Displace filter moves colors in an image by entering percentage values into the Horizontal Scale and Vertical Scale option boxes. At 100 percent, black and white areas in the dmap each have the effect of moving colors 128 pixels. That's 1 pixel per each brightness value over or under medium gray. You can isolate the effect of a single-channel dmap vertically or horizontally — or ignore the first or second channel of a two-channel dmap—by entering 0 percent into the Horizontal or Vertical option box respectively.

Figure 17-33 shows the effect of distorting an image exclusively horizontally (top row) and vertically (bottom row) at each of three percentage values: 5 percent, 15 percent, and 30 percent. In each case, I used the two-channel dmap from Figure 17-31.

Figure 17-32: Use these options to specify the degree of distortion, how the filter matches the displacement map to the image, and how it colors the pixels around the perimeter of the selection.

Figure 17-33: The results of applying the Distort filter exclusively horizontally (top row) and exclusively vertically (bottom row) at 5 percent (left column), 15 percent (middle), and 30 percent (right).

✦ **Displacement Map:** If the dmap contains fewer pixels than the image, you can either scale it to match the size of the selected image by selecting the Stretch to Fit radio button or repeat the dmap over and over within the image by selecting Tile. Figure 17-34 shows a small two-channel dmap that contains radial gradations. In the first column, I stretched the dmap to fit the image. In the second column, I tiled the dmap. To create both examples in the top row, I set the Horizontal Scale and Vertical Scale values to 10 percent. To create the bottom-row examples, I raised the values to 50 percent.

Figure 17-34: Using a small, two-channel dmap (offset top left), I stretched the dmap to fit (left column) and tiled it (right column) at 10 percent (top row) and 50 percent (bottom row).

✦ **Undefined Areas:** These radio buttons let you tell Photoshop how to color pixels around the outskirts of the selection that are otherwise undefined. By default, the Repeat Edge Pixels radio button is selected, which repeats the colors of pixels around the perimeter of the selection. This can result in extreme stretching effects, as shown in the middle example of Figure 17-35. To repeat the image inside the undefined areas instead, as demonstrated in the final example of the figure, select the Wrap Around option.

Tip

The Repeat Edge Pixels setting was active in all displacement map figures prior to Figure 17-35. In these cases, I frequently avoided stretching effects by coloring the edges of the dmap with medium gray and gradually lightening or darkening the brightness values toward the center.

Figure 17-35: After creating a straightforward, single-channel displacement map (left), I applied the filter subject to two different Undefined Areas settings: Repeat Edge Pixels (middle) and Wrap Around (right).

After you finish specifying options in the Displace dialog box, press Return to display the Open dialog box, which enables you to select the displacement map saved to disk. Only native Photoshop documents show up in the scrolling list.

Using Displacement Maps

So far, all the displacement maps demonstrated involve gradations of one form or another. Gradient dmaps distort the image over the contours of a fluid surface, like a reflection in a fun-house mirror. In this respect, the effects of the Displace filter closely resemble those of the Pinch and Spherize filters described in the last chapter. But the more functional and straightforward application of the Displace filter is to add texture to an image.

Creating texture effects

Figure 17-36 shows the results of using the Displace filter to apply nine of the patterns from the Displacement Maps folder inside the Plug-Ins folder. Color Plate 17-2 shows the effects of applying four of the patterns to color images. Introduced in Chapter 10, this folder contains repeating patterns that Adobe designed especially with the Displace filter in mind.

As shown in the figure and color plate, most of these patterns produce the effect of viewing the image through textured glass — an effect known in high-end graphics circles as *glass refraction*. Those few patterns that contain too much contrast to pass off as textured glass — including Fragment layers, Mezzo effect, and Schnable effect — can be employed to create images that appear as if they were printed on coarse paper or even textured metal.

12-sided   Crumbles   Fragment layers

Mezzo effect   Random strokes   Rectangular tiles

Schnable effect   Streaks pattern   Twirl pattern

Figure 17-36: These are examples of applying nine patterns from the Displacement Maps folder with the Displace filter at 10 percent horizontally and vertically.

Cross-Reference

To view each of the textures from the Displacement Maps folder on its own, see Figure 10-18 in the "Creating patterns and textures" section of Chapter 10. Like Figure 17-36, Figure 10-18 is labeled so that you can easily match texture and effect.

Tip

When using a repeating pattern — including any of the images inside the Displacement Maps folder — as a dmap, be sure to select the Tile radio button inside the Displace dialog box. This repeats the dmap rather than stretching it out of proportion.

I also explained in Chapter 10 that you can create your own textures from scratch using filtering effects. I specifically described how to create a stucco texture by applying the Add Noise filter three times in a row to an empty image and then using the Emboss filter to give it depth. (See the "Using filters" item in the "How to create patterns" section.) This texture appears in the first example of Figure 17-37. I applied the texture at 2 percent and 10 percent to create the windblown middle and right examples in the figure.

Figure 17-37: After creating a stucco texture with the Add Noise and Emboss filters (left), I applied the texture as a displacement map at 2 percent (middle) and 10 percent (right).

The stucco pattern is only one of an infinite number of textures that you can create using filters. In fact, stucco is a great base texture on which to build. For example, to create the wavy texture that starts off the first row of Figure 17-38, I softened the stucco texture by applying the Gaussian Blur filter with a 0.3-pixel radius. I then applied the Ripple filter twice with the Large option selected and an Amount value of 100. That's all there was to it.

To create the second texture in the figure, I applied the Crystallize filter at its default Cell Size value of 10. Believe me, I could go on creating textures like this forever, and more importantly, so could you. The images in the second and third columns of Figure 17-38 show the results of applying the textures with the Displace filter at 2 percent and 10 percent respectively.

In the final analysis, any pattern you design for use with the rubber stamp tool is equally applicable for use with the Displace filter. Furthermore, of the two options — rubber stamp and Displace — the latter is more likely to yield the kind of textured effects that will leave your audience begging, pleading, and scraping for more.

Figure 17-38: After creating two textures with the Add Noise, Emboss, and Ripple filters (first column), I applied the textures as displacement maps at 2 percent (middle) and 10 percent (right).

Displacing an image onto itself

I throw this technique in just for laughs. Personally, I can't get enough of *Dr. Strangelove*. That's why I call this the *Make My Day at the Atomic Café* effect. Warning: This effect features simulated melting Egyptian carvings. If you find them unnerving, you have a very soft stomach.

The Make My Day at the Atomic Café effect involves nothing more than using an image as its own displacement map. First, make sure that the image you want to distort is saved to disk in the native Photoshop 2.0 format. Then choose Filter ➪ Distort ➪ Displace, specify the desired settings, and select the version of the image saved to disk. Figure 17-39 shows three applications of this effect, once applied at 10 percent exclusively horizontally, the next at 10 percent vertically, and the last at 10 percent in both directions.

Figure 17-39: See Egypt, have a blast. Here I applied the
pharaoh image as a displacement map onto itself at
10 percent horizontally (left), 10 percent vertically (middle),
and 10 percent in both directions.

As a variation, save the image in its original form. Then choose Image ⇨ Adjust ⇨
Invert (⌘-I) and save the inverted image to disk under a different name. Open the
original image and use the Displace filter to apply the inverted image as a
displacement map. Figure 17-40 shows some results.

Figure 17-40: The results of applying an inverted version
of the pharaoh as a displacement map onto the original
image at 10 percent horizontally (left), 10 percent vertically
(middle), and 10 percent in both directions.

If you really want to blow an image apart, apply Horizontal Scale and Vertical Scale
values of 50 percent or greater. The first row of Figure 17-41 shows a series of 50
percent applications of the Displace filter. I took the liberty of sharpening each
image to heighten the effect. In the second row, I applied the filter and used Filter ⇨
Fade to lower the Opacity value to 10 percent. In this way, I retained the detail of
the original image while still managing to impart a smidgen of sandblasting.

Figure 17-41: The results of displacing the pharaoh image with itself at 50 percent horizontally, 50 percent vertically, and 50 percent in both directions (top row), followed by the same effects faded using the Fade command (bottom row).

Using the Filter Factory

If you've made it this far through the chapter, I just want to say one thing about the Filter Factory: It's extremely powerful and capable of doing far, far more than any filter I've described so far. But it's also difficult to use — so difficult, in fact, that it makes everything I've discussed in the previous pages look incredibly easy and transparently obvious. The Filter Factory tests the abilities of the most experienced Photoshop user.

Cross-Reference

Before you can use Filter Factory, you must install the Filter Factory plug-in in your Plug-Ins folder. The Filter Factory is included only on the Photoshop CD-ROM and does not install during the normal installation process. Open the CD-ROM and look for the Filter Factory folder inside the Optional Plugins folder, which is in the Other Goodies folder. Then copy the folder to the Plug-Ins folder on your hard drive and restart Photoshop.

Choose Filter ⇨ Synthetic ⇨ Filter Factory to display the Filter Factory dialog box, shown in Figure 17-42. By any account, I think this has to be the scariest dialog box ever put before a Photoshop user. Yours is probably even more scary. The R option box contains a little *r,* the G option box contains a little *g,* and the B option box contains a little *b.* Throw in a few arbitrarily named slider bars, and you have the perfect formula for striking terror in the unsuspecting image-editor's heart.

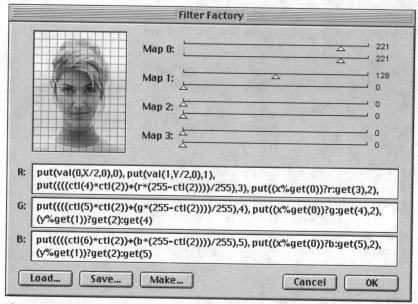

Figure 17-42: The Filter Factory dialog box containing the formulas for adding a series of grid lines to an image. The formula in the R option box is partially cut off because it's too long to fit on two lines.

Note   If the command is dimmed, it's because you're not in the RGB mode. Like the Lens Flare and Lighting Effects filters, Filter Factory is applicable to RGB images only.

Now I need to make something perfectly clear: There's no way I can describe every nuance of programming a custom filter with the Filter Factory in less than 100 pages. So to keep the story short and sweet, I'll explain the most important functions and variables, walk you through the process of creating a moderately amusing effect, and show you how to save your work as a fully-functioning filter. If you're serious about using the Filter Factory, I suggest that you also read the sparse PDF documentation that Adobe includes on its CD-ROM. It isn't the kind of thing you simply read through and ingest immediately, and some of the formulas are inaccurate (in my version, anyway), but it at least lists all the variables, operators, and functions permitted in the programming language. You may also want to load the settings that I've included on my CD-ROM and study my work. If you find a useful operation, feel free to copy it and paste it into a filter of your own. It's not stealing; it's research.

How the Factory works

To use this filter, you enter formulaic *expressions* into the R, G, and B option boxes. Each option box represents what you're doing to the red, green, or blue color channel. You can also integrate the slider bars at the top of the dialog box into your formulas. When you convert the formulas into a filter, you can specify which slider bars to include in the filter's own dialog box, enabling the user to modify the settings. You don't have to use the slider bars, but without them you get a single-shot filter like Photoshop's Sharpen More or Facet effects.

Tip

The Load and Save buttons enable you to load formulas from disk or save them for later use or editing. If you've had a long hard day and it's time to go home — or you're already home and you want to go to bed — don't forget to save the formulas to disk. Every time you restart Photoshop, the Filter Factory reverts to its original useless values of *r, g,* and *b.*

The Make button creates a filter, as I cover in more detail later in this chapter. The problem is, you can't open a filter with the Filter Factory once you've created it. So if you ever want to modify a setting or two — and believe me, you will — be sure to save the settings separately using the Save button. I recommend saving filters and settings under the same name in different folders to eliminate as much confusion as possible.

The expressions

Like the Custom filter, the Filter Factory evaluates each pixel in each channel one at a time and then finishes up by sending a new brightness value to that pixel. So in the following discussions, I'll take advantage of that same acronym I used earlier in this chapter — PBE, to indicate the *pixel being evaluated.*

You change the brightness of the PBE using three kinds of expressions — *variables, operators,* and *functions.* Here's the scoop on each.

Variables

There are two kinds of values that you can enter into a Filter Factory option box — hard and fast numbers, such as 3 and 17, and *variables.* The latter are single letters that represent values that are forever changing. The *r* that first appears in the R option box, for example, represents the brightness value that currently occupies the PBE in the red channel. So by entering *r* in the R option box, you tell Photoshop to change the red PBE to its current color, which is no change whatsoever. It's just Adobe's way of creating a clean slate for you in which to work.

All variables reset to a new value every time the filter advances from one pixel to the next. The most important variables are as follows:

✦ **r, g, and b:** The brightness value currently assigned to the PBE in the red channel is r. The green value of the PBE is g; the blue value is b. Why the heck would you want access to any of these values? Why, to mix them, of course. For example, if you enter $(r*g)/255$ in the R option box — that's all you have to enter — you multiply the red value by the green value, divide the result by 255, and put the result in the filtered red channel. The final product is identical to copying the contents of the green channel, pasting it onto the red channel, and choosing the Multiply overlay mode. Try it out and see.

✦ **c:** This variable represents the brightness value of the PBE in the current channel, whatever that may be. In the R option box, c is identical to r. So the equation $(c*g/255)$ means $(r*g/255)$ in the R channel and $(b*g/255)$ in the B channel.

✦ **x and y:** The horizontal coordinate of the PBE is saved to x. This value is measured in pixels from the left edge of the image. The vertical coordinate is y, as measured from the top of the image. These values are useful for shifting pixels around or mixing neighboring pixels together (as you can with the Custom command).

✦ **X and Y:** The total width of the image is X, the total height is Y. So $X - x$ calculates the distance from the PBE to the right edge.

You can also use other variables: The letter m, for example, measures the distance from the PBE to the exact center of the image, and d is the angle from the PBE to the center pixel (measured from 0 to 1,024, so that 255 is equivalent to 90 degrees). But r, g, b, c, x, y, X, and Y are the variables you'll use most often.

Operators

Operators include arithmetic signs, such as plus and minus, as well as relational symbols, such as < and >. They also include logical operations. For example, ? tells the Filter Factory to complete the following operation only if the previous expression holds true, and if it is false, to complete the operation after the colon (:). For example, the expression $x<(X/2)?r:g$ means that if the PBE is inside the left side of the image, color it with the red channel value. If not, color it with the green value. The following are the most important operators:

✦ **+, - , *, and /:** These symbols stand for plus, minus, multiply, and divide. The Filter Factory always handles multiply and divide operations before plus and minus operations. So the equation $4+8/2$ equals 8, not 6.

✦ **%:** Use the percentage sign to retain the remainder from a division equation. For example, $11\%4$ equals 3.

✦ **(and):** Parentheses tell the Filter Factory to complete the equation inside the parentheses before completing others. The equation $(4+8)/2$ equals 6 because 4 and 8 are added before dividing by 2.

✦ **<, >, <=, and >=:** These symbols mean less than, greater than, less than or equal to, and greater than or equal to. All four are used primarily within conditional operations like the one I mentioned at the beginning of this section.

✦ **==, =!:** Two equal signs in a row mean equal to. An equal sign and an exclamation point mean not equal to. Again, use these inside conditional operations.

✦ **?:** Here's the conditional operation, as I explained earlier.

Again, these aren't all the possible operators, just the best of them. But I should mention one additional operator: The comma separates phrases in an expression, sort of like a period separates sentences. The phrase after the final comma is the one that the Filter Factory applies to the PBE. All previous phrases are used for calculation purposes only. You can see how this works in the step-by-step example that's coming up right after the discussion of functions.

Functions

All functions are composed of three letters followed by numbers, variables, and equations inside parentheses. For example, *abs(x − X)* finds the absolute value of the equation inside the parentheses, which means that you get a positive result whether the answer to the equation is positive or negative. (Because negative brightness values simply become black, this can be useful.)

Rather than simply listing the functions, I'll explain them in groups. First, there are the two functions that use holding cells. In typical programming, you store the results of incremental equations in variables, but in the Filter Factory, variables are used by the filter only. You get ten numbered cells, ranging from 0 to 9. The two functions that work with cells are *put,* to place a number inside a cell, and *get,* to retrieve it. It's sort of like copying and pasting with 10 tiny Clipboards. The expression *put(r+b,0)* puts the result of the equation *r+b* into cell 0. Conversely, *put(r+b,1)* puts it in cell 1, and so on. The expression *get(0)/2* would retrieve the result of *r+b* and divide it by 2.

The function *src* retrieves information about a specific pixel in your image. For example, *src(x+5,y+5,0)* returns the brightness of the pixel five pixels to the right and five pixels down from the PBE. What is that last *0* for? That tells the function to get the value from the red channel. The green channel is *1,* the blue channel is *2,* and mask channels are *3* through *9.*

Similar to src, *rad* finds out the brightness value of a pixel in a certain channel based on its distance and direction from the center of the image. For example, if you enter *rad(d − 16,m − 16,0)* into the red channel, you rotate the contents of the channel 16 increments (about 6 degrees) counterclockwise and distort its center outward. The upcoming step-by-step example uses this function.

The function *rnd* generates a random number between two extremes, which is great for creating noise. The expression *rnd(r,g)* generates a random value between the red brightness value of the PBE and the green brightness of the PBE.

Evaluating the sliders

These next functions — *ctl* and *val* — get their own headline because they're so important. They evaluate how a user of your filter sets the slider bars. The function *ctl* simply retrieves the setting of a specified slider bar. There are eight slider bars in all, numbered 0 to 7 from top to bottom. (The sliders labeled Map 0 are therefore sliders 0 and 1; Map 1 includes sliders 2 and 3; and so on.) Each slider can be adjusted from 0 to 255. So if the first slider bar is set to 128, the function *ctl(0)* retrieves the number 128. You can then change the impact of your filter by moving the slider in real time. For example, if you enter *r*ctl(0)/255* in the R option box, you multiply the red value of the PBE by the setting of the top slider divided by 255. This makes the red channel black when the slider is set to 0, normal when the slider is set to 255, and darker shades when set to any increment in between.

The *val* function evaluates the setting of a slider bar within a specified range. For example, *val(0,15, –15)* takes the setting of the top slider, translates it to 15 when it's at 0, and translates it to –15 when it's at 255. As you can see, this function lets you translate the data within any specified range, even making the low values high and vice versa. This is useful when you don't want the entire range of data from 0 to 255 to mess up the results of your equations.

Touring the factory

Okay, now for a little hands-on action. The steps will be short and straightforward, but the results are both useful and interesting. I encourage you to try these steps out. Even if you've been sitting there with your jaw hanging open throughout the entire chapter, even if you haven't the slightest idea what you're doing, you'll be able to create a fully-functioning filter.

The steps show you how to create the Rotator filter included on the CD-ROM at the back of the book. For a sneak peek at the havoc you can wreak with this filter, look at Color Plate 17-3. Talk about your incentives!

Steps: Creating a Filter Inside the Factory

1. **Open an RGB image or convert some other image to the RGB mode.** This filter yields interesting results even when applied to grayscale images converted to RGB.

2. **Choose Filter ➪ Synthetic ➪ Factory.** Set all the slider bars back to 0, just in case somebody's been fooling around with them.

3. **Enter *rad(d − (4*ctl(0)),m,0)* into the R option box.** The first argument in the expression — *d − (4*ctl(0))* — subtracts four times the value of the top slider bar from the angle variable *d*. Why four times? Because the slider only offers 256 increments, and the filter measures a full circle in 1,024 increments — 256 times 4 equals 1,024, thus enabling you to translate the slider values to a full circle.

   Meanwhile, *d* is the angle of the current pixel from the center and m is the distance from the pixel to the center. So *rad(d − (4*ctl(0)),m,0)* tells the filter to lift the brightness from the pixel in a counterclockwise direction from the PBE. The result is that the red channel rotates in the opposite direction, clockwise. Drag the slider bar and you'll see that this is true.

4. **Insert the phrase − *ctl(4)/2* after the *m* so that the expression reads *rad(d − (4*ctl(0)),m − ctl(4)/2,0).*** You'll use the second and third slider bars — *ctl(1)* and *ctl(2)* — for rotating the other two channels. But I think that I'd like to use the fifth slider bar for distorting the image. Why not the fourth channel? Well, because the first three sliders are going to be devoted to rotation. The distortion slider will be logically different, so it might be nice to create a blank space between the rotation and distortion sliders. Not using slider four is the way to do it.

   By changing the expression to *rad(d − (4*ctl(0)),m − ctl(4)/2,0)*, you tell Photoshop to subtract half the value from the fourth slider from the distance-from-center variable, thus shoving the pixels outward as you drag the fifth slider bar (the top of the two labeled Map 2). Give it a try.

5. **Copy the R expression and paste it into G.** Select the entire expression in the R option box, copy it by pressing ⌘-C, tab to the G option box, and press ⌘-V to paste. Then change the *ctl(0)* function to *ctl(1)* and the final number after the comma from a *0* to a *1*, so that it reads *rad(d − (4*ctl(1)),m − ctl(4)/2,1)*. Now the expression takes rotation data from the second slider bar and lifts its colors from the green channel. The result is a rotating green channel.

6. **Tab to the B option box and press ⌘-V again.** Change *ctl(0)* to *ctl(2)* and change the final *0* to a *2*. The result is *rad(d − (4*ctl(2)),m − ctl(4)/2,2)*. Just to make sure that you haven't fallen behind, Figure 17-43 shows all three expressions exactly as they should appear.

Tip

By the way, a little yellow triangle to the left of the R, G, or B option boxes is Photoshop's way of telling you your formula contains some sort of error — a missing parenthesis or some other faux pas.

(continued)

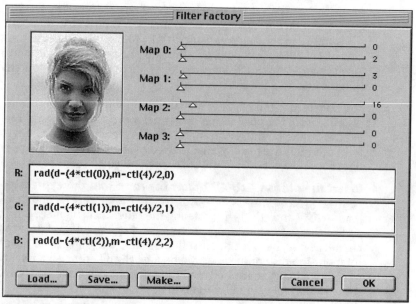

Figure 17-43: These three expressions let you rotate the three color channels independently using the first three slider bars and distort the image using the fifth slider.

7. **Click on the Save button and save your settings to disk.** You may want to use the name *Rotator.afs* to show that it's a Filter Factory file. (For some reason, *afs* is the accepted suffix for settings files.)

8. **Adjust the sliders to set the defaults.** Before you turn this sucker into its own filter, you need to be sure that the sliders are set how as want them to appear by default. Every time you open the new filter for the first time during a Photoshop session, these slider values will appear as they do now. You may want to set all sliders to 0 so that the user starts from square one, but it's completely up to you.

9. **Click on the Make button to convert your code into a filter.** Clicking on Make displays the dialog box shown in Figure 17-44. Enter the submenu in which you want the filter to appear in the Category option box. If you want it to appear with the rest of the *Photoshop Bible* filters, enter Tormentia. Enter the name of the filter, Rotator, in the Title option box. Then enter copyright and author information in the next two option boxes. (Go ahead, give yourself credit. You've earned it.)

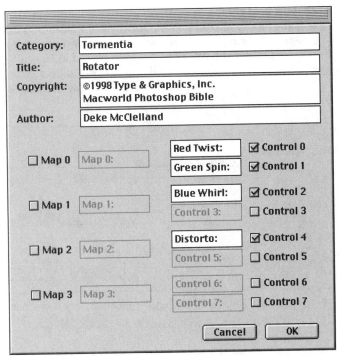

Category:	Tormentia
Title:	Rotator
Copyright:	©1998 Type & Graphics, Inc. Macworld Photoshop Bible
Author:	Deke McClelland

☐ Map 0 ⬜ Map 0:

☐ Map 1 ⬜ Map 1:

☐ Map 2 ⬜ Map 2:

☐ Map 3 ⬜ Map 3:

Red Twist: ☑ Control 0
Green Spin: ☑ Control 1
Blue Whirl: ☑ Control 2
Control 3: ☐ Control 3
Distorto: ☑ Control 4
Control 5: ☐ Control 5
Control 6: ☐ Control 6
Control 7: ☐ Control 7

[Cancel] [OK]

Figure 17-44: Click on the Make button to display this dialog box, which lets you name your filter, assign it to a submenu, and select the slider bars that you want to appear in the final dialog box.

10. **Select a Control check box for every slider you want to appear in your final filter.** The Control check boxes along the right side represent the slider bars inside the Filter Factory dialog box. Select the check boxes for Control 0, Control 1, Control 2, and Control 4. Then name them appropriately. My suggested names appear in Figure 17-44, but they may be a little too clever for your tastes.

Caution

Watch out: The Filter Factory enables you to select any of the slider check boxes, whether they were used in your formulas or not. If you're not careful, you can activate a slider bar that has no function.

11. **When you're finished, press Return.** You're asked to specify the location of the filter. To keep things tidy, you'll probably want to put it in the Filters folder inside the Plug-Ins folder, but anywhere in the Plug-Ins folder is okay.

12. **Press Escape to leave the Filter Factory dialog box.**

(continued)

13. **Quit Photoshop and relaunch it.** Open an RGB image—like the Filter Factory itself, any filter you create in the factory is applicable to RGB images only—and choose your newest command, Filter ➪ Tormentia ➪ Rotator. The dialog box should look something like the one shown in Figure 17-45. Notice the gaps between the Blue Whirl and Distorto sliders. Nice logical grouping, huh? Feel free to drag the controls and apply the filter as much as you want. It's alive!

Figure 17-45: The new Rotator filter complete with its four slider bars.

To see a demonstration of your powerful new filter, check out Color Plate 17-3, in which I applied the filter six times at various settings. The top row shows the effect of rotating the channels to different degrees with the Distorto option set to 0. The bottom row shows the same rotation values, but with the Distorto slider turned up to various volumes. It's not the most practical filter on earth, but it's diverting. You might even find something to do with it.

By the way, those sliders have a tendency to move around after you finish dragging them. It's very irritating. If you're interested in achieving an exact value, click at the location where you want to move the slider triangle. The triangle jumps in place. Then click, click, click to get it right where you want it.

If you want practical filters, check out the ones I've included on the CD-ROM. Most are much more complicated than the one you created in the steps, but they all use the variables, operators, and functions described in this chapter. Open the settings files to take a look at my code. (Just click on the Load button inside the Filter Factory dialog box.)

To whet your appetite, take a look at Color Plate 17-4, which shows all but one of the Tormentia filters applied to that poor surfer woman whose nose I mushed in the previous color plate. (The one filter not shown is my Channel Mixer, which was so cruelly usurped by Photoshop 5, as you may recall from my tearful account in Chapter 6. I guess I just don't have the heart to show it any more.)

Color Plate 17-4 shows only a few sample applications, many of them using the default slider bar settings. Obviously, jillions of other variations are possible. Have loads of fun.

✦   ✦   ✦

Corrections, Composites, and the Web

Mapping and Correcting Colors

What Is Color Mapping?

Color mapping is just a fancy name for shuffling colors around. For example, to map Color A to Color B simply means to take all the A-colored pixels and convert them to B-colored pixels. Photoshop provides several commands that enable you to map entire ranges of colors based on their hues, saturation levels, and, most frequently, brightness values.

Color effects and corrections

Why would you want to change colors around? For one reason, to achieve special effects. You know those psychedelic horror movies that show some guy's hair turning blue while his face turns purple and the palms of his hands glow a sort of cornflower yellow? A grayscale version of this very effect appears in the second example of Figure 18-1. Although not the most attractive effect by modern standards — you may be able to harvest more tasteful results if you put your shoulder to the color wheel — psychedelic qualifies as color mapping for the simple reason that each color shifts incrementally to a new color.

But the more common reason to map colors is to enhance the appearance of a scanned image or digital photograph, as demonstrated in the third example in Figure 18-1. In this case, you're not creating special effects — you're just making straightforward color adjustments, known in the biz as *color corrections*. Scans are never perfect, no matter how much money you spend on a scanning device or a service bureau. They can always benefit from tweaking and subtle adjustments, if not outright overhauls, in the color department.

Figure 18-1: Nobody's perfect, and neither is the best of scanned photos (left). You can modify colors in an image to achieve special effects (middle) or simply fix the image with a few well-targeted color corrections (right). Too bad Photoshop hasn't delivered on its promised Remove Excessive Jewelry filter.

Keep in mind, however, that Photoshop can't make something from nothing. In creating the illusion of more and better colors, most of the color-adjustment operations that you perform actually take some small amount of color *away* from the image. Somewhere in your image, two pixels that were two different colors before you started the correction change to the same color. The image may look 10 times better, but it will in fact be less colorful than when you started.

It's important to keep this principle in mind because it demonstrates that color mapping is a balancing act. The first nine operations you perform may make an image look progressively better, but the tenth may send it into decline. There's no magic formula; the amount of color mapping you need to apply varies from image to image. But if you follow my usual recommendations — use the commands in moderation, know when to stop, and save your image to disk before doing anything drastic — you should be fine.

The good, the bad, and the wacky

Photoshop stores all of its color mapping commands under the Image ➪ Adjust submenu. These commands fall into three basic categories:

✦ **Color mappers:** Commands such as Invert and Threshold are quick-and-dirty color mappers. They don't fix images, but they can be useful for creating special effects and adjusting masks.

✦ **Easy color correctors:** Brightness/Contrast and Color Balance are true color correction commands, but they sacrifice functionality for ease of use. If I had my way, these commands would be removed from the Image ⇨ Adjust submenu and thrown in the dust heap.

✦ **Expert color correctors:** The third, more complicated variety of color correction commands provide better control, but they take a fair amount of effort to learn. Levels, Curves, and Hue/Saturation are examples of color correcting at its best and most complicated.

This chapter contains little information about the second category of commands for the simple reason that some of them are inadequate and ultimately a big waste of time. There are exceptions of course — Auto Levels is a decent quick fixer, and Variations offers deceptively straightforward sophistication — but Brightness/Contrast and Color Balance sacrifice accuracy in their attempt to be straightforward. They are as liable to damage your image as fix it, making them quite dangerous in a dull, pedestrian sort of way. I know because I spent my first year with Photoshop relying exclusively on Brightness/Contrast and Color Balance, all the while wondering why I couldn't achieve the effects I wanted. Then, one happy day, I spent about a half an hour learning Levels and Curves, and the quality of my images skyrocketed. So wouldn't you just rather learn it right in the first place? I hope so, because the die is cast.

Quick Color Effects

Before we get into all the high-end gunk, however, I'll take a moment to explain the first category of commands, all of which happen to occupy one of the lower sections in the Image ⇨ Adjust submenu. These commands — Invert, Equalize, Threshold, and Posterize — produce immediate effects that are either difficult to duplicate or not worth attempting with the more full-featured commands.

Invert

When you choose Image ⇨ Adjust ⇨ Invert (⌘-I), Photoshop converts every color in your image to its exact opposite, as in a photographic negative. As demonstrated in Figure 18-2, black becomes white, white becomes black, fire becomes water, good becomes evil, dogs romance cats, and the brightness value of every primary color component changes to 255 minus the original brightness value.

Caution

By itself, the Invert command is not sufficient to convert a scanned color photographic negative to a positive. Negative film produces an orange cast that the Invert command does not address. After inverting, you can use the Variations command to remove the color cast. Or avoid Invert altogether and use the Levels command to invert the image. Both Variations and Levels are explained later in this chapter.

Original   Invert

Figure 18-2: An image before the advent of the Invert command (left) and after (right).

Image ➪ Adjust ➪ Invert is just about the only color mapping command that retains every single drop of color in an image. (The Hue/Saturation command also retains colors under specific conditions.) If you apply the Invert command twice in a row, you arrive at your original image.

When you're working on a full-color image, the Invert command simply inverts the contents of each color channel. This means that the command produces very different results when applied to RGB, Lab, and especially CMYK images. Color Plate 18-1 shows the results of inverting a single image in each of these modes. The RGB and Lab images share some similarities, but you'll find all kinds of subtle differences if you study the backgrounds and the basic colors of the faces.

Inverting in CMYK is much different. Typically, the Invert command changes much of a CMYK image to black. Except in rare instances — such as in night scenes — the black channel contains lots of light shades and few dark shades. So when you invert the channel, it becomes extremely dark. To reverse this effect, I inverted only the cyan, magenta, and yellow channels in the right example of Color Plate 18-1. (I did this by inverting the entire image and then going to the black channel — ⌘-4 — and pressing ⌘-I again.) Though this approach is preferable to inverting the black channel, it prevents the blacks in the hair and shadows from turning white (which would be the only portions even remotely light had I inverted the black channel as well).

Note

Just so you know, when I refer to applying color corrections in the CMYK mode, I mean applying them after choosing Mode ➪ CMYK Color. Applying corrections in the RGB mode when View ➪ Preview ➪ CMYK is active produces the same effect as when CMYK Preview is not selected; the only difference is that the on-screen colors are curtailed slightly to fit inside the CMYK color space. You're still editing inside the same old red, green, and blue color channels, so the effects are the same.

Cross-Reference

As I mentioned back in Chapter 12, inverting the contents of the mask channel is the same as applying Select ⇨ Inverse to a selection outline in the marching ants mode. In fact, this is one of the most useful applications of the filter. If you're considering inverting a color image, however, I strongly urge you to try out the SuperInvert filter contained in the Tormentia folder on the CD at the back of this book. It permits you to invert each channel independently and incrementally. Any setting under 128 lessens the contrast of the channel; 128 makes it completely gray; and any value over 128 inverts it to some degree.

Equalize

Equalize is the smartest and at the same time least useful of the Image ⇨ Adjust pack. When you invoke this command, Photoshop searches for the lightest and darkest color values in a selection. Then it maps the lightest color in all the color channels to white, maps the darkest color in the channels to black, and distributes the remaining colors to other brightness levels in an effort to evenly distribute pixels over the entire brightness spectrum. This doesn't mean that any one pixel will actually appear white or black after you apply Equalize; rather, that one pixel in at least one channel will be white and another pixel in at least one channel will be black. In an RGB image, for example, the red, green, or blue component of one pixel would be white, but the other two components of that same pixel might be black. The result is a higher contrast image with white and black pixels scattered throughout the color channels.

If no portion of the image is selected when you choose Image ⇨ Adjust ⇨ Equalize, Photoshop automatically maps out the entire image across the brightness spectrum, as shown in the upper right example of Figure 18-3. However, if you select a portion of the image before choosing the Equalize command, Photoshop displays a dialog box containing the following two radio buttons:

- ✦ **Selected Area Only:** Select this option to apply the Equalize command strictly within the confines of the selection. The lightest pixel in the selection becomes white, the darkest pixel becomes black, and so on.

- ✦ **Entire Image Based on Area:** If you select the second radio button, which is the default setting, Photoshop applies the Equalize command to the entire image based on the lightest and darkest colors in the selection. All colors in the image that are lighter than the lightest color in the selection become white, and all colors darker than the darkest color in the selection become black.

The bottom two examples in Figure 18-3 show the effects of selecting different parts of the image when the Entire Image Based on Area option is in force. In the left example, I selected a dark portion of the image, which resulted in over-lightening of the entire image. In the right example, I selected an area with both light and dark values, which boosted the amount of contrast between highlights and shadows in the image.

Original　　　　　　　　　Equalize

Equalize based on selection

Figure 18-3: An image before (top left) and after (top right) applying the Equalize command when no portion of the image is selected. You can also use the brightness values in a selected region as the basis for equalizing an entire image (bottom left and right).

The problem with the Equalize command is that it relies too heavily on some pretty bizarre automation to be of much use as a color correction tool. Certainly, you can create some interesting special effects. But if you'd prefer to automatically adjust the colors in an image from black to white regardless of the color mode and composition of the individual channels, choose Image ➪ Adjust ➪ Auto Levels (⌘-Shift-L). If you want to adjust the tonal balance manually and therefore with a higher degree of accuracy, the Levels and Curves commands are tops. I explain all of these commands at length later in this chapter.

Threshold

I touched on the Threshold command a couple of times in previous chapters. As you may recall, Threshold converts all colors to either black or white based on their brightness values. When you choose Image ➪ Adjust ➪ Threshold, Photoshop displays the Threshold dialog box shown in Figure 18-4. The dialog box offers a single option box and a slider bar, either of which you can use to specify the medium brightness value in the image. Photoshop changes any color lighter than the value in the Threshold option box to white, and changes any color darker than the value to black.

Figure 18-4: The histogram in the Threshold dialog box shows the distribution of brightness values in the selection.

The dialog box also includes a graph of all the colors in the image—even if only a portion of the image is selected. This graph is called a *histogram.* The width of the histogram represents all 256 possible brightness values, starting at black on the left and progressing through white on the right. The height of each vertical line in the graph demonstrates the number of pixels currently associated with that brightness value. Therefore, you can use the histogram to gauge the distribution of lights and darks in your image. It may seem weird at first, but with enough experience, the histogram becomes an invaluable tool, permitting you to corroborate the colors that you see onscreen.

Tip

Generally speaking, you achieve the best effects if you change an equal number of pixels to black as you change to white (and vice versa). So rather than moving the slider bar to 128, which is the medium brightness value, move it to the point at which the area of the vertical lines to the left of the slider triangle looks roughly equivalent to the area of the vertical lines to the right of the slider triangle.

The upper left example in Figure 18-5 shows the result of applying the Threshold command with a Threshold Level value of 120 (as in Figure 18-4). Although this value more or less evenly distributes black and white pixels, I lost a lot of detail in the dark areas.

As you may recall from my "Using the High Pass filter" discussion in Chapter 15, you can use Filter ➪ Other ➪ High Pass in advance of the Threshold command to retain areas of contrast. In the upper left image in Figure 18-5, I applied the High Pass filter with a radius of 1.0 pixel, followed by the Threshold command with a value of 125. In the two bottom images, I first chose an effects filter — Filter ➪ Artistic ➪ Watercolor on the left and Filter ➪ Sketch ➪ Bas Relief on the right. Then I applied High Pass with a radius of 1.0 pixel followed by the Threshold command.

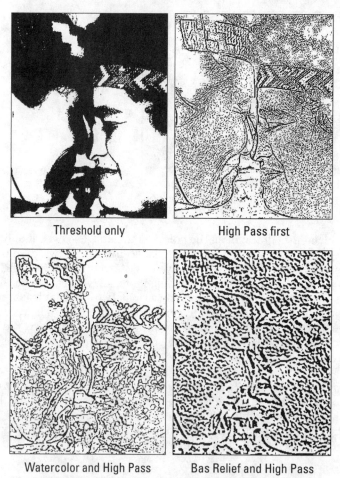

Threshold only   High Pass first

Watercolor and High Pass   Bas Relief and High Pass

Figure 18-5: By itself, the Threshold command tends to deliver flat results (top left). To better articulate the detail, apply High Pass and other filters prior to choosing Threshold.

If the Threshold effects in Figure 18-5 are a bit austere, first clone the image to a layer and then mix the layer with the underlying original. Figure 18-6 shows all the effects from Figure 18-5 applied to layers subject to the Overlay blend mode and 50 percent Opacity. In each example, the translucent selection helps to add contrast and reinforce details in the original image.

Figure 18-6: The Threshold operations from Figure 18-5 applied to separate layers, blended with the Overlay mode and an Opacity value of 50 percent.

Note

You can compare the before and after effects of any color correction command that includes a Preview check box in its dialog box by turning the check box off and then mousing down on the title bar. If the Video LUT Animation option in the Display & Cursors panel of the Preferences dialog box is active (as by default), turning the Preview check box off causes Photoshop to apply the Threshold settings to the entire screen. Unfortunately, Photoshop applies the effect separately to each color channel, creating a series of brightly colored areas that bear little resemblance to the actual black-and-white effect. To get a realistic picture of your image, leave the Preview check box turned on.

If you want to achieve a colorful Threshold effect like the one that appears when using Video LUT Animation, try applying the Threshold command independently to each color channel. In an RGB image, for example, press ⌘-1 and then apply Image ⇨ Adjust ⇨ Threshold. Then press ⌘-2 and repeat the command, and press ⌘-3 and do it again. Color Plate 18-2 shows examples of what happens when I apply High Pass (with a Radius value of 3.0) and Threshold to independent color channels in the RGB, Lab, and CMYK modes. To soften the transitions and avoid trapping problems, I resampled each image up and down a couple of times, as described back in the "Anti-aliasing an image" section of Chapter 15.

Posterize

The Posterize command is Threshold's rich cousin. Whereas Threshold boils down an image into two colors only, Posterize can retain as many colors as you like. However, you can't control how colors are mapped, as you can when you use Threshold. The Posterize dialog box does not provide a histogram or slider bar. Instead, Posterize automatically divides the full range of 256 brightness values into a specified number of equal increments.

To use this command, choose Image ⇨ Adjust ⇨ Posterize and enter a value into the Levels option box. The Levels value represents the number of brightness values that the Posterize command retains. Higher values result in subtle color adjustments; lower values produce more dramatic effects. The first example in Figure 18-7 shows an image subject to a Levels value of 8.

By now, you may be thinking, "By golly, if Posterize is so similar to Threshold, I wonder how it works when applied after the High Pass filter?" Well, you're in luck, because this is exactly the purpose of the second example in Figure 18-7. Here I chose the High Pass filter and entered 3.0 for the Radius. Then I applied the Posterize command with the same Levels value as before (8).

Now, just in case you've tried this same effect on your full-color image and thought, "Yech, this looks terrible — half the color just disappeared," the key is to apply High Pass and Posterize to a layered version of the image and then mix the effect with the underlying original. Color Plate 18-3 shows the results of applying the High Pass filter with a Radius of 3.0 and the Posterize command with a setting of 8 to the layered clone, and then compositing layer and underlying original using each of three overlay modes from the Layers palette. The Luminosity option applies only the lights and darks in the layered image, allowing the colors in the underlying image to show through; Hard Light strengthens the light and dark shades; and Hue applies the colors from the layer with the saturation and brightness values from the original. After flattening each image, I increased the saturation of the colors using Image ⇨ Adjust ⇨ Hue/Saturation (⌘-U), which I discuss in an upcoming section.

Posterize   High Pass first

Figure 18-7: An image subject to the Posterize command with
a Levels value of 8 (left). You can retain more detail in an image
by applying the High Pass filter before using Posterize (right).

Quick Corrections

Photoshop offers two quick-correctors under the Image ⇨ Adjust submenu that I
want to discuss before entering into the larger world of advanced color correction.
Both are single-shot commands that alter your image without any dialog boxes or
special options. The first, Desaturate, sucks the saturation out of a selection and
leaves it looking like a grayscale image. The second, Auto Levels, automatically
increases the contrast of an image according to what Photoshop deems to be the
ideal brightness values.

Sucking saturation

There's little reason to apply the Desaturate command to an entire image; you can
just as easily choose Image ⇨ Mode ⇨ Grayscale to accomplish the same thing and
dispose of the extra channels that would otherwise consume room in memory and
on disk. I know of only two reasons to sacrifice all colors in the RGB mode:

✦ You want to retain the option of applying RGB-only filters, such as Lens Flare,
   Lighting Effects, and anything created with the Filter Factory.

✦ You intend to downsize the colors using Image ⇨ Mode ⇨ Indexed Colors and
   save the final image in the GIF format for use on the World Wide Web (as I
   discuss in Chapter 20).

But mostly, you'll use Desaturate to rob color from discrete selections or independent layers, neither of which the Grayscale mode can accommodate. For example, in Color Plate 18-4, I used Select ⇨ Color Range to select all of the pumpkin except the eyes and mouth and a few speckly bits here and there. (I could have used the quick mask mode to tweak the selection and get it just right, but it didn't strike me as particularly important in this case.) I then applied Image ⇨ Adjust ⇨ Desaturate (⌘-Shift-U) to achieve the first example. To create the top-right pumpkin, I chose Filter ⇨ Fade Desaturate and changed the Opacity value to 50 percent, bringing back some of the original colors from the full-color original and achieving an only slightly desaturated pumpkin.

Tip

In case you missed that last paragraph, you can use Filter ⇨ Fade (⌘-Shift-F) to back off the effects of any command under the Image ⇨ Adjust submenu. As always, the Fade command is available immediately after you apply the color correction; if you so much as alter a selection outline, Fade goes dim.

Desaturate isn't the only way to suck colors out of an image. You can also invert the colors and mix them with their original counterparts to achieve a slightly different effect. The bottom row of Color Plate 18-4 shows what I mean. In the lower left example, I applied Invert (⌘-I) to my same Color Range selection. Then I pressed ⌘-Shift-F, changed the Opacity setting to 50 percent, and — here's the important part — selected Color from the Mode pop-up menu.

Note that the inverted and mixed colors are slightly different from the desaturated tones in the pumpkin above. When set to the Color blend mode, the colors in the inverted image should theoretically cancel out the colors in the underlying original. However, the Invert command doesn't change the saturation of the pixels, so the saturation of the inverted and original pixels are the same. As a result, some colors from the underlying image are allowed to show through, as the bottom left image shows.

The bottom right example shows what happened when I changed the Opacity to 70 percent, thus favoring the inverted colors. Why'd I do that? Maybe I just like blue pumpkins. Or more likely, I had a fourth spot to fill in the figure, and a blue pumpkin seemed like the guy to fill it.

Note

By the way, you might be wondering why Adobe selected ⌘-Shift-U as the keyboard shortcut for Desaturate. Well, Desaturate is actually a renegade element from the Hue/Saturation command, which lets you raise and lower saturation levels to any degree you like. The shortcut for Hue/Saturation is ⌘-U — for *hUUUe*, don't you know — so Desaturate is ⌘-Shift-U.

Auto contrast correction

Image ⇨ Adjust ⇨ Auto Levels (⌘-Shift-L) goes through each color channel and changes the lightest pixel to white, changes the darkest pixel to black, and stretches out all the shades of gray to fill out the spectrum. In Figure 18-8, I started with a drab and murky image. But when I applied Auto Levels, Photoshop pumped up the lights and darks, bolstering the contrast. Although I would argue that the corrected image is too dark, it's not half bad for an automated, no-brainer command that you just choose and let rip.

Figure 18-8: A grayscale image before (left) and after (right) applying the Auto Levels command.

Unlike the Equalize command, which considers all color channels as a whole, Auto Levels looks at each channel independently. So as with the Invert command, the active color mode has a profound effect on Auto Levels. Color Plate 18-5 shows our friendly jack o' lantern prior to color corrections, followed by the same image corrected with Auto Levels in the RGB, Lab, and CMYK modes. Quite frankly, the RGB image is the only one that's acceptable. The Lab image is far too orange, and the CMYK image is too dark, thanks to the exaggeration of the black channel. Auto Levels has also darkened the cyan channel, turning the pumpkin a bright red that one rarely sees in today's sincere pumpkin patches.

Like Invert, Equalize, and other automatic color mappers, Auto Levels is designed specifically for use in the RGB mode. If you use it in CMYK, you're more likely to achieve special effects than color correction.

Note

The Auto Levels command serves the same purpose and produces the same effect as the Auto button in the Levels dialog box. You shouldn't really rely on either. What you *should* do is read the rest of this chapter and learn about the bigger and better color correction commands.

Hue Shifting and Colorizing

The following sections cover commands that are specifically designed to change the distribution of colors in an image. You can rotate the hues around the color spectrum, change the saturation of colors, adjust highlights and shadows, and even tint an image. Two of these commands — Hue/Saturation and Selective Color — are applicable exclusively to color images. The other two — Replace Color and Variations — can be applied to grayscale images, but are not the best solutions. Although both permit you to select specific ranges of brightness values that you want to edit, they apply their corrections with less finesse than either the Levels or Curves commands (discussed toward the end of the chapter).

Tip

Before I go any further, I should mention one awesome little bit of advice. Remember that ⌘-Option-F redisplays the last filter dialog box so that you can tweak the effect? Well, a similar shortcut is available when you're applying color corrections. Press the Option key when choosing any of the commands described throughout the rest of this chapter to display that command's dialog box with the settings last applied to the image. If the command has a keyboard equivalent, just add Option to restore the last settings. ⌘-Option-U, for example, brings up the Hue/Saturation dialog box with the settings you last used.

Using the Hue/Saturation command

The Hue/Saturation command provides two functions. First, it enables you to adjust colors in an image according to their hues and saturation levels. You can apply the changes to specific ranges of colors or modify all colors equally across the spectrum. And second, the command lets you colorize images by applying new hue and saturation values while retaining the core brightness information from the original image.

This command is perfect for colorizing grayscale images. I know, I know, Woody Allen wouldn't approve, but with some effort, you can make Ted Turner green with envy. Just scan him and change the Hue value to 140 degrees.

When you choose Image ⇨ Adjust ⇨ Hue/Saturation (⌘-U), Photoshop displays the Hue/Saturation dialog box, shown in Figure 18-9. Before I explain how to use this dialog box to produce specific effects, let me briefly introduce the options, starting with the three option boxes and then moving to the other options:

✦ **Hue:** The Hue slider bar measures colors on the 360-degree color circle, as explained back in the "HSB" section of Chapter 5. You can adjust the Hue value from negative to positive 180 degrees. As you do, Photoshop rotates the colors around the Hue wheel. Consider the example of flesh tones. A Hue value of +30 moves the flesh into the orange range; a value of +100 makes it green. Going the other direction, a Hue of −30 makes the flesh red, and −100 makes it purple.

When the Colorize check box is selected, Hue becomes an absolute value measured from 0 to 360 degrees. A Hue value of 0 is red, 30 is orange, and so on, as described in Chapter 5.

Figure 18-9: The Hue/Saturation dialog box as it appears when editing all colors in a layer (top) or just a specific range of colors (bottom).

✦ **Saturation:** The Saturation value changes the intensity of the colors. Normally, the Saturation value varies from –100 for gray to +100 for incredibly vivid hues. The only exception occurs when the Colorize check box is active, in which case saturation becomes an absolute value, measured from 0 for gray to 100 for maximum saturation.

✦ **Lightness:** You can darken or lighten an image by varying the Lightness value from negative to positive 100.

Because this value invariably changes *all* brightness levels in an image to an equal extent — whether or not Colorize is selected — it permanently dulls highlights and shadows. I advise that you avoid this option like the plague and rely instead on the Levels or Curves command to edit brightness and contrast.

✦ **Edit:** The Edit pop-up menu controls which colors in the active selection or layer are affected by the Hue/Saturation command. If you select the Master option, as by default, Hue/Saturation adjusts all colors equally. If you prefer to adjust some colors in the layer differently than others, choose one of the other Edit options or press the keyboard equivalent — ⌘-1 for Reds, ⌘-2 for Yellows, and so on.

Each of the Edit options isolates a predefined range of colors inside the image. For example, the Reds option selects the range measured from 345 to 15 degrees on the Hue wheel. Naturally, if you were to modify just the red pixels and left all non-red pixels unchanged, you'd end up with some jagged transitions in your image. So Photoshop softens the edges with 30 degrees of fuzziness at either end of the red spectrum (the same kind of fuzziness described in the "Using the Color Range command" section of Chapter 12).

You can apply different Hue, Saturation, and Lightness settings for every one of the color ranges. For example, to change all reds in an image to green and all cyans to gray, do like so: choose the Reds option and change the Hue value to +50, then choose Cyans and change the Saturation value to −100.

✦ **Color ramps:** There are two ways to track changes made to colors in the Hue/Saturation dialog box. One way is to select the Preview check box and keep an eye on the changes in the image window. The second way is to observe the color ramps at the bottom of the dialog box. The first ramp shows the 360-degree color spectrum; the second ramp shows what the color ramp looks like after your edits.

✦ **Range controls:** You can also use the color ramps to broaden or narrow the range of colors affected by Hue/Saturation. When you choose any option other than Master from the Edit pop-up menu, a collection of color range controls appears between the color ramps. The range bar identifies the selected colors, but it also permits you to edit them.

Figure 18-10 shows the color range controls up close and personal. Here's how they work:

• Drag the central range bar to move the entire color range.

• To broaden or narrow the color range without affecting the fuzziness, drag one of the two lighter-colored fuzziness bars.

• Drag the vertical range control (labeled in Figure 18-10) to change the range while leaving the fuzziness points fixed in place. This means expanding the range and condensing the fuzziness, or vice versa.

• Drag the triangular fuzziness control to lengthen or contract the fuzziness independently of the color range.

Figure 18-10: After defining a basic range using the Edit pop-up menu, use the color range controls to modify the range or the fuzziness.

By default, red is the central color in the color ramps with blue at either side. This is great when the range is red or some other warm color. But if you're working with a blue range, the controls get split between the two ends. To move a different color to the central position, ⌘-drag in the color ramp. The spectrum revolves around the ramp as you drag.

✦ **Eyedroppers:** To lift a color range from the image window, click inside the image window with the eyedropper cursor. (The cursor automatically changes to an eyedropper when you move it outside the Hue/Saturation dialog box.) Photoshop centers the range on the exact color on which you click.

To expand the range to include more colors, Shift-click or drag in the image window. To remove colors from the range, Option-click or drag in the image. You can also use the alternative plus and minus eyedropper tools, but why bother. Shift and Option do the job just fine.

✦ **Load/Save:** As in all the best color correction dialog boxes, you can load and save settings to disk in case you want to reapply the options to other images. These options are especially useful if you find a magic combination of color-correction settings that accounts for most of the color mistakes produced by your scanner.

✦ **Colorize:** Select this check box to apply a single hue and a single saturation level to the entire selection or layer, regardless of how it was previously colored. (Notice that Photoshop 5 sets the Saturation to 25 percent by default, a much more satisfactory setting than the previous overblown default of 100 percent.) All brightness levels remain intact, although you can adjust them incrementally using the Lightness slider bar (a practice that I strongly advise against, as I mentioned earlier).

Color ranges are not permitted when colorizing. The moment you select the Colorize check box, Photoshop dims the Edit pop-up menu and sets it to Master.

✦ **Restore:** You can restore the options in the Hue/Saturation, Levels, and Curves dialog boxes to their original settings by Option-clicking on the Reset button (the Cancel button changes to Reset when you press the Option key). Or simply press Option-Escape.

To track the behavior of specific colors when using Hue/Saturation or any of Photoshop's other powerful color adjustment commands, display the Info palette (F8) before choosing the Hue/Saturation command. Then move the cursor inside the image window. As shown in Figure 18-11, the Info palette tracks the individual RGB and CMYK values of the pixel beneath the cursor. The number before the slash is the value before the color adjustment; the number after the slash is the value after the adjustment.

Figure 18-11: When you move the eyedropper outside a color adjustment dialog box and into the image window, the Info palette lists the color values of the pixel beneath the cursor before and after adjustment.

In Photoshop 5, you don't have to settle for just one color readout. Shift-click in the image window to add up to four fixed color samples (like those created with the color sample tool, described in Chapter 5). To move a color sample once you've set it in place, Shift-drag it.

In the case of the Hue/Saturation dialog box, you can set color sample points only when the Edit pop-up menu is set to Master. After you set the samples, then select some other options from the pop-up menu to modify a specific range.

Adjusting hue and saturation

All right, now that you know how the copious Hue/Saturation options work, it's time to give them a whirl. One caveat before I launch into things: Grayscale figures won't help you one whit in understanding the Hue/Saturation options, so I'll be referring you to three color plates. You may want to take a moment to slap a Post-it note on the page that contains Color Plates 18-6, 18-7, and 18-8 before you begin reading so that you can easily flip back and forth between text and figures.

Changing hues

When the Colorize check box is inactive, the Hue slider bar shifts colors in an image around the color wheel. It's as if the pixels were playing a colorful game of musical chairs, except that none of the chairs disappear. If you select the Master option and enter a value of +60 degrees, for example, all pixels stand up, march one sixth of the way around the color wheel, and sit down, assuming the colors of their new chairs. A pixel that was red becomes yellow, a pixel that was yellow becomes green, and so on. The top row of Color Plate 18-6 shows the result of applying various Hue values to a single image. Note that in each case, all colors in the image change to an equal degree.

Note

As long as you select only the Master option and edit only the Hue value, Photoshop retains all colors in an image. In other words, after shifting the hues in an image +60 degrees, you can later choose Hue/Saturation and shift the hues –60 degrees to restore the original colors.

If you select any Edit option other than Master, the musical chairs metaphor breaks down a little. All pixels that correspond to the selected color range move while pixels outside the color range remain seated. The pixels that move must sit on the non-moving pixels' laps, meaning that you sacrifice colors in the image.

For example, I edited the images in the second row of Color Plate 18-6 by applying Hue values exclusively while the Cyan option was selected. (In other words, I didn't apply Hue changes in combination with any other color range.) All pixels that fell inside the cyan range shifted to new hues; all non-cyan pixels remained unchanged. Despite the fact that the Hue values in each column of the color plate are identical, the colors in the horse changed less dramatically when Cyan was selected than when I used the Master option. Even the pixels in the primarily cyan areas contain trace amounts of blue and green, which are excluded from the Cyan range.

Changing saturation levels

When I was a little kid, I loved watching my grandmother's television, because she kept the Color knob cranked at all times. The images leapt off the screen, like they were radioactive or something. Way cool. Well, the Saturation option works just like that Color knob. I don't recommend that you follow my grandmother's example and send the saturation for every image through the roof, but it can prove helpful for enhancing or downplaying the colors in an image. If the image looks washed out, try adding saturation; if colors leap off the screen so that everybody in the image looks like they're wearing neon makeup, subtract saturation.

Note

Just as the Saturation option works like the Color knob on a TV set, the Hue value serves the same purpose as the Tint knob, and the Lightness value works like the Brightness knob. So you see, your mother was quite mistaken when she told you that sitting on your butt and staring at the TV wasn't going to teach you anything. Little did she know, you were getting a head start on electronic art.

The top row of Color Plate 18-7 shows the results of applying Saturation values when the Master option is selected. As you can see, all colors in the image fade or are fortified equally. However, by applying the Saturation values to specific color ranges only, you can selectively fade and fortify colors, as demonstrated in the second row of the color plate. The lower left image in the color plate shows the result of selecting every color range except Cyan and Blue and lowering the Saturation to −100, which translates to no saturation whatsoever. The result is that all colors outside the cyan and blue ranges turn gray. In the lower right image, I lowered the Saturation for the Cyan and Blue options to −100 and raised the saturation of all other color ranges to +50, thus eliminating the image's most prominent colors and enhancing the remaining weaker ones.

The Saturation option is especially useful for toning down images captured with low-end scanners and digital cameras, which have a tendency to exaggerate certain colors. Back in the early years, I used to work with an Epson ES-300C. Although a good device for its time, it would digitize flesh tones in varieties of vivid oranges and red. I couldn't for the life of me figure out how to peel the colors off the ceiling until I tried the Saturation option in the Hue/Saturation dialog box. By selecting the Red color range and dragging the slider down to about −50, I was usually able to eliminate the problem. You can, too.

Correcting out-of-gamut colors

Another common use for the Saturation option is to prepare RGB images for process-color printing. As I explained in Chapter 5, many colors in the RGB spectrum are considered "out of gamut," meaning that they fall outside the smaller CMYK color space. Photoshop now provides a means for recognizing such colors while remaining inside the RGB color space. Choose View ➪ Gamut Warning (⌘-Shift-Y) to color all out-of-gamut colors with gray (or some other color that you specify using the Preferences command). The pixels don't actually change to gray; they just appear gray on-screen as long as the command is active. To turn View ➪ Gamut Warning off, choose the command again.

How do you eliminate such problem colors? Well, you have three options:

✦ Let Photoshop take care of the problem automatically when you convert the image by choosing Image ➪ Mode ➪ CMYK Color. This tactic is risky, because Photoshop simply cuts off colors that are outside the gamut and converts them to their nearest CMYK equivalents. What was once an abundant range of differently saturated hues becomes abruptly flattened, like some kind of cruel buzz haircut. Choosing View ➪ Preview ➪ CMYK (⌘-Y) while working in the RGB color space gives you an idea of how dramatic the buzz can be. Sometimes the effect is hardly noticeable, in which case no additional attention may be warranted. Other times, the results can be disastrous.

✦ Another method is to scrub away with the sponge tool. In Chapter 8, I discussed how much I dislike this alternative, and despite the passage of ten chapters, I haven't changed my mind. Although it theoretically offers selective control — you just scrub at areas that need attention until the gray pixels created by the Gamut Warning command disappear — the process leaves too much to chance and frequently does more damage than simply choosing Image ➪ Mode ➪ CMYK Color.

✦ The third and best solution involves the Saturation option inside the Hue/Saturation dialog box.

No doubt that last item comes as a huge surprise, given that I decided to broach the whole out-of-gamut topic in the middle of examining the Saturation option. But try to scoop your jaw up off the floor long enough to peruse the following steps, which outline the proper procedure for bringing out-of-gamut colors back into the CMYK color space.

Steps: Eliminating Out-of-Gamut Colors

1. **Create a duplicate of your image to serve as a CMYK preview.** Choose Image ➪ Duplicate to create a copy of your image. Then choose View ➪ Preview ➪ CMYK or press ⌘-Y. This image represents what Photoshop will do with your image if you don't make any corrections whatsoever. It's good to have around for comparative purposes.

2. **Return to your original image and choose Select ➪ Color Range.** Then select the Out Of Gamut option from the Select pop-up menu and press Return. You have now selected all the nonconformist anti-gamut pixels throughout your image. These radicals must be expunged.

3. **To monitor your progress, choose View ➪ Gamut Warning to display the gray pixels.** Oh, and don't forget to press ⌘-H to get rid of those pesky ants.

4. **Press ⌘-U to display the Hue/Saturation dialog box.**

5. **Lower the saturation of individual color ranges.** Don't change any settings while Master is selected; it's not exacting enough. Rather, experiment with specifying your own color ranges and lowering the Saturation value. Every time you see one of the pixels change from gray to color, it means that another happy pixel has joined the CMYK collective. You may want to shout, "It's pointless to resist the invasion of the gamut snatchers!" and laugh mockingly just to make your work more entertaining.

(continued)

6. **When only a few hundred sporadic gray spots remain on screen, click on the OK button to return to the image window.** Bellow imperiously, "You may think you have won, you little gray pixels, but I have a secret weapon!" Then choose Image ⇨ Mode ⇨ CMYK Color and watch as Photoshop forcibly thrusts them into the gamut.

Mind you, the differences between your duplicate image and the one you manually turned away from the evils of RGB excess will be subtle, but they may prove enough to produce a better looking image with a more dynamic range of colors.

Avoiding gamut-correction edges

The one problem with the previous steps is that the Color Range command selects only the out-of-gamut pixels without even partially selecting their neighbors. As a result, you desaturate out-of-gamut colors while leaving similar colors fully saturated, an effect that may result in jagged and unnatural edges.

Tip

One solution is to insert a step between Steps 2 and 3 in which you do the following: Change the Tolerance value in the Magic Wand Options palette to, say, 12. Next, choose Select ⇨ Similar, which expands the selected area to incorporate all pixels that fall within the Tolerance range. Finally, choose Select ⇨ Feather and enter a Feather Radius value that's about half the Tolerance — in this case, 6.

This solution isn't perfect — ideally, the Color Range option box wouldn't dim the Fuzziness slider when you choose Out Of Gamut — but it does succeed in partially selecting a few neighboring pixels without sacrificing too many of the out-of-gamut bunch.

Colorizing images

When you select the Colorize check box in the Hue/Saturation dialog box, the options perform differently. Returning to that wonderful musical chairs analogy, the pixels no longer walk around a circle of chairs; they all get up and go sit in the same chair. Every pixel in the selection receives the same hue and the same level of saturation. Only the brightness values remain intact to ensure that the image remains recognizable.

The top row of Color Plate 18-8 shows the results of shifting the hues in an image in two different directions around the color wheel. In each case, the Colorize option is turned off. The second row shows similar colors applied separately to the blue and nonblue portions of the image using the Colorize option. (Because you can't specify color ranges in the Hue/Saturation dialog box when Colorize is on, I selected the blue regions using the Color Range command prior to choosing the Hue/Saturation command.) The colors look similar within each column in the color plate. However, the Hue values are different in the shifted images than those in the colorized images because the shifted colors are based on relative adjustments while the colorized changes are absolute.

In most cases, you'll only want to colorize grayscale images or bad color scans. After all, colorizing ruins the original color composition of an image. For the best results, you'll want to set the Saturation values to somewhere in the neighborhood of 25 to 75. All the colors in the second-row images in Color Plate 18-8 err on the high side, with Saturation values of 80.

Tip

To touch up the edges of a colorized selection, change the foreground color to match the Hue and Saturation values that you used in the Hue/Saturation dialog box. You can do this by choosing the HSB Sliders command from the Color palette menu, and entering the values into the H and S option boxes. Set the B (Brightness) value to 100 percent. Next, select the paintbrush tool and change the brush mode to Color (Shift-Option-C). Then paint away.

Shifting selected colors

The Replace Color command allows you to select an area of related colors and adjust the hue and saturation of that area. When you select Image ⇨ Adjust ⇨ Replace Color, you get a dialog box much like the Color Range dialog box. Shown in Figure 18-12, the Replace Color dialog box varies in only a few respects: It's missing the Select and Selection Preview pop-up menus and it offers three slider bars, taken right out of the Hue/Saturation dialog box.

In fact, this dialog box works exactly as if you were to select a portion of an image using Select ⇨ Color Range and edit it with the Hue/Saturation command. You don't have as many options to work with, but the outcome is the same. The Replace Color and Color Range dialog boxes even share the same default settings. If you change the Fuzziness value in one, the default Fuzziness value of the other changes as well. It's like they're identical twins or something.

So why does the Replace Color command even exist? Because it allows you to change the selection outline and apply different colors without affecting the image in any way. Just select the Preview check box to see the results of your changes on screen, and you're in business.

The top row of Color Plate 18-9 shows two effects created by selecting an area and changing the Hue value to +148 and the Saturation value to –12 (as in Figure 18-12). In the first example, I selected the pumpkin face by setting the Fuzziness value to 40 and clicking and Shift-clicking a few times with the eyedropper tool. In the right example, I clicked just once in the area behind the pumpkin and changed the Fuzziness to 200, the maximum setting. I was able to experiment freely without once leaving the dialog box or redrawing the selection outline.

Figure 18-12: The Replace Color dialog box works like the Color Range dialog box described back in Chapter 12, with a few Hue/Saturation options thrown in.

If you're not clear on how to use all the options in the Replace Color dialog box, read the "Using the Color Range command" section in Chapter 12. It tells you all about the eyedropper tools and the Fuzziness option.

Shifting predefined colors

The Selective Color command permits you to adjust the colors in CMYK images. You can use the command when working on RGB or Lab images, but because it permits you to adjust the levels of cyan, magenta, yellow, and black inks, Selective Color makes more sense in the CMYK color space.

Frankly, I'm not very keen on this command. For general image editing, the Variations command provides better control and more intuitive options. Adobe created the Selective Color command to accommodate traditional press managers who prefer to have direct control over ink levels rather than monkeying around with hue, saturation, and other observational color controls. If Selective Color works for you, great. But don't get hung up on it if it never quite gels. You can accomplish all this and more with the Variations command, described in the next section.

Choosing Image ⇨ Adjust ⇨ Selective Color brings up the dialog box shown in Figure 18-13. To use the dialog box, choose the predefined color that you want to edit from the Colors pop-up menu and then adjust the four process-color slider bars to change the predefined color. When the Relative radio button is selected, you add or subtract color, much as if you were moving the color around the musical chairs using the Hue slider bar. When you select Absolute, you change the predefined color to the exact value entered into the Cyan, Magenta, Yellow, and Black option boxes. The Absolute option is therefore very much like the Colorize check box in the Hue/Saturation dialog box.

Figure 18-13: Select a predefined color from the Colors pop-up menu and adjust the slider bars to change that color.

If you examine it closely, you'll notice that the Selective Color dialog box is very much like the Hue/Saturation dialog box. You have access to predefined colors in the form of a pop-up menu instead of radio buttons, and you can adjust slider bars to alter the color. The key differences are that the pop-up menu lets you adjust whites, medium grays (Neutrals), and blacks — options missing from Hue/Saturation — and the slider bars are always measured in CMYK color space.

The bottom row of Color Plate 18-9 includes two examples that show how this dialog box works. To create the first, I chose Red from the Colors pop-up menu and dragged the Cyan slider bar all the way up to +100 percent and the Yellow slider all the way down to –100 percent. I also selected the Relative radio button, which retains a lot of pink in the pumpkin's face. To create the second example, I reapplied the same colors but selected the Absolute radio button, making the entire pumpkin purple. I also chose Black from the Colors pop-up menu and dragged the Black slider to –100 percent.

Tip

As I mentioned at the outset, the Selective Color command produces the most predictable results when you're working on a CMYK image. When you drag the Cyan slider triangle to the right, for example, you're actually transferring brightness values to the cyan channel. However, you have to keep an eye out for a few anomalies, particularly when editing Black. In the CMYK mode, areas of your image that appear black include not only black, but also shades of cyan, magenta, and yellow, resulting in what printers call a *rich black* (or *saturated black*). Therefore, to change black to white, as I did in the lower right example of Color Plate 18-9, you have to set the Black slider to –100 percent and also set the Cyan, Magenta, and Yellow sliders to the same value.

Using the Variations command

The Variations command is at once Photoshop's most essential color correction function and its funkiest:

✦ On one hand, you can adjust hues and luminosity levels based on the brightness values of the pixels. This gives you a selective degree of control unmatched by Hue/Saturation. You can also see what you're doing by clicking on little thumbnail previews (see Figure 18-14), which takes much of the guesswork out of the correction process.

✦ On the other hand, the Variations dialog box takes over your screen and prevents you from previewing corrections in the image window. Furthermore, you can't see the area outside of a selection, which proves disconcerting when making relative color adjustments.

Variations is therefore best suited to correcting an image in its entirety. Here's how it works: To infuse color into the image, click on one of the thumbnails in the central portion of the dialog box. The thumbnail labeled More Cyan, for example, shifts the colors toward cyan. The thumbnail even shows how the additional cyan will look when added to the image. In case you're interested in seeing how these thumbnails actually affect a final printed image in the CMYK color space, check out Color Plate 18-10.

Now notice that each thumbnail is positioned directly opposite its complementary color. More Cyan is across from More Red, More Blue is across from More Yellow, and so on. In fact, clicking on a thumbnail not only shifts colors toward the named color but away from the opposite color. For example, if you click on More Cyan and then click on its opposite, More Red, you arrive at the original image.

Figure 18-14: Click on the thumbnails to shift the colors in an image; adjust the slider bar in the upper right corner to change the sensitivity of the thumbnails; and use the radio buttons to determine which part of an image is selected.

Note

Although this isn't exactly how the colors in the additive and subtractive worlds work—cyan is not the empirical opposite of red—the colors are theoretical opposites, and the Variations command makes the theory a practicality. After all, you haven't yet applied the color to the image, so the dialog box can calculate its adjustments in a pure and perfect world. Cyan and red ought to be opposites, so for the moment, they are.

To control the amount of color shifting that occurs when you click on a thumbnail, move the slider triangle in the upper right corner of the dialog box. Fine produces very minute changes; Coarse creates massive changes. Just to give you an idea of the difference between the two, you have to click on a thumbnail about 40 times when the slider is set to Fine to equal one click when it's set to Coarse.

The radio buttons at the top control which colors in the image are affected. Select Shadows to change the darkest colors, Highlights to change the lightest colors, and Midtones to change everything in between.

Note

In fact, if you're familiar with the Levels dialog box — as you will be when you read "The Levels command" section later in this chapter — the first three radio buttons have direct counterparts in the slider triangles in the Levels dialog box. For example, if you click on the Lighter thumbnail while the Highlights option is selected in the Variations dialog box, you perform the same action as moving the white triangle in the Levels dialog box to the left — that is, you make the lightest colors in the image even lighter.

The Saturation radio button lets you increase or decrease the saturation of colors in an image. Only one thumbnail appears on either side of the Current Pick image — one that decreases the saturation, and another that increases it. The Variations command modifies saturation differently than Hue/Saturation — where Hue/Saturation will push the saturation of a color as far as it will go, Variations attempts to modify the saturation without changing overall brightness values. As a result, an image saturated with Hue/Saturation will look lighter than one saturated with Variations.

As you click on the options — particularly when modifying saturation — you may notice that weird colors spring up inside the thumbnails. These brightly colored pixels are gamut warnings, highlighting colors that exceed the boundaries of the current color space. For example, if you're working in the RGB mode, these colors extend beyond the RGB gamut. Although the colors won't actually appear inverted as they do in the dialog box, it's not a good idea to exceed the color space because it results in areas of flat color, just as when you convert between the RGB and CMYK spaces. To view the thumbnails without the weirdly colored pixels, turn off the Show Clipping check box. (Incidentally, this use of the word *clipping* — Photoshop's third, in case you're counting — has nothing to do with paths or masks.)

Enhancing colors in a compressed image

Now that you know every possible way to adjust hues and saturation levels in Photoshop, it's time to discuss some of the possible stumbling blocks. The danger of rotating colors or increasing the saturation of an image is that you can bring out some very unstable colors. Adjusting the hues can switch ratty pixels from colors that your eyes aren't very sensitive to — particularly blue — into colors that you're eye sees very well — reds and greens. Drab color can also hide poor detail, which becomes painfully obvious when you make the colors bright and vivid.

Consider the digital photograph featured in Color Plate 18-11. Snapped in Boston's Copley Square with a Kodak DC50 digital camera, the original image at the top of the color plate is drab and lifeless. If I used the Hue/Saturation command to pump up the saturation levels, a world of ugly detail rises out of the muck, as shown in the second example. (Obviously, I've taken the saturation a little too high, but only to demonstrate a point.) The detail would have fared no better if I had used the Variations command to boost the saturation.

Unstable colors may be the result of JPEG compression, as in the case of the digital photo. Or you may have bad scanning or poor lighting to thank. In any case, you can fix the problem using our friends the Median and Gaussian Blur commands, as I explain in the following steps.

If you find yourself working with heavily compressed images on a regular basis, you may want to record these steps with the Actions palette, as explained in Chapter 3. Unlike the "Adjusting the Focus of Digital Photos" steps back in Chapter 15, you won't want to apply these steps to every digital photograph you take — or even most of them — but they come in handy more often than you might think.

Steps: Boosting the Saturation of Digital Photos

1. **Select the entire image and copy it to a new layer.** It seems like half of all Photoshop techniques begin with ⌘-A and ⌘-J.

2. **Press ⌘-U to display the Hue/Saturation dialog box.** Then raise the Saturation value to whatever setting you desire. Don't worry if your image starts to fall apart — that's the whole point of these steps. Pay attention to the color and don't worry about the rest. In the second example in Color Plate 18-11, I raised the Saturation to +80.

3. **Choose Filter ⇨ Noise ⇨ Median.** As you may recall from the last module, Median is the preeminent JPEG image fixer. A Radius value of 4 or 5 pixels works well for most images. You can take it even higher when working with resolutions of 200 ppi or more. I used 5. This destroys the detail, but that's not important. The color is all that matters.

4. **Choose Filter ⇨ Blur ⇨ Gaussian Blur.** As always, the Median filter introduces its own edges. And this is one case where you don't want to add any edges whatsoever. So blur the heck out of the layer. I used a Radius of 4.0, just 1 pixel less than my Median Radius value.

5. **Select Color from the blend mode pop-up menu in the Layers palette.** Photoshop mixes the gummy, blurry color with the crisp detail underneath. I also lowered the Opacity to 70 percent to produce the third example in Color Plate 18-11.

My image was still a little soft, so I applied the digital-photo sharpening steps from Chapter 15. After flattening the image, I pressed ⌘-A and ⌘-J again to copy it to yet another new layer. Then I applied the Median, Gaussian Blur, and Unsharp Mask filters, flattened the image one last time, and sharpened the image to taste. The finished result appears at the bottom of Color Plate 18-11. Although a tad bit too colorful — Boston's a lovely city, but it's not quite this resplendent — the edges look every bit as good as they did in the original photograph, and in many ways better.

Making Custom Brightness Adjustments

The Lighter and Darker options in the Variations dialog box are preferable to the Lightness slider bar inside the Hue/Saturation dialog box, because you can specify whether to edit the darkest, lightest, or medium colors in an image. But neither command is adequate for making precise adjustments to the brightness and contrast of an image. Photoshop provides two expert-level commands for adjusting the brightness levels in both grayscale and color images:

✦ The Levels command is great for most color corrections. It lets you adjust the darkest values, lightest values, and midrange colors with a minimum of fuss and a generous amount of control.

✦ The Curves command is great for creating special effects and correcting images that are beyond the help of the Levels command. Using the Curves command, you can map every brightness value in every color channel to an entirely different brightness value.

Note

There seems to be a controversy brewing in the back rooms of some print houses and art shops over which command is better, Levels or Curves. Based on a few letters I've received over the years, it seems that some folks consider Curves to be the command for real men and Levels suitable only for color-correcting wimps.

Naturally, this is a big wad of hooey. Levels provides a histogram, which is absolutely essential for gauging the proper setting for black and white points. Meanwhile, Curves lets you map out a virtually infinite number of significant points on a graph. The point is, both commands have their advantages, and both offer practical benefits for intermediate and advanced users alike.

There's no substitute for a good histogram, so I prefer to use Levels for my day-to-day color correcting. If you can't quite get the effect you want with Levels, or you know that you need to map specific brightness values in an image to other values, then use Curves. The Curves command is the more powerful function, but it is likewise more cumbersome.

The Levels command

When you choose Image ⇨ Adjust ⇨ Levels (⌘-L), Photoshop displays the Levels dialog box shown in Figure 18-15. The dialog box offers a histogram, as explained in the "Threshold" section earlier in this chapter, as well as two sets of slider bars with corresponding option boxes and a few automated eyedropper options in the lower-right corner. You can compress and expand the range of brightness values in an image by manipulating the Input Levels options and then mapping those brightness values to new brightness values by adjusting the Output Levels options.

Figure 18-15: Use the Levels dialog box to map brightness values in the image (Input Levels) to new brightness values (Output Levels).

The options in the Levels dialog box work as follows:

✦ **Channel:** Select the color channel that you want to edit from this pop-up menu. You can apply different Input Levels and Output Levels values to each color channel. However, the options along the right side of the dialog box affect all colors in the selected portion of an image regardless of which Channel option is active.

✦ **Input Levels:** Use these options to modify the contrast of the image by darkening the darkest colors and lightening the lightest ones. The Input Levels option boxes correspond to the slider bar immediately below the histogram. You map pixels to black (or the darkest Output Levels value) by entering a number from 0 to 255 into the first option box or by dragging the black slider triangle. For example, if you raise the value to 55, all colors with brightness values of 55 or less in the original image become black, darkening the image as shown in the first example of Figure 18-16.

You can map pixels at the opposite end of the brightness scale to white (or the lightest Output Levels value) by entering a number from 0 to 255 into the last option box or by dragging the white slider triangle. If you lower the value to 200, all colors with brightness values of 200 or greater become white, lightening the image as shown in the second example of Figure 18-16. In the last example of the figure, I raised the first value and lowered the last value, thereby increasing the amount of contrast in the image.

One of my favorite ways to edit the Input Levels values is to press the up and down arrow keys. Each press of an arrow key raises or lowers the value by 1. Press Shift with an arrow key to change the value in increments of 10.

Figure 18-16: The results of raising the first Input Levels value to 55 (left), lowering the last value to 200 (middle), and combining the two (right).

✦ **Gamma:** The middle Input Levels option box and the corresponding gray triangle in the slider bar (shown highlighted in Figure 18-17) represent the gamma value, which is the brightness level of the medium gray value in the image. The gamma value can range from 0.10 to 9.99, with 1.00 being dead-on medium gray. Any change to the gamma value has the effect of decreasing the amount of contrast in the image by lightening or darkening grays without changing shadows and highlights. Increase the gamma value or drag the gray slider triangle to the left to lighten the medium grays (also called *midtones*), as in the first and second examples of Figure 18-18. Lower the gamma value or drag the gray triangle to the right to darken the medium grays, as in the last example in the figure.

You can also edit the gamma value by pressing the up and down arrow keys. Pressing an arrow key changes the value by 0.01, while pressing Shift-arrow changes the value by 0.10. I can't stress enough how useful this technique is. I rarely do anything except press arrow keys inside the Levels dialog box anymore.

Figure 18-17: To create the spotlighting effects you see here, I selected the circular areas, inversed the selection, and applied the values shown in this very dialog box.

Figure 18-18: The results of raising (left and middle) and lowering (right) the gamma value to lighten and darken the midtones in an image.

Tip

✦ **Output Levels:** Use these options to curtail the range of brightness levels in an image by lightening the darkest pixels and darkening the lightest pixels. You adjust the brightness of the darkest pixels — those that correspond to the black Input Levels slider triangle — by entering a number from 0 to 255 into the first option box or by dragging the black slider triangle. For example, if you raise the value to 55, no color can be darker than that brightness level (roughly 80 percent black), which lightens the image as shown in the first example of Figure 18-19. You adjust the brightness of the lightest pixels — those that correspond to the white Input Levels slider triangle — by entering a number from 0 to 255 into the second option box or by dragging the white slider triangle. If you lower the value to 200, no color can be lighter than that brightness level (roughly 20 percent black), darkening the image as shown in the second example of Figure 18-19. In the last example of the figure, I raised the first value and lowered the second value, thereby dramatically decreasing the amount of contrast in the image.

You can fully or partially invert an image using the Output Levels slider triangles. Just drag the black triangle to the right and drag the white triangle to the left past the black triangle. The colors flip, whites mapping to dark colors and blacks mapping to light colors.

Figure 18-19: The result of raising the first Output Levels value to 55 (left), lowering the second value to 200 (middle), and combining the two (right).

✦ **Load/Save:** You can load and save settings to disk using these buttons.

✦ **Auto:** Click on the Auto button to automatically map the darkest pixel in your selection to black and the lightest pixel to white, as if you had chosen Image ⇨ Adjust ⇨ Auto Levels. Photoshop actually darkens and lightens the image by an extra half a percent just in case the darkest and lightest pixels are statistically inconsistent with the rest of the image.

To enter a percentage of your own, Option-click on the Auto button (the button name changes to Options). This displays two additional options, Black Clip and White Clip. Enter higher values to increase the number of pixels mapped to black and white; decrease the values to lessen the effect. Figure 18-20 compares the effect of the default 0.50 percent values to higher values of 2.50 and 9.99 percent. As you can see, raising the Clip value produces higher contrast effects.

| 0.50% Clips | 2.50% Clips | 9.99% Clips |

Figure 18-20: The default effect of the Auto button (left), the effect of the Auto button after raising the Clip values (middle), and the effect of the Equalize filter (right).

Note

Any changes made inside the Auto Range Options dialog box also affect the performance of the Auto Levels command. At all times, the effects of the Auto button and Auto Levels command are absolutely identical.

✦ **Eyedroppers:** Select one of the eyedropper tools in the Levels dialog box and click on a pixel in the image window to automatically adjust the color of that pixel. If you click on a pixel with the black eyedropper tool (the first of the three), Photoshop maps the color of the pixel and all darker colors to black. If you click on a pixel with the white eyedropper tool (last of the three), Photoshop maps it and all lighter colors to white. Use the gray eyedropper tool (middle) to change the exact color on which you click to medium gray and adjust all other colors in accordance. For example, if you click on a white pixel, all white pixels change to medium gray and all other pixels change to even darker colors.

Tip

One way to use the eyedropper tools is to color-correct scans without a lot of messing around. Include a neutral swatch of gray with the photograph you want to scan. (If you own a Pantone swatch book, Cool Gray 5 or 6 is your best bet.) After opening the scan in Photoshop, choose the Levels command, select the gray eyedropper tool, and click on the neutral gray swatch in the image window. This technique won't perform miracles, but it will help you to distribute lights and darks in the image more evenly. You then can fine-tune the image using the Input Levels and Output Levels options.

✦ **Preview:** Select this option to preview the effects of your settings in the image window. The effect of turning Preview off depends on the setting of the Video LUT Animation check box in the Display & Cursors panel of the Preferences dialog box (⌘-K, ⌘-3). When Video LUT Animation is inactive, turning off Preview simply displays the image prior to choosing the Levels command. When Video LUT Animation is active, turning off Preview applies the Levels settings to the entire screen. Click and hold on the title bar to see the original image prior to the correction, release to again apply the settings to the entire screen.

I discussed why I hate Video LUT Animation back in Chapter 2 — it applies adjustments to both selected and deselected areas in an image alike, and the preview is inaccurate in the Lab and CMYK modes. But there is one good thing about Video LUT Animation:

Tip

With Video LUT Animation turned on and the Preview check box turned off, you can preview the exact pixels that will turn to black or white in the image window. Just Option-drag the black or white triangle in the Input Levels slider bar. When Option-dragging the black handle, all pixels that appear some color other than white will change to black. When Option-dragging the white handle, look for the pixels that are not black to change to white.

To give you a sense of how the Levels command works, the following steps describe how to improve the appearance of an overly dark, low-contrast image such as the first example in Color Plate 18-12. Thanks to natural lighting and the dark color of the stone, this statue of Thomas Jefferson is hardly recognizable. Luckily, you can bring out the highlights using Levels.

Steps: Correcting Brightness and Contrast with the Levels Command

1. **Press ⌘-L to display the Levels dialog box.** The histogram for the Jefferson image appears superimposed in white in front of the great man's chest. As you can see, most of the colors are clustered together on the left side of the graph, showing that there are far more dark colors than light.

2. **Press ⌘-1 to examine the red channel.** Assuming that you're editing an RGB image, ⌘-1 displays a histogram for the red channel. The channel-specific histograms appear below Jefferson, colorized for your viewing pleasure.

3. **Edit the black Input Levels value as needed.** Drag the black slider triangle to below the point at which the histogram begins. In the case of Jefferson, you can see a spike in the histogram about a half pica in from the left side of the graph. I dragged the black triangle directly underneath that spike, changing the first Input Levels value to 14, as you can see in the red histogram on the right side of Color Plate 18-12.

4. **Edit the white Input Levels value.** Drag the white slider triangle to below the point at which the histogram ends. In the color plate, the histogram features a tall spike on the far right side. This means a whole lot of pixels are already white. I don't want to create a flat hot spot, so I leave the white triangle alone.

5. **Edit the gamma value.** Drag the gray triangle to the gravitational center of the histogram. Imagine that the histogram is a big mass, and you're trying to balance the mass evenly on top of the gray triangle. Because my histogram is weighted too heavily to the left, I had to drag the gray triangle far to the left, until the middle Input Levels value changed to 2.40, which represents a radical shift.

6. **Repeat Steps 2 through 5 for the green and blue channels.** Your image probably has a significant preponderance of red about it. To fix this, you need to edit the green and blue channels in kind. The graphs on the right side of Color Plate 18-12 show how I edited my histograms. Feel free to switch back and forth between channels as much as you like to get everything just right.

7. **Press ⌘-tilde (~) to return to the composite RGB histogram.** Once you get the color balance right, you can switch back to the composite mode and further edit the Input Levels. I typically bump up the gamma a few notches—to 1.2 or so—to account for dot gain.

   You may notice that your RGB histogram has changed. Although the histograms in the individual color channels remain fixed, the composite histogram updates to reflect the red, green, and blue modifications. I've superimposed the updated histogram in white on the corrected Jefferson on the right side of Color Plate 18-12. As you can see, the colors are now better distributed across the brightness range.

8. **Press Return to apply your changes.** Just for fun, press ⌘-Z a few times to see the before and after shots. Quite the transformation, eh?

Tip

If you decide after looking at the before and after views that you could do a better job, undo the color correction and press ⌘-Option-L to bring up the Levels dialog box with the previous settings intact. Now you can take up where you left off.

The Curves command

If you want to be able to map any brightness value in an image to absolutely any other brightness value—no holds barred, as they say at the drive-in movies—you want the Curves command. When you choose Image ⇨ Adjust ⇨ Curves (⌘-M), Photoshop displays the Curves dialog box, shown in Figure 18-21, which offers access to the most complex and powerful color correction options on the planet.

Figure 18-21: The Curves dialog box lets you distribute brightness values by drawing curves on a graph.

Quickly, here's how the options work:

✦ **Channel:** Surely you know how this option works by now. You select the color channel that you want to edit from this pop-up menu. You can apply different mapping functions to different channels by drawing in the graph below the pop-up menu. But, as is always the case, the options along the right side of the dialog box affect all colors in the selected portion of an image regardless of which Channel option is active.

✦ **Brightness graph:** The brightness graph is where you map brightness values in the original image to new brightness values. The horizontal axis of the graph represents input levels; the vertical axis represents output levels. The *brightness curve* charts the relationship between input and output levels. The lower left corner is the origin of the graph (the point at which both input and output values are 0). Move right in the graph for higher input values, up for higher output values. Because the brightness graph is the core of this dialog box, upcoming sections explain it in more detail.

Tip

By default, a trio of horizontal and vertical dotted lines crisscross the brightness graph, subdividing it into quarters. For added precision, you can divide the graph into horizontal and vertical tenths. Just Option-click inside the graph to toggle between tenths and quarters.

✦ **Brightness bar:** The horizontal brightness bar shows the direction of light and dark values in the graph. When the dark end of the brightness bar appears on the left — as by default when editing an RGB image — colors are measured in terms of brightness values. The colors in the graph proceed from black on the left to white on the right, as demonstrated in the left example of Figure 18-22. Therefore, higher values produce lighter colors. This is my preferred setting, because it measures colors in the same direction as the Levels dialog box.

If you click on the brightness bar, white and black switch places, as shown in the second example of the figure. The result is that Photoshop measures the colors in terms of ink coverage, from 0 percent of the primary color to 100 percent of the primary color. Higher values now produce darker colors. This is the default setting for grayscale and CMYK images.

Figure 18-22: Click on the brightness bar to change the way in which the graph measures color: by brightness values (left) or by ink coverage (right).

✦ **Curve tools:** Use the curve tools to draw the curve inside the brightness graph. The point tool (labeled in Figure 18-23) is selected by default. Click in the graph with this tool to add a point to the curve. Drag a point to move it. To delete a point, ⌘-click on it.

The pencil tool lets you draw free-form curves simply by dragging inside the graph, as illustrated in Figure 18-23. This pencil works much like Photoshop's standard pencil tool. This means you can draw straight lines by clicking at one location in the graph and Shift-clicking at a different point.

Figure 18-23: Use the pencil tool to draw free-form lines in the brightness graph. If the lines appear rough, you can soften them by clicking on the Smooth button.

✦ **Input and Output values:** The Input and Output values monitor the location of your cursor in the graph according to brightness values or ink coverage, depending on the setting of the brightness bar. In Photoshop 5, you can modify the Input or Output value when working with the point tool. Just click on the point on the graph you want to adjust, then enter new values. The Input number represents the brightness or ink value of the point before you entered the Curves dialog box; the Output number represents the new brightness or ink value.

Photoshop 5 also lets you change the Output value from the keyboard. Click on the point you want to modify. Then press the up or down arrow key to raise or lower the Output value by 1. Press Shift-up or down arrow to change the Output value in increments of 10. Note that these techniques — and ones that follow — work only when the point tool is active. (You can't change points with the pencil tool.)

Naturally, when editing multiple graph points from the keyboard, it's helpful to be able to activate the points from the keyboard as well. To advance from one point to the next, press ⌘-Tab. To select the previous point, press ⌘-Shift-Tab. To deselect all points, press ⌘-D.

✦ **Load/Save:** Use these buttons to load and save settings to disk.

Okay, here's *the* weirdest tip in all of Photoshop. It's not very practical, but it's about as wild as you can get. You can use a gradation as a Curves map. First, click on the Edit button in the Gradient Tool Options palette, select one of the more garish gradients, like Spectrum. Then ⌘-click on the Save button to save the gradient as a map settings file. Next, bring up the Curves dialog box (⌘-M), click on the Load button, open the saved gradation, and stand back and watch the fireworks.

In the psychedelic Color Plate 18-13, I cloned Constantine to a new layer and applied a heavy dose of Gaussian Blur. Then I used the Curves command to apply one of three gradient maps. In the bottom row, I mixed each of the fantastic images with its underlying original using the Color blend mode.

✦ **Smooth:** Click on the Smooth button to smooth out curves drawn with the pencil tool. Doing so leads to smoother color transitions in the image window. This button is dimmed except when you use the pencil tool.

✦ **Auto:** Click on this button to automatically map the darkest pixel in your selection to black and the lightest pixel to white. Photoshop throws in some additional darkening and lightening according to the Clip percentages, which you can edit by Option-clicking on the button.

✦ **Eyedroppers:** If you move the cursor out of the dialog box into the image window, you get the standard eyedropper cursor. Click on a pixel in the image to locate the brightness value of that pixel in the graph. A circle appears in the graph, and the input and output numbers list the value for as long as you hold down the mouse button, as shown in the first example in Figure 18-24.

The other eyedroppers work as they do in the Levels dialog box, mapping pixels to black, medium gray, or white. For example, the second image in Figure 18-24 shows the white eyedropper tool clicking on a light pixel, thereby mapping that value to white, as shown in the highlighted portion of the graph below the image. (Photoshop maps the value to each color channel independently. So when editing a full-color image inside the Curves dialog box, you'll have to switch channels to see the results of clicking with the eyedropper.) You can further adjust the brightness value of that pixel by dragging the corresponding point in the graph, as demonstrated in the last example of the figure.

The eyedropper tools aren't the only way to add points to a curve from the image window. Photoshop 5 adds two keyboard tricks that greatly simplify the process of pinpointing and adjusting colors inside the Curves dialog box. Bear in mind, both of these techniques work only when the point tool is active.

Figure 18-24: Use the standard eye-dropper cursor to locate a color in the brightness graph (left). Click with one of the eyedropper tools from the Curves dialog box to map the color of that pixel in the graph (middle). You then can edit the location of the point in the graph by dragging it (right).

✦ To add a color as a point along the Curves graph, ⌘-click on a pixel in the image window. Photoshop adds the point to the channel displayed in the dialog box. So if the RGB composite channel is visible, the point is added to the RGB composite curve. If the Red channel is visible, Photoshop adds the point to the red graph and leaves the green and blue graphs unchanged.

✦ To add a color to all graphs, regardless of which channel is visible in the Curves dialog box, ⌘-Shift-click on a pixel in the image window. In the case of an RGB image, Photoshop maps the red, green, and blue brightness values for that pixel to each of the red, green, and blue graphs in the Curves dialog box. The RGB composite graph will show no change — switch to the individual channels to see the new point.

Continuous curves

All discussions in the few remaining pages of this section assume that the brightness bar is set to edit brightness values (in which case the gradation in the bar lightens from left to right). If you set the bar to edit ink coverage (the bar darkens from left to right), you can still achieve the effects I describe, but you must drag in the opposite direction. For example, if I tell you to lighten colors by dragging upward, then you would drag downward. In a world backward live the people ink coverage.

When you first enter the Curves dialog box, the brightness curve appears as a straight line strung between two points, as shown in the first example of Figure 18-25, mapping every input level from black (the lower left point) to white (the upper right point) to an identical output level. If you want to perform seamless color corrections, the point tool is your best bet because it enables you to edit the levels in the brightness graph while maintaining a continuous curve.

To lighten the colors, click near the middle of the curve with the point tool to create a new point and then drag the point upward, as demonstrated in the second example of Figure 18-25. To darken the image, drag the point downward, as in the third example.

Figure 18-25: Create a single point in the curve with the point tool (left) and then drag it upward (middle) or downward (right) to lighten or darken the image evenly.

Create two points in the curve to boost or lessen the contrast between colors in the image. In the first example of Figure 18-26, I created one point very near the white point in the curve and another point very close to the black point. I then dragged down on the left point and up on the right point to make the dark pixels darker and the light pixels lighter, which translates to higher contrast.

In the second example of the figure, I did just the opposite, dragging up on the left point to lighten the dark pixels and down on the right point to darken the light pixels. As you can see in the second image, this lessens the contrast between colors, making the image more gray.

In the last example in Figure 18-26, I bolstered the contrast with a vengeance by dragging the right point down and to the left. This has the effect of springing the right half of the curve farther upward, thus increasing the brightness of the light pixels in the image.

Figure 18-26: Create two points in the curve to change the appearance of contrast in an image, whether by increasing it mildly (left), decreasing it (middle), or boosting it dramatically (right).

Arbitrary curves

You can create some mind-numbing color variations by adjusting the brightness curve arbitrarily, mapping light pixels to dark, dark pixels to light, and in-between pixels all over the place. In the first example of Figure 18-27, I used the point tool to achieve an arbitrary curve. By dragging the left point severely upward and the right point severely downward, I caused dark and light pixels alike to soar across the spectrum.

If you're interested in something a little more subtle, try applying an arbitrary curve to a single channel in a color image. Color Plate 18-14, for example, shows an image subject to relatively basic color manipulations in the red and green channels, followed by an arbitrary adjustment to the blue channel.

Although you can certainly achieve arbitrary effects using the point tool, the pencil tool is more versatile and less inhibiting. As shown in the second example of Figure 18-27, I created an effect that would alarm Carlos Castaneda just by zigzagging my way across the graph and clicking on the Smooth button.

Figure 18-27: These arbitrary brightness curves were created using the point tool (left) and the pencil tool (right).

In fact, the Smooth button is an integral part of using the pencil tool. Try this little experiment: Draw a bunch of completely random lines and squiggles with the pencil tool in the brightness graph. As shown in the first example of Figure 18-28, your efforts will most likely yield an unspeakably hideous and utterly unrecognizable effect.

Next, click on the Smooth button. Photoshop automatically connects all portions of the curve, miraculously smoothing out the color-mapping effect and rescuing some semblance of your image, as shown in the second example of the figure. If the effect is still too radical, you can continue to smooth it out by clicking additional times on the Smooth button. I clicked on the button twice more to create the right image in Figure 18-28. Eventually, the Smooth button restores the curve to a straight line.

Figure 18-28: After drawing a series of completely random lines with the pencil tool (left), I clicked on the Smooth button once to connect the lines into a frenetic curve (middle) and then twice more to even out the curve, thus preserving more of the original image (right).

Adjustment Layers

Every one of the commands I've discussed in this chapter is applicable to a single layer at a time. If you want to correct the colors in multiple layers, you have to create a special kind of layer called an *adjustment layer*. Adjustment layers are layers that contain mathematical color correction information. The layer applies its corrections to all layers below it, without affecting any layers above.

You can create an adjustment layer in one of two ways:

✦ Choose Layer ⇨ New ⇨ Adjustment Layer.

✦ ⌘-click on the page icon at the bottom of the Layers palette.

Either way, Photoshop displays the New Adjustment Layer dialog box shown in Figure 18-29. This dialog box contains the standard Name, Opacity, and Mode options that accompany any kind of layer. But you also get a Type pop-up menu, which offers some of Photoshop's most important color correction commands. Select the kind of color correction that you want to apply from the menu, and press Return.

Figure 18-29: The New Adjustment Layer dialog box, as it appears normally (top) and with Type pop-up menu unfurled (bottom).

Photoshop then displays the dialog box for the selected correction (unless you choose Invert, which does not offer a dialog box). Change the settings as desired and press Return as you normally would. The completed color correction appears as a new layer in the Layers palette. In Figure 18-30, for example, I've added a total of three adjustment layers. Photoshop marks adjustment layers with half-black circles so that you can readily tell them apart from image layers.

Figure 18-30: Here I've created three layers of color correction in front of a single background image.

The advantages of layer-based corrections

Now at this point, you might think, "Big whoop. You can apply corrections to multiple layers. That doesn't seem like such a great feature." Not only would that be an unkind assessment of adjustment layers — hey, computer code has feelings too — but an inaccurate assessment as well. Here are a few reasons adjustment layers are so great:

✦ **Forever editable:** So long as the adjustment layer remains intact — stored in the native Photoshop format, of course — you can edit the color correction over and over again without damaging the underlying pixels. Unlike standard color corrections, which alter selected pixels directly, adjustment layers have no permanent effect on the pixels whatsoever. On the slightest whim, you can double-click on the layer name in the palette to bring up the color correction dialog box, complete with the settings that are currently in force. Tweak the settings as the mood hits you and press Return to make changes on the fly. You can't get any more flexible than this.

✦ **Versatile layer masking:** You can also adjust the affected area to your heart's content. An adjustment layer covers the entire image like an adjustable wall-to-wall carpet. You modify the affected area by painting inside the layer. The layer doesn't contain any pixels of its own, so painting in an adjustment layer changes its layer mask. Paint with black to remove the correction from an area, use white to paint the correction back in.

Tip

In fact, if a selection is active when you create a new adjustment layer, Photoshop automatically creates a layer mask according to the selection outline. For example, in Color Plate 18-15, I selected the topiary dinosaur before creating the Levels layer. Photoshop thoughtfully converted my selection into a mask, as labeled in Figure 18-30. And like any layer mask, I can edit it well into the future without any adverse side effects.

✦ **Reorder your corrections:** As with any layers, you can shuffle adjustment layers up and down in stacking order. For example, if you decide you don't want the correction to affect a specific layer, just drag the adjustment layer to a level in the Layers palette below the layer you want to exclude. If you're juggling multiple adjustment layers, as in Figure 18-30 and Color Plate 18-15, you can shuffle the adjustment layers to change the order in which they're applied. This includes the standard reordering keyboard shortcuts, ⌘-[and ⌘-].

✦ **Fade corrections:** You can fade a standard color correction right after you apply it using Filter ⇨ Fade. But you can fade a correction applied with an adjustment layer any old time. Just change the Opacity and blend mode settings in the Layers palette.

✦ **Correct with blend modes:** Some folks prefer to correct overly light or dark images using blend modes. Take an image, copy it to a new layer, and apply the Multiply mode to darken the layer or Screen to lighten it. The problem with this trick is that it increases the size of the image in memory. Duplicating the image to a new layer requires Photoshop to double the size of the image in RAM.

Tip

Adjustment layers permit you to apply this same technique without adding pixels to RAM. Create a new adjustment layer with the Levels option selected. After the Levels dialog box comes up, press Return to ignore it. Now select Multiply or Screen from the blend mode pop-up menu in the Layers palette. The adjustment layer serves as a surrogate duplicate of the layers below it, mocking every merged pixel. And it doesn't add so much as a K to the file size. It's an image-editing miracle — layers without the pain.

Correcting a flat image using layers

Although many artists will use this new feature to edit multilayer compositions, adjustment layers are equally applicable to flat photos. Originally printed in the February 1996 issue of *Macworld* magazine, Color Plate 18-15 shows how I corrected an image shot with a Polaroid PDC-2000 using a total of three color corrections, layered one on top of the other. (Much of this text also comes from that same article.) At first glance, the original photo on the left side of the color plate is a textbook example of what happens if you ignore backlighting. But as you have probably figured out by now, an image that appears black may actually contain several thousands of colors just itching to get out. Adjustment layers make it easier than ever to free these colors and make them fully visible to the world.

Because my image was in such rotten shape, I decided to start with the expert Curves command. I ⌘-clicked on the new layer icon and selected Curves from the Type pop-up menu. Then I used the pencil tool in the Curves dialog box to draw a radical upswing on the left side of the graph, dramatically lightening the blacks right out of the gate. I clicked on the Smooth button a few times to even out the color transitions, as demonstrated in the second example in Color Plate 18-15.

All this lightening resulted in some very washed-out colors (a typical side effect), so I created a second adjustment layer using the Hue/Saturation command. By raising the Saturation value, I quickly breathed a little enthusiasm into these tired old hues — a sufficient amount, in fact, to make it clear how soft the focus was. So I went back to the original image layer and applied the Unsharp Mask filter. Had it not been for the advent of adjustment layers, I would have either had to sharpen the image before color correcting it, making it impossible to accurately gauge the results, or sharpen the image after correcting, which might bring out compression artifacts and other undesirable anomalies. With adjustment layers, however, I can sharpen and correct at the same time, giving no operation precedence over the other.

The hedge monster remained a little dark, so I selected it with the Color Range command and then created a third adjustment layer for the Levels command. Using Levels, I quickly enhanced the brightness and contrast of the green beast, bringing him out into the full light of day. As I mentioned earlier, Photoshop automatically generated a layer mask for my selection, which appears as a tiny white silhouette in the Layers palette.

To be fair, I should mention that adjustment layers are not an original invention for Photoshop. Just as Painter/X2 offered bitmapped layers more than a year before Photoshop, Live Picture introduced correction layers two years prior to the arrival of Photoshop. Live Picture's layers also permit you to temporarily sharpen, blur, and distort underlying pixels, three operations that are currently beyond Photoshop's reach. Although Adobe made no changes to adjustment layers in Version 5, my guess is that Photoshop will continue to grow in this direction in the future. The day you can apply filters with adjustment layers is the day the feature will be complete. (Photoshop 6 perhaps? We can only hope.)

✦ ✦ ✦

The Wonders of Blend Modes

Mixing Images Together

There must be 50 ways to combine and compare differently colored pixels in Photoshop. So far, we've seen how you can smear and blur pixels into each other, select pixels using other pixels, layer pixels in front of pixels, compare a pixel to its neighbors using automated filters, and map the colors of pixels to other colors. Any time that you edit, mask, composite, filter, or color correct an image, you're actually breeding the image with itself or with other images to create a new and unique offspring.

This chapter explores the final and ultimate experiment in Photoshop's great genetics laboratory. *Blend modes*, also called *calculations*, permit you to mix the color of a pixel with that of every pixel in a straight line beneath it. A single blend mode is as powerful as a mask, a filter, and a color map combined, and best of all, it's temporary. So long as one image remains layered in front of another, you can replace one calculation with another as easily as you change a letter of text in a word processor.

To appreciate the most rudimentary power of blend modes, consider Figure 19-1. The first image shows a terrestrial thrill seeker composited in front of the Apollo crew's old stomping grounds. Both layers are as opaque as if you had cut them out with scissors and glued them together. (Granted, you'd have to be very skilled with scissors.) The anti-aliased edges of the parachute mix slightly with the moon pixels below them. But beyond that, every pixel is a digital hermit, steadfastly avoiding interaction.

The second image in Figure 19-1 paints a different picture. Here I've created several clones of the parachute and moon and mixed them together using Photoshop's considerable array of calculation capabilities. Although I used just two images, I composited them onto ten layers, only one of which — the background layer — was fully opaque. I don't know if it's moon men invading earth or the other way around, but whatever it is, it wouldn't have been possible without blend modes and their ilk.

Figure 19-1: Layers permit you to combine images from different sources (left), but blend modes permit you to mix images together to create intriguing if sometimes unexpected interactions (right).

Photoshop gives you three ways to mix images:

✦ **The Layers palette:** You can combine the active layer with underlying pixels using the Opacity value and blend mode pop-up menu, both members of the Layers palette. Figure 19-2 shows these two illustrious items in the context of the layers list for Figure 19-1. To learn everything there is to know about the Opacity value and blend mode pop-up menu, read the next section.

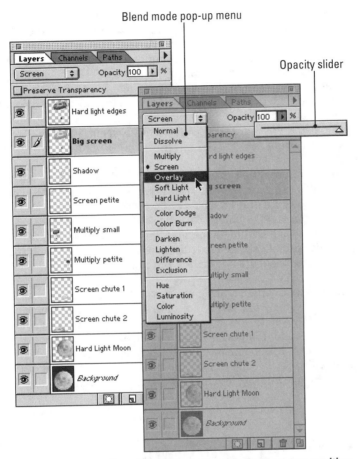

Figure 19-2: The list of layers in the Invasion Moon composition, with the blend mode pop-up menu proudly displayed on the right.

✦ **The Blend If sliders:** You can double-click on a layer name in the Layers palette to display the Layers Options dialog box. Many of the options in this dialog box are found elsewhere, but the two slider bars at the bottom are unique. They allow you to drop colors out of the active layer and force colors to show through from layers below. This is one of Photoshop's oldest, finest, and least used features, as I discuss later in the "Dropping Out and Forcing Through" section.

✦ **Channel operations:** The so-called channel operations permit you to combine two open images of identical size, or one image with itself. Photoshop offers two commands for this purpose, Image ➪ Apply Image and Image ➪ Calculations. Unusually complex and completely lacking in sizing and placement functions, these commands provide access to two unique blend modes named Add and Subtract. Simply put, unless a technique involves the Add or Subtract mode, or you want to clone two images into a third image window, you can mix images with greater ease, flexibility, and feedback using the Layers palette. For more on this lively topic, see the "Using Channel Operation Commands" section later in this chapter.

Blend modes are not Photoshop's most straightforward feature. There may even come a time when you utter the words, "Blend modes are stupid." They demand a generous supply of experimentation, and even then they'll fool you. I was a math major in college (with a double-major in art, for what it's worth), so I well understand the elementary arithmetic behind Photoshop's calculations. And yet, despite roughly a decade of experience with blend modes in Photoshop and other programs, I am frequently surprised by their outcome.

The key, therefore, is to combine a basic understanding of how blend modes and other compositing features work with your natural willingness to experiment. And now that Photoshop 5 permits you to switch blend modes from the keyboard, you can experiment more easily than ever. Sometime when you don't have a deadline looming over your head, take some multilayered composition you have lying around and hit it with a few calculations. Even if the end result is a disaster that you wouldn't share with your mother, let alone a client, you can consider it time well spent.

Using Opacity and Blend Modes

This is not the first time in this book that I've touched on the Opacity value or the blend mode pop-up menu. And given that the Layer palette's blend modes mimic the brush modes (both in name and in function) as I discussed in "The 18 paint tool modes" section near the end of Chapter 8, we're covering some familiar territory. But you'll soon find that there's a significant difference between laying down a single color with a brush, and merging the hundred or so thousand colors that inhabit a typical layer. This difference is the stuff of the following pages.

Incidentally, both the Opacity and blend mode options are dimmed when working on the background layer or in a single-layer image. There's nothing underneath, so there's nothing to mix. Naturally, this goes double when editing black and white and indexed images or when editing masks, since neither of these circumstances supports layers.

The Opacity setting

The Opacity value is the easiest of the layer mixers to understand. It permits you to mix the active layer with the layers below in prescribed portions. It's sort of like mixing a drink. Suppose you pour one part vermouth and four parts gin into a martini glass. (Any martini enthusiast knows that's too much vermouth, but bear with me on this one.) The resulting beverage is ⅕ vermouth and ⅘ gin. If the vermouth were a layer, you could achieve the same effect by setting the Opacity to 20 percent. This implies that 20 percent of what you see is vermouth and the remaining 80 percent is underlying gin.

When any selection or navigation tool is active, you can change the Opacity setting for a layer from the keyboard. Press a single number key to change the Opacity in 10-percent increments. That's 1 for 10 percent, 2 for 20 percent, up to 0 for 100 percent — in order along the top of your keyboard. If you have the urge to be more precise, press two keys in a row to specify an exact two-digit Opacity value.

Yes, I know, I already mentioned the previous tip in Chapter 13, but it bears repeating. Besides, here's something I didn't mention. In Photoshop 5, the old Opacity slider bar has gone into hiding. Click on the arrowhead to the right of the Opacity value to display the slider bar. Then drag the triangle to change the value. Or press the up and down arrows to nudge the triangle along. Press Shift with the arrow key to nudge in 10-percent increments. Press Return to confirm the slider setting. Press Escape to cancel and restore the previous setting.

The blend modes

Photoshop 5 offers a total of 17 blend modes. That's actually two down from Version 4. Thanks to the diminished role of floating selections, Behind and Clear are now officially ex-modes. Once upon a time — circa Photoshop 3 and earlier — Behind and Clear were quite useful for slipping floaters behind layers and cutting movable holes. But they became significantly more cumbersome in Version 4. Let us take a moment of silence to mourn their passing.

While the Behind and Clear modes are no longer available for layers, they are still available for use with the Line and Paintbucket tools and the Edit ⇨ Fill and Edit ⇨ Stroke commands.

Okay, enough of that. The remaining 17 modes — Normal through Luminosity — are still alive and well, so I suppose we should count our blessings. As you read through my upcoming discussions, you can check out examples of the blend modes both in the accompanying grayscale figures and in Color Plate 19-1. The grayscale figures show the results of compositing the two images shown in Figure 19-3. The thinker is on top, the sunset is on bottom. The color plate features a series of Saturns layered against the stormy gaseous planet of Jupiter. Although the planets aren't to scale — I understand that both bodies are several times larger than this book, for example — they do a fair job of showing the effects of Photoshop's modes.

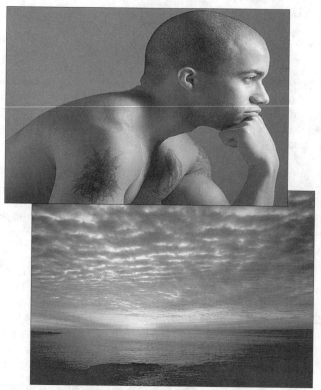

Figure 19-3: To demonstrate the effects of Photoshop's blend modes, I composited the thinker (top) against a sunset background (bottom). In each case, the blend mode is applied to the thinker.

In Photoshop 5, you can access every one of the blend modes from the keyboard by pressing Shift-Option-plus a letter. Some letters make perfect sense — Shift-Option-N for Normal, for example — others are a bit of a stretch — Shift-Option-I for Dissolve. Whether predictable or not, I list the letter in parentheses with each blend mode description.

One more note: Every so often, I allude to a little something called a *composite pixel*. By this I mean the pixel color that results from all the mixing that's going on in back of the active layer. For example, your document may contain hoards of layers with all sorts of blend modes in effect, but as long as you work on, say, Layer 23, Photoshop treats the image formed by Layers 1 through 22 as if it were one flattened image filled with a bunch of static composite pixels.

Cool? Keen. So without any further notes and clarifications, here they are, the 17 blend modes, in order of appearance:

✦ **Normal (N):** In combination with an Opacity setting of 100 percent, this option displays every pixel in the active layer normally regardless of the colors of the underlying image. When you use an Opacity of less than 100 percent, the color of each pixel in the active layer is averaged with the composite pixel in the layers behind it according to the Opacity value.

✦ **Dissolve (I):** This option specifically affects feathered or softened edges. If the active layer is entirely opaque with hard edges, this option has no effect. But when the edges of the layer are feathered, the Dissolve option randomizes the pixels along the edges. The first two images in Figure 19-4 compare a feathered layer subjected to the Normal and Dissolve modes. Dissolve also randomizes pixels when the Opacity value is set below 100 percent, as demonstrated in the final example in the figure.

Normal feather   Dissolve feather   70% Dissolve

Figure 19-4: Here I applied Normal (left) and Dissolve (middle) to a layer with heavily feathered edges. The final example shows the effect of Dissolve when I reduce the Opacity value to 70 percent. (The superimposed characters indicate the keyboard shortcuts Shift-Option-N for Normal, Shift-Option-I for Dissolve, and 7 for 70 percent opacity.)

✦ **Multiply (M):** To understand the Multiply and Screen modes, you have to use a little imagination. So here goes: Imagine that the active layer and the underlying image are both photos on transparent slides. The Multiply mode produces the same effect as holding those slides up to the light, one slide in front of the other. Because the light has to travel through two slides, the outcome is invariably a darker image that contains elements from both images. An example of the Multiply blend mode appears in Figure 19-5.

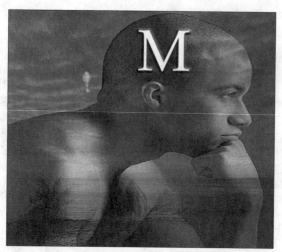

Figure 19-5: The Multiply blend mode produces the same effect as holding two overlapping transparencies up to the light. It always results in a darker image.

✦ **Screen (S):** Still have those transparent slides from the Multiply analogy? Well, place them both in separate projectors and point them at the same screen and you'll get the same effect as Screen. Rather than creating a darker image, as you do with Multiply, you create a lighter image, as demonstrated in Figure 19-6 and Color Plate 19-1.

You can use the Screen blend mode to emulate film that has been exposed multiple times. Ever seen Thomas Eakin's pioneering *Jumping Figure,* which shows rapid-fire exposures of a naked man jumping from one location to another? Each shot is effectively screened onto the other, lightening the film with each and every exposure. The photographer was smart enough to limit the exposure time so as not to overexpose the film; likewise, you should only apply Screen when working with images that are sufficiently dark so that you avoid overlightening.

✦ **Overlay (O), Soft Light (F), and Hard Light (H):** You just can't separate these guys. All three multiply the dark colors in the active layer and screen the light colors into the composite pixels in the layers below. But they apply their effects to different degrees. Overlay favors the composite pixels while Hard Light favors the layered pixels. (In fact, the two are direct opposites.) Soft Light is a washed out version of Hard Light that results in a low-contrast effect.

The left-hand examples in Figure 19-7 show each Overlay, Soft Light, and Hard Light applied to the thinking fellow. I then duplicated the thinker layer with the blend mode still in force to get the effects on the right. As these examples demonstrate, the modes effectively tattoo one image onto the image behind it. Even after multiple applications of the thinker layer, the sunset image still shows through as if the thinker were appliquéd on.

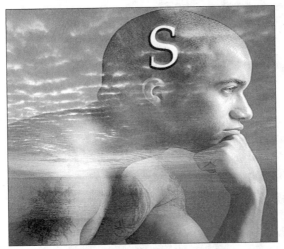

Figure 19-6: The Screen mode produces the same effect as shining two projectors at the same screen. It always results in a lighter image.

I recommend starting with the Overlay mode any time you want to mix both the active layer and the layers behind it to create a reciprocal blend. By this, I mean a blend that mixes the colors evenly without eliminating any of the detail in either layer. After you apply Overlay, vary the Opacity to favor the composite pixels. I've said it before and I'll say it again, Overlay is Photoshop's most practical blend mode, the one you should always try first.

If you can't quite get the effect you want at lower Opacity settings, switch to the Soft Light mode and give that a try. On the other hand, if the Overlay mode at 100 percent seems too subtle, switch to Hard Light. You can even clone the layer to darn well emblazon the layer onto its background, as in the bottom right image in Figure 19-7.

Overlay   x 2

Soft Light   x 2

Hard Light   x 2

Figure 19-7: The results of the Overlay, Soft Light, and Hard
Light blend modes as they appear when applied to a single
version of the thinker layer (left) and a second thinker layer (right).

✦ **Color Dodge (D):** When you apply the Color Dodge mode, each color in the layer becomes a brightness value multiplier. Light colors like white produce the greatest effect and black produces no effect. As a result, Color Dodge is Photoshop's most dramatic whitening agent, the equivalent of applying bleach to colored fabric. When applied to the thinker in Figure 19-8, Color Dodge exaggerates the sunset, resulting in a rougher effect than either Screen or the upcoming Lighten.

Figure 19-8: Color Dodge uses the active layer to bleach the pixels in the layer below. There is nothing subtle about this effect.

✦ **Color Burn (B):** If Color Dodge is bleach, then Color Burn is the charred surface of burnt toast. It uses the colors in the active layer to reduce brightness values, resulting in a radical darkening effect. Like Color Dodge, the Color Burn mode results in a radical, high-contrast effect, as shown in Figure 19-9. You may also want to sneak a peek at Color Plate 19-1, which illustrates how both Color Dodge and Color Burn sap the colors out of the active layer more surely than any other blend mode except Luminosity. If you want high-contrast stamping effects, these are the blend modes to use.

✦ **Darken (K):** When you select this option, Photoshop applies colors in the active layer only if they are darker than the corresponding pixels below. Keep in mind that Photoshop compares the brightness levels of pixels in a full-color image on a channel-by-channel basis. So although the red component of a pixel in the active layer may be darker than the red component of the underlying composite pixel, the green and blue components may be lighter. In this case, Photoshop would assign the red component but not the green or blue, thereby subtracting some red and making the pixel slightly more turquoise. Compare the predictable grayscale example in Figure 19-10 to its more challenging color counterpart in Color Plate 19-1.

Figure 19-9: Color Burn seers an image charcoal black. No other darkening mode is this severe.

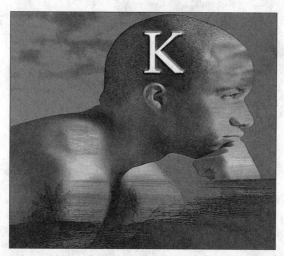

Figure 19-10: The same active layer subject to the Darken blend mode. Only those pixels in the thinker layer that are darker than the pixels in the underlying sunset remain visible.

✦ **Lighten (G):** If you select this option, Photoshop applies colors in the active layer only if they are lighter than the corresponding pixels in the underlying image. Again, Photoshop compares the brightness levels in all channels of a full-color image. Examples of the Lighten blend mode appear in Figure 19-11 and Color Plate 19-1.

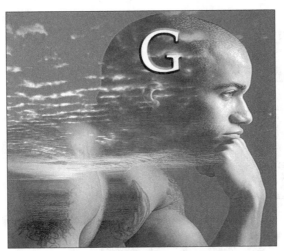

Figure 19-11: Our friend the thinker subject to the Lighten blend mode. Only those pixels in the selection that are lighter than the pixels in the underlying sunset remain visible.

✦ **Difference (E) and Exclusion (X):** Difference inverts lower layers according to the brightness values in the active layer. White inverts the composite pixels absolutely, black inverts them not at all, and the other brightness values invert it to some degree in between. In the first example of Figure 19-12, the light sunset shows through the black pixels at the back of the thinker's head, while the light areas along the front of the man's face invert the sky and clouds.

Exclusion works just like Difference, except for one, er, difference. Shown in the second example of Figure 19-12, Exclusion sends medium colored pixels to gray, creating a lower contrast effect, much as Soft Light is a low-contrast version of Hard Light.

Cross-Reference

One of my favorite uses for the Difference and Exclusion modes is to create a "Difference sandwich", in which you slide a filtered version of an image on a layer between two originals. I explain this technique and others in the upcoming section "Sandwiching a filtered image."

✦ **Hue (U):** The Hue mode and the following three blend modes make use of the HSL color model to mix colors between active layer and underlying composite. When you select Hue, Photoshop retains the hue values from the active layer and mixes them with the saturation and luminosity values from the underlying image. An example of this mode appears in the right column of Color Plate 19-1.

Note

I don't include grayscale figures for the Hue, Saturation, Color, and Luminosity blend modes for the simple reason that these modes affect color images only. In fact, all four options are dimmed when editing a grayscale document.

Difference

Exclusion

Figure 19-12: When you apply the Difference mode (top), white pixels invert the pixels beneath them, while black pixels leave the background untouched. The Exclusion mode (bottom) performs a similar effect, but instead of inverting medium colors, it changes them to gray.

✦ **Saturation (T):** When you select this option, Photoshop retains the saturation values from the active layer and mixes them with the hue and luminosity values from the underlying image. This mode rarely results in anything but very subtle effects, as demonstrated by the bright orange Saturn in Color Plate 19-1. You'll usually want to apply it in combination with some other blend mode. For example, after applying a random blend mode to a layer, you might duplicate the layer and then apply the Saturation mode to either boost or downplay the colors, much like printing a gloss or matte coating over the image.

✦ **Color (C):** This option combines hue and saturation. Photoshop retains both the hue and saturation values from the active layer and mixes them with the luminosity values from the underlying image. Because the saturation portion of the Color mode has such a slight effect, Color frequently produces an almost identical effect to Hue. For example, the Hue and Color versions of Saturn in Color Plate 19-1 are very similar, with the former appearing only slightly less bright than the latter.

✦ **Luminosity (Y):** The Luminosity blend mode retains the lightness values from the active layer and mixes them with the hue and saturation values from the underlying image. An example of this mode appears in the lower right corner in Color Plate 19-1. Here Saturn appears every bit as clearly defined as the Normal example in the upper left corner, but it assumes the orange color of its Jupiterian background. So just as the Color mode uses the layer to colorize its background, the Luminosity mode uses the background to colorize the layer.

The best way to get a feel for blend modes is to give them a whirl. Just start whacking the Shift-Option-key combos and see what you come up with. A handful of keys won't produce any effect. The beginning of the alphabet contains the motherload of shortcuts. Of the first 15 letters (up through and including O), only A, J, and L go unused. That's BO – JL. The other good ones are S, T, U, X, and Y, which just happens to spell "Stuxy." Summing up, the magic formula is:

BO – JL + Stuxy

Remember that and you're golden.

Blend mode madness

Remember that scene in *Amadeus* where Mozart is telling the king about some obscure opera that he's writing — "Marriage of Franz Joseph Haydn" or something like that — and he's bragging about how many folks he has singing on stage at the same time? Remember that scene? Oh, you're not even trying. Anyway, you can do that same thing with Photoshop. Not with melody or recitative or anything like that, but with imagery. Just as Mozart might juggle several different melodies and harmonies at once, you can juggle layers upon layers of images, each filtered differently and mixed differently with the images below it.

Predicting the outcome of these monumental compositions takes a brain the magnitude of Mozart's. But screwing around with different settings takes no intelligence at all, which is where I come in.

The hierarchy of blend modes

The most direct method for juggling multiple images is "sandwiching." By this I mean placing a heavily filtered version of an image between two originals. This technique is based on the principal that most blend modes — all but Multiply, Screen, Difference, and Exclusion — change depending on which of two images is on top.

For example, Figure 19-13 shows two layers, A and B, and what happens when I blend them with the Overlay mode. When the leaf is on top, as in the third example, the Overlay mode favors the woman; but when the woman appears on the top layer, the Overlay mode favors the leaf.

Layer A   Layer B   Overlay, B on A   Overlay, A on B

Figure 19-13: After establishing two layers, woman and leaf, I placed the leaf on top and applied Overlay to get the third image. Then I switched the order of the layers and applied the Overlay mode to the woman to get the last image.

As I mentioned earlier, the Overlay mode always favors the lower layer. Its opposite, Hard Light, favors the active layer. Therefore, I could have achieved the exact effect shown in the third example of Figure 19-13 by placing the leaf underneath and setting the woman layer to Hard Light. Flip-flop the layers and apply Hard Light to the leaf to get the last example.

Other blend modes have opposites as well. Take the Normal mode, for example. When you apply Normal, whichever image is on top is the one that you see. However, if you change the Opacity, you reveal the underlying image. At 50 percent Opacity, it doesn't matter which image is on top. The color of every pair of pixels in both images is merely averaged. So an inverse relationship exists. If the filtered image is on top, an Opacity setting of 25 percent produces the same effect as if you reversed the order of the images and changed the Opacity to 75 percent.

The other obvious opposites are Color and Luminosity. If I were to position the green leaf in front of the woman and apply Color, the woman would turn green. The very same thing would happen if I placed the woman in front and applied Luminosity.

The moral of this minutia is that the order in which you stack your layers is as important as the blend modes you apply. Even filters that have no stacking opposites — Soft Light, Color Dodge, Hue, and others — will produce different effects depending on which layer is on top. Just for your general edification, Figure 19-14 and possibly more enlightening Color Plate 19-2 show a few examples.

Figure 19-14: Examples of a few additional blend modes with the leaf on the front layer (top row) and the woman in front (bottom row).

Sandwiching a filtered image

When you sandwich a filtered image between two originals — which, as you may recall, is what all this is leading up to — you can lessen the effect of the filter and achieve different effects than those I discussed in Chapter 15. Layers and blend modes give you the flexibility to experiment as much as you want and for as long as you please.

In Color Plate 19-3, I copied the woman's face to a new layer, then I applied Filter ➪ Sketch ➪ Charcoal with the foreground color set to dark purple and the background color set to green. The top row of images in the color plate show what happened when I used three different blend modes — Hard Light, Color, and Difference — to mix the Charcoal image with the underlying original.

I next cloned the background layer and moved it above the Charcoal layer, so that the filtered image resided between two originals, creating a sandwich. The originals are the bread of the sandwich, and the Charcoal layer is the meat (or the eggplant, for you vegetarians). The bottom row demonstrates the effects of applying each of three blend modes to the top slice of bread, which interacts with the blend mode applied to the Charcoal meat shown above. For example, in the second column, I applied the Hard Light mode to the filtered image to achieve the top effect. Then I created the top layer and applied the Soft Light mode to get the bottom effect.

Creating a Difference sandwich

Ask your local deli guy, and he'll tell you that everyone has a favorite sandwich. Where blend modes are concerned, my favorite is the Difference sandwich. By applying Difference to both the filtered layer and the cloned original on top, you effectively invert the filter into the original image, and then reinvert the image to create a more subtle and utterly unique effect.

Figure 19-15 and Color Plate 19-4 show a small sampling of the several thousand possible variations on the Difference sandwich theme. In the top rows of both figures, I've vigorously applied a series of standard filters — so vigorously, in fact, that I've pretty well ruined the image. But no fear. By stacking it on top of the original, cloning the original on top of it, and applying the Difference mode to both layers, you can restore much of the original image detail, as shown in the bottom examples of the two figures. (I corrected the colors of the images by adding an adjustment layer on top of the sandwich, but otherwise you see the effects in their raw form.)

Note

A few notes about the Difference sandwich. First of all, the effect doesn't work nearly so well if you start reducing the Opacity values. Second, try using the Exclusion mode instead of Difference if you want to lower the contrast. And finally, Difference is one of those few blend modes that produces the same effect regardless of how you order the layers. This means you can filter either the middle layer or the bottom layer in the sandwich and get the exact same effect. But the top layer must be the original image.

Dropping Out and Forcing Through

When you double-click on a layer name in the Layers palette, Photoshop displays the Layer Options dialog box shown in Figure 19-16. In addition to permitting you to name a layer, change the Opacity value, and select a blend mode, you can drop out pixels in the active layer and force through pixels from lower layers according to their brightness values.

Gaussian Blur · · · · · Radial Blur · · · · · High Pass

Filtered image

Inside sandwich

Figure 19-15: Three different filtering effects as they appear on their own (top row) and when inserted into a Difference sandwich (bottom row).

Layer Options

Name: Layer in the Iron Mask

OK

Cancel

Options

Opacity: 100 % Mode: Difference

☑ Preview

Blend If: Gray ⌘~

This Layer: 0 255

Underlying: 0 255

Figure 19-16: When editing a layer, you can access a dialog box of options to selectively mix the colors in the active layer with the colors in the image below.

For the record, the Layer Options dialog box offers the following seven options:

✦ **Name:** Use this option box to change the layer name that appears in the Layers palette.

✦ **Opacity:** Enter a value to change the translucency of the active layer. This option works identically to the Opacity value in the Layers palette.

✦ **Mode:** Here's where you select one of the 17 blend modes you could already access in the Layers palette pop-up menu.

✦ **Blend If:** Select a color channel from the Blend If pop-up menu to apply the effects of the slider bars beneath the menu to one color channel independently of the others. When the Gray option is active, as it is by default, your changes affect all color channels equally. (To my knowledge, this is the only instance where Gray means all color channels; elsewhere, Gray means a gray composite, just like Gray ought to mean.) Just for the record, the Opacity value and Mode option affect all channels regardless of the color channel you select from Blend If.

✦ **This Layer:** This slider bar lets you exclude ranges of colors according to brightness values in the active layer. When you exclude colors by dragging the black triangle to the right or the white triangle to the left, the colors disappear from view.

✦ **Underlying:** This slider forces colors from the underlying layers to poke through the active layer. Any colors not included in the range set by the black and white triangles cannot be covered and are therefore visible regardless of the colors in the active layer.

✦ **Preview:** Select the Preview check box to continually update the image window every time you adjust a setting.

The slider bars are far too complicated to explain in a bulleted list. To find out more about these options as well as the Blend If pop-up menu, read the following sections.

Color exclusion sliders

The first slider bar, This Layer, hides pixels in the active layer according to their brightness values. You can abandon dark pixels by dragging the left slider triangle or light pixels by dragging the right slider triangle. Figure 19-17 shows examples of each.

✦ To create the first example, I first set the blend mode to Screen. Then I dragged the left slider bar until the value immediately to the right of the *This Layer* label read 170, thereby hiding all pixels whose brightness values were 170 or lower.

✦ To create the second example, I changed the blend mode to Multiply. I reset the left slider triangle to 0 and dragged the right slider triangle to 120, which hid those pixels with brightness values of 120 or higher.

Screen, This Layer: 170, 255

Multiply, This Layer: 0, 120

Figure 19-17: Two examples of modifying the blend mode and This Layer settings inside the Layer Options dialog box.

Drag the triangles along the Underlying slider bar to force pixels in the underlying layers to show through, again according to their brightness values. To force dark pixels in the underlying image to show through, drag the left slider triangle; to force light pixels to show through, drag the right slider triangle.

Here's how I achieved the effects in Figure 19-18:

> ✦ To achieve the effect in the top example in Figure 19-18, I started off by applying the Hard Light mode. (Those blend modes, they're keepers.) Then I dragged the left slider triangle until the first Underlying value read 140. This forced the pixels in the sunset that had brightness values of 140 or lower to show through.

   ✦ In the second example, I changed the blend mode to Overlay. Then I dragged the right Underlying slider triangle to 150, uncovering pixels at the bright end of the spectrum.

Hard Light, Underlying: 140, 255

Overlay, Underlying: 0, 150

Figure 19-18: Here I changed the Underlying slider bar settings to force through the darkest (top) and lightest (bottom) pixels in the sunset.

Bear in mind, every single adjustment made inside the Layer Options dialog box is temporary. The slider bars hide pixels, they don't delete them. So long as the layer remains intact, you can revisit Layer Options and restore hidden pixels or hide new ones.

Fuzziness

The problem with hiding and forcing colors with the slider bars is that you achieve some pretty harsh color transitions. Both Figures 19-17 and 19-18 bear witness to this fact. Talk about your jagged edges! Luckily, you can soften the color transitions by abandoning and forcing pixels gradually over a fuzziness range, which works much like the Fuzziness value in the Color range dialog box, leaving some pixels opaque and tapering others off into transparency.

To taper off the opacity of pixels in either the active layers or the underlying image, Option-drag one of the triangles in the appropriate slider bar. The triangle splits into two halves, and the corresponding value above the slider bar splits into two values separated by a slash, as demonstrated in Figure 19-19.

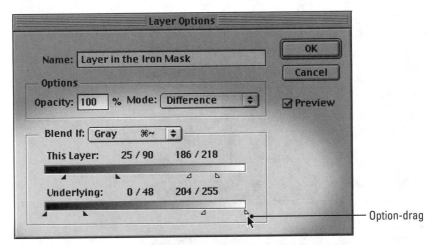

Figure 19-19: Option-drag a slider triangle to split it in half. You can then specify a fuzziness range across which brightness values will gradually fade into transparency.

The left triangle half represents the beginning of the fuzziness range — that is, the brightness values at which the pixels begin to fade into or away from view. The right half represents the end of the range — that is, the point at which the pixels are fully visible or invisible.

Figure 19-20 shows some fuzziness applied to the This Layer slider. Here are the specifics:

✦ In the top example of Figure 19-20, I set the blend mode to Multiply. I left the first This Layer triangle set to 0. I Option-dragged the second triangle to split it. And I moved the left half of the split triangle to 55 and the right half to 128. The result is a gradual drop off. All pixels with brightness values of 0 to 55 are opaque, the pixels become gradually more translucent from 56 to 127, and pixels brighter than 128 are transparent.

✦ Next, I duplicated my layer and switched the blend mode to Screen. After splitting the first slider triangle with an Option-drag, I set one half of the triangle to 128 and the other to 220. I dragged both halves of the second This Layer triangle back to 255. The darkest pixels are transparent, they fade into view from 129 to 219, and become opaque from 220 on up. As shown in the second example in Figure 19-20, the result is a perfect blending of Multiply and Screen, with the sunset showing through in the gray areas.

Multiply, This Layer: 0, 55/128

Duplicate layer, Screen, This Layer: 128/220, 255

Figure 19-20: By Option-dragging a This Layer slider triangle, you can create gradual transitions between the opaque and transparent portions of a layer.

Using the Underlying slider is a bit trickier. It typically works best when you're trying to force through very bright or dark details, like the highlights in the sunset sky and the shadows in the water. It also helps to work with a foreground layer that has lots of flat areas of color for the background to show through. Here's what I did to create Figure 19-21:

✦ For starters, I applied Filter ⇨ Other ⇨ High Pass to my thinker layer, as in the first example of Figure 19-21. This created lots of gray areas for the underlying pixels to shine through.

✦ I applied the radical Color Dodge mode to this layer. I left the first Underlying triangle at 0. Then I split the second one and moved the left half to 80 and the right half to 200. This forced through the darkest pixels, fading out as they got lighter.

✦ Next, I duplicated the layer, applied the Color Burn mode, and fiddled with the Underlying triangles until the values read 100/150 and 180/255.The result is a vibrant composition that nicely sets off the thinker's tattoos.

Color channel options

The options in the Blend If pop-up menu are applicable exclusively to the settings you apply using the This Layer and Underlying slider bars. When you work with a grayscale image, the Blend If pop-up menu offers one option only—Black— meaning that the Blend If option has no effect on grayscale editing. However, when you work in the RGB, CMYK, or Lab mode, you can hide and force ranges of pixels based on the brightness values of a single color channel.

To do so, select a color channel from the Blend If pop-up menu and then set the slider triangles as desired. Each time you select a different Blend If option, the slider triangles change to the positions at which you last set them for that color channel.

Using Channel Operation Commands

Image ⇨ Apply Image and Image ⇨ Calculations provide access to Photoshop's *channel operations,* which composite one or more channels with others according to predefined mathematical calculations. Although once hailed as Photoshop's most powerful capabilities, channel operations have been eclipsed by the standard and more accessible functions available from the Layers and Channels palettes. One day, I suspect Adobe will scrap Apply Image and Calculations altogether. But until that day, I will dutifully document them both.

High Pass filter

Color Dodge, Underlying: 0, 80/200

Duplicate layer, Color Burn, Underlying: 100/150, 180/255

Figure 19-21: After combining a High Pass effect with the radical Color Dodge and Color Burn blend modes, I used the Underlying slider bar to force through pixels from the background so the sunset and ocean didn't get lost.

The Apply Image and Calculations commands allow you to merge one or two identically sized images using 12 of the 17 blend modes discussed earlier plus two additional modes, Add and Subtract. In a nutshell, the commands duplicate the process of dragging and dropping one image onto another (or cloning an image onto a new layer), and using the blend mode and Opacity settings in the Layers palette to mix the two images together.

Although Apply Image and Calculations are more similar than different, each command fulfills a specific — if not entirely unique — function:

✦ **Apply Image:** This command takes an open image and merges it with the foreground image (or takes the foreground image and composites it onto itself). You can apply the command to either the full-color image or one or more of the individual channels.

✦ **Calculations:** The Calculations command works on individual channels only. It takes a channel from one image, mixes it with a channel from another (or the same) image, and puts the result inside an open image or in a new image window.

The primary advantage of these commands over other, more straightforward compositing methods is that they allow you to access and composite the contents of individual color channels without a lot of selecting, copying and pasting, cloning, floating, and layering. You also get two extra blend modes, Add and Subtract, which may prove useful on a rainy day.

The Apply Image and Calculations commands provide previewing options, so that you can see how an effect will look in the image window. But thanks to the sheer quantity of unfriendly options offered by the two commands, I suggest that you use them on a very occasional basis. The Calculations command can be a handy way to combine masks and layer transparencies to create precise selection outlines. And Apply Image is good for compositing images in different color models, such as RGB and Lab (as I explain in the "Mixing images in different color modes" section later in this chapter).

But if your time is limited and you want to concentrate your efforts on learning Photoshop's most essential features, then feel free to skip Apply Image and Calculations. I assure you, you won't be missing much.

The Apply Image command

Channel operations work by taking one or more channels from an image, called the *source,* and duplicating them to another image, called the *target.* When you use the Apply Image command, the foreground image is always the target, and you can select only one source image. Photoshop then takes the source and target, mixes them together, and puts the result in the target image. Therefore, the target image is the only image that the command actually changes. The source image remains unaffected.

When you choose Image ➪ Apply Image, Photoshop displays the dialog box shown in Figure 19-22. Notice that you can select from a pop-up menu of images to specify the Source, but the Target item — listed just above the Blending box — is fixed. This is the active layer in the foreground image.

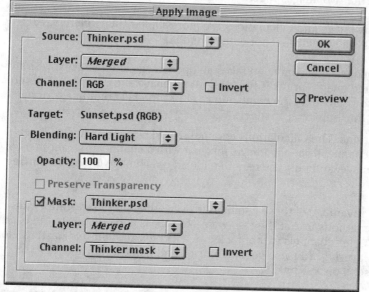

Figure 19-22: The Apply Image command lets you mix one source image with a target image and make the result the new target.

If this sounds a little dense, just think of it this way: The source image is the floating selection and the target is the underlying original. Meanwhile, the Blending options are the blend modes pop-up menu and Opacity value in the Layers palette.

Using the Apply Image command is a five-step process. You can always simply choose the command and hope for the best, but you'll get the most use out of it if you do the following:

Steps: Applying the Apply Image Command

1. **Open the two images that you want to mix.** If you want to mix the image with itself to create some effect, just open the one image.

2. **Make sure that the two images are exactly the same size, down to the last pixel.** Use the crop tool and Image Size command as necessary. (You don't have to worry about this step when mixing an image with itself.)

3. **Inside the target image, switch to the channel and layer that you want to edit.** If you want to edit all channels, press ⌘-tilde (~) to remain in the composite view.

   When you're editing a single channel, I strongly advise you to display all channels on-screen. For example, after pressing ⌘-1 to switch to the red channel, click in front of the RGB item in the Channels palette to display the eyeball icon and show all channels. Only one channel is active, but all are visible. This way, you can see how your edits inside the Apply Image dialog box will affect the entire image, not just the one channel.

4. **Select the portion of the target image that you want to edit.** If you want to affect the entire image, don't select anything.

5. **Choose Image ⇨ Apply Image and have at it.**

Obviously, that last step is a little more difficult than it sounds. That's why I've put together the following list to explain how all those options in the Apply Image dialog box work:

✦ **Source:** The Source pop-up menu contains the name of the foreground image as well as any other images that are both open and exactly the same size as the foreground image. If the image you want to merge is not available, you must not have been paying much attention to Step 2. Press Escape to cancel, then resize and crop as needed, choose Image ⇨ Apply Image, and try again.

✦ **Layer:** This pop-up menu lists all layers in the selected source image. If the image doesn't have any layers, Background is your only option. Otherwise, select the layer that contains the prospective source image. Select Merged to mix all visible layers in the source image with the target image.

✦ **Channel:** Select the channels that you want to mix from this pop-up menu. Both composite views and individual color and mask channels are included. Keep in mind that you'll be mixing these channels with the channels that you made available in the target image before choosing the command.

   For example, if the target image is an RGB image shown in the full-color composite view, and you choose RGB from the Channel pop-up menu in the Apply Image dialog box, Photoshop mixes the red, green, and blue channels in the source image with the corresponding red, green, and blue channels in the target image. However, if you switched to the red channel before choosing Apply Image and then selected the RGB option, the program mixes a composite grayscale version of the RGB source image with the red channel in the target and leaves the other target channels unaffected.

✦ **Selection, Transparency, and Layer Mask:** If a portion of the source image is selected, the pop-up menu offers a Selection option, which lets you apply the selection outline as if it were a grayscale image, just like a selection viewed in the quick mask mode. If you selected a specific layer from the Layer pop-up menu, you'll find a Transparency option that represents the transparency mask. If the layer includes its own layer mask, a Layer Mask option also appears.

None of the three options is particularly useful when you work in the composite view of the target image; you'll usually want to apply the Selection, Transparency, or Layer Mask option only to a single channel, as described in "The Calculations command" section toward the end of this chapter. (For an exception, see the upcoming tip.)

✦ **Invert:** Select this check box to invert the contents of the source image before compositing it with the target image. This option permits you to experiment with different effects. The last example in Color Plate 19-5, for example, shows one use for the Invert check box. I inverted the *b* channel before compositing it with the RGB image to create an early dawn effect.

✦ **Target:** You can't change this item. It merely shows which image, which channels, and which layers are being affected by the command.

✦ **Blending:** This pop-up menu offers access to 12 of the blend modes I discussed in "The remaining 17 blend modes" section earlier in this chapter. The Dissolve, Hue, Saturation, Color, and Luminosity options are missing. Two additional options, Add and Subtract, are discussed in the "Add and Subtract" section later in this chapter.

✦ **Opacity:** By now, I gather you're well aware of how this one works.

✦ **Preserve Transparency:** When you're editing a layer in the target image — that is, you activated a specific layer before choosing Image ⇨ Apply Image — the Preserve Transparency check box becomes available. Select it to protect transparent portions of the layer from any compositing, much as if the transparent portions were not selected and are therefore masked.

✦ **Mask:** Select this option to mask off a portion of the source image. I already mentioned that you can specify the exact portion of the target image you want to edit by selecting that portion before choosing the Apply Image command. But you can also control which portion of the source image is composited on top of the target through the use of a mask. When you select the Mask check box, three new pop-up menus and an Invert check box appear at the bottom of the Apply Image dialog box. For complete information on these options, see the upcoming "Compositing with a mask" section.

Mixing images in different color modes

Tip

Throughout my laborious explanations of all those options in the Apply Image dialog box, I've been eagerly waiting to share with you the command's one truly unique capability. Image ⇨ Apply Image is the only way to composite images in different color modes without setting the modes to match. For example, you could mix the lightness channel from a Lab image with each of the channels from an RGB image, or mix the green channel from an RGB image with each of the channels in a CMYK image. By contrast, if you were to simply drag and drop a Lab image into an RGB image, Photoshop would automatically convert the image to the RGB color space, which would result in a very different effect.

To help make things a little more clear, Color Plate 19-5 shows four examples of an image composited onto itself using the Hard Light blend mode. The first example shows the result of selecting the RGB image as both source and target. As always, this exaggerates the colors in the image and enhances contrast, but retains the same basic color composition as before.

The other examples in the color plate show what happened when I duplicated the image by choosing Image ⇨ Duplicate, converted the duplicate to the Lab mode (Mode ⇨ Lab Color), and then composited the Lab and RGB images together. To do this, I switched to the RGB image, chose Image ⇨ Apply Image, and selected the Lab image from the Source pop-up menu. In the top right example, I chose Lightness from the Channel pop-up menu, which mixed the lightness channel with all three RGB channels. And in the bottom left image, I chose *b* from the Channel pop-up menu and selected the Invert check box, which inverted the *b* channel before applying it. For the final, moderately psychedelic effect in Color Plate 19-5, I used the Lab image as the destination. I switched to the Lab image, chose the Apply Image command, selected the RGB image as the Source, and select Blue from the Channel pop-up menu.

Compositing with a mask

The Mask option in the Apply Image dialog box provides a method for you to import only a selected portion of the source image into the target image. Select the Mask check box and choose the image that contains the mask from the pop-up menu on the immediate right. As with the Source pop-up menu, the Mask menu lists only those images that are open and happen to be the exact same size as the target image. If necessary, select the layer on which the mask appears from the Layer pop-up menu. Then select the specific mask channel from the final pop-up menu. This doesn't have to be a mask channel; you can use any color channel as a mask.

After you select all the necessary options, the mask works like so: Where the mask is white, the source image shows through and mixes in with the target image, just as if it were a selected portion of the floating image. Where the mask is black, the source image is absent. Gray values in the mask mix the source and target with progressive emphasis on the target as the grays darken.

If you prefer to swap the masked and unmasked areas of the source image, select the Invert check box at the bottom of the dialog box. Now, where the mask is black, you see the source image; where the mask is white, you don't.

The first example in Color Plate 19-6 shows a mask viewed as a rubylith overlay with the image. To make the mask, I selected the background with the Color Range command, inversed the selection, and saved the result as a separate channel. In the other examples in the color plate, I again composited the RGB and Lab versions of the image — as in the previous section — using Photoshop's most outrageous blend modes. No matter how dramatically the Apply Image command affected the thinker, his background remained unscathed, thanks to the mask. If the Mask option had not been turned on, the background would have changed with the mode, turning light blue for Color Dodge, black for Color Burn, and deep red for Difference.

You can even use a selection outline or layer as a mask. If you select some portion of the source image before switching to the target image and choosing Image ⇨ Apply Image, you can access the selection by choosing Selection from the Channel pop-up menu at the very bottom of the dialog box. Those pixels from the source image that fall inside the selection remain visible; those that do not are transparent. Use the Invert check box to inverse the selection outline. To use the boundaries of a layer selected from the Layer pop-up menu as a mask, choose the Transparency option from the Channel menu. Where the layer is opaque, the source image is opaque (assuming that the Opacity option is set to 100 percent, of course); where the layer is transparent, so too is the source image.

Add and Subtract

The Add and Subtract blend modes found in the Apply Image dialog box (and also in the Calculations dialog box) work a bit like the Custom filter that I discussed in Chapter 17. However, instead of multiplying brightness values by matrix numbers and calculating a sum, as the Custom filter does, these modes add and subtract the brightness values of pixels in different channels.

The Add option adds the brightness value of each pixel in the source image to that of its corresponding pixel in the target image. The Subtract option takes the brightness value of each pixel in the target image and subtracts the brightness value of its corresponding pixel in the source image. When you select either Add or Subtract, the Apply Image dialog box offers two additional option boxes, Scale and Offset. Photoshop divides the sum or difference of the Add or Subtract mode by the Scale value (from 1.000 to 2.000) and then adds the Offset value (from negative to positive 255).

If equations will help, here's the equation for the Add blend mode:

Resulting brightness value = (Target + Source) ÷ Scale + Offset

And here's the equation for the Subtract mode:

Resulting brightness value = (Target − Source) ÷ Scale + Offset

If equations only confuse you, just remember this: The Add option results in a destination image that is lighter than either source; the Subtract option results in a destination image that is darker than either source. If you want to darken the image further, raise the Scale value. To darken each pixel in the target image by a constant amount, which is useful when applying the Add option, enter a negative Offset value. If you want to lighten each pixel, as when applying the Subtract option, enter a positive Offset value.

Applying the Add command

The best way to demonstrate how these commands work is to offer an example. To create the effects shown in Figures 19-23 and 19-24, I began with the thinker and sunset shown way back in Figure 19-3.

After switching to the Sunset image and choosing Image ➪ Apply Image, I selected the Thinker image from the Source pop-up menu. (I happened to be working with flat, grayscale images, so I didn't have to worry about the Layer and Channel options.) I selected the Add option from the Blending pop-up menu and accepted the default Scale and Offset values of 1 and 0, respectively, to achieve the first example in Figure 19-23. The thinker went blindingly white, much lighter than he would under any other blend mode, even Color Dodge. To improve the quality and detail of the image, I changed the Scale value to 1.2 to slightly downplay the brightness values and entered an Offset value of –60 to darken the colors uniformly. The result of this operation is the more satisfactory image shown in the second example of the figure.

Add, Scale: 1, Offset: 0

Figure 19-23: Two applications of the Add blend mode from the Apply Image command, each subject to different Scale and Offset values.

Add, Scale: 1.2, Offset: -60

Applying the Subtract command

To create the first example in Figure 19-24, I selected the Subtract option from the Blending pop-up menu, once again accepting the default Scale and Offset values of 1 and 0, respectively. This time, the thinker turned pitch black because I subtracted the light values of his face from the light values in the sky, leaving no brightness value at all. Meanwhile, the thinker's hair had virtually no effect on the sunset because the hair pixels were very dark and in some cases black. Subtracting black from a color is like subtracting 0 from a number — it leaves the value unchanged.

The result struck me as too dark, so I lightened it by raising the Scale and Offset values. To create the second image in Figure 19-24, I upped the Scale value to 1.2, just as in the second Add example, which actually darkened the image slightly. Then I raised the Offset value to 180, thus adding 180 points of brightness value to each pixel. This second image is more likely to survive reproduction with all detail intact.

The Calculations command

Though its options are nearly identical, the Calculations command performs a slightly different function than Apply Image. Rather than compositing a source image on top of the current target image, Image ⇨ Calculations combines two source channels and puts the result in a target channel. You can use a single image for both sources, a source and the target, or all three. The target doesn't have to be the foreground image (although Photoshop previews the effect in the foreground image window). And the target can even be a new image. But the biggest difference is that instead of affecting entire full-color images, the Calculations command affects individual color channels only. Only one channel changes as a result of this command.

Choosing Image ⇨ Calculations displays the dialog box shown in Figure 19-25. Rather than explaining this dialog box option by option — I'd just end up wasting 35 pages and repeating myself every other sentence — I'll attack the topic in a less structured but more expedient fashion.

When you arrive inside the dialog box, you select your source images from the Source 1 and Source 2 pop-up menus. As with Apply Image, the images have to be exactly the same size. You can composite individual layers using the Layer menus. Select the channels you want to mix together from the Channel options. In place of the full-color options — RGB, Lab, CMYK — each Channel menu offers a Gray option, which represents the grayscale composite of all channels in an image.

Subtract, Scale: 1, Offset: 0

Subtract, Scale: 1.2, Offset: 180

Figure 19-24: Two applications of the Subtract command on the images from Figure 19-23, one subject to Scale and Offset values of 1 and 0 (left) and the other subject to values of 1.2 and 60 (right).

The Blending pop-up menu offers the same 14 blend modes — including Add and Subtract — that are found in the Apply Image dialog box. But it's important to keep in mind how the Calculations dialog box organizes the source images when working with blend modes. The Source 1 image is equivalent to the source when using the Apply Image command (or the floating selection when compositing conventionally); the Source 2 image is equivalent to the target (or the underlying original). Therefore, choosing the Normal blend mode displays the Source 1 image. The Subtract command subtracts the Source 1 image from the Source 2 image.

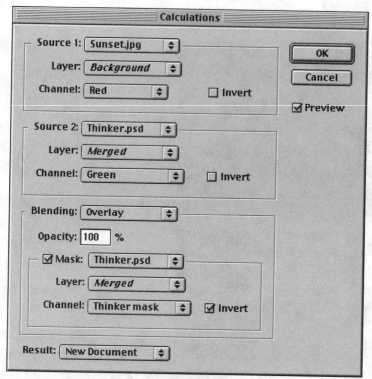

Figure 19-25: Use the Calculations command to mix two source channels and place them inside a new or existing target channel.

Half of the blend modes perform identically regardless of which of the two images is Source 1 and which is Source 2. The other half — including Normal, Overlay, Soft Light, and Hard Light — produce different results based on the image you assign to each spot. But as long as you keep in mind that Source 1 is the floater — hey, it's at the top of the dialog box, right? — you should be okay.

Tip

The only one that throws me off is Subtract, because I see Source 1 at the top of the dialog box and naturally assume that Photoshop will subtract Source 2, which is underneath it. Unfortunately, this is exactly opposite to the way it really works. If you find yourself similarly confused and set up the equation backwards, you can reverse it by selecting both Invert options. Source 2 minus Source 1 results in the exact same effect as an inverted Source 1 minus an inverted Source 2. (After all, the equation (255 – Source 1) – (255 – Source 2), which represents an inverted Source 1 minus an inverted Source 2, simplifies down to *Source 2 – Source 1*. If math isn't your strong point, don't worry. I was just showing my work.)

As you can in the Apply Image dialog box, you can specify a mask using the Mask options in the Calculations dialog box. The difference here is that the mask applies to the first source image and protects the second one. So where the mask is white, the two sources mix together normally. Where the mask is black, you see the second source image only.

The Result option determines the target for the composited channels. If you select New Document from the Result pop-up menu, as in Figure 19-25, Photoshop creates a new grayscale image. Alternatively, you can stick the result of the composited channels in any channel inside any image that is the same size as the source images.

Combining masks

As described for the Apply Image command, Selection, Transparency, and Layer Mask may be available as options from any of the Channel pop-up menus. But here they have more purpose. You can composite layer masks to form selection outlines, selection outlines to form masks, and all sorts of other pragmatic combinations.

Figure 19-26 shows how the Calculations command sees selected areas. Whether you're working with masks, selection outlines, transparency masks, or layer masks, the Calculations command sees the area as a grayscale image. So in Figure 19-28, the white areas are selected or opaque, and the black areas are deselected or transparent.

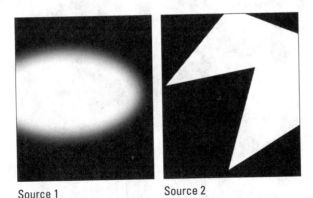

Source 1　　　　　Source 2

Figure 19-26: Two selections expressed as grayscale images (a.k.a. masks). The left image is the first source, and the right image is the second.

Assuming that I've chosen Image ⇨ Calculations and selected the images using the Source 1 and Source 2 options, the only remaining step is to select the proper blend mode from the Blending pop-up menu. Screen, Multiply, and Difference are the best solutions. The top row in Figure 19-27 shows the common methods for combining selection outlines. In the first example, I added the two together using the Screen mode, just as in the previous steps. In fact, Screening masks and adding selection outlines are exact equivalents. To subtract the Source 1 selection from Source 2, I inverted the former (by selecting the Invert check box in the Source 1 area) and applied the Multiply blend mode. To find the intersection of the two masks, I simply applied Multiply without inverting.

Screen (add)　　　Invert + Multiply (subtract)　　Multiply (intersect)

Invert + Screen　　　Difference　　　Invert + Difference

Figure 19-27: Starting with the masks shown in Figure 19-28, I combined them in traditional (top row) and nontraditional (bottom row) ways using the Calculations command.

But the Calculations command doesn't stop at the standard three — add, subtract, and intersect. The bottom row of Figure 19-27 shows three methods of combining selection outlines that are not possible using keyboard shortcuts. For example, if I invert the Source 1 mask and combine it with the Screen mode, I add the inverse of the elliptical selection and add it to the polygonal one. The Difference mode adds the portion of the elliptical selection that doesn't intersect the polygonal one and subtracts the intersection. And inverting Source 1 and then applying Difference retains the intersection, subtracts the portion of the polygonal selection that is not intersected, and inverts the elliptical selection where it does not intersect. These may not be options you use every day, but they are extremely powerful if you can manage to wrap your brain around them.

Depending on how well you've been keeping up with this discussion, you may be asking yourself, "Why not apply Lighten or Add in place of Screen, or Darken or Subtract in place of Multiply?" The reason becomes evident when you combine two soft selections. Suppose that I blurred the Source 2 mask to give it a feathered edge. Figure 19-28 shows the results of combining the newly blurred polygonal mask with the elliptical mask using a series of blend modes. In the top row, I added the two selection outlines together using the Lighten, Add, and Screen modes. Lighten results in harsh corner transitions, while Add cuts off the interior edges. Only Screen does it just right. The bottom row of the figure shows the results of subtracting the elliptical mask from the polygonal one by occasionally inverting the elliptical mask and applying Darken, Subtract, and Multiply. Again, Darken results in sharp corners. The Subtract mode eliminates the need to invert the elliptical marquee, but it brings the black area too far into the blurred edges, resulting in an overly abrupt interior cusp. Multiply ensures that all transitions remain smooth as silk.

The reason for the success of the Screen and Multiply modes is that they mix colors together. Lighten and Darken simply settle on the color of one source image or the other — no mixing occurs — hence the harsh transitions. Add and Subtract rely on overly simplistic arithmetic equations — as I explained earlier, they really just add and subtract brightness values — which result in steep fall-off and build-up rates; in other words, there are cliffs of color transition where there ought to be rolling hills. Both Screen and Multiply soften the transitions using variations on color averaging that makes colors incrementally lighter or darker.

Lighten   Add   Screen

Invert + Darken   Subtract   Invert + Multiply

Figure 19-28: When adding softened selections (top row) and subtracting them (bottom row), the Screen and Multiply modes provide the most even and continuous transitions.

✦   ✦   ✦

Creating Graphics for the Web

The World of Web Imagery

The Internet may well be the most chaotic, anarchic force ever unleashed on the planet. It has no boundaries, it has no unifying purpose, it is controlled by no one, and it is owned by everyone. It's also incomprehensibly enormous, larger than any single government or business entity on the planet. If the ten richest men in the world pooled their resources, they still couldn't purchase all the computers and cables that keep the Internet alive. In terms of pure size and volume, the Web makes the great thoroughfares of the Roman empire look like a paper boy's route.

As a result, it's impossible to get a bead on the World Wide Web. With several million hands in the pie, and several million more hands groping for a slice, the Web is as subject to casual comprehension as are the depths of the oceans, the infinity of the cosmos, or the meaning of life. And the Web mutates faster than any of those forces. Something just changed while you were reading the last sentence. An important new Web technology hit the market during the sentence you're reading now. It's enough to drive any sane human bonkers.

Fortunately, I'm not altogether sane, so I find the Web quite intriguing. Even so, whatever I write today will very likely change by the time you read this. We may all have the Internet cabled into our homes, animation and video images may rule the day, and the Web as I presently know it may be stone cold dead. All of this will happen gradually, of course — even lightning-fast changes take some time to occur. And were a new technology to come along that combined the power of Java, the versatility of HTML, and the ease of use of a bar of soap, every one of the untold millions of Web content providers would continue to create their millions of different pages in millions of different ways. The most brilliant of technologies is forever mitigated by the willingness of humans to adapt to it.

I include the preceding by way of a disclaimer for the general thesis of this chapter, which is simply this: Bitmapped graphics rule the Web. Sure, text-based content, file libraries, and hyperlinks are the main stock and trade of the Internet, but the graphics are what make the Web intelligible and invite us to come back for more. Graphics have brought the masses to the Web, images account for 90 percent of all Web graphics, and Photoshop is the world's number one image editor. As a result, Photoshop has become as inextricably linked to the Web as Netscape Navigator, Adobe PageMill, RealAudio, and a hundred other programs. It's just another happy accident in Photoshop's runaway success.

The smaller, the speedier

If you have any experience with the Web, then you know that small images are speedy images. By "small," I don't mean small in physical size (although that often helps). I mean small in terms of disk space. A 20K image that fills your screen takes less time to download and display than a 50K file no larger than a sticky note. It's the act of getting the data through the cables and phone lines that takes the time; by comparison, the time it takes your browser software to interpret the data is insignificant.

Therefore, the main focus of this chapter is file size. How can you squish the finest graphics you're capable of creating into the smallest amount of disk space with the least amount of sacrifice? This is the single most important challenge facing Web artists today. And while the Web-wide world is certain to change by the time you read this, I have a sneaking suspicion that small and speedy will remain the watchwords for some time to come.

Preparing screen images

Many Web artists come from a background in print media, and while much of what you've learned while preparing printed photographs is equally applicable to online artwork, there are differences. Foremost among them, you never need worry about converting images to the CMYK color space. All Web graphics are RGB (or a subset of indexed colors or gray values). This is extremely good news, because it means that for once in the history of electronic publishing, what you see on-screen is really, truly what you're going to get.

Well, almost. Ignoring the differences in the ways people perceive colors and the variances in ambient light from one office or study to the next, there are measurable differences between monitors. Some monitors produce highly accurate colors, others — especially older screens — are entirely unreliable. But more importantly, some screens display images more brightly than others.

For example, the typical Macintosh user with an Apple-brand monitor is cursed with a very bright screen. Apple monitors — and many non-Apple brands developed for the Mac — are calibrated to a gamma of 1.8. Meanwhile, most PC monitors are calibrated to 2.2, which is roughly equivalent to a standard television.

Note

Higher gamma values translate to darker displays because they indicate degrees of compensation. That is, an image has to be lightened only to 1.8 on the Mac to look as light as an image corrected to 2.2 on the PC.

Figure 20-1 shows a test image subjected to various brightness settings. The upper left example shows how the image looks when corrected for a typical Macintosh screen. The upper right example shows that very same image displayed on a typical PC monitor. Most of the folks who visit your Web page are seeing the darker of the two images.

The solution is to strike a compromise. Choose Image ➪ Adjust ➪ Levels (⌘-L) and raise the gamma (the middle Input Levels value) to between 1.2 and 1.25. Although the result will look a tad bit washed out on your screen, it'll look better on most monitors. The bottom two examples in Figure 20-1 show what happens when I raise the gamma to 1.25 and display the image on a Mac screen (left) and a PC screen (right). A little light on one, a little dark on the other, but ultimately an equitable compromise.

Photoshop 5.0

You can use File ➪ Color Settings ➪ RGB Setup to preview how your image will look on a foreign monitor. Assuming your monitor is properly calibrated using Gamma or a similar calibration tool (as explained in Chapter 6), here's what you do: Choose the RGB Setup command. Make sure the two check boxes — Preview and Display Using Monitor Compensation — are turned on. Then select an option from the RGB pop-up menu. Select the Apple RGB option to check out the view on a typical Mac screen, choose sRGB to preview the image on a typical PC. Photoshop updates the image in the background. When you finish appraising the situations, press Escape to return to your previous screen settings.

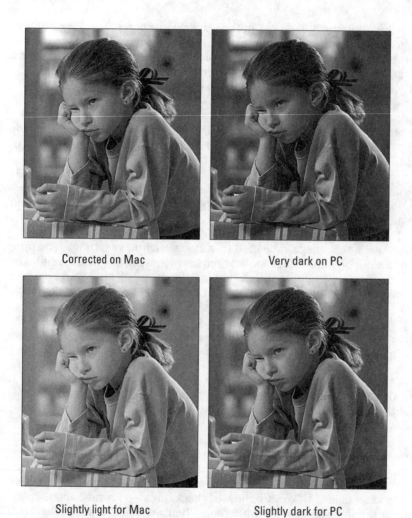

Corrected on Mac　　　　　　　Very dark on PC

Slightly light for Mac　　　　　Slightly dark for PC

Figure 20-1: Although most Web images are prepared on the Mac, they are more often viewed on PCs. Therefore, Mac users have to be aware that PC screens are typically darker.

More rules of Web imagery

Here are a few more items to remember when creating Web graphics:

✦ **Resolution doesn't matter:** Regardless of the Resolution value you enter into the Image Size dialog box, the Web browser displays one image pixel for every screen pixel (unless you specify an alternative image size in your HTML file). All that counts, therefore, is the pixel measurements — the number of pixels wide by the number of pixels tall.

✦ **GIF, JPEG, and PNG:** GIF and JPEG are the file formats of choice for Web graphics. GIF supports just 256 colors, so it's better for high-contrast artwork and text. JPEG applies lossy compression, so it's better for photographs and other continuous-tone images. The upstart format is PNG, which is essentially a 24-bit version of GIF designed for small full-color images that you don't want to compress.

✦ **Indexing colors:** Before you can save an image in the GIF format, you have to reduce the number of colors to 256 or fewer. Photoshop uses a technique called *indexing,* which reassigns colors according to a fixed index, which serves much the same purpose as the index in the back of this book.

✦ **Use the Save a Copy command:** To keep your file sizes as small as possible, choose File ➪ Save a Copy (⌘-Option-S) and select the Exclude Non-Image Data check box. This dumps the previews, color settings, file info, and all other data that isn't absolutely necessary to display the image on screen. This one operation can shave as much as 10K off a typical image, and that's a big savings on the Internet.

By recognizing which formats to use when, and how best to reduce colors, you can better ensure that visitors to your Web site will spend less time sitting on their hands and more time enjoying your site. I explain the fine points of the file formats and color indexing in the following sections.

Saving JPEG Images

When it comes to saving photographic images, no format results in smaller file sizes than JPEG. As explained in gory detail in Chapter 4, the JPEG format decreases the file size by applying a lossy compression scheme that actually redraws details in the image. Inside the JPEG Options dialog box, select lower Quality settings to put the screws to the image and squish it as low as it will go. But in doing so, you also sacrifice image detail. (Revisit the first color plate in this book, Color Plate 4-1, to see an example of JPEG compression at work.)

Just to show you how well the JPEG format works, Figure 20-2 shows a series of images saved in the JPEG and GIF formats, along with their file sizes. The original file consumed 62K in memory. Yet by lowering the Quality setting to Medium, I was able to get the file size down to 28K on disk. To accomplish similar savings using the GIF format, I had to reduce the color palette to 3 bits, or a mere 8 colors. (For the record, this same file saved in the PNG format consumed 63K on disk.) As you can plainly see in the enlarged details, applying JPEG compression has a less destructive effect on the appearance of the image than reducing the color palette.

JPEG

Maximum (8), 43K High (6), 34K Medium (3), 28K

GIF

8 bits/pixel, 71K 5 bits/pixel, 44K 3 bits/pixel, 26K

Figure 20-2: JPEG compression produces smaller file sizes with less impact than reducing the color palette and saving in GIF. The number in parentheses indicates the Quality value entered into the JPEG Options dialog box.

Tip

When judging small differences in file size, be sure to select the file at the Finder desktop and choose File ➪ Get Info (⌘-I). Then check the Size item listed in bytes. For example, the Size item in Figure 20-3 reads *33K on disk (16,551 bytes)*. The value in parentheses is the true reading, accurate to the byte. The first value — in this case, 33K — is measured in drive blocks, which are the smallest parcels of disk that the system can write to. This makes for a misleading measurement that is invariably larger than the actual file size, and that grows in proportion to the capacity of the hard drive (or drive partition). The value listed in the Size column inside a directory window, and the value Photoshop shows in the Open dialog box, are likewise measured in drive blocks. Whatever you do, don't believe the size listed in the preview box in the bottom left corner of the image window. This is the size of the image in memory, but where Web graphics are concerned, all that counts is the size of the file on disk.

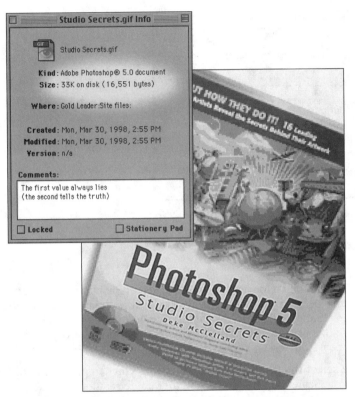

Figure 20-3: To gauge the true size of a file—accurate to the byte—select it at the desktop level, press ⌘-I, and observe the value in parentheses.

When you save a JPEG image, Photoshop displays the JPEG Options dialog box shown in Figure 20-4. Here's how the options contained inside affect Web images:

✦ **Image Options:** Use the Quality option to specify the amount of compression applied to your image. Lower values mean smaller file sizes and more JPEG compression gook. Many experts say Medium (3) is the best setting for Web graphics, but I think it looks pretty awful, especially on-screen. I prefer a Quality value of 5 or better.

✦ **Format Options:** Most Web browsers support two variations on the JPEG format. The so-called *baseline* (or *sequentially displayed*) format displays images in line-by-line passes on-screen. The *progressive* JPEG format displays an image on-screen in multiple passes, permitting visitors to your page to get an idea of how an image looks right off the bat, without waiting for the entire image to arrive.

Figure 20-4: Select the Baseline Optimized or Progressive radio button when saving a JPEG image for use on the Web.

To save a baseline image for use on the Web, select Baseline Optimized. This format includes better Huffman encoding that makes the file even smaller than Baseline ("Standard"). You can generally reduce the file size by 5 to 10 percent using this option. Select the Progressive option to save an image that gradually appears on-screen in passes.

✦ **Scans:** If you select the Progressive radio button, you can pick a number of passes from the Scans pop-up menu. A higher value results in a faster display of the initial image on your page, but it also takes longer to display completely on screen because of all the incremental refreshing (although some browsers are smart enough not to redisplay individual JPEG scans if they already have received data for subsequent ones). A medium value of 4 is probably best, but it doesn't particularly matter.

There's a fair amount of debate over whether or not you should use progressive JPEG (and other incremental display options such as GIF interlacing). Certainly, some older Web browsers don't support progressive JPEG files, but that's not much of a problem these days. More controversial, some artists believe that progressive JPEGs are somehow tacky, because they have a rough appearance in the first few passes.

If that bothers you, and you don't want the viewer to see your image until it's in its final form, then select Baseline Optimized. But if you want my opinion, that would be doing your visitors a disservice. By providing an immediate, unfinished pass at your image, you're giving the viewer an early right of refusal. And that's what the Web's all about — providing the viewer with the tools of page customization and navigation. I mean, heck, guests can turn your graphics completely off if they want to. If you get too hung up on making your visitors see things your way, you'll go bonkers. Too many things are out of your control.

Preparing and Saving GIF Images

So much for JPEG, now on to GIF. The GIF format came into being during a time when only the super savvy owned 1200-bps modems. It supports a maximum of 8 bits per pixel (256 colors), and it uses LZW compression, just like TIFF. GIF comes in two varieties, known by the snappy monikers 87a and 89a, with the latter supporting transparent pixels.

Frankly, GIF is getting a little long in the tooth. Most online pundits figure PNG will replace GIF in the next few years. But for the time being, GIF is an extremely popular and widely supported format. And despite its obvious limitations, it has its uses. GIF is a much better format than JPEG for saving high-contrast line art or text. Figure 20-5 shows two versions of the same image; the top image was saved in the JPEG format, and the bottom one was saved in GIF. As you can see, the JPEG compression utterly ruins the image. And I had to reduce the Quality setting to 0 — the absolute minimum — to get the file size down to 16K. Meanwhile, saving the image in the GIF format sacrificed no detail whatsoever and resulted in a file size of 18K. GIF's LZW compression is well suited to high-resolution artwork with large areas of flat color.

Figure 20-5: The JPEG format creates weird patterns in high-contrast images (top) and saves relatively little space on disk. Meanwhile, GIF keeps the sharp edges very much intact (bottom).

But before you can save a color image in the GIF format, you have to reduce the number of colors using Image ➪ Mode ➪ Indexed Color. The following section explains how this command works.

Using the Indexed Color command

Choose Image ➪ Mode ➪ Indexed Color to display the dialog box shown in Figure 20-6. This command permits you to strip an image of all but its most essential colors. Photoshop then generates a color look-up table (or LUT) which describes the few remaining colors in the image. The LUT serves as an index, which is why the process is called *indexing*.

Figure 20-6: Use the Palette options to select the kinds of colors that remain in the image. Use the Color Depth option to specify how many colors remain.

Photoshop 5 has greatly improved upon its indexing capabilities. The program not only generates better colors, it also permits you to preview effects before you apply them. So turn that Preview check box on and keep an eye on the image window.

For some reason, Photoshop doesn't let you index grayscale, Lab, or CMYK images. If the Indexed Color command is dimmed, choose Image ➪ Mode ➪ RGB to convert the image to the RGB mode and then choose Image ➪ Mode ➪ Indexed Color.

Don't expect to be able to edit your image after indexing it. Most of Photoshop's functions — including the gradient tool, all the edit tools, and the filters — refuse to work. Others, like feathering and the paintbrush and airbrush tools, produce undesirable effects. If you plan on editing an 8-bit image much in Photoshop, convert it to the RGB mode, edit it as desired, and then switch back to the indexed color mode when you finish.

Now that I've gotten all the warnings and special advice out of the way, the following sections explain how to use the options inside the Indexed Color dialog box. Enjoy.

Specifying the palette

The first pop-up menu — Palette — tells Photoshop how to compute the colors in the look-up table. Most of the time, you'll want to select the Adaptive option, as in Figure 20-6. But just so you're prepared to be all you can be, the following list explains how each of the options works:

✦ **Exact:** If the image already contains fewer than 256 colors, the Exact option appears by default. This only occurs if you've created an extremely high-contrast image — such as a screen shot — or you're working from an image that originally started out as grayscale. If Exact is selected, just press Return and let the command do its stuff. No sense messing with a good thing.

✦ **System:** Photoshop offers two System options, which are used by the Macintosh and Windows operating systems. The only reason to select either of these options is if you want to add a bit of imagery to the system. For example, it's a good idea to select the System (Macintosh) option when creating a background pattern, a custom file icon,or some other item that appears at the desktop level. Color Plate 20-1 shows examples of a 24-bit image downsized to the Mac and Windows system palettes.

✦ **Web:** Just to make things as confusing as possible, Web browsers subscribe to their own variety of color palette. According to folklore, this 216-color LUT is an intersection of colors found in the Mac and Windows system palettes. But in fact, the Web palette includes those 216 colors whose R, G, and B values are divisible by 51. That means each primary color can be set to 0, 51, 102, 153, 204, or 255. Calculate all possible combinations, and you get 216 colors.

When displaying an image on an 8-bit screen, the browser invariably changes all colors to those in the Web palette. Therefore, converting your colors to the Web palette ensures that what you see on your screen is what your guests see as well. But for most folks, I still argue in favor of Adaptive. An image with an adaptive palette will look far better on 16-bit and better monitors, and these days, high-color screens are in the majority. (The notable exceptions are portables, which often max out at 8-bit screens. But these LCD screens hardly do your color graphics justice, so it seems silly to let such lowest-common-denominator concerns dictate your work.)

✦ **Uniform:** This is the dumbest option of them all. It merely retains a uniform sampling of colors from the spectrum. I've never heard of anyone finding a use for it — but as always, I welcome your suggestions.

✦ **Adaptive:** This option selects the most frequently used colors in your image, which typically delivers the best possible results. Because it ignores all system and Web palettes, images downsized with Adaptive look best on high-color monitors, as I mentioned above. To demonstrate just how much better they look, the bottom row of Color Plate 20-1 shows three images subject to the Adaptive palette at various Color Depth settings. Even with a mere 64 and 16 colors, the middle and right images look as good or better than the 256-color system-palette images above them.

You can influence the performance of the Adaptive option by selecting an area of your image before choosing the Indexed Color command. Photoshop will then favor the selected area when creating the palette. For example, before indexing the image in Color Plate 20-1 down to the 8-color palette (bottom right), I selected the fellow's face to avoid losing all the flesh tones.

✦ **Custom:** Select this option to load a look-up table from disk. This is useful when creating multimedia content, but rarely serves any purpose for Web graphics. You can save a custom palette using Image ➪ Mode ➪ Color Table, as I explain in this chapter.

✦ **Previous:** This option uses the last look-up table created by the Indexed Color command. If you're trying to create a series of high-contrast graphics that you want to look as homogenous as possible, then this is the option to use. The Previous option is dimmed unless you have used the Indexed Color command at least once during the current session.

Color depth

Select a value from the Color Depth pop-up menu to specify the number of colors you want to retain in your image. Fewer colors results in smaller GIF files. I generally start with 6 bits/pixel, which results in 64 colors. With the Preview check box turned on, I can see the effect of this palette in the image window. If the image looks okay, I try 5 bits/pixel; if not, I try 7 bits/pixel. It's all a matter of getting the colors as low as they can go without becoming ugly. The bottom row in Color Plate 20-1 shows examples of the same image with 256, 64, and 16 colors.

Like all computer programs, Photoshop measures color in terms of *bit depth*. As I've mentioned elsewhere in this book, an 8-bit image translates to 256 colors. Photoshop computes this figure by taking the number 2 and multiplying it by itself the number of times specified by the bit depth. 24-bit means 2 to the 24th power, which is 16 million; 4-bit means 2 to the 4th power, which is 16. You don't need to know this to select an option from a pop-up menu — Photoshop constantly keeps you apprised of the number of colors in the Colors option box — but sometimes it's nice to know what the program's up to.

Dither

Use the Dither pop-up menu to specify how Photoshop distributes the indexed colors throughout the image:

✦ **None:** If you select None, Photoshop maps each color in the image to its closest equivalent in the look-up table, pixel for pixel. This results in the harshest color transitions. But as I'll explain in a moment, it is frequently the preferable option.

✦ **Pattern:** This option is available only if you select System (Macintosh) from the Palette options. And even then, you should avoid the Pattern option like the plague. It dithers colors in a geometric pattern, which is altogether ugly.

Look to the lower left example of Figure 20-7 and the middle image in Color Plate 20-2 for examples.

✦ **Diffusion:** The Diffusion option dithers colors randomly to create a naturalistic effect, as shown in the lower right example of Figure 20-7 and the last image in Color Plate 20-2.

After looking at Figure 20-7 and Color Plate 20-2, you might be inclined to think that Diffusion is the option of choice. Not necessarily. In most cases, None is the better option. First of all, None results in smaller GIF files (as Color Plate 20-2 shows). Because LZW is better suited to compressing uninterrupted expanses of color, harsh transitions mean speedier images. Second, if a guest views your page on an 8-bit monitor, the system will dither the image automatically (assuming you selected Adaptive from the Palette pop-up menu). System dithering on top of Diffusion dithering gets incredibly messy; system dithering on its own, however, is acceptable.

Color Matching

Photoshop 5.0

In the past, Photoshop has done an average to poor job of maintaining decent colors in an indexed image, which was one of the reasons third-party GIF plug-ins were so popular. But Photoshop 5 fairs much better. Even if you never mess with the new Color Matching controls, you'll see your GIF images improve in quality.

Then again, I see no reason to avoid the Color Matching options. They're ridiculously easy to use. The Faster and Better check boxes permit you to adjust the quality of the color reduction. Faster is supposedly faster, and Better is typically better at maintaining colors in gradations and smooth color transitions. But I would give them both a try. When editing small images, neither option takes more than a couple of seconds to preview. So try out both and go with the one that looks best.

The Preserve Exact Colors check box is available only when the Diffusion option is selected from the Dither pop-up menu. When turned on, this option turns off dithering inside areas of flat color that exactly match a color in the active palette. Say that you've created some text in a Web-safe color. The text is antialiased, but the letters themselves are flat color. By selecting Web from the palette pop-up menu and selecting the Preserve Exact Colors check box, you tell Photoshop to dither around the edges of the letters, but leave the interiors undithered.

As I mentioned before, I recommend you avoid dithering whenever possible, in which case Preserve Exact Colors is dimmed. But if you decide to dither, it's a good idea to turn Preserve Exact Colors on. Even if you can't see a difference on your screen, it may show up on another.

Original   None

Pattern   Diffusion

Figure 20-7: The results of converting an image (upper left) to the System palette using each of the three Dither options, None, Pattern, and Diffusion.

Editing indexed colors

As I said earlier, Adaptive is generally the best choice when creating Web graphics, because it scans each image for its most essential colors. But even the Adaptive option doesn't get things 100 percent right. On occasion, Photoshop selects some colors that look wildly off base.

To replace all occurrences of one color in an indexed image with a different color, choose Image ➪ Mode ➪ Color Table. The ensuing Color Table dialog box, shown in Figure 20-8, enables you to selectively edit the contents of the LUT. To edit any color, click on it to display the Color Picker dialog box. Then select a different color and press Return to go back to the Color Table dialog box. Then press Return again to close the Color Table dialog box and change every pixel colored in the old color to the new color.

Figure 20-8: Use the Color Table dialog box to modify the colors in an indexed image.

The Color Table dialog box also enables you to open and save palettes and select predefined palettes from the Table pop-up menu. What the Color Table dialog box doesn't let you do is identify a color from the image. For example, if you're trying to fix a color in your image, you can't display the Color Table dialog box, click on the color in the image, and have the dialog box show you the corresponding color in the look-up table. The only way to be sure you're editing the correct color — and be forewarned, this is a royal pain in the behind — is to slog through the following steps, which begin before you choose Image ➪ Mode ➪ Color Table.

Steps: Editing a Specific CLUT Color

1. **Use the eyedropper tool to click on the offending color in the image.** This makes it the foreground color.

2. **Click on the foreground color icon to display the specs for the color in the Color Picker dialog box.** Write down the RGB values on a handy piece of paper, the palm of your hand, or a bald friend's scalp. (Don't edit the color inside the Color Picker dialog box at this time. If you do, you just change the color without changing any pixel in the image associated with that color.) Press Escape to leave the dialog box.

3. **Choose Image ⇨ Mode ⇨ Color Table.**

4. **Click on a color that looks like it might be the right one.** After the Color Picker appears, compare the color's RGB numbers to those you wrote down. If they match, boy, did you ever luck out. Go ahead and edit the color as desired. If the RGB values don't match, press the Escape key to return to the Color Table dialog box and try again. And again. And again.

Tip

To create a *color ramp* — that is, a gradual color progression — drag rather than click on the colors in the palette to select multiple colors at a time. Photoshop then displays the Color Picker dialog box, enabling you to edit the first color in the ramp. After you select the desired color and press Return, the Color Picker reappears, this time asking you to edit the last color in the ramp. After you specify this color, Photoshop automatically creates the colors between the first and last colors in the ramp in even RGB increments.

Saving the completed GIF image

When it comes time to save your GIF image, you can save it in either the GIF87a or 89a format. To save a GIF87a image — where all pixels are opaque — choose File ⇨ Save As and select the CompuServe GIF option from the Format pop-up menu. After you press Return, Photoshop presents you with two options, Normal and Interlaced. If you want the Web browser to display the image in incremental passes — similar to a progressive JPEG image — select the latter. Otherwise, select Normal.

Tip

But it's generally a better idea to save the indexed image as a GIF89a file. GIF89a is a more efficient format with better compression, which means it results in smaller files. GIF89a also supports transparent pixels, thereby permitting you to see through portions of the image to the Web page background pattern, or to other images in a Dynamic HTML file.

Choose File ➪ Export ➪ GIF89a Export to display the similarly named dialog box shown in Figure 20-9. Here you'll find an Interlace check box, which you can turn on or off as desired. There's also a Caption check box which lets you save a caption created with File ➪ File Info. The only purpose for this is to let image cataloging programs search for the file by keywords. The caption does not appear in the HTML file.

Figure 20-9: Click with the eyedropper cursor to make colors in the image transparent, as I have with the pixels outside the man's face.

All this is very well and good, but the real purpose of the GIF89a Export dialog box is to make pixels transparent:

✦ Click on a pixel in the image preview, or on one of the swatches in the color palette below, to make that color transparent. Keep clicking to add more transparent colors. Photoshop surrounds the transparent color swatches with heavy outlines.

✦ ⌘-click on a color to bring it back from transparency and return it to opacity again.

✦ You can scroll the preview by pressing the spacebar and dragging inside it. Zoom by ⌘-spacebar-clicking, and Option-spacebar-clicking.

✦ By default, Photoshop changes the transparent pixels to gray. But if gray is a popular color in your image, this may make it difficult to edit the image later. Because Photoshop has no method for expressing GIF transparency — the checkerboard method only works for native Photoshop files — the transparent pixels appear gray in color when you open and edit the image. So I recommend that you take the extra precaution of changing the transparent pixels to some way-out color, like bright yellow or green. To do this, click on the swatch labeled Transparency Index Color (just below the check boxes) and select a new color in the Color Picker.

Tip

If your image contains a mask channel, you can use the mask to define the transparent areas in the image. Just select the mask name from the Transparency From pop-up menu in the GIF89a Export dialog box. The black areas of the mask translate to transparency; the white areas are opaque. Keep in mind that GIF can handle just two levels of opacity — on and off, with no room for translucency. So if the mask includes gray pixels, the dark gray pixels become transparent and the light gray pixels become opaque.

Cross-Reference

For examples of transparent pixels, you might want to check out my site at *http://www.dekemc.com*. Every single graphic includes some transparent pixels, permitting the drop shadows and other gradual elements to blend in with the background.

Third-Party JPEG and GIF Alternatives

Photoshop's own GIF and JPEG export modules are pretty good, but third-party replacements from Digital Frontiers (*www.digfrontiers.com*) and BoxTop Software (*www.boxtopsoft.com*) suggest that there's ample room for improvement. The CD at the back of the book includes demonstrations of these filters so you can arrive at your own conclusions, but here's the skinny:

Digital Frontier's $150 HVS WebFocus includes separate modules for exporting JPEG and GIF images, both featured in Figure 20-10. The HVS JPEG module includes a live preview that updates when you change settings. (The preview isn't entirely accurate — you can't know the exact effects of JPEG compression until the final compression is applied — but it's a heck of a lot better than no preview at all.) HVS JPEG also estimates the size of the saved image, a terrific help when deciding how much compression to apply.

But if HVS JPEG is helpful, HVS ColorGIF is essential. First, ColorGIF gives you precise control over dithering. Instead of simply turning dithering on or off, as Photoshop lets you do, you can adjust the dithering incrementally, thereby permitting you to soften edges without speckling flat areas of color, whether the flat colors are found in the palette or not. ColorGIF also lets you adjust threshold and gamma settings to prepare images for display on foreign monitors. You can establish settings and preview the results inside a single dialog box. And like HVS

JPEG, ColorGIF estimates the size of the saved file. Frankly, ColorGIF is a must for anyone who's serious about Web graphics.

Figure 20-10: The HVS JPEG and ColorGIF plug-ins permit you to apply and preview effects inside a single dialog box, as well as predict file size before saving.

A less expensive solution is the $70 ProJPEG and PhotoGIF bundle from BoxTop. ProJPEG does most of what HVS JPEG does, and with a simpler interface. PhotoGIF filter shares ColorGIF's ability to gradually dither an image, but it lacks the screen calibration options and you have to preview your settings in a separate dialog box. Still, at half the price of WebFocus, you may be able to live with those limitations.

Oh, and in case you were considering worrying about compatibility, don't. The JPEG and GIF formats are sufficiently standardized that your on-line guests will never know where your images came from. An image saved with HVS JPEG or ColorGIF can be opened on another machine by Photoshop without HVS. The same holds true for the BoxTop plug-ins as well.

Saving PNG Images

As I write this, the newest Web image format is the *Portable Network Graphics* format, or PNG (pronounced *ping*). Developed by a panel of independent graphics experts, PNG was designed specifically to outperform and ultimately replace GIF. It supports 24-bit and 48-bit images, it permits you to include mask channels for gradual transparency control, and — perhaps most importantly — PNG is not patented. Starting in 1995, Unisys, the developer of GIF, began to charge royalties to Web software developers. PNG, meanwhile, is free for all, which is why some folks claim PNG unofficially stands for "PNG, Not GIF."

PNG files are typically larger than comparable JPEG or GIF images because a PNG file does not include JPEG's lossy compression, and it can contain more colors than a GIF image. (The exception is when you save a grayscale or indexed PNG file, which is frequently smaller than the same file saved in GIF.) So PNG is generally best suited to small images — buttons and thumbnails — with fine details that you don't want mangled by JPEG compression.

Photoshop supports any RGB, grayscale, or indexed image in the PNG format. PNG doesn't support layers (of course), but it does permit you to include a single mask channel. Assuming the browser supports extra PNG channels, the mask defines the opacity and transparency of the image on the page. PNG graphics can even be translucent (as defined by gray areas in the mask channel), a terrific advantage over GIF and JPEG.

When you save a PNG image, Photoshop displays the dialog box shown in Figure 20-11. Here you can select the kind of interlacing and compression that you want to apply:

✦ **Interlace:** The PNG format offers the strangely named "Adam7" interlacing. Adam7 draws your image on screen in seven passes, drawing the image in blocks and filling in the pixels between blocks. If you want interlacing, select Adam7. If you don't, turn it off.

✦ **Filter:** These options permit you to specify the way in which Photoshop applies PNG's special *zlib* compression scheme. This particular scheme compresses data in blocks, and the Filter options let you specify the way in which the blocks are calculated. Even when armed with this knowledge, only one option, None, makes any sense. It turns off the compression. The other options permit you to tweak the compression for the minimum possible file size.

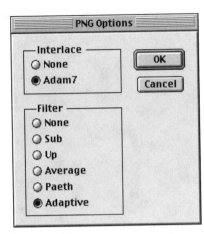

Figure 20-11: When saving a PNG file, Photoshop offers you some very peculiar options found nowhere else in the program.

See, GIF's LZW compression can actually lead to an increase in file size in some cases. To avoid this, PNG gives you a sufficient number of compression options to ensure smaller files. You can certainly experiment with the options to see which one gives you the smallest results. But unless you're absolutely obsessed by small file size — we're talking about saving a few hundred bytes at most — just select Adaptive and let the compression do its magic without your help.

Before you rush out to save an image to the PNG format, however, bear in mind that support is thus far spotty. As I write this, neither Netscape Navigator nor Internet Explorer directly support PNG. If you want to include a PNG image on your page, your guests will have to install a third-party plug-in, such as Siegel and Gale's PNG Live. I live in hope that this will change. I imagine that PNG support might become fairly universal by, say, the year 2001. But in the meantime, the format is more interesting than practical.

✦ ✦ ✦

Appendixes

Preparing the Soil

Because I write for a handful of trade magazines and spend far too much of my time staring at CRT and LCD screens, friends and neighbors naturally enjoy subjecting me to computer questions. (I believe I know how the surgeon at a party feels listening to strangers complain about their ailments.) One of the most common questions I hear is, "Should I upgrade my computer?" Folks read a blurb about the newest, slickest, sexiest CPU and wonder if it might help them to work faster or better. For the typical user, I generally advise against it. If your work primarily involves routine word processing or number crunching, then much of the power of the latest greatest system will be wasted on you. Sure, you'll see some speed boost, but I sincerely doubt it'll be significant enough to warrant the investment.

But graphic artists are not typical computer users. Image editing applications, drawing and publishing programs, authoring applications, off-line video editors, and other graphics and media programs require lots and lots of horsepower. A single brushstroke in Photoshop may entail several thousand mathematical computations, and they have to happen in the second or two it takes you to drag the brush across the screen. If you're using Photoshop 5, you already own a Power Macintosh running System 7.5 or later. But you also need a sizable chunk of RAM, a fast hard drive, a decent monitor, and a 4MB or better video board to maximize your productivity and creative potential.

In past editions of this book, I explained how to install Photoshop on your computer, which is really not necessary. The Photoshop installer is painstakingly straightforward, both familiar to anyone who's ever installed anything and altogether implicit for anyone who hasn't.

The fact is, any half-wit can take the baby (Photoshop) and put it in the crib (your computer). The trick is to get the crib ready in the first place so the baby grows up happy, healthy, and tolerably obedient. So rather than tell you what you already know, this appendix spells out the stuff you don't. Here's how you create the ideal digital nest.

The Best of the Best

For the sake of simplicity, I'll start at the top and work my way down. If you want to make it easy on yourself and you have $5,000 to $6,000 budgeted for a new machine, then the best cribs for Photoshop come from Umax (*www.umax.com*) and Intergraph (*www.intergraph.com*). Both companies make top-of-the-line computers designed especially with graphic artists in mind.

As I write this, the fastest Macintosh OS computer is the SuperMac S900Base from Umax which comes pre-equipped with a 267MHz MaxPowr Pro+ board from Newer Technology (*www.newertech.com*). Not only was this the first Power PC 750 chip out on the market, but it's considerably faster than anything that Apple has released thanks to a larger Level 2 cache. Umax also provides fast hard drive and networking configurations, and its technical support is superb. I had a hard drive melt down recently, and Umax sent a guy to my office to replace it.

The fastest PC for Photoshop is the ExtremeZ 2D Graphics Workstation from Intergraph. Equipped with two 300MHz Pentium II processors, fast networking and hard drives, and Windows NT, this computer sizzles. As an added incentive, ExtremeZ is a great solution for folks who work in a Macintosh environment or do a lot of business with Mac artists. The ExtremeZ comes preconfigured with PC MacLAN from Miramar Systems (*www.miramarsys.com*), which enables Macs and PCs to share data over an Ethernet-based AppleTalk network. You also get MacOpener from DataViz (*www.dataviz.com*), which reads Macintosh-formatted Zips, floppies, and other media.

Note

Some of you might take objection to my mentioning a PC in a Mac book. But I have no idea what kind of computer you'll be using in the future, and hopefully, neither do you. Quite frankly, it doesn't pay to be married to one platform or the other, and the successful artist will always be the one that can turn on a dime. For the record, the Mac offers better color matching, plug-and-play networking, support for dual monitors, no-rules file naming, and more robust file management. Meanwhile, Windows NT offers protected memory, better multitasking, dynamic memory allocation, more stable Internet access, and all the benefits of the dominant industry platform. Many of the Mac's advantages are likely to be addressed by Microsoft's Windows 98, and many of Windows' advantages are likely to be addressed by Apple's Rhapsody. Apple's biggest downside is that many lack faith in the long-term prospects of its platform, and Microsoft's biggest problem is that many of its core functions remain obscenely difficult to use. But after more than a decade of working with both platforms — in the name of full disclosure, I've made more money off the Mac, but I've sold more books to PC users — I see the Mac and

PC operating systems growing closer and closer together. Whichever one you choose, I can assure you, they are quite comparable.

Bear in mind, the specific machines I mentioned—the S900Base and ExtremeZ—are merely the fastest machines at this moment in time. Clearly, faster computers may have come along by the time you read this. But I will enthusiastically endorse both Umax and Intergraph products to any artist. My impression is that both companies are behind electronic designers for the long haul.

Hardware Specifics

Naturally, you may find reason to ignore my advice about Umax and Intergraph and go with a vendor that provides you with a better deal. Or you may prefer to upgrade your existing computer rather than purchase a new one. In this case, you need to acquaint yourself with the most important hardware issues, as itemized in the following sections.

RAM

Photoshop gobbles up RAM with a voracious appetite. To use Photoshop, your computer must be equipped with at least 16MB of RAM, but that's just enough to get the program to run. Some folks recommend 32MB; I say no less than 64MB. (Until recently, one of my computers was equipped with 32MB of RAM—I like to keep one machine configured at the low end—but I finally lost patience with the poky pace of the program.)

The reason for Photoshop's extreme RAM requirements is simple. Because RAM has no moving parts (and because of its proximity to the CPU), the CPU can access data in RAM several hundred times faster than it can access data off the hard drive. This means Photoshop works fastest when the entire image fits inside RAM. Images are very big, so Photoshop needs lots of RAM.

Just how much of a difference can RAM make? When editing a 5MB image, Photoshop runs faster on a 100MHz Pentium equipped with 128MB of RAM than a 300MHz dual-processor Pentium II machine with just 16MB of RAM. And you can pick up a used 100MHz Pentium for less than half the price of a PII. The relatively low cost of RAM—as I write this, a 64MB upgrade costs about $200—makes it far and away the least expensive way to accelerate Photoshop.

To figure out how much RAM you need, I recommend the following formula: Take the size of the average image you edit and multiply it times 20. Suppose that you spend most of your time editing 5MB Photo CD images. You probably work with 10 or so layers at a time, so the image balloons to 25MB to 30MB. By default, Photoshop's History palette tracks the last 20 operations, so the image expands to 50MB to 60MB. You want to be able to open other images, so you need another 10MB to 20MB of wiggle room. And of course, Photoshop isn't the only application on your hard drive, so toss in another 20MB to accommodate the operating system and other programs. The net result, 5MB times 20, or 100MB.

If you mostly work with quarter-page artwork or Web images, then your average file size is under 3MB and 64MB of RAM should suit you just fine. If you make your living creating 20MB full-page magazine artwork, then you should consider equipping your machine with 300MB to 400MB of RAM. For what it's worth, both of my primary machines are equipped with 256MB of RAM, which I would argue is on the high end of what most working artists need.

The Macintosh operating system lets you add *virtual memory* to the physical RAM supply. Virtual memory is space on the hard disk that mimics RAM and permits you to run more applications at a time. However, Photoshop offers its own more efficient virtual memory in the form of its scratch disk scheme (explained in Chapter 2), and using Apple's virtual memory on top of Photoshop's may gum up the works and slow down the program, depending on which version of the system software you use.

✦ Under OS 7.6 and earlier, the system's virtual memory hinders Photoshop. Therefore, it is imperative that you open the Memory control panel (which you can access from the Apple menu) and turn off the Virtual Memory option. Then restart your Mac.

✦ Apple retooled its virtual memory under OS 8 and again under OS 8.1. The memory management is so dramatically improved, in fact, that Adobe now officially recommends that users leave the Memory control panel's Virtual Memory check box turned on. Personally, I generally leave it off, but it's quite possible I'm just being superstitious. Old habits die hard.

In order for your 64MB or more of RAM to do you any good, you have to assign some of that big stash of memory to Photoshop. First, quit all applications including Photoshop. Then choose About This Computer from the Apple menu and note the Largest Unused Block value. (I'll use 45.3 as an example.) This tells you how much RAM is left over after the operating system loads. Grab a calculator and multiply that value by 0.75 (33.975) and round it off to the nearest MB (34). This represents the amount of free RAM you should assign to Photoshop — about 75 percent, might as well be generous. Next, locate and select the Photoshop application icon. Press ⌘-I (or choose File ➪ Get Info) to bring up the Info dialog box. Enter the value from your calculator in the Preferred Size option box. This value is measured in K instead of MB, so add three zeros at the end of it (34000). Then click on the close box in the upper left corner. Now you're ready to roll.

Hard drives

The second most important element in enhancing or diminishing Photoshop's performance is the hard drive. Images take up a lot of room, so a large hard drive is essential. But the drive also needs to be fast. Regardless of how much RAM you have, Photoshop has to build a scratch file on disk every time you open an image. And when the image gets larger than usual—as images are bound to do on occasion—Photoshop will need to refer to that scratch disk space on a regular basis.

The two most common varieties of hard drive connections are IDE and SCSI. IDE is rare in Macs but common in PCs. SCSI is more expensive, but it's also substantially faster. Both the machines I recommended at the outset of this chapter—the S900Base and ExtremeZ—come equipped with internal SCSI, which means that all drives connected inside and outside the machine rely on SCSI. Still, it's a good idea to ask for SCSI (pronounced *scuzzy*) by name, regardless of what kind of computer you buy. If you find a bargain on an IDE machine, fine. But be aware that Photoshop won't be able to open and save images nearly as fast as it would if you had SCSI.

There are lots of variations on SCSI, culminating in Ultra SCSI. If money is no object and you want Photoshop to run at top speed even when accessing scratch files, then look into RAID drives. A RAID configuration permits Photoshop to access two or more drives at once, which accelerates disk operations by 50 percent or more.

I can't imagine running Photoshop 5 on anything less than a 2GB internal drive. For the best results, equip your machine with 4GB to 8GB of internal hard drive space. I also recommend you partition drives into 1GB to 2GB blocks. (You can only partition the drive when initializing it, which you do before putting any data on the drive.) Try to keep one of the drives as empty as possible and set that to your primary scratch disk using File ➪ Preferences ➪ Plug-Ins & Scratch Disks.

Monitors

Where monitors are concerned, your primary criteria are size and tube. Size is easy. Buy the biggest monitor you can get your hands on. Some experts recommend 17-inch tubes over 21-inch tubes because the focus tends to be sharper. But I'd go as large as you can afford. Bigger monitors mean bigger pixels and that typically translates to less eye strain, particularly when editing fine details and reading option names and the like. Personally, I would rather pay a little extra money to protect my eyeballs, which are indisputably more difficult to replace that a CRT tube.

Choosing a tube is a bit more complicated. Speaking very generally, there are two basic varieties of CRT (cathode-ray tube)—tridot (also known as *shadow mask*) and Trinitron (*aperture grille*). If you look closely at a tridot screen, you can see a trio of dots—red, green, and blue—merging to form colors on the screen. The effect is analogous to a printed halftone pattern, except that the dots are much smaller and don't overlap. Colors on a Trinitron screen are arranged in vertical strips, uninterrupted from the top of the screen to the bottom. If you look very closely at the screen, you can see fine breaks between the columns of color, but it's virtually impossible to see any variance between the red, green, and blue phosphors.

I know a lot of folks who work with tridot screens and have no problem with them. But if you ask me, even the best tridot is awful. The screen image is softer, and the screen itself bows outward horizontally and vertically, resulting in greater distortion. A Trinitron screen is significantly sharper, and while it bows slightly horizontally, it's absolutely flat vertically. Trinitron screens also happen to cost more, but they're well worth it.

Tip

As a word to the wise, be sure to purchase a multisync monitor that you can easily port over to a PC if the need ever arises. (Ask if the monitor provides a VGA connection.) You can use any PC monitor with the Mac with the aid of an inexpensive adapter. But plugging an Apple monitor into a PC is significantly more difficult. (The only difference between PC and Mac monitors is connectivity, so you're not losing anything by getting a cross-platform device.)

Another criteria worth considering is screen calibration. If you're willing to part with $3,000 or so, you can purchase a professional-level monitor with hardware calibration. I've been using Radius (*www.radius.com*) PressView monitors for years now, and they are splendid devices. But as I write this, the PressView is available exclusively for the Mac. (It is possible to connect a PressView to a PC, but the calibration hardware won't work.) A cross-platform solution comes from Mitsubishi (*www.mitsubishi.com/display*) in the form of the SpectraView 1000. Both the PressView and SpectraView include Diamondtron screens (Mitsubishi's aperture grille tube) and both include calibration hardware and software. I have more experience with the PressView series, but after working with a SpectraView for a couple of weeks, it strikes me as every bit as good.

Video boards

Computer novices often believe that the number of colors and pixels that they see on screen is a factor of the monitor. But a typical monitor is just a big dumb tube that does what the computer tells it to do. And the part of the computer that's in charge of pixels and colors is the video board.

Video boards are measured based on the amount of VRAM (video RAM) that they provide. These days, most boards provides 4MB or 8MB of VRAM, although you can still find low-end boards equipped with just 2MB. More VRAM means more color at higher resolutions:

✦ A 2MB board provides 16 million colors up to 832 × 624 pixels. If you raise the resolution beyond that, you have to drop the number of on-screen colors to 32 thousand colors.

✦ 4MB of VRAM permits you to display 16 million colors at resolutions up to 1,152 × 870 pixels.

✦ Most boards top out at 8MB of VRAM, which permits 16 million colors up to 1,600 × 1,200 pixels.

To change the number of colors and pixels visible on screen, bring up the Monitors & Sound control panel and select a setting from each of the Color Depth and Resolution lists. Most likely, you'll be permitted to change settings on the fly. But depending on your video board, you may be asked to restart your computer.

Note

Digital color is measured in bits. And the number of colors that your video board can display at once is called the *bit depth*. Where 2-D images are concerned, the highest bit depth is 24-bit, which means that each pixel requires 24 bits of data. A bit can be one of two values — 0 or 1 — so a string of 24 bits can express 2 to the 24th power = 16,777,216 values. Hence, 24-bit video translates to 16 million colors. That's enough colors to assign a different color to every one of the $1,600 \times 1,200$ pixels made available by an 8MB video board.

The CPU speed

The last item you should concern yourself with when buying a new computer is the CPU speed. The CPU type is important; it's always a good idea to stay on top of the newest chip technology, whether it's a PowerPC 750 or a Pentium II. But differences in clock speed — measured in MHz — are costly and largely overrated. At the present, the price difference between a computer with a 233MHz chip and one with that same chip in its 266MHz incarnation is about $500. That's enough to buy about 128MB of RAM, which will go a lot farther toward accelerating Photoshop than a few measly clicks in the clock speed. Don't get me wrong, if you have the money, you might as well buy the best. But if you're on the budget, buy the computer that's one or two notches behind the fastest machine on the block. Very likely, you'll never notice the difference.

✦   ✦   ✦

Photograph Credits

The images used in this book came from all kinds of sources. The following list cites the figures or color plates in which a photograph appears. Following the figure number is the name of the photographer and the company from which the photo was licensed. In each case, the photographer holds the copyright. If the photograph comes from a CD collection, the product name appears in italics, along with or instead of a photographer, and the company holds the copyright. If no company is listed, the photo was licensed from the photographer directly.

To all who contributed their photography, my heartfelt thanks.

Images	Photographer/Product	Company
Figures 2-3, 2-5, and 2-11	*Space Exploration*	Digital Stock
Figure 2-9	*Natural World*	Digital Stock
Figure 2-10	*V. 1, Business & Industry*	PhotoDisc
Figure 3-1	*V. 76, Body Beautiful*	Digital Stock
Figure 4-1	*Urban Graffiti*	Digital Stock
Figure 4-3	Me, with a Polaroid PDC-2000 digital camera	
Figures 4-6 and 4-7	*V. 81, Senior Living*	Digital Stock
Figure 4-14	Me, with a Hitachi MP-EG1Adigital video camera	
Figure 4-16	*V. 11, Retro Americana*	PhotoDisc

(continued)

Images	Photographer/Product	Company
Figure 4-18	*World War II*	Digital Stock
Figure 4-23	*Urban Graffiti*	Digital Stock
Figures 4-25, 4-26, and 4-28	*Urban Graffiti*	Digital Stock
Figure 4-29	*V. 19, Agriculture*	PhotoDisc
Color Plate 4-2	*V. 9, Holidays & Celebrations*	PhotoDisc
Figures 5-6, 5-8, and 5-9	Me, with a Polaroid PDC-2000 digital camera	
Figure 5-12	*V. 86, Animals in Motion*	Digital Stock
Figures 6-10 through 6-12 and 6-15	*Water Sports*	Digital Stock
Color Plate 6-1	*V. 32, World Religions*	PhotoDisc
Color Plates 6-2 through 6-4	*Water Sports*	Digital Stock
Figure 7-4	*V. 11, Retro Americana*	PhotoDisc
Figure 7-5	Denise McClelland	
Figures 7-12 and 7-14	Mark Collen	
Color Plates 7-1 and 7-2	Mark Collen	
Figure 7-16	Me, with a Kodak DC40 digital camera	
Figure 8-5	*Signature Series 16, Everyday People*	PhotoDisc
Figures 8-6 through 8-8, 8-29, and 8-30	Russell McDougal	
Figures 8-13, 8-14, and 8-22	*V. 5, World Commerce & Travel*	PhotoDisc
Figure 8-15	*V. 12, Food & Dining*	PhotoDisc
Color Plate 8-1	*V. 12, Food & Dining*	PhotoDisc
Color Plates 8-2 through 8-4	*Fine Art Series 1, European Paintings*	PhotoDisc
Figures 9-2 and 9-3	*V. 30, Contemporary Cuisine*	PhotoDisc
Figures 9-4, 9-11, 9-24, and 9-26 (dog)	*Object Series 18, Everyday Animals*	PhotoDisc
Figures 9-4, 9-11, 9-24, and 9-26 (hydrant)	Me, with a Polaroid PDC-2000 digital camera	
Figures 9-6 and 9-7	*V. 11, Retro Americana*	PhotoDisc

Images	Photographer/Product	Company
Figures 9-24 through 9-26 (fly)	V. 8, Bugs & Butterflies	MetaCreations
Color Plate 9-1	V. 30, Contemporary Cuisine	PhotoDisc
Color Plate 9-2	Signature Series 14, Cultural Arts	PhotoDisc
Figures 10-2 through 10-5, 10-16, and 10-28	Denise McClelland	
Figures 10-6 and 10-7	Russell McDougal	
Figures 10-8 through 10-11	Ed Long	
Figures 10-12 through 10-15	Michael Probst	Reuter
Figures 10-21 through 10-24	V. 23, Far Eastern Business & Culture	PhotoDisc
Figures 10-30 through 10-32	Maps & Globes	Digital Stock
Color Plate 10-1	Ed Long	
Figure 11-1 (ant)	V. 8, Bugs & Butterflies	MetaCreations
Figures 11-3, 11-4, 11-18, 11-19 through 11-22, 11-24 through 11-28, 11-35, and 11-37	V. 4, Technology & Medicine	PhotoDisc
Figure 11-7	V. 16, US Landmarks and Travel	PhotoDisc
Figures 11-8 through 11-10	Russell McDougal	
Figures 11-11, and 11-30 through 11-32	V. 4, Technology & Medicine	PhotoDisc
Figures 11-13 through 11-17	V. 4, Technology & Medicine	PhotoDisc
Figure 11-20 (face)	V. 5, World Commerce & Travel	PhotoDisc
Color Plate 11-1	V. 16, US Landmarks and Travel	PhotoDisc
Figures 12-1 and 12-2	Sport & Leisure	Digital Stock
Figures 12-3 through 12-10	V. 4, Technology & Medicine	PhotoDisc
Figures 12-12 through 12-14 (capitol)	Washington D.C.	Digital Stock
Figures 12-12 and 12-14 (lava)	Fire & Ice	Digital Stock
Figures 12-15, 12-17, 12-20 through 12-22	Washington D.C.	Digital Stock

(continued)

Images	Photographer/Product	Company
Figures 12-24 through 12-29	Children & Teens	Digital Stock
Color Plate 12-1	Sport & Leisure	Digital Stock
Color Plate 12-2 (capitol)	Washington D.C.	Digital Stock
Color Plate 12-2 (lava)	Fire & Ice	Digital Stock
Color Plate 12-3 (girl)	Children & Teens	Digital Stock
Color Plate 12-3 (background)	Southern California	Digital Stock
Figure 13-1 (x-ray)	V. 29, Modern Technologies	PhotoDisc
Figures 13-1, 13-29 through 13-31	Object Series 15, InfoMedia	PhotoDisc
Figures 13-2, 13-6 through 13-10, 13-12 through 13-14, 13-32	Object Series 15, InfoMedia	PhotoDisc
Figures 13-16 through 13-25	V. 6, Nature & the Environment	PhotoDisc
Figures 13-34 through 13-36	Children & Teens	Digital Stock
Figures 13-37 and 13-38	Me, with a Polaroid PDC-2000 digital camera	
Color Plate 13-1 (painting)	Fine Art Series 1, European Paintings	PhotoDisc
Color Plate 13-1 (fruit)	V. 83, Food & Ingredients	Digital Stock
Color Plate 13-2	Me, with a Polaroid PDC-2000 digital camera	
Figure 14-1	Microscape Backgrounds	Digital Stock
Figures 14-2 through 14-4	Vintage Lifestyle Classics	Digital Stock
Figure 14-3	Background Series 2: Industrial Sidestreets	PhotoDisc
Figures 14-14 through 14-18 (clock)	V. 89, Conceptual Still Life	Digital Stock
Figures 14-14 through 14-18 (eel)	Undersea Life	Digital Stock
Figures 15-1 through 15-7, 15-20, 15-23, 15-25 through 15-27, 15-29, 15-30, 15-36, 15-39, 15-40, and 15-42	Italy	Digital Stock

Images	Photographer/Product	Company
Figures 15-8 through 15-13, 15-17 through 15-19, 15-21, 15-31, 15-37, and 15-41	V. 23, Far Eastern Business & Culture	PhotoDisc
Figures 15-14 through 15-16, and 15-32	World War II	Digital Stock
Figure 15-22	V. 5, World Commerce & Travel	PhotoDisc
Figures 15-33 through 15-35	Object Series 15, InfoMedia	PhotoDisc
Figure 15-35 (zebra pattern)	Nick Koudis, Background Series 5, Wackgrounds	PhotoDisc
Figures 15-43 through 15-45	Me, with a Kodak DC40 digital camera	
Color Plates 15-1 and 15-2	Italy	Digital Stock
Color Plates 15-3 through 15-5	V. 89, Conceptual Still Life	Digital Stock
Color Plate 15-6	V. 5, World Commerce & Travel	PhotoDisc
Figure 16-1	Central Europe	Digital Stock
Figures 16-2 through 16-5, 16-7 through 16-9, 16-12, 16-15, 16-21, 16-22, and 16-39	V. 5, World Commerce & Travel	PhotoDisc
Figures 16-6, 16-13, 16-14, 16-16, 16-23, 16-27, 16-30, and 16-46	Italy	Digital Stock
Figures 16-10 and 16-11	V. 11, Retro Americana	PhotoDisc
Figures 16-31 and 16-32	Maps & Globes	Digital Stock
Figure 16-40	Textures & Backgrounds	Digital Stock
Figures 16-41 through 16-43 and 16-45	Landscapes	Digital Stock
Color Plates 16-1 through 16-4, and 16-10	V. 9, Holidays & Celebrations	PhotoDisc
Color Plate 16-5	V. 7, Business & Occupations	PhotoDisc
Color Plate 16-7	Mark Collen	
Color Plates 16-8 and 16-9	Landscapes	Digital Stock
Color Plate 16-11	Antistock	Digital Stock

(continued)

Images	Photographer/Product	Company
Figures 17-1, 17-42, 17-43, and 17-45	*V. 82, Travel & Romance*	Digital Stock
Figures 17-3 through 17-31, and 17-33 through 17-41	*V. 5, World Commerce & Travel*	PhotoDisc
Color Plates 17-1 and 17-2	*Flowers*	Digital Stock
Color Plates 17-3 and 17-4	*V. 82, Travel & Romance*	Digital Stock
Figure 18-1	*V. 25, Government & Social Issues*	PhotoDisc
Figures 18-2, 18-3, 18-5 through 18-7, 18-16, 18-18 through 18-20, 18-24 through 18-28	*V. 5, World Commerce & Travel*	PhotoDisc
Figures 18-8, 18-12, and 18-14	*V. 9, Holidays & Celebrations*	PhotoDisc
Color Plates 18-1 through 18-3, and 18-6 through 18-8	*Antistock*	Digital Stock
Color Plates 18-4, 18-5, 18-9, and 18-10	*V. 9, Holidays & Celebrations*	PhotoDisc
Color Plate 18-11	Me, with a Kodak DC50 digital camera	
Color Plate 18-12	*V. 25, Government & Social Issues*	PhotoDisc
Color Plate 18-13	*Italy*	Digital Stock
Color Plate 18-14	*V. 5, World Commerce & Travel*	PhotoDisc
Color Plate 18-15	Me, with a Polaroid PDC-2000 digital camera	
Figure 19-1 (parachute)	*Active Lifestyles 2*	Digital Stock
Figure 19-1 (moon)	*Space & Exploration*	Digital Stock
Figures 19-3 through 19-12, 19-17, 19-18, 19-20, 19-21, 19-23, and 19-24 (thinker)	*Children & Teens*	Digital Stock
Figures 19-3 through 19-12, 19-17, 19-18, 19-20, 19-21, 19-23, and 19-24 (sunset)	*Sunsets, Skies, & Weather*	Digital Stock
Figures 19-13 through 19-15 (woman)	*V.28, People, Lifestyles, & Vacations*	PhotoDisc
Figures 19-13 and 19-14 (leaf)	*V.26, Homes & Gardens*	PhotoDisc
Color Plate 19-1	*Space & Exploration*	Digital Stock

Images	Photographer/Product	Company
Color Plates 19-2 through 19-4 (woman)	V.28, People, Lifestyles, & Vacations	PhotoDisc
Color Plate 19-2 (leaf)	V.26, Homes & Gardens	PhotoDisc
Color Plates 19-5 and 19-6	Children & Teens	Digital Stock
Figure 20-1	V. 35, Business Today	PhotoDisc
Figure 20-2	Indigenous Peoples	Digital Think
Figures 20-7 and 20-9	V. 5, World Commerce & Travel	PhotoDisc
Figure 20-10	Animals & Wildlife	Digital Think
Color Plates 20-1 and 20-2	V. 5, World Commerce & Travel	PhotoDisc

Using the CD-ROM

The CD-ROM attached to the back cover of this book contains an extensive collection of photographs, artwork, and plug-ins that you can use with Photoshop. The CD works with both Macs and PCs, regardless of which version of this book you have purchased. On the Mac, you need to be running System 7.5 or later. On the PC, you need Windows 95, 98, or NT 4 or later. (The CD will not function properly under Windows 3.1 or earlier.)

To view the photographs and artwork contained on the CD, you will need Photoshop or some other image editor. You will also need Photoshop to take advantage of the filters contained in the Plug-Ins folder. The remaining files — including artist biographies and documentation — are provided in one of three formats:

+ **Text-only (.txt) files:** You can open these in SimpleText or a word processor.

+ **Acrobat (.pdf) documents:** To open a .pdf file, you'll need Acrobat Reader or Acrobat Exchange from Adobe. Most folks already have Acrobat Reader, but if you don't, you can download it from *www.adobe.com*.

+ **Web (.html) pages:** To open these documents, you need access to a Web browser such as Netscape Navigator (*www.netscape.com*) or Microsoft Internet Explorer (*www.microsoft.com*).

The *Photoshop 5 Bible* CD does not contain any of the software required to read these formats. However, this shouldn't be a problem because most computers come preconfigured with the software you need.

Note   One final note before we get underway: This CD does not contain the Photoshop 5 application. Photoshop retails for nearly $1,000 (about $600 on the street), so it's unrealistic to expect a copy of the software for the $49.99 or less you paid for this book. This book has just two purposes: A) to educate digital artists and, more importantly, B) to prop up youngsters who are too short to reach the table. If you want Photoshop, you have to buy it from Adobe.

Opening the CD

To access the images and artwork included on the CD-ROM, start by inserting the CD into your CD-ROM drive. The CD icon, called Ph5 Bible, appears on your desktop. Double-click on the Ph5 Bible icon to open the CD-ROM. The window pops open and displays the following items:

✦ **AboutThisCD:** This file duplicates some of the text from this appendix. But because I'm the kind of person who would pop the CD into the drive before ever cracking open the book, I thought it might be a good idea to include a "read me" file for impatient people like me.

✦ **Artist Gallery:** This folder contains nearly 150MB of original imagery from 16 of the finest artists working with Photoshop today. The artists cover a broad range of styles and techniques, and you can get some great ideas from looking at their work. Note that these images belong to the artists who created them. Feel free to view them on screen, but under no condition should you integrate an image from this folder into your own work, post an image on the Internet, or in any way pass it off as your own. Thanks.

✦ **Digital Cameras:** Over the years, I've had the opportunity to use virtually every midrange digital camera that's come down the pike. I get a lot of e-mail about cameras, so I figured I'd help you make your own decision by judging the snapshots for yourself. This folder contains hundreds of images shot with 27 cameras from 14 different vendors. This time, I'm the copyright holder. I don't really care what you do with the photos in the privacy of your own home, but please don't reproduce them or post them online.

✦ **DigitalThink:** This folder contains a sample lesson from DigitalThink, a Web-based training company that offers interactive classes in Photoshop and Illustrator written by yours truly. You can check out their entire catalog of courses at *www.digitalthink.com*.

✦ **PC MacLAN:** Available to Windows users only, this folder contains a demonstration version of Miramar's PC MacLAN, the easiest solution for networking Macintosh and PC computers. This is the software I use in my office, so I can attest that it works great. (If you're viewing the CD on a Mac, you will not see this folder.)

✦ **Plug-ins:** This folder contains a wide range of Photoshop plug-ins from scads of different vendors, including such luminaries as Alien Skin, Andromeda, and Extensis. Most of the plug-ins are limited demonstration versions that give you ample chance to try out the software before you buy. But many of the vendors have graciously shared one or two fully functional plug-ins that are exclusive to this book. You can use them right off the CD without paying another dime. I can proudly say that I know of no other Photoshop book that includes so much free software, and of such excellent caliber.

✦ **Stock Photos:** This folder contains a total of 48 high-resolution images from the titans of digital stock photography, PhotoDisc and Digital Stock. Not coincidentally, every one of these photographs is featured in the figures in this book, so you can follow along with the exercises and techniques exactly as I describe them.

The following sections explain the contents of each of these folders in depth.

Artists Gallery

These folders contain images created by 16 of the finest Photoshop artists working today. I'm hear to tell you, some of this stuff will blow your socks off. In alphabetical order, the artists include Robert Bowen, Ron Chan, Mark Collen, Katrin Eismann, Helen Golden, Wendy Grossman, Dorothy Krause, Bonny Lhotka, Kent Maske, Judith Moncrieff, Bud Peen, Jeff Schewe, Karin Schminke, Gordon Studer, Richard Tuschman, and Nanette Wylde. All images are provided as inspirational material only; they are not for commercial use and the artists retain all copyrights to their work.

The easiest way to peruse the artwork is to use the Image Database.fdb file included in the Artists Gallery folder. To open this file, you must install Portfolio by double-clicking on the Install Portfolio alias. Provided by Extensis, this demonstration version of Portfolio will run for 60 days. After that, you'll have to either purchase Portfolio from Extensis or do without.

After you install Portfolio, double-click on the Image Database.fdb file to open it. (When Portfolio asks you for a serial number, click on the Demo button.) The utility then shows you a long list of thumbnails. To view the thumbnails by artist, press ⌘-K to bring up the Keyword palette then double-click on the name of an artist in the list.

If you like, you can view a full-size image by double-clicking on its thumbnail. But for ideal viewing, you'll want to open the image in Photoshop. Inside Photoshop, choose File ➪ Color Settings ➪ RGB Setup and set the RGB pop-up menu to SMPTE-240M. (This of course assumes your monitor is properly calibrated or characterized, as explained in Chapter 6.) Then open the image you want to view.

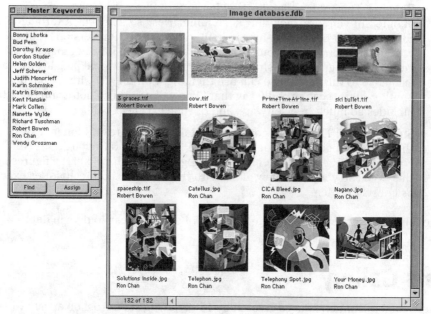

Figure C-1: Press ⌘-K to bring up the Keyword palette, then double-click on an artist's name to view his or her work.

Cross-Reference

Each artist folder contains a short biography of the artist. You can open the biography in your favorite word-processor. To find out more about how these artists create their work, I recommend you take a look at another book I've written called *Photoshop Studio Secrets*. Printed in full color, this book examines the work of 16 artists including many of those included in the Gallery folder — namely Robert Bowen, Ron Chan, Katrin Eismann, Bud Peen, Jeff Schewe, Karin Schminke, and Gordon Studer.

Digital Cameras

In 1994, Apple introduced the QuickTake 100, the first camera to shoot 24-bit 640 by 480-pixel digital photographs for less than $1,000. I was fortunate enough to review that camera for *Macworld* magazine and have continued to review succeeding midrange cameras ever since, amassing a library of more than 6,000 snapshots to date.

As with any category of hardware, some midrange cameras are great and others are awful. What's unusual is how much disagreement there is from one publication to the next. I can't tell you how many times I've felt generous awarding a camera two stars, and then read a four-star review in another trade publication. It's truly bewildering.

It goes without saying that I'm right and the other reviewers are raving lunatics. But it occurred to me that you might like the chance to see a few hundred sample images shot with these cameras and make up your own mind. That's what this folder is all about. The images are grouped by vendor — Kodak, Olympus, Polaroid, and so on — and then divided by camera model. In all, 27 different cameras are represented with four to eight examples from each.

I corrected the brightness and focus of the images in an effort to make them look their best. After all, Photoshop gives me control over the digital darkroom and I'd be remiss not to take minimal advantage of it. But I didn't do any retouching, nor did I crop the images, so the pixels you see are the ones the camera captured. You should also know that I captured almost all of the photographs at the maximum image size permitted by the camera. (The exceptions are the images shot with the Agfa ePhoto and Polaroid PDC-2000. These are shown at second-to-highest resolution, which yielded sharper results due to unique internal interpolation schemes afforded by the two devices.) The Casio QV-10A squeaks by with the cheesiest and tiniest pictures, measuring just 320 by 240 pixels. The Olympus D-340L weighs in with the biggest and the best, at 1280 by 960 pixels. As shown in Figure C-2, a D-340L picture is big enough to hold 16 snapshots captured with the QV-10A.

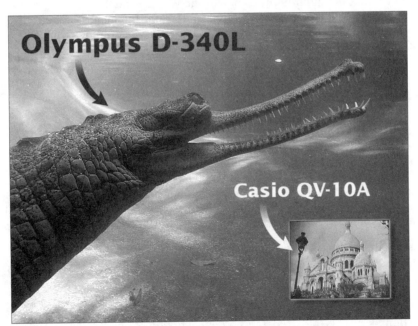

Figure C-2: An image shot at the San Diego Zoo with the Olympus D-340L compared with one shot in Paris (inset) with the Casio QV-10A. Both images are printed at 300 ppi.

Bear in mind, image quality isn't the only measure of a camera. For example, the Minolta Dimage V takes reasonably good pictures, but it's a pain in the neck to work with. By contrast, the pictures taken with the Fuji DS-7 are fair to average, but the camera is a dream to use. For complete information about each camera—and future models that come out after the release of this book—see my reviews at *www.macworld.com*. Most of the cameras work the same on Windows, so the reviews should be equally applicable to PC folks.

Again, you can peruse the photographs by opening the Image Database.fdb file in the Digital Cameras folder. (If you haven't yet installed Portfolio, double-click on the Install Portfolio icon. When asked for a serial number, click on the Demo button.) Then press ⌘-K to view the Keywords palette and double-click on the name of the camera that you're interested in. For ideal viewing of the full-size photograph, open the images in Photoshop. Be sure the RGB Setup environment is set to SMPTE-240M and that your monitor is properly calibrated with Gamma or some other utility.

DigitalThink

This folder contains HTML files from DigitalThink, a company that offers on-line training in Java, C++, and other topics over the World Wide Web. They also have a first-rate course on Photoshop and an even better one on Illustrator, both designed by me. To learn more about these and other training opportunities from DigitalThink, open the index.html document in your favorite Web browser.

Plug-Ins

The contents of this folder vary depending on whether you're using a Mac or a PC. On the Mac, the Plug-Ins folder contains filters from 12 different vendors. On the Windows side, 11 vendors are represented. This is because two vendors—ImageXpress and Vivid Details—create plug-ins for the Mac only and another vendor—Ulead—is exclusively Windows. The remaining vendors—Alien Skin, Altamira Group, Andromeda, BoxTop Software, Chroma Graphics, Digital Frontiers, Extensis, Wacom, and Xaos Tools—are cross-platform.

All told, the Plug-Ins folder includes more than 50 pieces of software. Each plug-in includes documentation on the CD that explains what it does and how it works. So rather than itemize each program, here's a quick summary of the highlights to get you started:

✦ **Alien Skin:** This folder contains a demo version of Eye Candy 3.0, the splendid special effects suite from Alien Skin. As a special gift to *Photoshop 5 Bible* readers, Alien Skin also includes Eye Candy LE 2.1, which includes the fully functioning filters Glass and Swirl, two of my personal favorites. All hail Alien Skin.

✦ **Altamira Group:** Altamira has provided a demonstration version of Genuine Fractals, which rewrites pixels using fractal math to create what amounts to resolution-independent images. For example, you can export a 20MB letter-sized image to the FIF format, and then import it as a 100MB poster-sized image without measurable degradation in quality. Meanwhile, the image takes up as little as 1MB of disk. It's wonderful technology for expert users. To use the filters, add the filters to Photoshop's Plug-Ins folder, restart Photoshop, and experiment with the commands in the Filter ➪ Import and File ➪ Export submenus.

✦ **Andromeda:** Andromeda Software has generously provided samples of six of its special effects and 3-D filter collections. Among these is a fully functioning demo of Series 4, Techtures, an excellent texture creation and manipulation laboratory, which also happens to be available exclusively to *Photoshop 5 Bible* readers. Just double-click on the Install utilities to add these plug-ins to Photoshop.

✦ **BoxTop Software:** BoxTop specializes in plug-ins that export and optimize Web graphics. On the Windows side, you'll find three demo plug-ins. Each program is fully functional for 30 days, then rather than expiring, it merely slows down. Frankly, that's pretty darn generous. On the Mac side, you'll find several more demos, along with a few freebies, including one — PhotoGIF Lite — which is available exclusively to *Photoshop 5 Bible* readers.

✦ **Chroma Graphics:** This folder contains three traditional demos, no freebies. But I decided to include the filters anyway because they automate one of the most complicated operations in Photoshop, masking. You can't save your work with any of these demos, but at least you can get a sense for how the filters work.

✦ **Digital Frontiers:** Like BoxTop, Digital Frontiers specializes in plug-ins for exporting and optimizing Web graphics. But unlike BoxTop, all of its filters are cross-platform. As a special service for *Photoshop 5 Bible* readers, Digital Frontiers has provided a free and fully functioning copy of HVS ColorGIF. For more information about this and other Digital Frontiers plug-ins, see Chapter 20.

✦ **Extensis:** This folder includes four Photoshop plug-ins — Mask Pro, PhotoTools, Intellihance, and PhotoFrame — plus two stand-alone applications, PhotoAnimator and Portfolio. Definitely check out Mask Pro, which automates complex masking, and Portfolio, which lets you assemble catalogs of your images. (If you ever encounter a dialog box that requests a serial number, just click on the Demo button and you can use the software for free for 30 days.)

✦ **ImageXpress:** Available on the Mac only, this folder contains demonstration versions of Alius and ScanPrepPro. Alius is a first-rate posterization filter, ScanPrepPro is perhaps the most highly rated module for scanning images into Photoshop. Both are worth a look. The installation is a little tricky, so be sure to read the documentation supplied in the folder. Enter "Trial" as the serial number to use either plug-in free for 7 days.

✦ **Tormentia:** This is the collection of eight filters that I created using the Filter Factory, as explained in Chapter 17. Every single one of them is fully functional, free, and cross-platform. To install the filters, drag them into Photoshop's Plug-Ins folder. To learn what each of these filters does, read the Torment.txt file included in the Tormentia folder.

✦ **Ulead:** If you Windows folks were starting to feel peeved about the absent filters from BoxTop and ImageXpress, here's your chance to get even. This folder contains a grand total of 14 plug-ins and stand-alone utilities from Ulead, and every one of them is available exclusively for Windows. Many of the plug-ins are fully functioning shareware, and one program — Gale10.exe — installs a free version of GIF Animator Lite, exclusively available to *Photoshop 5 Bible* readers.

✦ **Vivid Details:** Available only for Macintosh users, this folder contains a demonstration version of Test Strip. This excellent plug-in is ideal for anyone who owns a color proofing or output device and wants to be able to compare side-by-side color variations. Test Strip eliminates the guesswork of printing reliable color and it's extremely easy to use. What more could you ask?

✦ **Wacom:** Every one of the eight plug-ins in this folder is free and fully functional. Just drag the filters into Photoshop's Plug-Ins folder, restart Photoshop, and you're ready to go. The catch is that they only work if you own a Wacom drawing tablet. If you have a tablet, you're good to go; if not, visit *www.wacom.com*.

✦ **Xaos Tools:** This folder includes two items. One is a utility that installs Total Xaos (pronounced *chaos*), which is a collection of three demo plug-ins — the brush laboratory Paint Alchemy, the 3-D type creation filter Type Caster, and the texture-creation filter Terrazzo. As a special gift to *Photoshop 5 Bible* readers, Xaos has also thrown in 32 "luminous texture" images from the company's commercial Fresco collection. If a bunch of textures strikes you as a mite dull, open one or two in Photoshop and you'll quickly change your mind.

Caution

Remember, after installing a plug-in from any of the vendors listed above, you must quit Photoshop and relaunch the program in order to load the plug-ins into RAM. Most plug-ins only work if an image is open.

Stock Photos

The idea behind the Stock Photos folder is to provide you access to the original images featured in this book. That way, you can edit the images as you read along. The Stock Photos folder contains two subfolders named after the vendors who contributed photographs to the *Photoshop 5 Bible*, Digital Stock and PhotoDisc. Each subfolder contains another folder called High-rez images. Inside, you'll find 24 high-resolution images from the book.

I've provided an Image Database.fdb file so you can find the file you're looking for without too much scrambling. As I explained in the "Artists Gallery" section, you can open this file with Portfolio from Extensis. If you haven't installed Portfolio, double-click on the Install Portfolio icon. When asked for a serial number, click on the Demo button. (The demo will last you 60 days.) Then open the Image Database.fdb file and press ⌘-K to view a list of keywords that will help you locate the desired image. Once you've found the image you're looking for, open it up in Photoshop. (These images are too large to open in Portfolio, and besides, Photoshop is where you want to do your editing.)

By way of an endorsement, you can rely on both Digital Stock and PhotoDisc for their vast libraries of high-quality stock photography. If you're looking for an image, one or the other is bound to provide what you need. For more information, or to search for photographs on-line according to subject, consult the companies' Web sites at *www.digitalstock.com* and *www.photodisc.com*.

✦   ✦   ✦

Index

(continued)

IDG BOOKS WORLDWIDE, INC.
END-USER LICENSE AGREEMENT

<u>Read This</u>. You should carefully read these terms and conditions before opening the software packet(s) included with this book ("Book"). This is a license agreement ("Agreement") between you and IDG Books Worldwide, Inc. ("IDGB"). By opening the accompanying software packet(s), you acknowledge that you have read and accept the following terms and conditions. If you do not agree and do not want to be bound by such terms and conditions, promptly return the Book and the unopened software packet(s) to the place you obtained them for a full refund.

1. <u>License Grant</u>. IDGB grants to you (either an individual or entity) a nonexclusive license to use one copy of the enclosed software program(s) (collectively, the "Software") solely for your own personal or business purposes on a single computer (whether a standard computer or a workstation component of a multiuser network). The Software is in use on a computer when it is loaded into temporary memory (i.e., RAM) or installed into permanent memory (e.g., hard disk, CD-ROM, or other storage device). IDGB reserves all rights not expressly granted herein.

2. <u>Ownership</u>. IDGB is the owner of all right, title, and interest, including copyright, in and to the compilation of the Software recorded on the disk(s)/CD-ROM. Copyright to the individual programs on the disk(s)/CD-ROM is owned by the author or other authorized copyright owner of each program. Ownership of the Software and all proprietary rights relating thereto remain with IDGB and its licensors.

3. <u>Restrictions on Use and Transfer</u>.

   (a) You may only (i) make one copy of the Software for backup or archival purposes, or (ii) transfer the Software to a single hard disk, provided that you keep the original for backup or archival purposes. You may not (i) rent or lease the Software, (ii) copy or reproduce the Software through a LAN or other network system or through any computer subscriber system or bulletin-board system, or (iii) modify, adapt, or create derivative works based on the Software.

   (b) You may not reverse engineer, decompile, or disassemble the Software. You may transfer the Software and user documentation on a permanent basis, provided that the transferee agrees to accept the terms and conditions of this Agreement and you retain no copies. If the Software is an update or has been updated, any transfer must include the most recent update and all prior versions.

4. **Restrictions on Use of Individual Programs.** You must follow the individual requirements and restrictions detailed for each individual program Appendix C of this book, "Using the CD-ROM." These limitations are contained in the individual license agreements recorded on the disk(s)/CD-ROM. These restrictions may include a requirement that after using the program for the period of time specified in its text, the user must pay a registration fee or discontinue use. By opening the Software packet(s), you will be agreeing to abide by the licenses and restrictions for these individual programs. None of the material on this disk(s) or listed in this Book may ever be distributed, in original or modified form, for commercial purposes.

5. **Limited Warranty.**

   (a) IDGB warrants that the Software and disk(s)/CD-ROM are free from defects in materials and workmanship under normal use for a period of sixty (60) days from the date of purchase of this Book. If IDGB receives notification within the warranty period of defects in materials or workmanship, IDGB will replace the defective disk(s)/CD-ROM.

   (b) **IDGB AND THE AUTHOR OF THE BOOK DISCLAIM ALL OTHER WARRANTIES, EXPRESS OR IMPLIED, INCLUDING WITHOUT LIMITATION IMPLIED WARRANTIES OF MERCHANTABILITY AND FITNESS FOR A PARTICULAR PURPOSE, WITH RESPECT TO THE SOFTWARE, THE PROGRAMS, THE SOURCE CODE CONTAINED THEREIN, AND/OR THE TECHNIQUES DESCRIBED IN THIS BOOK. IDGB DOES NOT WARRANT THAT THE FUNCTIONS CONTAINED IN THE SOFTWARE WILL MEET YOUR REQUIREMENTS OR THAT THE OPERATION OF THE SOFTWARE WILL BE ERROR FREE.**

   (c) This limited warranty gives you specific legal rights, and you may have other rights which vary from jurisdiction to jurisdiction.

6. **Remedies.**

   (a) IDGB's entire liability and your exclusive remedy for defects in materials and workmanship shall be limited to replacement of the Software, which may be returned to IDGB with a copy of your receipt at the following address: Disk Fulfillment Department, Attn: Macworld Photoshop 5 Bible, IDG Books Worldwide, Inc., 7260 Shadeland Station, Ste. 100, Indianapolis, IN 46256, or call 1-800-762-2974. Please allow 3-4 weeks for delivery. This Limited Warranty is void if failure of the Software has resulted from accident, abuse, or misapplication. Any replacement Software will be warranted for the remainder of the original warranty period or thirty (30) days, whichever is longer.

(b) In no event shall IDGB or the author be liable for any damages whatsoever (including without limitation damages for loss of business profits, business interruption, loss of business information, or any other pecuniary loss) arising from the use of or inability to use the Book or the Software, even if IDGB has been advised of the possibility of such damages.

(c) Because some jurisdictions do not allow the exclusion or limitation of liability for consequential or incidental damages, the above limitation or exclusion may not apply to you.

7. **<u>U.S. Government Restricted Rights</u>.** Use, duplication, or disclosure of the Software by the U.S. Government is subject to restrictions stated in paragraph (c) (1) (ii) of the Rights in Technical Data and Computer Software clause of DFARS 252.227-7013, and in subparagraphs (a) through (d) of the Commercial Computer—Restricted Rights clause at FAR 52.227-19, and in similar clauses in the NASA FAR supplement, when applicable.

8. **<u>General</u>.** This Agreement constitutes the entire understanding of the parties and revokes and supersedes all prior agreements, oral or written, between them and may not be modified or amended except in a writing signed by both parties hereto which specifically refers to this Agreement. This Agreement shall take precedence over any other documents that may be in conflict herewith. If any one or more provisions contained in this Agreement are held by any court or tribunal to be invalid, illegal, or otherwise unenforceable, each and every other provision shall remain in full force and effect.

HIGH-IMPACT DESIGNS
START WITH HIGH-QUALITY IMAGES.

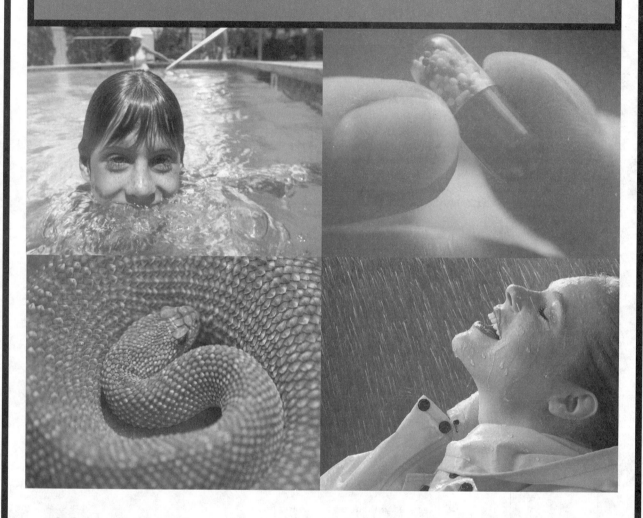

Digital Stock offers thousands of outstanding, royalty-free stock images on CD ROM. Each high-resolution image is drum-scanned and perfect for everything from multimedia to full-page print. A disc of 100 images is just $249. Order our Starter Pak and receive a Catalog Disc and Catalog Book for just $19.95. Call 1-800-545-4514 or visit our web site.

We're the Best Way to Learn Photoshop. Just Ask Deke.

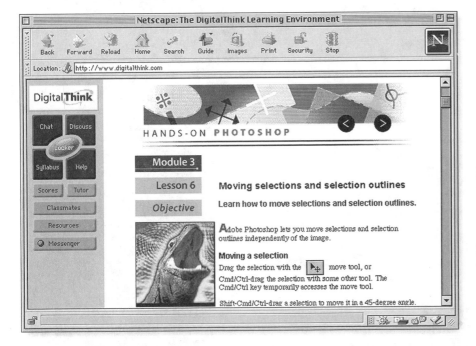

DigitalThink courses are taught completely over the Web and let you learn what you want, when you want.

Deke McClelland, author of *The MacWorld Photoshop 5.0 Bible,* is on the World Wide Web with **Hands-On Photoshop,** an all new online course from DigitalThink.

DigitalThink is the only Adobe Authorized Learning Provider (AALP) for online training. Our courses teach you how to get the most out of Adobe Photoshop®, Adobe Illustrator®, Java Programming, the Internet, and more.

Learn anytime you want, from wherever you have a Web connection. DigitalThink courses give you live tutors, chat sessions with experts, interactive quizzes, discussion boards, and more.

If you can't get online, you can still sample DigitalThink's learning environment. Deke has

included a lesson from **Hands-On Photoshop** on his CD-ROM in the back of this book.

Not convinced? Come to the DigitalThink site at **http://www.digitalthink.com** to take a FREE demo of a Web-based course. Then sign up for **Hands-On Photoshop** at a 10% discount.

DigitalThink. Simply the best way to learn Adobe Photoshop. Just ask Deke.

www.digitalthink.com

Royalty-free Stock Photography on CD-ROM or On-Line from PhotoDisc

- Over 35,000 photos available

- Pay no royalty fees

- Technically superior

- Delivered overnight

- Or download hi-res images from the Internet instantly

Call for a free catalog!

1 800 528 3472

http://www.photodisc.com

The Biggest Difference In The SpectraView Display System Is There Is No Difference.

Computers that work the way you do.

▸ With all the power and value of any PC, plus the ease-of-use of a Mac, the J700 is designed to be your complete business solution... at a price that will fit into any company's budget.

- **Fast and Powerful**
- **Expandable & Upgradeable**
- **Advanced Design**

▸ The SuperMac "S" series computers are the ideal workstations for high-end graphic design, digital video or internet server, requiring maximum possible CPU power, ultimate system throughput, fastest networking and highest system expandability. When it comes time to work with large files in programs like Photoshop, no other computer even comes

- **Ultimate Expandability**
- **Totally Upgradeable**
- **Advanced Design**

▸ The SuperMac "C" series comes with built-in graphics and lots of cool software to help you get your work done fast! Starting with the MacOS, we've added all the latest high-tech tools available - covering just about everything you can use a small office or home office (SOHO) computer for.

- **Fast, Powerful Mac OS**
- **Expandable & Upgradeable**
- **Easy-to-use & Affordable**

  ▸ All the features of the S900 with an additional second processor card!

Dual Processor

Two processors give you the earth-shattering performance you need.

NOW AVAILABLE!

  UMAX® **Computer Corporation**

Illustrator 7
Studio Secrets™
0-7645-4026-2
$49.99

Official Kai's Power Tools®
Studio Secrets™
0-7645-4002-5
$44.99

Please send this order form to:

IDG Books Worldwide, Inc.
Attn: Order Entry Dept.
7260 Shadeland Station,
Suite 100
Indianapolis, IN 46256
(800) 762-2974

ORDER FORM

Qty	ISBN	Title	Price	Total
	0-7645-4038-6	Painter 5 Studio Secrets™	$49.99	
	0-7645-3134-4	Photoshop® and Illustrator Synergy Studio Secrets™	$49.99	
	0-7645-4028-9	Photoshop® 4 Studio Secrets™	$49.99	
	0-7645-4026-2	Illustrator 7 Studio Secrets™	$49.99	
	0-7645-4002-5	Official Kai's Power Tools® Studio Secrets™	$44.99	

Shipping & Handling Charges

	Description	First book	Each add'l. book	Total
Domestic	Normal	$4.50	$1.50	$
	Two Day Air	$8.50	$2.50	$
	Overnight	$18.00	$3.00	$
International	Surface	$8.00	$8.00	$
	Airmail	$16.00	$16.00	$
	DHL Air	$17.00	$17.00	$

*For large quantities call for shipping & handling charges.
**Prices are subject to change without notice.

Subtotal _____

CA residents add
applicable sales tax _____

IN and MA
residents add 5%
sales tax _____

CT, FL and NJ
residents add 6%
sales tax _____

IL residents add
6.25% sales tax _____

PA residents add
7% sales tax _____

WA residents add
8.2% sales tax _____

NY, TN and TX
residents add 8.25%
sales tax _____

Shipping _____

Total _____

Ship to:

Name _____

Company _____

Address _____

City/State/Zip _____ Daytime Phone _____

Payment: ☐ Check to IDG Books (US Funds Only)
☐ Visa ☐ Mastercard ☐ American Express

Card # _____ Expires _____ Signature _____

IDG BOOKS
WORLDWIDE

Installation Instructions

To access the images and artwork included on the CD-ROM, start by inserting the CD into your CD-ROM drive. The CD icon, called Ph5 Bible, appears on your desktop. Double-click on the Ph5 Bible icon to open the CD-ROM. The window pops open and displays the following items:

- ✦ **AboutThisCD:** This file duplicates some of the text from this appendix. But because I'm the kind of person who would pop the CD into the drive before ever cracking open the book, I thought it might be a good idea to include a "read me" file for impatient people like me.

- ✦ **Artist Gallery:** This folder contains nearly 150MB of original imagery from 16 of the finest artists working with Photoshop today. The artists cover a broad range of styles and techniques, and you can get some great ideas from looking at their work. Note that these images belong to the artists who created them. Feel free to view them on screen, but under no condition should you integrate an image from this folder into your own work, post an image on the Internet, or in any way pass it off as your own. Thanks.

- ✦ **Digital Cameras:** Over the years, I've had the opportunity to use virtually every midrange digital camera that's come down the pike. I get a lot of e-mail about cameras, so I figured I'd help you make your own decision by judging the snapshots for yourself. This folder contains hundreds of images shot with 27 cameras from 14 different vendors. This time, I'm the copyright holder. I don't really care what you do with the photos in the privacy of your own home, but please don't reproduce them or post them on-line.

- ✦ **DigitalThink:** This folder contains a sample lesson from DigitalThink, a Web-based training company that offers interactive classes in Photoshop and Illustrator written by yours truly. You can check out their entire catalog of courses at *www.digitalthink.com*.

- ✦ **PC MacLAN:** Available to Windows users only, this folder contains a demonstration version of Miramar's PC MacLAN, the easiest solution for networking Macintosh and PC computers. This is the software I use in my office, so I can attest that it works great. (If you're viewing the CD on a Mac, you will not see this folder.)

- ✦ **Plug-ins:** This folder contains a wide range of Photoshop plug-ins from scads of different vendors, including such luminaries as Alien Skin, Andromeda, and Extensis. Most of the plug-ins are limited demonstration versions that give you ample chance to try out the software before you buy. But many of the vendors have graciously shared one or two fully functional plug-ins that are exclusive to this book. You can use them right off the CD without paying another dime. I can proudly say that I know of no other Photoshop book that includes so much free software, and of such excellent caliber.

- ✦ **Stock Photos:** This folder contains a total of 48 high-resolution images from the titans of digital stock photography, PhotoDisc and Digital Stock. Not coincidentally, every one of these photographs is featured in the figures in this book, so you can follow along with the exercises and techniques exactly as I describe them.